Parallel Processing
for Supercomputers
and Artificial Intelligence

McGraw-Hill Series in Supercomputing and Parallel Processing

Consulting Editor
Kai Hwang, *University of Southern California*

Hwang/Briggs: *Computer Architecture and Parallel Processing*
Hwang/DeGroot: *Parallel Processing for Supercomputers and Artificial Intelligence*
Quinn: *Designing Efficient Algorithms for Parallel Computers*

Related McGraw-Hill Books on Artificial Intelligence

Allen: *Anatomy of LISP*
Davis and Lenat: *Knowledge-Based Systems in Artificial Intelligence*
Nilsson: *Problem-Solving Methods in Artificial Intelligence*
Rich: *Artificial Intelligence*

ISBN	AUTHOR	TITLE
0-07-001404-3	Allerhand (Ranade, Ed.)	*Knowledge-Based Speech Pattern Recognition*
0-07-023437-X	Girard et al.	*Building Expert Systems Using Rule Based Shells*
0-07-026909-2	Hart	*Knowledge Acquisition for Expert Systems*
0-07-031606-6	Hwang, DeGroot	*Parallel Processing for Supercomputers and Artificial Intelligence*
0-07-037476-7	Levine et al.	*Comprehensive Guide to AI and Expert Systems Using Turbo Pascal*
0-07-044088-3	Murray, Murray	*Expert Systems in Data Processing*
0-07-053614-7	Rolston	*Principles of Artificial Intelligence and Expert Systems Development*
0-07-061573-X	Stock (paper)	*AI Theory and Applications in the VAX Environment*
0-07-852109-2	Thompson, Thompson	*MicroExpert (Software for IBM PC)*

Parallel Processing for Supercomputers and Artificial Intelligence

Editors

Kai Hwang
University of Southern California
Los Angeles, California

Doug DeGroot
Texas Instruments
Dallas, Texas

McGraw-Hill Publishing Company

New York St. Louis San Francisco Auckland
Bogotá Hamburg London Madrid Mexico
Milan Montreal New Delhi Panama
Paris São Paulo Singapore
Sydney Tokyo Toronto

Library of Congress Cataloging-in-Publication Data

Parallel processing for supercomputers and artificial intelligence /
  editors in chief, Kai Hwang, Douglas DeGroot.
      p. cm.
    Includes bibliographies and index.
    ISBN 0-07-031606-6
    1. Parallel processing (Electronic computers)   2. Supercomputers.
  3. Artificial intelligence.   I. Hwang, Kai.   II. DeGroot, Doug.
  QA76.5.P31485   1989
  004'.35--dc19   88-31875
                                                                      CIP

1234567890   DOC/DOC   89432109

ISBN 0-07-031606-6

*The editors for this book were Theron Shreve and Martha Gleason, the
designer was Naomi Auerbach, and the production supervisor was
Dianne Walber. This book was set in Century Schoolbook. It was composed by the McGraw-Hill Publishing Company Professional & Reference Division composition unit.*

Printed and bound by R. R. Donnelley & Sons Company.

*For more information about other McGraw-Hill materials,
call 1-800-2-MCGRAW in the United States. In other
countries, call your nearest McGraw-Hill office.*

Contents

Chapter 3   Design Requirements of Concurrent Lisp Machines   69
Robert H. Halstead, Jr.   *MIT Laboratory for Computer Science*

**Chapter 4   Design Issues of Multiprocessors for Artificial
           Intelligence**   107
Benjamin W. Wah   *University of Illinois at Urbana*
Guo-jie Li   *Chinese Academia Sinica*

Part 2   Advanced Computer Architectures   167

Chapter 5   Compute-Intensive Processors and Multicomputers   169
John L. Gustafson *Sandia National Laboratories*

Part 3 Parallel Processing Software   367

Chapter 10   Parallel Programming Environment and Software Support 369
Kai Hwang   *University of Southern California*
Doug DeGroot   *Texas Instruments*

Chapter 11   Automatic Vectorization, Data Dependence, and
                   Optimizations for Parallel Computers   409
Michael Wolfe   *Oregon Graduate Center*

Part 4   New Computing Technologies   523

Contributors

Raymond Chowkwanyun *Symult Systems Corporation,[†] Monrovia, CA 91016* (CHAPS. 7, 9).

Doug DeGroot *Computer Science Center, Texas Instruments, Inc., Dallas, TX 75265* (CHAPS. 10, 13).

Jack B. Dennis *Laboratory for Computer Science, Massachusetts Institute of Technology, Cambridge, MA 02139* (CHAP. 14).

Jack J. Dongarra *Mathematics and Computer Science Division, Argonne National Laboratory, Argonne, IL 60439* (CHAP. 8).

Jeff Fier *Symult Systems Corporation,[†] Monrovia, CA 91016* (CHAP. 6).

Dennis Gannon *Computer Science Department, Indiana University, Bloomington, IN 47405* (CHAP. 12).

Joydeep Ghosh *Department of Electrical and Computer Engineering, University of Texas, Austin, TX 78712* (CHAP. 7).

John L. Gustafson *Parallel Processing Division, Sandia National Laboratories, Albuquerque, NM 87123* (CHAP. 5).

Robert H. Halstead, Jr. *Laboratory for Computer Science, Massachusetts Institute of Technology, Cambridge, MA 02139* (CHAP. 3).

Alan Hinds *Computer Services, Argonne National Laboratory, Argonne, IL 60439* (CHAP. 8).

Kai Hwang *Department of Electrical Engineering-Systems, University of Southern California, Los Angeles, CA 90089* (CHAPS. 2, 7, 9, 10, 16).

Walter J. Karplus *Department of Computer Science, University of California, Los Angeles, CA 90024* (CHAP. 1).

S. Y. Kung *Department of Electrical Engineering, Princeton University, Princeton, NJ 08544* (CHAP. 15).

Guo-jie Li *Institute of Computing Technology, Academia Sinica, Beijing, People's Republic of China* (CHAP. 4).

Yin L. Shih *Symult Systems Corporation,[†] Monrovia, CA 91016* (CHAP. 6).

Scott T. Toborg *Space and Communications Group, Hughes Aircraft Company, El Segundo, CA 90009* (CHAP. 16).

Benjamin W. Wah *Department of Electrical and Computer Engineering, University of Illinois, Urbana, IL 61801* (CHAP. 4).

Ko-Yang Wang *Department of Computer Science, Purdue University, West Lafayette, IN 47907* (CHAP. 12).

Michael Wolfe *Oregon Graduate Center—CSE, Beaverton, OR 97006* (CHAP. 11).

[†]Formerly AMETEK Computer Research Division.

Preface

The need to solve ever more complex problems continues to outpace the ability of the world's fastest and most powerful computers to execute the required programs within acceptable time periods. And it is becoming increasingly difficult to design and build more powerful computers, even with the continuing advances in microelectronics technology. Parallel processing continues to hold the promise of a solution. By connecting a number of powerful computer processors together into a single system and having these connected processors cooperate to solve a single problem that exceeds the ability of any one of the processors, we hope to be able to solve problems that are at present beyond our reach.

Today, very few aspects of society and daily life remain which are not in one way or another significantly impacted by the presence of computers somewhere in the cycle, and demands for increasing capability and higher performance are continually being placed on these computers. As a consequence, a growing number of computing practitioners are turning to parallel processing to solve their problems, and fields which only recently began using computers are already turning to the promises held forward by parallel processing. The result has been a deluge of recent research, application results, and commercial endeavors.

Significant breakthroughs have occurred on several fronts. In particular, one of the most promising, in our opinion, has been the emerging success in combining the fields of supercomputing with artificial intelligence. This combination is occurring in a number of ways, and with a number of different approaches using a number of different technologies. For example, expert systems technology is beginning to be applied to the incredibly complicated task of automatically performing program transformations on highly numeric programs in order to derive the optimal execution of that program on a given parallel, scientific supercomputer. In another area, the data dependence work that has so long been a hallmark of vector processing and Fortran is now finding a home in parallel symbolic languages based on Lisp and Prolog. Dataflow architectures and execution models, an active area of parallel processing research for 20 years now, are beginning to be increasingly applied to artificial intelligence problems, and a number of dataflow processors have been designed specifically for symbolic and artificial intelligence computing. While parallel processing has a long history in scientific computing, its role in artificial intelligence is really only now emerging. As is typical in such situations, the more the new borrows and learns from the old, the more the new has to offer the old.

Because of this trend and its successes, and because of the increasing interdependence of the research activities in these two major areas of parallel computing, we felt it not only timely but also important to produce this reference and study text. We hope you find it of value. The text is designed to be used either as a reference book by computer professionals or as a textbook by graduate students studying parallel processing, advanced computer architecture, supercomputers, or AI machines.

The text is divided into four parts. In Part 1, Principles of Parallel Computation, we address several design issues of parallel processors for vector processing, artificial intelligence, and supercomputing. Four chapters are presented. Walter Karplus first discusses design alternatives and applications for both vector processors and multiprocessors. Kai Hwang then provides a detailed classification of existing supercomputers based on a number of performance and cost characteristics. Next, a thorough analysis of the major design requirements of concurrent Lisp machines is provided by Bert Halstead. The final chapter in this section, by Benjamin Wah, provides a thorough analysis of several of the most important design issues of multiprocessors for artificial intelligence applications.

In Part 2, Advanced Computer Architectures, we begin with John Gustafson's analysis of the major issues in design philosophy, architectural techniques, algorithms, applications, and performance metrics of compute-intensive applications. These issues are then considered with respect to hypercube-based computers. Yin Shih and Jeff Fier then describe and analyze several major hypercube architectures and present major applications that have been successfully executed in hypercube systems. Kai Hwang, Raymond Chowkwanyun, and Joydeep Ghosh then discuss the issues of parallel architectures, technological bases, and knowledge engineering requirements for developing high-performance parallel processors for artificial intelligence. Jack Dongarra and Alan Hinds then present a detailed comparison of the execution speeds of the Cray X-MP-4, the Fujitsu VP-200, and the

Hitachi S-810/20 vector processing computers. Raymond Chowkwan-yun and Kai Hwang describe the architectural supports for concurrent Lisp execution using a dynamic load balancing approach.

In Part 3, Parallel Processing Software, we begin with Kai Hwang and Doug DeGroot's discussions of the requirements for effective environments and software support for parallel processing. Michael Wolfe describes the process of using data dependence analysis to achieve automatic vectorization of a program by a compiler. A research effort aimed at providing an expert system for use in automatic program restructuring techniques used by compilers for vectorization and parallelization of scientific code is then described by Ko-Yang Wang and Dennis Gannon. The last chapter in this part of the text is Doug DeGroot's description of a technique for use in ensuring the proper sequencing of side-effect computations in a parallel logic programming model.

The last section, Part 4, is New Computing Technologies. Jack Dennis reports on the emerging use of dataflow architectures for artificial intelligence. S.Y. Kung then presents methodologies for mapping computational graphs onto systolic and wavefront arrays, as well as discussing system design issues. In our final chapter, Scott Toborg and Kai Hwang discuss some current explorations in the areas of optical computing and artificial neural network technologies.

Preparing a comprehensive text such as this is always a major undertaking, as technology and science rarely sit still long enough to collect a representative "snapshot" in time of the important research activities within an area, seemingly no matter how restricted in scope. And to exacerbate the problem, our friends, who kindly consented to contribute to this volume, are some of the very same people who are creating these changes. To them all, we are deeply indebted for this opportunity to be of service. It is indeed an honor to include our works with theirs. Finally, we would like to thank Jenine E. Abarbanel of USC, Martha Gleason, Dianne Walber, Theron Shreve, and the production staff of McGraw-Hill Publishing Company for their efforts in the timely production of this book.

Kai Hwang

Doug DeGroot

Parallel Processing
for Supercomputers
and Artificial Intelligence

Principles of Parallel Computation

1

Vector Processors and Multiprocessors

Walter J. Karplus

University of California, Los Angeles, CA

1.1 The Quest for Speed

Since the end of World War II, the requirements of engineers and scientists for ever more powerful digital processors has been one of the principal driving forces in the development of digital computers. The attainment of high computing speeds has always been one of the most, if not the most, challenging requirement. High speed becomes of paramount importance in several distinct classes of application including the following.

1.1.1 Simulation of distributed parameter systems

Many phenomena of interest to scientists and engineers are characterized by mathematical models in the form of simultaneous partial differential equations. In order to solve these equations by digital computer techniques, the space/time continuum is represented by discretely spaced points, and the partial differential equations are discretized using finite difference or finite element approximations. The smaller the discretization intervals, the greater is the number of discretely spaced points, and the smaller is the truncation error. In order to attain desired accuracies in many situations, the finite difference models may contain hundreds of thousands of grid points in the space domain. An algebraic equation must be solved at each point for each time level. Particularly where the partial differential equations are nonlinear and where implicit algorithms must be used to avoid computational instability, the solution of such systems of algebraic equations presents truly formidable problems. Even with the best available supercomputers, computing runs lasting many hours are not uncommon.

1.1.2   Real-time simulation of dynamic systems

In the simulation of many aerospace, electromechanical, and chemical processes, the physical system is modeled by sets of simultaneous nonlinear ordinary differential equations. It is frequently important in such simulations to be able to connect real-world hardware and/or human operators to the simulator in order to explore the functioning of the overall system under realistic conditions. For example, in flight simulations using cockpit trainers, the computer implementing the mathematical model of the aircraft is connected in a closed loop with a mock-up cockpit and a flight table. The simulation run is divided into discrete intervals termed *time frames*. At the beginning of each time frame, the computer receives as inputs the latest settings of all pilot controls and environmental variables; at the end of the time frame, the computer reads out new values to the flight table actuators so as to produce the required translations and rotations of the cockpit. The frame time must be short enough so as to obviate undesirable sampling errors, which would lead to erroneous and unrealistic behavior. It is therefore necessary in the single time frame, which may be as short as 1 ms, to solve the mathematical model of the entire aircraft, that is, to integrate all of the simultaneous differential equations over one time step. In some aircraft such as helicopters and vertical lift-off planes the complexity of the mathematical model is such that the speed requirements exceed the capabilities of even the most powerful of the contemporary sequential digital computers.

1.1.3   Signal processing of sampled data

Many computer applications involve the digitizing of analog signals and the processing of the resulting samples. Most frequently this processing entails the application of various mathematical transformations, such as the fast Fourier transform (FFT), in order to facilitate auto- and cross-correlations. Particularly important application areas include acoustic signal processing in antisubmarine warfare, speech recognition, seismic prospecting for underground petroleum deposits, and image processing of radar signals and medical x-rays (CT scanners). In many of these applications, input data arrive at very high rates, and the processed outputs must be generated very rapidly in order to be useful.

Ever since the introduction of electronic digital computers, the quest for high speed has focused on overcoming the limitations imposed by the so-called von Neumann bottleneck. In conventional sequential digital computers, a single memory buffer serves as the only gate between the high-speed memory and the central processing unit. This makes it necessary to organize all computational tasks in a strictly sequential fashion, so that the more complex the computing task the more time-consuming the computations. Although advances in hardware technology have led to continuing increases in the speed of individual arithmetic operations, these have been greatly overshadowed by the increasing complexity of many simulation problems. Two major innovations in the hardware design of digital computers have permitted the circumventing of the von Neumann bottleneck so as to attain high speeds: pipelining and parallelism. The implementation of these techniques has given rise to a number of distinct families of high-speed digital computers including supercomputers, peripheral array processors, and multiprocessors.

1.2 Supercomputers and Minisupercomputers

Stimulated primarily by the requirement for large-scale simulations of distributed parameter systems, major digital computer manufacturers in the United States and Japan undertook to develop systems intended to dwarf existing sequential computers in performance as well as in cost. Known collectively as supercomputers, these large systems have now reached an advanced stage in their evolution. The first supercomputer to become operational was ILLIAC IV, which consisted of an array of 64 processing elements, each containing an arithmetic and logic unit as well as local memory. Although this machine did not fulfill the expectations of its designers, it proved to be an invaluable testing ground for many architectural ideas. During the mid-1970s the focus in the development of supercomputers shifted away from arrays of processing elements and toward pipelining.

In a pipeline architecture, arithmetic operations are broken down into successive stages, and separate hardware units are provided for carrying out the computations of each stage. Two major pipeline-oriented supercomputers of the 1970s were the Control Corporation Data STAR-100 and the Texas Instruments ASC. These computers are known as vector processors since they function efficiently only if the arithmetic operations to be performed are vectorized, that is, arranged as continuous streams of data. Although these vector processors are remarkably fast in certain situations, it proved very difficult in practical simulation problems to arrange the computations to be performed in sufficiently long vectors so as to derive a maximum benefit from the pipelines. The first supercomputer to win widespread acceptance was the Cray-1, developed by Cray Research, Incorporated, and first installed in 1976. This unit contains both vector and scalar sections, the latter serving for sequential computations which cannot conveniently be vectorized. This machine set the pattern for numerous other supercomputers with a similar approach to high-speed computations. These include the well-known products of the Control Data Corporation in the United States and the Hitachi, Fujitsu, and Nippon Electric corporations in Japan. The design of contemporary supercomputers is discussed in Chap. 2. While supercomputers are unequaled in providing high speed for scientific computations, their high cost generally makes them suitable for only very large computing centers and facilities. Only very rarely are such computers dedicated to a single user or application. Although supercomputers present a considerable "economy of scale," there are many users who prefer a less expensive, albeit less powerful, version of these machines over which they can exercise complete control.

In the late 1970s a new class of computing devices designed to meet this need began to appear on the market. These systems were called *array processors,* a misleading designation, since neither are they designed for processing multidimensional arrays of numbers nor do they consist of arrays of processing elements. They are actually relatively small scale vector processors and are intended to function as peripheral devices for sequential digital computers. For this reason they are frequently termed *peripheral array processors* or *attached array processors.* They communicate with a conventional host digital computer through a direct memory access or other input/output channel and enhance the performance of the host with the aid of extensive internal parallelism and pipelining. By the mid-1980s, over two dozen different manufacturers were competing for the signal processing and simulation market for these devices [Karplus 82, 84, 87].

A second approach to the attainment of high speed at a relatively moderate cost entails the networking of microcomputers to form multiprocessor simulation systems. Fashioning networks of general-purpose digital computers so as to attain greater speed through parallelism has been a tantalizing prospect for many years. A number of networks destined for applications such as image processing and dynamic simulation were proposed in the 1970s and early 1980s but did not emerge from the experimental or prototype stage. Only in the mid-1980s did multiprocessing finally come into its own. The resulting multiprocessors along with vector processors, patterned after supercomputers but much less expensive, provide very viable alternatives to supercomputers and are often called *minisupercomputers.* Typically, minisupercomputers strive to achieve 25 percent of the performance of a Cray 1S at 10 percent of the cost.

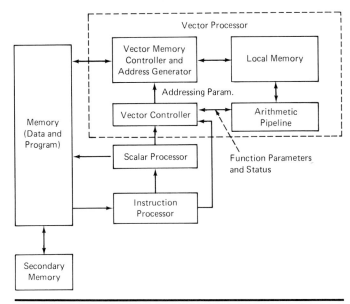

Figure 1.1   Vector processor organization.

1.3   Vector Processors: Design Alternatives

A number of contemporary minisupercomputers attain high speed primarily through pipelining. These devices have a vector processor architecture similar in many respects to that of supercomputers, such as the Cray 1. The basic organization of such a computer is shown in Fig. 1.1 [Wu 85]. It consists of an instruction processor to fetch and decode instructions, a vector processor for processing streams of data, and a scalar processor for dealing with that portion of the computing task which is not amenable to vectorization.

Of particular importance in the design of vector processors is pipelining arithmetic operations. As an example of a typical pipelining operation, consider the performance of floating-point addition in a computer with an instruction cycle time of 50 ns. Assume that it is desired to add the numbers 987 and 65.4, represented in floating-point form as $(+.9870 + 03)$ and $(+.6540 + 02)$. The sequential addition of these numbers involves four distinct operations:

1. Align (modify) the exponents: $(+.6540 + 02) \rightarrow (+.0654 + 03)$.

2. Add the mantissas: $(+.9870) + (+.0654) \rightarrow +1.0524$.

3. Normalize: $(+ 1.0524 + 03) \rightarrow (+.10524 + 04)$.

4. Round off the result: $(+ .10524 + 04) \rightarrow (+.1052 + 04)$.

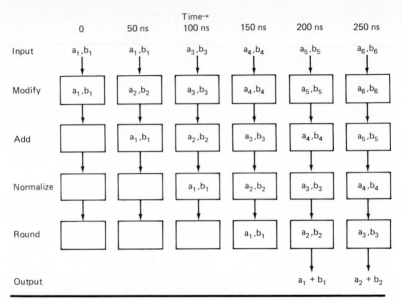

Figure 1.2 Pipelined addition of two vectors.

Using a conventional sequential computer, the addition of two floating-point numbers therefore requires four instruction cycles. In a pipeline realization, each of these four operations is performed by a separate hardware unit. Assume that the characteristics of the electronic circuits are such that the slowest of these operations requires less than 50 ns. It is then possible to pass data from one unit to the next and to commence work on a new pair of inputs every 50 ns. Once the pipeline is full, a new sum will appear at the output of the pipeline every 50 ns. This is illustrated in Fig. 1.2, where summations are to be performed on two streams of numbers $a_1, a_2,\ldots, a_n$ and $b_1, b_2,\ldots, b_n$.

At time $t = O$, the first pair of numbers to be added, a_1 and b_1, enter the pipeline, and 200 ns later, the sum $a_1 + b_1$ emerges from the pipelined adder. At that time each element in the pipeline is simultaneously operating on a different pair of numbers. Provided that the streams a and b are sufficiently long to keep the pipeline filled for a substantial length of time, the pipeline adder provides the same throughput as a single adder with a 50-ns addition time, or four times as rapidly as a conventional adder. There exist numerous alternative approaches to the realization of vector computers with the general organization of Fig. 1.1 These include the following.

Instruction processor.   In order to make optimum use of the arithmetic pipeline elements, careful attention must be paid to fetching instructions from the program memory, the temporary storage of these instructions, the analysis of each instruction to determine whether it demands scalar or vector processing, and the transmission of the instruction to the appropriate processor. Many of these functions can be effectively pipelined within the instruction processor, and a variety of buffering and look-ahead techniques can be used.

Scalar processor. A variety of architectures and technologies are available for the realization of this unit. It may process data in fixed-point or floating-point form, and it may be provided with the registers for the storage of intermediate results, for example.

Arithmetic pipeline. The pipelining approach described above for a floating-point adder can be applied to the realization of many other arithmetic functional elements. Most vector processors contain at least one floating-point adder and one floating-point multiplier. Some also contain division and square root units. In some processors, so-called multifunction units (which are capable of being automatically configured to execute a variety of functions) are provided. A vector processor may contain a multiplicity of pipelined adders, multipliers, and other functional units. Some of these may be used for scalar or for vector processing, as required, and as determined by the instruction processor.

Local memory. A memory unit within the vector processor is vital for buffering the information flow between the main memory and the arithmetic pipelines. Many alternatives exist as to the manner in which this buffering operation is implemented.

1.4 Peripheral Array Processors: Design Alternatives

The discussion of this class of devices is complicated by the absence of standard terminology. The term *array processor* is sometimes used to describe systems composed of arrays of processing elements, systems designed to facilitate the processing of vectors, systems designed to process arrays of numbers, and systems designed to process data originating from arrays of points in the space and time domains. For the purpose of the present discussion, however, the term *peripheral array processor* is applied only to a computing device which manifests all of the following features:

1. It is designed to operate in concert with a conventional computer, the host, so as to enhance its performance in certain numerical applications.

2. It is coupled to the host computer through a host interface unit, so that it acts as a peripheral.

3. It achieves high performance through the use of parallelism and/or pipelining.

4. Its arithmetic section contains at least one adder and one multiplier capable of operating concurrently.

5. It can be programmed by the users so as to perform a variety of computing tasks.

Most contemporary peripheral array processors embody the functional units shown in Fig. 1.3. A wide variety of design alternatives exist [Karplus 81].

Host interface.   Peripheral array processors may be designed to support only one brand or one model of host computer. Alternatively, interface units may be provided so as to permit the peripheral array processor to enhance the performance of a wide variety of mainframes, minicomputers, and microcomputers.

Memory hierarchy.   All peripheral array processors include a program memory, which is loaded by the host computer prior to the start of the computing task. Typically each program word is in microcode and includes instructions to each of the other functional units. The data memory may accommodate 32- or 64-bit word formats, or it may be byte-addressable. Interleaving may be provided so as to permit more rapid memory access. Scratch pad units in the form of rapid access registers may be available for intermediate computational results.

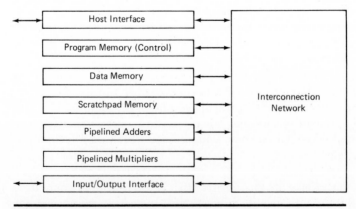

Figure 1.3   Peripheral array processor organization.

Pipelined arithmetic units. An assortment of adders, multipliers, and occasionally dividers and square root units, may be provided. Generally these employ floating-point arithmetic, although integer arithmetic units may also be available.

Input/output interface. This unit permits direct access to network busses, mass memories, and analog/digital and digital/analog converters. Input/output operations may be accomplished by "cycle stealing," or provision may be made for simultaneous processing and input/output.

Interconnection network. A wide variety of bus structures may be used, or a crossbar switch may be employed.

The characteristics of commercially available peripheral array processors are summarized in Table 1.1.

1.5 Minisupercomputers: Vector Processors

The success and widespread acceptance of supercomputers, such as the Cray 1, has encouraged a number of manufacturers to introduce computers patterned upon these supercomputers but providing more favorable cost/performance ratios. The minisupercomputers falling in this class provide full 64-bit floating-point arithmetic and include powerful vector pipelines as well as high-performance scalar units. Their software systems include Fortran compilers which automatically divide instructions among the vector and scalar units so as to take maximum advantage of available pipelining and parallelism. Listed in Table 1.2 are seven minisupercomputers falling in this class and introduced in 1985 and 1986. Most of them represent attempts to provide approximately 25 percent of the performance of a Cray 1S at approximately 10 percent of the cost. The actual performance of most of these computers in one significant benchmark study is included in Table 1.4. Although similar in general approach and objectives, each of these vector processors has some unique features that distinguish it from its competitors.

The products of Alliant Computer Systems Corporation are geared to providing a relatively high level of multiprocessing as well as vector processing. The basic computational engine is the computational unit (CU) implemented in custom NMOS VLSI including a floating-point adder, two floating-point multipliers, two floating-point dividers and one integer multiplier. The system is expandable to include up to twenty CUs. The most widely used system, the FX/8, contains eight computational units.

The Control Data Corporation's Cyberplus features a unique dual ring structure. One ring allows for the transfer of data from one pro-

TABLE 1.1 Examples of Peripheral Array Processor Products

Manufacturer	Model number	Host computer	Instruction cycle time, ns	Data word size, bits	Number of adders	Number of multipliers	Microprogram size, bits	Execution time for 1024-point complex FFT, ms
Analogic	AP-500	DEC-VAX	160	32	1	1	n/a	4.6
Computer Design and Applications	MSP-3000	DEC-VAX	200	32	1	1	96	13.0
Control Data Corp.	MAP-III	CDC Cyber 205	150	32	4	4	123	n/a
CSP, Inc.	Minimap	Many	125	32	1	1	64	7.8
CSP, Inc.	MAP-300	Many	125	32	2	2	64	4.5
CSP, Inc.	MAP-6400	Many	125	64	2	2	64	n/a
Data General	AP/130	Eclipse	200	32	1	1	132	8.7
Floating Point Systems	FPS-5000	Many	167	38	1	1	64	4.7
IBM	3838	IBM 370	100	32	4	4	68	2.9
Numerix (CNR)	MARS-432	Many	100	32	2	1	128	1.7
Signal Processing Systems	SPS-81	Many	167	16	2	1	96	3.0
Sperry Corp. (Datawest)	APS	Univac 1100/80	100	36	8	4	120	n/a
Star Tech. Inc.	ST-100	Many	40	32	2	2	208	0.86

TABLE 1.2   Examples of 64-Bit Vector Processors

Manufacturer	Model	Cycle time, ns	Maximum theoretical throughput, MFLOPS
Alliant Computer Systems	FX/1, FX/8	170	94
Control Data Corp.	Cyberplus	21	65/processor
Convex Computer Corp.	C-1	100	20
Culler Scientific Systems Corp.	PSC	200	5
Floating Point Systems, Inc.	FPS 164 (M64/145)/MAX	167	341
	FPS 264 (M64/60)	54	38
Scientific Computer Systems	SCS-40	45	44

cessor on the ring to another, while the second ring supports communications between the processing elements and the control processor or host computer. The basic Cyberplus processor contains 14 independent functional units as well as an instruction control unit. This processor can be enhanced by additional 32- and 64-bit floating-point arithmetic units including one adder, one multiplier, and one divide/square root unit.

The Convex Computer Corporation's C-1 has a scalar unit and two vector pipelines. The scalar unit is a 64-bit microprogrammed processor. The vector processing unit consists of three independent microprogrammed processors. One controls loads, stores, and vector edit; the second controls vector addition and logical operations; and the third controls vector multiplication and division. The vector processing unit works in conjunction with the scalar processing unit, thereby permitting concurrent vector and scalar operations. For data types of 32 bits, such as single-precision floating-point data, two elements can be stored during a single clock cycle. This doubles the performance for vector operations with data types of 32 bits or less.

The Culler Scientific Systems Corporation's PSC consists of a kernel processor which runs the Unix operating system and a number of user processors (UPs). The UPs perform the actual computations. Each UP consists of an address subsystem and an arithmetic system, which operate concurrently. The arithmetic processor unit consists of one arithmetic and logic unit (ALU), a multiplier, and high-speed memories and registers.

The M64 series of Floating Point Systems, Inc., includes a variety of 64-bit products. The M64/145 is very similar to the FPS 164. The rationale for the design of this computer is discussed in Chap. 5. An unusual feature of this minisupercomputer is the optional MAX extension. The MAX units are vector processors especially designed to accelerate matrix operations. These accelerators plug into slots normally employed by memory units. The user is therefore able to trade speed for storage capacity. The M64/60, formerly the FPS 264, is similar in structure to the M64/145 but is realized in emitter-coupled logic (ECL) and is therefore considerably faster. The MAX option is not available on the M64/60.

The Scientific Computer Systems' SCS-40 is a microcoded machine which uses emulation and table lookup instruction decode methods. The microcode emulates the Cray X-MP instruction set. This bit-for-bit emulation enables programs operating on a Cray to run without modification on the SCS-40.

In addition to the computers mentioned above, there are a number of 64-bit vector processors which evolved from 32-bit peripheral array processors. These include the MAP-6400 of CSP, Inc., and the NMX-464 of Numerix Corporation.

1.6 Multiprocessors: Design Alternatives

Contemporary multiprocessor systems manifest a wide variety of architectural approaches and innovative concepts. No fully satisfactory taxonomy of multiprocessors has as yet appeared in the literature. It is possible, however, to identify a number of fundamental design alternatives to aid in the classification of available multiprocessors and to better understand their relative advantages and limitations [Hockney 7].

Program control.   One of the oldest and still most widely used methods of classifying multiprocessor systems was developed by Flynn [72]. In a conventional sequential computer, at any instant of time, there can be but a single command in the command register, and this command can effect an arithmetic or logical operation upon a single datum stored in the accumulator. Such a machine organization is termed *single-instruction stream, single-data stream,* or SISD. In one widely used approach to parallelism, a multiplicity of concurrently operating processing elements is provided, where each processing element consists of an ALU and a memory unit. The arithmetic and memory units are interconnected to form a network or an array. The system contains only one program control unit which can activate any or all of the arithmetic units. Each active element of the array performs the same arithmetic or logic operation under command of the control unit. Of course, each arithmetic element may be operating on different data in executing the instruction resident in the control unit. For this reason, this type of structure is termed *single-instruction stream, multiple-data stream,* or SIMD. In the third approach to machine organization, each processing element contains a control unit as well as an ALU and memory unit. The elements of the network can therefore function as full-fledged independent digital computers, and during any instruction cycle each processing element can carry out a different arithmetic or logic operation. For this reason systems of this type are termed *multiple-instruction stream, multiple-data stream,* or MIMD.

Interconnection methods. The technique selected to connect the processing elements forming an MIMD system to each other and to peripheral devices is a major factor in determining the performance of the multiprocessor. A number of basic alternatives in network topology exist [Feng 84]. The first major distinction to be considered is whether the interconnections are to be dynamic or static.

In a dynamic interconnection network, switches are provided so that processing elements, memory modules, and peripheral devices can be connected to each other under program control. Dynamic approaches involve single-stage and multistage switching including the shuffle exchange networks. The crossbar switch is another widely used example of a dynamic interconnection medium. The most widely used method of connecting processing elements, memory units, and peripherals to each other is the bus structure. In this method all elements share a single connection medium and employ a variety of techniques such as token passing or time-sliced broadcasting to assure that messages are received correctly. In other static interconnection networks, the processing elements are arranged in multidimensional patterns and permanently connected to each other. Static network topologies include such one- and two-dimensional structures as the ring, the star, the nearest neighbor mesh, and the systolic array. Of concern in selecting a specific topology is the time (in instruction cycles) required to pass information among elements that are not adjacent to each other. The *hypercube,* illustrated in Fig. 1.4, is one approach to minimizing the "maximum distance" between processing elements in large networks. The number of processing elements N is made equal to a power of 2, and each processing element is connected to $\log_2 N$ nearest neighbors. For $N = 4$ and $N = 8$, the hypercube configurations are the square and the cube, respectively. For large numbers of processing elements, the networks take on complex configurations termed higher-dimensional hypercubes. Chapter 6 is devoted to hypercube systems and their applications.

Form of information exchange. Many multiprocessor systems employ so-called shared memories. In such systems, the processing elements have access to common memory resources and exchange data among each other by successive record and read operations on designated memory locations. This approach may lead to serious resource conten-

Hypercube Dimensions

Dimension	Nodes	Channels/Node	Channels	Topology
0 D	1	0	0	
1 D	2	1	1	
2 D	4	2	4	
3 D	8	3	12	
4 D	16	4	32	

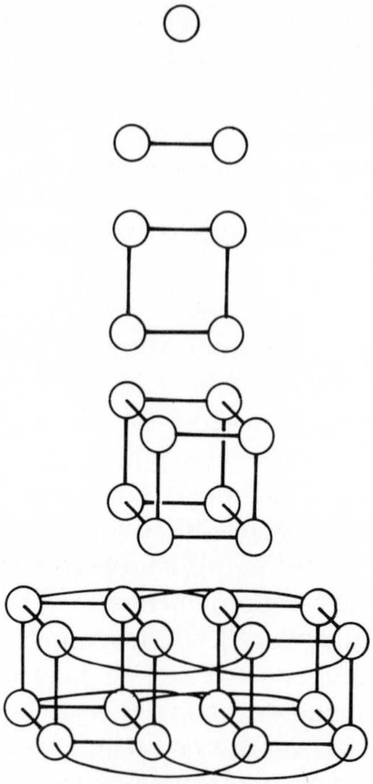

Figure 1.4 The hypercube topology.

tion problems when the data traffic becomes large. To alleviate this problem, a number of contemporary multiprocessor systems employ rapid-access or cache units to act as buffers for frequently used memories. A major alternative to shared memories are the so-called message-passing systems. Here, each processing element has local memory of its own, but no shared memory units exist. Instead data to be exchanged are transmitted as messages between two processing elements.

Processing element granularity. The number of processing elements available in present-day multiprocessors ranges widely. Some contain as few as two parallel elements while others contain many thousands. A multiprocessor system is considered small if the number of processing elements is 16 or less. Multiprocessors with from 16 to 1024 elements are large. Multiprocessors with more than 1024 elements are sometimes termed massive.

System software.   In order to make effective use of multiprocessor systems, it is necessary to ensure that all of the processing elements are gainfully employed as much of the time as possible. Additionally it is necessary to minimize the time devoted to interprocessor communications and housekeeping. For large simulation problems, the overall program must be partitioned so as to permit the allocation of portions of it to the different processing elements. An allocation algorithm must then be employed to direct each of the partitions (or program modules) to specific processing elements. Additionally, the entire program and dataflow must be carefully scheduled and synchronized. The combined   partitioning-scheduling-synchronization   problems   are among the most challenging in the implementation of simulation models on multiprocessor systems. Optimum strategies in this regard tend to be highly problem and hardware specific. Chapter 10 is devoted to a discussion of software supports for parallel processing.

Programming languages.   It is essential that adequate application programming tools be made available to the user of multiprocessor systems. Often it is desired to implement, on a multiprocessor, simulation programs which were originally designed to be executed on a sequential computer. In many application areas these programs are massive, and a reprogramming effort would be exceedingly time consuming and expensive. Since most of the early simulation programs were written in Fortran, multiprocessor systems which do not have available an efficient Fortran compiler are at a serious disadvantage. More modern languages such as Pascal, Ada, and C are favored by present-day programmers; therefore the demand for compilers of these languages exists. In the lumped parameter area, higher-level programming languages have been proposed, and in some instances implemented [Fadden 84, Makoui 87].

1.7   Minisupercomputers: Multiprocessors

Commercially available multiprocessor systems are presented in Table 1.3. Five of these systems employ shared memories as the principal means of information exchange between processing elements. These include

Alliant Computer Systems Corporation, FX/8

Elxsi, 6400

Encore Computer Corporation, Multimax

Flexible Computer Corporation, Flex/32

Sequent Computer Systems, Inc., Balance 8000

TABLE 1.3 Examples of Tightly Coupled and Loosely Coupled Multiprocessors

Manufacturer	Model number	Maximum number of processing elements	Topology	Interprocessor communication	Processor technology	Operating system	Languages supported	Approximate cost, K $
Alliant	FX/8	8	Crossbar and bus	Shared memory	Weitek 1064/5	Unix	Fortran 77 Pascal C	300–750
AMETEK	System 14	256	Hypercube	Message passing	Intel 80287		Fortran 77 C	840
BBN	Butterfly	128	Butterfly switch	Message passing	MC 68000	Unix	Lisp C	800
ELXSI	6400	12	Bus	Shared memory	ECL	Unix Embos Cobol	Fortran 77 Pascal C	400 for 1 processing element
Encore	Multimax	20	Bus	Shared memory	NS 32032/32081	Unix	Fortran 7 Pascal C	
Flexible	Flex/32	20	Bus	Shared memory	NS32032/32081	Unix	Fortran 77 C	0.36 per processing element
Intel	iPSC	128	Hypercube	Message passing	Intel 80286/80287	Xenix	Fortran C	520
NCUBE	NCUBE	1024	Hypercube	Message passing		Unix	Fortran 77 C	
Sequent	Balance 8000	12	Bus	Shared memory	NS 32032/32081	Unix	Fortran 77 Pascal C	220

Among the loosely coupled multiprocessor systems that employ message passing as the primary mode of information exchange, the BBN Advanced Computers Inc.'s Butterfly is unique in that it uses custom-designed VLSI chips to create a switchboard which provides all processors with equal access to one another and expands modularly to match increasing processing power. The switching system permits one processor to communicate directly with another, using packet addresses to transport data. The other loosely coupled multiprocessors all employ the hypercube topology and are discussed in detail in Chap. 6. They include

AMETEK, System 14

Floating Point Systems, Inc., T-Series

Intel Corporation, iPSC

NCUBE, NCUBE/ten

1.8 Performance Measures

The specification or selection of a digital computing device generally involves the consideration of a variety of engineering tradeoffs including particularly speed, accuracy, precision, reliability, and cost. For computation-intensive, scientific computations, performance is virtually synonymous with speed. In signal processing, the speed with which arithmetic operations can be performed determines the rate at which an incoming stream of data can be processed; speed also determines whether the desired outputs, such as processed images, can be generated rapidly enough to be useful. In the simulation of dynamic systems, computing speed determines the minimum frame time, the time required to advance the solution of a system of nonlinear differential equations by one step. The rational choice of a specific computational approach and a specific hardware device requires the availability of suitable performance measures and evaluation criteria to determine in advance the extent to which computational objectives can be met.

The problems of performance measurement and performance prediction are among the most difficult and complex subjects in computer science and have been subjected to a great deal of study over the years. The most widely used performance prediction methods for digital computer systems involve the analysis of multiple-access, time-shared systems and utilize probabilistic approaches and queuing theory. These methods are primarily useful in situations where computational tasks (customers) arrive at unknown times and demand an unknown amount of service. Statistical models are employed to characterize these tasks and the manner in which they compete for computing resources. By contrast, in signal processing and in simulation the computing tasks are generally known fairly precisely in advance. Inputs arrive only at predictable instants of time, and the required data processing tasks are likewise known in advance. Data-dependent operations, such as IF instructions, occur very rarely. It is possible, therefore, to configure the hardware and software systems to operate optimally in performing the specific required tasks. For this reason, probabilistic performance evaluation methods are of little value in assessing vector processors and multiprocessors when used for large-scale scientific problems.

A variety of techniques have been employed to evaluate vector processors and multiprocessors. These fall into the following five major categories:

- Maximum theoretical throughput
- Operations mix
- Kernel tasks
- Benchmark problems
- Complete implementations

The performance measurement methods are listed above in order of the amount of effort a user must expend to develop meaningful information. Thus, the generation of maximum theoretical throughput data requires only a relatively superficial reference to vendor brochures, while the complete implementation of a signal processing or simulation task may require a programming effort so expensive and time consuming that it would be impractical to repeat it using a number of different completing processors. Most often, acquisition and implementation decisions are made using a combination of the first three of the above methods, as described in more detail below.

Maximum theoretical throughput. This performance figure is based upon the number of arithmetic operations or instructions that can be executed by the device, provided that it is programmed in such a way that all arithmetic computational units are usefully occupied all of the time. Most often this figure is expressed as millions of floating-point operations per second, or MFLOPS. Although such maximum throughput figures provide very general yardsticks for comparing different processors, it must be realized that they are highly unrealistic from the user's point of view. In practical situations, it is rarely possible to program a vector processor or multiprocessor so as to utilize over 30 or 40 percent of its maximum computing capability. Moreover, memory contentions, input/output problems, housekeeping and operating system considerations constitute the real limitations upon computational throughput. In the Dongarra benchmark described below none of the supercomputers, minisupercomputers, or mainframes attained even 20 percent of the maximum theoretical throughput.

Operations mix.   Over the years a variety of so-called scientific mixes have been proposed as a measure of computer performance. These mixes are generally based upon empirical studies of the occurrence of the various computational operations such as addition, multiplication, logical operations, memory fetches, etc., in scientific programs. In the early days of digital computing, the Gibson mix was widely used to evaluate sequential computers. This mix is a weighted average of instruction times so as to reflect the frequency of usage of various operations in scientific computing. Subsequently, Knuth [71] developed a somewhat different mix based upon the observation of a large number of Fortran programs at the Stanford Computing Center. In Great Britain the Central Computer Agency [Curnow 76] developed a more elaborate and presumably more meaningful instruction mix, the Whetstone mix, by observing the frequency of various operations in Algol 60 implementations of a set of carefully designed benchmark problems.

Kernel tasks.   In this approach to performance evaluation, the time required to perform a reasonably complex computational task is employed as a yardstick. In order to be effective, this so-called kernel task should be one that occurs frequently in programs and that can be considered to be of key importance in determining the computational throughput of the entire program. In many signal processing tasks, incoming time series are converted to the frequency domain using the fast Fourier transform (FFT) algorithm. In image processing applications (such as radar and computer-aided tomography), and in seismic data analysis, among others, each complete data processing operation entails the execution of thousands of FFTs, followed by the execution of thousands of inverse FFTs. For example, processing a synthetic aperture radar (SAR) image may require in excess of five hundred thousand 2048-point complex FFTs. The speed with which typical FFTs can be executed is therefore a meaningful and useful performance measure, and most vendors of array processors for signal processing provide information to that end. In Table 1.1, the time required by various array processors to perform the 1024-point complex FFTs is included. These figures must be used with considerable caution since no accepted standards exist as to the manner in which to obtain these figures. In practical applications, there are wide differences among the various array processor models in the overhead times which must be added to the basic FFT times to account for initialization and various housekeeping operations. The Dongarra benchmarks described in the following section are actually measures of kernel tasks, since the solution of the system of 100 linear algebraic equations is but a part of the overall task of solving partial differential equations.

Benchmarks.   From the user's point of view, a much more meaningful performance measure is based upon the implementation of benchmark problems on different computers and a detailed comparative analysis of speed, accuracy, precision, programmability, hardware costs, software development costs, etc. Of course, the major difficulty with this approach is that the user must carry out the implementation on his or her own and may not attain optimally effective programs. Manufacturers very rarely provide direct assistance in benchmarking; therefore, the user is compelled to expend considerable time and effort in order to become sufficiently expert in programming a variety of different devices.

1.8.1   Partial differential equations

By far the most extensive and impressive kernel experiments have been conducted under the direction of J. Dongarra at the Argonne National Laboratory [Dongarra 87]. The Dongarra *benchmarks* are designed to compare the performance of a wide variety of computers when solving systems of linear algebraic equations programmed in Fortran. Over the past decade, the LINPACK software package developed at Argonne National Laboratory has become one of the preferred tools for dealing with dense matrix problems using floating-point arithmetic and 64-bit (full-precision) and 32-bit (half-precision) formats. The benchmark selected consists of 100 simultaneous linear algebraic equations which are strongly coupled so that the characterizing matrix is dense rather than sparse. This benchmark was run under different conditions on over one hundred different computer systems ranging from the Nippon Electric Corporation SX-2 to the Apple MacIntosh.

The results of this study for the computer systems mentioned in the preceding section are shown in Table 1.4. In general, the objective of the study was to observe how well the computers process the LINPACK program without any modification or reprogramming. Since the solution of linear equations entails the repeated application of Fortran arrays of identical size, the Fortran DO loops in LINPACK are "unrolled," i.e., expressed by N consecutive algebraic statements (where N is the number of equations). In order to permit the Fortran compilers of a number of the computer systems to perform properly, these lines of LINPACK were "rolled," i.e., replaced by simple Fortran loops. The utilization of LINPACK entails very frequent calls of the so-called basic linear algebra subprograms (BLAS). In the experi-

TABLE 1.4   Performance of Selected Supercomputers and Minisupercomputers in Executing Linear Algebraic Equations Benchmark

| Manufacturer | Model | Speed relative to Cray 1S | | | |
| | | 64-bit precision | | 32-bit precision | |
		All Fortran	Coded BLAS	All Fortran	Coded BLAS
Cray	1S	1.0	0.22		
Alliant	FX/8 (8 CEs)	1.6	1.1	1.6	1.3
Alliant	FX/1 (8 CEs)	7.5	6.2	7.8	6.1
Convex	C-1	4.2	3.7	3.0	2.5
CSPI	MAP-6430	10	8.4		
ELXSI	6400	12	8.7	10	7.5
Encore	Multimax	298		233	
FPS	264(M64/60)	2.2	1.2		
Numerix	NMX 432			14	3.5
SCS	40	1.5			
Sequent	Balance 8000	208	185	162	148

SOURCE: Dongarra [3].

ments the performance of most of the computers was investigated under two conditions: using Fortran only and replacing the BLAS with the assembly language code of the specific machine. No other attempts were made to exploit the special hardware features of the computers.

An interesting footnote to the Dongarra benchmark studies was provided by Alliant Computer Systems Corporation. In LINPACK, each pass through the BLAS subprogram is independent of other passes. These passes can therefore be processed in parallel. The Alliant compiler, however, did not until recently automatically provide for the parallel execution of subroutines. In order to initiate parallel execution, the programmer had to insert a directive in the Fortran program. This entailed an inspection by the programmer of the program to be run and of its data dependencies. If a given routine could be executed in parallel, the programmer needed only to insert a single statement in the Fortran program. The importance of including such a directive is illustrated in Fig. 1.5, which shows the Alliant FX/8 performance using one through eight processing elements. Performance figures are provided for the BLAS coded in assembly language and in standard Fortran. The dotted curves show the relative speed of solving the benchmark problem without the use of the directive, while the solid curves show the performance for the same problem with the addition of the single compiler directive statement. These results highlight the importance of making relatively simple concessions to the special features of multiprocessor systems.

It should be recognized that the Dongarra benchmarks are meaningful primarily in considering the application of minisupercomputers

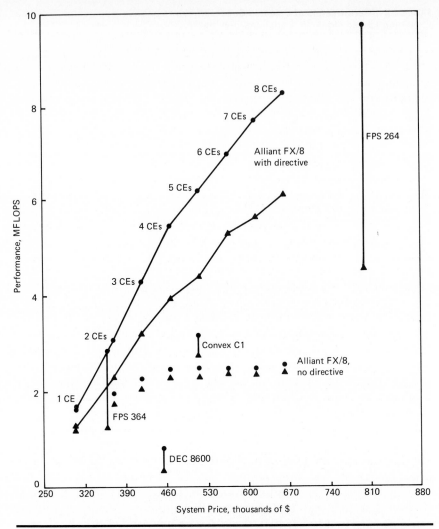

Figure 1.5   Performance of early version of Alliant multiprocessors with and without directive statement. Reported LINPACK results for October 11, 1985. Note: Higher number s (symbol: •) are for coded BLAS. Lower numbers (symbol: ▲) are for compiled Fortran. (*Courtesy of Alliant Computer Systems, Corp.*)

to solve dense matrix problems. Large systems of simultaneous algebraic equations arise in the solution of finite difference and finite element approximations of the partial differential equations characterizing distributed parameter systems. The matrices in that area, however, are often very sparse, and specialized sparse matrix algorithms may then be preferred to the LINPACK routines of the benchmark.

1.8.2 Ordinary differential equations

No comprehensive kernel task or benchmark studies relating to the treatment of lumped parameter systems and ordinary differential equations have as yet been reported. In many of the more challenging real-time simulation problems, the most time-consuming calculations in each time frame are the generation of nonlinear functions of two or more independent variables. Function generation involves extensive table lookups of stored functions and interpolation. In this case, the manner in which the function generation tasks are parceled out to the processing elements of a multiprocessor system is of key importance in determining whether real-time simulation speeds can be attained. The Network II.5 Program introduced in 1983 by CACI Products Co. has been reported to be particularly useful for problems of that type [Cheung 86]. This software package accepts a user-specified computer software and hardware description, simulates the execution of the software and provides performance statistics and records of hardware contention and utilization.

Network II.5 has three types of building blocks for the specification of the hardware comprising multiprocessor systems: processing elements, data storage devices, and data transfer devices. The characteristics of the processing elements are defined by their instruction cycle times and their instruction sets. Processing instructions are designed to model arithmetic and logic operations. Since Network II.5 does not actually execute the program, the only difference among processing instructions is the execution time, which is specified for each operation in terms of the number of required instruction cycles. Message instructions are used to indicate interprocessor data transfers. Each message is specified by its name, a destination processing element, the number of bits to be transferred, and a list of buses that may be used.

The program whose execution is to be simulated by Network II.5 is divided into software modules. Each module contains a list of instructions which link the hardware and software. Network II.5 makes available three different types of reports during the simulation. Periodic reports provide hardware utilization statistics at any time during the simulation; the narrative trace generates a detailed list of every event during the simulation; and snapshots show the status of the entire system at user-specified times. After the simulation, the user may request time-line diagrams which indicate the busy and idle periods of each hardware device. In this way the performance of multiprocessor systems employing different components and architectures may be compared as to the speed with which they execute specific simulation problems.

1.8.3 Artificial intelligence†

Performance measurements for artificial intelligence (AI) machines differ fundamentally from those for computers oriented toward numerical computation. This is because AI programs are highly data dependent, so it is difficult to predict which computer will perform best on any given data set and program. The architectures of AI systems are discussed in detail in Chap. 7. When benchmarking AI machines it is necessary to probe further and have a good understanding of what the benchmark is accomplishing. This requires a detailed profile of the basic machine operations that the benchmark is exercising. Users should adjust the benchmark results for any discrepancies in the mix of operations with the mix found in their own applications.

For Lisp machines the Gabriel suite [Gabriel 85] of benchmark tests is now widely accepted as a standard benchmark. Selected results from these benchmark tests are shown in Table 1.5. Within some quarters of the AI community there is a feeling that the Gabriel benchmarks are outdated and embody a style of programming that was more prevalent 10 years ago rather than modern programming style.

The four benchmarks for which results are shown in Table 1.5 are Tak, Boyer, Browse, and Traverse. As a functionally oriented language, Lisp makes heavy demands on the function-calling capabilities of an implementation. Tak generates many function calls and is a good test of the extent of overhead incurred by an implementation in setting up function calls. Boyer is a theorem-proving program. The inner loop of this program is unification, which is also the inner loop process of the Prolog language. Browse performs pattern-matching operations indicative of the inner loop operations found in expert systems. Traverse is a graph traversal program.

In Table 1.5, the notation IFU shown with the Symbolics machine refers to the optional instruction fetch unit. The Symbolics, Lambda, Dandelion, Dolphin, and Dorado are dedicated Lisp machines, and the tests were written in Common Lisp. The S1 is a supercomputer running its own implementation of Lisp. The IBM 3081, the Cray X-MP2, and the VAX ran codes written in Portable Standard Lisp.

As already mentioned, a full understanding of the benchmark requires a profile of the machine operations which the benchmark exercises. A precise profile for Boyer is not available. Gabriel indicates that it performs approximately three-quarters of a million CARs, a half million each of CDRs, NULLs and ATOMs, and a quarter million CONSs. These list accessing functions make up the bulk of the Lisp

---

†Section 1.8.3 was contributed by Raymond Chowkwanyun, Symult Systems Corporation, Monrovia, California.

TABLE 1.5   Performance of Lisp Machine Benchmarks

a. Benchmark Results for Tak	
Machine	Time, s
Symbolics 3600 + IFU	0.43
Lambda	0.19
Dandelion	1.67
Dolphin	3.84
Dorado	0.52
S1	0.29
IBM 3081	0.11
Cray X-MP2	0.04
VAX 11-780	0.83

b. Profile of Tak	
Item	Count
Calls to Tak	63,609
1 −	47,706
Total	111,315

c. Benchmark Results for Boyer	
Machine	Time, s
Symbolics 3600 + IFU	9.40
Lambda	10.60
Dandelion	119.00
Dolphin	132.40
Dorado	30.28
S1	10.03
IBM 3081	4.60
Cray X-MP2	3.35
VAX 11-780	41.27

d. Benchmark Results for Browse	
Machine	Time, s
Symbolics 3600 + IFU	23.94
Lambda	19.70
Dandelion	300.00
Dolphin	331.60
Dorado	94.40
S1	10.20
IBM 3081	6.30
Cray X-MP2	8.36
VAX 11-780	50.27

e. Profile of Browse	
Item	Count
CAR	1,319,800
EQ	755,700
NULL	504,100
CDR	483,400
CONS	239,200
CHAR1	226,800
NCONC	69,000
Return	600
Total	3,598,600

f. Benchmark Results for Traverse	
Machine	Time, s
Symbolics 3600 + IFU	35.34
Lambda	48.40
Dandelion	181.00
Dolphin	299.00
Dorado	63.90
S1	30.10
IBM 3081	9.89
Cray X-MP2	N/A
VAX 11-780	72.35

g. Profile of Traverse	
Item	Count
MARK	3,083,000
NULL	3,082,750
CDR	3,057,750
CAR	3,057,750
SETF	175,000
1 +	25,000
Total	12,481,250

Source: Gabriel [85].

operations performed. The statistics shown in Table 1.5 parts *d* and *e* are for the inner loop operation of Browse, which is pattern matching. Pattern matching accounts for over 99 of this program's operations.

Work is currently being done on parallel implementations of Lisp at several research sites. Published work includes an implementation of a distributed operating system with dynamic load balancing to support parallel Lisp on a hypercube multicomputer as described in Chap. 9 and in Hwang [87]. The hypercube is equipped with 16 processors, and initial results with Tak indicate that speedups on the order of 13 are possible. This work is being extended to Boyer, Browse, and Traverse. Further work has also been done on the Cray implementation of Portable Standard Lisp, and the new timings are shown in Table 1.6 alongside the old timings for Boyer and Browse [Anderson 87].

TABLE 1.6   Results for Portable Standard Lisp 3.4 on a Cray X-M-P

Benchmark	Old Timing, s	New Timing, s
Boyer	3.4	0.9
Browse	8.4	1.3

SOURCE: Anderson [87].

1.9   The Changing Simulation Environment

The increasing availability of relatively low cost alternatives to supercomputers promises in the coming years to effect significant changes in the manner in which simulations are conducted. During the past decade, as the size of simulation models has increased, particularly in the partial differential equation area, more and more challenging simulations have been shifted to supercomputers. The early 1980s saw the rise of the centralized supercomputer facility. In the United States most of these facilities employ a Control Data Corporation Cyber 205 or one of the products of Cray Research, Inc. Often located in university or U.S. government laboratory settings these very expensive and powerful systems can be accessed remotely by scientists and engineers with large simulation problems to be solved. Until well into the mid-1980s, these large systems provided an economy of scale unattainable with other scientific computers, and they permitted the treatment of problems with computational requirements that would be excessive on any but a supercomputer. The advent of minisupercomputers is already effecting a fundamental change in this picture. In some respects this phenomenon is similar to events that occurred a decade earlier when minicomputers first became popular.

Throughout the 1960s and well into the 1970s, most large-scale scientific computations were carried out on large mainframe computers such as the IBM 360 series, the Control Data Corporation 6600 and

7600, and the Sperry Univac. These multimillion dollar systems usually processed large scientific problems in the batch mode, and users had to adapt themselves to the scheduling and accounting algorithms of the centralized computer facility. The introduction of minicomputers such as the Digital Equipment Corporation's PDP-11 and VAX series, the Xerox Data Systems' Sigma series, and numerous others started a trend toward decentralization. Since these minicomputers were generally marketed at a cost less than 10 percent of that of mainframes, it became possible for individual research groups or organizational subunits to acquire a scientific computer of their own. Frequently these groups found that the more casual operating environment possible with a dedicated machine facilitated considerable economies in personnel and maintenance costs. The cost/performance figures for a minicomputer facility eventually became very favorable compared to that of the large mainframe facilities. More important, however, these minicomputers came under the complete control of the user and provided a marked improvement in flexibility and availability. Ultimately many scientific users came to treasure their independence from a centralized computing facility more than any economic considerations.

The cost of the minisupercomputers of the mid-1980s bears a similar relationship to that of the supercomputers, i.e., a ratio of at least 1:10. More important, the cost of these minisupercomputer facilities may well be within the reach of many research groups, projects, or academic departments. And again, the possibility of owning a dedicated and decentralized computer can be expected to prove very attractive to many scientists and engineers. The complete availability of such a dedicated facility makes possible a mode of interactive scientific computing that is very difficult to duplicate when using a centralized supercomputer.

The emergence of multiprocessors and moderately priced vector processors has already had notable effects upon the manner in which simulations of lumped and distributed parameter systems are conducted. The trend in the direction of minisupercomputers can be expected to accelerate during the late 1980s and to affect most simulation and signal processing activities as well as most individuals engaged in the modeling instrumentation and control of scientific and engineering systems.

Bibliography

[Anderson 87]   J.W. Anderson, W.F. Galway, R.R. Kessler, H. Melenk, and W. Neun. "Implementing and Optimizing Lisp for the Cray." *IEEE Software,* vol. 4, pp. 74–83, July 1987.

[Cheung 86]   S. Cheung, J.W. Carlyle, and W.J. Karplus. "Asynchronous Distributed Simulation of a Communications Network." *Proceedings of the Summer*

Computer Simulation Conference, Society for Computer Simulation, Reno, Nevada, pp. 147–152, July 1986.

[Curnow 76]   H.J. Curnow and B.A. Wichmann. "A Synthetic Benchmark." *The Computer Journal,* vol. 19, pp. 43–49, February 1976.

[Dongarra 87]   J.J. Dongarra and I.S. Duff. "Performance of Various Computers Using Standard Linear Equation Software in a FORTRAN Environment." *Simulation,* vol. 49, pp. 51–62, August 1987.

[Fadden 84]   E.J. Fadden. "The System 10 Plus: Broader Horizons." In W.J. Karplus (ed). *Peripheral Array Processors,* Simulation Series, vol. 14, no. 2, pp. 53–67, Society for Computer Simulation, San Diego, CA, 1984.

[Feng 84]   T. Feng. "A Survey of Interconnection Networks." In K. Hwang (ed). *Supercomputers: Design and Applications.* IEEE Computer Society Press, Silver Springs, MD, 1984.

[Flynn 72]   M.J. Flynn. "Some Computer Organizations and Their Effectiveness." *IEEE Trans. Computers,* vol. C-21, pp. 948–960, September 1972.

[Gabriel 85]   R.P. Gabriel. *Performance and Evaluation of Lisp Systems.* MIT Press, Cambridge, MA, 1985.

[Hockney 81]   R.W. Hockney and C.R. Jesshope. *Parallel Computers.* Adam Hilger, Bristol, UK, 1981.

[Hwang 84]   K. Hwang and F.A. Briggs. *Computer Architecture and Parallel Processing.* McGraw-Hill, New York, NY, 1984.

[Hwang 87]   K. Hwang and R. Chowkwanyun. *Dynamic Load Balancing Methods for Message-Passing Multicomputers.* Technical Report CRI-87-04, Electrical Engineering Systems, University of Southern California, Los Angeles, CA, 1987.

[Karplus 81]   W.J. Karplus and D. Cohen. "Architectural and Software Issues in the Design and Application of Peripheral Array Processors." *IEEE Computer,* vol. 14, pp. 11–17, September 1981.

[Karplus 82]   W.J. Karplus (ed). *Peripheral Array Processors,* Simulation Series, vol. 11, no. 1, Society for Computer Simulation, San Diego, CA, 1982.

[Karplus 84]   W.J. Karplus (ed). *Peripheral Array Processors,* Simulation Series, vol. 14, no. 2, Society for Computer Simulation, San Diego, CA, 1984.

[Karplus 87]   W.J. Karplus (ed). *Multiprocessor and Array Processors,* Simulation Series, vol. 18, no. 2, Society for Computer Simulation, San Diego, CA, 1987.

[Knuth 71]   D.E. Knuth. "An Empirical Study of FORTRAN Programs." *Software: Practice and Experience,* vol. 1, no. 2, pp. 105–133, April–June 1971.

[Makoui 87]   A. Makoui and W.J. Karplus. "ALI: A CSSL-Multiprocessor Software Interface." *Simulation,* vol. 49, pp. 63–71, August 1987.

[Wu 85]   C. Wu (ed). "Multiprocessor Technology." *IEEE Computer* (special issue), vol. 18, pp. 6–108, June 1985.

2

Exploiting Parallelism in Multiprocessors and Multicomputers

Kai Hwang

University of Southern California, Los Angeles, CA

2.1   Supercomputer Architectural Advances

Supercomputers are defined as the fastest computers at any point of time. Compared to today's mainframes, supercomputers are 10 to 1000 times faster in effective speed. To characterize them numerically, today's supercomputers typically have a performance of hundreds of MFLOPS (millions of floating-point operations per second) with a word length of 64 bits and a main memory capacity of millions of words [Hwang 87a]. The definition of a supercomputer varies with time. The obvious trend is that we are demanding future super-computers to be faster and more intelligent. In this chapter, we classify supercomputers by their performance and cost ranges. Advanced architectures and parallel programming requirements of these supercomputers will be studied in subsequent chapters.

2.1.1   Evolution of modern supercomputers

As illustrated in Fig. 2.1, the evolution of supercomputer architectures follows an increasing trend of more hardware and software functions built into a system. The skewed tree demonstrates that most of today's supercomputers are designed with look-ahead techniques, functional parallelism, and pipelining at various levels; they use explicit vectors and explore parallel processing in *single-instruction and multiple-data streams* (SIMD) or *multiple-instruction and multiple-*

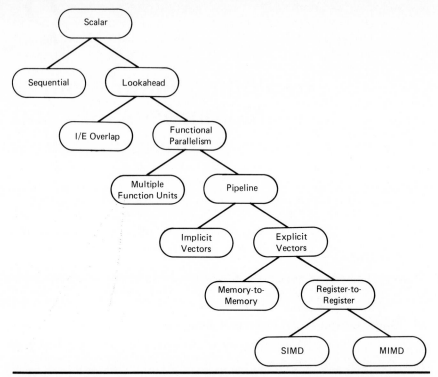

Figure 2.1 Architectural evolution of supercomputers from sequential scalar processing to concurrent vector/scalar multiprocessing. I/E = instruction fetch/decode and execution; SIMD = single-instruction stream and multiple-data streams; MIMD = multiple-instruction streams and multiple-data streams.

data streams (MIMD) mode [Flynn 72]. Most supercomputers support concurrent scalar and vector processing with multiple functional units in a uniprocessor or multiprocessor system. We reserve the terms *multiprocessors* for shared-memory multiple-processor systems and *multicomputers* for loosely coupled, multiple-processor systems with distributed local memories. Other authors may use multiprocessor for both types of MIMD machines. We divide vector processors into two subclasses: *register-to-register* architectures, which are being adapted for almost all supercomputers [Hwang 84] and minisupers [Karplus 87]; and *memory-to-memory* architecture, such as that used in the Cyber 205.

Supercomputer performance is often measured in terms of MFLOPS or *millions of instructions per second* (MIPS). MFLOPS reflects the number-crunching capability of a computer and is often tied to 64- or 32-bit floating point results. The measure of MIPS indicates the instruction execution rate of a computer including the mixture of arithmetic, logic, and program control instructions. The relationship between MFLOPS and MIPS varies with different machines and program mixes. In a typical supercomputer containing scalar, vector, and control instructions, 1 MIPS implies anywhere between 0.5 and 10 MFLOPS of performance. However, this is by no means universally true for all computers.

We often use a range to indicate the expected performance of a supercomputer. The real performance for a given application program often approaches the low end of the range, if the problem is not skillfully programmed with sufficient software support. The peak speed of a machine sets the absolute upper bound in performance. There is no such a term as "average" performance, because it means very little to average the performance of different application programs. The performances and cost ranges of three classes of commercial supercomputers are given in Table 2.1. The *full-scale supers* are the most expensive class, represented by Cray, ETA, and Fujitsu systems, for example. the *near supers* are the high-end mainframes such as the IBM 3090/VF, CDC Cyberplus, Connection Machines, etc. The *minisupers* are the low-cost parallel/vector computers represented by Alliant and Convex systems, etc. The *superminis* do not qualify as supercomputers. We list them here only as a reference point. Note that minisupers tend to have much higher MFLOPS/MIPS ratios than superminis. According to today's standard, a machine is qualified as a supercomputer if it can perform 10 to 1000 MFLOPS in typical scientific or engineering computations [Dongarra 86].

TABLE 2.1   Supercomputer Classes and Performance/Cost Ranges

Class	Peak performance	Cost	Representative systems
Full-scale supercomputers	200 ~ 2400 MFLOPS, >500 MIPS	$2–25 million	Cray 2, Cray X-MP, NEC SX-1/SX-2, Fujitsu VP 200, ETA-10, IBM GF11
Near supers (high-end mainframes)	50 ~ 500 MFLOPS, > 50 MIPS	$1–4 million	IBM 3090/VF, Loral MPP, CDC Cyberplus, Univac 1194/ISP, Connection Machine, BBN Butterfly
Minisuper-computers (minisupers)	10 ~ 100 MFLOPS, > 10 MIPS	$100,000–1.5 million	Alliant FX/8, Convex C-1, SCS-40, Elxsi 6400, Encore/Multimax, iPSC, FPS 164 Max, T-Series, Warp
Superminis (not a class of supercomputers; listed as a reference point)	< 0.5 MFLOPS, < 5 MIPS	$20,000–400,000	VAX 8600, IBM 4300, IBM 9370, VAX/780, Pyramid

2.1.2   Advanced architectural choices

Since supercomputers are mainly used to perform numerical computations in science and engineering, most are equipped with scalar and vector hardware units that can operate in parallel. The architectures of modern supercomputers are divided into five categories based on their interconnect and operational structures as summarized in Table 2.2. The key features of these architectural choices are characterized below.

Multipipelined uniprocessors.   Most vector supercomputers start as a pipelined uniprocessor containing multiple functional units. The memory-to-memory architecture demands much wider memory bandwidth and longer instructions, which favors only the processing of long vectors. For short vectors or scalars, the performance could be very poor, as experienced in the Cyber 205. On the contrary, the register-to-register architecture performs much better with a scalar/vector mix. Most pipelined vector machines choose this architecture, ranging from Cray 1 to Convex C1 and SCS-40, etc. The Alliant FX/1 uses a cache-based, register-to-register architecture, which is a compromise between the two extremes. Multiple data streams can be executed by multiple functional pipelines simultaneously, even if there is only one instruction stream in the system [Ortega 85].

SIMD processor arrays.   SIMD machines are parallel processors which operate synchronously in lockstep under the same control unit. Physically, the *processing elements* (PEs) form a processor array such as

TABLE 2.2   An Architectural Taxonomy of Supercomputers

Architecture	Representative systems
Uniprocessors with multiple functional units and vector hardware options	Alliant FX/1; IBM 3090; CDC 7600; FPS 164/264/364; Convex C-1; Cray 1; Cray X-MP/1; Cyber 205; Amdahl 500, 1100, 1200, 1400; (also Fujitsu VP-50, 100, 200, 400); Hitachi S-810; NEC SX-1; SX-2; SCS-40
SIMD processor arrays or attached processors	Loral MPP; ICL/DAP; FPS 164/MAX; Connection Machine; IBM GF11
Shared-memory multiprocessor systems	Cray X-MP/2,4; Cray 2; Alliant FX/8; Encore/Multimax; Elxsi 6400; Sequent 8000; Cray 3; IBM 3090/400 VF; Univax 1194/ISP
Distributed-memory multicomputers	iPSC; AMETEK 14; NCUBE; BBN Butterfly; CDC Cyberplus; Culler PSC; FPS T-Series; Warp
Hierarchical or reconfigurable systems	Cedar, ETA-10, IBM RP3

the mesh architecture in ILLIAC IV, Loral MPP, IBM GF11 [Beetam 85], and ICL/DAP [Hockney 81], or the hypercube architecture in the Connection Machine [Hillis 85]. Since these machines are often used in processing large-scale arrays of data, they are often called *array processors*. The FPS 164/Max [Charlesworth 86] belongs to this class. Up to 15 matrix algebra accelerators (MAXs) are attached to an FPS 164 and operate in an SIMD mode. Most SIMD array processors are special-purpose machines, applied mainly to signal and image processing [Levialdi 85]. The Connection Machine is presented in Sec. 7.4.2. The IBM GF11 is discussed in Sec. 2.2.3.

Shared-memory multiprocessors. Shared-memory multiprocessors are tightly coupled MIMD machines using shared memory among multiple processors. The interconnect architecture falls essentially into one of two classes: *bus-connected* and *directly connected*. Most minisupers choose the bus-connected structure, in which multiple microprocessors, parallel memories, network interfaces, and device controllers are tied to the same contention bus [Bell 85]. For example, the Elxsi 6400 uses a high-speed, 64-bit bus with a bandwidth of 320 Mbytes/s [McGrogan 87]. The directly connected architectures include the *crossbar, partially connected graphs,* and *multistage networks* [Chin 84]. Most high-cost supers and high-end mainframes use direct interconnects [Dongarra 86]. We choose to present the multiprocessor of Univac 1100/94, Cray X-MP, Alliant FX/8, and OMP in this chapter. In Chap. 10, we discuss the IBM 3090/400 multiprocessor.

Distributed-memory multicomputers. This class of computers corresponds to loosely coupled MIMD systems with distributed local memories attached to multiple processor nodes. The popular interconnect topologies include the *hypercube, ring, butterfly switch, hypertrees,* and *hypernets*. Message passing is the major communication method among the computing nodes in a multicomputer system. Most multicomputers are designed to be scalable in performance. The BBN Butterfly switch is a multistage network [BBN 86] through which processors can access each other's local memories. The ring architecture, as demonstrated by the CDC Cyberplus in Sec. 2.2.2, requires less hardware. The hypernets [Hwang 87b] offer a compromise in hardware demand between hypertrees [Goodman 81] and hypercubes [Fox 86, Graham 87]. Hypernets are treated in Sec. 7.5.1 as a connectionist architecture for AI systems. Communication efficiency and hardware connectivity are the major concerns in the choice of a cost-effective multicomputer architecture. In Chap. 6, various hypercube multicomputers are presented and evaluated. The BBN Butterfly processor is discussed in Sec. 7.5.2.

Hierarchical and reconfigurable supercomputers. A hybrid architecture can be obtained by combining both shared memory and message passing for interprocessor communications. Several research multiprocessor systems belong to this category, such as the Cedar [Kuck 86] and the ETA-10 [ETA 86]. Hierarchical memory is built into the system. The approach is to apply *macro dataflow* at the level of processor clusters and to use *control flow* within each processor. Therefore, parallelism is exploited at multiple levels, even with different computing models. The OMP [Hwang 89] was proposed to have a partially shared memory architecture especially designed for supporting large-grain scientific computations. Other parallel machines have been reviewed in Ortega [85] for solving partial-differential equations (PDEs). The ETA-10, a multiprocessor using a hierarchy of fast memories, is discussed in Sec. 2.3.2.

Representative supercomputers and high-end mainframes are summarized in Table 2.3. Presently, the Cray X-MP, Cray 2, Cyber 205, and ETA-10 are the only full-scale supercomputers manufactured in the United States. The Cray 3 is still under development. The HEP is no longer in production. All Japanese-made supercomputers are uniprocessors equipped with multiple functional pipelines. All of the multiprocessor supercomputers use shared memory. The IBM 3090 and Univac 1190 series are both multiprocessors with shared memory and vector hardware. The largest CDC Cyberplus is a loosely coupled multicomputer with 64 processors using distributed memory. The Connection Machine, the MPP, the Butterfly Processor, the Cedar, the IBM GF11, and IBM RP3 all emphasize a high degree of parallelism ranging from 256 to 64K processing elements. The IBM machines, RP3 and GF11, and the Cedar are research prototypes, still under development. The CM, MPP, and GF11 all emphasize massive parallelism. Existing full-scale supercomputers consist of at most 16 processors, each equipped with extensive scalar/vector hardware; some research supercomputer projects are challenging a system with hundreds of processors, each of which is essentially a 32-bit microprocessor equipped with some vector accelerators. Worldwide, there were about 300 supercomputers in use by late 1988.

Table 2.4 summarizes various minisupercomputers. Most minisupercomputers are made from off-the-shelf 32-bit microprocessors. The Convex C-1 and SCS-40 are essentially baby Crays. Most multiprocessor minisupers are bus-connected with shared memory. Four multicomputer minisupers (iPSC, AMETEK, NCUBE, and FPS T-Series) choose the hypercube architecture with distributed memory. Minisupers represent a new startup computer industry. The sustained performance data are difficult to accumulate with a limited number of

TABLE 2.3 Supercomputers and High-End Mainframe Systems

System model	Architecture configuration[1]	Max. no. of processors[2]	Processor type[3]	Max. memory capacity[4]	Peak performance[5]	Remarks[6]
Cray X-MP/4	MP with SM and direct connect	4 processors	Custom ECL	16 Mwords in CM 128 Mwords in SSD	840 MFLOPS	Shared registers among 4 processors
Cray 2	MP with SM and direct connect	4 processors, 1 IOP	Custom ECL	256 Mwords	2 GFLOPS	16 kwords/LM/ processor
Cray 3	MP with SM	16 processors	GaAs/ECL	2 Gwords	16 GFLOPS	Under development
Cyber 205	UP with scalar processor and 4 vector pipes	1 processor	Custom CMOS	4 Mwords	400 MFLOPS	MM architecture
ETA-10	MP with SM	8 processors, 18 IOPs	Custom	256 Mwords	10 GFLOPS	Under development
Fujitsu VP-200	UP with multiple pipelines	1 processor	Custom ECL	32 Mwords	533 MFLOPS	Also Amdahl
NCE SX-2	UP with 16 functional pipes	1 processor	Custom	32 Mwords	1.3 GFLOPS	16 pipes divided into 4 identical sets
Hitachi S-810	UP with multiple pipelines	1 processor	Custom	32 Mwords	840 MFLOPS	Host scalar processor
HEP-1	MP with SM and switch network	16 processors	Custom	256 Mwords	160 MFLOPS	MIMD pipelining
IBM 3090/400/VF	MP with SM and direct connect	4 processors	Custom TCM	2 Gbytes in CM 16 Tbytes in EM	480 MFLOPS	Vector facility optional
Univac 1194/ISPx2	MP with SM and direct connect	4 processors, 4 IOPs, 2 ISPs	Custom	16 Mwords	67 MFLOPS	ISP contains vector hardware

TABLE 2.3   Supercomputers and High-End Mainframe Systems (Continued)

System model	Architecture configuration[1]	Max. no. of processors[2]	Processor type[3]	Max. memory capacity[4]	Peak performance[5]	Remarks[6]
CDC Cyberplus	MC with DM and ring connect	64 processors	Custom	512 kwords per processor	65 MFLOPS and 620 MIPS per processor	Up to 3 rings among processors
Connection Machine	SIMD with DM hypercube embedded in a global mesh	64K PEs	VLSI/CMOS gate arrays	32 Mbytes	1000 MIPS, 250 MFLOPS	Available 1985
BBN Butterfly	MP with SM via butterfly switch network	256 processors	M68020, custom coprocessor	128 Mwords	256 MIPS	Available 1985
Goodyear MPP	SIMD 128 × 128 mesh with DM	16K PEs	CMOS/SOS, 8 PEs per chip	128 Mbytes	470 MFLOPS	Available 1983 (bit slice PEs)
IBM GF11	SIMD with a reconfigurable Benes network	576 PEs	Custom floating-point processor	2 Mbytes/processor; 1.1 Gbytes total	20 MFLOPS/processor; 11 GFLOPS	Under development
IBM RP3	MP with SM/DM and fast network	512 processors	32-bit RISC	128 Mwords	800 MFLOPS; 1300 MIPS	Under development
Cedar	Hierarchical MP with Sm	256 processors	Alliant FX clusters	256 Mwords	3.2 GFLOPS	Under development (prototype 32 processors)

[1]MP = multiprocessor, MC = multicomputer, SM = shared memory, DM = distributed memory (local memory), UP = uniprocessor.

[2]CE = computational elements, IP = interactive processor, IOP = I/O processor, ISP = integrated scientific processor, CN = computer nodes, PE = processing elements.

[3]TCM = thermal conduction module, RISC = reduced instruction set computer.

[4]A word has 64 bits; CM = central memory, EM = extended memory, SSD = solid-state device.

[5]MFLOPS = million floating-point operations per second (64-bit precision), MIPS = million instructions per second.

[6]RR = register-to-register, and MM = memory-to-memory.

Source: Hwang [87a].

38

TABLE 2.4 Minisupercomputers for Parallel/Vector/Multiprocessing

System model	Architecture configuration[1]	Max. no. of processors[2]	Processor type[3]	Max. memory capacity[4]	Peak performance[5]	Remarks[6]
Alliant FX/8	MP with SM and bus connect	8 CEs, 12 IPs	Gate array, M68010	4 Mwords	94 MFLOPS, 35.6 MIPS	Shared cache, RR architecture
Elxsi 6400	MP with SM and bus connect	12 processors	ECL/LSI custom	192 Mbytes	156 MIPS	
Encore/ Multimax	MP with SM and bus connect	20	NS32032	16 Mwords	35 MIPS	
Balance 21 000	MC with SM and vus connect	30	NS32020/32081	48 Mbytes	2 MFLOPS, 21 MIPS	
Flexible /32	MC with DM and VME buses	20 per cabinet	NS32020, M68020	20 Mwords	3.5 MIPS per processor	
Convex C-1 XP	UP with vector hardware	4 processors, 5 IOPs	CMOS/VLSI gate array	16 Mwords	20 MFLOPS, 25.5 MIPS	Multiple I/Os (Crayetts)
SCS-40	UP with multiple pipes	1	ECL/LSI	4 Mwords	18 MIPS, 44 MFLOPS	Vector hardware Cray-compatible
iPSC-VX	MC with DM and hypercube	128 CNs	Intel 80286, 80287	4.5 Mbytes per processor	20 MFLOPS per processor	Multiple I/Os and memory options
NCUBE/10	MC with DM and hypercube	1024	Custom VLSI	20 Mwords	500 MFLOPS, 2000 MIPS	
FPS T	MC with DM and hypercube	4096	CMOS transputer	128 Mwords per node	16 MFLOPS and 7.5 MIPS per processor	

TABLE 2.4 Minisupercomputers for Parallel/Vector/Multiprocessing (*Continued*)

System model	Architecture configuration[1]	Max. no. of processors[2]	Processor type[3]	Max. memory capacity[4]	Peak	Remarks[6]
FPS 164/MAX	SIMD array of 15 MAXs	1 processor, 15 MAXs	Custom with Weitek MAXs	16 Mwords	341 MFLOPS	Newly named as FPS M64/145
ICL-DAP	SIMD lockstep array processor	64 × 64 mesh	Custom bit-slice	8 Mbytes	16 MFLOPS	ICL 2900 host
Warp	Linear systolic array	10	Custom	80 Mwords	100 MFLOPS	Link to a host

[1]MP = multiprocessor, MC = multicomputer, SM = shared memory, DM = distributed memory (local memory), UP = uniprocessor.

[2]CE = computational elements, IP = interactive processor, IOP = I/O processor, ISP = integrated scientific processor, CN = computer nodes, PE = processing elements.

[3]TCM = thermal conduction module, RISC = reduced instruction set computer.

[4]A word has 64 bits; CM = central memory, EM = extended memory, SSD = solid-state device.

[5]MFLOPS = million floating-point operations per second (64-bit precision), MIPS = million instructions per second.

[6]RR = register-to-register, and MM = memory-to-memory.

Source: Hwang [87a].

users. However, due to the high performance/cost ratio, minisupers may penetrate the scientific community quickly. For those machines listed in Table 2.4, the total number of installations was estimated to be around 1000 by late 1988. However, the number could multiply in the next few years. Key features listed include the *degree of parallelism* (number of processors in the system), *processor type, memory capacity, interconnect architecture,* and *peak performance* for characterizing both classes of supercomputers.

2.2 Concurrency in Multiprocessors and Multicomputers

This section deals with resource management for parallel computers and their concurrency control techniques. These issues will greatly affect the degree of parallelism, the resource utilization rate, and thus the system throughput. Resource management includes the scheduling of multiple processors and functional units, memory allocation and accesses, and I/O activity control. Concurrency refers to the simultaneous execution of multiple software processes in a computer system. It combines *vectorization* and *multitasking* in a multiprocessing environment. Multiprocessing techniques address three critical issues: *partitioning, scheduling,* and *synchronization* [Gajski 85]. Various concurrency control techniques will pave the way to developing advanced software tools for balanced parallel processing. We introduce these advanced techniques for exploiting parallelism with hardware and software approaches.

2.2.1 Processor scheduling and activity control

Parallel techniques for multiple processor scheduling and concurrent activity control are presented below with four advanced system features: the *MIMD pipelining* as introduced in HEP-1, the *activity control mechanism* developed in the Univac ISP system, the *scoreboard* approach in Cyberplus, and the *lockstep* mechanism in the IBM GF11. These concurrency control techniques will be discussed in subsequent chapters. The HEP-1 was designed as a tightly coupled multiprocessor consisting of 16 processors and up to 128 memory modules that are interconnected via a pipelined packet-switching network [Smith 81]. Parallelism is exploited at the process level within each processor. The system allows 50 user processes to be concurrently created in each processor. Fifty instruction streams are allowed per processor, with a maximum of $50 \times 16 = 800$ user instruction streams in the entire HEP system.

The pipelined HEP executes multiple instruction streams over multiple data streams. For example, while an *add* is in progress in one process, a *multiply* can be executing in another, a *divide* in a third, and a *branch* in a fourth. Instructions being executed concurrently are independent of each other. Thus, fill-in parallelism increases processor utilization. Arbitrarily structured parallelism is applicable to codes that do not vectorize well. The concepts of packet-switched data forwarding [Chin 84] and of MIMD pipelining [Jordan 83, Jordan 86] make HEP very attractive for solving PDE problems described by sparse matrices. MIMD pipelining allows various execution phases of instructions from different process streams to be mixed through the same pipeline unit, whereas conventional pipelining receives instructions from only a single stream.

There are four central processors and four I/O processors in the Univac 1100/94 (Fig. 2.2). Two *integrated scientific processors* (ISPs) are attached to form a supercomputer, because each ISP is equipped with high-speed hardware for scalar and vector arithmetic computations. Sixteen million words of main storage are shared by 10 processors through multiple data paths as shown in Fig. 2.2. The major architectural advantage of this system lies in its availability, reliability, and maintainability [Sperry 85] due to its modular construction. What interests us here is the control of concurrent activities in the system. An *activity* is the unit of work scheduled for the ISP. Each activity is explicitly dispatched by the 1100/94 system.

Three activity control mechanisms are used in an ISP: the *mailbox,* the *status register,* and the *processor control box.* The mailbox is used

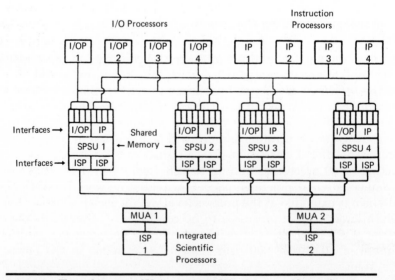

Figure 2.2   The architecture of Univac 1100/94/ISP. (*Courtesy of Sperry Corp.*)

to convey information between the 1100/94 system and the ISPs. Each ISP has a mailbox occupying 8 words in the shared memory. When an activity is initiated, it contains a pointer to the processor control box assigned for the activity. At activity termination, the mailbox is loaded with the contents of the hardware status register to report the termination status. The control box, also residing in the shared memory, contains information needed to process the activity. Another method is to use the *scoreboard* originally used in CDC 7600 series to match ready-to-run instructions with the available functional units in the processor.

Dynamic scheduling of concurrent processes depends on run-time conditions. Optimal schedules are computationally intractable. However, there are many heuristics one can select, such as *first-in–first-out, round-robin, shortest-process-first,* or *least-memory-demand-first,* etc. [Gajski 85, Hwang 84]. Static scheduling can be made at compile time, and it is easier to implement but potentially results in poor processor utilizations. The *trace scheduling* [Fisher 81] of loop-free code offers such an approach. The trace scheduling compiler generates code blocks that can be executed in parallel without going through vectorization. The above mechanisms have been practiced in many commercial machines. Other new approaches include data-driven and demand-driven mechanisms which have been proposed in developing dataflow [Dennis 80] and reduction machines, respectively. At present, these new mechanisms are still in the research stage.

2.2.2 Interprocessor communications schemes

Processors form the major working force in a supercomputer. Information items communicating among multiple processors include synchronization primitives, status semaphores, interrupt signals, variable-size messages, shared variables, and data values. Interprocessor communications are achieved essentially by four methods: *shared variables, message passing, marker passing,* and *value passing.* These methods are implemented with shared memory, shared registers, communication buffers, concurrency control or interrupt buses, interprocessor connection rings, or networks as summarized in Table 2.5. Various interconnection networks for parallel processing have been summarized in Siegel [84].

Shared variables are often stored in the common memory shared by many processors. Many tightly coupled multiprocessors use shared memory as a major means of communication between processors such as the Cray series and in the Encore/Multimax multiprocessor [Bell 85]. Besides shared central memory, the ETA-10 uses a communication buffer for fast transfer of information among central processors and I/O processors [ETA 86]. Tagged shared variables are used for

TABLE 2.5   Interprocessor Communication Schemes in Modern Supercomputers

System model	Hardware supporting structures	Communication mechanisms
Cray X-MP	Shared memory, shared register clusters	Semaphore and shared variables
ETA-10	Communication buffer, shared memory	Shared variables and synchronization functions
HEP-1	Shared memory	Tagged variables
iPSC	Hypercube interconnect	Message passing (packet switched)
Cyberplus	Multiple rings	Message passing (packet switched)
Multimax	Common bus/shared memory	Data transfer via bus
Alliant FX/8	Concurrency control bus, shared cache/memory	Synchronization via special bus
Connection Machine	Hypercube/mesh connections	Maker/message passing
Boltzmann machine	AI machine using virtual connections	Value passing
BBN Butterfly	Butterfly switching network	Shared variables in distributed memory
IBM RP3	Multistage network	Shared variables and message passing
IBM GF11	SIMD network	SIMD broadcasting
FLEX/32	Multiple bus and shared memory	Message passing
Elxsi 6400	Bus and shared memory	Message passing
FPS T-Series	Hypercube/transputer	OCCAM channel commands

synchronizing concurrent processes in the HEP [Smith 81]. Using shared memory for large data movement between processors, the Cray X-MP uses clusters of shared registers for direct communications of semaphores or status information between processors as illustrated in Fig. 2.3. If not properly handled, synchronization may become a major barrier to parallel processing [Axelrod 86].

For an n-processor Cray X-MP, the shared registers can be clustered into $n + 1$ nondisjoint clusters of processors [Chen 85]. Each cluster has eight 24-bit shared addresses, eight 64-bit shared scalar and 32 one-bit semaphore registers. These shared registers allow direct passing of scalar data and semaphores between two, three, or four processors per cluster. There are four ports to each cluster for the four CPUs

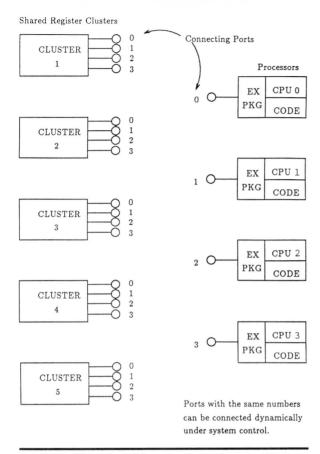

Figure 2.3   Clustering of shared registers for inter-CPU communications in the Cray X-MP-4.

in the X-MP/4 system. The COS operating system dynamically allocates the clusters to CPUs. An allocated cluster may be accessed by the CPU in either user mode or supervisor mode. Any number of processors (two, three, or four) can be clustered together to perform multiple tasks of a single job. Such a dynamic multitasking is the key improvement of the X-MP over the Cray 1.

Message passing is popular among loosely coupled, distributed-memory multicomputers, such as the hypercube-structured iPSC [Graham 87], FPS T-series [Hawkinson 87], NCUBE [Palmer 87], and the ring-structured Cyberplus [Ferrante 87]. Passing messages of arbitrary sizes and performing complex operations on these messages demand quite powerful node processors. The hypercube topology has the advantage of being uniformly structured with $\log_2 N$ diameter. However, for a very large number of processor-memory nodes (N), the

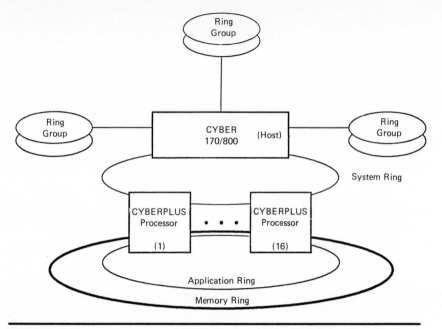

Figure 2.4 Interprocessor communication structure in the CDC Cyberplus parallel processing system.

contention and traffic congestion problems may introduce appreciable communication overhead among the nodes. The CDC Cyberplus chooses a less costly multiring structure for packet-switched message passing among the processors as illustrated in Fig. 2.4.

The Cyberplus ring structure differs from the bus structure in Multimax [Bell 85], Elexi 6400 [McGrogan 87], and Sequent 8000 [Sequent 85] in that the ring carries $2n$ data packets simultaneously in the ring which links n processors. The traditional system bus can carry only one data element at a time. The Cyberplus configuration consists of a maximum of four ring groups with 16 Cyberplus processors (accelerators) per group. Each group has two rings: the 16-bit *system ring* provides communications between the Cyberplus processors and the host Cyber processor, say a CDC Cyber 180/990; and the 16-bit *application ring* provides direct communications between the Cyberplus processors themselves.

Each Cyberplus processor has 14 functional units for memory accesses and integer operations plus an optional 5 floating-point units. The 19 functional units can operate in parallel under the coordination of a scoreboard which helps set up the crossbar to direct the flow of data among the functional units and initiate the simultaneous operation of all functional units in each machine cycle of 21 ns. This implies that each Cyberplus processor can potentially perform 620 MIPS and up to 98 MFLOPS.

Besides the dual rings, an additional *memory ring* can be added to provide direct memory-to-memory communications among Cyberplus processors and between two 64-bit memories. Sustained data transfer rates of 100 to 800 Mbytes/s are built into the system. This multiring scheme offers direct processor-to-processor and memory-to-memory communications, which are highly desirable features in a parallel system. In Alliant FX/8 (Fig. 2.5), a *concurrency control bus* is used for synchronizing activities in different processors [Alliant 87].

In a *marker passing* system, the communication among processing cells (often with RISC or bit-slice structures) is done by passing single-bit markers. Each processing cell can handle a few marker bits with simple boolean operations. These cells are connected by a hypercube such as in the Connection Machine [Hillis 85], in which all cells operate in lockstep synchronously under one external control. The markers in a collection represent entities with a common property and are identified in a single broadcast, thus synchronization can be avoided. *Value passing* systems pass around continuous numbers and perform simple arithmetic operations on these values. Multiple values arriving at a processor simultaneously are combined into a single value; hence contention will not happen and synchronization is unnecessary. Neural networks and Boltzmann machines have been proposed to use this scheme [Fahlman 87]. The marker passing and value passing are primarily used in AI-oriented processing as discussed in Chaps. 4 and 7.

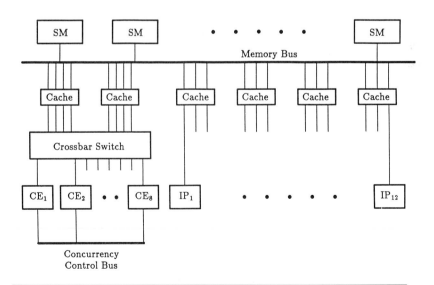

Figure 2.5   The architecture of the Alliant FX/8 system with 8 computational elements and 12 interactive processors. CE = computational elements; IP = interactive processors; SM = shared-memory modules.

2.2.3   Reconfigurable interconnection networks

Two recent approaches to constructing reconfigurable interconnection networks are discussed: one is the IBM GF11 using a *reconfigurable multistage network* for inter-PE communications in an SIMD mode, and the other is the *programmable crossbar network* proposed with the pipeline nets for constructing dynamically reconfigurable systolic arrays.

The IBM GF11 is a modified SIMD computer conceived primarily for the numerical solution of problems in quantum chromodynamics [Beetam 85]. As illustrated in Fig. 2.6, the machine incorporates 576 floating-point processors, each with its own 2 Mbytes of memory and capable of 20 MFLOPS, giving the total machine over 1 Gbytes of memory and a peak processing speed of more than 11 GFLOPS. The floating-point processors are interconnected by a high-speed Benes network, a nonblocking network capable of realizing configurations incorporating any permutation of the processors. Using this network, GF11 can be programmed to assume a number of different topologies, such as a rectangular mesh of any dimension and size, a torus, a hexagonal mesh, or some irregular organization matching with a special problem. A central controller is used to broadcast instructions to all processors and the interconnection network, and also to communicate with a host computer.

The GF11 architecture is shown in Fig. 2.6. Each stage of the Memphis switch consists of 24 crossbar switches. The middle stage is connected to the outer stages by "perfect shuffle" fixed interconnections. By suitable configurations of the crossbars it is possible to realize any permutation of the 576 inputs. All data paths are 9 bits wide: 8 data bits plus a parity bit. The data rate on each path is 20 Mbytes/s; for 576 processors the aggregate data rate is 11.5 Gbytes/s. The 24-24 crossbar switching is accomplished using a high-speed semicustom CMOS gate array.

For most applications, only a few switch configurations are required. For example, if the application involves a two-dimensional mesh where only nearest neighbors are important, just four configurations are needed: send north, send south, send east, and send west. A four-dimensional torus requires only eight. The GF11 network allows up to 1024 distinct configurations, enough to cover a wide variety of applications and allow easy communication with nonadjacent neighbors.

An efficient compound vector processing technique has been developed at the University of Southern California [Hwang 89] based on multipipeline networking. This new technique is generalized from the pipeline chaining in Cray supercomputers and systolic arrays introduced in recent years. A *pipeline net* can be viewed as a programmable

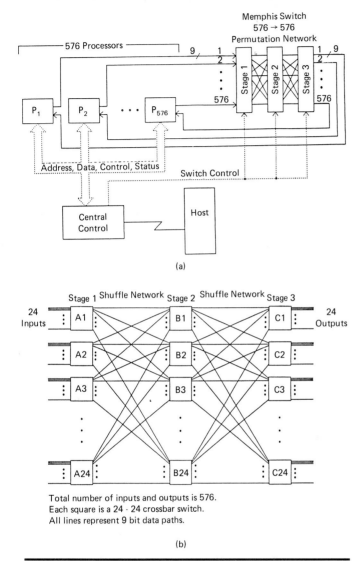

Figure 2.6 The architecture of the IBM GF11. (*a*) GF11 architecture; (*b*) the reconfigurable switching network.

systolic array, which can be dynamically reconfigured to evaluate various vector compound functions. In other words, pipeline nets exploit parallelism in user program graphs with the efficient use of multiple functional pipelines in a vector supercomputer. The reconfigurability of a pipeline net provides the flexibility in implementing most Livermore loops, matrix algebra, complex arithmetic, polynomial evaluation, and signal/image processing algorithms.

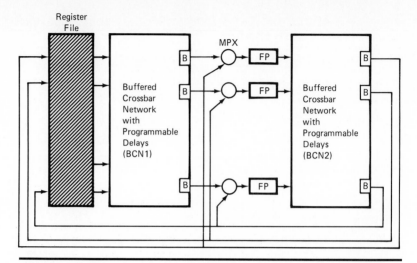

Figure 2.7   The logical structure of a pipeline net showing interconnecting multiple functional pipelines with buffered crossbar networks having programmable   delays.   FP = functional   pipeline;   MPX = multiplexer, B = programmable delays (buffer). [Hwang 88]

The concept of pipeline net is briefly introduced in Fig. 2.7. Two buffered crossbar switches are used to provide dynamic interconnections among the *functional pipelines* (FPs). All FPs are multifunctional, and they do not have to operate in lockstep. In other words, different functions can be performed by different FPs at the same time. The buffers are attached at the output ports of the crossbar switch, and these buffers are programmable in the sense that noncompute delay can be inserted at any data path to be established by the crossbar switches.

The pipeline net supports arbitrary connections among the FPs. Regular local connections as necessary in a static systolic array are no longer a structural constraint in a pipeline net. However, the systolic flow of data through a pipeline net is preserved, the same as in a systolic array. For example, when two operand streams arrive at a certain pipeline unit, they may have traversed through different data paths with unequal delays. These path delays must be equalized in order to have the correct operand pairs arriving at the right place at the right time. Delay matching is handled by the programmable crossbar switches. In this sense, we consider a pipeline net as a *dynamic* systolic array, which uses a two-level pipelining structure; i.e., all processing cells (the FPs) are themselves pipelined and the buffered crossbar connections are also pipelined. Detailed comparisons of *pipe-*

line nets, systolic arrays, and *switch latches* (the Chip project [Snyder 82]) have been given in Hwang [88].

2.3 Parallel Memory and I/O
Multiprocessing

In this section, we study the memory and I/O requirements in supporting parallel processing on a supercomputer. Innovative multimemory organizations and their access methods are evaluated. Then we examine how I/O bandwidth can be widened with the use of multiple I/O processors.

2.3.1 Memory hierarchy and access methods

Besides being faster in speed, supercomputers must have large physical memory space. The early supers, like Cray 1, use physical memory only in a single-user batch-processing mode. Most second-generation supers and minisupers are adapting Unix in an interactive mode, which implies that virtual memory becomes necessary for multiple users to share the memory space, besides using only physical main memory. Memory hierarchy, allocation schemes, and accessing methods in ETA-10 [ETA 86], Cedar [Kuck 86], IBM RP3 [Pfister 85], and OMP [Hwang 88*a*] are examined below. The memory structure in these systems represents state-of-the-art approaches to establishing efficient physical memory and extremely large virtual space for the next generation of supercomputers.

The ETA-10 system is a shared-memory multiprocessor super-computer, extended from the earlier CDC Cyber 205. The architecture of ETA-10 is shown in Fig. 2.8. The system consists of 8 central processors and up to 18 I/O processors under the coordination of a service processor and is targeted to have a peak performance of 10 GFLOPS. All 27 processors have access to the large shared memory and the communication buffer. The memory hierarchy is shown in Fig. 2.8*b*. Essentially, there are four levels of memory. The large register file is managed by the compilers running on ETA-10. The central processor memory is local to each CPU. The shared memory (256 Mwords or 2 Gbytes) sets the limit of the physical space for active files. The disk storage, with a capacity as large as trillions of bytes, is controlled by the I/O units. Virtual memory space consists of 248 logical addresses. All user programs and a large portion of the ETA-10 system code run in this space. Acting as a mechanism for interprocessor communications, the communication buffer is not a direct part of the virtual memory support system. Instead, it provides fast locking and synchronizing functions.

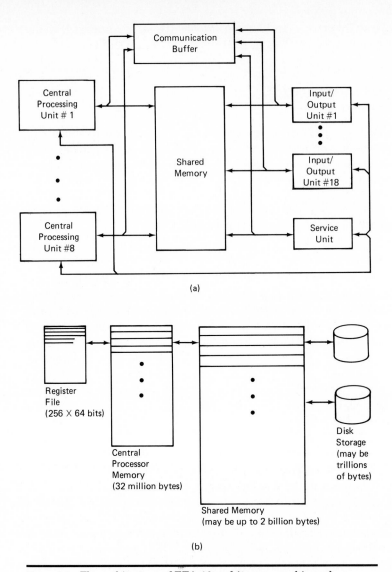

Figure 2.8   The architecture of ETA-10 and its memory hierarchy.
(*a*) System components; (*b*) memory hierarchy.

The Cedar system is one of the largest supercomputer projects under development in a university environment [Kuck 86]. Figure 2.9 shows the hierarchical structure of the Cedar. Multiple levels of parallelism and dynamic adaptability to run-time conditions are the key features of this supercomputer. The main objective of the project is to demonstrate that parallel processing can deliver high performance across a wide range of applications. The system is targeted to use eight clus-

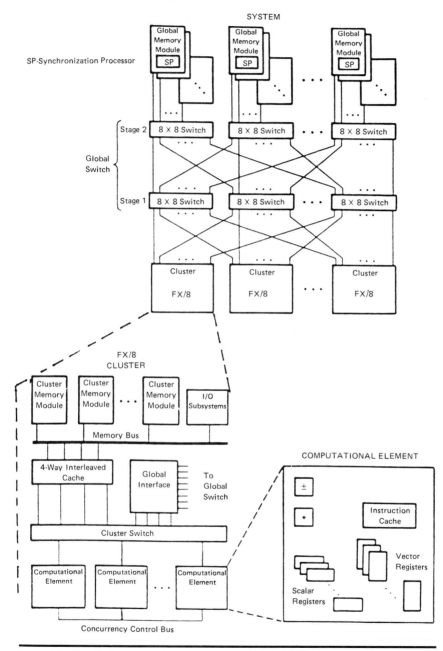

Figure 2.9 The Cedar research supercomputer prototype. [Kuck 86]

ters of processors; each cluster is currently built with the Alliant FX/8 processors running Unix. The global memory is shared by all clusters through the two-stage global switches. These are two sets of unidirectional crossbar switches which are pipelined with input buffers. *Within each cluster, there are three additional levels of memories: the registers* in the computational element, the *interleaved caches,* and the *cluster memories.*

Communications among all levels are done through the cluster switch, the cluster memory bus, and the intercluster global switches. The global memory is used for intercluster shared data and synchronization, for streaming long-vector access, and as a fast backup memory for cluster memory. Besides the standard FX/8 hardware, the University of Illinois has developed the *global interface unit* within each cluster, the *global switch,* and the *global memory.* It would be interesting to check the performance data once the prototype is complete. An *interactive supercompiler* is being developed for Cedar, which is partially discussed in Chap. 11. The target applications of Cedar include the simulation of aerodynamic flows, dynamic structural analysis, oil explorations, etc.

The *Research Parallel Processing Prototype* (RP3) is being undertaken at the IBM Watson Research Center [Pfister 85] in conjunction with the New York University Ultracomputer Project [Gottlieb 83, Schwartz 80]. This experimental project aims at investigating the hardware and software aspects of highly parallel computations. The RP3 is an MIMD system consisting of 512 state-of-the-art 32-bit microprocessors with a RISC architecture and a fast interconnection network (Fig. 2.10). The full configuration will provide 1300 MIPS or 800 MFLOPS, if fully utilized. The system will run on a modified version of BSD 4.2 Unix operating system. The RP3 can be configured as a shared-memory system, as a message-passing system with localized memories, or as mixtures of these two paradigms. Furthermore, the system can be partitioned into completely independent submachines by controlling the degree of memory interleaving.

Figure 2.10*b* shows how the global address space is distributed across the processors in the RP3. Part of each local memory is allocated to form the global memory. True local memory is accessed via the cache without going through the interconnection network. The dynamic partitioning of memory is determined at run time. Moving the local/global boundary to the far right makes RP3 a pure shared-memory machine like the ultracomputer. Moving it to the far left makes it a pure local-memory multicomputer using message passing. Intermediate boundary positions provide a mixed mode of computation. The architecture allows shared-memory-oriented applications to allocate private data locally to improve efficiency, while message-oriented applications use the global memory to balance the work load.

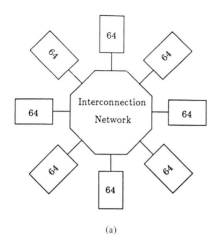

(a)

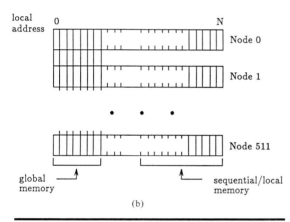

(b)

Figure 2.10 The IBM RP3 architecture. (*a*) RP3
with 64* 8 = 5/2 processors; (*b*) dynamic memory allocation.

A *hot spot* is said to occur at a memory module if it receives more than
the average number of memory references from the processors. Hot
spots are expected to occur, typically at shared-memory locations
which contain synchronization mechanisms, shared data, common
queues, etc. [Norton 85].

Recently, a new MIMD multiprocessor architecture has been proposed independently by the two research groups at the University of
Southern California and Princeton. We call the architecture an *orthogonal multiprocessor* (OMP) as shown in Fig. 2.11. An OMP consists of n processors and n^2 memory modules connected with n orthogonally used buses. OMP is considered a partially shared memory

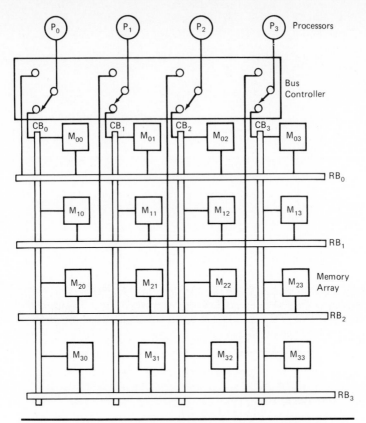

Figure 2.11 The orthogonal multiprocessor (OMP) architecture for $n = 4$ processors. RB = row bus, CB = column bus. [Hwang 89]

multiprocessor. Memory module M_{ij} is shared by only two processors P_i and P_j. Each of the diagonal modules serves as a local memory, i.e. M_{ii} is accessible only by P_i. The organization enables parallel accesses of row memories or of column memories by all processors simultaneously. A bus controller coordinates the switching between the row buses (RB_i) and the column buses (CB_i). The processors access the mesh of memories orthogonally. This is particularly attractive in implementing those parallel algorithms which have the orthogonal memory access patterns, such as are often found in matrix arithmetic, signal and image processing, linear programming, and the solution of PDE problems. These and other applications of the OMP architecture for parallel processing can be found in Hwang [89] and Scherson [88].

2.3.2 I/O multiprocessing and front end

Many supercomputing tasks are I/O-bound, especially those in a real-time environment. High-speed CPU operations alone cannot solve such I/O-bound problems efficiently. We have chosen the I/O architectures in Cray 2, ETA-10, Convex C-1, and Alliant FX/8 to discuss how parallel processing can be applied to solve the I/O bottleneck problem. The I/O problems can be greatly alleviated with the use of larger central memory. What we wish to achieve is to transform I/O-bound problems into CPU-bound ones with the practice of concurrent I/O operations.

In Cray 2 [Cray 85], a *foreground processor* is used to handle all operating system (OS) and I/O functions. Four communication channels are used to connect the foreground processor to four background processors, peripheral controllers, and common memory. Data traffic travels directly between the controllers and the common memory of 256 Mwords. This I/O section greatly alleviates the communication bottleneck with the outside world. Cray 2 uses an interactive OS based on the Unix System V. Forty peripheral devices can be attached to these high-speed I/O channels. In ETA-10, 18 I/O processors are used to perform concurrent I/O operations as described in Fig. 2.8.*a*.

In the Alliant FX/8 (see Fig. 2.5), 12 *interactive processors* (IPs) are used to offload the computational complex by executing interactive user jobs, I/O, and other OS activities in parallel. Each IP is built around a Motorola 68012 microprocessor on a multibus card. The IP interfaces with the IP cache which provides access to global memory and to I/O devices via the multibus. A multibus *direct-memory access* (DMA) device can transfer data at 1.96 Mbytes/s. High system I/O throughput is achieved with multiple IPs. Each IP can sustain a bandwidth of 3.92 Mbytes/s to its associated cache.

In Convex C-1, five intelligent *channel control units* (CCUs) are attached to a high-speed bus. Each CCU is an autonomous I/O processor with its own local memory and cache. OS functions are distributed between the central processor and the CCUs. Interrupts and device driver routines are executed by the CCUs. The multibus I/O processor can support up to 18 controllers for a total of up to 80 device controllers. The high-speed parallel interface taps the user with an 80-Mbytes/s I/O bandwidth. The *service processor unit* (SPU) controls diagnostic program execution, initializes the CPU's functional units, and handles the OS functions.

The I/O architectures in the above systems indicate a clear trend in using multiple I/O channels in modern supercomputers. To match with the high I/O data transfer rate, the I/O processors must use high-speed cache (such as in the C-1 and FX/8) or communication buffer (as in the ETA-10 and Cray 2). These buffer memories form a staged memory system all the way from device controllers to the central memory. Concurrent I/O processing demands the use of a large number of I/O processors or communication channels. The *front end* is often a host computer that is used to support OS and I/O operations and to coordinate the operations between the back-end CPUs and the I/O subsystem.

2.4   Process Migration and Load Balancing

In this section, we discuss load balancing for multicomputers with distributed local memory attached to each processor. A *computer node* in a multicomputer consists of a processor and its local memory and I/O ports. Multiple computer nodes, or simply *nodes,* are linked by an interconnection structure such as a point-to-point network or a bus. There is no shared memory between the nodes. A multicomputer uses a distributed problem-solving paradigm characterized by localized computation and the use of message passing for internodal communication. All nodes work in common to solve the same problem under a *distributed operating system.* This is distinguished from a *network operating system,* which links computers that typically work on independent problems. Such a multinode architecture can be found in such architectures as the Intel iPSC, Connection Machine, and FPS T-Series.

In practice it is often true that the number of processes in a multicomputer exceeds the number of processors available. Thus a fundamental problem of distributed supercomputing is the effective allocation of processes to processors in order to achieve a balanced performance. Load balancing addresses this problem directly by providing a self-scheduling mechanism by which the multicomputer can allocate a large number of processes to multiple processors automatically and efficiently. The purpose of load balancing is to promote better processor utilization, greater throughput, and faster response times. The need for load balancing arises when some processors in the system have heavy processing loads while other processors sit idle. When such a situation arises the load balancer will move some processing load from the busy to the idle processors.

2.4.1   Process migration requirements

The first issue to consider when designing a load-balancing system is the measure of load index to be used. Load measures that have appeared in the literature include *processing time, communications time, memory utilization,* and *the number of processes* [Lin 86]. Alternative measures of system load include *CPU idle time* and *the number of page faults.* The selected load measure will in turn determine what is considered an *idle* and a *busy* node. The classification of a node as idle or busy can be varied by changing the *threshold* load level that divides idle and busy nodes. The application domain will determine the appropriate load measure and threshold level.

After a program is started, there will be an initialization period during which the system load will build as processes are spawned and migrated to other processors. Load balancing is not an efficient way to accomplish the initial distribution of processes to processors, because the dynamic load balancing mechanism will not be triggered until the system load builds up. Predictive heuristics base load-balancing decisions on estimates of the future resource utilization of processes. Real-time deadlines occur in industrial control systems such as nuclear power plants and in military applications. In such systems, certain tasks must be performed exactly once in a given time cycle of fixed duration, and other tasks must be scheduled around these priority tasks. System stability may prevent tasks from being perpetually circulated by the load balancing system and never executed. Three requirements for dynamic load balancing through process migration are identified below:

1. The load of the system is expected to be unevenly distributed between processor nodes. The processor population needs to be split into idle and busy nodes; otherwise there will be no sense of load migration. What is considered idle or busy depends on the specific load index and threshold levels selected for each implementation. The system should have passed the initialization stage. Static (compile-time) load balancing methods can be used during the initialization.

2. The load incurred by subroutine calls during the execution of a program should be unpredictable. Applications whose subroutine loads can be predicted are best handled by static time load balancing techniques at compile time. Such static techniques avoid the runtime overhead inherent in any dynamic load-balancing system. However the static techniques cannot be used when the load is unpredictable. This is when a dynamic load balancing method should be used.

3. What is migrated during process migration? Both executable code and the binding context for the code could be migrated. In some systems a policy of complete code copying is employed so that a copy of every subroutine exists on every node. In this case there is no need for code migration. It is only necessary to send a message invoking the procedure to be migrated together with its context. This context consists simply of the state of all global variables. However, in some cases these objects could occupy several megabytes so that a significant overhead could be incurred in migration. One solution is to implement faster internodal communications with fast switches and high bandwidth interconnections. Another solution is to employ functional languages which have no binding context and hence avoid this problem altogether.

2.4.2 Dynamic load-balancing methods

In *dynamic load balancing,* processes are allocated to processors at run time. Processes automatically migrate from heavily loaded processors to lightly loaded ones. By attaining a well-balanced load, we can achieve better processor utilization and thus higher performance. For programs with unpredictable run-time resource utilization, dynamic load balancing is more desirable because it allows the system to continuously adapt to rapidly changing run-time conditions. Three dynamic load-balancing methods are introduced below.

The receiver-initiated method is initiated by the receiving processor using a drafting approach. Each receiving node sends requests for work and exchanges load information only with neighboring processors. A process can migrate only once to avoid the possibility of circulating processes. The local and external loads can be in one of three states. An *H-load* node is a candidate for migrating processes. An *N-load* node does not participate in load balancing. An *L-load node* requests work from H-load nodes in its neighborhood using a *drafting protocol* [Ni 85], such as using a draft age which is determined by the number of active processes handled by the processor. The drafting node will request a process from the node with the highest draft age among those responding. This is a very conservative policy, where migration only takes place after a lengthy drafting protocol.

The *sender-initiated method* is based on a *gradient* approach, in which the roles of the idle and busy processors are reversed, so that the busy processors initiate the load balancing [Lin 86]. The system exerts some control over the behaviors of the nodes by setting the neighborhood diameter and a static systemwide *threshold T*. The threshold serves dual purposes: First, a node will begin exporting processes only when its local load exceeds the threshold. Second, the threshold determines the load information propagated by the node in a lightly loaded system. The sender-initiated method has the advantage of immediately beginning process migration as soon as a node enters a heavily loaded state. There is no necessity to wait for lightly loaded nodes to engage in a lengthy protocol before migration begins. Once the system is saturated, this method becomes useless.

The receiver-initiated method acts in favor of heavily load systems, in which the network traffic can be minimized by restricting to, at most, one migration per process. The sender-initiated method is in favor of lightly loaded systems in which the load balancing process converges much faster. The *hybrid load-balancing method* uses the receiver-initiated drafting when the system load becomes excessive and uses the sender-initiated scheme when the system load is light. Intuitively, this hybrid method will result in better balanced loads among the node processors.

The hybrid method requires a distributed mechanism to manage the switching between sender-initiated and receiver-initiated modes of operation. Each node operates in either the sender-initiated or receiver-initiated mode depending on its local environment. All nodes are initialized to sender-initiated mode. A node will switch to receiver-initiated mode when more than a threshold number of its neighbors become heavily loaded. We refer to this threshold as the *hybrid threshold H* to distinguish it from the threshold value *T* that defines low and heavy load. If the number of heavily loaded neighbors falls below the hybrid threshold, the node switches back to sender-initiated mode.

In Chap. 9, the application of the hybrid load-balancing method for concurrent Lisp execution of AI-oriented Gabriel benchmarks is presented. Detailed software implementation of the hybrid load balancer, multicomputer hardware support, and some necessary OS functions are discussed there. Performance benchmark results, obtained on an Intel hypercube computer at the University of Southern California, Laboratory for Parallel and Distributed Computing, suggest that the hybrid method is indeed better for balancing unpredictable workload in a parallel computer [Chowkwanyun 88].

2.5   Performance Issues and Answers

Basic issues effecting the performance of today's parallel/vector processing systems are evaluated below for the best answers. Then we call for the consolidation of a new science of parallel computation. This new science will serve as the foundation for the future development of high-performance computers. Multidisciplinary cooperation is needed to achieve this goal.

2.5.1   Critical issues to achieve high performance

We summarize below the critical issues affecting the performance of supercomputers. Answers to these issues will be treated in subsequent chapters. Here, we enumerate them in order to acquaint our readers with the essential issues discussed in subsequent chapters.

Concurrent languages for parallel, vector, and symbolic processing. Existing programming languages need to be enriched for efficient implementation of parallel algorithms on modern computers. Extended language features are needed to exploit parallelism in either numerical or symbolic processing applications. Detailed treatments of these issues are given in Chaps. 4, 7, 9, 10, and 11, and, in particular, Sec. 10.2.1.

Vectorizing, parallelizing, and trace-scheduling compilers for automatic program optimization. Automatic vectorization, multitasking, and multiprocessing are needed to reduce the burdens of using parallel computers. These issues are treated in Chaps. 9, 10, 11, and 12.

Design and analysis of parallel algorithms and data structures. Sequentially coded algorithms cannot exploit parallelism. We have to modify the algorithms for parallel machines. These issues are treated in Sec. 10.4.1 and Chaps. 6, 8, and 14.

User-friendly parallel programming environment to be created. Besides languages, compilers, and algorithms, we need to create run-time software supports to maximize the resource utilization and thus to achieve higher system throughput. This topic is treated in Sec. 10.5 as well as in Chaps. 3 and 13.

Program partitioning and time-space tradeoffs for parallel processing. Software developers must divide problems into manageable chunks and ensure efficient communications between computing componants. In other words, divide-and-conquer-in-parallel is the key strategy in programming parallel processors. These topics are treated in Chaps. 2, 4, 8, 9, 10, 12, and 13.

Load balancing and resource allocation in parallel computers. Static load balancing at compile time is only appropriate for the well-partitioned problem with predetermined program behavior. For data-dependent parallelism, one must develop dynamic load balancing for run-time resource optimization. This is treated in Sec. 2.4 and Chaps. 6, 7, and 9.

Memory bandwidth and capacity planning in a hierarchy. The memory bandwidth must match with the multiprocessing bandwidth. Furthermore, capacity planning in a memory hierarchy plays a crucial role in dealing with large-scale scientific or AI applications. These are discussed in Chaps. 2, 3, 4, 6, and 7, and in particular, Sec. 2.3.1.

I/O multiprocessing and miscellaneous OS functions. I/O bound problems can be attacked with multiple I/O channels or I/O processors. Besides I/O parallelism, one must also develop other operating system functions to support parallel scheduling, communication synchronization, automatic process migration, load balancing, file management,

I/O supervision, and system performance monitoring. Chapters 2, 7, 8, and 10 have treated these issues.

Graphics and visualization on parallel supercomputers. High performance also implies high-resolution color graphics display of computing results. In a network environment, the resources and large database must be shared with low communication overhead. These issues are addressed in Chaps. 4, 7, 8, and 10.

Exploiting parallelism in AI computations. Both Lisp and Prolog machines demand a high degree of parallelism. These are studied in Chaps. 3, 4, 7, 9, and 13. The dataflow approach to AI is worthy of further experimentation as suggested in Chap. 14.

Exploring new computing technologies and new computing models. New technologies for supercomputing and AI include GaAs circuits, integrated optics, artificial neural networks, and superconducting connections, etc. New computing models include dataflow, reduction, connectionism, neural networks, and others. These new approaches, which are still in the research domain, are discussed in Chaps. 14, 15, and 16.

2.5.2 Toward a science of parallel computation

We have evaluated state-of-the-art supercomputer architectures and their concurrency control techniques. The intention is to bring together important issues and evaluate the best answers for higher performance. New research findings and high-risk hardware/software approaches are being transferred to the computer industry slowly. However, low-cost supercomputing is becoming a major driving force in high-tech markets. This has triggered the thought of personal supercomputers for the future.

The rise of the computer industry in producing minisupers, mainframe extensions, array processors, scientific workstations, AI machines, optical computers, and artificial neurocomputers has had a great impact on the development of future supercomputers. We conclude with the following observations: First, new technologies, innovative architectures, and more exotic computers will appear. Second, the cost of future supercomputers must be affordable in general-purpose applications. Third, a new generation of programmers must be trained to use supercomputers effectively. Fourth, we envision the emerging science of parallel computation, which serves as the foundation of supercomputing [Hwang 87a] and artificial intelligence [Uhr 87].

The way parallel computation is practiced today is quite ad hoc and lacks both theoretical foundations and engineering methodologies. In the past two decades, there have been growing demands for interdisciplinary communications toward the development of a new science of parallel computation. To develop such a scientific discipline, we may have to go through three phases: *exploratory, paradigmatic,* and *postparadigmatic.* The exploratory phase encourages competing paradigms to go through experimentation, observation, and classification stages, which are primarily driven by internal forces. The paradigmatic phase will produce different paradigms that organize the field. Research will focus on the accepted paradigms that are driven by both internal and external forces. The last phase must be based on well-tested theories of parallel computation. The discipline must be exploited to solve the real problems in society. At this stage the research will be driven largely by external forces.

At present, the state of parallel computation is still in the exploratory and paradigmatic phases. Gorden Bell has noted: "Many theories have been invalidated, stagnant, and sterile because of the lack of parallel computers. The core program in parallelism should provide the impetus so that all basic mathematical theory, hardware machines and operating systems, languages, algorithms and applications are inherently parallel within a decade." This clearly indicates the need of multidiscipline interactions. In fact, most research organizations and funding agencies are encouraging research in parallelism to be applied to supercomputing, automation, robotics, intelligent systems, knowledge engineering, scientific simulations, engineering designs, and distributed communications.

Multidiscipline interactions are demanded in parallel supercomputing. Four groups of professionals should be involved, namely, *theoreticians, experimentalists, computational scientists,* and *application engineers* [Rodrigue 80]. Applications drive the development of particular parallel processing software. The barriers lie in partial systems, confirmation bias, and lack of performance spectrum and project database. Comparative analysis is needed to determine the effectiveness, robustness, efficiency, extensibility, economy, ease of use, reliability, and maintainability of parallel systems and to broaden their application domains. Of course, we need the cooperation between academic and industrial communities to distribute new discoveries and to publish key concepts, principles, paradigms, and prescriptive terminologies. This could become one of the major thrusts in computer science/engineering education. The lack of vision in pushing this thrust area may slow down the future progress in science and technology.

Bibliography

[Alliant 87]   *Alliant FX/Series: Product Summary.* Alliant Computer Systems Corp., Acton, MA, June, 1987.

[Axelrod 86]   T.S. Axelrod. "Effects of Synchronization Barriers on Multiprocessor Performance." *Parallel Computing,* vol. 3, no. 2, pp. 129–140, May 1986.

[BBN 86]   *Butterfly Parallel Processor Overview.* BBN Labs., Inc., Version 1, March 1986.

[Beetam 85]   J. Beetam, M. Denneau, and D. Weingarten. "The GF11 Supercomputer." *Proceedings of the 12th Annual International Symposium on Computer Architecture,* pp. 108–115, June 1985.

[Bell 85]   C.G. Bell. "Multis: A New Class of Multiprocessor Computer." *Science,* vol. 228, pp. 462–467, 1985.

[Charlesworth 86]   A.L. Charlesworth and J.L. Gustafson. "Introducing Replicated VLSI to Supercomputing: The FPS-164/MAX Scientific Computer." *IEEE Computer,* vol. 19, no. 3, pp. 10–23, March 1986.

[Chen 85]   S.S. Chen. "Cray X-MP-4 Series." Cray Research Presentations, August 1985.

[Chin 84]   C.Y. Chin and K. Hwang. "Packet Switching Networks for Multiprocessors and Dataflow Computers." *IEEE Trans. Computers,* vol. C-33, pp. 991–1003, November 1984.

[Chowkwanyun 88]   R. Chowkwanyun and K. Hwang. "Concurrent Lisp Execution of AI-Oriented Gabriel Benchmarks with Hybrid Load Balancing." *Tech. Rep. CRI 88-29.* University of Southern California, Los Angeles, CA, May 1988.

[Cray 85]   *The Cray 2 Computer Systems.* Tech. Brochure, Cray Research Inc., 1985.

[Dennis 80]   J.B. Dennis. "Dataflow Supercomputer." *IEEE Computer,* vol. 13, no. 11, pp. 48–56, November 1980.

[Dongarra 86]   J.J. Dongarra. "A Survey of High Performance Computers." *Digest of Papers: IEEE Computer Society COMPCON,* pp. 8–11, Spring 1986.

[ETA 86]   *ETA-10 System Overview: Introduction.* Tech. Note, Publ. 1006, Revision A, ETA Systems, February 1986.

[Fahlman 87]   S.E. Fahlman and G.E. Hinton. "Connectionist Architectures for Artificial Intelligence." *IEEE Computer,* vol. 20, pp. 100–109, January 1987.

[Ferrante 87]   M.W. Ferrante. "Cyberplus and Map V Interprocessor Communications for Parallel and Array Processor Systems." In W.J. Karplus (ed). *Multiprocessors and Array Processors,* pp. 45–54, Simulation Councils, Inc., San Diego, CA, January 1987.

[Fisher 81]   J.A. Fisher. "Trace Scheduling: A Technique for Global Microcode Compaction." *IEEE Trans. Computers,* vol. C-30, no. 7, pp. 478–490, July 1981.

[Flynn 72]   M.J. Flynn. "Some Computer Organizations and Their Effectiveness." *IEEE Trans. Computers,* vol. C-21, pp. 948–960, September 1972.

[Fox 86]   G. Fox. "Questions and Unexpected Answers in Concurrent Computation." Tech. Rep. No. CP-288. Cal Tech Concurrent Computation Program, California Institute of Technology/Jet Propulsion Labs, Pasadena, CA, June 1986.

[Gajski 85]   D. Gajski and J.K. Pier. "Essential Issues in Multiprocessor Systems." *IEEE Computer,* vol. 18, no. 6, pp. 9–28, June 1985.

[Goodman 81]   J.R. Goodman and C.H. Sequin. "Hypertree: A Multiprocessor Interconnection Topology." *IEEE Trans. Computers,* vol. C-30, no. 12, pp. 923–933, December, 1981.

[Gottlieb 83]   A. Gottlieb, R. Grishman, R. Kruskal, C.P. McAalifte, K.P. Randolph, and M. Snir. "The NYU Ultracomputer-Designing an MIMD Shared Memory Parallel Computer." *IEEE Trans. Computers,* vol. C-32, no. 2, pp. 175–189, February 1983.

[Graham 87]   J. Graham and J. Rattner. "Expert Computation on the iPSC Concurrent Computer." In W.J. Karplus (ed). *Multiprocessors and Array Processors,* pp. 167–176, Simulation Councils, Inc., San Diego, CA, January 1987.

[Hawkinson 87]   S. Hawkinson. "The FPS T Series: A Parallel Vector Super Computer." In W.J. Karplus (ed). *Multiprocessors and Array Processors,* pp. 147–156, Simulation Councils, Inc., San Diego, CA, January 1987.

[Hillis 85]   W.D. Hillis. *The Connection Machine.* MIT Press, Cambridge, MA, 1985.

[Hwang 84]   K. Hwang (ed). *Supercomputers: Design and Applications.* IEEE Computer Society Press, Silver Spring, MD, August 1984.

[Hwang 87a]   K. Hwang. "Advanced Parallel Processing with Supercomputer Architectures." *Proceedings of the IEEE,* pp. 1348–1379, October 1987.

[Hwang 87b]   K. Hwang and J. Ghosh. "Hypernet: A Communication-Efficient Architecture for Constructing Massively Parallel Computers." *IEEE Trans. Computers,* December 1987.

[Hwang 88]   K. Hwang and Z. Xu. "Pipeline Nets for Compound Vector Supercomputing." *IEEE Trans. Computers,* pp. 32–47, January 1988.

[Hwang 89]   K. Hwang, P.S. Tseng, and D. Kim. "An Orthogonal Multiprocessor for Large-Grain Scientific Computations." *IEEE Trans. Computers,* January 1989.

[Jordan 83]   H.F. Jordan. "Performance Measurement of HEP-A Pipelined MIMD Computer." *Proceedings of the 10th Annual Symposium on Computer Architecture,* pp. 207–212, June 1983.

[Jordan 86]   H.F. Jordan. "Structuring Parallel Algorithms in an MIMD, Shared Memory Environment." *Parallel Computing,* pp. 93–110, May 1986.

[Karplus 87]   W.J. Karplus (ed). *Multiprocessors and Array Processors.* The Society of Computer Simulation, San Diego, CA, January 1987.

[Kuck 86]   D.J. Kuck, E.S. Davidson, D.H. Lawrie, and A.H. Sameh. "Parallel Supercomputing Today and the Cedar Approach." *Science,* vol. 231, pp. 967–974, February 1986.

[Lin 86]   F.C. Lin and R.M. Keller. "Gradient Model: A Demand-Driven Load Balancing Scheme." *IEEE Conference on Distributed Systems,* pp. 329–336, 1986.

[McGrogan 87]   S.K. McGrogan. "Modifying Algorithms to Achieve Greater than Linear Performance Improvements on the ELXSI 6400 Multiprocessor." In W.J. Karplus (ed). *Multiprocessors and Array Processors,* pp. 103–110, Simulation Councils, Inc., San Diego, CA, January 1987.

[Ni 85]   L.M. Ni, C. Xu, and T.B. Gendreau. "A Distributed Drafting Algorithm for Load Balancing." *IEEE Trans. on Computers,* vol. SE-11, no. 10, pp. 1153–1161, October 1985.

[Norton 85]   V.A. Norton and G.F. Pfister. "A Methodology for Predicting Multiprocessor Performance." *Proceedings of the 1985 International Conference on Parallel Processing,* pp. 772–781, August 1985.

[Ortega 85]   J.M. Ortega and R.G. Voigt. "Solution of PDEs on Vector and Parallel Computers." *SIAM Review,* vol. 27, pp. 149–240, June 1985.

[Palmer 87]   J.F. Palmer. "The NCUBE Family of Parallel Supercomputers." In W.J. Karplus (ed). *Multiprocessors and Array Processors,* pp. 177–187, Simulation Councils, Inc., San Diego, CA, January 1987.

[Pfister 85]   G.F. Pfister, W.C. Brantley, D.A. George, S.L. Harvey, W.J. Kleinfelder, K.P. McAuliffe, E.A. Melton, V.A. Norton, and J. Weiss. "The IBM Research Parallel Processor Prototype (RP3): Introduction and Architecture." *International Conference on Parallel Processing,* pp. 764–771, August 1985.

[Rodrigue 80]   G. Rodrigue, E.D. Giroux, and M. Pratt. "Perspective on Large-Scale Scientific Computation." *IEEE Computer,* pp. 65–80, October 1980.

[Scherson 88]   I.D. Scherson and Y. Ma. "Orthogonal Access Multiprocessing: An Architecture for Numerical Applications." *J. of Parallel and Distributed Computing,* December 1988.

[Schwartz 80]   J.T. Schwartz. "Ultracomputers." *ACM Trans. Programming Languages and Systems,* pp. 484–521, April 1980.

[Sequent 85]   *Balance 8000 System Technical Summary.* Sequent Computer Systems, Inc., Beaverton, OR, December 1985.

[Siegel 84]   H.J. Siegel. *Interconnection Networks for Large-Scale Parallel Processing.* Lexington Books, Boston, MA, 1984.

[Smith 81]   B.J. Smith. "Architecture and Applications of the HEP Multiprocessor Computer System." *Real-Time Signal Processing IV,* vol. 298, pp. 241–248, August 1981.

[Snyder 82]   L. Snyder. "Introduction to the Configurable, Highly Parallel Computer." *IEEE Computer,* vol. 15, pp. 47–64, January 1982.

[Sperry 85]   Sperry Corporation. *Sperry Integrated Processor System.* P.O. Box 64942, St. Paul, MN 55164, 1985.

[Uhr 87]   L. Uhr. *Parallel Multicomputer Architectures for Artificial Intelligence.* Wiley Interscience, New York, NY, 1987.

Design Requirements for Concurrent Lisp Machines

Robert H. Halstead, Jr.

MIT Laboratory for Computer Science, Cambridge, MA

3.1 Introduction

Major increases in computing power in the future are likely to be achieved by exploiting concurrency. The challenges of concurrent computing for symbolic applications differ in several ways from the better understood challenges of concurrent numerical computing. Several languages derived from Lisp have been proposed as vehicles for concurrent symbolic computing. This chapter surveys these languages and then identifies 11 challenges to architects of concurrent Lisp machines. One promising architectural response to these challenges features simple "smart memory" operations executed directly in memory modules, along with multiple register sets in each processing module that can be used to reduce the cost of procedure invocation, process creation, and context switching. Other aspects of concurrent Lisp machines are also treated in Chaps. 4, 7, and 9.

Because of limitations due to the laws of physics, it is widely believed that future breakthroughs in high-performance computing must come from learning how to use concurrency. Up to now, the greatest amount of activity in this area has been in the area of numerical computing. Progress in high-performance symbolic computing has lagged behind. Two major reasons for this are that numerical computing is currently more important economically and that numerical computing is richer in algorithms which are relatively easy to analyze and parallelize. Many numerical programs use vectors and matrices extensively to represent data; loops with numerical indices and predictable behavior are also common. These properties of the typical numerical program can be used effectively in relatively simple architectures to generate concurrency through pipelining as in the Cray series of machines [Russell 78] or other parallel structures such as the Cosmic Cube [Seitz 85] or the Alliant FX/8.

Symbolic computing seems less orderly and predictable than numerical computing because the sequence of operations performed is usually more data-dependent than with numerical computing. Consequently, the relatively straightforward techniques for generating concurrency that have been successful in many numerical programs are less successful in symbolic programs [Lee 85]. On the other hand, a growing body of work outlines other techniques that show promise for parallel symbolic computing [Halstead 86b, Steele 86]. The preeminent programming language for symbolic computing today is Lisp, so a machine capable of using concurrency to achieve high performance in executing a Lisplike language would be an attractive delivery vehicle for these new ideas. Consequently, this chapter explores the design of concurrent Lisp machines.

The design of a computer does not occur in a vacuum; the programming languages and application programs that the computer is intended to support must be considered. Therefore, we begin in Sec. 3.2 with a survey of current ideas on how to use concurrency with Lisp and a discussion of some properties of symbolic programs. We continue in Sec. 3.3 with an analysis of concurrent Lisp machine design requirements, ultimately identifying 11 challenges a concurrent Lisp machine must meet. Section 3.4 then discusses some high-level design issues in a relatively architecture independent way, after which Sec. 3.5 deepens the exploration by means of an example. Finally, Sec. 3.6 assesses progress to date and discusses where more work needs to be done. The picture that emerges is of a young field where there are many more questions than answers; however, the picture also includes many exciting ideas which, although not yet worked out in detail and tested, show great promise of future progress.

3.2 Concurrent Lisp Languages

There is no unanimity on the question of what a concurrent Lisp language should look like. Proposed Lisplike languages for programming parallel machines run the gamut from unmodified Common Lisp through a variety of Lisp dialects with added operators for producing and controlling parallelism.

A common characteristic of virtually all proposed concurrent Lisp languages is that they use a *shared-memory* model of data: data objects (such as Lisp cons cells) created during execution are considered to belong to the whole concurrent program, rather than to any particular process or processor. Whether or not the underlying machine has a shared-memory architecture, any part of a concurrent Lisp program can access any data to which it can obtain a pointer. This can be done without any explicit operations in the program to copy data from one domain or location to another, and without any syntactic distinction between access to "locally created" and "remotely created" objects. Not only is there no syntactic distinction between local and remote accesses, but the programmer is encouraged, to the first order, to treat all accesses as having approximately equal cost. Thus, it is assumed that access times to data stored at different places in the machine do not differ so significantly from each other that the location of data should be taken into account when a program is written. This philosophy contrasts with that of languages such as Communicating Sequential Processes [Hoare 78], where strongly different linguistic constructs and, implicitly, performance characteristics are associated with operations local to a process and communication between processes. *Prototype* concurrent Lisp language implementations may not adhere to the shared-memory ideal, but virtually all concurrent Lisp projects have as an ultimate objective an implementation that achieves this ideal.

Beyond this shared characteristic, Lisp languages proposed for programming concurrent machines diverge. The proposed languages fall into three major groups: unmodified sequential Lisps, Lisps with all side-effect primitives removed, and Lisps including both side-effect primitives and explicit concurrency primitives.

3.2.1 Unmodified sequential Lisps

A combination of compile-time and ɪun-time analysis can be used to discover portions of an unmodified sequential Lisp program that may be executed concurrently without changing the program's result from that which would have been produced by sequential execution. Side effects are the chief concern in either kind of analysis. At compile time, interprocedural analysis can show which pairs of procedures interact via side effects. Noninteracting procedures (or other groups of code) that are not related by data dependencies can then be scheduled for execution in parallel. The Bath Concurrent Lisp Machine [Marti 83] exemplifies this approach.

An alternative technique that relies more on run-time analysis begins by dividing each program into *atomicity blocks*. These blocks are executed in parallel, using concurrency control methods that borrow heavily from the theory of running concurrent atomic transactions against a database. Blocks are executed concurrently, but the side effects performed by a block are only tentative until the block "commits." Blocks commit in the order in which a sequential computer would have executed them. If the currently committing block has performed a side effect on a value already read by a not yet committed block, the uncommitted computation is invalid and must be aborted and performed again. Several different mechanisms for detecting and handling such conflicts are plausible [Katz 86, Knight 86]. Mixtures of these run-time strategies with automated compile-time analysis are also plausible.

Both compile-time and run-time methods function best when side effects are rare. If side effects are numerous, compile-time analysis will have difficulty finding pairs of modules that can run safely in parallel; run-time methods will suffer a high rate of aborting and reexecuting of blocks if interactions due to side effects are common. Fortunately, a "nearly functional" programming style, using few side effects, is well supported in Lisp. Lisp's **let** construct obviates most uses of side effects for saving intermediate results. Lisp's **do** and **loop** constructs (or equivalent use of tail-recursive procedures [Abelson 84] in a tail-recursive Lisp dialect such as Scheme [Rees 86]) allow loops to be expressed without explicit use of side effects. Looping and saving intermediate results account for most of the side effects in programs written in conventional algebraic languages (as well as many avoidable side effects in typical Lisp programs). Interestingly, since side effects are not needed for performing these functions in Lisp, it is actually quite feasible to delay teaching side effects to students of Lisp until they have already written many powerful programs in a side-effect-free sublanguage of Lisp [Abelson 84]. In practice, the use of side effects in Lisp can be limited to cases where mutability is a fairly integral part of the description of an algorithm, for example, an algorithm that traverses a graph, leaving a mark at each node that has been visited.

When a compile-time analyzer is used to find parallelism in an unmodified sequential Lisp program, one may imagine the analyzer's output to take the form of a Lisp program in a target language that includes side effects and explicit concurrency. The Lisp languages discussed in Sec. 3.2.3 would be suitable target languages for this task, and thus any concurrent Lisp machine adept at executing programs in those languages would suffice for parallel execution of sequential Lisp programs after compile-time analysis as well. Run-time mechanisms for concurrent execution of unmodified sequential Lisp programs seem to require some specialized hardware support [Knight 86], but the costs and potential performance benefits of such approaches are still largely unexplored. Due to the reasons outlined in this paragraph, we do not explicitly consider concurrent architecture for unmodified sequential Lisps any further in this chapter.

3.2.2 Side-effect-free Lisps

A second approach to concurrent Lisp execution takes the more radical approach of modifying Lisp by removing *all* primitives capable of causing side effects. The removal of side effects eliminates most of the difficulties of compile-time and run-time analysis discussed above, but at the expense of requiring fundamental redesign of algorithms depending on side effects, such as the graph-marking example mentioned above. The costs and benefits of this "functional programming" approach are currently the subject of great debate; however, it is notable that no current and widely known proposal for concurrent Lisp execution follows this path. The concept has honorable historical roots in the pioneering work of Friedman and Wise [Friedman 78], but the vast majority of functional programming advocates today seem to operate outside of the Lisp world [Ackerman 79, Arvind 78, Backus 78, McGraw 83, Turner 79].

3.2.3 Lisp with explicit concurrency

Contrasting with the approaches discussed in the two preceding sections, where compile-time or run-time analysis finds concurrency in an apparently sequential program, is a sizable family of Lisp dialects that incorporate concurrency explicitly in their semantics, including Multilisp [Halstead 85, Halstead 86b], QLisp [Gabriel 84], Connection Machine Lisp [Steele 86], and Symmetric Lisp [Ahuja 86]. These languages all include some side-effect primitives (without side effects, we are operating in the functional programming world, and automated analysis is easy enough that there is little need for explicit concurrency primitives allowing the user to specify what to do in parallel). The properties of languages in this family may be better understood by considering some specific questions:

- How is concurrency created (what are the "fork" primitives)?
- What are the synchronization primitives (for both "joining" and mutual exclusion)?
- How expensive are the concurrency primitives, and hence what granularity of tasks is encouraged?
- What other changes to Lisp (e.g., addition of new data types) have been made to support and facilitate the use of the chosen concurrency mechanisms?

It is unwise to consider concurrent Lisp machine architecture without understanding the answers to these questions, because many concurrent Lisp languages employ somewhat unconventional constructs for expressing parallelism. Many of the languages have a straightforward *fork-join* construct that effectively means, "Perform this set of computations concurrently, and continue only when all of them have finished." However, much of the power and interest of concurrent Lisps comes from additional constructs of two types: (1) facilities for manipulating not yet computed values (pioneered in Baker [77] and Knueven [76]), such as Multilisp's *futures* and QLisp's eager evaluation; and (2) novel data types that facilitate concurrent access to large sets of data, such as the *xappings* of Connection Machine Lisp. Programming languages for future concurrent Lisp machines will probably include both kinds of features, and even a programming environment without programmer-specified concurrency would probably use these ideas to some extent at lower levels of its implementation.

Multilisp's futures are essentially placeholders for values that are being computed. In Multilisp, the basic forking primitive creates both a future and a "child" task whose purpose is to compute a value for the future. The future is immediately returned to the parent task, which can continue execution using the future as a placeholder for the value that will ultimately be computed by the child task. When the child task finishes, the value V that it computed will be assigned to the future in such a way that the future *mutates* into V; it is as if the future had always really been V. We say that the future is initially *unresolved,* or *undetermined,* and later *resolves* to V. Futures are a concurrency primitive because execution of the parent task can resume while V is concurrently being computed.

The result of supplying an unresolved future as an operand to some operation depends on the nature of the operation. For *nonstrict* operations, such as passing parameters to procedures, returning values from procedures, and building data structures, the parent task need not wait until V is known; the future is sufficient information to allow computation to proceed. For *strict* operations, such as comparisons, arithmetic, and selection of elements from a data structure, an unresolved future is not a good enough operand; a task that attempts such an operation on a future must wait until the future resolves.

We say that strict operations *touch* their operands; touching an operand causes the touching task to be suspended if the operand is an unresolved future. Touching is the join operation corresponding to the fork operation in which a future is created; but futures are very different from a simple fork-join construct, where the forking and joining operations are statically given in the program text: the joining due to futures is highly dynamic and depends completely on the run-time details of when and in what order strict operators are applied to operands. This "delayed join" property of futures makes them quite successful in exposing parallelism in symbolic applications, because symbolic computing is especially rich in nonstrict operations that rearrange data but do not require information about it.

Many programs obtain parallelism by using futures at an extremely fine level of granularity [Halstead 85, Halstead 86*b*]. The very fine grained tasks in these programs are no longer than the body of a typical short Lisp procedure. In order for such programs to execute efficiently, futures must be a very efficient mechanism. In current implementations, creating and using a future costs about four times as much processor time as calling and returning from a procedure [Halstead 86b]. It should be possible to reduce this cost by better performance tuning of the implementation, a necessary step if very fine-grained use of futures is to be made practical.

The *xappings* of Connection Machine Lisp are a completely different mechanism from futures. A xapping can be viewed as a function whose domain and range are both subsets of the universe of Lisp objects. Equivalently, a xapping can be seen as a set of ordered pairs *index → value,* where *index* is an element of the function's domain and *value* is an element of its range. A *xet* is a special kind of xapping which is just the identity xapping over some domain that need not be the entire universe of Lisp objects. A xet can be used like a mathematical set.

Parallelism in Connection Machine Lisp occurs through "xapping application," where a xapping F whose range consists of functions is applied to a sequence of other xappings $A_1, A_2, \ldots, A_N$ whose ranges consist of argument values. The application produces a result xapping containing all elements of the form $i \to f_i(a_{1i}, a_{2i}, \ldots, a_{Ni})$, where the function xapping F contains an element $i \to f_i$ and each of the argument xappings A_k contains an element $i \to a_{ki}$. The elements of the result xapping can all be computed in parallel.

As a simple, if contrived, example, suppose the xapping **populations** contains {**Albania→3046000 Andorra→43000 Angola→7948000 Argentina→30708000**}, the xapping **areas** contains {**Argentina→1065189 Andorra→188 Algeria→918497 Albania→11100**}, and the xapping **operator** contains {**Afghanistan→/ Andorra→/ Argentina→/ Angola→/**}. Then (**operator populations areas**) would evaluate to the xapping {**Andorra→228.72 Argentina→28.83**} (with both quotients calculated concurrently) since xapping application implicitly intersects the domains of the xappings involved, and **Andorra** and **Argentina** are the only domain elements common to all three xappings. Since it is common to want to apply the same function (say→/) to all available elements of the argument xappings, Connection Machine Lisp includes an operator α such that α *f* extends *f* into a xapping containing elements *i→f* for every possible index *i*. Thus (α / **populations areas**) would yield {**Albania→274.41 Andorra→228.72 Argentina→28.83**}. Connection Machine Lisp has many other features not discussed here, including a **xunion** primitive for taking the *union,* rather than the intersection, of domain elements, and a β operator that allows xapping elements to be merged in various ways and given new indices. Much more interesting examples can be given using these primitives, but this would take us too far afield.

We see that parallelism using xappings arises rather directly out of "bushiness" in *data* structures, whereas parallelism using futures is more a function of bushiness in a program's data dependency graph—its *control* structure. Xappings provide a natural representation of sparse data objects, such as sparse matrices or polynomials, and often allow parallel algorithms on such objects to be expressed in an especially elegant form.

The beginning of a xapping application is essentially a fork, whose matching join must occur before execution proceeds beyond the application. Xapping application thus comes much closer than futures to a conventional static fork-join construct. Depending on the nature of the function being applied, each computation of an element of a result xapping may be a very fine grained task, increasing the importance of efficient realization of the fork and join components of xapping application. However, the pragmatics of efficiently performing the intersection of domains of function and argument xappings can be troublesome on conventional computer architectures. As in the case of the fine-grained use of futures, it seems that performance tuning and possibly the aggressive use of unconventional computer system components such as content-addressable memories holds the key to efficient execution of xapping applications that generate fine-grained tasks.

The *delayed join* property of futures helps expose parallelism by extending the overlap between concurrent tasks until the last possible moment, often giving each concurrent task the chance to spawn yet more tasks before pausing for synchronization. Xapping application is a less powerful parallelism generator in this respect, since, as defined in Connection Machine Lisp, a join occurs before proceeding beyond the application. However, it is not difficult to imagine a combination of xapping application with delayed join (perhaps the elements of the result xapping would initially appear as futures) that could be an extremely powerful parallelism generator. Although such a combination of properties sounds interesting, no such language has yet been proposed publicly.

3.2.4 Sources of parallelism

Algorithms may have opportunities for concurrency at any of several levels of granularity, ranging from short sequences of primitive operations to large program modules. These opportunities are multiplicative: if the application of medium- or fine-grain parallelism within a module is sufficient to occupy m processors, and furthermore n of these modules can be executed in parallel, then mn processors can be used efficiently to execute the program as a whole (unless contention for shared resources imposes a smaller limit). Thus opportunities for concurrency should be exploited at all levels if execution on a highly parallel machine is desired.

We have already seen that constructs such as futures and xappings exploit parallelism that comes from somewhat different sources—bushy data structures vs. bushy control structures. To a considerable extent these are merely two sides of the same coin, although in many applications one viewpoint may be more natural than the other. In any case, deeper insight can be obtained by considering another classification of sources of concurrency in programming: *mandatory work* vs. *speculative parallelism*. The mandatory work style starts with a suitably chosen sequential program and then relaxes some of the precedence constraints in that program to produce opportunities for executing some operations concurrently. This style of parallel programming is supported by futures, xapping application, and the fork-join constructs of other languages. A concurrent program written in the mandatory work style executes precisely the same set of operations as its sequential counterpart: only the scheduling of operations is different. Language constructs may differ in their effectiveness at relaxing precedence constraints and may therefore be more or less useful in support of the mandatory work style, but the basic equivalence between the sets of operations performed by sequential and mandatory work parallel programs remains.

The mandatory work style contrasts with the speculative style, where parallelism is obtained by eagerly spawning tasks before it is certain that their results will be needed. In many artificial intelligence programs, as well as in other applications, multiple approaches to solve a class of problems may exist. For any particular problem, some of the approaches may work very quickly, while others may fail altogether. It is therefore desirable to be able to attempt several approaches in parallel but also to be able to terminate the execution of extra attempts when one of them produces an answer. Even outside the domain of artificial intelligence, searching often provides opportunities for speculative parallelism, such as in the use of branch-and-bound techniques for problems such as the traveling salesman problem.

Mandatory work parallelism is of "higher quality" than speculative parallelism because scheduling is less critical, and, except for process management overhead, no extra operations are performed during parallel execution. Assuming that the original sequential algorithm is efficient, the mandatory work approach represents a kind of lower bound: it may be possible to increase concurrency beyond that available in a mandatory work program by adding speculative operations, but these operations represent an overhead that is only justified if the increase in parallelism outweighs the extra work done. To exploit concurrency at all levels and from all sources, both mandatory work and speculative parallelism should be used, and therefore both need to be supported by parallel programming languages; however, tools for expressing speculative parallelism cannot replace good constructs for mandatory work parallelism.

Scheduling of mandatory operations is not very critical because all mandatory operations must be done eventually, so *any* mandatory operation that is ready to be performed may be executed with reasonable confidence that it will not be wasted work. Scheduling is much more critical in the presence of speculative parallelism. Usually, some speculative tasks have a higher potential payoff than others. Low-payoff speculative tasks should not be executed in preference to high-payoff speculative tasks or mandatory tasks. The only time to execute speculative tasks is when processing resources would otherwise go idle; they should not take resources away from more important tasks.

Futures and xappings are fairly effective for exposing mandatory work parallelism, but neither gives the information needed to properly schedule speculative tasks. In some cases, the scheduling of tasks could be dictated by associating numerical priorities with the tasks, but the general problem of what tools to give the programmer for use in specifying the scheduling of speculative tasks remains an interesting question for research.

3.2.5 Summary

Although a great variety of concurrent Lisp languages have been proposed, they fall into three general categories: unmodified sequential Lisps with compile-time or run-time concurrency extraction, side-effect-free Lisps, and Lisp dialects with explicit concurrency primitives. All three categories take a shared-memory view of data, but the categories diverge in many other respects. The third category of languages is the subject of by far the largest amount of research activity and the greatest progress toward usable systems. Two interesting concurrency-generating primitives used in this category of languages are Multilisp's *futures* and Connection Machine Lisp's *xappings*. Since each of these primitives seems best at exploiting parallelism from certain kinds of sources, a language including both looks attractive; however, neither primitive addresses the requirements of speculative parallelism, an area where further study is needed.

3.3 Challenges to the Concurrent Lisp Machine Architect

Computer architecture is often as much art as science, and only rarely is there a single, obviously optimal architectural solution to a problem. So it is with architecture for executing parallel Lisp. There is a large, multidimensional space of possible designs, with decisions to be made at levels ranging from what sort of parallel Lisp computational model to support, through several alternatives for the overall machine organization, to detailed questions of processor and memory organization. It is best to begin by reviewing the characteristics of parallel Lisp programs. These characteristics can then be used as a guide in navigating through the large design space of possible architectures.

The challenge to the concurrent Lisp machine architect is to provide good support for the operations most commonly performed by parallel Lisp programs. The characteristics of these programs are similar in some ways to those of the much better understood family of sequential programs expressed in the Fortran, Algol, Pascal, or Ada varieties of algebraic programming languages, but sequential programs in algebraic languages differ from concurrent Lisp programs in many ways. Some of these are due to differences between Lisp and algebraic languages, some are due to differences between sequential and parallel execution, and some are due to the combination of these two factors. Each of these differences challenges the architect to respond with some deviation from traditional computer design.

3.3.1 Challenges from Lisp

The characteristic qualities of typical Lisp programs can be summarized in two phrases: *late binding* and *less arithmetic*. These characteristics come in part from the programming style made possible and encouraged by Lisp, and in part from the symbolic application domain for which most Lisp programs are written. Probably "late binding" is due principally to Lisp itself, while "less arithmetic" is more due to the symbolic application domain, but both factors really contribute to both characteristics.

The principal function of a symbolic program may be broadly stated as the reorganization of a set of data so that the relevant information in it is more useful or easier to extract. Examples of primarily symbolic algorithms include sorting, compiling, database management, symbolic algebra, expert systems, and other artificial intelligence applications. The sequence of operations in symbolic programs is often highly data dependent and less amenable to compile-time analysis than in the case of numerical computation [Lee 85]. The structure of symbolic computations generally seems to lend itself less well to analysis of loops—the major focus in parallelizing numerical computation—and favors recursions on composite data structures such as trees, lists, and sets as the major source of concurrency. The lesser emphasis of typical Lisp programs on arithmetic is associated with a greater emphasis on searching and data structure access ("chasing pointers"). Thus high-performance arithmetic capabilities are less important than high performance in accessing memory.

The late-binding aspect of typical Lisp programs has several manifestations. Many Lisp operators are generic: the type of their operands need not be declared at compile time and may not be known until run time. Storage reclamation in Lisp is not explicit but is performed automatically by a garbage collector; therefore, the lifetime of an object allocated from storage is often not obvious at compile time and may not be known until run time. Finally, as mentioned above, Lisp's reduced emphasis on loops with numerical indices, in favor of pointer chasing, makes the flow of control in a program harder to predict at compile time.

An often noted property of Lisp programs is the high frequency of procedure calls and, in object-oriented extensions of Lisp such as Flavors [Moon 86], the high frequency of method invocations; about 1 out of every 14 instructions executed in a set of benchmark Lisp programs has been found to be either a procedure call or return [Taylor 86]. Therefore, procedure and method invocation need to be streamlined if Lisp execution is to be efficient.

To summarize, Lisp programs tend to be especially characterized by (1) the use of tagged data and generic operations; (2) memory-intensive pointer chasing; (3) frequent procedure and method invocation; and (4) garbage collection (this item gets rather more interesting in the presence of complications like virtual memory [Moon 84] and concurrency). Finally, (5) sophisticated compile-time analysis is likely to be somewhat less successful than usual. These characteristics challenge the architect to devise unique mechanisms for the efficient support of Lisp programs on concurrent Lisp machines just as on sequential ones.

3.3.2 Challenges from concurrency

Whether of Lisp or some other language, parallel execution poses three kinds of challenges that we must not neglect: efficient communication of data, economical creation of processes, and economical synchronization. Although these are general challenges of parallel computation, the use of Lisp often gives them a particular form.

Given the shared-memory flavor of most proposed concurrent Lisp languages, the most pressing requirement in the data communication area is for high performance on unanticipated requests for small quantities of data. Some computing systems can compensate for long latencies in the delivery of requested data by delivering large quantities of data in each transaction. This technique is used both in networking and in dealing with secondary storage media such as disk and tape in order to maintain an acceptable bandwidth even though the latency for individual operations is long. Such an approach works well where data requirements are predictable, so that a block of data can be requested while a previous block is being processed, or at least so that a large amount of relevant data can be included in each block. Where data requirements are hard to predict, as is frequently the case in Lisp, a communication system should be designed primarily for efficient short transfers, even at the expense of reduced performance for large block transfers.

If any given datum is stored in one place only, then there is likely to be a heavy load on the communication system as that datum is accessed from different places. One way to reduce this load is to cache duplicate copies of data at different places in the system. Since most languages for concurrent Lisp programming include side effects, some complexity and cost are involved in keeping all copies of an object consistent. Resolving these issues in a satisfactory way is one of the most important challenges to the concurrent Lisp machine architect.

Creation of processes needs to be fairly inexpensive in a concurrent Lisp machine, since we expect to do a lot of it. It is difficult to discuss this topic in general without getting into the details of a particular architecture, because processes may have very different implementations on different architectures. However, a few general points can be noted. One is simply that processes must, in fact, be created dynamically in nearly all concurrent Lisp models, in contrast to some other parallel computing models [Hoare 78] in which all tasks are created at the beginning of a program execution. A second point is that tasks, once created, must be assigned to processors and then scheduled for execution. In keeping with the general late-binding character of Lisp, it is usually not feasible to resolve the assignment and scheduling decisions before run time.

Synchronization appears in different forms according to the concurrent Lisp model that is used, but it always appears in some form. We can divide synchronization requirements into two general categories: precedence and mutual exclusion. Precedence constraints apply when a consumer of some data must make sure the production of that data has finished. Mutual exclusion constraints arise out of shared resources that can only support one user at a time, such as physical input/output devices and objects on which complex operations must be performed atomically. Both categories of synchronization are needed for concurrent Lisp languages with side effects, but precedence constraints are likely to be the more important category since, if a "nearly functional" programming style is used, side effects to shared objects should be much less frequent than the use of values produced by other tasks.

Synchronization potentially involves waiting, and waiting can waste resources. The architect's goal is to minimize the waste of resources due to synchronization delays, as well as to make synchronization efficient in the case where a check shows no waiting is needed. Synchronization checks can be very frequent; for example, in

Multilisp, a synchronization check is made every time a value is touched, since any value might be a future. When synchronization checks are so frequent, they must be very quick. Ideally, most synchronization checks show that no waiting is needed, and execution continues (this appears to be the case in Multilisp [Halstead 85]). When waiting occurs, however, its cost must be controlled. Though aesthetically displeasing, "busy-waiting" is as good as any other approach when the resources it occupies would otherwise go idle. When there is no work for a processor to do, it might as well busy-wait, as long as its busy-waiting does not load the communication system with requests that delay useful work. However, the best solution of all is to find other useful work for a processor any time its current task needs to wait.

3.3.3   Challenges from concurrent symbolic algorithms

A special category of challenges arises because the kinds of concurrency most likely to be found in symbolic applications are not exactly like those available in common numerical programs. These challenges come not just from the symbolic application domain, nor from parallel execution alone, but rather from the combination of the two. Discussion of these challenges is necessarily somewhat speculative, since there has been very little experience with parallel symbolic computing. Furthermore, we must beware of the limitations of generalization; although the "typical" symbolic program may differ from the "typical" numerical program in certain ways, particular symbolic and numerical programs may not differ much at all. Nevertheless, it is useful to examine these challenges as best we can.

One likely attribute of parallel symbolic computing is a greater need for speculative parallelism than in the numerical case. A common paradigm in numerical computing is mapping an operation over a vector or other aggregate of values. Generally, the operation really does need to be performed on every one of the values and is programmed that way even on a sequential computer. This is a good opportunity for mandatory work parallelism. Many symbolic applications depend more heavily on searching. Parallelism can be used in searching by exploring several alternatives concurrently, but a search programmed sequentially may do less work because it can stop as soon as the first instance of the thing searched for is found. In a parallel search, it may be desirable to assign different priorities to the exploration of different alternatives and to terminate exploration of parallel branches when one branch succeeds. These are the earmarks of speculative parallelism, suggesting that the combination of parallelism and symbolic computing will challenge us to support speculative parallelism well.

Also arising from this combination is a challenge to devise new data types that both are useful for symbolic computing and are powerful concurrency generators. For example, the programmer of a symbolic application will frequently want to manipulate an object conceived of abstractly as a set. Lisp makes possible various concrete implementations of sets in terms of lower-level primitives such as lists, but mapping an operation to run concurrently over the elements of a list is not the most efficient way to spawn large amounts of parallel computation. This is because the operations cannot all be initiated at the same time; operations on elements near the end of the list can start only after a sequential scan of a large part of the list. This problem can be ameliorated considerably by representing sets as trees rather than lists. Then the spawning of operations can follow the structure of a tree and reach all elements much more quickly; however, there is still a logarithmic start-up time before the actual operations on elements begin, and the programmer must be concerned with details such as making sure that trees remain balanced.

A higher-level primitive data type that represents the original abstraction more directly may be a more attractive solution. For example, a set might be represented as a *xet,* a special instance of a xapping. The use of higher-level primitives such as xappings takes certain decisions (e.g., whether to use a linear or treelike data structure) out of the programmer's hands and puts them into the hands of the language implementor. This makes it possible to use innovative implementations (e.g., storing xappings in a content-addressable memory) without requiring changes to the source program. Rapidly selecting "interesting" members of a set and concurrently initiating some operation on each selected element is an example where innovative implementations may have more impact on the performance of parallel Lisp machines than on sequential ones. Therefore, new, higher-level, primitive data types that support symbolic computing well and allow such implementations promise to be more important on parallel machines than on sequential ones.

3.3.4 Summary

Before proceeding, we gather in one list all of the concurrent Lisp machine design challenges discussed in the preceding sections. Each challenge in the list is presented as a statement that is expected to be generally true of concurrent Lisp programs, requiring efficient implementation of some operation or restricting the designer's range of options (e.g., by reducing the benefits likely to be obtained by compile-time analysis). Each challenge is identified by a number and mnemonic short name used subsequently to refer to it.

C1 *(run-time typing):*   Tagged data and generic operations are common.

C2 *(procedure calling):*   Procedure and method invocations are frequent.

C3 *(garbage collection):*   Garbage collection is important.

C4 *(late binding):*   Less reliance can be placed on compile-time analysis.

C5 *(pointer chasing):*   Pointer chasing is a common program structure.

C6 *(small data transfers):*   Unanticipated small data transfers are frequent.

C7 *(replication of data):*   Some data need to be replicated for faster access.

C8 *(frequent process creation):*   Process creation is frequent.

C9 *(frequent synchronization):*   Synchronization operations are frequent.

C10 *(speculative parallelism):*   Speculative parallelism is important.

C11 *(concurrency generators):*   New data types may be more effective concurrency generators than traditional Lisp data types.

3.4   Important Concurrent Lisp Machine Design Decisions

The variety of different possible concurrent architectures for Lisp defies any attempt to devise a simple framework that contains them all, but the answers to five major design questions determine many of the details that follow. The five questions are

1. What are the goals and metrics of success of the machine? In particular, what scale of machine is contemplated?

2. What is the overall physical organization of the machine?

3. How are data addressed, and what strategies are used to cache or replicate data for faster access and reduced communication traffic?

4. How is storage allocated and what strategy is used for garbage collection?

5. What strategies are used to ensure that the utilization of each element in the system is a high enough fraction of its capacity? In par-

ticular, how are lengthy delays in the transit of data from one part of the machine to another masked or prevented?

3.4.1 Scale of the machine

The first question is both the most fundamental and in many ways the most difficult. Data caching, for example, looks like a very different problem according to whether a machine is intended to exploit tenfold or thousandfold parallelism. Although the question cannot be answered precisely here, machines with approximately hundredfold parallelism look like a bold enough step, given our current inexperience with such machines. Accordingly, we do not indulge in speculation about the design of machines with thousandfold parallelism or more.

3.4.2 Overall organization

Generally, MIMD architectures [Flynn 66] seem more natural for concurrent Lisp machines than SIMD architectures such as the Connection Machine [Hillis 85]. Certainly all of the concurrent Lisp languages discussed in Sec. 3.2 have a MIMD flavor, in that they can be used to spawn a large number of processes doing essentially different computations. It is possible to perform such calculations on a SIMD machine by sequencing the machine through all the different kinds of operations that one or more processors are ready to perform, temporarily disabling all processors that are not waiting to perform the currently scheduled operation; however, we do not pursue this approach, because, except in special cases, it is likely to lead to very low processor utilization, as most processors will spend most of the time disabled.

Considering only MIMD architectures, we still face a bewildering array of choices. However, in almost all cases, we can envision a machine as a collection of processing modules and memory modules, interconnected by some communication medium. Hence we can identify three somewhat separable components of design: processor architecture, memory architecture, and communication architecture. Frequently, the communication medium will exhibit some locality, so the cost of communication between "neighboring" processing and memory modules will be less than the cost of "long-distance" communication between modules not located in the same neighborhood.

3.4.3 Addressing, caching, and replication

One of the overall organizational questions transcending this division into separable components of design is that of how and where data are stored and accessed. The simplest way to use memory would be to give each memory location in the machine a unique physical address, such as the concatenation of a memory module's unique identifier and the location's address within the memory module. All memory access requests would refer to the unique physical address of the memory location to be accessed and therefore could presumably be routed easily through the communication medium to their destination. This is essentially the strategy used by the Concert implementation of Multilisp [Halstead 85]. The classic difficulty with this solution is that it is not always possible to place a single copy of an object so that it can be accessed cheaply from all processors that need to access it. If long-distance accesses are frequent, considerable performance may be lost compared to the situation in which the accesses are fairly local. Furthermore, if an object is written seldom or never, as is very often the case, it is possible to reduce the number of long-distance accesses by making several replicated copies of the object and caching them where they are needed. This is advantageous in two ways: accesses can be performed faster, which improves processor efficiency, and the average access traverses a smaller region of the communication medium, resulting in less communication load.

Whenever objects are replicated, the addressing mechanisms of the machine must be able to select a suitable instance of a replicated object toward which to direct each access. Some mechanisms for replication are mentioned in Sec. 3.5.3. The difficulty of replication depends on which of the following two alternatives are tried:

1. Replicate only read-only objects.

2. Replicate read-only *and* read/write objects.

The former solution is simpler, but its applicability is limited. It is relatively easy for a compiler to detect the read-only nature of executable code and of local variables that are initialized but never subsequently reassigned. Simply being able to cache these two kinds of objects can eliminate many long-distance accesses. The exact number of accesses eliminated in this manner in any real concurrent Lisp language has yet to be measured, and depends, moreover, on many implementation details such as how executable code is represented, as well as program-specific details such as how common read-only variables are. Nevertheless, it is reasonable to estimate a reduction in nonlocal accesses by a factor of four as a result of exploiting these read-only caching opportunities. As in many other computer systems, caching executable code is especially easy and valuable.

Identifying additional kinds of objects as read-only, and hence as candidates for easy replication, is harder, even though writing into already existing objects is not common in Lisp programming and will probably be even less common in concurrent Lisp programs because of the software engineering difficulties of writing parallel programs with

side effects. It is usually very difficult for a Lisp compiler or program
analyzer to track down all accesses to a given object and verify that no
write operations could possibly be performed on it. Therefore, run-
time caching methods powerful enough to handle read/write objects
are probably needed if additional kinds of objects are to be replicated.
These methods require a solution to the "cache coherence" problem—
finding all replicated copies of an object to be written and either eliminating them or updating them so that discrepancies do not arise between copies of the object.

As mentioned above, one advantage of replication is a reduction in
load on the communication medium. Another, complementary memory system design option to reduce communication load is *smart memory,* which implements frequently used operations at a higher level
than simple reads and writes. Such operations can reduce communication traffic by performing, entirely in a memory module, compound
operations that would otherwise need to be performed by several
transactions between a processor and memory. The best candidates for
such higher-level memory operations are those that require several
memory accesses but a minimum of computation and can be conducted
entirely within one memory module without the involvement of third
parties. Section 3.5.3 discusses this question further and gives some
examples.

3.4.4 Storage allocation and garbage collection

Lisp depends on the ability to allocate storage dynamically and to automatically reclaim unused storage through garbage collection. In a
multiprocessor, both operations take on new dimensions. In a system
with multiple memory modules, a conveniently located module with
available storage must be chosen every time some storage needs to be
allocated. Decisions such as selecting the best memory module for a
particular purpose probably need to be made at a higher level than
hardware, but hardware can help by efficiently propagating status information such as which modules currently have storage available.
Hardware can also help optimize the process of claiming space in a
storage module that may be concurrently receiving claims from many
sources.

In garbage collection, the high-level decisions can be even more
complex than in storage allocation and probably should be implemented in software, but some well-designed hardware assistance can
make the low-level, "inner loop" steps much more efficient [Moon 84].
A suggestive example of a garbage collector for a concurrent Lisp is
that used in the Concert implementation of Multilisp, which is an incremental, copying garbage collector [Halstead 85]. A *garbage collec-*

tion cycle of this garbage collector copies all accessible objects from old locations (in *oldspace*) to new ones (in *copyspace*). When an object is copied into copyspace, its pointers to other objects in oldspace must eventually be converted to point to the images of those objects in copyspace.

Each processor alternates between short periods of computing, or *mutating,* and garbage collection activity, or *scavenging.* A single garbage collection cycle is composed of many such alternations. During each period of scavenging, a processor scans a region of copyspace, looking for pointers to objects in oldspace. When such a pointer is found, the object pointed to is *transported* to copyspace and the oldspace pointer is replaced by a pointer to the transported copy. (If the object pointed to has already been transported, the transporting step is skipped and a pointer to the already transported copy is used.) A final requirement of the usual incremental garbage collection algorithms is that mutating (as opposed to scavenging) processors should never see oldspace pointers; thus, if a mutating processor tries to read a location containing an oldspace pointer, a *transporter trap* occurs and the oldspace object is transported before execution continues.

A nonincremental *stop-and-copy* garbage collection algorithm can also be used in a concurrent Lisp machine, as in Butterfly Lisp [Courtemanche 86]. In this case, when the need for a garbage collection cycle is sensed, all processors suspend computing and cooperate on garbage collection. Only after all garbage collection is complete can any of the processors resume computing. A third variation on the theme of garbage collection on a multiprocessor is *on-the-fly* garbage collection, which dedicates certain (perhaps specialized) processors to scavenge full-time while the other processors compute full-time [Dijkstra 76].

Stop and copy is probably the simplest garbage collection scheme, since it is the only one in which mutating processors are not exposed to intermediate states of the garbage collector. Incremental garbage collection is probably the most complex of the three, since the other two can be viewed as special cases of incremental garbage collection arising from particular decisions about how to schedule processors between mutation and scavenging. On the other hand, the full generality of incremental garbage collection, with each processor able to switch between the two kinds of activity, seems little more complex than on-the-fly garbage collection, since the complexity of ensuring correct interaction between processors engaged in mutation and scavenging exists in both cases.

Although incremental garbage collection is the most complex, it is also the most flexible in the allocation of processor time, since each processor is free to switch between mutation and scavenging as needed. This flexibility takes some pressure off the garbage collector's load-balancing mechanisms. Efficient operation of a stop-and-copy garbage collector requires a very even distribution of work among the processors during scavenging to avoid large amounts of idle time caused by processors that finish scavenging early. This has been difficult to achieve in some early prototypes of parallel stop-and-copy garbage collectors [Courtemanche 86]. In on-the-fly garbage collection, unless the level of necessary garbage collection activity is estimated very accurately in advance, either scavenger processors will need to wait at times for mutator processors to generate more garbage, or vice versa. Using an incremental garbage collector, both of these load-balancing problems can be solved adaptively, simply by switching processors between scavenging and mutation as needed. Thus although incremental garbage collection is somewhat more complex, it has the potential to respond to changing conditions in a much more forgiving way.

Incremental garbage collection looks the most desirable due to its adaptability, but it is a complex algorithm. We can conclude that the best path for a concurrent Lisp machine is to support certain low-level operations necessary for incremental garbage collection, such as transporter traps, with special hardware features as needed, but to leave the overall control of garbage collection in the hands of software.

3.4.5 Latency avoidance and latency tolerance

However a concurrent Lisp machine is organized, even with replication or caching, sometimes there will be a relatively long distance between a processor and data that it wishes to access. There will always be some cache misses, causing occasional communication latencies one or two orders of magnitude longer than the time taken by a cache hit.

Challenges **C5** (pointer chasing) and **C6** (small data transfers) paint a picture of a multiprocessor tied together by exchange of rather fine grained messages (e.g., "Read a word from memory."). Many message exchanges will be needed in such an architecture to perform a useful computation; therefore, the communication medium must deliver messages quickly. But quick delivery of messages is worth little if sending or receiving messages is expensive. Perhaps due to the special-purpose nature of memory modules, it is not too hard to imagine how simple requests like read and write can be pipelined through a *memory module* without excessive delay or complexity, but efficient message processing by *processors* is not as simple.

In many message-passing multiprocessors based on conventional microprocessors, the cost in processor time of sending a message is high—at least a substantial fraction of a millisecond. A cost of this magnitude cannot be tolerated if the granularity of messages is as small as we have been assuming. The generating and sending of messages has to be much more closely coupled to the processor's instruction set. In effect, the cost of sending a message has to be much closer to the cost of a cache miss on a conventional computer than to the cost of a page fault. Therefore, just as with cache misses, there is no time to invoke software mechanisms; the generation of messages must be implemented in hardware when needed to access an item of data.

A primary architectural question concerns what a processor does after sending a message. The simplest option is for it to just wait until a response is received. If messages are sent frequently and message transmission latency is significant, then a processor using this policy will experience a lot of idle time. Both of these assumptions are likely to be true, despite our best efforts to reduce message transmission *frequency* through caching and reduce transmission *latency* through clever communication architecture. We can accept the high level of processor idle time, or we can try to reduce it by finding other things for the processor to do while waiting for a response to a message.

Accepting a high level of processor idle time is not as foolish as it might seem. Focusing on processor utilization as a measure of computational efficiency is a habit left over from the days of large and very costly processors. This habit becomes less justifiable as processor hardware becomes a smaller fraction of a computer system. If, for example, a system's hardware is devoted in equal proportions to processor, memory, and communications, why is high processor utilization any more desirable a goal than high memory utilization or high communication utilization?

The important yardstick is not processor utilization; it is system cost/performance. A variant of the law of diminishing returns applies to computer systems (as well as many other kinds of systems): beyond a certain point, the cost of trying to eliminate waste (in this case, processor idle time) is higher than the cost of the waste itself. Therefore, the optimum point in system cost/performance is a point where there is some waste of every kind of resource in the system. The right question to ask is whether the cost of a method for reducing resource waste pays for itself by increasing the overall performance/cost ratio of the system.

The question of whether or not to accept high levels of processor idle time can thus be rephrased as a question about available methods to reduce the idle time. What methods for reducing idle time are available, what are their costs, and how do the costs compare with the increase in system performance that they provide? One way to reduce idle time is for a processor to be able to continue executing after issuing a memory request, without waiting immediately for the response, as in the PIPE processor [Goodman 85]. This is an excellent way to mask latency if the processor does not in fact need to examine the response immediately. When a processor can operate in an "oblivious" mode, i.e., the sequence of memory locations it accesses is independent of the contents of those locations, it can issue a large number of memory requests to be serviced concurrently. It is then likely that, by the time all the requests have been issued, the responses have begun to arrive and processing can continue uninterrupted.

Unfortunately, the common Lisp paradigm of pointer chasing is the antithesis of oblivious execution. Pointer chasing frequently features long chains of memory accesses where the address of each access is calculated from the value returned by the immediately preceding access. This paradigm leaves a task little work to do between issuing a memory access request and receiving the response. One way to keep a processor busy when a task blocks awaiting a message response is to switch to executing a different task. This policy incurs the cost of a context switch; therefore, that cost must be substantially less than the expected message response latency. A strategy of this sort was used by the Denelcor HEP-1 processor, which switched between tasks on an instruction-by-instruction basis [Kowalik 85, Smith 78]. The context switching cost was essentially zero because every task could have its own registers and program counter—in short, its own processor state—loaded into the processor at the same time. Switching to a new task simply consisted of changing the contents of a task ID register, directing the processor's attention toward a different set of processor state registers.†

Both the PIPE approach and the HEP-1 approach to latency-tolerant processor architecture attempt to increase the utilization of certain central parts of a processor (such as the arithmetic and logic unit) by adding additional state to the processor and more mechanisms to coordinate a greater variety of concurrent activities in the processor. A judgment of the worth of these approaches depends on the cost of these mechanisms and the extent to which they increase utilization of the central parts of the processor. These factors depend on many details of the machine and therefore can be evaluated only in a more concrete context.

3.4.6 Summary

The answers to five major design questions affect the design of many parts of a concurrent Lisp machine. These questions concern scale,

---

† Operation of the HEP-1 was actually somewhat more complicated than this, because instruction execution was pipelined. At every clock tick, the instruction issued to fill the next pipeline slot would come from some runnable task that did not already have an instruction in the pipe. Combining instruction-by-instruction task switching and pipelining is probably a good idea for a concurrent Lisp machine as well but is not especially relevant to the present discussion.

overall organization, replication of data, garbage collection, and latency avoidance and tolerance. Based on the design challenges summarized in Sec. 3.3.4 and other considerations, some general answers to these questions can be given. Given the current state of knowledge, a scale somewhere between tenfold and thousandfold parallelism looks the most prudent for a next step. The most promising overall organization seems to be MIMD. No one scheme for replication of data stands out, but replication of known read-only objects promises many advantages. Extending replication to read/write objects invites the cache coherence problem but promises substantial further advantages in the case of concurrent Lisp. Among garbage collection algorithms, incremental garbage collection is the most complex, but it is also the most flexible in allocation of processing resources and therefore is preferred. Finally, communication latency should be minimized by streamlining the communication medium and designing the processor to reduce the cost of sending and receiving messages. Nevertheless, communication delays will still be significant and hinder full utilization of processors. Although the costs of increasing processor utilization may outweigh the benefits, processor designs that allow processing to continue during communication latency look promising.

3.5   An Example

To illustrate in more detail the issues involved in concurrent Lisp machine design, we can consider the design of a hypothetical machine, currently under study in the author's laboratory. The machine represents an educated "best guess" at the outlines of an effective design, because very few of the detailed design choices are supported by a quantitative analysis of costs and benefits. This lack of data is regrettable and illustrates the infancy of this field. Unfortunately, many design decisions can be discussed only in a somewhat concrete setting; it is hoped that the reader will find some useful insights in the sections that follow, even though many of the design decisions need to be evaluated using much more quantitative data than are currently available.

3.5.1   Overall organization

We picture the hypothetical machine as being composed of clusters, each containing a processor and a memory element. Each cluster is connected to a communication subnet through which it communicates with other clusters. There are several choices in how clusters could be connected internally, as shown in Fig. 3.1. In Fig. 3.1a, there is a direct path between a cluster's processor and memory, as well as a path

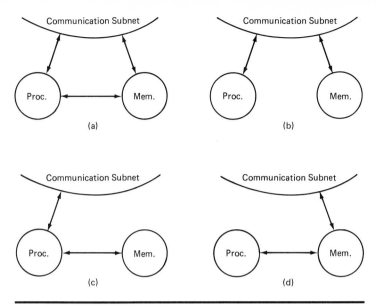

Figure 3.1   Cluster organization alternatives for example machine.

from each to the subnet. In Fig. 3.1*b,* the direct path from processor to memory has been removed, so the processor must use the subnet even to reach the memory in its own "cluster." This organization weakens the clustering bonds considerably, but if the subnet is fast enough and provides a reasonably short path between a cluster's processor and memory, it might serve as an adequate substitute for the direct link. Among the four structures in Fig. 3.1, this is perhaps the closest analog to contemporary shared-memory multiprocessors [Matelan 85, Rodgers 85]. Figure 3.1*c* is derived from Fig. 3.1*a* by removing a different link—the direct link between memory and the subnet. Therefore, in this organization, all traffic to a memory must go through the memory's associated processor. Of the structures shown in Fig. 3.1, this is perhaps the closest cousin to contemporary message-passing multiprocessors [Seitz 85]. Finally, Fig. 3.1*d* is derived from Fig. 3.1*a* by removing yet a different link—the direct link between the processor and the subnet, forcing all communication to or from a processor to go through its associated memory. This structure probably would not exist in its pure form without some enhancement of the memory's capabilities.

Figures 3.1*b, c,* and *d* are all subsets of Fig. 3.1*a.* Although the organization of Fig. 3.1*a* is therefore probably the most expensive to build, it is simpler to discuss since no indirect paths need to be defined. Since there is little evidence to guide the selection of the most desirable simplification among Figs. 3.1*b, c,* and *d,* we select Fig. 3.1*a* as the organization for our example machine; at various points we comment on the effect of selecting one of the others instead.

3.5.2 The communication subnet

The design of the communication subnet is left largely unspecified in Fig. 3.1. In accordance with challenge **C6** (small data transfers), it should be able to accept relatively short messages (30 to 100 bits) and deliver them with very low latency. We may imagine the most common kind of operation on the communication subnet to be a read operation by a processor P from a memory M in a different cluster. Such an operation would begin with P transmitting a message containing

- An operation code identifying the request as a read and possibly giving further information such as the number of bits to read.
- The address of the target location in M.
- And a "return address" identifying $P,$ to which M should send the response.

Upon receiving a read request, M would perform the read operation and send a message containing

- An operation code identifying the message as a response to a read request.
- The return address.
- And the data read.

This kind of *request-response* protocol is familiar from split-transaction buses and multiprocessors such as the BBN Butterfly [BBN 82, Crowther 85, Rettberg 79] or the IBM RP3 [Pfister 85] that are built around communication subnets similar to that proposed here. Write operations could be handled in a very similar way. Operations more elaborate than a simple read or write can also be performed in this manner; subsequent sections give some examples.

The use of the subnet for operations such as reading individual words from the memories of remote clusters underscores the importance of quick message delivery. To reduce the cost of remote references, we may hope to exploit some level of locality of reference, though the amount of locality available in concurrent Lisp programs has yet to be quantified. Indeed, the first level of locality is the private processor-memory link of Fig. 3.1*a,* which avoids the cost of the message protocol for intracluster references. Since we can hope that only a small minority of requests will fall into the long-distance category, it may not be necessary to have extremely fast delivery of messages from a cluster to every other cluster; however, many interesting concurrent Lisp programs have a fairly fine granularity of parallelism [Halstead 86b], implying very frequent interprocessor communication at least on a local level, which must be done efficiently. A traditional local area network medium such as Ethernet [Metcalfe 76] has neither the bandwidth nor the low latency to satisfy this need. Instead, we need a subnet whose bandwidth and latency properties are much closer to those of the system bus of a conventional computer.

Many technologies can be employed to build such a subnet. For a limited number of clusters, something very close to a conventional bus would probably serve. For more clusters, a hierarchical collection of buses organized as in Concert [Anderson 82, Halstead 86a] or Cm* [Gehringer 82] could serve; alternatively, a switching network as in the Butterfly or RP3 machines could be used. Finally, a "myria-processor" organization [Halstead 81] could also be employed. An important objective is that, although the delay in delivering messages may be variable, in the best case (communication between neighboring clusters, no transmission delays due to congestion in the subnet) the delay approaches the speed of communication between a processor and main memory in a conventional computer system. If this is true, we can approach shared-memory performance characteristics using message-passing technology, though we must remember that the worst-case and best-case message delay may differ by an order of magnitude or more.

The choice of subnet technology should really be an engineering decision, based on data indicating which organization can deliver messages in the most cost-effective fashion, taking into account the observed locality properties of concurrent Lisp programs. The choice of subnet topology is subordinate to the technology choice, and thus we are a long way from having enough information to specify it. Since so much data remain to be collected and studied before informed choices about subnet organization can be made, we leave the choices unspecified for now. Fortunately, provided a subnet meets the objective given in the previous paragraph, other aspects of concurrent Lisp machine design are only weakly coupled to details of subnet organization.

3.5.3 Memory organization

The principal memory design issues concern ways of reducing communication traffic. As discussed in Sec. 3.4.3, this can be done through (1) replication and (2) high-level smart-memory functions. The difficulty of implementing replication depends on the scale of our example machine. For small-scale machines, on the order of 10 clusters or fewer, a shared bus can be used as the communication subnet and *snoopy cache* techniques can be used for cache coherence [Goodman 83, Sweazey

86]. When the number of clusters is increased by an order of magnitude, such a solution is no longer practical. It should be possible to generalize existing snoopy cache protocols to work on a hierarchy of buses instead of a single shared bus, but the details of this potential solution have not been worked out. Alternatively, *reference trees* [Halstead 78, Halstead 79] could be used, although there are many questions about the efficiency of reference tree mechanisms in practical situations. A final solution, planned for the RP3 [Pfister 85] and proposed or implemented in many other systems, is to allow replication only of read-only objects, leaving a compiler (or the programmer) responsible for distinguishing read-only from read/write objects.

An example of a higher-level smart-memory operation is an atomic compare and swap that checks the contents V of a location L for equality to a test datum T, and if $V = T$, writes a new value V' into L. Whether or not the write occurs, V is returned to the requesting processor. Such an operation directly implements the **replace-if-eq** operation of Multilisp [Halstead 85] as well as comparable operations in other languages. In the absence of this high-level memory operation, **replace-if-eq** would have to be implemented by using a sequence of lower-level operations to lock the location L, read out its value, write back the value V' if necessary, and finally unlock L. This sequence would require four requests and four responses, even in the absence of contention for locking the location L. A primitive compare-and-swap memory operation can thus save considerable message traffic if **replace-if-eq** is used frequently.

An especially flexible family of synchronization operations on memory may be implemented if each memory location has a *full/empty bit*† in addition to its other contents. A write operation on a memory location can be defined to set the location's full/empty bit, indicating that the location is full. A read request that finds an empty location can be held by the memory module, waiting for the location to become full, or a rejection message can be sent back to the originating processor, indicating the read could not be performed because the target location was empty. (The two strategies are best for different situations. Holding the request is best if locations are rarely empty and usually remain empty for only a short period; however, if many locations remain empty for long periods, then holding requests could burden a memory module with a long backlog of held requests. In this case, rejection messages are better.) Successful read operations can leave a location either full or empty, as indicated by the request type. Using full/empty bits, a read-modify-write operation on a memory location can be performed just by reading the location, leaving it empty, and

† Used in the HEP-1 [Kowalik 85, Smith 78].

then writing back the new value. Although the two memory requests required, for example, by the full/empty-bit method of performing a compare-and-swap operation are more than the one required for a specialized compare-and-swap request, the full/empty-bit mechanism generalizes to handle a much broader class of operations than compare and swap.

As the preceding two paragraphs illustrate, synchronization is one area in which higher-level memory operations can be useful. Another often-mentioned opportunity for high-level memory operations to assist is garbage collection. For the reasons given in Sec. 3.4.4, we consider incremental garbage collection. Two ways in which memory modules might help are (1) handling transporter traps, and (2) scavenging copyspace for pointers into oldspace. We can hope to avoid bothering a processor with these operations and to avoid the message traffic that would result from a processor performing these operations using intercluster references. A memory module would transport an object whenever needed to prevent a read request from returning a pointer to an oldspace object; scavenging could be scheduled for otherwise idle time occurring between requests to the memory module.

Unfortunately, both of these operations can require copying objects from oldspace to copyspace. In general, this copying operation is complex—objects can have many different formats, requiring different copying procedures—and copying may involve several memory modules, since an object to be copied may not be located in the same memory module that notices a need to copy it. Such ambitious smart-memory functions can cause problems. If a memory module undertakes a potentially time-consuming transporter operation, can the transporter operation be preempted by simple read and write requests? If preemption does not occur, a large number of read and write requests might queue up at a memory module occupied with a time-consuming operation. The memory module could become a performance bottleneck by delaying response to a large number of simple requests from many sources, all of which would be forced to wait for the smart-memory operation to complete. Allowing preemption avoids this problem but complicates memory design.

Further complications occur if a smart-memory operation requires interaction with other modules. If a memory module M_1 needs to send a read request to another memory module M_2 in order to complete a smart-memory operation at M_1 (e.g., to transport an object stored in M_2), the round-trip message delay will add to the time that M_1 takes to finish the operation. Again, preemption offers a way out by allowing M_1 to process other requests while it waits, but at the expense of added memory module complexity.

Especially when every memory module has a processor tightly coupled to it, it makes more sense to assign algorithmically complicated memory functions to a processor. A general characterization of the ideal higher-level operation to be performed directly by a memory module is that the operation should be computationally simple (to avoid complex hardware that duplicates the capabilities of processors), guaranteed to be of short duration (to avoid requiring preemption), and not require requests to be made to other modules (again to avoid needing preemption). Therefore, it is probably not desirable to delegate the transporter and scavenger functions in their entirety to the memory modules. However, memory modules may still be able to provide some simple functions that will streamline the handling of common cases. For example, a *block copy* operation could speed up transporting objects, and a *block scan* could be used to advantage by a scavenger algorithm running on a remote processor.

Memory modules may also be able to provide more novel services. For example, in response to challenge **C11** (concurrency generators), memory modules might include content-addressable memories and accept requests to search for matches to a given pattern and report back the matching data, or even create and queue up a Lisp task for each match. Although care would have to be taken that such an operation not violate the criteria discussed above by being too time-consuming, operations of this sort might be useful, for example, in efficiently implementing xapping applications. Probably our imagination is the most serious constraint to the set of useful smart-memory operations that can be devised without violating the above criteria.

Thus the principal memory design questions involve replication (and the associated problem of knowing where to find a copy of an object) and the selection of suitable smart-memory operations. Smart-memory operations, in turn, begin to blur the distinction between memory and processing functions, calling into question the conventional ideas about the distribution of work between processors and memories. As a result, the big picture cannot be discussed until processor organization has been considered as well.

3.5.4   Processor organization

In the context of our example machine, there are many processor design concerns. The processors should perform well for generic operations on tagged data, procedure invocation, task creation, task queuing, and scheduling. Additionally, processors should tolerate communication latency well. Several of these requirements (procedure invocation, task switching, and latency tolerance) involve context switching of one sort or another, so we can expect efficient context manipulation and switching to be important features of our processor.

There are too many processor design options to consider each at length here; however, we outline one example solution as an illustration of the possibilities. One way to achieve fast context switching is to have multiple register sets, or *contexts,* as the HEP-1 does [Kowalik 85, Smith 78], so that each instruction fetched can be from any one of a set of eligible tasks, with no penalty for switching from one task to another. This ability to have several tasks on "hot standby" enables the processor to tolerate latency by switching to a different task whenever a task blocks waiting for a message. We refer to a register set as a *physical context* since it is physically moved in and out of processor registers, in distinction to the possibly larger *logical context,* which includes task-specific information that remains in memory and is referenced there.

When a task blocks awaiting a message, it is reasonable to assume that it will not remain blocked for a long time. However, a task may block for long periods of time for other reasons (e.g., waiting for a future to resolve). A task that is blocked for a long time is using an expensive resource if it stays loaded into a processor's register set. If other runnable tasks exist, it is advantageous to unload a blocked task from the processor registers and replace it with a runnable task that can be used to help mask latency. Since achieving the highest degree of parallelism in concurrent Lisp programs often requires heavy use of synchronization constructs such as futures, it is important to reduce the cost of blocking of a task by a synchronization construct as much as possible. Thus it is desirable to minimize the amount of work involved in saving or restoring a context. This argues in favor of minimizing the size of physical contexts. On the other hand, if physical contexts are too small, extra processor time will be spent accessing those parts of a logical context that cannot be held in processor registers. This tradeoff—a large physical context speeds execution but slows context loading and unloading, while a small physical context speeds loading and unloading at the expense of slower execution—is a familiar one in processor architecture. The proper design point can be found only by measuring the performance of actual programs with several different physical context sizes.

Invoking a procedure or method amounts to pushing an old context on a stack of suspended contexts and creating a new context for execution of the procedure or method. One way to speed up this process is through the *register window* technique that has been tried on several research processors [Patterson 85, Taylor 86]. These processors have room for several physical contexts so that old contexts can usually remain where they are and a fresh set of registers can be used as the new physical context for procedure execution. This technique eliminates most memory accesses for saving and restoring contexts at procedure calls and returns. It is interesting to contemplate merging this mechanism for keeping multiple contexts within a processor with the hot standby mechanism previously discussed. In the merged mechanism, both calling a procedure and creating a task would begin by locating a free physical context, created if necessary by saving the contents of some currently loaded context in memory. At any point in time, some of a processor's physical contexts would be runnable and some would be suspended. Of the suspended contexts, some would be waiting for a message from the communication subnet, some would be waiting for a future to resolve, and some would be waiting for a called procedure to return. The net effect would be similar to that of register windows, but without the stack discipline on allocating contexts or moving them between memory and processor registers.

A processor structure of this sort, which makes it very inexpensive to create and execute short-lived tasks, could be used to let a processor help implement customized smart-memory operations on the memory module in its cluster. Such an operation would be requested by means of a message to the *processor,* rather than to the memory module. Receipt of the message would cause a short-lived task to be created in the processor, which could access the memory module directly to perform the requested operation. Finally, the task could send back any needed response message and terminate. Implemented in this way, smart-memory operations could benefit from fast context switching mechanisms already included in the processor for other reasons and thereby avoid falling under the constraints on smart-memory operations discussed in the previous section. This flexibility opens the way for even higher level smart-memory operations and a further blurring of the distinction between processor and memory operations.

A capability to create and switch between tasks efficiently is important, but it is only a building block. On top of this foundation there must be a bookkeeping system for keeping track of runnable and suspended tasks, so that a processor with unused capacity can find a suitable task to run, and an overloaded processor can shed some load. Especially if speculative parallelism causes tasks to have different priorities, it is important to ensure that, at any given moment, most of the tasks being executed are among the highest-priority runnable tasks. To ensure this, processors will have to exchange status information so that a processor running only low-priority tasks has a way of knowing that higher-priority runnable tasks exist elsewhere. The strategic decisions about scheduling are probably complex enough to be best left to software, but special processor design features could be useful in facilitating the exchange of status information and redistribution of tasks.

A final requirement for processor design for a concurrent Lisp machine is that it be able to manipulate tagged data and perform generic operations efficiently. This same requirement exists in systems for executing sequential Lisps, and there has been considerable debate over the value of hardware support for tagged data and generic operations.

A sensible approach, however, seems to be that taken by the SPUR processor [Taylor 86], which supports tagged data and generic operations in a basic way without wiring much detailed information about the Lisp type system into the hardware. Although one can still question the value of even this level of support, the value is probably greater for a concurrent Lisp using futures than for a sequential Lisp; this is because a natural implementation for futures is as a new data type *FUTURE* normally invisible to the programmer. All strict primitive operations become generic, handling an operand of type *FUTURE* by finding its value (or suspending the current task if the future is still unresolved) and using that value as the real operand.

Processor organization is clearly the aspect of concurrent Lisp machine design featuring the largest number of possible design philosophies and the smallest supply of hard data to guide the choice. Evaluating the approaches proposed in this section and working out their details will require a great deal of further work. Nevertheless, particularly in the area of context management, the preceding paragraphs outline a promising and little-tried approach to meeting several of the processing requirements for efficient concurrent Lisp execution.

3.5.5 Summary and discussion

Our example architecture consists of clusters composed of processor and memory modules tightly coupled to each other. Clusters are interconnected by a communication subnet through which they can exchange messages. Messages can range from simple read and write requests, through higher-level smart-memory operations, to arbitrary processor-to-processor communications. The subnet is fast enough to deliver messages between neighboring clusters at a speed comparable to that of contemporary system buses.

The most unconventional feature of the example architecture is the ability of processors to switch between multiple loaded contexts on an instruction-by-instruction basis. This mechanism offers a potential solution to several problems: latency tolerance, cheap creation of short-lived tasks, efficient procedure and method invocation, and implementation of sophisticated smart-memory operations.

It is appropriate at this point to review the success of the example architecture in meeting the challenges laid down in Sec. 3.3.4. Challenges **C2** (procedure calling), **C5** (pointer chasing), **C6** (small data transfers), and **C8** (frequent process creation) are addressed by storing multiple contexts in the processor. **C3** (garbage collection), **C9** (frequent synchronization), and **C11** (concurrency generators) can be addressed by defining suitable smart-memory operations, though many details remain to be worked out. **C1** (run-time typing) can be addressed by a processor architecture specialized to manipulate tagged data efficiently (along with a memory architecture allowing tagged data to be stored efficiently). **C4** (late binding) is a general commentary on the late-binding character of Lisp and is addressed in part by each of the mechanisms just mentioned. The two challenges about which the least substantive comments have been made are **C7** (replication of data) and **C10** (speculative parallelism). **C7** needs to be addressed in the memory architecture, perhaps through one of the mechanisms discussed at the beginning of Sec. 3.5.3. **C10** is the challenge about which we know the least, since good speculative parallelism features have yet to be worked out even at the language level. Further definitions of responses to this challenge will have to await further research.

3.6 Conclusion

Concurrent Lisp machine design is a wide-open area for research. Two prerequisites for defining a concurrent Lisp machine architecture are definition of a concurrent Lisp language and collection of a set of representative benchmark programs of realistic size. The concurrent Lisp research community appears to have reached consensus on some issues, such as the shared-memory model of access to data, but not on many other questions, such as the sources of concurrency to be exploited or the linguistic means for exploiting them. Furthermore, there is a serious scarcity of representative, realistic programs whose properties can guide the tuning of parameters of a concurrent Lisp architecture. As a result, this chapter has been forced to discuss concurrent Lisp machine design at a somewhat abstract and speculative level. Even so, it has been possible to identify several generic design requirements and discuss the potential advantages of certain unconventional architectural solutions. Before the real worth of any of these ideas can be known, however, they and their competitors must be worked out in much more detail and tested against a set of representative benchmarks. This is the largest single task toward which the concurrent Lisp research community must now orient itself.

Acknowledgments

The Parallel Processing Group in the MIT Laboratory for Computer Science provided the environment in which the ideas discussed in this article germinated. Thanks are due to past and present members of the group too numerous to list by name, who labored selflessly to build the Concert multiprocessor and the Multilisp implementation, and who also helped sharpen many of the ideas presented here. Thanks are due also to Doug DeGroot for his careful reading of the manuscript, his suggestions, and his encouragement.

Bibliography

[Abelson 84]   H. Abelson and G. Sussman. *Structure and Interpretation of Computer Programs.* MIT Press, Cambridge, MA, 1984.

[Ackerman 79]   W. Ackerman and J. Dennis. *VAL—A Value-Oriented Algorithmic Language.* LCS TR-218, MIT Laboratory for Computer Science, Cambridge, MA, 1979.

[Ahuja 86]   S. Ahuja, N. Carriero, and D. Gelernter. "Linda and Friends." *IEEE Computer,* vol. 19, no. 8, pp. 26–34, August 1986.

[Anderson 82]   T. Anderson. *The Design of a Multiprocessor Development System.* Technical Report TR-279, MIT Laboratory for Computer Science, Cambridge, MA, September 1982.

[Arvind 78]   K. Gostelow, Arvind, and W. Plouffe. *An Asynchronous Programming Language and Computing Machine.* Report TR114a, University of California, Irvine, CA, 1978.

[Backus 78]   J. Backus. "Can Programming be Liberated from the von Neumann Style? A Functional Style and its Algebra of Programs." *Comm. ACM* vol. 21, no. 8, pp. 613–641, August 1978.

[Baker 77]   H. Baker and C. Hewitt. "The Incremental Garbage Collection of Processes." Memo 454, MIT Artificial Intelligence Laboratory, Cambridge, MA, December 1977.

[BBN 82]   BBN. "Development of a Voice Funnel System: Quarterly Technical Report." BBN Reports no. 4845 (January 1982) and no. 5284 (April 1983), Bolt, Beranek, and Newman, Cambridge, MA.

[Courtemanche 86]   A. Courtemanche. *MultiTrash, a Parallel Garbage Collector for MultiScheme.* S.B. Thesis, MIT E.E.C.S. Department, Cambridge, MA, January 1986.

[Crowther 85]   W. Crowther, J. Goodhue, E. Starr, R. Thomas, W. Williken, and T. Blackadar. "Performance Measurements on a 128-Node Butterfly Parallel Processor." *1985 International Conference on Parallel Processing,* pp. 531–540, St. Charles, IL, August 1985.

[Dijkstra 76]   E. Dijkstra, et al., "On-the-fly Garbage Collection: An Exercise in Cooperation." *Language Hierarchies and Interfaces.* (*Lecture Notes in Computer Science,* vol. 46). Springer-Verlag, Berlin, 1976.

[Flynn 66]   M.J. Flynn. "Very High-Speed Computing Systems." *Proc. IEEE,* vol. 54, no. 12, pp. 1901–1909, December 1966.

[Friedman 76]   D. Friedman and D. Wise. "CONS Should Not Evaluate its Arguments." In S. Michaelson and R. Milner (eds). *Automata, Languages, and Programming,* pp. 257–284, Edinburgh University Press, Edinburgh, 1976.

[Friedman 78]   D. Friedman and D. Wise. "Aspects of Applicative Programming for Parallel Processing." *IEEE Trans. Comp.,* vol. C-27, no. 4, pp. 289–296, April 1978.

[Gabriel 84]   R.P. Gabriel and J. McCarthy. "Queue-Based Multi-Processing Lisp." *1984 ACM Symposium on Lisp and Functional Programming,* pp. 25–44, Austin, TX, August 1984.

[Gehringer 82]   E.F. Gehringer, A.K. Jones, and Z.Z. Segall. "The Cm* Testbed." *IEEE Computer,* vol. 15, no. 10, pp. 40–53, October 1982.

[Goodman 83]   J.R. Goodman. "Using Cache Memory to Reduce Processor-Memory

Traffic." *Tenth International Symposium on Computer Architecture,* pp. 124–131, Stockholm, June 1983.

[Goodman 85]   J.R. Goodman, J. Hsieh, K. Liou, A. Pleszkun, P. Schechter and H. C. Young. "PIPE: A VLSI Decoupled Architecture." *12th International Symposium on Computer Architecture,* pp. 20–27, Boston, June 1985.

[Halstead 78]   R. Halstead. "Object Management on Distributed Systems." *Seventh Texas Conference on Computing Systems,* pp. 7-7–7-14, Houston, TX, October 1978.

[Halstead 79]   R. Halstead. *Reference Tree Networks: Virtual Machine and Implementation.* Technical Report TR-222, MIT Laboratory for Computer Science, Cambridge, MA, July 1979.

[Halstead 81]   R. Halstead. "Architecture of a Myriaprocessor." *IEEE COMPCON Spring 81,* pp. 299–302, San Francisco, February 1981.

[Halstead 85]   R. Halstead. "Multilisp: A Language for Concurrent Symbolic Computation." *ACM Trans. on Prog. Languages and Systems,* vol. 7, no. 4, pp. 501–538, October 1985.

[Halstead 86a]   R. Halstead, T. Anderson, R. Osborne, and T. Sterling. "Concert: Design of a Multiprocessor Development System." *13th Annual Symposium on Computer Architecture,* pp. 40–48, Tokyo, June 1986.

[Halstead 86b]   R. Halstead. "Parallel Symbolic Computing." *IEEE Computer,* vol. 19, no. 8, pp. 35–43, August 1986.

[Hillis 85]   D. Hillis. *The Connection Machine.* MIT Press, Cambridge, MA, 1985.

[Hoare 78]   C.A.R. Hoare. "Communicating Sequential Processes." *Comm. ACM,* vol. 21, no. 8, pp. 666–677, August 1978.

[Katz 86]   M. Katz. *ParaTran: A Transparent, Transaction Based Runtime Mechanism for Parallel Execution of Scheme.* S.M. Thesis, MIT E.E.C.S. Department, Cambridge, MA, May 1986.

[Knight 86]   T. Knight. "An Architecture for Mostly Functional Languages." *1986 ACM Conference on Lisp and Functional Programming,* pp. 105–112, Cambridge, MA, August 1986.

[Knueven 76]   P. Knueven, P. Hibbard, and B. Leverett. "A Language System for a Multiprocessor Environment." *Fourth International Conference on the Design and Implementation of Algorithmic Languages,* pp. 264–274, Courant Institute of Mathematical Studies, New York, June 1976.

[Kowalik 85]   J.S. Kowalik. *Parallel MIMD Computation: HEP Supercomputer and Its Applications.* MIT Press, Cambridge, MA, 1985.

[Lee 85]   G. Lee, C. Kruskal and D. Kuck. "An Empirical Study of Automatic Restructuring of Nonnumerical Programs for Parallel Processors." *IEEE Trans. Computers,* vol. C-34, no. 10, pp. 927–933, October 1985.

[Marti 83]   J. Marti and J. Fitch. "The Bath Concurrent Lisp Machine." *EUROCAM '83. (Lecture Notes in Computer Science).* Springer-Verlag, Berlin, 1983.

[Matelan 85]   N. Matelan. "The Flex/32 Multicomputer." *12th Annual Symposium on Computer Architecture,* pp. 209–213, Boston, June 1985.

[McGraw 83]   J. McGraw, et al. *SISAL—Streams and Iteration in a Single-Assignment Language.* Language Reference Manual (version 1.0). Lawrence Livermore National Laboratory, Livermore, CA, July 1983.

[Metcalfe 76]   R. Metcalfe and D. Boggs. "Ethernet: Distributed Packet Switching for Local Computer Networks." *Comm. ACM,* vol. 19, no. 7, pp. 395–404, July 1976.

[Moon 84]   D. Moon. "Garbage Collection in a Large Lisp System." *1984 ACM Symposium on Lisp and Functional Programming,* pp. 235–246, Austin, TX, August 1984.

[Moon 86]   D. Moon. "Object-Oriented Programming with *Flavors." Proc. ACM OOPSLA '86 Conference,* pp. 1–8, September 1986.

[Patterson 85]   D. Patterson. "Reduced Instruction Set Computers." *Comm. ACM,* vol. 28, no. 1, pp. 8–21, January 1985.

[Pfister 85]   G. Pfister, W. Brantley, D. George, S.L. Harvey, W. Kleinfelder, K. McAuliffe, E. Melton, V. Norton, and J. Weiss. "The IBM Research Parallel Processor Prototype (RP3): Introduction and Architecture." *1985 International Conference on Parallel Processing,* pp. 764–771, St. Charles, IL, August 1985.

[Rees 86]   J. Rees and W. Clinger (eds). "Revised Report on the Algorithmic Language Scheme." *ACM SIGPLAN Notices,* vol. 21, no. 12, pp. 37–79, December 1986.

[Rettberg 79]   R. Rettberg, et al. "Development of a Voice Funnel System: Design Report." BBN Report no. 4088, Bolt, Beranek, and Newman, Cambridge, MA, August 1979.

[Rodgers 85]   D. Rodgers. "Improvements in Multiprocessor System Design." *12th Annual Symposium on Computer Architecture,* pp. 225–231, Boston, June 1985.

[Russell 78]   R.M. Russell. "The Cray-1 Computer System." *Comm. ACM,* vol. 21, no. 1, pp. 63–72, January 1978.

[Seitz 85]   C.L. Seitz. "The Cosmic Cube." *Comm. ACM,* vol. 28, no. 1, pp. 22–33, January 1985.

[Smith 78]   B.J. Smith. "A Pipelined, Shared Resource MIMD Computer." *Proc. International Conference on Parallel Processing,* 1978.

[Steele 86]   G.L. Steele and W.D. Hillis. "Connection Machine Lisp: Fine-Grained Parallel Symbolic Processing." *1986 ACM Conference on Lisp and Functional Programming.* pp. 279–297, Cambridge, MA, August 1986.

[Sweazey 86]   P. Sweazey and A.J. Smith. "A Class of Compatible Cache Consistency Protocols and Their Support by the IEEE Futurebus." *13th Annual Symposium on Computer Architecture,* pp. 414–423, Tokyo, June 1986.

[Taylor 86]   G. Taylor, P. Hilfinger, J. Larus, D. Patterson, and B. Zorn. "Evaluation of the SPUR Lisp Architecture." *13th Annual Symposium on Computer Architecture,* pp. 444–452, Tokyo, June 1986.

[Turner 79]   D. Turner. "A New Implementation Technique for Applicative Languages." *Software—Practice and Experience,* vol. 9, no. 1, pp. 31–49, January 1979.

4

Design Issues of Multiprocessors for Artificial Intelligence

Benjamin W. Wah

University of Illinois, Urbana, IL

Guo-jie Li

Academia Sinica, Beijing, People's Republic of China

4.1 Introduction

In recent years, artificial intelligence (AI) techniques have been widely used in various applications, such as natural-language understanding, computer vision, and robotics. As AI applications move from the laboratories to the real world and as AI software grows in complexity, the computational throughput and cost are increasingly important concerns. The conventional von Neumann computers are not suitable for AI applications because they were designed mainly for sequential and deterministic numeric computations. Extensive efforts have been devoted to investigate and develop efficient AI architectures [Wah 86]. This chapter provides a state-of-the-art assessment of AI-oriented systems and discusses the major issues involved in such designs. Chapter 7 discusses various architectural classes of AI machines with case studies.

4.1.1 Characteristics of AI computations

To develop a special-purpose computer to support AI applications, the requirements of these applications must be fully understood. Many conventional numeric algorithms are well analyzed, and bounds on their computational performance have been established. In contrast, many AI applications are characterized by symbolic processing, nondeterministic computations, dynamic execution, large potential for parallel and distributed processing, management of extensive knowledge, and an open system.

Symbolic processing.   Data are generally processed in symbolic form in AI applications. Primitive symbolic operations, such as comparison, selection, sorting, matching, logic set operations (union, intersection, and negation), contexts and partitions, transitive closure, and pattern retrieval and recognition, are frequently used. At a higher level, symbolic operations on patterns such as sentences, speech, graphics, and images may be needed.

Nondeterministic computations.   Many AI algorithms are nondeterministic; that is, it is impossible to plan in advance the procedures to execute and to terminate with the available information. This is attributed to a lack of knowledge and a complete understanding of the problem; it may result in exhaustively enumerating all possibilities when the problem is solved or in a controlled search through a solution space.

Dynamic execution.   With a lack of complete knowledge and anticipation of the solution process, the capabilities and features of existing data structures and functions may be defined and new data structures and functions created while the problem is actually being solved. Further, the maximum size for a given structure may be so large that it is impossible to allocate the necessary memory space ahead of time. As a result, when the problem is solved, memory space and other resources may have to be dynamically allocated and deallocated, tasks may be dynamically created, and communication topology may be dynamically changing.

Large potential for parallel and distributed processing.   In parallel processing of deterministic algorithms, a set of necessary and independent tasks must be identified and processed concurrently. This class of parallelism is called AND-parallelism. In AI processing, the large degree of nondeterminism offers an additional source of parallel processing. Tasks at a nondeterministic decision point can be processed in parallel. This latter class is called OR-parallelism.

Knowledge management.   Knowledge is an important component in reducing the complexity of solving a given problem; more *useful* knowledge means less exhaustive searching. However, many AI problems may have very high inherent complexity, hence the amount of useful knowledge may also be exceedingly large. Further, the knowledge acquired may be fuzzy, heuristic, and uncertain in nature. The representation, management, manipulation, and learning of knowledge are, therefore, important problems to be addressed.

Open system.   In many AI applications, the knowledge needed to solve the problem may be incomplete because the source of the knowledge is unknown at the time the solution is devised, or the environment may be changing and cannot be anticipated at design time. AI systems should be designed with an open concept and allow continuous refinement and acquisition of new knowledge.

In general, there are two basic approaches to improving the computational efficiency of processing AI tasks: having heuristic knowledge to guide searches and using faster computers. In the following sections, these approaches are discussed.

4.1.2   Heuristic searches

The key performance-related feature of AI computations is their nondeterminism, which results from a lack of complete understanding of the solution process. In other words, when a problem becomes well understood and can be solved by a deterministic algorithm, we usually cease to consider it "intelligent," although the problem may still be symbolic [Simon 86].

The starting point of conventional computations is deterministic algorithms, whereas efficient deterministic algorithms to solve a given AI problem are a result of the knowledge accumulated and the gradual refinement of the computations. This involves the succinct choice of an appropriate knowledge-representation scheme, the learning mechanisms to acquire the related knowledge, and a suitable architecture to support the computations. Good heuristics designed from previous experience may allow a complex problem to be solved efficiently, even on a serial processor.

Since the mid-1960s, it has become apparent to the AI community that inference alone is often inadequate to solve real-life problems. To enhance the performance of AI algorithms, they must be augmented with knowledge and metaknowledge of the problem domain in addition to formal reasoning methods. *Metaknowledge* refers to the control information to guide the search. This realization gave birth to *knowledge engineering* and *knowledge-based systems,* the field of applied AI [Feigenbaum 83]. Since knowledge stored in any knowledge-based system may be incomplete and inaccurate, combinatorial searches are still needed.

4.1.3 Faster technologies and parallel processing

An AI computer system must support both knowledge-based management and heuristic searches. Faster technologies and parallel processing are means to improve the computational efficiency. For many applications, such as natural-language understanding and computer vision, the current achievable performance is much lower than that needed. For example, according to the Defense Advanced Research Project Agency's (DARPA) strategic computing proposal, it was estimated that an equivalent of 1 trillion von Neumann computer operations per second were required to perform the vehicle-vision task at a level that would satisfy the long-range objective of the Autonomous Vehicle Project [Spectrum 83]. At best, current sequential computers of reasonable cost achieve processing rates below 100 million operations per second, which implies at least 10^4 times improvement in performance is required.

Newer technologies can help in designing faster computers. For example, using GaAs high-electron-mobility transistors (HEMTs), it was estimated that for a computer with over 500,000 gates operating at 77 K and 15 levels per pipeline stage, the cycles times would be 2.7 ns with 5 W and 3200 gates per chip, and 2.0 ns with 20 W and 5200 gates per chip, respectively [Amdahl 87]. In contrast, a liquid-cooled Cray 2 supercomputer built using emitter-coupled logic (ECL) technologies has 8 levels per pipeline stage, more than 500,000 gates, and operates at 300 K and 4.1 ns per cycle. The delay of one ECL gate level is approximately translated into 1.5 GaAs HEMT gate levels; hence, correcting the cycle time of the Cray 2 supercomputer into HEMT technologies and 15 levels results in a 5.1-ns cycle time for the Cray 2 computer. In short, there is a factor of 2 in using the newer technologies available today.

Another way to decrease the cycle time is to reduce the interconnect delay. It was estimated that with GaAs HEMTs operating at a 2-ns cycle time, the switching, fan-out, and interconnect delays were approximately 2 percent, 10.5 percent, and 87.5 percent of the cycle time, respectively [Amdahl 87]. Although superconductivity can be used to reduce the interconnect delays, it is less desirable with GaAs technologies, due to the high impedance in the gates, and more desirable with ECL technologies. When combined, these newer technologies available today may allow one to two orders of magnitude improvement in the cycle times of computers.

The trend in designing AI computers has been toward applying faster technologies and parallelism to process computation-intensive

AI tasks. Examples of parallel AI systems currently available or under research/development include ALICE, Aquarius, Butterfly, Concurrent Lisp machine, Connection Machine, DADO, FAIM-1, FFP, iPSC, Japanese Fifth-Generation Computer System (FGCS), NETL, NON-VON, Rediflow, SOAR, SPUR, and ZMOB [Wah 86]. Some of these computers, such as the Aquarius, Butterfly, iPSC, and ZMOB, were designed for both numeric and symbolic processing.

Recently, there is another trend to design small-grain massively parallel architectures for AI applications. These architectures are sometimes called *connectionist systems;* they are composed of a very large number of simple processing elements. Knowledge of a given entity in such systems is distributed on a number of processing elements and links, and each processor or link may be shared by multiple entities. The use of connections rather than memory cells as the principal means to store information leads to the name *connectionism* [Fahlman 87]. The resemblance to neurons in a brain also results in the term *neural networks.* Connectionist and neural systems are discussed in Chap. 16. Many computers can simulate connectionist systems. An example is the Connection Machine developed by Thinking Machines Inc., which can perform neural-network simulations two to three orders of magnitude faster than serial machines of comparable cost [Hillis 85, Waltz 87].

The high performance of many parallel AI computers is achieved through associative processing and *data-level parallelism.* This approach is suitable for operations on large databases, such as sorting, set operations, statistical analysis, and associative pattern matching. Yet data-level parallelism is not intelligent enough. For general AI applications involving heuristic searches, control-level parallelism should be involved. Unfortunately, early experience with multiprocessor architectures for Hearsay-II [Fennell 77], Eurisko [Lenat 84], OPS5 [Forgy 84], and others has led to a belief that parallel AI programs will not have a speedup of more than one order of magnitude. A possibly revolutionary approach to designing parallel languages and systems for AI processing may be needed.

One misconception in parallel processing is to use the total computing power of a parallel system to characterize the rate at which a given AI application is processed. Due to the nondeterminism in AI computations, a high computing power does not always imply a shorter completion time. Since most AI applications involve heuristic searches, resources may be devoted to fruitless searches, which use more computing power but do not help to decrease the time to find a solution. In fact, anomalies may happen such that increasing the degree of parallelism may even increase the completion time in nondeterministic searches [Wah 85, Li 87, Li 86a]. What is important is how to allocate resources so only useful tasks are performed. The question of solving an AI problem in a parallel processing environment is still largely unanswered.

Another misconception about parallel processing is that it can be used to extend the solvable problem size of AI problems. Due to the high complexity of AI problems, parallel processing is useful *in improving the computational efficiency*, but *not in extending the solvable problem size* [Wah 85]. For example, a problem of size N and complexity N^k can be solved in N^k time units by a sequential processor. Assuming that N processors are used, X, the new problem size that can be solved in the same amount of time, satisfies the following equation:

$$N*N^k = X^k$$

The left-hand side of the above equation represents the total computing power in N^k units of time with N processors, and the right-hand side represents the number of operations to be performed in solving a problem of size X. Solving the above equation yields

$$X = N^{1+1/k}$$

Table 4.1 summarizes the results for other instances. It is assumed that the size of the problem solved by a sequential processor is N, that the number of parallel processors ranges from 1 to 2^N, that linear speedup is achievable, and that the same amount of time is allocated to both sequential and parallel processing. The first column of Table 4.1 shows the complexities of solving the problem optimally, and the other columns show the corresponding sizes of the same problem that can be evaluated in the same amount of time for various number of processors. The extension in problem size is minimal when the problem involved is complex. This is evident in the last row in which the problem solved has exponential complexity. In this case only a logarithmic increase in problem size is achieved when a polynomial num-

TABLE 4.1   Relative Problem Sizes Solvable in a Fixed Amount of Time Assuming Linear Speedup†

Complexity to find optimal solution	Number of processors					
	1	N	N^2	N^3	N^k	2^N
N	N	N^2	N^3	N^4	N^{k+1}	$N2^N$
N^2	N	$N^{1.5}$	N^2	$N^{2.5}$	$N^{k/2+1}$	$N2^{N/2}$
N^3	N	$N^{1.33}$	$N^{1.67}$	N^2	$N^{k/3+1}$	$N2^{N/3}$
N^k	N	$N^{1+1/k}$	$N^{1+2/k}$	$N^{1+3/k}$	N^2	$N2^{N/k}$
2^N	N	$N + \log N$	$N + 2 \log N$	$N + 3 \log N$	$N + k \log N$	$2N$

†When sequential processing is used, problem size is N.

ber of processors are used, and a linear increase results with an exponential number of processors.

In essence, parallel processing alone cannot circumvent the difficulty of combinatorial explosion. The power of multiprocessing should not be overemphasized and must be combined with heuristic information to solve complex AI problems. Currently, methods for combining heuristic information and massive parallelism are still largely unknown. The publication in 1985 of the Sixth-Generation Computing System development proposal shows a serious intention in Japan to go beyond the current FGCS activities and address the AI aspects of computations [Agency 85].

4.1.4 Design issues of parallel AI architectures

The essential issues in designing a computer system to support a given AI application can be classified into the representation level, the control level, and the processor level. The *representation level* deals with the knowledge and methods used to solve a given AI problem and the means to represent it. Design issues related to the representation level are discussed in Sec. 4.2. The *control level* is concerned with the detection of dependencies and parallelism in the algorithmic and program representations of the problem. Design issues related to the control level are presented in Sec. 4.3. The processor level addresses the hardware and architectural components needed to evaluate the algorithmic and program representations. Issues related to the processor level are discussed in Sec. 4.4. Examples of issues in each level are shown in Table 4.2.

Developing an AI architecture requires solutions to many issues in each level. Yet some of these issues are still open at this time. In this chapter, we do not provide an exhaustive survey of all reported projects and their relevant issues. Instead, we discuss some important issues concerning the three levels and illustrate the solutions with a number of representative systems.

4.2 Representation Level

Since 1950, knowledge-representation schemes have been widely discussed in the literature [Brachman 85, Dreyfues 86]. The representation level is an important element in the design process and dictates whether or not the given problem can be solved in a reasonable amount of time. Although various paradigms have been developed, most existing knowledge-representation methods and AI languages were designed for sequential computations, and the requirements of parallel processing were either not taken into account or were only secondary considerations. Moreover, many designers of AI computers

TABLE 4.2   Examples of Issues in Designing AI Computers
_____

Representation level:
  Choosing an appropriate knowledge representation
  Representing metaknowledge
  Acquiring and learning domain knowledge and metaknowledge
  Representing knowledge in a distributed fashion
  Declaring parallelism in AI languages

Control level:
  Analyzing data dependencies
  Synchronization
  Maintaining consistency
  Partitioning AI problems
  Deciding granularity of parallelism
  Dynamic scheduling and load balancing
  Efficient search strategies
  Tradeoffs on using heuristic information
  Predicting performance and linear scaling

Processor level:
  Defining computational models
  Developing methods to pass information
  Designing hardware for overhead-intensive operations
  Designing interconnection structure for load balancing and communication of
    guiding and pruning information
  Managing large memory space
_____

start with a given language or knowledge-representation scheme;
hence the representation level is already fixed. Research in designing
AI computers has focused on automatic methods of detecting detect
parallelism and providing hardware support for time-consuming operations in a given representation but has not aided users much in collecting and organizing knowledge or in designing efficient algorithms.

4.2.1 Domain-knowledge representations

Domain knowledge refers to objects, events, and actions. From an implementation point of view, the criteria to evaluate a representation
scheme for a multiprocessing system are its declarative power, the degree of knowledge distribution, and its structuralization.

Declarative vs. procedural representations. The major knowledge-
representation paradigms used today can roughly be classified into declarative and procedural ones, although most practical representation
schemes combine features from both. Declarative representations specify
static knowledge, while procedural ones include static knowledge as well
as the control information that operates on this static knowledge. Horn
clauses (or even first-order logic), semantic networks, and rule-based production systems are examples of declarative representations, while Lisp

programs are procedural representations. Frames combine both declarative and procedural information to represent structured knowledge. Attached to each frame is various heuristic information, such as a procedure on using the information in the frame.

A declarative approach allows hiding procedural control-flow information, thereby resulting in an easily created, modified, and understood knowledge representation. Declarative representations are referentially transparent; that is, the meaning of a whole can be derived solely from the meaning of its parts and is independent of its historical behavior. This may significantly increase program productivity because of its user orientation and user friendliness.

Declarative representations offer higher potential for parallelism than procedural ones for the same problem, because a declarative representation specifies tasks as a set, while a procedural representation may overconstrain the order of execution by the implicit order of statements. Parallel versions of procedural representations, such as parallel Lisp programs, achieve a limited amount of concurrency, while relying on programmers to specify the parallel tasks [Halstead 84, Halstead 88]. However, parallelism in a declarative representation may be restricted by the implementation of the language translators. For example, interpreters for rule-based production systems can be viewed as pattern-directed procedure invocations. Although pattern matching may provide a rich source of parallelism, the match-select-act cycle is a bottleneck and restricts the potential parallelism. Fewer restrictions are seen in the implementation of logic programming and semantic networks. This is the key reason behind the Japanese FGCS project's choosing logic as the basic representation. It has also been reported that if 256K processing units were used, the Connection Machine, using a semantic-network representation, can execute four orders of magnitude faster than a sequential Lisp machine with respect to a number of object-recognition problems [Flynn 85].

A disadvantage of declarative representations is that their nondeterminism is usually associated with a large search space that may partly counteract the gains of parallel processing; whereas procedural schemes allow the specification and direct interaction of facts and heuristic information, hence eliminating wasteful searches. A tradeoff between the degree of parallelism and the size of the search space must be made in designing a representation scheme.

Distributed-knowledge representations. A second criterion to use in evaluating a representation scheme is its degree of distribution. In a local representation, each concept is stored in a distinct physical device, and each device may be shared among multiple concepts. Although this simplifies their management, the knowledge will be lost if the device fails. Most current AI systems adopt the local representations.

Recently, distributed representations have been proposed. In this scheme, a piece of knowledge is represented by a large number of units and distributed among multiple physical devices, and each device is shared among multiple knowledge entities. The resulting system is more robust because the failure of one physical device may cause some but not all information to be lost in multiple knowledge entities. Neural networks [Hopfield 82] and the Boltzmann machine [Hinton 84] are examples in this class. The proposed Boltzmann machine consists of a very large network of binary-valued elements that are connected to one another by bidirectional links with real-value weights. The weight on a link represents a weak pairwise constraint between two hypotheses. A positive weight indicates that the two hypotheses tend to support one another, while a negative weight suggests that the two hypotheses should not both be accepted. The quality of a solution is then determined by the total cost of all constraints it violates.

Another interesting distributed knowledge-representation scheme, called sparse distributed memory (SDM), has been proposed by Kanerva [Kanerva 86]. The SDM has a 1000-bit address to model a *random* sample of 2^{20} physical locations. Given a 1000-bit read/write address, the locations in the SDM that are within 450 bits of this address are selected associatively. Statistically, nearly 1000 memory locations will be selected. The word read is a statistical reconstruction by a majority rule. The SDM model was designed with an analogy to the human brain and can perform pattern computations such as looking up patterns similar to a given pattern and generating a pattern that is an abstraction of a given set of similar patterns [Denning 86]. Although it is much simplified with respect to the human brain, its concept may lead to a new class of computers suitable for pattern computations.

Distributed representations are generally fault-tolerant in that within a large parallel network with a few faulty units, the remaining pattern is still usable. This property is very attractive for wafer-scale integration. The disadvantage of distributed representations is that they are hard for an outside observer to understand and modify, so automatic learning schemes must be employed. An open problem at this time is to combine local and distributed representations by decomposing a large knowledge base into partitions and using a local representation for each.

Structuralization of knowledge. A third criterion to use in evaluating knowledge-representation schemes is their structuralization, which is related to the inference time and the amount of memory space required to store the knowledge.

In general, the more structured a knowledge representation is, the less inference time and the more memory space are needed. An experimental comparison of efficiency has been reported for four kinds of knowledge-representation schemes for a pilot expert system, namely, the simple production system, structured production system, frame, and logic [Niwa 84]. It was found that the volume of the knowledge base was different for the four schemes. In one instance, both production systems have 263 rules and 15K characters, the frame system has 213 frames and 29K characters, and the logic system has 348 clauses and 17K characters. The memory space required by the frame system is the largest because some related pieces of knowledge have to be replicated in different frames. Since at most one conclusion is allowed in each Horn clause, the space of the logic system is larger than that of the production systems. The experimental results also show that, with respect to forward and backward reasoning, the frame system is the fastest, while the logic system is the slowest. The efficiency of the frame system is relatively insensitive to the size of the knowledge base because related pieces of knowledge are connected to one another by pointers, thereby limiting searches. Inference time for the simple production system is moderately sensitive to changes in the size of the knowledge base, while that for the logic system is markedly sensitive to changes in size.

Structured knowledge representations are usually desirable as long as the memory space needed is reasonable. To achieve this end, metaknowledge may be included in the knowledge base to reduce the search overhead needed. There are two problems in using metaknowledge. First, it consumes more memory space and may increase the overheads in memory management and communication. Second, metaknowledge in a poorly understood domain may be fallible and may lead the search in the wrong direction, thereby increasing the total search time. Theoretical studies and experimental comparisons are urgently needed to address this space-time tradeoff.

4.2.2   Metaknowledge representations

Metaknowledge includes the extent and origin of domain knowledge of a particular object, the reliability of certain information, the possibility that an event will occur, and the precedence constraints. In other words, metaknowledge is knowledge about domain knowledge. Metaknowledge can be considered to exist in a single level or in a hierarchy [Bowen 85]. In a hierarchical form, metaknowledge is used to decide which domain-dependent actions to perform, while *metametaknowledge* is the control knowledge about metaknowledge.

Higher level metaknowledge is commonsense knowledge known to humans.

The use of metaknowledge allows one to express the partial specification of program behavior in a declarative language, hence making programs more aesthetic, simpler to build, and easier to modify. It facilitates incremental system development; that is, one can start from a search-intensive program and incrementally add control information until a possibly search-free program is obtained. Last, many knowledge-representation schemes and programming paradigms, such as logic, frames, semantic networks, and object-orient programming, can be integrated with the aid of metaknowledge [Genesereth 83a, Bowen 85a].

Metaknowledge can be classified as deterministic and statistical according to the correctness and efficiency considerations.

Deterministic metaknowledge.   Deterministic metaknowledge is related to the correct execution of the algorithm. Metaknowledge about precedence relationships results from a better understanding of the problem; this helps reduce the resource and time complexities. For instance, to solve the problem of sorting a list, it is necessary to analyze the problem, find the appropriate representation, and evaluate the necessary tasks. A list of n elements can be sorted by searching in parallel in $O(\log n!)$ average time $(= O(n \cdot \log n))$ one of the $n!$ permutations that contain the sorted elements; however, an algorithm such as Quicksort contains functionally dependent subtasks and can sort the list in $O(n \cdot \log n)$ average time using one processor. In general, the more deeply we understand the problem to be solved, the larger is the set of necessary precedence constraints and the more efficient is the solution to the problem.

Many AI languages allow programmers to specify the sequence of executions in a serial computer, but the metaknowledge to specify the correct execution in a multiprocessing environment is incomplete or missing. In programs written in pure declarative languages, the static aspects of the represented knowledge are stressed, while the controls are left to the compiler/interpreter. For instance, in a logic program, a clause "a : − a_1, a_2, a_3." means that 'a' is true, if 'a_1,' 'a_2,' and 'a_3' are true, but nothing about their functional dependencies is represented. The sequence of executions in a serial computer is correct because a definite search order is imposed, but the precedence relationships among subgoals are unknown to the scheduler in a multiprocessor.

In a number of AI languages, such as Prolog, the type and meaning of variables and functions are dynamic and query-dependent and cannot be completely specified at compile time. To use metaknowledge in this regard, the semantic meaning of subgoals and operations can be specified, which can be interpreted as precedence relationships by the scheduler at run time. In logic programming, the method to represent semantic information in a general and efficient way is still open.

The *metarules* used must be sufficient and precise such that all precedence relationships can be derived unambiguously and easily. An important consideration is the scope within which metarules can be applied. Commonsense metarules should be included to operate on more specific metarules specified by the programmers. Using the metarules, the interpreter/compiler generates the necessary synchronization primitives.

Several researchers have addressed the above problem. Gallaire and Lasserre used metaknowledge expressed as a general or special control strategy in a Prolog-like interpreter [Gallaire 82]. In their approach, metaknowledge is made explicit through metarules, each of which describes an action to be undertaken by the interpreter whenever the interpreter focuses its attention on an object involved in the metarule. In LP, a Prolog equation-solver learning system [Silver 86], control information is expressed in a declarative representation, and inference is performed at the metalevel. Search at the object level is replaced by search at the metalevel. Research is necessary to provide a practical method to unambiguously specify the needed synchronization through metaknowledge.

Statistical metaknowledge.   Statistical metaknowledge can be used to enhance the computational efficiency of an AI program. Warren used a simple heuristic and reordered only the goals of compound queries written in pure Prolog [Warren 81]; even so, he typically obtained query speedups of an order of magnitude. The probability of a subgoal's success and the associated search cost have been found to be useful in guiding the search of logic programs [Li 85, Gooley 88]. In general, clauses in Prolog with the same head should be ordered such that those likely to succeed with a smaller expected search cost are searched first. In contrast, subgoals within a clause should be ordered such that those likely to fail with a smaller expected search cost are searched first.

In many expert systems, the *belief* and other measurements of accuracy of the information have been widely used. For example, in MYCIN, the *confidence factor* (CF) is used to decide among alternatives during a consultation session [Buchanan 84]. A CF of a rule is a measurement of the association between premises and actions. A positive CF indicates that the evidence confirms the hypothesis, while a negative CF indicates disconfirming evidence.

The representation of metaknowledge about uncertainty is an active topic in AI. Several methods, such as Fuzzy logic and Dempster-Shafer theory, are studied currently. The proper choice is still unclear.

4.2.3   AI languages and programming

Conventional imperative languages are inefficient and complex to program for symbolic and pattern processing; hence, the design of AI programming languages has had a central role in the history of AI research. Frequently, new ideas in AI were accompanied by a new language that was natural for expressing the ideas.

To enhance programmer productivity and take full advantage of parallel processing, declarative languages have been designed for AI programming. Function-oriented, logic-oriented, and object-oriented languages are the major programming paradigms today. Lisp is an early and widely used functional language; it is characterized by symbolic computations, representation of information by lists, and recursion as the only control mechanism. Numerous imperative features have been incorporated into different dialects of Lisp, so most Lisp programs are not actually declarative, but a large enough subset allows declarative programming to be done.

Hybrids of programming paradigms have been developed. One simple approach to combining features from two languages is to provide an interface between the two. Examples include Loglisp [Robinson 82], Funlog [DeGroot 85a], and OIL [Davis 85]. Providing features from multiple languages within a single unified framework, such as Lambda Prolog, has also been proposed. A different approach called *narrowing* involves replacing pattern matching in functional languages by unification [Reddy 85]. Logic programs can then be expressed as functions. Recently, three commercial programming tools, KEE, ART, and LOOPS, have been introduced, which provide a mechanism to allow multiple paradigms to be used in a program.

New AI languages feature large declarative power, symbolic processing constructs, representing information by lists, and using recursion as the only control mechanism. These languages differ in their expressive power, their ease of implementation, and their ability to specify parallelism and to include heuristic knowledge. A language-oriented AI computer will inherit all the features and limitations of the language it implements. It should be noted that no single paradigm is appropriate for all problems, because one language may be more "natural" than another depending on the requirements and the personal view. Hence, intelligent systems should allow multiple styles, including function-oriented, object-oriented, and logic-oriented paradigms.

Expressive power vs. ease of implementation. Functional languages, such as pure Lisp [McCarthy 78], Backus's FP [Backus 82], HOPE [Bailey 85], and VAL [McGraw 80], share many features with logic languages, including their declarative nature, reliance on recursion, and potential for execution parallelism. Yet they have vital individual features as well. First, in functional programs, input and output variables are fixed, while in logic programs, the modes of variables are query-dependent. For example, the statement $z = plus(x,y)$ in a functional program implies that x and y are inputs and z is output. In contrast, in a logic program, the goal sum (X,Y,Z) has eight possible combinations of modes of variables X, Y, and Z. For instance, (in, out, in) means that $Y = Z - X$. Second, in a functional program, only constant and constructor functions can appear in the output, while in a logic program, logic variables can be used as output. Third, pure functional programs are deterministic, and no search is needed, while logic programs are inherently nondeterministic and require searches. Finally, functional programming provides the ability to write high-order functions; that is, a function can be passed as an argument. In contrast, Prolog is a first-order language, although some logic programming languages are not.

The first three properties, especially the nondirectionality, make logic languages more expressive in the sense that a single logic program corresponds to several functional programs. Moreover, logic and functional programs are executed using *resolution* and *reduction* (or *term rewriting*), respectively. Note that resolution can use input information implicit in the patterns to cut down the size of the set to be examined. For example, to solve the append subgoal append([P], [Q,R], [1,2,3]), resolution makes no distinction between inputs and outputs and uses the input information (length of the lists) to select the appropriate clauses and produce bindings for the variables involved. However, in the corresponding functional formulation ([P], [Q,R]) = split([1,2,3]), all possible splits of [1,2,3] are produced, and the one that splits the list into [P] and [Q,R] will be selected. The above example illustrates that reduction can lead to overcomputation as compared to resolution.

The crucial disadvantage of functional programming lies in the difficulty of representing inherent nondeterminism in AI problems. Although the recursive formulation and the leftmost-outermost reduction of functional programs enable depth-first searches naturally, it is difficult to write a heuristic search program with a pure functional language since heuristic searches are inherently history-sensitive. In fact, best-first-search programs written in Lisp include a lot of "setq" and "prog" statements, which are not pure functional primitives [Winston 84]. Due to their less expressive power for representing nondeterminism and their inefficiency in dealing with large data structures, pure functional languages are unsuitable for general AI applications.

Although logic languages are more expressive, their implementations, especially in a parallel processing environment, are more difficult due to the nondirectionality of variables. The dynamic nature of modes requires run-time analysis. In contrast, the run-time behavior of functional programs is much simpler to control than that of logic programs, particularly in a parallel context. Techniques, such as graph reduction and dataflow, have been developed for the parallel evaluation of functional languages. Furthermore, Lisp has only a few primitive operators and provides unique list structures to compound data objects. These features simplify the implementation of Lisp compilers/interpreters. In fact, Scheme, a dialect of Lisp, has been implemented in a single chip [Sussman 81]. The implementation, however, may be complicated by the dynamic nature of Lisp programs and primitives with side effects introduced in practical functional languages. Dynamic features, such as random accesses to linked lists, garbage collection, frequent function calls, and dynamic binding of functions, incur extensive run-time overheads.

Obviously, it would be advantageous if the simple controls of functional languages could be implemented in the more expressive logic languages. Considerable efforts have been devoted to combine functional and logic programming [DeGroot 85a]. One approach to simplifying logic languages is to introduce directionality of modes of variables [Reddy 85]. This method degrades its expressive power to that of first-order functional languages. Others attempt to extend functional languages to achieve the expressive power of logic languages but retain most of the underlying functional simplicity. An example is HOPE with unification [Darlington 85]. Unfortunately, up to now, a language that has good expressive power and yet is flexible enough for parallel execution does not exist. Efforts are needed in this direction.

Specification of parallelism.   Since parallel processing was not a consideration when most existing AI languages, such as Lisp and Prolog, were designed, the precedence restrictions implicit in a sequential execution order cannot be detected easily in a parallel execution. To extend these languages in a parallel processing environment, explicit primitives may have to be included.

In a pure functional language (dataflow language), the meaning of an expression is independent of the history of computations performed prior to the evaluation of this expression. Precedence restrictions occur as a result of function application. Notions such as side effects do not exist; hence all arguments and distinct elements in a dynamically created structure can be evaluated concurrently. For example, to compute the average of numbers in a list s, (1.(2.(3.nil))), using the function

average(s) = div(sum(s), count(s)), the computations of sum(1.(2.(3.nil)))
and count(1.(2.(3.nil))) can proceed concurrently. It has been reported
that implementations of functional languages on parallel computers
seem easier than on sequential ones [Darlington 84].

Note that Lisp and many of its dialects are not pure functional languages. Referential transparency is lost in most Lisp languages due to
side effects. The precedence restrictions are represented not only in
function calls but also in procedures.

Several parallel Lisp languages have been proposed and implemented. Multilisp, developed by Halstead, has been implemented on a
128-processor Butterfly computer. Concurrency in Multilisp can be
specified by means of the **pcall** and **future** constructs [Halstead 86a].
pcall embodies an implicit fork-join. For example, (**pcall** A B C) results in the concurrent evaluation of expressions A, B, and C. The
form (**future** X) immediately returns *future* (a pseudo value) for X and
creates a task to concurrently evaluate X, hence allowing concurrency
between the computation and the use of X. When the evaluation of X
yields a value, it replaces the *future*. The **future** construct is good in
expressing mandatory parallelism but is quite expensive in the current Multilisp implementation.

Another parallel Lisp language, Concurrent Lisp [Sugimoto 81], is
extended from Lisp 1.5 and has three additional primitive functions to
specify concurrency: Starteval for process activation, and CR (critical
region function) and CCR (conditional critical region function) for mutual exclusion. A multiprocessing program written in Concurrent Lisp
is a set of cooperating sequential processes, each of which evaluates its
given form. Similar to P/V primitives, CR and CCR have enough
power to express process interactions.

In Parlog, a parallel logic programming language [Clark 84b], every argument has a mode declaration that states whether the argument
is input (?) or output ($\wedge$). For example, in the following statements:

mode merge(?,?,$\wedge$).

merge([U|X],y,[U|Z])←merge(X,Y,Z).

the first two lists are merged to form the result. In Concurrent Prolog
[Shapiro 83], a read-only annotation (?) is used. For example,

merge([U|X],Y,[U|Z])←merge(X?,Y,Z).

indicates that X must have a value before merge(X?,Y,Z) can be invoked. Another way to specify the concurrency is to use different symbols to distinguish between parallel AND and sequential AND, such
as "," and "&" in Parlog. Guarded clauses are used in Parlog and
Concurrent Prolog to partly specify parallelism. A guarded clause has
a format h :- g | b., where g is the *guard* of the clause and b is its *body*.
Subgoals in the body can only be evaluated when all subgoals in the

guard have succeeded and values bound have been committed to the body.

It is clear that the above approach for specifying parallelism by users detracts from the objective of declarative programming, which separates logic from control, or "what" from "how." Both mode declarations in Parlog and read-only annotations in Concurrent Prolog impose a fixed execution order on subgoals, which may be inefficient in parallel processing. On the other hand, distinguishing the guard from the body cannot completely specify the precedence relationships because subgoals in the guard and body may be dependent. The use of guards is also complicated by a lack of general methodology for selecting subgoals in the guard. Moreover, precedence relationships are a partial order, so the distinction between sequential AND and parallel AND, which are linear orders, is insufficient to specify all precedence relationships. Last, owing to the nondeterministic behavior of AI programs, users cannot always specify the parallelism perfectly. A desirable parallel AI language should allow its compiler to detect the parallelism and schedule parallel executions as efficiently as possible.

Object-oriented languages. *Object-oriented programming* holds promise as a framework for concurrent programming that can be extended to databases and knowledge bases. The prediction that "object-oriented programming will be in the 1980s what structured programming was in the 1970s" [Rentsch 82] is becoming a reality. The first object-oriented language was Smalltalk [Goldberg 83]. A variety of object-oriented languages include Loops [Stefik 86], Actor [Agha 86], CommonObjects [Snyder 85], and many others [Wegner 86]. Recently, CommonLoops was suggested as a standard for object-oriented extensions to Common Lisp by the Lisp community [Bobrow 85].

Object-oriented programming has been used to express different concepts, but the concept of an object is the common feature in these languages. Objects are entities that combine the properties of procedures and data. Object-oriented programming replaces the conventional operator-operand concept by messages and objects. All actions in an object-oriented program result from sending messages among objects. A selector in the message specifies the operation to be performed. An object responds to messages using its own procedures (called *methods*) for performing operations. Message sending supports *data abstractions,* a concept that is necessary but not sufficient for the language to be object-oriented. Object-oriented languages must additionally support the management of data abstractions using *abstract data types* and the composition of abstract data types through *inheritance.* Inheritance is used to define objects that are almost like other objects. In fact, object-oriented programming should be characterized by the nature of its type mechanisms rather than the nature of its communication mechanisms; that is, object-oriented programming can be defined as

$$Object-oriented\ programming = data\ abstraction + data\ types$$
$$+ type\ inheritance$$

Object-oriented programming is a paradigm for organizing knowledge domains while allowing communications. Concurrent models, operating systems, and coordination tools are built from low-level objects, such as processes, queues, and semaphores. Hewitt's Actor model is a formalization of the ideas of object-oriented languages; in his model an actor is the analog of a class or type but has the added effects of parallelism [Hewitt 77]. Computations in the Actor model are partial orders of inherently parallel events having no assignment commands. The language Act3, based on the Actor model, combines the advantages of both object-oriented and functional programming [Agha 85]. To support object-oriented programming, appropriate objects representing data structures should exist at the hardware level as machine data-structure types. This gives birth to the *Datatype Architecture* [Giloi 85]. The Apiary network architecture is based on the Actor model [Hewitt 80, Hewitt 84].

A major problem in the representation level lies in the large amount of knowledge needed to define a good representation and the imprecise nature of this knowledge. Efforts have been directed at the automatic acquisition of domain knowledge and metaknowledge and toward the design of a language that is more expressive and yet easy to implement in a parallel processing environment. The design of a systematic method to generate alternate representations is particularly desirable. The methodology should start with the problem specification, use automated tools to transform the problem specifications into problem representations, compare alternate representations, and use metaknowledge to guide the generation of different representations.

4.3 Control Level

There are four basic issues regarding the control level of computer-system design. Maintaining a consistency of knowledge is important because incomplete and inconsistent knowledge is often dealt with in AI computations. Because multiprocessing is widely used in AI computations, related issues include the decomposition of a problem (or program) into subproblems, the synchronization of cooperating processes, and the scheduling of processes for efficient execution. Although the design issues for the control level are similar to those for traditional multiprocessing systems, AI problems often start with different representations; hence their solutions for the control level may be very different from traditional ones.

4.3.1 Consistency maintenance

Traditional logic is *monotonic* because new axioms are only added to the list of provable theorems and never cause any to be withdrawn. However, knowledge-based systems on changing real-world domains have to cope with the maintenance of consistent deduction. Classic symbolic logic lacks the tools to deal with inconsistencies caused by new information. *Nonmonotonic reasoning* has been developed to deal with this problem [Winograd 80].

Early attempts at consistency maintenance evolved around the explicit manipulation of statements. The major system developed was STRIPS, which dealt with the manipulation of blocks of various sizes, shapes, colors, and locations by a robot [Fikes 71]. In STRIPS, the entire database is searched for inconsistencies when the robot moves a block. *System-applied inference* refers to a system in which the architecture provides a mechanism to automatically maintain the consistency of the database. The widely publicized system of this nature was Microplanner [Sussman 70]. In Microplanner, the operators of STRIPS are replaced by "theorems." There is no automatic inference mechanism, and the programmer is required to encode all possible implications of a theorem. An improvement to STRIPS is Doyle's truth maintenance system (TMS), in which the reasons for beliefs are recorded and maintained, and these beliefs can be revised when discoveries contradict assumptions [Doyle 79]. To attach a justification to a fact, a TMS is designed with a goal that efficiently links consequences and their underlying assumptions. In TMS, each relation has an associated IN and OUT node. The statement at this node is true if the statements in the IN list are known to be true and the statements in the OUT list are not true.

A different approach to handle consistency maintenance was adopted in designing the IBM YES/MVS expert system that operates on a System 370 computer under the MVS operating system [Schor 86]. This expert system is used to schedule a real-time system in which contradiction occurs between the changed facts and the previous consequences. The system removes inconsistent deductions and computes new consequences in accordance with the changed facts. The consistency maintenance mechanism has three parts: recognition of inconsistencies, modification of the resultant state to remove inconsistencies and rededuce consistent consequence, and hidden control to ensure that all inconsistencies are detected and corrected properly.

Experience on the design of YES/MVS shows a pitfall in which correcting an inconsistency may cause another inconsistency, which in the process of being corrected reintroduces the first inconsistency. It was also found that knowledge represented in a style for consistency maintenance turned out to be quite modular, and maintaining it has been easier than initially expected.

Nonmonotonic logic has been demonstrated to be feasible but inefficient to implement in a large system. To allow the system to be used in real time, hardware support has to be provided on the time-consuming operations. Fundamental operations such as standard database functions may have to be implemented in hardware. The management of a virtual memory system to support frequent additions and deletions in a TMS is an important design issue. The maintenance of the appropriate storage organization such that locality is maintained among relations affecting each other is a nontrivial problem. Finally, parallel processing may introduce additional problems of consistency; efficient parallel architectures to process concurrent queries have to be investigated.

4.3.2   Partitioning

In parallel computations, determining the granularity, or the minimum size of a subproblem that should be computed by a single processor, depends on the inherent parallelism in the problem to be solved. Partitioning can be implemented at different levels. At the higher levels, a complex AI problem is partitioned into several functional tasks, each of which is processed by a functionally distributed computer system. At the lower levels, the control graph of the program is partitioned into atomic operations, each of which can be processed independently.

Partitioning can be performed by users at design time or compilers at compile time or processors at run time. In the first method, programmers use a parallel language to specify and partition problems. These languages can define parallel tasks and the associated data communications. Design issues of parallel languages were discussed in Sec. 4.2.3. In this section, we discuss static and dynamic partitioning.

Inherent parallelism and granularity.   The proper granularity of parallelism should be determined from the inherent parallelism in the problem and the communication overheads involved in synchronization and scheduling. In general, finding the optimal granularity is difficult; however, the degree of parallelism inherent in the problem may provide useful information to guide the design of the architecture.

An example to illustrate the choice of the proper granularity is-shown in the design of parallel rule-base systems. Forgy et al. observed that each OPS5 production, when it fires, manipulates a few (usually 2 to 3) working memory elements and affects only a small number (20 to 30) of productions [Forgy 84]. According to this analysis, it appears that only limited speedups are available and that massive parallelism may not be needed. To improve the degree of parallelism, further efforts should be devoted (1) to investigate parallel match algorithms, (2) to design efficient partitioning strategies, and (3) to develop techniques to rewrite sequential OPS5 programs into versions more suitable for parallel processing.

Gupta estimated that the hardware utilization will be around 2 percent if the Rete match algorithm is mapped directly onto the DADO architecture [Gupta 84]. He recommended partitioning OPS5 production rules into 32 subsets to exploit the modest amount of production-level parallelism.

Based on Gupta's algorithm, Hillyer and Shaw studied the execution of production systems on the NON-VON computer, a heterogeneous system with 32 large processor elements (LPEs) and 16K small processor elements (SPEs) [Hillyer 86]. Each SPE has 64 bytes of RAM to store a condition-element term. The large number of SPEs, which can be viewed as an active memory of LPEs, perform intraproduction tests in a massively associative fashion. The performance is predicted at a rate of more than 850 productions fired per second using hardware comparable in cost to a VAX-11/780. This shows that two orders of magnitude of speedup is achievable by properly partitioning production systems.

The partitioning algorithm used may have significant effects on performance. If a majority of node activations occur within a single partition, then the performance will not be good. Some researchers have reported heuristics for partitioning production systems, such as assigning productions that are sensitive to the same context, goal, or task, to different processors in a round-robin fashion. However, preliminary results have shown that these strategies do not bring significant improvement as compared to random partitioning [Oflazer 84]. The efficiency of intelligent partitioning strategies using knowledge previously known remains an open question.

In a multiprocessing system, it is hoped that equal-sized tasks are distributed evenly to all processing units. The above example, however, has shown that this may be impractical because the problems to be solved may have irregularly structured control-flow and dataflow graphs and data-dependent workloads. In practice, efficient heuristic methods may have to be used to partition the task graph into granules that can be executed in parallel. Important related issues to be studied in this case are the design of heterogeneous architectures and the dynamic distribution of workload.

Compiler detection of parallelism.   Based on the data dependencies in a program, a compiler may be able to detect the parallel modules in it and partition the program at compile time. An example is the postcompiler of FAIM-1, called an *allocator,* which performs dataflow analysis on the procedural code and inference connectivity analysis on the logic behavior in order to statically distribute the fragments to the processing elements [Anderson 87]. Similar work has been done on partitioning programs for numeric applications [Kuck 86].

Detection of parallelism in logic programs has centered on detecting AND-parallelism and OR-parallelism. AND-parallelism in logic programs involves the simultaneous execution of subgoals in a clause. Due to shared variables, concurrent execution of two or more subgoals in a clause may result in binding conflicts. Detection of AND-parallelism is based on the analysis of *input-output modes* of arguments in a subgoal. The input and output variables in a logic program denote the direction of binding transfers during unification, in a way similar to the input and output arguments in procedure calls. However, an argument in a logic program can be in the input mode in one instance and in the output mode in another, or may remain unbound. This dynamic behavior prohibits a complete static analysis. Previous research, therefore, developed methods either to provide primitives for users to specify the modes or to automatically assign modes to arguments that can be analyzed at compile time and leave the rest to be resolved at run time.

Approaches to compile-time detection of AND-parallelism have followed two basic approaches:

1. *Restricted AND-Parallelism.*   DeGroot describes a technique that restricts the allowable parallel execution of logic programs to certain, well-defined fork-join type execution graphs [DeGroot 84]. Such graphs can be expressed with a recursive execution graph expression language. Each graph expression contains a conditional, run-time test used to see if the expression can be executed in parallel or if it must execute sequentially. When expressions execute in parallel, inner expressions recursively test subsequent conditions at run time to see if they too may execute in parallel or if they must execute sequentially. The resulting behavior is similar to a downward-branching tree attached to an upward-branching tree, similar to the traditional fork-join paradigm. By restricting parallel execution to this form, DeGroot's restricted AND-parallelism (RAP) model can be efficiently implemented in an extended Warren Abstract-Machine for Prolog [Hermemegildo 88]. DeGroot also describes an efficient typing algorithm that can be used to reduce the cost of the run-time checks as detailed in Chap. 13.

2. *Static-Data Dependency Analysis.*   Chang, Despain, and DeGroot studied another model which does not restrict the types of

parallel behavior but instead restricts the dynamic behavior of the Prolog clauses to a single behavior [Chang 85, DeGroot 85b]. Unlike DeGroot's original model, which can achieve multiple parallel execution behaviors for a given clause, the static data-dependency model uses a global program dataflow analysis to select a single, worst-case behavior for each clause. In this way, no run-time tests are required, as they are in the RAP model; however, this reduced run-time cost is traded for potentially greater parallelism. The global dataflow analysis determines when two or more terms are coupled through shared variables. Like DeGroot's model, no two subgoals are allowed to execute in parallel if they share coupled terms. Because the condition of being coupled is a dynamic state, the static data-dependency model simply assumes the worst case; that is, if two terms are ever coupled, then it is assumed that they are always coupled.

Other heuristic methods of checking types at compile time are also possible. Tung and Moldovan have also investigated a number of heuristics to infer the modes of a given variable and mark all possible input/output modes of arguments in the clauses [Tung 86].

Compiler detection of parallelism has the advantages of reduced run-time overhead and programming efforts. Its disadvantage is that it may not be able to detect all the inherent parallelism in a highly expressive AI language and may have to be combined with user declaration and dynamic detection. The restrictions of compiler detection are briefly summarized below.

Special cases. The extraction of parallelism from data-dependency analysis is based on the assumption that if two subgoals do not share any unbound variable then they can be executed concurrently. This assumption is not true in some special features of the language, such as outputs in Prolog. A solution to this problem is proposed in Chap. 13.

Procedural dependencies. A procedural dependency exists between two subgoals if their execution order is fixed by their semantics. For example, in the following clause:

a(X): − test_for_ok(X), work_on(X).

the subgoal "test_for_ok(X)" must be executed first. Note that the subgoals in this example cannot be executed concurrently even if X is grounded, because the second subgoal may contain meaningless, inaccurate, or unbound work unless the first subgoal is true. In declarative languages such as Prolog, it is difficult to specify the semantics of subgoals without specifying its explicit control for parallelism. A solution to this problem is proposed in Chap. 13.

Exponential complexity. It may be difficult to define all possible combinations of modes at compile time because they grow exponentially with the number of potential output variables.

Dynamic detection of parallelism. Many data dependencies in a highly expressive AI language cannot be resolved until run time. For example, a subgoal p(X,Y) in a logic program may be called as p(X,X), which is a coupling dependency on a query with coupled terms introduced at run time. This dependency cannot be detected at compile time. Due to the dynamic nature of AI computations, an AI computer should provide a mechanism to map the program and data onto hardware dynamically.

In general, the computational model can be represented as a token-flow graph with four kinds of nodes: AND-decomposition, OR-decomposition, AND-join, and OR-join. The tokens passed along the edges can be demand tokens, data tokens, or control tokens. Conery and Kibler described an AND/OR-process system based on a producer-consumer model that dynamically monitors variables and continually develops data-dependency networks to control the order of execution of subgoals, never allowing two potential procedures with the same variable to be executed in parallel [Conery 85]. An ordering algorithm, called a *connection rule,* is used to dynamically determine a generator for each unbound variable. When a subgoal is completed, it is checked to ensure that it did produce all variable bindings it was supposed to; otherwise, the ordering algorithm is evaluated again. Improvements were made to the above scheme to further reduce the run-time overhead and extract more parallelism [Lin 86, Kim 86].

Since dynamic partitioning must be repeatedly executed at run time, it may reduce the performance gains and could even produce negative gains. The tradeoff between static partitioning by an intelligent compiler and dynamic partitioning by a sophisticated operating system is an important issue to be addressed in parallel AI processing. Dynamic partitioning is closely related to dynamic scheduling, and related issues will be discussed in a subsequent section.

Bottleneck analysis. An important issue in partitioning is to evenly decompose the problem, so bottlenecks in performance do not exist. It is easy to see that if a bottleneck requires a fraction of the total computations, then the speedup cannot be more than the reciprocal of this fraction, regardless of how the rest is partitioned. It is well known that the performance bottleneck of an application executing on a vector computer is its scalar code. Similarly, the performance bottleneck of a parallel AI computation is its sequential part (sequential inference or I/O). An important problem is to find the bottleneck in the problem to be solved.

Experience with designing the FIDO vision system at Carnegie-Mellon University has shown that an unbalanced partitioning algorithm can substantially degrade the performance [Klinker 86]. Adding Warp, a systolic system with a peak processing rate of 100 MFLOPS, to a host (a Sun computer and three "stand-alone processors") seems to only double or triple the speed of the FIDO loop. This means that Warp is definitely underutilized; functions on the stand-alone processors, either in preprocessing or postprocessing in using the Warp array, take up a substantial amount of time. It is expected that proper partitioning of vision algorithms will improve its performance significantly.

4.3.3 Synchronization

Synchronization refers to the control of deterministic aspects of computations, while scheduling handles mainly the nondeterministic aspects. The objective of synchronization is to guarantee the correctness of parallel computations such that the results of execution in parallel are the same as those of a sequential execution; that is, the parallel execution is serializable. In some nondeterministic problems, the generation of the same set of results as a sequential execution may not be necessary. For example, a user may wish to obtain a small subset of answers from a large set; the particular answers obtained do not have to be the same in the serial and parallel cases. In this case requirements on synchronization can be relaxed in parallel processing.

Many synchronization primitives used in AI processing are the same as those used in conventional computers. Examples include semaphores, test-and-set, full/empty bits, fetch-and-add, and synchronization keys. In addition, new or extended concepts related to synchronization have been introduced by AI researchers, such as the blackboard and actors. In this section, we will survey the synchronization of AI computations in the control and data levels and mechanisms using shared memory and message passing.

Two levels of synchronization.   In procedural languages, if a statement precedes another statement in the program, the implication is that this statement should be executed before the second statement if the two statements share common variables; that is, control-level synchronization is implicit when data-level synchronization is needed. This implicit execution order may overspecify the necessary precedence constraints in the problem.

On the other hand, if the tasks are specified as a set using a declarative language, then control-level synchronization is absent, and they can be processed concurrently if they do not share common variables. If they have common variables but are semantically independent, then they can be processed sequentially in an arbitrary order to maintain data-level synchronization.

The difficulty of specifying control-level synchronization when tasks are semantically dependent is a major problem in declarative languages such as Prolog. For example, the decomposition of a set into two subsets in Quicksort must be performed before the subsets are sorted. Hence, the tasks for decomposition and for sorting are both semantically dependent and data-dependent. To overcome this problem, programmers are provided with additional tools, such as specifying the input/output modes of variables in a Prolog program, to specify control-level synchronization. These primitives may have side effects and may not be able to completely specify all control-level synchronization in all situations. These problems may have to be dealt with at run time until sufficient information is available.

In general, process activations and deactivations can be considered as control-level synchronization, while passing arguments in procedure calls can be considered as data-level synchronization. Both methods can be implemented through a shared memory or by message transfers.

Shared memory.   In tightly coupled multiprocessor systems, synchronization is done through a shared memory. Examples of such existing and proposed AI computers include the Aquarius [Despain 85], Concurrent Lisp machine [Sugimoto 83], Concert Multilisp machine [Halstead 86b], and Parallel Inference Engine [Goto 84]. In what follows, we discuss synchronization using blackboards and show methods using shared variables in logic programs.

Blackboard.   Historically, the *blackboard* model was developed for abstracting features of the HEARSAY-II speech-understanding system [Erman 80]. The model is usually viewed as a problem-solving framework; however, we discuss only its control aspect here. The model consists of three major components: a knowledge source, a blackboard data structure, and control. The knowledge to solve the problem is partitioned into knowledge sources that are kept independently. The data needed to solve the problem concerned include input data, partial solutions, alternatives, and final solutions, which are kept in a global database, the blackboard. The blackboard can be divided into multiple blackboard panels that correspond to the hierarchy of solution space. Knowledge sources result in changes in the blackboard, which lead to a solution to the problem. Communications and interactions among knowledge sources take place solely through the blackboard. A monitor is needed to ensure that no more than one knowledge source can change the blackboard at one time. There are a set of control modules that monitor changes in the blackboard and decide the appropriate action to take next. The sequence of knowledge-source invocations is dynamic.

The blackboard model provides a useful framework for diverse types of knowledge to cooperate in solving a problem and has been used for many AI applications. Its implementation is similar to that of a critical section in operating systems. In the pure model, the solution is built one step at a time. Currently, extensive research on concurrent access to blackboards is conducted.

Hayes-Roth has proposed a more powerful *blackboard control architecture* in which control information (metaknowledge) is also stored and updated on a separated control blackboard [Hayes-Roth, 85]. This approach adapts to complex control plans as a whole. Operational strategies, heuristics, and scheduling rules can change repeatedly in the course of problem solving.

Synchronization via shared-memory variables. Although Lisp contains a "pure function" subset, it also supports many functions with side effects, such as *rplaca, rplacd, set,* and input/output functions. These side effects, which result from procedural dependencies and global (or free) variables, resemble problems in conventional parallel languages. In fact, some shared-memory multiprocessors, such as Concert and Butterfly, support both Multilisp, Simultaneous Pascal, and other parallel languages [Halstead 86*b*]. Multilisp provides a simple method to wait for values generated in the future. However, as in other languages, procedure activations in Multilisp may not be well nested, and an activation can terminate before another activation it contains. This exception-handing problem has to be addressed in programming the system [Halstead 85].

Pure Prolog is a single-assignment language. Under this restriction, the distinction between a shared-memory variable and a communication channel vanishes. Since a logic variable is not allowed to be rewritten through side effects, conventional hardware-synchronization mechanisms, such as test-and-set, full/empty-bit method, and fetch-and-add, are no longer needed in multiprocessing pure logic programs [Lindstrom 84]. The popular strategy taken now is to provide the programmer with a mechanism to delay process reduction until enough information is available so that a correct decision can be made. Currently, the Concurrent Prolog group is concentrating their efforts on Flat Concurrent Prolog, a subset of Concurrent Prolog. In Guarded Horn Clause (GHC) [Ueda 85], ICOT's current choice for Kernel Language 1, OR-parallelism was eliminated from Concurrent Prolog, and a strict synchronization rule that suspends a subgoal if it tries to write in the parent environment is adhered. This rule made the read-only annotation somewhat superfluous. Although it simplifies the implementation of GHC, some expressive power is lost due to a weaker notion of unification [Takeuchi 86].

Joins. As similar to conventional *fork-join* primitives, static joins can be used for synchronization in parallel AI processing. For example, in multiprocessing logic programs, a parent node can activate its children in parallel, and each child begins producing all possible answers. The parent waits for each child to complete, collects their answers, computes the "join" of their answers, and passes the entire set of results as its answer. This approach uncovers the greatest AND-parallelism in a logic program but is efficient only if the program consists mostly of deterministic procedures and clauses; that is, most variables have only a single binding. For nondeterministic AI problems, joins are impractical because the nondeterminism increases the uncertainty whether a given AND node should be evaluated. Note that if joins are computed dynamically, that is, a parent node collects separate answers from each child as they are produced, then the data-level synchronization employed forms a pipelined computation called *dynamic joins*. This scheme is discussed later with respect to synchronization in semantic networks.

Message passing. In passing messages, a communication channel between the sender and receiver processes is required. Synchronization via messages can be achieved through software protocols or specialized hardware. Many existing and proposed AI computers pass around messages of arbitrary complexity and perform complex operations on them. The computing elements are complex, and the communication costs are high. Alternatives to passing messages are discussed in this section.

Message passing in production systems. Reasoning using forward chaining in production systems has different behavior from reasoning using backward chaining. The behavior in forward chaining is illustrated in OPS5, whose interpreter repeatedly executes a match-select-act cycle. In the match phase, all rules whose conditions are satisfied by the current content of the working memory are selected. This is called the *conflict set*. In the select phase, conflict resolution is performed to select one of the productions in the conflict set. In the act phase, the working memory is modified according to the action part of the selected rule. Although the three phases can overlap in a multiprocessing environment, synchronization must be performed to ensure that the result is consistent with that of a sequential execution; that is, all changes in the conflict set must be known prior to the completion of conflict resolution in the next cycle.

Synchronization in the efficient Rete interpreter for OPS5 is based on a dataflow graph, which can be viewed as a collection of tests that progressively determine the productions ready to fire. Inputs to the graph consist of changes to the working memory encoded in tokens. Output tokens specify changes that must be made to the conflict set. Tokens are sent via messages in a multiprocessing system.

Marker passing and value passing.   Marker passing has been studied as an alternative to message passing. In such systems, communications among processors are in the form of single-bit markers. An important characteristic is that there is never any contention: if many copies of the same marker arrive at a node at once, they are simply ORed together. The order of markers to be passed is determined by an external host.

Marker passing is suitable for systems implementing semantic networks. Nodes in the semantic network are mapped to processors in the system. An example of such a system is NETL [Fahlman 79]. A basic inference operation in semantic networks is set intersection. Analogous to dynamic joins in databases, set intersections are implemented using data-level synchronization. If an object with n properties is searched, then n commands are sequentially broadcast to all corresponding links, the associated nodes are marked, and the node with n markers reports its identity to the controller. Marker passing is adequate for many recognition problems; however, it may not be sufficient to handle general AI problems. The Connection Machine was originally developed to implement marker passing to retrieve data from semantic networks, but its current version has more powerful processing units that can manipulate address pointers and send arbitrary messages.

In value passing, continuous quantities or numbers are passed around the system, and simple arithmetic operations are performed on these values. Like marker-passing systems, there is no contention in value passing: if several values arrive at a node via different links, they are combined arithmetically, and only one combined value is received. In this sense, value-passing systems can be considered as an analog computer. Examples of value-passing systems are the Boltzmann machine [Fahlman 83], and other "neural" computation systems [Hopfield 85].

Marker-passing systems do not gracefully handle recognition problems in which the incoming features may be noisy. These problems can be better handled by a value-passing system in which each connection has an associated scalar weight that represents the confidence on the incoming values. Many iterative-relaxation algorithms that have been proposed for solving low-level vision and speech-understanding problems are ideally suited to value-passing architectures.

Object-oriented and actor approaches. In the object-oriented approach, and in particular, the Actor model, an actor is a virtual computing unit that is defined by its behavior when messages are received. Actors communicate via point-to-point messages that are buffered by a mail system. The behavior of an actor consists of three kinds of actions: (1) communicating with specific actors of known mail addresses; (2) creating new actors; and (3) specifying a replacement that will accept the next message. Actor languages avoid the assignment command but allow actors to specify a *replacement*. Replacements can capture history-sensitive information, while allowing concurrent evaluation of data-independent expressions [Agha 86]. Message passing in actors, which can be viewed as a parameter-passing mechanism, differs from both call-by-value and call-by-reference.

4.3.4 Scheduling

Scheduling is the assignment of ready tasks to available processors. It is especially important when there is nondeterminism in the algorithm. Scheduling can be static or dynamic. Static scheduling is performed before the tasks are executed, while dynamic scheduling is carried out as the tasks are executed. The actions to be performed in scheduling include (1) determination of dependent tasks, (2) static reordering of tasks at compile time, (3) dynamic selection of tasks at run time when free processors are available, and (4) determination of the number of processors to solve a given class of problems cost-effectively. All schedules can be considered as a search strategy based on a search tree or search graph [Pearl 84].

Identifying dependencies. Parallel scheduling of AI programs is complicated by their dynamic functional and shared-variable dependencies and the high expressive power of many AI languages. Due to high expressive power, the same program can be used to represent many different dependencies, each of which may be scheduled differently. Identifying dependencies at compile time is also difficult due to the dynamic and nondeterministic nature of executions.

If functional dependencies exist among tasks, then the scheduler must find these dependencies dynamically; if there are only shared-variable dependencies and no functional dependencies, then the scheduler has to compare the merits of all possible schedules. Both examples are not practical because of the high dynamic overhead. As discussed earlier, solutions to detect dependencies are not satisfactory at this time.

A viable approach is to identify the possible dependencies at compile time, statically order all sibling nodes in a search tree for each case, and schedule them according to a parallel depth-first strategy. A simple method was proposed by Warren [81], which orders the subgoals in a clause according to the number of possible solutions generated under the given subgoal. Our experimental simulations indicated that the worst-case evaluation time resulting from this method can be worse than the case without reordering, but the best-case time can be 2 to 30 times better. Warren's method does not consider the effects of backtracking, the possible dependencies among subgoals and clauses, and the overhead of finding the solutions. We have proposed a method to represent the effects of backtracking as an absorbing Markov chain [Li 86b]. By assuming that sibling nodes are independent, they are reordered to minimize the total expected search cost of the program. Heuristics have been developed to reorder subgoals when they are dependent and have side effects. Our preliminary simulations indicated that the performance is substantially better than that of Warren's method.

Selection strategies.   Suppose in the course of evaluating an AI program, n active tasks and m processors are available, $1 \leq m < n$. The ideal scheduling algorithm should select m active tasks such that this decision will minimize the expected computational time. It is difficult to design such an optimal selection algorithm because (1) the metrics to guide the search are estimated heuristically and may be fallible, (2) the metrics may be dynamically changing during the search, and (3) problem-dependent precedence restrictions may exist that cannot be detected at compile time. As a result, unexpected anomalies may occur when parallel processing is applied.

The potential parallelism in an AI computation can be classified into two types: deterministic parallelism and nondeterministic parallelism. *Deterministic parallelism* refers to the concurrent execution of two or more units of computations, all of which are necessary for the completion of the given job. The computational units can be tasks, processes, and/or instructions. Since all units of computation, which are performed concurrently, have "AND" relations, this kind of parallelism is traditionally called AND-parallelism. *Nondeterministic parallelism* refers to the search of multiple potential solutions in parallel. Since all potential solutions have "OR" relations, this kind of parallelism is traditionally called OR-parallelism.

Although AND-parallelism is treated as deterministic and OR-parallelism as nondeterministic in conventional studies, the selection of descendents of an AND task to evaluate is also nondeterministic, because the aim is to select one that fails as soon as possible. Hence, scheduling is important for tasks that are nondeterministic but may not be specific with respect to AND- or OR-parallelism.

In nondeterministic searches, heuristic information to guide the scheduler in selecting nondeterministic tasks is more important than the design of parallel processors, because the number of processors is almost always smaller than the number of processable tasks.

As an example, in selecting nodes to evaluate in a branch-and-bound search tree, which is an OR tree with lower-bound values to guide the search, the problem is reduced to finding the m smallest number from n numbers. Table 4.3 shows the results obtained by

TABLE 4.3   Selecting the m Smallest Numbers from n Numbers

Approach	Time complexity in each iteration	Space/hardware complexity for selection	Accuracy of selection
Multistage selection net-work	$O(\log m \cdot \log n)$	$O(n \cdot \log^2 m)$	1.0
Single-stage network	$O(m)$	$O(n)$	1.0
No-wait policy	$O(1)$	$O(m)$	0.63

three architectural approaches. In the first approach, a multistage selection network was designed to perform the selection exactly [Wah 84]. In the second approach, a single-stage ring network was used to shuffle the nodes until a complete selection was obtained [Wah 84b]. In the third approach, a *no-wait policy* was applied. It was recognized that the heuristic information to guide the search might not be always accurate. Hence, the most promising task in local memory was always evaluated in each cycle, while the fetch of the more promising tasks from other processors was initiated. It was found that on the average, a minimum of 63 percent of the desirable tasks to be selected were selected by the no-wait policy without any additional overhead on selection, assuming that the m most promising tasks were randomly distributed among the processors [Wah 84b, Wah 85].

The management of the large memory space to store the heuristic information and the large number of intermediate nodes in the search tree is another difficult problem to solve. A tradeoff must be made to decide for a given amount of heuristic information and a given architectural model, whether the amount of heuristic information should be increased or decreased, and how effective should the new heuristic information be.

The memory space required to store enough heuristic information to avoid backtracking is often prohibitive. For example, assume that all solution trees of a complete binary AND/OR tree with n levels are equally likely. The leaves are assumed to be OR nodes and are at level 0, while the root is an AND node and is at level n. We have that $f(n)$, the total number of solution trees, satisfy the following recurrence:

$$f(n) = \begin{cases} 1 & n = 0 \ \text{or} \ n = 1 \\ 4f^2(n - 2) & n \geq 2 \end{cases}$$

$$= 2^{2(2^{n/2}-1)} \tag{4.1}$$

For $n = 0$, there is only one node; hence there is one solution tree. For $n = 1$, the root is an AND node with two descendents (see Fig. 4.1a). Again, this represents one solution tree. For the general case, each node in level $n - 2$ has $f(n - 2)$ solution trees (see Fig. 4.1b). A solution tree for the root at level n consists of picking two nodes in level $n - 2$, a total of four combinations. Each pair of nodes selected in level $n - 2$ represents two solution trees, all possible combinations of which will yield a new solution tree. This is depicted in Fig. 4.1b.

Since all solution trees are equally likely, the entropy I of the heuristic information to guide the search at the root such that a correct decision is always made without backtracking is

$$I = \sum_{j=1}^{f(n)} \frac{1}{f(n)} \ \log_2 \ f(n)$$

$$= 2 \ (2^{n/2} - 1) \tag{4.2}$$

which is exponential with respect to the height of the tree.

To manage the large memory space incurred by the storage of intermediate subproblems that may lead to solutions, we have investigated three alternatives to support branch-and-bound algorithms with a best-first search, the results of which are displayed in Table 4.4. In a direct implementation, the best-first search was implemented on an existing virtual-memory system, a VAX-11/780 computer running 4.2

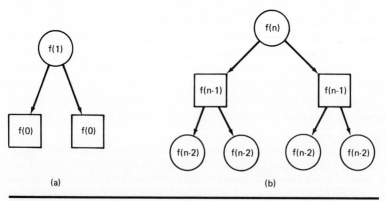

(a)   (b)

Figure 4.1 (a) A binary AND/OR tree with two levels; (b) a binary AND/OR tree with n levels. (Circles represent AND nodes; boxes represent OR nodes.)

TABLE 4.4   Relative Times to Complete a Branch-and-Bound Algorithm for Various Memory-Management Techniques

Approach	0/1 integer programming problems	0/1 knapsack problems
Direct implementation	1	1
Modified virtual memory	0.6	0.1
No-wait policy	0.1	0.001

BSD UNIX. In the second approach, a modified virtual memory with specialized fetch and replacement policies was designed to adapt to the characteristics of the search algorithm. In the third approach, the no-wait policy discussed above was used to select subproblems in the main memory without waiting for the most promising subproblem to be accessed from the secondary memory. Again, the no-wait policy is superior in performance [Yu 88].

The nondeterministic nature of computations and the fallibility of heuristic guiding may lead to anomalies of parallelism. When n processors are used to solve the problem, the resulting speedup as compared to a single processor may be less than 1, greater than $n,$ or between 1 and n. The reasons for this anomalous behavior are due to (1) ambiguity in the heuristic information, (2) more than one solution node, and (3) approximation and dominance tests [Li 84]. As a result, subtrees searched under serial processing will be terminated, and the search will be misled into a different part of the search tree.

In summary, scheduling is important when there is nondeterminism in the problem. Good heuristic metrics to guide the search are usually difficult to design and depend on statistics such as success probabilities, search costs, and problem-dependent parameters. Tradeoffs must be made among the dynamic overhead incurred in communicating the heuristic-guiding information, the benefits that would be gained if this information led the search in the right direction, and the granularity of tasks. In practice, the merits of heuristic guiding are not clear, since the heuristic information may be fallible. As a result, some AI architects do not schedule nondeterministic tasks in parallel. The excessive overhead coupled with the fallibility of heuristic information also leads some designers to apply only static scheduling to AI programs.

Pruning. Pruning can be considered as a negative form of heuristic guiding which guides the search to avoid subproblems that will never lead to better or feasible solutions. Pruning is useful in both backward and forward chaining. In backward reasoning, problems are decomposed into smaller subproblems and evaluated independently. There are usually redundant evaluations of the same task in different parts of the search tree when the search trees are recursive. Likewise, in forward reasoning, the more primitive facts are reduced to form more general facts until the query is satisfied. Unnecessary results are generated because it is not clear which reduction will lead to a solution of the problem.

Pruning in search problems can be carried out by dominance relations. When a node P_i dominates another node P_j, it implies that the subtree rooted at P_i contains a solution with a value no more (or no less) than the minimum (or maximum) solution value of the subtree rooted at P_j.

As an example, consider two assignments, P_1 and P_2, on the same subset of objects to be packed into a knapsack in the 0/1 knapsack problem. If the total profit of the objects assigned to the knapsack for P_1 exceeds that of P_2 and the total weight of the objects assigned in P_1 is less than that of P_2, then the best solution expanded from P_1 dominates P_2.

When parallel processing is used, it is necessary to keep the set of *current dominating nodes* (denoted by N_d) in memory [Wah 85]. These are nodes that have been generated but not yet dominated. In general, N_d can be larger than the set of active nodes. A newly generated node P_i has to be compared with all nodes in N_d to see whether P_i or any nodes in N_d are dominated.

If N_d is small, it can be stored in a bank of global data registers. However, centralized comparisons are inefficient when N_d is large. A large N_d should then be partitioned into m subsets, $N_d^0, \ldots, N_d^{m-1}$, and distributed among the local memories of the m processors. A subproblem $P_{i,j}$ generated in processor i is first compared with N_d^i; any subproblems in N_d^i, dominated by $P_{i,j}$ are removed. If $P_{i,j}$ is not dominated by a subproblem in N_d^i, it is sent to a neighboring processor and the process repeats. If it has not been dominated by any node in N_d, $P_{i,j}$ eventually returns to processor i and is inserted into N_d^i.

There are several problems associated with the use of dominance tests in AI applications. First, dominance relations are very problem dependent and cannot be derived by a general methodology. Most dominance relations have been developed for dynamic programming problems. To derive a dominance relation in a search process, a dominance relation is hypothesized and a proof is developed to show that the dominance relation is correct. Some progress has been made in using learning-by-experimentation to derive dominance relations for dynamic programming problems [Yu 86]. However, automatic proof techniques are largely missing. Moreover, learning-by-experimentation is applicable if there are a very small number of dominance relations that are used frequently in the problem. In many AI applications coded in Prolog, there are a large number of dominance relations, each of which is used infrequently in the program. Some special cases can be solved, such as finding redundant computations in recurrences [Chen 87]. For the general situation, it is sometimes difficult to find these dominance relations without human ingenuity. Second, many dominance relations are related to the semantics of the applications. A good language to represent semantics is missing at this time. Last, the overhead of applying dominance relations is usually very high, and sequential and parallel implementations will incur prohibitive overhead.

Granularity of parallelism.   When a parallel computer system with a large number of processors is available, it is necessary to determine the granularity of parallelism, that is, the size of tasks that will be executed as an indivisible unit in a processor. Since many AI problems can be represented by AND/OR trees, some processors have to be idle when nodes close to the root are evaluated. The proper number of processors should be chosen to match the inherent parallelism in the problem to be solved.

The proper granularity is a function of the problem complexity, the shape of the AND/OR tree, and the distribution of processing times of tasks. Many of these parameters are dynamically changing and data-dependent, and only special instances can be analyzed [Li 86c]. An important functional requirement for parallel processing of AI programs is the ability to dynamically distribute the workload. For a system with a small granularity, an efficient interconnection network is required to transfer data and control information. In a loosely coupled system with a coarse grain, an effective load-balancing mechanism is also needed.

4.4   Processor Level

The VLSI technology that has flourished in the past 10 years has resulted in the development of many special-purpose computers for AI processing. Architectures for AI processing can be classified into the microlevel, macrolevel, and system-level architectures. Microlevel and macrolevel architectures are discussed in the next two sections. Sections 4.4.3 through 4.4.7 briefly discuss the system-level architectures. A taxonomy of architectures implementing AI systems is discussed in Chap. 7.

4.4.1   Microlevel architectures

The microlevel architectures consist of architectural designs that are fundamental to applications in AI. In the design of massively parallel AI machines [Fahlman 83], some of the basic computational problems recognized are set intersection, transitive closure, contexts and partitions, best-match recognition, Gestalt recognition, and recognition under transformation. These operations may not be unique to AI, and many exist in other applications as well. Due to the simplicity of some of these operations, they are usually implemented directly in hardware, especially in systolic arrays. Many other basic operations can also be implemented in VLSI. Examples include sorting and selection, computing transitive closure, string and pattern matching, selection from secondary memories, dynamic programming evaluations, proximity searches, and unification.

Some AI languages such as Lisp differ from traditional machine languages in that the program/data storage is conceptually an unordered set of linked record structures of various sizes, rather than an ordered, indexable vector of numbers or bit fields of a fixed size. The instruction set must be designed according to the storage structure [Steele 80]. Additional concepts that are well suited for list processing are the tagged-memory [Moon 87] and stack architectures.

4.4.2 Macrolevel architectures

The macrolevel is an intermediate level between the microlevel and the system level. In contrast to the microlevel architectures, macrolevel architectures are (possibly) made up of a variety of microlevel architectures and perform more complex operations. However, they are not considered a complete AI system but can be taken as more complex supporting mechanisms for the system level. The architectures can be classified into those that manage data, such as dictionary machines, database machines, and structures for garbage collection, and those that search.

A dictionary machine is an architecture that supports the insertion, deletion, and searching for membership, extremum, and proximity of keys in a database [Schmeck 85]. Most designs are based on binary-tree architectures; however, designs using radix trees and a small number of processors have been found to be preferable when keys are long and clustered [Fisher 84].

Database machines depend on an architectural approach that distributes the search intelligence into the secondary and mass storage and relieves the workload of the central processor. Extensive research has been carried out in the past decade on optical and mass storage, back-end storage systems, and database machines. Earlier database machines developed were mainly directed toward general-purpose relational database management systems. Examples include the DBC, DIRECT, RAP, CASSM, associative array processors, text retrieval systems, and CAFS [Hsiao 79, Langdon 79, Babb 82]. Nearly all current research on database machines to support knowledge databases assumes that the knowledge database is relational, hence research is directed toward solving the disk paradox [Boral 83] and enhancing previous relational database machines by extensive parallelism [Tanaka 84, Muraka 84, Shibayama 84, Sakai 84]. Commercially available database and back-end machines have also been applied to knowledge management [Kellogg 83, Neches 84].

Searching is essential to many applications, although unnecessary combinatorial searches should be avoided. The suitability of parallel processing to searching depends on the problem complexity, the problem representation, and the corresponding search algorithms. Parallel algorithms and architectures to support divide-and-conquer, branch-and-bound, and AND/OR-graph search have been developed [Wah 85].

Extensive research has been carried out in supporting dynamic data structures in a computer with a limited memory space. *Garbage collection* is an algorithm that periodically reclaims memory space no longer needed by the users [Cohen 81]. This is usually transparent to the users and could be implemented in hardware, software, or a combination of both. For efficiency reasons, additional hardware such as stacks and reference counters are usually provided.

4.4.3 Functional-programming-oriented system-level architectures

The objective of writing a functional program is to define a set of (possibly recursive) equations for each function [Darlington 84]. Data structures are handled by introducing a special class of functions called *constructor functions*. This view allows functional languages to deal directly with structures that would be termed "abstract" in more conventional languages. Moreover, functions themselves can be passed around as data objects.

The design of the necessary computer architecture to support functional languages thus centers around the parallel evaluation of functional programs (function-oriented architectures) and the mechanisms of efficient manipulation of data structures (list-oriented architectures).

In *function-oriented architectures,* the design issues center on the physical interconnection of processors, the method used to "drive" the computation, the representation of programs and data, the method to invoke and control parallelism, and the optimization techniques [Vegdahl 84]. Desirable features of such architectures should include a multiprocessor system with a rich interconnection structure, the representation of list structures by balanced trees, and hardware supports for demand-driven execution, low-overhead process creation, and storage management.

Architectures to support functional-programming languages can be classified as uniprocessor architectures, tree-structured machines, data-driven machines, and demand-driven machines. In a uniprocessor architecture, besides the mechanisms to handle lists, additional stacks to handle function calls and optimization for redundant calls and array operations may be implemented [Steel 79, Turner 79, Castan 82]. Tree-structured machines usually employ lazy evaluations but suffer from the bottleneck at the root of the tree [Mago 85, Davis 79, O'Donnell 81]. Dataflow machines are also natural candidates for executing functional programs and have tremendous potential for parallelism. However, the issue of controlling parallelism remains unresolved. A lot of the recent work has concentrated on demand-driven machines that are based on reduction machines on a set of load-balanced (possibly virtual) processors [Treleaven 82a, Darlington 83, Kluge 83, Keller 84a, Keller 84b, Clarke 80, Treleaven 80].

List-oriented architectures are architectures designed to efficiently support the manipulation of data structures and objects. Lisp, a mnemonic for "list processing language," is a well-known language to support symbolic processing. There are several reasons why Lisp and list-oriented computers are really needed. First, to relieve the burden on the programmers, Lisp was designed as an untyped language. The computer must be able to identify the types of data, which involves an enormous amount of data-type checking and the use of long strings of instructions at compile and run times. Conventional computers cannot do these efficiently in software. Second, the system must periodically perform garbage collection and reclaim unused memory at run time. This amounts to around 10 to 30 percent of the total processing time in a conventional computer. Hardware implementation of garbage collection is thus essential. Third, due to the nature of recursion, a stack-oriented architecture is more suitable for list processing. Last, list processing usually requires an enormous amount of space, and the data structures are so dynamic that the compiler cannot predict how much space to allocate at compile time. Special hardware to manage the data structures and the large memory space would make the system more efficient [Fitch 80, Deering 85].

The earliest implementation of Lisp machines were the PDP-6 computer and its successors the PDP-10 and PDP-20 made by the Digital Equipment Corporation [McCarthy 78]. The half-word instructions and the stack instructions of these machines were developed with Lisp's requirements in mind. Extensive work has been done for the DEC system 10s and 20s on garbage collection to manage and reclaim the memory space used.

The design of Lisp machines was started at MIT's AI Laboratory in 1974. CONS, designed in 1976 [Knight 74], was superseded in 1978 by a second-generation Lisp machine, the CADR. This machine was a model for the first commercially available Lisp machines, including the Symbolics LM2, the Xerox 1100 Interlisp workstation, and the Lisp Machine, Inc., Series III CADR, all of them delivered in 1981. The third-generation machines were based on additional hardware to support data tagging and garbage collection. They are characterized by the Lisp Machines, Inc.'s Lambda supporting Zetalisp and LMLisp; the Symbolics 3600 supporting Zetalisp, Flavors, and Fortran 77; the Xerox 1108 and 1132 supporting Interlisp-D and Smalltalk; and the Fujitsu FACOM Alpha Machine, a back-end Lisp processor supporting Maclisp. Most of the Lisp machines support networking using Ethernet. The LMI Lambda has a NuBus developed at MIT to produce a modular, expandable Lisp machine with multiprocessor architecture.

A single-chip processor to support Lisp has been implemented in the MIT SCHEME-79 chip [Sussman 81]. Other experimental computers to support Lisp and list-oriented processing have been reported [Griss 77; Taki 79; Goto 79; Deutsch 78; Nagao 79; Greenfeld 81; Sansonnet 80, 82a, 82b; Puttkamer 83]. These machines usually have additional hardware tables, hashing hardware, tag mechanisms, and list processing hardware, or are microprogrammed to provide macroinstructions for list processing. A Lisp chip built by Texas Instruments (TI) implements over half a million transistors on a 1-cm^2 chip for 60 percent of the functions in a TI Explorer. The implementation on a single chip results in five times improvement in performance [Matthews 87]. Experimental multiprocessing systems have been proposed to execute Lisp programs concurrently [Williams 78; McKay 80; Model 80; Guzman 81; Sugimoto 81, 83; Hill 86]. Dataflow processing is suitable for Lisp because these programs are generally data-driven [Yamaguchi 84, 83; Amamiya 82, 84]. Other multiprocessing architectures to support list processing have been proposed and developed [Coghill 79, Hewitt 80, Giloi 82, Treleaven 82a, Diel 84].

Architectures have also been developed to support object-oriented programming languages. First developed in 1972 by the Xerox Corporation, Smalltalk is recognized as a simple but powerful way of communicating with computers. At MIT, the concept was extended to become the Flavors system. Special hardware and multiprocessors have been proposed to directly support the processing of object-oriented languages [Plotkin 83, Ishikawa 84, Suzuki 84, Ungar 84].

Owing to the different motivations and objectives of various functional-programming-oriented architectures, each machine has its own distinct features. For example, the Symbolics 3600 [Moon 87] was designed for an interactive program development environment where compilation is very frequent and ought to appear instantaneous to the user. This requirement simplified the design of the compiler and results in only a single-address instruction format, no indexed and indirect addressing modes, and other mechanisms to minimize the number of nontrivial choices to be made. On the other hand, the aim in developing SOAR [Ungar 84] was to demonstrate that a reduced instruction set computer (RISC) could provide high performance in an exploratory programming environment. Instead of microcode, SOAR relied on software to provide complicated operations. As a result, more sophisticated software techniques were used.

4.4.4 Logic and production-oriented system-level architectures

Substantial research has been carried out on parallel computational models of utilizing AND-parallelism, OR-parallelism, and stream parallelism in logical inference systems, production systems, and others. The basic problem of their exponential complexity remains open at this time.

Sequential Prolog machines using software interpretation, emulation, and additional hardware support such as hardware unification and backtracking [Tick 84] have been reported. Single-processor systems for production systems using additional data memories [Lenat 77] and a RISC architecture [Forgy 84] have been studied.

New logic programming languages suitable for parallel processing have been investigated. In particular, the use of predicate logic [Emden 82]; extensions of Prolog to become Concurrent Prolog [Shapiro 83], Parlog [Clark 84a], and Delta-Prolog [Pereira 84]; and parallel production systems [Uhr 79] have been developed. One interesting parallel language is systolic programming, which is useful as an algorithm design and programming methodology for high-level-language parallel computers [Shapiro 84].

Several prototype multiprocessor systems for processing inference programs and Prolog have been proposed, some of which are currently under construction. These systems include multiprocessors with a shared memory [Borgwandt 84]; ZMOB, a multiprocessor of Z80s connected by a ring network [Weiser 85]; Aquarius, a heterogeneous multiprocessor with a crossbar switch [Despain 85]; and MAGO, a cellular machine implementing a Prolog compiler that translates a Prolog program into a formal functional program [Koster 84]. Techniques for analyzing Prolog programs such that they can be processed on a dataflow architecture have been derived [Bic 84, Hasegawa 84, Irani 84, Ito 85, Amamiya 86]. An associative processor has been proposed to carry out propositional and first-order predicate calculus [Dilger 83].

DADO is a multiprocessor system with a binary-tree interconnection network that implements parallel production systems [Stoflo 87].

Non-Von is another tree architecture to evaluate production systems at a lower level of granularity [Shaw 87].

4.4.5   Distributed problem-solving systems

Knowledge in an AI system can sometimes be represented in terms of semantic nets. Several proposed and experimental architectures have been developed. NETL [Fahlman 79], and its generalization to THISTLE [Falhman 83], consists of an array of simple cells with marker-passing capability to perform searches, set-intersections, inheritance of properties and descriptions, and multiple-context operations on semantic nets. Thinking Machine Inc.'s Connection Machine is a cellular machine with 65,536 processing elements. It implements marker passing and virtually reconfigures the processing elements to match the topology of the application semantic nets [Hillis 85]. Associative processors for processing semantic nets have also been proposed [Moldovan 84].

Some AI architectures are based on frame representations and may be called object-oriented architectures. For example, the *Apiary* developed at MIT is a multiprocessor actor system [Hewitt 80]. An efficient AI architecture may also depend on the problem-solving strategy. A general form called connectionist architectures evolve from implementing neurons in brains [Fahlman 87]. The basic idea of the *Boltzmann machine* is the application of statistical mechanics to constrained searches in a parallel network [Hinton 84]. The most interesting aspect of this machine lies in its domain-independent learning algorithm [Askley 85].

Including control in stored knowledge results in a distributed problem-solving system. These systems are characterized by the relative autonomy of the problem-solving nodes, a direct consequence of the limited communication capability. With the proposed formalism of the Contract Net, contracts are used to express the control of problem solving in a distributed processor architecture [Smith 81]. Related work in this area includes Petri-net modeling [Pavlin 83], distributed vehicle-monitoring testbed [Lesser 83], distributed air-traffic control system [Cammarata 83], and modeling the brain as a distributed system [Gevins 83, Fritz 84].

4.4.6   Hybrid systems

It has been suggested that a combination of Lisp, Prolog, and an object-oriented language such as Smalltalk may be a better language for AI applications [Takeuchi 83]. This approach can be carried out in two ways. First, multiple AI languages can be implemented using microprogramming on the same computer, so programs written in these languages can be executed independently. For example, Prolog is available as a secondary language on some Lisp machines. A version of a Prolog interpreter with a speed of 4.5 kilologic inferences per second (KLIPS) has been developed for Lisp Machine's Lambda. A second approach is to design a language that combines the desirable features from several AI languages into a new language. Some of the prototype multiprocessors, such as ZMOB and MAGO, were developed with a flexible architecture that can implement object-oriented, functional, and logic languages. FAIM-1, a multiprocessor connected in the form of a twisted hex-plane topology, was designed to implement the features of object-oriented, functional, and logic programming in the OIL programming language [Anderson 87]. Currently, a parallel version of Scheme similar to MultiLisp is being implemented. HOPE, a hybrid functional and logic language, is currently being implemented on ALICE [Smith 83].

4.4.7   Fifth-generation computer projects

The Fifth-Generation Computer System (FGCS) project was started in Japan in 1982 to further the research and development of the next generation of computers. It was conjectured that computers of the next decade will be used increasingly for nonnumeric data processing such as symbolic manipulation and applied AI. The goals of the FGCS project are

1. To implement basic mechanisms for inference, association, and learning in hardware.

2. To prepare basic AI software in order to utilize the full power of the basic mechanisms implemented.

3. To implement the basic mechanisms for retrieving and managing a knowledge base in hardware and software.

4. To use pattern recognition and AI research achievements in developing user-oriented people-machine interfaces.

5. To realize supporting environments for resolving the software crisis and enhancing software production.

The FGCS project is a marriage between the implementation of a computer system and the requirements specified by applications in AI, such as natural-language understanding and speech recognition. Specific issues studied include the choice of logic programming over functional programming; the design of the basic software systems to support knowledge acquisition, management, learning, and the intelligent interface to users; the design of highly parallel architectures to support inferencing operations; and the design of distributed-function architectures that integrate VLSI technology to support knowledge databases [Treleaven 82*b*, Kawanobe 84, Uchida 85].

A first effort in the FGCS project has been to implement a sequential inference machine, or SIM [Yokoi 84]. Its first implementation consists of two medium-performance machines for software development known as the Personal Sequential Inference machine (PSI) and Cooperative High-Speed Inference machine (CHI) [Taki 84]. The PSI and CHI have been further implemented in custom LSIs into PSI-II and CHI-II. The PSI-II has been found to have a performance that ranges from 100 to 333 KLIPS for various benchmark programs. Another architectural development is on the knowledge-base machine, Delta [Murakami 85].

The current efforts in the intermediate stage are directed at the parallel inference machine, or PIM, and the multi-PSI computers [Murakami 85]. As an intermediate target, PIM-I is being built now. It consists of about 100 processing elements, with a total speed of 10 to 20 MLIPS including overhead caused by the operating system for PIM, PIMOS. Eight processing elements with private caches in a cluster are connected through a shared memory, and a switching network is used to connect the clusters. Each processing element will be implemented in standard-cell VLSI chips. The machine language is KL1-B, based on GHC [Sato 87]. Last, the development of the basic software system acts as a bridge to fill the gap between a highly parallel computer architecture and knowledge information processing [Furukawa 84]. The PIMOS was designed as a single unified operating system to control the parallel hardware [Taki 86]. It will be built on the multi-PSI (version 2) system that is currently being developed. Each PE consists of a PSI-II with a 16-MW main memory and interfaces to the mesh interconnection network. The KL1-B interpreter is implemented in firmware and is expected to attain a speed of 100 to 150 KLIPS [Ichiyoshi 87].

In the final stage, a parallel computer with about 1000 PEs and attaining 100 MLIPS to 1 GLIPS is expected to be built. Although the projects are progressing well, there is the recognition that more research on exploiting intelligence is needed rather than on brute-force parallelism. The proposal of the Sixth-Generation Computer System Project is an indication of efforts in this direction [Agency 85].

The Japanese FGCS project has stirred intensive responses from other countries. The British project is a 5-year, $550 million cooperative program between government and industry that concentrates on software engineering, intelligent knowledge-based systems, VLSI circuitry, and people-machine interfaces. Hardware development has focused on ALICE, a Parlog machine using dataflow architectures and implementing both HOPE, Prolog, and Lisp [Smith 83]. The European Commission started the $1.5 billion, 5-year European Strategic Program for Research in Information Technologies (Esprit) in 1984 [FGCS 84]. The program focuses on microelectronics, software technology, advanced information processing, computer-integrated manufacturing, and office automation. In the United States, the most direct response to the Japanese FGCS project was the establishment of the Microelectronics and Computer Technology Corporation in 1983 [Spectrum 83]. The project has an annual budget of $50 to $80 million per year. It has a more evolutionary approach than the revolutionary approach of the Japanese and would yield technology that the corporate sponsors can build into advanced products in the next 10 to 12 years. Meanwhile, other research organizations have formed to develop future computer technologies of the United States in a broader sense. These include DARPA's Strategic Computing and Survivability, the semiconductor industry's Semiconductor Research Corporation, and the Microelectronics Center of North Carolina [Spectrum 83].

4.5   Design Decisions of AI-Oriented Computers

The appropriate methodology to design an AI computer should utilize a top-down design approach: functional requirements should be developed from the problem requirements, which are mapped into hardware based on technological constraints. Similar to the design of conventional computers, a bottom-up design approach is not adequate since special requirements of the applications may not be satisfied. Before a design decision is made, it is important to understand the applicability of the system to a class of problems and to then strive for high performance in a prototype implementation. Thus knowing that an m-processor system gives a k-fold increase in performance over a single processor is more important than knowing the maximum instruction rate of a prototype. Proper understanding and analysis of the problem is probably more important than applying brute-force parallelism randomly in the design.

The issues classified in Table 4.2 provide a view to the sequence of design decisions made in developing a special-purpose computer to support AI processing. The various approaches can be classified as top-down, bottom-up, and middle-out.

Top-down design decisions.   This approach starts by defining, specifying, refining, and validating the requirements of the application; devising methods to collect the necessary knowledge and metaknowledge; choosing an appropriate representation for the knowledge and metaknowledge; studying problems related to the control of correct and efficient execution with the given representation scheme; identifying functional requirements of components; and mapping these components into software and microlevel, macrolevel, and system-level architectures subject to technological and cost constraints. The process is iterative. For example, the representation of knowledge and the language features may be changed or restricted when it is discovered that the functional requirements found cannot be mapped into a desirable and realizable system with the given technology and cost. In some projects, the requirements may be very loose and span across many different applications. As a result, the languages and knowledge-representation schemes used may be oriented toward general-purpose usage. The Japanese FGCS project is an attempt to use a top-down approach to design an integrated user-oriented intelligent system for a wide spectrum of applications.

Bottom-up design decisions.   In this approach, the designers first design the computer system based on a computational model, such as dataflow, reduction, and control flow, and the technological and cost limitations. Possible extensions of existing knowledge-representation schemes and languages developed for AI applications are implemented. Finally, AI applications are coded using the representation schemes and languages provided. This is probably the most popular approach to apply a general-purpose or existing system for AI processing. However, it may result in inefficient processing, and the available representation schemes and languages may not satisfy the application requirements completely. The ZMOB and Butterfly multiprocessor are examples in this class.

Middle-out design decisions.   This approach is a shortcut to the top-down design approach. It starts from a proven and well-established knowledge-representation scheme or AI language (most likely developed for sequential processing) and develops the architecture and the necessary modifications to the language and representation scheme to adapt to the application requirements and the architecture. This is the approach taken by many in designing special-purpose computers for AI processing. It may be subdivided into top-first and bottom-first, although both may be iterative. In a top-first middle-out approach, studies are first performed to modify the language and representation scheme to make it more adaptable to the architecture and computational model. Primitives may be added to the language to facilitate parallel processing. Nice features from several languages may be combined. The design of the architecture follows. ALICE and FAIM-1 are examples of architectures designed using this approach. In the bottom-first middle-out approach, the chosen language or representation scheme is mapped directly into architecture by providing hardware support for the overhead-intensive operations. Applications are implemented using the language and representation scheme provided. LISP computers are examples designed with this approach.

4.6   The Future

Although many AI computers have been proposed or built, Lisp computers are probably the only architecture that have had widespread use for solving real AI problems. This is probably due to the large investment in software for many applications coded in Lisp. At present, there is no comprehensive methodology for designing parallel AI computers. Research on AI in the past three decades and the recent experience in building AI computers have led to a view that the key issue of an AI system lies in understanding the problem rather than efficient software and hardware. In fact, most underlying concepts in AI computers are not new and have been used in conventional systems. For example, hardware stack and tagged memory were proposed before they were used in Lisp computers. However, the above argument does not imply that research on hardware and architectures is not necessary.

To support efficient processing of AI applications, research must be done in developing better AI algorithms, better AI software management methods, and better AI architectures. The development of better algorithms can lead to significant improvements in performance. Many AI algorithms are heuristic in nature, and upper bounds on performance to solve these problems have not been established as in traditional combinatorial problems. As a consequence, the use of better heuristic information, based on commonsense or high-level meta-knowledge and better representation of the knowledge, can have far greater improvement in performance than improved computer architecture. Automatic learning methods to aid designers in systematically acquiring and managing new knowledge to be available in the future are very important.

Better AI software management methods are essential in developing more efficient and reliable software for AI processing. AI systems are usually open and cannot be defined based on a closed-world model. The language must be able to support the acquisition of new knowledge and the validation of existing knowledge. Probabilistic reasoning, fuzzy knowledge, and nonmonotonic logic may have to be supported. The verification of the correctness of an AI program is especially difficult due to the imprecise knowledge involved and the disorganized way of managing knowledge in a number of declarative languages and representation schemes. Traditional software engineering design methodologies must be extended to become knowledge engineering to accommodate the characteristics of knowledge in AI applications. Automatic programming is important to aid designers to generate the AI software from specifications.

The role of parallel processing and innovative computer architectures lies in improving the processing time of solving a given AI problem. It is important to realize that parallel processing and better computer architectures cannot be used to overcome the exponential complexity of exhaustive enumeration (unless an exponential amount of hardware is used) and are not very useful to extend the solvable problem space. For a problem with a size that is too large to be solved today by a sequential computer in a reasonable amount of time, it is unlikely that it can be solved by parallel processing alone, even if a linear speedup can be achieved. The decision to implement a given algorithm in hardware depends on the complexity of the problem it solves and its frequency of occurrence. Problems of low complexity can be solved by sequential processing or in hardware if they are frequently encountered; problems of moderate complexity should be solved by parallel processing; and problems of high complexity should be solved by a combination of heuristics and parallel processing.

In many AI systems developed today, tasks and operations implemented in hardware are those that are frequently executed and have polynomial complexity. These tasks or operations are identified from the languages or the knowledge-representation schemes supported. The architectural concepts and parallel processing schemes applied may be either well-known conventional concepts or new concepts for nondeterministic and dynamic processing. The role of the computer architects lies in choosing a good representation, recognizing overhead-intensive tasks to maintain and learn metaknowledge, identifying primitive operations in the languages and knowledge-representation schemes, and supporting these tasks in hardware and software.

Acknowledgment

This research was supported by the National Aeronautics and Space Administration under contract NCC 2-481.

Bibliography

[Agency 85]   Agency, Science and Technology. *Promotion of Research and Development on Electronic and Information Systems That May Complement or Substitute for Human Intelligence.* Science and Technology Agency, Tokyo, 1985.

[Agha 86]   G. Agha. *Actor: A Model of Concurrent Computation in Distributed Systems.* MIT Press, Cambridge, MA, 1986.

[Amamiya 86]   M. Amamiya, M. Takesue, R. Hasegawa, and H. Mikami. "Implementation and Evaluation of a List-Processing-Oriented Data Flow Machine." *Proc. 13th Annual International Symposium on Computer Architecture,* pp. 10–19, Tokyo, June 1986.

[Amdahl 87]   G.M. Amdahl. "Tampered Expectations in Massively Parallel Processing and Semiconductor Industry." Keynote Address, Second International Conference on Supercomputing, Santa Clara, CA, May 1987.

[Anderson 87]   J.M. Anderson, W.S. Coates, A.L. Davis, R.W. Hon, I.N. Robinson, S.V. Robison, and K.S. Stevens. "The Architecture of FAIM-1." *Computer,* vol. 20, no. 1, pp. 55–65, January 1987.

[Askley 85]   D.H. Askley, G.E. Hinton, and T.J. Sejnowski. "A Learning Algorithm for Boltzmann Machines." *Cognitive Science,* vol. 9, no. 1, pp. 147–169, 1985.

[Babb 82]   E. Babb. "Joined Normal Form: A Storage Encoding for Relational Databases." *Trans. on Database Systems,* vol. 7, no. 4, pp. 588–614, ACM, December 1982.

[Backus 82]   J. Backus. "Function-Level Computing." *Spectrum,* vol. 19, no. 8, pp. 22–27, August 1982.

[Bailey 85]   R. Bailey. "A Hope Tutorial." *Byte,* vol. 10, no. 8, pp. 235–258, August 1985.

[Bic 84]   L. Bic. "Execution of Logic Programs on a Dataflow Architecture." *Proc. 11th Annual International Symposium on Computer Architecture,* pp. 290–296, June 1984.

[Bobrow 85]   G. Bobrow, et al. "CommonLoops: Merging Common Lisp and Object-Oriented Programming." *Tech. Rep.* ISL-85-8, Xerox Palo Alto Research Center, August 1985.

[Boral 83]   H. Boral and D. DeWitt. "Database Machine: An Idea Whose Time has Passed?" *Database Machines,* pp. 166–167, Springer-Verlag, Berlin, 1983.

[Borgwardt 84]   P. Borgwardt. "Parallel Prolog Using Stack Segments on Shared-Memory Multiprocessors." *Proc. International Symposium on Logic Programming,* pp. 2–11, February 1984.

[Bowen 85]   K. Bowen. "Meta-Level Programming and Knowledge Representation." *New Generation Computing,* vol. 3, no. 4, pp. 359–383, 1985.

[Brachman 85]   R. Brachman and H. Levesque (eds). *Readings in Knowledge Representation.* Morgan Kaufmann, Los Altos, CA, 1985.

[Buchanan 84]   B.G. Buchanan and E.H. Shortliffe. *Rule-Based Experts Programs: The MYCIN Experiments of the Stanford Heuristic Programming Project.* Addison-Wesley, Reading, MA, 1984.

[Cammarata 83]   S. Cammarata, D. McArthur, and R. Steeb. "Strategies of Cooperation in Distributed Problem Solving." *Proc. 8th International Joint Conference on Artificial Intelligence,* pp. 767–770, William Kaufman, Los Altos, CA, August 1983.

[Castan 82]   M. Castan and E.I. Organick. "M3L: An HLL-RISC Processor for Parallel Execution of FP-Language Programs." *Proc. 9th Annual Symposium on Computer Architecture,* pp. 239–247, 1982.

[Chang 85]   J.H. Chang, A.M. Despain, and D. DeGroot. "AND-Parallelism of Logic Programs Based on a Static Data Dependency Analysis." *Proc. COMPCON Spring,* pp. 218–225, 1985.

[Chen 87]   H.-Y. Chen and B.W. Wah. "The "RID-REDUNDANT"' Procedure in C-Prolog." *Proc. International Symposium on Methodologies for Intelligent Systems,* Charlette, NC, October 1987.

[Clark 84a]   K. Clark and S. Gregory. "PARLOG: Parallel Programming in Logic." Research Rep. DOC 84/4, Imperial College, London, England, 1984.

[Clark 84b]   K. Clark and S. Gregory. "Note on System Programming in PARLOG." *Proc. International Conference on Fifth-Generation Computer System,* pp. 299–306, 1984.

[Clarke 80]   T. Clarke, P. Gladstone, C. Maclean, and A. Norman. "SKIM—The S, K, I Reduction Machine." Conf. Record of Lisp Conference, Stanford University, Menlo Park, CA, 1980.

[Cohen 81]   J. Cohen. "Garbage Collection of Linked Data Structures." *Computing Surveys,* vol. 13, no. 3, pp. 341–367, September 1981.

[Conery 85]   J.S. Conery and D.F. Kibler. "AND Parallelism and Nondeterminism in

Logic Programs." *New Generation Computing,* vol. 3, no. 1, pp. 43–70, 1985.

[Darlington 83]   J. Darlington and M. Reeve. "ALICE and the Parallel Evaluation of Logic Programs." Preliminary Draft, Dept. of Computing, Imperial College of Science and Technology, London, England, June 1983.

[Darlington 84]   J. Darlington. "Functional Programming." In F.B. Chambers, D.A. Duce, and G.P. Jones (eds). *Distributed Computing,* Academic Press, London, 1984.

[Darlington 85]   J. Darlington, A.J. Field, and H. Pull. "The Unification of Functional and Logic Languages." Tech. Report, Imperial College, London, England, February 1985.

[Davis 79]   A.L. Davis. "A Data Flow Evaluation System Based on the Concept of Recursive Locality." *Proc. National Computer Conference,* pp. 1079–1086, 1979.

[Davis 85]   A.L. Davis and S.V. Robison. "The FAIM-1 Symbolic Multiprocessing System." *Proc. COMPCON,* pp. 370–375, Spring 1985.

[Deering 85]   M.F. Deering. "Architectures for AI." *Byte,* pp. 193–206, April 1985.

[DeGroot 84]   D. DeGroot. "Restricted AND-Parallelism." *Proc. International Conference on Fifth Generation Computers,* pp. 471–478, November 1984.

[DeGroot 85a]   D. DeGroot and G. Lindstrom (eds). *Logic Programming.* Prentice-Hall, Englewood Cliffs, NJ, 1985.

[DeGroot 85b]   D. DeGroot and J.-H. Chang. "A Comparison of Two AND-Parallel Execution Models." *Hardware and Software Components and Architectures for the 5th Generation, AFCET Informatique,* pp. 271–280, Paris, March 1985.

[Denning 86]   P. Denning. "A View of Kanerva's Sparse Distributed Memory." RIACS Tech. Rep. TR-86.14, NASA Ames Research Center, Moffett Field, CA, June 1986.

[Despain 85]   A.M. Despain and Y.N. Patt. "Aquarius—A High Performance Computing System for Symbolic/Numeric Applications." *Proc. COMPCON,* pp. 376–382, February 1985.

[Deutsch 78]   P. Deutsch. "Experience with Microprogrammed Interlisp Systems." *Proc. MICRO,* vol. 11, November 1978.

[Diel 84]   H. Diel. "Concurrent Data Access Architecture." *Proc. International Conference on Fifth Generation Computer Systems,* pp. 373–388, 1984.

[Dilger 83]   W. Dilger and J. Muller. "An Associative Processor for Theorem Proving." *Proc. Symposium on Artificial Intelligence,* pp. 489–497, 1983.

[Doyle 79]   J. Doyle. "A Truth Maintenance System." *Artificial Intelligence,* vol. 12, no. 3, pp. 231–272, 1979.

[Dreyfus 86]   H. Dreyfus and S. Dreyfus. "Why Expert Systems Do Not Exhibit Expertise." *IEEE Expert,* vol. 1, no. 2, Summer 1986.

[Emden 82]   M.H. van Emden and G.J. de Lucena-Filho. "Predicate Logic as a Language for Parallel Programming." In S.-A. Tarnlund and K. Clark (eds). *Logic Programming,* pp. 189–198, Academic Press, New York, 1982.

[Erman 80]   L.D. Erman, F. Hayes-Roth, V.R. Lesser, and D.R. Reddy. "The Hearsay-II Speech-Understanding System: Integrating Knowledge to Resolve Uncertainty." *Computing Surveys,* vol. 12, no. 2, pp. 213–253, June 1980.

[Fahlman 79]   S. Fahlman. *NETL: A System for Representing and Using Real-World Knowledge.* Series on Artificial Intelligence, MIT Press, Cambridge, MA, 1979.

[Fahlman 83]   S.E. Fahlman and G.E. Hinton. "Massively Parallel Architectures for AI: NETL, THISTLE, and BOLTZMANN Machines." *Proc. National Conference on Artificial Intelligence,* pp. 109–113, 1983.

[Fahlman 87] S.E. Fahlman and G.E. Hinton. "Connectionist Architecture for Artificial Intelligence." *Computer,* vol. 20, no. 1, pp. 100–109, January 1987.

[Feigenbaum 83] E.A. Feigenbaum. "Knowledge Engineering: The Applied Side." In J.E. Hayes and D. Michie (eds). *Intelligent Systems: The Unprecedented Opportunity,* pp. 37–55, Ellis Horwood, Chichester, England, 1983.

[Fennell 77] R.D. Fennell and V.R. Lesser. "Parallelism in Artificial Intelligence Problem Solving: A Case Study of Hearsay-II." *IEEE Trans. Computers,* vol. C-26, no. 2, pp. 98–111, February 1977.

[FGCS 84] "ESPRIT: Europe Challenges U.S. and Japanese Competitors." *Future Generation Computer Systems,* vol. 1, no. 1, pp. 61–69, 1984.

[Fikes 71] R.E. Fikes and N.J. Nilsson. "STRIPS: A New Approach to the Application of Theorem Proving to Problem Solving." *Artificial Intelligence,* vol. 2, nos. 3 and 4, pp. 189–208, 1971.

[Fisher 84] A.L. Fisher. "Dictionary Machines with a Small Number of Processors." *Proc. 11th Annual International Symposium on Computer Architecture,* pp. 151–156, June 1984.

[Fitch 80] J. Fitch. "Do We Really Want a Lisp Machine?" *SEAS/SMC Annual Meeting, January 1980.*

[Flynn 85] A.M. Flynn and J.G. Harris. "Recognition Algorithms for the Connection Machine." *Proc. International Joint Conference on Artificial Intelligence,* pp. 57–60, 1985.

[Forgy 84] C. Forgy, A. Gupta, A. Newell, and R. Wedig. "Initial Assessment of Architectures for Production Systems." *Proc. National Conference on Artificial Intelligence,* pp. 116–120, August 1984.

[Fritz 84] W. Fritz and The Intelligent System. *SIGART Newsletter,* no. 90, pp. 34–38, October 1984.

[Furukawa 84] K. Furukawa and T. Yokoi. "Basic Software System." *Proc. International Conference on Fifth Generation Computer Systems,* pp. 37–57, 1984.

[Gallaire 82] H. Gallaire and C. Lasserre. "Metalevel Control For Logic Programs." In K.L. Clark and S.-A. Tarnlund (eds). *Logic Programming,* pp. 173–185, Academic Press, New York, 1982.

[Genesereth 83] M.R. Genesereth. "An Overview of Meta-Level Architecture." *Proc. National Conference on Artificial Intelligence,* pp. 119–124, 1983.

[Gevins 83] A.S. Gevins. "Overview of the Human Brain as a Distributed Computing Network." *Proc. International Conference on Computer Design: VLSI in Computers,* pp. 13–16, 1983.

[Giloi 82] W.K. Giloi and R. Gueth. "Concepts and Realization of a High-Performance Data Type Architecture." *International Journal of Computer and Information Sciences,* vol. 11, no. 1, pp. 25–54, 1982.

[Goldberg 83] A.J. Goldberg and D. Robson. *Smalltalk-80: The Language and Its Implementation,* Addison-Wesley, Reading, MA, 1983.

[Gooley 88] M.A. Gooley and B.W. Wah. "Efficient Reordering of Prolog Programs." *Proc. 4th International Conference on Data Engineering,* Los Angeles, February 1988.

[Goto 84] A. Goto, H. Tanaka, and T. Moto-oka. "Highly Parallel Inference Engine PIE—Goal Rewriting Model and Machine Architecture." *New Generation Computing,* vol. 2, no. 1, pp. 37–58, 1984.

[Goto 79] E. Goto, T. Ida, K. Hiraki, M. Suzuki, and N. Inada. "FLATS, A Machine for Numerical, Symbolic and Associative Computing." *Proc. 6th International Joint Conference on Artificial Intelligence,* pp. 1058–1066, August 1979.

[Greenfeld 81]   N. Greenfeld and A. Jericho. "A Professional's Personal Computer System." *Proc. 8th International Symposium on Computer Architecture,* pp. 217–226, 1981.

[Griss 77]   M. Griss and M. Swanson. "MBALM/1700: A Microprogrammed Lisp Machine for the Burroughs B1726." *Proc. MICRO-10,* 1977.

[Gupta 84]   A. Gupta. "Implementing OPS5 Production Systems on DADO." *Proc. International Conference on Parallel Processing,* pp. 83–91, 1984.

[Guzman 81]   A. Guzman. "A Heterarchical Multi-Microprocessor Lisp Machine." *Proc. Workshop on Computer Architecture for Pattern Analysis and Image Database Management,* pp. 309–317, November 1981.

[Halstead 85]   R. Halstead Jr. and J. Loaiza. "Exception Handling in Multilisp." *Proc. International Conference on Parallel Processing,* pp. 822–830, August 1985.

[Halstead 86a]   R. Halstead. "Parallel Symbolic Computing." *Computer,* vol. 19, no. 8, pp. 35–43, August 1986.

[Halstead 86b]   R. Halstead Jr., T. Anderson, R. Osborne, and T. Sterlig. "Concept: Design of a Multiprocessor Development System." *Proc. International Symposium on Computer Architecture,* pp. 40–48, June 1986.

[Hasegawa 84]   R. Hasegawa and M. Amamiya. "Parallel Execution of Logic Programs based on Dataflow Concept." *Proc. International Conference on Fifth Generation Computer Systems,* pp. 507–516, 1984.

[Hayes-Roth 85]   B. Hayes-Roth. "A Blackboard Architecture for Control." *Artificial Intelligence,* vol. 26, no. 3, pp. 251–321, July 1985.

[Hermenegildo 88]   M. Hermenegildo. *A Restricted AND-Parallel Execution Model and Abstract Machine for Prolog Programs.* Academic Press, New York, 1988.

[Hewitt 80]   C. Hewitt. "The Apiary Network Architecture for Knowledgeable Systems." *Conf. Record of Lisp Conference,* pp. 107–117, Stanford University, Menlo Park, CA, 1980.

[Hewitt 84]   C. Hewitt and H. Lieberman. "Design Issues in Parallel Architectures for Artificial Intelligence." *Proc. COMPCON Spring,* pp. 418–423, February 1984.

[Hillis 85]   W.D. Hillis. *The Connection Machine.* MIT Press, Cambridge, MA, 1985.

[Hillyer 86]   B.K. Hillyer and D.E. Shaw. "Execution of OPS5 Production Systems on a Massively Parallel Machine." *J. Parallel and Distributed Computing,* vol. 3, no. 2, pp. 236–268, 1986.

[Hinton 84]   G.E. Hinton, T.J. Sejnowski, and D.H. Askley. "Boltzmann Machine: Constraint Satisfaction Network that Learns." Tech. Rep., Carnegie-Mellon University, Pittsburgh, PA, 1984.

[Hopfield 85]   J. Hopfield and D. Tank. "'Neural' Computation of Decisions in Optimization Problems." *Biologic Cybernetics,* vol. 52, pp. 141–152, 1985.

[Hsiao 79]   D.K. Hsiao (ed.). "Special Issue on Database Machines." *Computer,* vol. 12, no. 3, March 1979.

[Ichiyoshi 87]   N. Ichiyoshi, T. Miyazaki, and K. Taki. "A Distributed Implementation of Flat GHC on the Multi-PSI." *International Conference on Logic Programming,* 1987.

[Irani 84]   K.B. Irani and Y.F. Shih. "Implementation of Very Large Prolog-Based Knowledge Bases on Data Flow Architectures." *Proc. 1st Conferences on Artificial Intelligence Applications,* pp. 454–459, December 1984.

[Ishikawa 84]   Y. Ishikawa and M. Tokoro. "The Design of an Object-Oriented Architecture." *Proc. 11th International Symposium on Computer Architecture,* pp. 178–187, 1984.

[Ito 85]   N. Ito, H. Shimizu, M. Kishi, E. Kuno, and K. Rokusawa. "Data-Flow Based Execution Mechanisms of Parallel and Concurrent Prolog." *New Generation Computing,* vol. 3, pp. 15–41, 1985.

[Kanerva 86]   P. Kanerva. *Parallel Structures in Human and Computer Memory.* RIACS Tech. Rep. TR-86.2, NASA Ames Research Center, Moffett Field, CA, January 1986.

[Keller 84]   R.M. Keller, F.C.H. Lin, and J. Tanaka. "Rediflow Multiprocessing." *Proc. COMPCON Spring,* pp. 410–417, 1984.

[Kellogg 83]   C. Kellogg. "Intelligent Assistants for Knowledge and Information Resources Management." *Proc. 8th International Conference on Artificial Intelligence,* pp. 170–172, William Kaufman, Los Altos, CA, 1983.

[Kim 86]   S. Kim, S. Maeng, and J.W. Cho. "A Parallel Execution Model of Logic Program Based on Dependency Relationship Graph." *Proc. International Conference on Parallel Processing,* pp. 976–983, August 1986.

[Klinker 86]   G. Klinker, E. Clune, J. Crisman, and J. Webb. "The Implementation of a Complex Vision System on Systolic Array Machine." Tech. Rep. Department of Computer Science, CMU, May 1986.

[Kluge 83]   W.E. Kluge. "Cooperating Reduction Machines." *IEEE Trans. Computers,* vol. C-32, no. 11, pp. 1002–1012, November 1983.

[Knight 74]   T. Knight. "The CONS Microprocessor," AI Working Paper 80, MIT, Cambridge, MA, November 1974.

[Koster 84]   A. Koster. "Compiling Prolog Programs for Parallel Execution on a Cellular Machine," *Proc. ACM'84 Annual Conference,* pp. 167–178, October 1984.

[Kuck 86]   D.J. Kuck, E.S. Davidson, D.H. Lawrie, and A.H. Sameh. "Parallel Supercomputing Today and the Cedar Approach," *Science,* pp. 967–974, February 1986.

[Langdon 79]   G.G. Langdon Jr. (ed). "Special Issue on Database Machines." *Trans. on Computers,* vol. C-28, no. 6, June 1979.

[Lenat 77]   D.B. Lenat and J. McDermott. "Less Than General Production System Architectures," *Proc. 5th International Joint Conference on Artificial Intelligence,* pp. 923–932, William Kaufman, Los Altos, CA, 1977.

[Lenat 84]   D.B. Lenat. "Computer Software for Intelligent Systems." *Scientific American,* vol. 251, no. 3, pp. 204–213, September 1984.

[Lesser 83]   V.R. Lesser and D.D. Corkill. "The Distributed Vehicle Monitoring Testbed: A Tool for Investigating Distributed Problem Solving Networks." *The AI Magazine,* pp. 15–33, Fall 1983.

[Li 84]   G.-J. Li and B.W. Wah. "Computational Efficiency of Parallel Approximate Branch-and-Bound Algorithms." *Proc. International Conference on Parallel Processing,* pp. 473–480, 1984.

[Li 85]   G.-J. Li and B.W. Wah. "MANIP-2: A Multicomputer Architecture for Evaluating Logic Programs." *Proc. International Conference on Parallel Processing,* pp. 123–130, June 1985.

[Li 86a]   G.-J. Li and B.W. Wah. "Coping with Anomalies in Parallel Branch-and-Bound Algorithms." *IEEE Trans. Computers,* vol. C-35, no. 6, pp. 568–573, June 1986.

[Li 86b]   G.-J. Li and B.W. Wah. "How Good Are Parallel and Ordered Depth-First Searches?" *Proc. of International Conference on Parallel Processing,* pp. 992–999, 1986.

[Li 86c]   G.-J. Li and B.W. Wah. "Optimal Granularity of Parallel Evaluation of AND Trees." *Proc. 1986 Fall Joint Computer Conference,* pp. 297–306, November 1986.

[Li 87]   G.-J. Li and B.W. Wah. *IEEE Trans. on Software Engineering*, "Computational Efficiency of Combinatorial OR-Tree Searches, 1987.

[Lin 86]   Y.-J. Lin and V. Kumar. "A Parallel Execution Scheme for Exploiting AND-Parallelism of Logic Programs." *Artificial Intelligence*, pp. 972–975, August 1986.

[Lindstrom 84]   G. Lindstrom and P. Panangaden. "Stream-Based Execution of Logic Programs." *Proc. International Symposium on Logic Programming*, pp. 168–176, February 1984.

[Mago 85]   G. Mago. "Making Parallel Computation Simple: The FFP Machine." *Proc. COMPCON Spring*, pp. 424–428, 1985.

[McCarthy 78]   J. McCarthy. "History of Lisp." *SIGPLAN Notices*, vol. 13, no. 8, pp. 217–223, 1978.

[McGraw 80]   J.R. McGraw. "Data Flow Computing: Software Development." *IEEE Trans. Computers*, vol. C-29, no. 12, pp. 1095–1103, 1980.

[McKay 80]   D. McKay and S. Shapiro. "MULTI—A Lisp Based Multiprocessing System." *Conf. Record of Lisp Conference*, Stanford University, Menlo Park, CA, 1980.

[Model 80]   M. Model. "Multiprocessing via Intercommunicating Lisp Systems." *Conf. Record of Lisp Conference*, Stanford University, Menlo Park, CA, 1980.

[Moldovan 84]   D.I. Moldovan. "An Associative Array Architecture Intended for Semantic Network Processing." *Proc. ACM'84 Annual Conference*, pp. 212–221, October 1984.

[Moon 87]   D.A. Moon. "Symbolics Architecture." *Computer*, vol. 20, no. 1, pp. 43–52, January 1987.

[Murakami 84]   K. Murakami, T. Kakuta, and R. Onai. "Architectures and Hardware Systems: Parallel Inference Machine and Knowledge Base Machine." *Proc. International Conference on Fifth Generation Computer Systems*, pp. 18–36, 1984.

[Murakami 85]   K. Murakami, T. Kakuta, R. Onai, and N. Ito. "Research on Parallel Machine Architecture for Fifth-Generation Computer Systems." *Computer*, vol. 18, no. 6, pp. 76–92, June 1985.

[Nagao 79]   M. Nagao, J.I. Tsujii, K. Nakajima, K. Mitamura, and H. Ito. "Lisp Machine NK3 and Measurement of Its Performance." *Proc. 6th International Joint Conference on Artificial Intelligence*, pp. 625–627, August 1979.

[Neches 84]   P.M. Neches. "Hardware Support for Advanced Data Management Systems." *Computer*, vol. 17, no. 11, pp. 29–40, November 1984.

[Niwa 84]   K. Niwa, K. Sasaki, and H. Ihara. "An Experimental Comparison of Knowledge Representation Schemes." *The AI Magazine*, pp. 29–36, Summer 1984.

[O'Donnell 81]   J.T. O'Donnell. "A Systolic Associative Lisp Computer Architecture with Incremental Parallel Storage Management." *Ph.D. Dissertation*, University of Iowa, Iowa City, IA, 1981.

[Oflazer 84]   K. Oflazer. "Partitioning in Parallel Processing of Production Systems." *Proc. International Conference on Parallel Processing*, pp. 92–100, 1984.

[Pavlin 83]   J. Pavlin. "Predicting the Performance of Distributed Knowledge-Based Systems: A Modeling Approach." *Proc. National Conference on Artificial Intelligence*, pp. 314–319, 1983.

[Pearl 84]   J. Pearl. *Heuristics: Intelligent Search Strategies for Computer Problem Solving*. Addison-Wesley, Reading, MA, 1984.

[Pereira 84]   L.M. Pereira and R. Nasr. "Delta-Prolog: A Distributed Logic Programming Language." *Proc. International Conference on Fifth Generation Computer Systems,* pp. 283–291, 1984.

[Plotkin 83]   A. Plotkin and D. Tabak. "A Tree Structured Architecture for Semantic Gap Reduction." *Computer Architecture News,* vol. 11, no. 4, pp. 30–44, September 1983.

[Puttkamer 83]   E. von Puttkamer. "A Microprogrammed Lisp Machine." *Microprocessing and Microprogramming,* vol. 11, no. 1, pp. 9–14, January 1983.

[Reddy 85]   U.S. Reddy. "On the Relationship Between Logic and Functional Languages." In D. DeGroot and E.G. Lindstrom (eds). *Logic Programming,* Prentice-Hall, Englewood Cliffs, NJ, 1985.

[Rentsch 82]   T. Rentsch. "Object Oriented Programming." *SIGPLAN Notices,* vol. 17, no. 9, pp. 51–57, September 1982.

[Robinson 82]   J. Robinson and E. Sibert. "LOGLISP: Motivation, Design, and Implementation." In K. Clark and S. Tarnlund (eds). *Logic Programming,* Academic Press, New York 1982.

[Sakai 84]   H. Sakai, K. Iwata, S. Kamiya, M. Abe, A. Tanaka, S. Shibayama, and K. Murakami. "Design and Implementation of Relational Database Engine." *Proc. Fifth Generation Computer Systems,* pp. 419–426, 1984.

[Sansonnet 80]   J.P. Sansonnet, M. Castan, and C. Percebois. "M3L: A List-Directed Architecture." *Proc. 7th Annual Symposium on Computer Architecture,* pp. 105–112, May 1980.

[Sansonnet 82a]   J. Sansonnet, D. Botella, and J. Perez. "Function Distribution in a List-Directed Architecture." *Microprocessing and Microprogramming,* vol. 9, no. 3, pp. 143–153, 1982.

[Sansonnet 82b]   J.P. Sansonnet, M. Castan, C. Percebois, D. Botella, and J. Perez. "Direct Execution of Lisp on a List-Directed Architecture." *Proc. Symposium on Architectural Support for Programming Languages and Operating Systems,* pp. 132–139, March 1982.

[Sato 87]   M. Sato, H. Shimizu, A. Matsumoto, K. Rokusawa, and A. Goto. "KL1 Execution Model for PIM Cluster with Shared Memory." *International Conference on Logic Programming,* 1987.

[Schmeck 85]   H. Schmeck and H. Schroder. "Dictionary Machines for Different Models of VLSI." *IEEE Trans. Computers,* vol. C-34, no. 5, pp. 472–475, May 1985.

[Schor 86]   M. Schor. "Declarative Knowledge Programming: Better Than Procedural." *Expert,* vol. 1, no. 1, pp. 36–43, Spring 1986.

[Shapiro 83]   E. Shapiro and A. Takeuchi. "Object Oriented Programming in Concurrent Prolog." *New Generation Computing,* vol. 1, no. 1, pp. 25–48, 1983.

[Shapiro 84]   E. Shapiro. "Systolic Programming: A Paradigm of Parallel Processing." *Proc. International Conference on Fifth Generation Computer Systems,* pp. 458–470, 1984.

[Shaw 87]   D.E. Shaw. "On the Range of Applicability of an Artificial Intelligence Machine." *Artificial Intelligence,* vol. 32, pp. 151–172, 1987.

[Shibayama 84]   S. Shibayama, T. Kakuta, N. Miyazaki, H. Yokota, and K. Murakami. "A Relational Database Machine with Large Semiconductor Disk and Hardware Relational Algebra Processor." *New Generation Computing,* vol. 2, no. 2, pp. 131–155, 1984.

[Silver 86]   B. Silver. *Mete-Level Inference: Representing and Learning Control Information in Artificial Intelligence.* North-Holland, Amsterdam, 1986.

[Simon 86]   H.A. Simon. "Whether Software Engineering Needs to Be Artificially Intelligent." *Trans. on Software Engineering,* vol. SE-12, no. 7, July 1986.

[Smith 83]   K. Smith. "New Computer Breed Uses Transputers for Parallel Processing." *Electronics,* pp. 67–68, February 24, 1983.

[Smith 81]   R.G. Smith and R. Davis. "Frameworks for Cooperation in DistributedProblem Solving." *Trans. on Systems, Man and Cybernetics,* vol. SMC-11, no. 1, pp. 61–70, January 1981.

[Snyder 85]   A. Snyder. "Report ATC-85-1, Software Technology Lab., Hewlett-Packard Lab." Object-Oriented Programming for Common Lisp, Palo Alto, CA, 1985.

[Spectrum 83]   "Special Issue on Tomorrow's Computers." *Spectrum* vol. 20, no. 11, pp. 51–58, 69, November 1983.

[Steel 79]   G. Steel and G. Sussman. "Design of Lisp-Based Processor, or SCHEME: A Dielectric Lisp or Finite Memories Considered Harmful, or LAMBDA: The Ultimate Opcode." AI Memo 514, MIT, Cambridge, MA, March 1979.

[Steele 80]   G.L. Steele Jr. and G.J. Sussman. "Design of a Lisp-Based Microprocessor." *Comm. of the ACM,* vol. 23, no. 11, pp. 628–645, November 1980.

[Stefik 86]   M. Stefik and G. Bobrow. "Object-Oriented Programming: Themes and Variations." *AI Magazine,* Spring 1986.

[Stoflo 87]   S.J. Stoflo. "Initial Performance of the DADO2 Prototype." *Computer,* vol. 20, no. 1, pp. 75–84, January 1987.

[Sugimoto 83]   S. Sugimoto, K. Agusa, K. Tabata, and Y. Ohno. "A Multi-Microprocessor System for Concurrent Lisp." *Proc. International Conference on Parallel Processing,* pp. 135–143, 1983.

[Sussman 70]   G. Sussman, T. Winograd, and E. Charniak. *Micro-planner Reference Manual.* Tech. Rep. AIM-203, MIT Press, Cambridge, MA, 1970.

[Sussman 81]   G.J. Sussman, J. Holloway, G.L. Steel Jr., and A. Bell. "Scheme-79—Lisp on a Chip." *Computer,* vol. 14, no. 7, pp. 10–21, July 1981.

[Suzuki 84]   N. Suzuki, K. Kubota, and T. Aoki. "SWORD32: A Bytecode Emulating Microprocessor for Object-Oriented Languages." *Proc. International Conference on Fifth Generation Computer Systems,* pp. 389–397, 1984.

[Takeuchi 83]   I. Takeuchi, H. Okuno, and N. Ohsato. "TAO—A Harmonic Mean of Lisp, Prolog, and Smalltalk." *SIGPLAN Notices,* vol. 18, no. 7, pp. 65–74, July 1983.

[Taki 79]   K. Taki, Y. Kaneda, and S. Maekawa. "The Experimental Lisp Machine." *Proc. 6th International Joint Conference on Artificial Intelligence,* pp. 865–867, August 1979.

[Taki 84]   K. Taki, M. Yokota, A. Yamamoto, H. Nishikawa, S. Uchida, H. Nakashima, and A. Mitsuishi. "Hardware Design and Implementation of the Personal Sequential Inference Machine (PSI)." *Proc. International Conference on Fifth Generation Computer Systems,* pp. 398–409, 1984.

[Taki 86]   K. Taki. "The Parallel Software Research and Development Tool: Multi-PSI System." *France-Japan Artificial Intelligence and Computer Science Symposium,* pp. 365–381, 1986.

[Tanaka 84]   Y. Tanaka. "MPDC-Massive Parallel Architecture for Very Large Databases." *Proc. International Conference on Fifth Generation Computer Systems,* pp. 113–137, 1984.

[Tick 84]   E. Tick and D.H.D. Warren. "Towards a Pipelined Prolog Processor." *New Generation Computing,* vol. 2, no. 4, pp. 323–345, 1984.

[Treleaven 80]   P. Treleaven and G. Mole. "A Multi-Processor Reduction Machine for User-Defined Reduction Languages." *Proc. 7th International Symposium Computer Architecture,* pp. 121–130, 1980.

[Treleaven 82a]   P.C. Treleaven and R.P. Hopkins. "A Recursive Computer Architecture for VLSI." *Proc. 9th Annual Symposium on Computer Architecture,* pp. 229–238, April 1982.

[Tung 86]   Y.-W. Tung and D. Moldovan. "Detection of AND-Parallelism in Logic Programming." *Proc. International Conference on Parallel Processing,* pp. 984–991, August 1986.

[Turner 79]   D.A. Turner. "A New Implementation Technique for Applicative Languages." *Software—Practice and Experience,* vol. 9, no. 1, pp. 31–49, 1979.

[Uchida 85]   S. Uchida. "Inference Machines in FGCS Project." *Proc. VLSI'87 International Conference,* IFIP TC-10, WG 10.5, August 1985.

[Ueda 85]   K. Ueda. "Guarded Horn Clauses." Tech. Rep. TR-103, ICOT, Tokyo, 1985.

[Uhr 79]   L.M. Uhr. "Parallel-Serial Production Systems." *Proc. 6th International Joint Conference on Artificial Intelligence,* pp. 911–916, August 1979.

[Ungar 84]   D. Ungar, R. Blau, P. Foley, D. Samples, and D. Patterson. "Architecture of SOAR: Smalltalk on RISC." *Proc. 11th Annual International Symposium on Computer Architecture,* pp. 188–197, 1984.

[Vegdahl 84]   S.R. Vegdahl. "A Survey of Proposed Architectures for the Execution of Functional Languages." *IEEE Trans. Computers,* vol. C-33, no. 12, pp. 1050–1071, December 1984.

[Wah 84a]   B.W. Wah and K.L. Chen. "A Partitioning Approach to the Design of Selection Networks." *IEEE Trans. Computers,* vol. C-33, no. 3, pp. 261–268, March 1984.

[Wah 84b]   B.W. Wah and Y.W.E. Ma. "MANIP—A Multicomputer Architecture for Solving Combinatorial Extremum-Search Problems." *IEEE Trans. Computers,* vol. C-33, no. 5, pp. 377–390, May 1984.

[Wah 85]   B.W. Wah, G.-J. Li, and C.F. Yu. "Multiprocessing of Combinatorial Search Problems." *Computer,* vol. 18, no. 6, pp. 93–108, June 1985.

[Wah 86]   B.W. Wah and G.-J. Li. *Tutorial on Computers for Artificial Intelligence Applications,* IEEE Press, 1986.

[Waltz 87]   D.L. Waltz. "Applications of the Connection Machine." *Computer,* vol. 20, no. 1, January 1987.

[Warren 81]   D.H.D. Warren. "Efficient Processing of Interactive Relational Database Queries Expressed in Logic." *Proc. 7th International Conference on Very Large Data Bases,* pp. 272–281, 1981.

[Wegner 86]   P. Wegner and B. Shriver (eds). "Special Issue on Object-Oriented Programming Workshop." *SIGPLAN,* vol. 21, no. 10, October 1986.

[Weiser 85]   M. Weiser, S. Kogge, M. McElvany, R. Pierson, R. Post, and A. Thareja. "Status and Performance of the ZMOB Parallel Processing System." *Proc. COMPCON Spring,* pp. 71–73, February 1985.

[Williams 78]   R. Williams. "A Multiprocessing System for the Direct Execution of Lisp." *Proc. 4th Workshop on Computer Architecture for Non-Numeric Processing,* August 1978.

[Winograd 80]   T. Winograd. "Extended Inference Modes in Reasoning by Computer Systems." *Artificial Intelligence,* vol. 13, pp. 5–26, 1980.

[Winston 84]   P.H. Winston and B. Horn. *Lisp,* 2nd ed., Addison-Wesley, Reading, MA, 1984.

[Yamaguchi 84]   Y. Yamaguchi, K. Toda, J. Herath, and T. Yuba. "EM-3: A Lisp-Based Data-Driven Machine." *Proc. International Conference on Fifth Generation Computer Systems,* pp. 524–532, 1984.

[Yokoi 84a]   T. Yokoi, S. Uchida, and ICOT Third Laboratory. "Sequential Inference Machine: SIM—Its Programming and Operating System." *Proc. Interna-*

tional Conference on Fifth Generation Computer Systems, pp. 70–81, 1984.

[Yu 86]   C.-F. Yu and B.W. Wah. "Learning Dominance Relations in Combinatorial Search Problems." *Proc. Computer Software and Applications Conference,* October 1986.

[Yu 88]   C.-F. Yu and B.W. Wah. "Efficient Branch-and-Bound Algorithms on a Two-Level Memory System." *IEEE Trans. Software Engineering,* vol. SE-14, no. 9, September 1988.

Advanced Computer Architectures

5

Compute-Intensive Processors and Multicomputers

John L. Gustafson

Sandia National Laboratories, Albuquerque, NM

5.1 Introduction

Compute-intensive processors are defined as those that have an unusual amount of arithmetic capability compared to other facilities. They are designed in such a way that floating-point calculations can be done as fast or faster than the operation of simply moving data to and from main memory. This class of processor includes the so-called array processors and attached processors, as well as some supercomputers.

The algorithms appropriate for such processors require special attention, since communication cost is high relative to computation cost, the opposite of most general-purpose computers. The sections that follow discuss the primary applications, design philosophy, architectural techniques, and appropriate algorithms of compute-intensive processors. There is also some discussion of the performance metrics associated with such processors. As an addendum, we apply the issues of compute/communicate ratios to hypercube-based multicomputers.

5.2 Applications of Array Processors

The following discussion is organized along historical lines. Compute-intensive processors began as single-precision subroutine processors and evolved into double-precision attached processors; the applications for such host-dependent machines have driven this change.

5.2.1 Seismic data processing

The array processors of the mid-1970s were born of the desire to better deal with the needs of the seismic data-processing industry. The petroleum industry relies on artificially induced seismic waves to infer underground geological formations. A delta function in space and time is approximated by striking the surface or setting off an explosion, and detectors on the surface record the next few seconds of wave displacement. The "inverse problem," that of deriving the probable structure that produced the waves, is underdetermined and very compute intensive; those few seconds of recording can take days of computer processing. In fact, it is common to archive the data so obtained and reexamine it using various methods over a period of years.

A large part of one stage of the problem involves two-dimensional fast Fourier transforms (FFTs), where one dimension is time and the other is the spatial dimension along which the detectors lie. Since it is representative, consider the problem from a system perspective: Suppose there are 128 detectors and 1024 discrete time measurements in a given time window. If the detectors produce 16-bit data, then the input data size is 256 kbytes for that time window, typically stored on magnetic tape. The operation of a forward FFT in the time dimension, then in the space dimension, applying a filtering operator, then doing inverse FFTs in both dimensions, requires approximately 23 MFLOPS. This represents 44 operations for every word of input data, a rather high ratio of computation to overall communication. If seismic tapes are to be processed at sustained rates of 1 Mbyte/s for both input and filtered output, say, then the processor (or processors) should be capable of sustaining around 44 MFLOPS in single precision when performing FFTs. The computational kernel is relatively simple and fits in a small program cache. Both vector arithmetic and parallelism are easily applied because of the repetitiveness and two-dimensional nature of the problem. Considering the precision of the input data, 32-bit arithmetic is quite adequate. This is a nearly ideal problem for compute-intensive array or attached processors, and a variety of such machines are currently offered that are highly optimized for this application.

5.2.2 Medical imaging

The problem of processing data from computerized tomography (CT) x-ray scanners is very similar to the seismic problem. Low-precision input data are processed with a large number of operations per data word, using small, unchanging computational kernels, and a modest data memory size of less than 1 Mword.

The difference between using a compute-intensive processor and a conventional processor can mean the difference between waiting 10 s and waiting half an hour for the brain scan of a person who has experienced a severe blow to the head. CT scanners soared in popularity once the time for computation was economically brought close to the time required for the scan itself, using compute-intensive processors.

At the time of writing, seismic and medical imaging uses are perhaps the most important applications of single-precision compute-intensive processors. Both applications are dominated by the Floating Point Systems AP-120B and its architectural descendants, and by the Star Technologies ST-100.

5.3   Applications of Attached Scientific Processors

In the mid-1970s, the only commercial machine capable of delivering nearly 10 MFLOPS with high precision was the CDC 7600. Since the architecture was general, its cost was many millions of dollars, and only a few were built. When array processors were first introduced, they offered the same potential MFLOPS as the CDC 7600 for about 1 percent of the price of that mainframe. The result was explosive interest in applying the new array processors to many applications only marginally suited to their architectural restrictions. Both vendors and customers attempted to circumvent the inherent limitations that gave rise to the cost efficiency.

Kenneth Wilson, a physicist at Cornell University, saw the AP-120B architecture as nearly ideal for his work on the Renormalization Group except for the lack of a Fortran compiler to ease the burden of explicitly programming each functional unit. A group at Cornell, led by D. Bergmark, produced a Fortran 66 subset compiler for the AP-120B which proved that high-level compilers for "horizontally microcoded" computers were both possible and practical.

At about the same time, R. C. Young, a mechanical engineer at General Atomic, saw the AP-120B architecture as potentially useful for the three-dimensional structural analysis problems that were out of the range of conventional machines. But the precision needed to be a bit higher, and some way had to be found to achieve the effect of a large virtual address space so that the many megawords representing the stiffness matrix could be handled without slowing computation. The latter problem he solved by using a block factorization technique that overlapped disk fetches with submatrix multiplications. As discussed in Sec. 5.5.4 below, $M \times M$ matrix multiples can perform M multiply-adds for every input data value, so a disk 50 times slower than the arithmetic unit (0.2 to 0.3 Mwords/s vs. 12 MFLOPS) can still keep pace once the stiffness matrix, stored with profile sparsity, has an average profile on the order of 50 elements (see Fig. 5.1).

Both Kenneth Wilson's and R. C. Young's efforts influenced the next generation of array processors, typified by the Floating Point

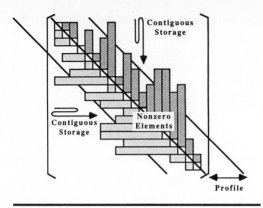

Figure 5.1   Profile matrix storage.

Systems (FPS) 164. The FPS 164 had full 64-bit precision words, more registers, a somewhat more complete crossbar between functional units to assist Fortran compilation, and greatly expanded memories throughout the system. Since it ran entire Fortran programs instead of subroutines, its environment resembled that of the Cray 1 more than that of the AP-120B, and the term *attached processor* was used to denote this distinction from *array processors*. The applications that follow are appropriate for *attached 64-bit processors*.

5.3.1 Structural analysis

Structural analysis is used to predict the behavior of objects ranging from tiny machine parts to bridges and large buildings. Its numerical methods are mature and are not confined to stress analysis but can also calculate heat flow or electromagnetic fields to very high accuracy. It relies on the *finite element method,* whereby the structure is broken into geometrically simple domains called *elements* for which an exact analytical solution exists. The global solution is found by mating element boundaries together in a consistent way, which amounts to the construction and solution of a large system of equations called the *global stiffness matrix*. For sufficiently large models, factoring the global stiffness matrix dominates run time.

With the exception of the matrix setup and factoring, structural analysis is very much a problem for *general-purpose* computers. A structural analysis program like MacNeal-Schwendler's MSC/ NASTRAN involves hundreds of thousands of lines of source code and spends much of its time moving data from disk to memory and back with very little arithmetic. Structural analysis environments must support interactive graphics terminals, data formatting, low-precision integer operations, archiving to disk and tape, and other functions for which very few compute-intensive processors are economical. The solution, then, is to combine a general-purpose computer with some sort of arithmetic enhancement to try to make the matrix solution time commensurate with the time spent on the rest of the task. IBM introduced its vector facility for the 3090 mainframe with this situation in mind, and attached processors such as the FPS 164 and FPS 264 can economically handle all but the preprocessing and postprocessing parts of the run, leaving those to an IBM or VAX host.

To illustrate the magnitude of the matrix solution step, suppose one wishes to model a cubical elastic body divided into cubical elements, 100 on a side. Each cube corner has three translational and three rotational degrees of freedom, so there are roughly 6×10^6 unknown quantities to be solved for. If the elements are numbered lexicographically, the matrix describing the system has a bandwidth on the order of 10^4, and the solution of the matrix for a single set of input forces takes about 10^{13} floating-point operations. A machine with an *effective* speed of 10 GFLOPS would therefore take 15 min to compute a single static response, and T times that if T time steps are desired for a dynamic analysis. So structural analysis is appropriate for compute-intensive processors, especially for the larger problems; the percentage of the total work spent in the matrix solution phase approaches 100 percent as problems grow large in the number of elements.

5.3.2 Analog circuit simulation

The SPICE circuit simulation emerged as a public-domain program from Berkeley around 1972 and has since undergone much modification and commercialization. Early users of SPICE soon discovered that it was not the least bit difficult to find relatively simple circuits for which SPICE runs appeared interminable on general-purpose machines.

SPICE does its own memory management from within Fortran, dimensioning all of the available memory as a single array and using integers as pointers to allocate and de-allocate regions of memory at run time. The dynamic sizing of arrays that this permits is essential for circuit simulation, since it is difficult to estimate memory requirements before the run begins. This memory management from Fortran severely burdens the memory bus of a computer, and speed with SPICE is all too frequently a function of the megabytes per second rating of the memory and the *latency* of the memory. Latency is critical because the memory management adds a level of indirection to the memory references. Pipelined memory is of little help for conventional

SPICE, which was written well before the advent of compute-intensive processors.

The elements of the circuit have current-voltage properties that require substantial calculation; a transistor element evaluation might involve several pages of source code containing exponentials, tests, branches, polynomial evaluations, and square roots. Machines with data caches such as the VAX perform relatively well on SPICE, since modeling each element means bringing in a small amount of memory and using just that memory intensively. The original version of SPICE makes no attempt to group devices by type so as to permit vectorized evaluation; vectorized versions for compute-intensive processors, such as the Cray and the FPS 264, group the devices, use conditional merges to replace branching, and work very well on large-scale circuits where there is a great deal of repetition of device type.

Analog circuit simulation spends most of its time alternating between the setup of a large, very sparse asymmetrical matrix and solving that matrix. An element of the matrix A_{ij} is nonzero if circuit element i is connected to circuit element j. Circuit elements such as diodes create asymmetries in the matrix, so the economies of symmetric matrix factoring are not available to most circuit models. Before factoring, there might be only five or six nonzeros per row of the matrix in a matrix several hundred elements on a side. A symbolic factoring determines where nonzeros will arise in solving and that symbolic factoring needs updating infrequently relative to the number of times the matrix is actually solved; the cost of accounting for the sparsity is amply repaid after a few iterations. This is a very different approach to matrix solving from the dense or banded systems discussed above; a profile-type approach, even on specialized hardware (see Sec. 5.6.2), does not seem to overcome the advantages of exploiting sparsity.

On a general-purpose processor, the division of time between matrix factoring and matrix setup (device property evaluation) is roughly half and half. On a compute-intensive processor, the division is more like 20 percent for the factoring and 80 percent for the setup. It is worth noting that a vectorized version of SPICE for the Cray 1 only achieves about 100 times the speed of the VAX-11/780, despite the much higher ratio (about 1000:1) in peak 64-bit arithmetic speed. Analog circuit simulation, even when substantially reorganized from the Berkeley version, is memory-intensive and best handled by compute-intensive processors that have a very short path to main memory.

5.3.3 Computational chemistry

There are many ways that computers can be used to simulate the behavior of chemical entities, ranging in complexity from a simple hydrogen-hydrogen bond to the dynamic behavior of a strand of DNA with dozens of component atoms. In general, the simpler problems are studied with *ab initio* methods based on the laws of quantum mechanics, whereas more complicated molecules must make use of approximations in order to render the problems computationally tractable. The electrons in a molecule have several energy states that can be approximated as a combination of *basis functions*. The basis functions are analogous to the polynomial terms in a Taylor series expansion, and when chosen appropriately form a complete set for describing the molecular bonds.

Ab initio methods compute the interaction of electron states, ignoring those below a certain energy threshold. With N basis functions, the number of interactions is $O(N^4)$. The interactions, or *Gaussian integrals,* typically number in the billions and must be stored on disk rather than in main memory. An $O(N^5)$ or $O(N^6)$ process, involving eigenvalue extraction, then produces the configuration of basis functions that best describes the molecule.

The process is well suited to compute-intensive processors, with one exception to the paradigm; the primary feature required other than 64-bit floating-point operations is the ability to move data quickly to and from secondary storage, with large secondary storage. Some compute-intensive processors can *recompute* the Gaussian integrals faster than they can be retrieved from disk, thereby eliminating the need for a large and fast secondary storage. There is also a need for logic and bit-packing operations, since the indices of an integral are usually packed into a word to save storage.

The processing of integrals usually involves repeated matrix multiplications, the canonical operation of compute-intensive processors. If the architecture can efficiently exploit sparsity, then there are great performance benefits, because a typical matrix in computational chemistry only has 10 percent nonzero elements. A 10 percent sparse–10 percent sparse matrix multiply requires, on the average, only 1 percent of the multiply-adds of a dense-dense matrix multiply, so the potential speedup is on the order of a hundredfold. One approach, known as *direct configuration interaction* (CI), consists almost entirely of matrix multiplication, which was a motivation for the FPS 164/MAX special-purpose architecture (see Sec. 5.6.2).

5.3.4 Electromagnetic modeling

For pure number crunching, few applications can compare with that of assessing the radar reflection of a metal object such as an aircraft. Because every point on the metal object acts both as a receiving antenna and a reradiating antenna, every point affects every other point, so the equations describing the problem are *dense.* It is not unusual to have to factor and solve a dense, complex-valued set of 20,000 equations in 20,000 unknowns, requiring over 20 trillion floating-point operations and over 6 billion bytes of (secondary) storage. The result of the computation is the cross section seen by a detector from various viewing angles.

Even the most highly specialized compute-intensive processor can be used efficiently on the radar cross-section application. The vectors are long, hundreds of operations are performed for every communication of data to or from disk, and the inner loop of the factoring is pure multiply-add arithmetic: a complex dot product. Setting up the matrix is a more scalar-intensive operation but is usually less than 1 percent of the total work. The problem *must* be done with 64-bit precision; the problem can be formulated as an ill-conditioned matrix of modest size or a numerically better-behaved matrix of the size mentioned above. In either case, less than 64-bit precision does not seem to lead to useful answers.

5.3.5 Seismic simulation

The oil exploration industry uses 32-bit processors to analyze seismic measurements and form hypotheses about what is underground. Because the problem is severely underdetermined, choosing from among many possible underground formations remains an art as much as a science. A natural method for checking the hypotheses is to ask a computer the following question: *If this particular structure describes what is underground, what would have been detected by the seismic sensors?* Answering this question requires a 64-bit simulation, the opposite of the data acquisition problem. It is conceptually simple. One describes the rock layers in the computer memory by position and refractive index, produces a point disturbance at the memory location representing the *shot point,* and then uses a difference equation to simulate the wave that propagates through the earth. The values in storage locations representing the surface of the earth simulate the displacements that would be recorded by seismic detectors.

In the *acoustic model,* there is only one degree of freedom at each discrete space point, representing pressure. A far more accurate method recognizes the earth as an elastic medium, with independent stresses and torques in every dimension. The elastic model uses principles from finite element methods but avoids factoring a global stiffness matrix at every time step; each degree of freedom can be computed *explicitly* from the nearby data of the previous time step, since stresses cannot propagate faster than the speed of sound in the medium. Problem size is usually limited by main memory size, since a fully elastic three-dimensional $N \times N \times N$ model requires two time steps in memory, each with $6N^3$ 64-bit words of main memory. Current supercomputers are inadequate for models with completely satisfactory fidelity. In general, the problem is ideally suited to the compute-intensive paradigm.

5.3.6 AI applications

The main AI applications for compute-intensive processors are in *recognizing* sounds and images. *Understanding* the sound or image is a very different problem, requiring more of a Lisp-type environment that is not at all dependent on arithmetic.

As an example, *speech recognition* involves both identification of phonetic sounds (independent of the speaker) and mapping those sounds to the most probable word in the language. Assessing the *meaning* of the speech is a separate phase, although feedback from that understanding can assist future recognition by adjusting probabilities and weighting factors assigned to raw input data.

Another example is satellite image processing. A large amount of arithmetic computation goes into refining data from satellites prior to being able to use AI methods to distinguish structures (e.g., airbases from highways, tanks from trucks). An array processor might well be coupled to a Lisp-specific computer to handle both parts of the task with specialized hardware.

Finally, an example of a compute-intensive AI application is the *Neocognitron* neural network model for visual pattern recognition developed by Nippon Telephone and Telegraph researchers [Fukushima 83]. It refines handwritten Arabic numerals described on a 19×19 array of pixels through 12 stages to a final 1×10 array representing digits 0 to 9. By "teaching" the network using a small number of distorted examples, the Neocognitron can accurately recognize a wide range of written numerals. Each "neuron" performs essentially a floating-point inner product followed by a binary decision, with a very high ratio of computation to communication. Since neurons are known to integrate information that is digital in amplitude but analog (best represented by floating-point numbers) in time, it seems likely that compute-intensive processors will play a role in AI applications based on neural networks.

5.4 Design Philosophy

General-purpose computers do surprisingly little *arithmetic*. The majority of instruction cycles in the world are spent *moving* data from one place to another without performing operations on them. A typical example is *word processing*. String comparison and computing the best location of text on a page are virtually the only arithmetic tasks involved; the rest of the work consists of moving information between keyboard, memory, display, printout, and mass storage. Most of the

TABLE 5.1   IBM 370 Instruction Frequencies

Instruction	Percent of total instructions
Branch on condition	20.2
Load from memory	15.5
Test under mask	6.1
Store to memory	5.9
Load register	4.7
Load address	4.0
Test register	3.8
Branch on register	2.9
Move characters	2.1
Load half-word	1.8

capital investment today in computers is in mainframes oriented toward business applications. These are used for searching through disks and tapes for information, sorting, and tracking events (such as banking transactions or airline reservations), all of which involve an occasional byte-level comparison or fixed-point (integer) calculation. But in fact arithmetic is relatively rare, and high-precision floating-point arithmetic is practically unused on such machines except in figuring compound interest. For good reasons, then, conventional computers are designed with the communication and storage of data foremost in mind. Table 5.1 illustrates this fact with a list of the most-used instructions on the venerable IBM 370 family [IBM 86]. This top 10 list accounts for 66 percent of the instruction usage on the IBM/370 but contains not a single mathematical operator. A similar study has been done for Digital Equipment's VAX-11/780 in Table 5.2.

TABLE 5.2   VAX-11/780 Instruction Frequencies

Instruction type	Percent of total instructions
Simple (moves, etc.)	83.6
Bit manipulation	6.92
Floating-point math	3.62
Call/return	3.22
System management	2.11
Character manipulation	0.43
Decimal instructions	0.03

Scientific and engineering applications are such a sharp contrast to this distribution of instruction usage that they demand an entirely different approach. These applications are typically heavily laden with arithmetic operations. When run on a general-purpose machine without floating-point hardware, most of the time will be spent in the software or firmware routines that combine basic integer operations to accomplish a floating-point operation. Time spent fetching data becomes negligible by comparison, leading to algorithms that minimize total work simply by minimizing the number of floating point operations.

Extensive hardware is necessary to reduce floating-point calculation time to a few processor clock cycles. Such hardware can roughly double the number of gates in a processor. Since doubling gate count might nearly double hardware cost, manufacturers of general-purpose computers prefer to leave out such hardware since most of their customers would never use it and would find such machines less cost-efficient for business tasks.

This dilemma has brought about the separation of computers into two classes: those optimized for business processing, typified by the mainframes built by International Business Machines, Unisys, and Digital Equipment; and those optimized for scientific processing, typified by mainframes built by Control Data and Cray Research. An alternative approach is a compute-intensive processor that attaches to a general-purpose mainframe to provide floating-point speed via an optional peripheral device. These attached processors, typified by those made by Floating Point Systems and Star Technologies, are able to leave out many hardware functions that are taken care of by the host processor, recovering cost efficiency that would otherwise be slightly worse than a solution based on a single scientific processor. Figure 5.2

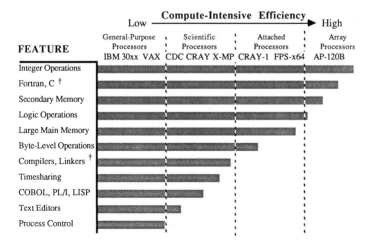

†"Fortran, C" might mean the availability of cross compilers that execute on a separate machine.
"Compilers, Linkers" means that the CPU runs all of its own program development tools.

Figure 5.2   Generality-efficiency tradeoff.

illustrates the tradeoff between generality and compute-intensive efficiency.

The Cray 1 is very nearly in the attached processor class, requiring a host processor to manage it but differing from attached processors in that it runs its own compiler and linker. At installations where Cray usage is heavily subsidized, complete time sharing and even text editing are done directly on the compute-intensive processor despite the very poor cost efficiency of that approach.

A glance at the instruction set for a general-purpose computer reveals operations for converting binary number representations to character representations, rotating and shifting the bits of words, and prioritized interrupt handling to assist in sharing machine resources among multiple users. Compute-intensive processors can have greatly simplified designs through the elimination of such instructions. Where necessary, those functions can be built somewhat inelegantly from other operations, just as some general-purpose processors build floating-point operations. A compute-intensive processor will typically have instructions such as floating-point multiply, add, subtract, reciprocal (not necessarily a divide), square root, and conversions between floating-point and integer representations.

Besides the presence or absence of instructions, compute-intensive processors have very unusual ratios of communication speed to computation speed. On general-purpose machines, it typically takes one or two orders of magnitude longer to perform a floating-point operation than to fetch or store the operands/result; on compute-intensive processors, the ratio is closer to unity. We will later discuss an example in which 248 floating-point operations occur (usefully) in the time required for a single memory reference. With a polynomial evaluation, computing the norm of a vector, or multiplying a matrix times a vector, the ratio of speed for

Memory reference : floating-point add : floating-point multiply

can in fact be 1:1:1. Most compute-intensive processors approximate this ratio. Examples include the FPS 264, the Cray 1 (but not the Cray X-MP), the Convex C-1, and the Alliant FX series. The Cray X-MP actually has multiple ports to main memory, making its ratio 3:1:1 and tending toward more general-purpose computing.

5.5 Architectural Techniques

Although the last 50 years of computer technology show steady and dramatic improvements in cost, size, speed, and packaging, history repeats itself with respect to computer *architecture*. The board-level processors of the 1970s rediscovered techniques of the mainframes of the

1960s, and in the 1980s those techniques have been discovered yet again in single-chip processors. For example, the concept of multiple pipelined functional units appeared in the CDC 6600 mainframe, then the AP-120B array processor, and today in chip sets such as the 2264/2265 from Weitek. Several vendors are currently working on consolidating a multiple-pipeline compute-intensive processor onto a single VLSI chip. The designers of compute-intensive processors, *whatever the technology or scale,* have repeatedly faced the same issues:

- How many different functional units should there be?
- How can they be controlled by an instruction stream?
- How much parallelism can be used by Fortran-type environments?
- How much main memory is needed to keep the processor busy?
- Can registers or cache successfully substitute for main memory?
- What is the optimal ratio of vector speed to scalar speed (pipeline length)?
- What is the ideal precision (32-bit, 64-bit, etc.)?

The following sections offer some arguments that have been used in successful designs, illustrating tradeoffs that must be made.

5.5.1 Functional units

The idea of multiple functional units dates back at least to the ATLAS computer of the early 1960s. Separate functional units for memory addressing and register-to-register operations are nearly universal. On a compute-intensive processor, one might envision so many different functional units that a Fortran expression such as

A(I,J) = 0.5* (SQRT(FLOAT(I/2))) *B(J) + 3.0/C(I,J)

could be evaluated efficiently by having a processor that contains a machine for the integer divide I/2, a machine for the FLOAT, a machine for the SQRT, two floating-point multipliers, a floating-point divider, a floating-point adder, and address calculation units for the (I,J) indexing, all capable of cooperating on this task. Hardware cost grows with the number of functional units, faster than linearly because of the need to heavily interconnect the functional units (the classic crossbar switch problem). Studies of compute-intensive kernels [Charlesworth 81] reveal that a typical mix of operation is weighted as follows:

Operation	Relative weight
Operand reference	7
Integer add/subtract	1 to 2
Integer multiply	<0.1
Floating-point add/subtract	1
Floating-point multiply	1
Divides	<0.1
Square roots	<0.1

It is an engineering heuristic that a processor is most cost efficient when no single part is a conspicuous bottleneck. Therefore, the preceding list implies that a well-balanced compute-intensive processor should have an integer adder, a floating-point adder/subtracter, and a floating-point multiplier, and should handle the other operations less directly. For example, divides can be accomplished (with a slight increase in rounding error) by fetching a reciprocal approximation of the denominator from a table in read-only memory, refining the precision with Newton-Raphson iterations (using the floating-point adder and multiplier), and finally multiplying by the numerator. This is perhaps an order of magnitude slower than an add or multiply but is acceptable for the typical mix of operations shown above.

The list also indicates that there should be the ability to fetch or store about seven operands for every time the floating-point multiplier and adder units complete an operation. But doing this from main memory is exactly the communication cost that compute-intensive processors seek to avoid. Since the adder and multiplier each take two inputs and produce one output, it is evident that at least six operand references are necessary to sustain anything close to the peak speed of the arithmetic. The solution usually makes use of registers and the interconnect between functional units rather than memory bandwidth, the most limited resource in a von Neumann design. For example, a processor could provide two register reads, two register writes, a main memory reference, a local "table memory" reference, and connect the output of one floating-point functional unit to the input of another, providing a total of seven operand references, of which only one actually burdens the main memory bus.

5.5.2 Processor control

When is such a processor supposed to obtain *instructions*, with memory tied up moving data? A separate program store is called for, either as a cache or a memory explicitly loaded by the user. Program caches can be much simpler than data caches, since there is usually no requirement to *write* to a program cache during a run, which eliminates the need for the cache to ever write anything back to main memory. They also can be fairly small, since compute-intensive applications usually involve small loops occupying less than 1K of program store. Opportunities to fill the cache from main memory arise whenever *serial data dependencies* allow the data reference unit to go idle. Alternatively, one can simply have a separate memory for program storage that must be loaded explicitly. Caches are characteristic of attached scientific computers that must run entire Fortran programs, whereas separate program stores are characteristic of array processors that concentrate on simple subroutines.

There is a price to pay for the multiple instruction units in the instruction word. The choice is to either *hard-wire* a set of basic operations such as dot product, vector add, etc., and use the instruction to select one of those basic operations, or else provide a *wide instruction word* that explicitly controls all of the functional units with parcels of bits within the instruction. Programming the latter has an analogy with the task of writing multipart musical harmony. The rules of western music place certain context-dependent restrictions on what notes can occur simultaneously, and voices enter the harmony depending on what has come before, just as incomplete crossbars limit what operations can be performed simultaneously, and just as loop iterations imply an order in which functional units can be invoked. Constructing a software pipeline for a simple vector operation can be every bit as difficult as writing a *canon* or *round*. Consider a loop for computing an inner product:

        DO 10 I = 1,N
    10 SUM = SUM + A(I) * B(I)

and the round, "Row, Row, Row Your Boat":

Fetch A(I)	*Row,*
Fetch B (I)	*Row,*
(Memory pipeline wait)	*Row, Your Boat,*
(Memory pipeline wait)	*Gently*
Multiply A (I) and B (I)	*Down the*
(Multiplier pipeline wait)	*Stream...*
(Multiplier pipeline wait)	*Merrily,*
Add product to SUM	*Merrily,*
(Adder pipeline wait)	*Merrily, Merrily,*
Test I = loop end?	*Life is*
(Comparison wait)	*but a*
Jump to beginning	*Dream.* (Repeat)

Both the program and the music have been arranged in such a fashion that a conflict-free *pipeline* can be established, as shown in Fig. 5.3.

Note that the role of the singers in the music above is *not* the usual one where each singer repeats the entire melody; the notes that occur are identical if each singer behaves as a functional unit for a single phrase. Whereas many people can write a melody, very few can write

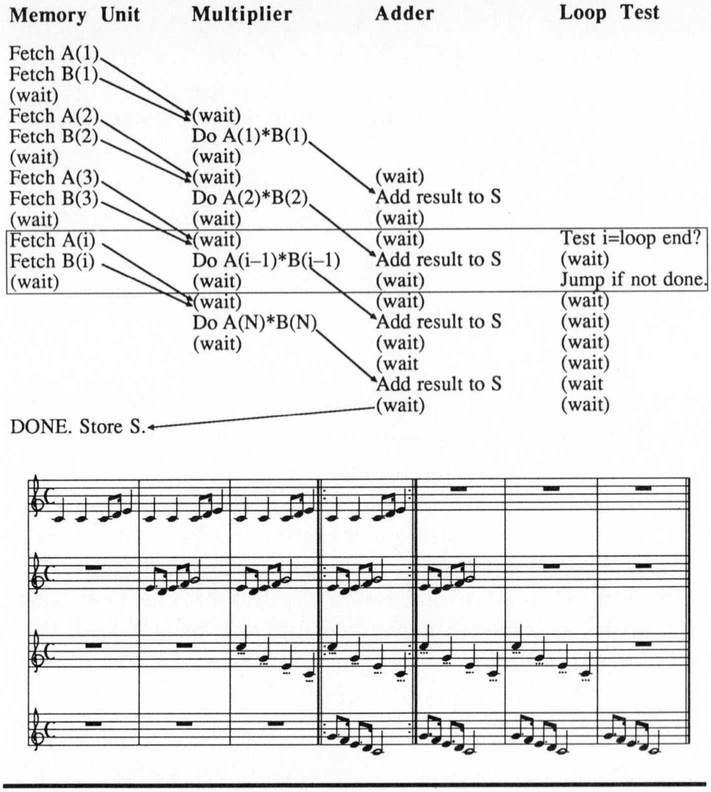

Memory Unit	Multiplier	Adder	Loop Test
Fetch A(1)			
Fetch B(1)			
(wait)			
Fetch A(2)	(wait)		
Fetch B(2)	Do A(1)*B(1)		
(wait)	(wait)		
Fetch A(3)	(wait)	(wait)	
Fetch B(3)	Do A(2)*B(2)	Add result to S	
(wait)	(wait)	(wait)	
Fetch A(i)	(wait)	(wait)	Test i=loop end?
Fetch B(i)	Do A(i–1)*B(i–1)	Add result to S	(wait)
(wait)	(wait)	(wait)	Jump if not done.
	(wait)	(wait)	(wait)
	Do A(N)*B(N)	Add result to S	(wait)
	(wait)	(wait)	(wait)
		(wait	(wait)
		Add result to S	(wait
		(wait)	(wait)
DONE. Store S.			

Figure 5.3   Software pipeline analogy.

multiple melodies that interlock properly as a fugue, and still fewer can create a melody that interlocks properly when overlapped with itself. For this reason, compute-intensive processors with simultaneous control of many functional units have the reputation of being much more difficult to program efficiently than conventional machines. Surprisingly, a Fortran compiler can generate conflict-free schemes such as that shown in Fig. 5.3. A pipelining compiler was first introduced in 1983 by Floating Point Systems [Touzeau 84]. The problem of scheduling the units for optimal efficiency is known to be NP-complete, so the current version of the compiler only performs a shallow search of the tree of possibilities. Empirically, this turns out to produce efficiency comparable to that of hand-tuned assembly code. This type of compiler is markedly different from "vectorizing compilers" targeted at vector processors.

On a vector processor, the type of loop shown above would be in microcode that the user can invoke but never alter. This greatly reduces the burden on the instruction bandwidth but restricts the set of operations. For example, to perform a *sparse* dot product of the form

```
    DO 10 I = 1, N
10  SUM = SUM + A(J(I)) * B(I)
```

is only slightly more work for a software-pipelined machine, but at least twice as hard for a vector machine that must construct the operation from a Vector Gather followed by a Vector Multiply-Reduction-Add. The compiler burden shifts to one of *recognizing* vector forms expressed as DO loops by template matching; the compiler must then attempt an efficient construct from the basic forms available on the machine. The hardware to manage vector forms is expensive, but so is programming assembly language on a software-pipelined machine. The argument has yet to be firmly settled in the community of computer users.

5.5.3 Parallelism and Fortran

Despite its historical development as a language for serial architectures, Fortran shows a fair amount of *functional* parallelism close to the surface. If a Fortran text is divided into *basic blocks,* that is, code segments bounded by subroutine calls or branches, then the program text implies a data dependency graph that can be extracted by an optimizing compiler. In the case of DO loops where iteration $n + 1$ is independent of iterations 1 to $n,$ there might well be as many concurrent operations in the data dependency graph as there are iterations of the loop. For example, the vector add

```
    DO 10 I = 1,N
 10  R (I) = A(I) + B(I)
```

involves N completely independent additions. Optimization for this goes hand-in-hand with the multiple functional unit idea, since the units can be scheduled at *compile* time. Many general-purpose computers use concurrency only at run time, where the processor looks ahead in the instruction stream and tries, for example, to prefetch operands that will soon be needed while some other operation is completing.

The philosophy in compute-intensive processors has traditionally been to put the burden on the compiler or other software tools such as libraries of vector operations, thereby lessening the amount of hardware needed to detect and make use of concurrency at run time. This affects the Edit-Compile-Link-Run-Debug cycle in which the user sits, because on small problems the time saved in the Run will be consumed by the additional time during the Compile. For this reason, attached processors and array processors are inherently less interactive than general-purpose computers when traditional programming languages are used.

5.5.4 Main memory

Asked why his computers do not have virtual memory, Seymour Cray reputedly once said, "In machines this fast, there's no use pretending you got something you ain't." Compute-intensive processors do not spend a great deal of time operating on any one page of memory, nor do they go for long periods without a memory reference during which a data cache can be moved to or from disk storage. Thus, the strategy is usually to have a large physical memory, making the best use of address bits by addressing *words,* even 64-bit words, rather than *bytes.*

How big should the main memory be? This is highly application de-pendent, but the answer stems from the need to amortize the time to load and unload the data for a particular problem. If it takes 5 s to load a program and its data set, then the computation should take at least as long. Although initialization grows linearly with the amount of memory to move, the amount of computation usually grows superlinearly. For example, an $N \times N$ matrix multiplication requires $2N^2$ input values but $2N^3$ operations; so for some sufficiently large N, the system will spend most of the time computing rather than com-municating data. As a specific example, suppose that the loading pro-ceeds at 0.1 Mword/s, and the compute-intensive processor can per-form 10 MFLOPS. If we require communication time to be roughly 1 percent of the total, then

$$\text{Load time} = \frac{\text{compute time}}{100}$$

which implies that

$$\frac{2N^2 \text{ words}}{0.1 \text{ Mwords/s}} = \frac{2N^3 \text{ operations}}{10 \text{ MFLOPS}} \times 1\%$$

This is satisfied when N is 10,000 words. This is quite a bit smaller than the typical memories of general-purpose processors, suggesting that for some applications, simple array processors can improve cost efficiency by reducing main memory size. Attached scientific comput-ers must have larger memories since they contain the entire applica-tion program (or large overlays of it), not just compute-intensive ker-nels, and must use physical memory rather than virtual memory for both program and data.

General-purpose computing is characterized by problems for which the number of computations grows proportionately to the amount of data. If desired run time is on the order of seconds, then a general-purpose processor capable of X operations per second should have about X words of memory. The above argument, however, shows that compute-intensive processors can often succeed with less than this. The Cray 1, for example, is capable of over 150 MFLOPS, yet has only 1 million words of memory. The reason behind this is that scientific computing is characterized by problems (such as matrix multiplication) for which the number of computations per data point grows much faster than the number of data points.

5.5.5 Registers

Since data caches appear difficult to make efficient for the whole spectrum of memory reference patterns used for compute-intensive processing, one must have a large set of registers close to the functional units. For example, the FPS 164 has 64 integer registers and 64 floating-point registers, with the capacity for several simultaneous reads and writes per clock cycle. The Cray 1 uses multiple vector registers, where each vector contains 64 floating-point elements to keep operands within a few nanoseconds of the functional units. Besides the obvious design difficulties and parts cost of having a large number of fast registers, state-save becomes much slower, making context switching a clumsy operation. Compute-intensive processors are thus *not* intended for time slicing between multiple users, at least not with time slices measured in milliseconds. (Hardware to partition registers as well as memory among multiple users is generally counter to compute-intensive design). They also have trouble with languages such as Ada and Pascal, for which subroutine calls require an extensive state-save.

5.5.6 Vector-scalar balance

A *vector operation* is repeated on a list of numbers; a *scalar operation* is on a single number (one-argument functions) or pair of numbers (two-argument functions). (Unfortunately, the terms "parallel operation" and "serial operation" are often mistakenly used as synonyms for vector operation and scalar operation.) Vector arithmetic is efficient because it allows the reuse of an instruction and it permits a hardware pipeline to process the vector in a manner analogous to an assembly line. An excellent survey of pipelining techniques and history can be found in Kogge [81].

If a pipelined functional unit has N stages, then a scalar operation on that unit will take N clock cycles to complete and be N times slower than the speed for long vectors where a result is completed every cycle. There will also be $N - 1$ latches between stages, and hence pipelined units are slower at scalar operations than simple scalar units. The tradeoff for the computer designer is to strike a balance that prevents either scalar-type or vector-type operations from showing up as a performance bottleneck.

Suppose, statistically, that $7F$ percent of an application is vector-oriented and the rest is scalar, as timed on a completely scalar processor. Then a machine that is three times faster at vector processing than scalar processing will spend equal time in both types of code, and neither will appear as a bottleneck. If the same functional unit performs both scalar and vector operations, then the use of three-stage pipelines is suggested. If 90 percent of the application is vector-oriented, one would wish for nine-stage pipelines, although there is a limit as to how finely one can pipeline tasks like multiplication and addition. One manufacturer of array processors, CSP Inc., discarded the idea of pipelining entirely, with the argument that scalar units are easier to compile to. FPS opted for pipeline lengths of 2 or 3 stages in the functional units of the AP-120B and FPS 164 processors, and the pipelines in the Cray 1 are up to 14 stages long. The memory pipeline on the original Cray 2 is roughly 60 stages long, which is perhaps a record. Applications are generally scalar-bound on such machines. The Cray machines generally fit the definition of a compute-intensive processor, since a scalar floating-point operation is faster than a memory reference, and vector memory bandwidth (full pipelines) is just fast enough to keep up with the peak speed of the vector floating-point functional units.

The current generation of VLSI floating-point parts uses mostly four-stage pipelines for the multiplier and adder. Note that it is convenient to have the number of stages be a power of 2, since if there are 2^n stages, then binary collapses can be efficiently done in n passes for reduction operations such as sums and inner products.

The term *array processor* stems from the fact that these small, simple compute-intensive processors are frequently used to perform highly repetitive operations on arrays of numbers, *but in fact the term is misleading*. Pipelines in array processors are shorter than in supercomputers, making them actually better adapted to scalars and short vectors, and to programs with recursion and branching. Perhaps "subroutine processor" would be a more accurate term, since the main distinction between array processors and supercomputers is the generality of their capabilities (as shown in Fig. 5.2.)

5.5.7 Precision

When floating-point operations are constructed in software from integer shifting and summing operations, 64-bit operations take almost twice as long as 32-bit operations. In hardware, 64-bit operations can be brought down to approximately the same length critical path by adding extra gates and increasing the width of data paths. But a machine with 64-bit words and only full-word addressing must have double the storage cost for a 32-bit application.

Attached processors have the additional problem that users are generally unwilling to tolerate the loss of either precision or dynamic range in passing data from the host to the attached processor. Therefore, an attached processor should have at least as many mantissa bits *and* at least as many exponent bits as every host to which it will be attached. In the AP-120B, this led to the choice of a 38-bit data word since there were so many floating-point formats in use by various vendors for single-precision (usually 32- or 36-bit) data. As more 32-bit machines standardize on the IEEE floating-point standard and 36-bit computers become less common, more attached processors are able to use VLSI parts based on the 32-bit IEEE format without incurring loss of precision or range through data transfer.

Required precision is a function of application. Some generalizations are listed below:

32-bit precision	64-bit precision
Most signal processing	Structural analysis (finite element methods)
Most image processing	
Lattice-gauge calculations	Circuit simulation (stiff ODEs)
Missile simulation (simple ODEs)	*Ab initio* computational chemistry
Most graphics (rendering)	Seismic simulation (forward modeling)
Seismic migration	High-order or hyperbolic finite difference schemes
Coarse-grid, elliptic finite difference schemes	Computational fluid dynamics
	Oil reservoir simulation

- Data acquired from physical phenomena (seismic data reduction, satellite image processing) rarely have more than four decimals of precision or four orders of magnitude dynamic range, and hence signal and image processing usually need no more than 32-bit precision.

- Lattice-gauge simulations are unusual among compute-intensive simulations in that errors accumulated using 32-bit arithmetic on small unitary matrices can be periodically removed by renormalizing to keep determinants close to unity.

- Missile simulation and other models involving ordinary differential equations (ODEs) with few degrees of freedom frequently have very stable numerical methods, and errors caused by use of single precision damp out over repeated timesteps.

- Rendering methods for generating photographic-quality simulated images (such as ray tracing) need only compute with the precision that will be relevant to a raster-scan display (about one part in 1000). An exception occurs when one must compute the intersection of nearly parallel plane sections, which is an ill-posed problem mitigated by the judicious use of 64-bit precision.

- Finite difference schemes for solving partial differential equations (PDEs) often have inherent numerical error proportional to some low power of the grid spacing. For instance, the usual five-point operator applied to an $n \times n$ grid only has accuracy proportional to $1/n^2$, so when n is increased, one usually runs out of memory and patience before one runs out of precision. This applies to static problems such as elliptic PDEs where errors do not propagate with time.

- Structural analysis methods use finite element methods, which are in principle far more accurate than typical finite difference methods. A large problem might lose seven or eight digits in the process of solving the global stiffness equations, however, so 64-bit precision or better is essential. The need for high precision is easily seen by considering the bending of a beam; although the overall bending might be quite significant, the strain on an element in the beam is perhaps one part in a million. Since the overall bending is computed by accumulating element strains, small errors caused by precision translate into major macroscopic errors.

- Analog circuit simulation can easily run into ill-posed sets of nonlinear ODEs for which high precision helps convergence. Iterations can get "stuck" on the jagged steps of 32-bit precision, even though they are far from the best solution of the nonlinear system.

- Computational chemistry involves the computation of eigenvalues (which represent energy levels of molecular orbitals) where the eigenvalues span many orders of magnitude, and operations on matrices where the sum of many small quantities is significant relative to a few large quantities; some computational chemists are even forced to use 128-bit precision, for which hardware support is rare.

- Electromagnetic wave modeling, used to simulate radar reflections from metal objects, is currently done using boundary integral techniques that give rise to very large ($10,000 \times 10,000$), dense systems of linear equations; since the bound on roundoff error is proportional to the number of equations times the relative error of the floating-point representation, 64-bit precision is preferred.

- Seismic simulation is a large hyperbolic PDE model, not to be confused with seismic migration. One is the inverse of the other. Fine-grid finite difference schemes involving multipoint operators can be accurate enough that single-precision floating-point error exceeds the error of the numerical method; hence double precision is needed.

- At first glance oil reservoir simulation appears feasible using 32-bit precision, since coarse grids are used; however, the methods repeatedly calculate pressure differences at adjacent grid points, where subtraction of large similar uncertain numbers removes many significant figures.

In summary, there are a variety of reasons why high-precision arithmetic might be needed by an application. As models become larger or more detailed, some low-precision applications are moving into the high-precision camp.

5.5.8 Architecture summary

Table 5.3 summarizes tradeoffs for various compute-intensive architectural techniques.

5.6 Appropriate Algorithms

The body of knowledge about numerical algorithms that has formed over the last 40 years has largely been based on the assumption that

TABLE 5.3   Architectural Tradeoffs

Method	Advantages	Disadvantages
Multiple functional units	Higher peak speed; better cost/performance; widely applicable	Extra hardware cost; complicated control needed; hard to program efficiently
Wide instruction word	Customizable to application; efficient compilation possible; allows fine-grain concurrency	Must decode at run time; high program bandwidth needed; optimal scheduling difficult
Virtual memory	Applications run regardless of actual memory configuration	Typically high cache miss rate greatly degrades performance
Large register set	Less memory speed burden; allows scratchpad-type programming at high speed	Expensive state-save; expensive hardware; slow context switching
Vector arithmetic	Much higher peak performance; somewhat higher typical performance	Complicated to build; pressures users to alter programs; reduced scalar speed
Many operations per instruction	Very high peak MFLOPS; less memory speed burden; rewards organized programs	Very application specific; pressures users to alter programs; poor at branching, calls
High-precision word size	Wider range of applications run satisfactorily; less roundoff expertise needed	Increased memory size needed; greatly increased hardware; waste on low-precision operations

calculation is expensive and memory references instantaneous and free. On general-purpose computers, this is still sometimes a good approximation to the truth; for example, personal computers (without coprocessors) typically take 100 to 1000 times as long to do a 64-bit floating-point multiplication as to simply fetch a 64-bit word from memory. Unfortunately, compute-intensive processors bring to ratio close to unity, so *traditional analysis of computational complexity is frequently inadequate when attempting to select an appropriate algorithm for attached processors or array processors.*

5.6.1 Dense linear equations

Consider the classic problem of solving a system of equations represented by $Ax = b$, where A is a dense, real, $n \times n$ matrix, x is the unknown n-long real vector, and b is a given n-long real vector. A typical implementation of Gaussian elimination might resemble algorithm A:

A1. For column $k = 1$ to $n - 1$:
A2. Find the element A_{ij} in the column with the largest magnitude (pivot).
A3. Exchange the row A_{i*} with row A_{k*} so the pivot is on the diagonal.
A4. For row $i = k + 1$ to n:
A5. Compute $R = A_{ik} / A_{kk}$.
A6. For row element $j = i$ to n:
A7. Compute $A_{ij} - R \cdot A_{kj}$ and store in the A_{ij} location.
A8. Next j.
A9. Next i.
A10. Next k.

The usual work estimate for this algorithm is $\frac{2}{3}n^3 + 2n^2 + O(n)$ floating-point operations. Line A7 is executed $\frac{1}{3}n^3$ times and constitutes the kernel of the algorithm. Now consider the *memory burden* imposed by that kernel. The computer must reference A_{ij}, A_{kj}, and then A_{ij} again for each multiply-add; R is easily held in a register. If a compute-intensive processor can only make one main memory reference per multiply-add, it will be limited to only one-third of peak speed in this algorithm. Furthermore, the references in the kernel use pointers to the two sets of locations $A_{ij} \ldots A_{in}$ and $A_{kj} \ldots A_{kn}$, which for column storage means incrementing pointers by a constant stride of n. This requires an integer addition, which is usually more expensive than increments by unity. In addition to the two constant strides, an integer add is needed to test the loop for completion, also limiting the kernel to one-third of peak.

The simple act of reordering the operations by changing loop nesting in the preceding algorithm can remove this problem. By arranging the loop over k to be the innermost loop, the kernel can be changed to an inner product, as shown below for the inner two loops:

B1. Save A_{ij} in a table memory, y_i (contiguous).
B2. For $j = i$ to n:
B3. Set $S = 0$.
B4. For $k = i$ to n:
B5. Set $S = S + y_k \cdot A_{kj}$
B6. Next k.
B7. Scale by diagonal pivots.
B8. Next j

The kernel, line B5, can keep S in a register and y_k in a vector register or table memory. The y_k quantities are used $O(n)$ times, effectively spreading the cost of the main memory reference to load them into the vector register. There is only *one* memory reference in the kernel, that of A_{kj}, that uses a contiguous stride through a column of matrix storage. Hence the kernel involves a register add, a floating-point multiply, and an integer comparison for the end-of-loop test. This can execute at near full speed on most compute-intensive processors; hence, there is at least one useful application that allows this type of computer to approach its claimed performance for periods of at least several seconds rather than just a burst of a few microseconds. A more detailed discussion of this problem can be found in Dongarra [84].

If the floating-point adder is pipelined with p pipeline stages, the S accumulation will actually be done as p subtotals moving through the pipeline. The inner product $y_* \cdot A_{*j}$ actually becomes a matrix-matrix multiply where y is a matrix with p rows, yielding p subtotals that are collapsed later. Note that this affects the floating-point roundoff error, since floating-point arithmetic is not associative.

5.6.2   An extreme example: The matrix algebra accelerator

In both dense matrix-matrix multiplication and dense matrix factoring, there are $O(n^3)$ floating-point operations and $O(n^2)$ words of data. It therefore appears possible for a processor to effectively perform $O(n)$ useful floating-point operations for every data word referenced from main memory. While the preceding example showed how matrix factoring can achieve a 1:1:1 ratio of fetches to multiplies to adds, it is in fact possible to use $m \times m$ block factoring to achieve a ratio of $1:m:m$. This led to the development by Floating Point Systems of a special-purpose computer originally called the FPS 164/MAX, which modified the FPS 164 architecture simply by adding arithmetic pipelines, not increasing main memory bandwidth. The effective speed on problems possessing an $m \times m$ submatrix structure can be increased by up to 31 times, the maximum concurrent multiplier-adders [Charlesworth 86]. Figure 5.4 shows a block diagram of the architecture.

Both matrix multiplication and matrix factoring involve at least $O(n^2)$ parallel tasks for $n \times n$ dense problems. The parallelism can be exploited to reduce memory bandwidth in two ways:

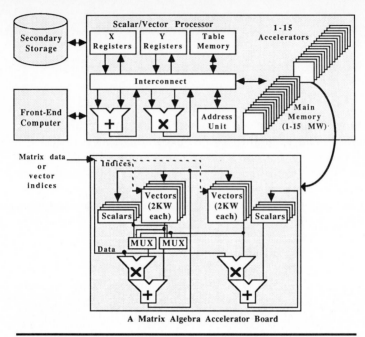

Figure 5.4   The FPS 164 Matrix Algebra Accelerator.

1. Reuse of data (temporal bandwidth reduction)
2. Broadcast of data (spatial bandwidth reduction)

In multiplying a matrix A times a matrix B, each column in B is used n times; hence the cost of moving a column to a fast local memory is amortized over many clock cycles. Every element in A is eventually applied to a corresponding element in n columns of B, so a broadcast of elements of A to those columns can accomplish useful work. Broadcasting takes the form of multiple processor boards, each mapped to a region of high memory, that can all respond simultaneously to some reserved set of addresses on the memory backplane. Not only does bandwidth reduction unburden the backplane, but it also permits the disk storage to keep pace with the arithmetic, which is essential to keep the computer busy for more than a few seconds.

The MAX allows up to 15 extra processor boards, each with 2 multiply-add pipelines, or 30 pipelines total. The scalar unit of the main processor participates in the column operations using its table memory as a column store, so the actual number of parallel pipelines is 31. Thus, the 11 MFLOPS pipeline in the FPS 164 can be supplemented to attain a peak of $11 \times 31 = 341$ MFLOPS on a highly restricted but very useful set of operations. A single memory reference is used for four multiply-adds per pipeline, so that 248 floating-point operations can be sustained with just one fetch! The full MAX configuration has been successfully used to solve dense linear systems as large as 20,000 × 20,000 elements in a little over 8 h.

5.6.3 Fourier transforms

Now consider the problem of evaluating the discrete Fourier transform on 64 complex data points. The usual operation count says that evaluating the sum

$$F(l) = \sum_{k=0}^{n-1} f(k)\omega^{kl}$$

directly requires $O(n^2)$ floating-point operations, whereas the fast Fourier transform (FFT) methods use $O(n \ln n)$ operations, a clear improvement. But the sum above is nothing more than a matrix-vector product, where the matrix elements are defined by $W_{kl} = \omega^{kl}$, and that matrix can be *reused* for many input functions $f(k)$. Because the MAX can easily do many vector-vector scalar products at once, the architectural parallelism can actually outweigh the algorithmic advantages of the FFT for small numbers of discrete points. The FPS 164, for example, must perform about 2000 floating-point operations for a radix-2 FFT on 64 points, requiring over 1300 clock cycles even when highly optimized. The matrix-vector product requires about 16,000 floating-point operations (multiply-add pairs), but it can be done with 16 concurrent complex dot product engines using the MAX, bringing the total time under 500 cycles. For larger Fourier transforms, one can simply build FFTs out of mixed radices ranging up to radix 64, using matrix-vector methods up to the crossover point and then switching to the factorization methods of the FFT.

This illustrates the flaw of conventional algorithm analysis, which ignores memory references in the work assessment. An FFT must eventually reference every storage location $O(\ln n)$ times, and those references cannot all be local; they stride up to halfway across the required storage. The matrix-vector product pays the price of redundant floating-point operations to reduce communication, so that every location of $f(k)$ need only be referenced *once*. In a hypothetical computer that can compute the parallel inner products with binary sum collapses in $O(\ln n)$ time, both methods are ultimately $O(\ln n)$ in the time complexity of memory accesses.

5.6.4 Finite difference methods

As a final example of algorithm choices affected by the use of compute-intensive architectures, consider the partial differential equations (PDEs) solved by discretizing time and space and applying a difference operator to approximate the differential operator. A typical case of a two-dimensional problem might resemble the following, in Fortran:

```
      DO 1 I = 2,N − 1
      DO 1 J = 2,N − 1
    1 F(I,J) = U*F(I,J) + V* (F(I − 1,J) + F(I + 1,J) + F(I,J − 1) + F(I,J + 1))
```

where U and V are predefined constants and F(I,J) is a two-dimensional array representing the physical state of the system. For hyperbolic PDEs, this type of equation might compute the next time step of the spatial state of the system; for elliptic PDEs, it might be a relaxation method that produces an F (I,J) that eventually becomes sufficiently close to the solution. In any case, the kernel involves 6 main memory references and 6 floating-point operations. The memory references are "nearest neighbor" in two dimensions, so the technique of *loop unrolling* can improve the ratio of arithmetic to memory references:

```
      DO 1 I = 2,N − 1
      DO 1 J = 2,N − 1,2
      F(I,J) = U*F(I,J) + V* (F(I − 1,J) + F(I + 1,J) + F(I,J − 1) + F(I,J + 1))
    1 F(I,J + 1) = U*F(I,J + 1) + V* (F(I − 1,J + 1) + F(I + 1,J + 1) + F(I,J)
        + F(I,J + 2))
```

Using registers for expressions that occur more than once, there are 10 memory references and 12 floating-point operations. More unrolling allows the ratio to approach 2:3 at the cost of register usage (and possibly exceeding the size of the program cache), which is one argument in favor of a large set of scalar registers. Computers with a 1:1:1 ratio of fetches to multiplies to adds can approach 50 percent of peak speed with no unrolling, or 66 percent with extensive unrolling.

An interesting contrast with either of the above methods is the one favored by highly vector-oriented computers. A vector computer might run the problem more efficiently in the following form, where TEMP is a vector register:

```
       DO 10 I = 2,N − 1
       DO 1 J = 2,N − 1,2
     1 TEMP(J)  = F(I − 1,J) + F(I + 1,J)
       DO 2 J = 2,N − 1
     2 TEMP(J)  = TEMP(J) + F(I,J − 1)
       DO 3 J = 2,N − 1
     3 TEMP(J) = (TEMP(J) + F(I,J + 1))*V
       DO 4 J = 2,N − 1
     4 F(I,J) = U*F(I,J) + TEMP(J)
    10 CONTINUE
```

If there is enough bandwidth to either memory or vector registers to keep the floating-point functional units busy, and if the vector operations shown are in the repertoire of the hardware that manages the arithmetic, then the preceding method can approach 75 percent of the peak MFLOPS rate of machines with one adder and one multiplier functional unit. On the other hand, if TEMP must reside in main memory, then this is a disastrous approach for memory-bound processors. There are twice as many memory references as in the "unvectorized" approaches, causing a multiply-add processor to achieve at most 25 percent of peak speed. This is why one occasionally observes the phenomenon that the Cray or Cyber type of processor does relatively better on the vectorized version of an application program, whereas the FPS type of processor does relatively better on the unvectorized version. This is a source of difficulty for the developers of application software, who naturally seek a simple-to-maintain single method that works well on a wide range of compute-intensive machines.

5.7 Metrics for Compute-Intensive Performance

Ultimately, the only performance questions of interest to a computer user are

1. How long will the application take to run?

2. How much will the run cost?

This assumes, of course, that answers are within required accuracy tolerance. On compute-intensive processors, there is usually a significant hurdle to answering the above questions by direct measurement. Architectures vary greatly, and only considerable conversion effort shows the performance that is ultimately possible. Since compute-intensive processors trade ease of use for cost/performance, predicting overall speed and cost (including reprogramming cost amortized over the useful life of the application) is a difficult proposition.

As a result, the industry has come to use simpler metrics that claim correlation with application performance. At the simplest (and most inaccurate) level are machine specifications such as clock speed, peak MFLOPS rating, millions of instructions per second (MIPS) rating, memory size and speed, disk size and speed, and base system price. An experienced user may find a linear combination of these that correlates well with performance and cost on the application of interest, but these metrics are generally the least useful. Comparisons of clock speeds or MIPS are meaningless unless the architectures being compared are practically identical, down to the machine instruction set.

A compromise is to use standard problems that are much simpler than a complete application but exercise a variety of dimensions of machine performance. Compute-intensive processors have their own set of industry-standard benchmarks, of which the following are examples (arranged in rough order of increasing complexity and usefulness at gauging performance):

- Matrix multiplication (no particular size).
- The 1024-point complex FFT.
- Whetstones (a synthetic mixture of operations designed to test scalar speed only).
- Solution of 100 equations in 100 unknowns, with partial pivoting.
- The Livermore Kernels (24 Fortran excerpts from application programs).
- The 4-bit adder simulation in the SPICE test suite.
- Solving structural analysis problem "SP3" in Swanson's ANSYS test suite.

To compare actual costs, it is similarly possible to estimate total computer cost by considering all hardware costs, software costs, facilities requirements, and conversion effort. The ultimate measure of cost can be determined by the price of the application run at a computer service bureau, which must determine charges accurately enough to remain in business and yet be competitive with alternatives. It is rare for compute-intensive processors to be compared using applications that exercise memory bandwidth or disk speed, for all the reasons stated in the introduction to this chapter. This is perhaps unfortunate, since they figure prominently in the performance of applications such as analog circuit simulation and large-scale structural analysis.

5.8   Addendum: Hypercube Multicomputers

Hypercubes [Fox 84, Seitz 84] have emerged as a commercially important class of multicomputers. In contrast with so-called dance hall architectures where a set of processors share a set of memories through a switching network, hypercube computers are built out of an ensemble of memory-processor pairs. Each processor-memory node is autonomous and contains communications channels to N other nodes. The channels form the topology of the edges of an N-dimensional cube, which has a number of desirable properties (see Chap. 6).

In practice, at least one channel is used for communication to a host or other I/O device, and the commercial hypercubes have all made this variation on the original prototype built at Caltech in the early 1980s.

Processors cooperate on a particular task by passing messages explicitly to one another; there is no shared memory in the system and hence no need to deal with the problem of multiple writes to a memory location. This latter problem is a major source of indeterminism and programming difficulty in shared memory designs. Both shared-memory and hypercube designs pay a cost for global memory accesses that grows logarithmically in the number of processor-memory pairs; the hypercube, however, rewards locality of memory accesses.

Replicated VLSI is ideal for the nodes of hypercube computers, now that VLSI density has reached the point where a complete processor can fit on a single chip. The early hypercubes used a mixture of small-, medium-, and large-scale integration to put a node on one or two boards. The implementation by NCUBE, Inc., integrates a complete VAX-style processor with floating-point arithmetic, 11 communications channel pairs, and an error-correcting memory interface, on a single chip. With no "glue logic," this chip plus six memory chips form a complete node with 512 kbytes of memory.

Available hypercubes tend to be either highly compute intensive or general-purpose. They are largely characterized by three times: communication time, memory-move time, and arithmetic time. The ratio of the last time to the first two determines how compute-intensive the design is.

Communication time is the time to send a message of length n across a single channel. There is a startup time which currently ranges from 18 to 3000 μs, followed by transmission at a rate which currently ranges from 1 to 10 μs/byte (based on 1987 product literature from AMETEK, Intel, NCUBE, and Floating Point Systems). The startup time is largely a function of the amount of protocol used by the software for error detection/correction and for automatic message forwarding to more distant nodes. Low startup times are critical when the application is fine-grained and cannot batch together transmitted data into longer structures. This is the communication analog of vector arithmetic.

Memory-move, or *gather-scatter,* time, is the time to move data within the memory of a single node. Usually, the communications channels use only a fraction of the memory bus, so moves within a single node are much faster by the reciprocal of that fraction. Currently, time to move a contiguous array from one location to another ranges from 0.1 to 2 μs/byte.

Arithmetic time is the time to do a floating-point operation (two inputs, one output) by whatever means is provided on the node. For 64-bit operands, the current range is rather wide: from 0.1 to 20 μs. The ratio of arithmetic time to communication time varies from about 1:100 or 1:200 for the FPS T Series or the Intel iPSC/VX, to about 1:1 for the NCUBE. The T Series and iPSC/VX are extremely compute intensive and use vector arithmetic managed by a microprocessor, whereas the NCUBE uses integrated scalar arithmetic.

The arguments of earlier sections regarding system balance apply here, with the added consideration of surface area. Ideally, each node communicates and computes at the same time, and sees no bottleneck from either activity. On the T Series or the iPSC/VX, every word brought over a channel must participate in over 100 floating-point operations if the arithmetic is to be kept busy. Suppose that the application is the synthetic seismic problem, modeling the wave equation in three dimensions. Each grid point requires 8 floating-point operations per time step in the simplest acoustic model. When the three-dimensional domain of the problem is partitioned into $n \times n \times n$ subdomains, one per processor, there will be $6n^2$ points on the "surface" and n^3 points on the "interior" of the node memory. Each time step will require the exchange of $6n^2$ words of data (both in and out) and will perform $8n^3$ floating-point operations, a ratio of $4/3n$. For optimum balance, this number should approximate the communication time-arithmetic time ratio. If this ratio is 100:1, then the two time steps in each node will require 2 million words, or 16 million bytes, *per node* just for the data.

This illustrates a growing problem in computer design: memory technology lags behind floating-point arithmetic technology by 2 years or more, so users must await fourfold or sixteenfold increases in commodity memory chip densities before the announced compute-intensive ensembles reach the minimum main storage needed for reasonable system balance. The advent of floating-point chip sets such as those made by AMD and Weitek have made it easy to add several MFLOPS of peak performance to an ordinary microprocessor. Everyone who does so soon notices that a 10 MFLOPS 64-bit engine unfortunately consumes 240 Mbytes/s and at least 10 MIPS for effective control. This brings to the fore all the issues discussed in previous sections: methods such as a large register set for reducing bandwidth, and vector instructions in microcode for reducing required MIPS. For high MFLOPS rates which do not compromise on bandwidth or control, the simplest solution is to have more nodes as in the NCUBE processor, highly integrated so that many nodes can be reliably put into a small space with small power requirements. The 500 MFLOPS rating of the 1024-node NCUBE is similar to that of the compute-intensive hypercubes, but very dissimilar in that those 500 MFLOPS are accompanied with 10 Gbytes of bandwidth and over 2000 MIPS of control; its node memory is capacious relative to the amount required for compute/communicate balance.

5.9 Concluding Comments

In the spectrum of computer architectures, compute-intensive designs may indicate the future of all designs. As switching devices become ever faster and cheaper relative to the wires that send the information, all computers may ultimately be able to regard arithmetic operations as free relative to the cost of moving data. The traditional measures of algorithmic work using floating-point operation counts may soon be just as misleading on general-purpose computers as they are on compute-intensive ones, as computer designers push closer to the physical limits imposed on the speed that information can travel.

The feature that will remain distinctive of compute-intensive designs is that they trade ease of use, interactivity, and generality for cost/performance. They are neither inferior nor superior to general-purpose computers; they simply have a different feature emphasis. The availability of computers that make this tradeoff will continue to bring large-scale scientific applications within the reach of users who would otherwise not be able to afford to do them.

Acknowledgments

The author obtained much of the information in this chapter while working on applications at Floating Point Systems, Inc. That experience was invaluable in providing a cross section of both compute-intensive architectures and compute-intensive applications of both academic and commercial importance. Alan Charlesworth, staff engineer at FPS, is in particular due much thanks for many hours of insightful discussion.

Bibliography

[IBM 86]   "IBM RT PC Computer Technology." IBM Form No. SA23-1057, p. 81, 1986.

[Charlesworth 81]   A.E. Charlesworth. "An Approach to Scientific Array Processing: The Architectural Design of the AP-120B/FPS-164 Family." *IEEE Computer,* vol. 14, no. 9, pp. 18–27, September 1981.

[Charlesworth 86]   A.E. Charlesworth and J.L. Gustafson. "Introducing Replicated VLSI to Supercomputing: The FPS-164/MAX Scientific Computer." *IEEE Computer,* vol. 19, no. 3, pp. 10–23, March 1986.

[Dongarra 85]   J. Dongarra, F. Gustavson, and A. Karp. "Implementing Linear Algebra Algorithms for Dense Matrices on a Vector Pipeline Machine." *SIAM Review,* vol. 26, no. 1, pp. 91–112, January 1985.

[Fox 84]   G.C. Fox and S.W. Otto. "Algorithms for Concurrent Processors." *Physics Today,* vol. 37, no. 5, pp. 50–58, May 1984.

[Kogge 81]   P.M. Kogge. *The Architecture of Pipelined Computers.* McGraw-Hill, New York, 1981.

[Seitz 84]   C.L. Seitz. "Concurrent VLSI Architectures." *IEEE Trans. Computers,* vol. C-33, no. 12, pp. 1247–1265, December 1984.

[Touzeau 84]   R. Touzeau. "A Fortran Compiler for the FPS-164 Scientific Computer." *Proc. SIGPLAN '84 Symposium on Compiler Construction.* ACM, June 1984, pp. 48–57.

[Fukushima 83]   K. Fukushima, S. Miyake, and T. Ito. "Neocognitron: A Neural Network Model for a Mechanism of Visual Pattern Recognition." *IEEE Trans. on Systems, Man, and Cybernetics,* vol. SMC-13, no. 5, pp. 826–832, September–October 1983.

6

Hypercube Systems
and Key Applications

Yin Shih and **Jeff Fier**

Symult Systems Corporation,† Monrovia, CA

6.1 Introduction

Since the earliest days of computers there has been an insatiable thirst for more computing power. While there are sometimes plateaus, as technology drives cost or performance to improved levels, new uses and greater demands become the norm. It has been noted that uniprocessor performance is approaching an asymptote of approximately 3×10^9 operations per second [Seitz 84b]. This includes the application of techniques such as multiple functional units and pipelining to uniprocessor design. If this holds true, what technological solutions are available to provide the performance of 10^{12} operations per second already being placed on some wish lists?

The approach now accepted is to avoid the limitation of uniprocessor performance by providing more processors. This approach has always been attractive to aggressive computer designers,‡ but advancing technology often put off the need to resort to this class of solutions. Now technology is up against some fundamental physical constraints. As a result, every high-performance processor proposed or constructed in the last few years has been a multiprocessor or parallel processor.

Many types of parallel processors have been proposed: shared memory and distributed memory, loosely coupled and tightly coupled, packet switching and message passing of data, fine grain and coarse grain, and so on. The design space is huge and large segments are unexplored. In recent years one particular set of design choices has stood

---

†Formerly AMETEK Computer Research Division.
‡For example, ILLIAC IV and ICL DAP.

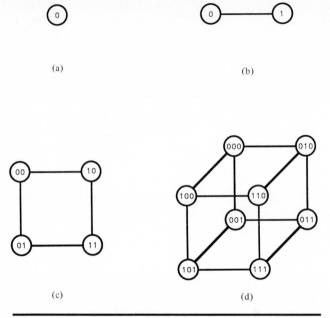

Figure 6.1 n-dimensional hypercube for $n = 0, 1, 2, 3$.

out as highly promising. This is the hypercube or boolean n-cube. These were first proposed in 1962 by Squire and Palais at the University of Michigan. Since that time, the idea resurfaced occasionally [Pease 77, Locanthi 80] until it was finally introduced in practice in 1983 by Seitz at Caltech [Seitz 85]. That first hypercube, called the Cosmic Cube, demonstrated a highly parallel and scalable processor architecture that achieved high processor efficiencies, often 80 to 90 percent, on many different types of problems.

A *hypercube* is a multiple-instruction/multiple-data, loosely coupled, distributed memory, message-passing concurrent computer. The hypercube derives its name from the direct connection network used to interconnect its processing elements or nodes. There are $N = 2^n$ nodes, each of which is connected by fixed communications paths to n other nodes. The value n is known as the dimension of the hypercube. If the nodes of the hypercube are numbered from 0 to $2^n - 1$, then the connection scheme can be defined by that set of edges that can be drawn between any two nodes whose numberings differ by one bit position in their binary representations (see Fig. 6.1).†

An extension to the basic hypercube scheme often designed into hypercubes is the addition of input/output (I/O) channels either as

---

†See also "Compute-Intensive Processors and Multicomputers" by J. L. Gustafson, Chap. 5 in this text, for more on hypercube computers.

unconnected edges of the hypercube or as distinct additions to the node. By making use of these channels it is possible to develop a highly parallel distributed I/O capability which scales appropriately with the processing capability.

The typical programming approach for hypercubes is to take a large problem and partition it into subproblems. These subproblems are assigned to hypercube nodes which then share results or cooperate through messages sent between the nodes. In the first-generation hypercubes,† the capability to treat the hypercube topology as one of its embedded network topologies, e.g., a mesh or ring, allows for programming flexibility for many physical, or otherwise regular, problems. This is especially true when trying to extract the maximum performance from the network. The regular structure of hypercubes also suggests strategies for resource allocation, i.e., cube partitioning for multiuser support, and graceful degradation for fault tolerance and recovery.

6.2   Example Hypercubes

Once the initial feasibility and promise of hypercube technology had been demonstrated at Caltech, the computer industry lost no time in commercializing hypercubes for the scientific and engineering community. Within the space of a year, four hypercubes became commercially available: the Intel iPSC, the AMETEK System 14, the NCUBE/10, and the FPS T Series.

6.2.1   AMETEK System 14

AMETEK, a large industrial firm, began development of hypercube computers in 1983. Its first hypercube product was the System 14 computer, introduced in mid-1985 [Colanna 86, Durham 86].

The System 14 is composed of from 16 to 256 nodes. Each node has CPU, memory, and network communication subsystem. The System 14 node is unique in that it is itself a multiprocessor unit. Figure 6.2 shows the node architecture for the System 14. The central processing capability is provided by an iAPX286/287, 16-bit microprocessor which provides approximately 1 million instructions per second (MIPS) of performance. There is an associated floating-point coprocessor which supports 32-, 64-, and 80-bit IEEE floating-point arithmetic with floating-point performance on the order of 50 thousand floating-point operations per second (KFLOPS). In addition, an I/O processing unit, an iAPX186, also a 16-bit microprocessor, has been included as

---

†See Sec. 6.4 for a discussion of possible second-generation capabilities.

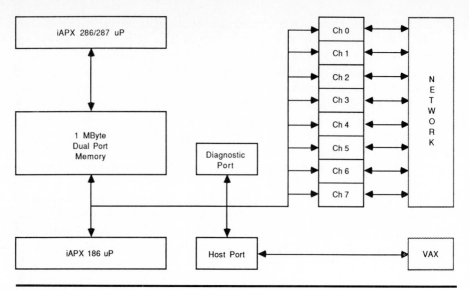

Figure 6.2   AMETEK S14 node architecture.

part of the system to reduce I/O processing loads on the central processor.

These two processing units share a 1-Mbyte dual ported main memory. Both microprocessors have instruction prefetch queues which allow simultaneous operation with the shared memory with only slight performance degradation. Hardware support of atomic read/write functions is provided for critical-section interlock management between the two local processors.

The hypercube network communication subsystem is composed of eight bidirectional serial communication channels. Data transfer rates on these channels are on the order of 10 μs/byte. There are two additional I/O channels supporting diagnostic functions or external connections.

Like most hypercubes of the first generation, the System 14 is not self-sufficient. These hypercubes are connected to a host computer which provides the user and program interface. This consists of the program development and maintenance environment and the user file system. The host in the case of the System 14 is a member of the VAX family of superminicomputers. The host operating system is UNIX. The System 14 allows for multiple host-hypercube channels.

The System 14 is supported by two operating systems. The first is called the *xtalline operating system* (XOS) and the second is called the *message auto-routing system* (MARS). XOS is a nonrouting nearest-neighbor-only message-passing operating system. Each message-passing operation is explicit and processor-node-referenced. Further, internode synchronization is explicit. The intention is that the machine architecture and topology be visible to the programmer (hence crystalline) and therefore has the fewest possible performance penalties and restrictions. It is an unforgiving operating system, but it does deliver all that is necessary for highly regular problems such as those that are commonly encountered in intensive numeric processing. MARS is the next step forward, with some corresponding increase in operating system overhead to provide for additional user amenities. Message passing under MARS is process-based and allows for asynchronous non-nearest-neighbor messages to be automatically routed by the operating system.

The software development environment includes all the tools available under the UNIX operating system. Macrolibraries and hypercube management utilities are supplied. Further tools include the support of an operating environment simulator which allows multiple nodes of the hypercube to be simulated by multiple processes under UNIX. A parallel debugger permits simultaneous debugging for any one or all of these processes. Language support is primarily for C, although a Fortran 77 compiler has been available in an unsupported form.

An interesting feature of the System 14 hypercube is its use of a dual processor configuration within each node. The second processor is intended to offload the primary processor from message management duty and thereby to obtain more CPU cycles for problem solution. However, this only makes sense under the right conditions. This feature was designed with a sophisticated multitasking operating system in mind. It was expected that a node would be running multiple tasks, and message operations could be treated like I/O operations, i.e., by blocking and causing a context switch to a task on the **ready** queue and posting the blocked process to a **wait** queue. The effect is to maximize CPU cycles at the expense of latency. In practice, however, most software for first-generation hypercubes runs with only one task per node. In this case, any task **wait** times subtract directly from CPU performance and the additional interprocessor synchronization costs result in a net detriment.

Limitations of the System 14 include the difficult programming and code efficiency issues of a segmented address architecture due to the use of the iAPX286. Another limiting factor is the lack of support for expansion of a node.

6.2.2 FPS T Series

FPS (Floating Point Systems) is a manufacturer of vector and array processors. In early 1986 FPS introduced their first hypercube product, the T Series computer [Gustafson 86, Durham 86]. In the design of the T Series, FPS capitalized on their strengths in vector processor architecture. The T Series is the first computer of this type with vector processing capabilities integrated into the architecture.

The T Series consists of from 8 to 4096 nodes. Nodes are combined in groups of 8 to form a module. Each module has an additional system unit which includes support for a disk, also configured with the module. Due to the high cost of a T Series node and the large number of cabinets necessary to make up the largest possible system, it is unlikely that systems with more than a few hundred nodes will ever be built. Early systems have ranged from 8 to 64 nodes.

Figure 6.3 shows the FPS T Series node architecture. The T Series node processor is an Inmos Transputer. The Transputer is a RISC-type (reduced instruction set computer) 32-bit microprocessor. Estimated performance is 7.5 MIPS. The Transputer acts as a control processor for the integral vector unit. The vector unit consists of an adder and a multiplier supported by vector registers. The adder has a 6-stage pipeline for 32- or 64-bit operations. The multiplier has a 5-stage pipeline for 32-bit operations and a 7-stage pipeline for 64-bit operations. Peak performance is 8 MFLOPS for each unit on 64-bit operations. Some operations may allow simultaneous use of both the adder and multiplier, so combined peak performance in such situations would be 16 MFLOPS. IEEE floating-point format is supported, but some portions of the standard are relaxed in the implementation.

The T Series node memory is 1 Mbyte in size, shared between the control processor and the vector unit. The control processor views the memory as a contiguous array of 256 kwords (32-bit words). The vector unit views the memory as two banks, the first bank being 256 vec-

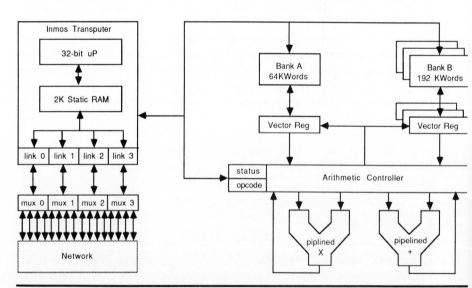

Figure 6.3 FPS T-Series node architecture.

tors and the second bank being 768 vectors (1024-byte vectors). Each bank interfaces to the vector unit through a 1-kbyte vector register. Each vector register is able to do a simultaneous load of all 1024 bytes in one memory cycle. On each floating-point cycle the vector registers are able to supply two operands to, and receive one result from, the adder or multiplier. With the vector registers buffering main memory for the vector unit, the control processor is able to access main memory while the vector unit is in operation. Overlapped operation is thus possible, e.g., the control processor could be performing scatter-gather operations to distribute the results of the past vector operation and to set up the next.

The T Series node implements hypercube communications in an unusual way. The Transputer on each node has four bidirectional serial communication channels; each channel is capable of supporting data transfer at a rate of 2 μs/byte. These 4 channels are then each multiplexed 4 ways, allowing up to 16 connections per node. Two of these channels are allocated to the system board, and two more are usually allocated to additional storage or I/O connections. The remaining 12 channels can then be wired into a hypercube of up to 12 dimensions, or 4096 nodes. However, the multiplexing of these channels is not transparent, i.e., the programmer sees only four active connections at one time. With one of these four dedicated to the system board, there are only three connections available for internode communication. Thus the T Series is really an ensemble of isolated or intersecting cubes (three-dimensional hypercubes), depending on multiplexer settings, and those allowed intersections conform to the hypercube topology.

Each T Series system unit acts both as an interface to the host system and as a file system for the eight nodes within its module. The system unit is connected to all nodes within its module through a daisy-chain scheme. A system unit is connected to all other system units through a ring network. Finally a microVAX host running under the VMS operating system manages the system boards through the ring network. The communication channels for these interconnections are still Transputer-based with the same performance as the internode channels.

The program development environment on the T Series is unusual. The Transputer was developed as a building block for parallel processing architectures. The systems and applications software environment was designed at the same time to fully take advantage of the capabilities that were planned for the hardware. The end result is that the Transputer uses a new programming language called Occam with messaging operations and parallel constructs built into the language. Despite the features of Occam, it has not been readily accepted in the U.S. programming community. More traditional languages such as Fortran and C are still preferred.

The most notable feature of the T Series computer is its integrated high-performance vector capability. However, the performance of the vector unit is so high that the communication channels may become a limiting factor to overall system performance. Further, the need to multiplex the communication channels between large numbers of nodes on the T Series is cumbersome to manage and adds significantly to communications overhead. While there are certainly arguments for variations from the boolean n-cube for a network topology, the need to explicitly configure the network to maintain connectivity can be considered retrogressive.

Though the T Series computer offers mass storage integrated within the system, there is no expansion beyond that capability.

6.2.3 Intel iPSC

Intel is a semiconductor and microcomputer products manufacturer. In early 1985 they announced the first commercial hypercube, the iPSC [Rosenberg 85, Durham 86]. Since that introduction, Intel has announced enhanced versions of their system called the iPSC-MX, with expanded memory, and the iPSC-VX, with vector capability [Ezsih 86, Durham 86].

Without extensions or enhancements the iPSC ranges from 32 to 128 nodes; with them it ranges from 16 to 64 nodes. The iPSC is organized in one to four packages of 32 slots each. Of the 32 slots, one of every two is assigned to an iPSC node. Every other slot may be another iPSC node, or it may be an expansion option extending the capabilities of the associated iPSC node.

The iPSC node processor is an iAPX286/287, a 16-bit microprocessor, and its associated floating-point coprocessor. The floating-point coprocessor supports both 32-, 64-, and 80-bit IEEE floating-point arithmetic. This same processor is also used in the AMETEK System 14 and the performance is equivalent.

There are 512 kbytes of memory on the iPSC node board. This memory is dual-ported, one port supporting the iAPX286/287 and the second port supporting eight communication channels. These channels on the iPSC node are based on an Ethernet communication IC. Seven are dedicated to the hypercube interconnection. The eighth is used to tie all nodes together into a global Ethernet. Each channel is driven at the Ethernet standard speed of 10 MHz with effective data transfer rates close to 2 μs/byte.

The MX expansion for the iPSC is a 4-Mbyte memory unit that can be inserted adjacent to each node after first depopulating every other node in a cabinet. The VX enhancement is configured similarly to the MX. The VX consists of a vector unit supporting 32- and 64-bit floating-point, vector program memory and vector data memory. Estimated peak performance for the vector unit is 6.67 MFLOPS for 64-bit operations and 20 MFLOPS for 32-bit operations. Vector program memory is 4 kwords and vector data memory is 128 kwords (both 64-bit words). Both vector program and data memory are dual-ported and mapped into the address space of the iPSC node processor.

The host is an Intel 286/310 microcomputer running under the XENIX operating system, a variant of UNIX. It is connected to the iPSC through an Ethernet tied to the global Ethernet channel of the hypercube.

The iPSC uses a message-passing, autorouting operating system. It is derived from, but not compatible with, the Cosmic Kernel operating system developed at Caltech for the Cosmic Cube. Programming support is provided for Fortran 77, C, and Lisp. Lisp requires the MX expansion to run.

The iPSC offers more node configuration flexibility than other existing hypercubes. Memory, processing performance, and hypercube dimension may be traded against each other. The iPSC is the first hypercube to support Lisp, which will become increasingly desirable as more efforts are made to apply hypercubes to artificial intelligence. However, the iPSC node processor suffers from a segmented address architecture which makes programming with large data structures difficult.

The use of a microcomputer for the host function limits the potential of the system in some ways. Direct user availability is low and the file system capacity is small, so there is always a connection to another computer system or network to provide additional support. And while the global Ethernet may appear to be a feature, its limited bandwidth and the lack of any compensating parallel or distributed I/O scheme makes it a bottleneck for system performance. Its primary strength is for message broadcast functions, but other hypercube systems are able to support message broadcasting without significant cost.

6.2.4 NCUBE

NCUBE is a start-up company founded expressly to develop a commercial hypercube. They introduced their first product, the NCUBE/10 in late 1985. They have since followed up with repackaged versions of their node processors such as the NCUBE/7 and the NCUBE/4 [Hayes 86, Durham 86].

When NCUBE set out to develop a hypercube computer, they took a radical approach and developed a hypercube node on an IC. As a result of this approach, a single node is only seven ICs: a CPU chip and six memory chips. This allows them to combine 64 nodes onto a single printed circuit board. Up to 16 of these high-density boards are combined to form their flagship product, the NCUBE/10, a 1024-node hypercube. Another product, the NCUBE/4, combines four of the unique NCUBE nodes onto a single IBM Personal Computer AT peripheral card. Up to four of these units may be configured in a PC, providing for a 16-node hypercube in a remarkably small package.

The NCUBE processor unit is all contained on one IC. It is comprised of a CPU, built-in floating-point support, memory controller support including error-correction/detection, and 11 bidirectional communication channels. The NCUBE CPU architecture is a proprietary 32-bit design. Claimed performance with a 10-MHz clock is 2 MIPS. Both 32- and 64-bit floating point is supported with IEEE standard format. Claimed performance is 300 KFLOPS in double precision and 500 KFLOPS in single precision.

Each NCUBE node has either 128 or 512 kbytes of memory. It is interesting to note that even though the CPU has a 32-bit architecture, the memory data path is only 16 bits wide.

Ten of the eleven NCUBE communication channels are allocated to the hypercube network, thus allowing up to 1024 nodes. The eleventh is dedicated to system I/O. Each channel consists of two links, one in each direction. Each link operates at 10 MHz with measured data transfer rates on the order of 2 μs/byte. Unlike communication channel designs in other hypercubes, where only one or a few channels can be active at a time, the NCUBE channels can all be active simultaneously.

The NCUBE I/O architecture, shown in Fig. 6.4, is very powerful. For every 128 nodes of the NCUBE system, an I/O unit slot is allocated. NCUBE makes full use of the eleventh communication channel coming from each node of the 128-node subcube. On every I/O unit, 8 channels on each of an additional 16 NCUBE processors dedicated to this I/O task are used to match the 128 system I/O channels coming from the hypercube. These 16 NCUBE processors are then able to move data to and from separate I/O unit memory. Aggregate hypercube-I/O unit bandwidth is claimed to be 90 Mbytes/s in each direction. Each I/O unit replicates this scheme on the hypercube connected side but may then specialize its function. For example, one type of I/O unit that implements the host computer function has an iAPX286, 4 Mbytes of memory, and peripheral support. Other I/O units provide support for a graphics frame buffer and an interhypercube channel.

NCUBE provides a proprietary UNIX-like operating system called AXIS which is resident on their host computer board. This operating system provides most of the functionality that users expect from UNIX. Resident on the nodes of the hypercube is an operating system called VERTEX. VERTEX is a fairly simple message-passing, autorouting operating system for hypercubes. Fortran 77 and C are supported languages.

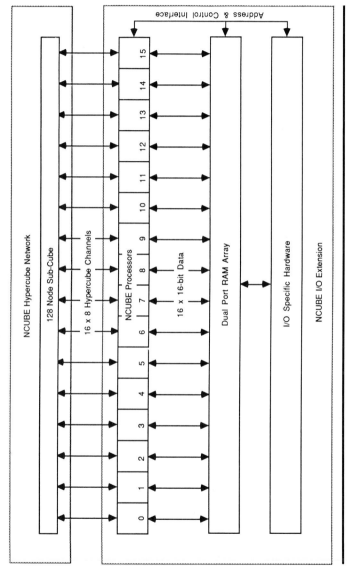

Figure 6.4 NCUBE I/O system architecture.

213

TABLE 6.1   **Hypercube System Characteristics†**

	AMETEK System 14	Intel iPSC (VX)	NCUBE	FPS T Series
Number of nodes	16–256	32–128 (16–64)	4–1024	8–4096
Peak performance:				
MIPS	200	100	2000	30,000
MFLOPS (double precision)	12	8 (424)	300	65,000
Maximum memory, Mbytes	256	64 (96)/(288)‡	512	4096
Host	VAX	286/310	286 host	MicroVAX
Host operating system	UNIX/Ultrix	XENIX	AXIS	VMS
Hypercube operating system	XOS/MARS	iPSC/OS	VERTEX	Occam

†Derived from published data sheets.
‡288 Mbytes maximum on iPSC-MX.

The most remarkable feature of the NCUBE system design is the high level of integration achieved through the use of commercial VLSI technology. This has the obvious advantage of small physical size. A less obvious advantage, but a major driving force behind the NCUBE design philosophy, is the increased reliability of large hypercubes due to reduced component count. Other strengths of the NCUBE system are the high-performance distributed I/O capability.

A limitation of the NCUBE design is the small amount of available memory, especially for a node processor of the given performance level. Even with memory capacity at the 512-kbyte limit, there is a demand for more memory. Due to its highly integrated architecture, there is no further memory or other expansion available on the NCUBE node.

6.2.5 Comparisons

Tables 6.1 and 6.2 summarize many of the features that were described in the previous section. These were derived from published data [Durham 86].

It is interesting to note the differences and similarities in the example hypercubes (see Table 6.1). With these four examples, we span a range of 4 to 4096 nodes and 8 to 65,000 MFLOPS. On the other hand, three out of the four offer a UNIX or UNIX-like host environment, two out of the four chose the same host computer, and two out of the four chose the same building-block processor.

TABLE 6.2   Node Characteristics†

	AMETEK System 14	Intel iPSC (VX)	NCUBE	FPS T Series
Processor	iAPX286/287	iAPX286/287	Custom	Transputer
Word size, bits	16	16	32	32
Clock rate, MHz	8	8	10	15
MFLOPS/Node (double precision)	0.05	0.06 (6.6)	0.3	16
Memory size, Mbytes	1	0.5 (1.5)	0.5	1
Channel rate, Mbits/s	3	10	10	20

†Derived from published data sheets

Closer examination of the individual node characteristics generally indicates conservatism in the node design (with the exception of vector units) of the various systems. Off-the-shelf microprocessors are preferred, as are generic dynamic random-access memories (RAMs) and moderate performance communication channels. There are good reasons for this. First, these parts are commonly available and are less expensive. This allows manufacturers to offer improved cost to performance ratios. Second, because large-scale hypercubes have large numbers of components, it is difficult to maintain acceptable levels of reliability, unless conservatively designed parts are used.

6.2.6 Performance measurements

Actual test results are provided in the following tables. Most of these results were generated at Oak Ridge National Labs or AMETEK Computer Research in the latter half of 1986, with some results as current as May 1987. Both the AMETEK and Intel systems were production level versions and were tested with current releases of operating system and compiler software. The NCUBE hardware, operating system, and compiler software used were current production releases, but the NCUBE system operated at 8 MHz rather than the specified 10 MHz. For a complete version of the test results see Dunnigan [87]. Because an FPS T Series was not available, test results of that system cannot be provided.

A series of standard benchmarks were applied to a node of each hypercube (see Table 6.3). The first test was the Sieve of Erastosthenes. This is primarily an integer operation test. Using the same microprocessor, the System 14 and iPSC generated comparable results. The NCUBE processor was not able to demonstrate a meaningful advantage, whereas it should have been 1.5 to 2 times faster according to claimed specifications.

The Dhrystone benchmark is a well-known test which exercises pro-

TABLE 6.3   Single Processor Performance (Measured)

	AMETEK System 14	Intel iPSC	NCUBE
Sieve, s	22.0	29.3	21.4
Dhrystone, s	35.9	55.9	43.7
Whetstone, s	5.3	5.6	2.5

cessor functions most likely to be needed for systems programming. The System 14 was surprisingly quick, due mostly, we think, to a compiler particularly good at pointer operations.

The Whetstone benchmark is an even better known test which exercises floating-point operations. In this test, the System 14 and the iPSC again demonstrated the equivalent capabilities of the two iAPX286/287 designs. The NCUBE processor demonstrated a more significant advantage than under the previous tests, but still less than expected.

On taking a closer look at the single-operation floating-point performance (see Table 6.4), confirmation of the results of the previous

TABLE 6.4   Claimed MFLOPS vs. Measured MFLOPS

	AMETEK System 14	Intel iPSC	NCUBE
Claimed, MFLOPS	50	60	300
Measured, MFLOPS	40	40	140 (175)

benchmarks is obtained. This test derived the cost of a single floating-point operation with operands kept in memory as opposed to register by looping on the operation many times and subtracting the cost of an equivalent null loop. The System 14 and the iPSC have a comparable floating-point performance which is close to their specifications. The NCUBE floating-point performance (with a calculated correction for a 10-MHz clock in parentheses) is significantly below the claimed performance. This may be because the cost of memory-based floating-point operations on the NCUBE processor is significantly higher than that for register-based floating-point operations. Since it has a faster floating-point unit but only uses memory technology comparable to the System 14 and the iPSC, the relative cost of referencing a memory-based operand compared to a register-based operand is much higher.

An especially critical area of hypercube performance is the design of the communication channels. The designs that are currently being used can be modeled simply with reasonable accuracy. The model assumes that all the processor and channel protocol overhead for starting and stopping the channel can be lumped into a single number.

TABLE 6.5 Communication Performance Model (measured)

	AMETEK System 14†	Intel iPSC	NCUBE
Overhead t_{oh}, μs	335	862	384
1/Rate t_r, μs/byte	9.5	1.8	2.6
Rate $1/t_r$ (asymptotic), kbytes/s	105	504	381

†AMETEK times measured by AMETEK.

This is simply overhead cost, or t_{oh}. Then it assumes that all those costs not accounted for in fixed overhead are paid on a per datum basis, i.e., a per byte cost t_r. The formula for calculating the time cost of an M-byte message is thus

$$T = t_{oh} + t_r M$$

The results of Table 6.5 were derived by measuring time costs for messages of varying lengths on the tested systems and then fitting the resulting data points to this model. The System 14 has a significantly lower t_{oh}, but a much higher t_r than the comparable iPSC model. This result suggests that the System 14 will give a better performance for problems that are naturally organized around short messages, whereas the iPSC will do better on those problems that can take advantage of long messages. The NCUBE performance appears to be good in comparison for either case.

It may be noted that none of the systems is able to achieve asymptotic rates that fully utilize the raw communications channel bandwidth quoted in their respective manufacturers' data sheets. Table 6.6 describes the utilization factors of the tested systems.

TABLE 6.6 Available Channel Bandwidth vs. Measured Utilizations

	AMETEK System 14	Intel iPSC	NCUBE
Available bandwidth, Mbits/s	3	10	8 (10)
Measured, Mbits/s	0.832	4.03	3.05 (3.81)
Efficiency	0.274	0.403	0.381 (0.381)

Another critical area of hypercube performance is the balance between computation and communication performance, i.e., what is the ratio of the cost of performing a transfer of a datum compared to the cost of performing a computation on that same datum? If the cost of sending a datum across the hypercube is too large, then that datum must be used many times in computation to amortize the cost of transfer. The number of times a datum is reused is highly problem dependent. Thus, decreasing relative communications costs increases the problem span for which the hypercube remains efficient. Conversely,

TABLE 6.7   Communication Performance Model (measured)

	AMETEK System 14†	Intel iPSC	NCUBE
Message time (double-precision transfer), μs	410	1120	401
Multiply time (double precision), μs	33.9	43.0	13.5
Communication/computation ratio	12	26	30

†AMETEK times measured by AMETEK.

if the time to send a datum is much less than the time to perform a computation, then performance is being wasted. In general, an ideal ratio would be 1:1, i.e., communication and computation are comparable. This allows a perfect overlap of data transfer with data computation.

This analysis is presented in Table 6.7 for the tested systems. On these systems all basic floating-point operations are roughly comparable, so a double-precision multiply was chosen as the test computation. The communication cost used is that for transferring a double-precision value. The numbers indicate that all three systems are short of the ideal. These systems take much longer to transfer a datum than they take to perform a computation. Thus, it is highly desirable in these systems to maintain a distinction between a local and an external datum reference. This inbalance is reduced significantly if the size of the datum increases, either because the datum is naturally larger or because a higher level structure is imposed on data of smaller size. With larger message sizes, t_{oh} is able to be amortized, with a corresponding reduction in per byte cost.

These results are sample data points which may give the reader a feeling for the considerations and tradeoffs that may go into designing or purchasing a hypercube computer. For the most part, these systems are highly complex and are early examples of this class of computer. It is expected that designers of these systems will continue to increase performance and achieve a better balance of system characteristics in future generations.

6.3   Applications on Hypercubes

Now that hypercubes have been available commercially for a few years, we are in a position to assess their suitability for realistic problems rather than benchmarks. Since Caltech built the original Cosmic Cube, it is only natural that they are a leader in this area. Table 6.8 contains a partial list of work completed or currently underway at Caltech and the Jet Propulsion Laboratory (JPL) [Fox 86].

TABLE 6.8 **List of Current or Completed Application Projects at Caltech/JPL**

Modeling neural networks

Image processing

Modeling the electromagnetic field in the brain

Chemical reaction dynamics

Chaotic motion in plasma physics

Structural analysis using multigrid

Incompressible Navier-Stokes solvers

Parallel shooting for ODEs

Vortex methods

Finite-difference solution of PDEs

Lattice gauge theory

Melting two-dimensional solids

Ion-induced sputtering

Grain dynamics

Ray tracing

Expert systems

Computer algebra

Computer chess

Dynamic load balancing

As might be expected, scientific applications dominate this list. But good progress has also been made in symbolic processing. Of particular note has been the effort to develop a competitive chess-playing program on the hypercube. The program presently evaluates about 20,000 positions per second under tournament conditions on a 64-node NCUBE hypercube. This is quite respectable when compared to the state-of-the-art Cray Blitz and Hitech which examine 100,000 and 200,000 positions per second, respectively. As of October 1986 the program/computer had achieved a rating of 1860 in tournament play.

With the advent of commercially available hypercubes, many other institutions have been able to play a leading role in hypercube research. Yale and Cornell are two of the leading university sites, and Oak Ridge National Laboratory, with both Intel and NCUBE processors, has also been at the forefront of this research. In addition to their investigation of parallel algorithms, the scientists at Oak Ridge have conducted a study to determine how well suited hypercubes are for general scientific computation [Heath 87a]. For this study, a representative set of applications used regularly throughout the laboratory was selected. The application areas studied were finite element fracture analysis, cascade simulation, geochemical contaminant transport, image analysis, molecular dynamics of polymers, density functional theory, and nonlinear magnetohydrodynamics.

In most cases, a team of researchers started with an existing sequential code and attempted to port it, or at least a major portion of it, to the hypercube. The results were quite impressive considering that only six staff-months were budgeted per application. Six of the seven projects resulted in efficient, working hypercube codes. In porting the codes, they found that parallelism arose naturally from the physical problems being addressed. In addition, they found that it was not the hypercube topology per se that was important. Rather, they usually made use of one of the embedded networks, such as a ring, or of the hypercube's close approximation to a fully connected network. They concluded their report by saying that they expect parallel processors to play an important role in everyday computing at Oak Ridge in the future and that more powerful second-generation versions of hypercubes, or other ensemble machines, are likely to be used.

In order to get a better idea of what is required to develop an application for a hypercube and what factors influence the success or failure of such an effort, we will now present in more detail some examples of the work we have performed in the Applications Group at AMETEK. The applications we will describe are separated flow simulations using the vortex method; transonic flow over an airfoil; fast Fourier transforms; implementations of the alternating direction implicit method; and solving matrix equations (i.e., LINPACK). The third and fourth examples involve new codes and algorithms developed specifically to achieve good performance on a hypercube. The first two are ports of full engineering applications codes that are used daily on sequential computers. As such, they should give a good indication of how well these machines perform in a realistic scientific computing environment. The last example is a classic benchmark for scientific computers. We include a theoretical discussion of its performance on a hypercube as a means of indicating where manufacturers of second-generation machines need to make improvements.

6.3.1 Separated flow simulations using the vortex method

In the vortex method, a fluid is represented by point (or finite area) vortices, and the flow is simulated by integrating the vorticity transport equation in a frame of reference which moves with the fluid. The method is of great interest because it can be used to simulate turbulent flows over arbitrary obstacles in the flow, something that the standard finite-difference methods based on the Euler or Navier-

Stokes equations cannot handle. A disadvantage to the method, however, is its great computational intensity. This stems from the long-range nature of the velocity interaction between vortices, which results in an $O(N^2)$ operation count.

In an effort to reduce the computational load, alternatives to this direct summation algorithm which only require $O(N \log N)$ operations have been proposed. The *vortex-in-cell* [Christiansen 73] is one such algorithm, but it too has its problems in that it tends to introduce nonphysical effects such as dissipation, dispersion, and anisotropy into the solution. These can be dealt with, but at increased cost. In view of this, another alternative which looks very attractive is parallel processing. With the potential for great increases in computing power, one has the option of using the more accurate direct-summation algorithm rather than methods that could introduce nonphysical side effects into the solution.

In order to investigate the viability of this option, Catherasoo [87] has ported a production vortex code developed at NASA's Ames Research Center [Spalart 83] to a hypercube. The sequential version of this code has been used quite effectively to study flows around stalled airfoils, helicopter blades, and cascades of blades.

In porting a code or algorithm to a hypercube, the key is deciding how the data are to be partitioned among the processors. For best efficiency one wants to distribute the work evenly among the processors. The majority of the work in the vortex method is due to the direct summation needed to calculate the force on each vortex. Since the amount of work per vortex is the same for each vortex and is independent of its position, one can ensure an even workload by assigning a vortex to any processor so long as the number of vortices in all processors is equal.

The tricky part of the parallelization is minimization of the interprocessor communications required to calculate the force. In this phase one only needs to use the embedded ring topology. We proceed as follows: First, each processor calculates the force on each of its vortices due to the rest of its vortices. Then all processors pass a copy of the positions and strengths of their vortices forward in the ring. Each node can now compute the contribution to the force on its particles due to this new set of vortices. Once this has been done, the process is repeated until the moving vortices have visited all the nodes and the total force has been computed.

As described above, this algorithm would require information to be passed one full cycle around the ring. But once the moving vortices have traveled halfway around the ring, each processor has seen the contribution from half the vortices. However, the processor directly across the ring has seen the complementary half of the vortices. Due to the extra hypercube connections, these two pieces of information can be combined with at most two more communication steps. This modification to the algorithm allows the work to be cut in half.

But there is more to the vortex method than just the direct summation calculation. The NASA Ames code consists of a setup stage and a main loop. In the setup stage, the problem geometry is defined and locations are calculated for vorticity creation points that lie on the surface of the body (or bodies) in the flow. These creation points are used to inject new vorticity into the flow at each time step, thus simulating the effect of viscosity. The strengths of the creation vortices are found by solving a system of linear equations derived from the boundary conditions on the body.

The linear system, which is called the *buffer matrix,* is factored by giving each processor a share of the matrix rows as if they had been dealt out like a deck of cards. The standard LU factorization with pivoting is performed, with each processor only working on the rows it has in its local memory. The only internode communications required are a global maximum to find the pivot element (which can be calculated by a fan-in to a single node) and a broadcast of the pivot row from the node holding it to all others (which is effected by a fan-out). In addition, the creation points are distributed evenly among the processors in order to guarantee a uniform workload when vorticity is introduced into the flow.

The main loop of the program consists of five sections: emit, move, absorb, merge, and share. In the emit section, new vorticity is injected into the flow at the creation points. In order to do this, each node must calculate its contribution to the stream function at each creation point based on the free-stream velocity and the vortices in that node. The contributions from all the nodes are summed using a fan-in, and then new right-hand sides for the vorticity creation equations are calculated. Since the buffer matrix has already been factored, only a backsolve is required, and this may be done in parallel as was the factorization.

The move section is just the direct summation calculation described above combined with a time integration of the vorticity transport equation. Once the new positions of the vortices have been calculated, the absorb routine removes from the flow those vortices that have impacted body surfaces. Each processor can check the positions of its vortices independently of the others, so this section of the code runs with essentially perfect efficiency.

Next, pairs of vortices are checked to determine whether they may be merged into one vortex. This operation can be used to keep the number of vortices down to a reasonable number, thus minimizing the $O(N^2)$ workload in the move section. This reduction comes with a price, however. The merging is done one vortex at a time, each calcu-

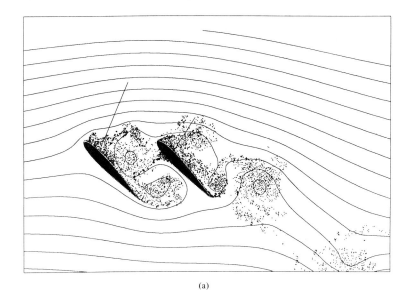

(a)

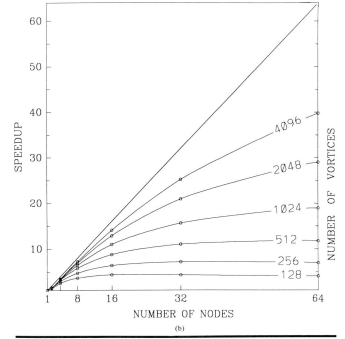

(b)

Figure 6.5   (*a*) Flow field around two NACA airfoils in tandem by the vortex method, T = 4.0 s; (*b*) speedup curves for the vortex method on an S14 hypercube for 32 creation points.

lation requiring a comparison with all other vortices in the flow to find the best merging partner. Intranode comparisons can of course be done in parallel, but a fan-in is required to find which vortex is the best overall merging partner.

Once vortices have been absorbed and merged, it is likely that the processors no longer hold equal numbers of them. The share routine reequilibrates the distribution by having each processor compare successively its number of vortices with that of its neighbors across each dimension of the hypercube. If the two numbers differ by more than one in a comparison, the node with the greater number sends half its excess to its neighbor, and then the next dimension is considered. After all dimensions have been compared, the vortices are once again equally distributed.

In order to determine the performance of the parallel implementation, the code has been applied to a typical model problem. This problem consists of calculating the flow over a pair of airfoils separated by one chord length. Figure 6.5*a* shows the flow field after 4.0 s. Here, the Reynolds number based on the airfoil chord is 1 million. To test the parallel performance, the problem was solved using numbers of processors varying from 1 to 64, and for a given run, the number of vortices in the flow was held constant by judicious use of merging. Figure 6.5*b* shows the speedup curves obtained on an AMETEK System 14 hypercube when 32 creation points were used.

Several characteristics typical of the performance of parallel machines can be seen from the speedup curves. First, the larger the problem, the better the speedup achieved. This is due to the diminishing percentage of total time consumed by communications as the amount of work increases. Second, there is a maximum number of processors that one should use for a given problem size since in exceeding that number, communication costs overwhelm the extra parallelism gained by using more processors. From Fig. 6.5, one can see that each node should have no fewer than about four to eight vortices. If a node has more than this, efficiencies as high as 85 percent are achieved. Most of the inefficiency seen here, however, is due to the merging step. If one considers only the move step, efficiencies in excess of 95 percent are typical.

Speedup curves indicate how effectively an algorithm can be run in parallel, but if one is to compare a hypercube to another computer, the desired data are the MFLOPS rates. Due to the large number of conditional calculations required by the vortex method, particularly in the merge section, a true MFLOPS rate is difficult to determine. But one can calculate a lower bound by counting the number of operations that are always performed and dividing this by the solution time. Table 6.9 shows the rates obtained on a 64-node System 14 for the model problem when 256 creation points were used and merging was turned

TABLE 6.9   Vortex Method Timings for an AMETEK System 14/64

Flow time, s	Number of vortices	MFLOPS
2.0	3376	1.648
4.0	6497	1.858
6.0	9780	1.940
8.0	13186	1.987
10.0	15828	2.014

off. Note that the rate increases as the number of vortices grows. Thus, hypercubes, like other architectures well suited for large-scale scientific computing, exhibit the very desirable property of providing more performance when it is needed most. For this problem, the single-node calculation rate is 32 KFLOPS, so that the machine is operating at 98 percent efficiency when the flow time has reached 10.0 s.

6.3.2   Transonic flow

A source of significant computing time today is the calculation of flows over aircraft. This problem area pushes the limits of modern computers in both computation speed and memory requirements. For example, the simulation of the full three-dimensional flow over an entire aircraft such as a Boeing 747 can require a computational grid of 500,000 to 1 million grid points. In single precision, this requires upward of 100 Mbytes of storage if one wants to keep the problem in core. Moreover, a typical transient simulation requires over 700 floating-point operations per grid point per time step, and several hundred to a few thousand time steps are needed to reach steady state.

Given such massive computing requirements, it is natural to turn to parallel processing for help. Hypercubes offer the potential to provide great amounts of memory at a reasonable cost. Furthermore, large numbers of nodes should allow the processing of all these data in a reasonable amount of time.

As a prototype for this kind of simulation, we consider porting to a hypercube [Bassett 87] one of the most popular transonic flow codes available, the FLO57 package written by Antony Jameson of Princeton University [Jameson 84]. The code calculates flows over wings and aircraft by solving the Euler equations using the finite volume method with explicit Runge-Kutta time stepping. Newer codes that use the full Navier-Stokes equations and implicit solvers are now beginning to appear, at least at research centers, but FLO57 has gained wide use in the aerospace community due to its accuracy and robustness. It can reliably be used to study flows over a wide range of geometries, and Mach numbers as great as 3.0 have been used. It offers a significant improvement over the still popular panel method codes, especially when strong shocks are encountered.

At first, it might appear that such a code would present serious load-balancing problems for parallel computers when one considers the very irregular geometries that are present. But this is not the case because the first section of the code maps the irregular shape of a wing or jet into a three-dimensional rectangular region. FLO57 uses an algebraic method to effect this transformation, and the code for this was ported in a completely straightforward manner.

Once this transformation is performed, the resulting grid is easily partitioned among multiple processors that are arranged as a three-dimensional grid themselves. As previously mentioned, one of the advantages of the hypercube interconnection topology is that one-, two-, and three-dimensional meshes are subsets of it. For this application we treat the hypercube as a three-dimensional mesh.

The finite volume method, like finite differences or elements, is a local procedure. That is, the solution for the next time step at a given grid point is calculated from the current time-step solutions in a small neighborhood of the grid point. Thus, if each processor is given a three-dimensional subset of the problem domain, most of the calculations can be made independently of the other processors. Only those grid points at the edges of the subdomains need worry about information from other processors. To provide storage for the neighboring edge information, the data array in each processor is made bigger by two elements in each dimension, and the edge data are stored around the surface of the processor's subdomain. To minimize the amount of edge data that must be communicated, the subdomains should generally be chosen to be as cubic as possible. This rectangular decomposition is one of the most commonly used partitionings in hypercube codes.

Putting such a partitioning into FLO57 was not anticipated to be too difficult, but it turned out to be easier than expected since the code had been written to run out-of-core on sequential machines. That is, anticipating insufficient memory to hold the entire problem at once, the code allowed for the problem to be broken into subdomains, each of which could be solved alone, with only a small amount of "glue" calculations required at the edges to piece the whole solution together. But this out-of-core partitioning is precisely the same type of partitioning one expected to use for the hypercube. This good fortune is not uncommon; other researchers have observed that out-of-core algorithms are easily ported directly to hypercubes. For example, this observation was made by researchers at Oak Ridge in their finite element fracture analysis.

Nevertheless, care still needed to be taken to assure that communications were not more costly than need be. The data for each processor are stored in a four-dimensional array (three dimensions for physical

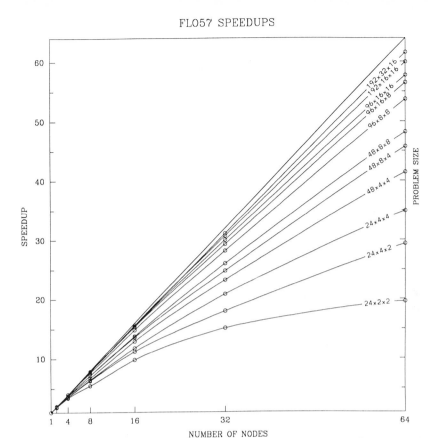

Figure 6.6 Speedup curves for FL057 on an AMETEK S14 hypercube.

space and one for time). Thus, most of the edges of the processor's subdomain are not in consecutive memory locations, so they must be copied through contiguous arrays before and after exchange with a neighboring node. Since this copying is directly proportional to the size of the message sent between nodes, it has the effect of showing up as a reduction in the hardware's per byte messaging rate. This reduction in effective communication speed can be minimized by using the processor's block move instruction.

Figure 6.6 shows the speedup curves for FLO57 run on an AMETEK System 14. They display the classic behavior that we have seen previously. Note that most of the problem sizes considered are quite small. The largest uses only 100,000 grid points, which is about the smallest size that would be used for a production run. For a detailed flow simulation, 500,000 to 1 million grid points is a more desirable range. For these larger problems we would see near perfect efficien-

TABLE 6.10   **FLO57 Performance Comparison**

$96 \times 16 \times 16$ grid	Cyber 205	AP 164	System 14/64
Time per iteration, s	1.85	18.45	8.57
MFLOPS	9.56	0.959	2.09

cies. One can convert the vertical scale on this graph to FLOPS by multiplying the speedup by 35 KFLOPS, which is the single-node speed of the processor on this application.

Since FLO57 is a widely used code, the literature offers us the opportunity to compare the hypercube performance to that of more conventional scientific processors. Table 6.10 shows the computation time and floating-point rates for a single time step of a model problem using a $96 \times 16 \times 16$ grid (the Cyber 205 and AP 164 times are taken from Agarwal [83]). As can be seen from the table, the first-generation hypercube is no match for the supercomputer in total performance, but given that the cost of the Cyber is about 50 times that of the hypercube, a factor of 5 advantage in speed does not look so great. And as we will see in Sec. 6.3.5, a hypercube with on-board array processors can compete quite favorably with today's supercomputers on this type of application.

6.3.3   Fast Fourier transforms

The fast Fourier transform (FFT) has become such an important algorithm in scientific computing that it would be conspicuous by its absence from even as short a review of applications as this one. But there are more reasons than mere popularity to include a discussion of the FFT here. As we shall soon see, FFTs on hypercubes demonstrate some very nice nonclassical performance characteristics.

Because the FFT algorithm is so well known, we will not spend time here to discuss it in detail. Suffice it to say that the key point to recall is that an array of 2^m complex numbers is transformed by performing a series of linear combinations of the array elements. The first set of linear combinations involves elements whose indices in the array differ only in the first bit of their binary representation; the second set involves elements whose indices differ only in their second bit; the third set those which differ in the third bit; and so on. The result of these linear combinations is an array containing the discrete Fourier transform in frequency space of the original array, although the order of the array elements has been somewhat scrambled. This reordering is usually of little concern, though, as it is undone when one returns to physical space with the inverse transform.

Recall that the hypercube connections can be created by joining together those nodes in the set $\{0, 1, \ldots, 2^n - 1\}$ whose node numbers differ by only 1 bit in their binary representations. In this description, nodes differing in the first bit are connected across the first dimension, those differing in the second bit are connected across the second dimension, and so on. In comparing this to the algorithm described above, we see that this set of connections is precisely what is needed to perform the FFT operations. Given an array of length 2^m to transform using 2^n hypercube nodes, we store the first 2^{m-n} elements in node 0, the next 2^{m-n} elements in node 1, and so forth. The first $m - n$ linear combinations can be performed entirely in the individual nodes. The remaining linear combinations will then require communications between the nodes, each occurring in succession across dimensions of the hypercube.

In the case where m is much larger than n, one would expect that this algorithm should be very efficient since the vast majority of the work is done with no internode communication. This is in fact the case. Walton [87] presents a theoretical derivation of the time required to perform an FFT on a hypercube:

$$T_{\text{FFT}} = \frac{5\delta M \ \log_2 \ M}{N} + \log_2 \ N \left(\alpha + \beta \frac{M}{N} \right)$$

where M = size of transform, 2^m
  N = number of nodes, 2^n
  δ = time required for addition or multiplication
  α = overhead associated with exchange of data between two processors
  β = time to exchange floating-point number exclusive of overhead

The classic behavior we have seen previously would lead us to believe that there should be a maximal number of processors one should use on the problem in order to achieve the greatest speedup. But by differentiating this formula with respect to N, one finds that, as long as α is not too large (less than about 100δ), the fastest FFT is achieved by using as many nodes as possible.

But how fast is this? Using the above formula we can make some estimates. Table 6.11 shows the times and MFLOPS rates that a 1024-node hypercube would achieve on a 1 million point transform for a variety of machine parameters. Of particular interest is line 6, since the advent of processors such as the Transputer or that found in the NCUBE/10 hypercube indicates that a machine with this kind of performance, in a small physical package, is feasible with today's technology.

Now, for real applications, 1 million point FFTs are of little interest unless they are in two dimensions. Fortunately, Table 6.11 is applica-

TABLE 6.11   Performance of 1 Million Point FFT on a 1024-Node Hypercube

μs α	β, Mbytes/s	δ, MFLOPS	Time, s	MFLOPS	Efficiency, %
100	10	0.5	0.210	500	97.6
10	10	0.5	0.209	502	98.0
100	20	0.5	0.208	504	98.5
10	20	0.5	0.207	507	99.0
100	10	1.0	0.107	975	95.3
10	10	1.0	0.107	984	96.1
100	20	1.0	0.105	994	97.1
10	20	1.0	0.105	1003	97.9
100	10	10.0	0.015	6837	66.8
10	10	10.0	0.014	7264	70.9
100	20	10.0	0.013	7891	77.1
10	20	10.0	0.012	8464	82.7

ble to that case since, as Walton [87] points out, the time for the one-dimensional FFT is an upper bound for the time of a two-dimensional transform of the same number of points. In fact, we should expect the time for two-dimensional transforms to be slightly better than those listed since they are more efficient in terms of internode communications.

6.3.4   Implementations of the alternating direction implicit method

The *alternating direction implicit* (ADI) method is a very popular technique for solving elliptic and parabolic partial differential equations. For reasons of stability, the time integration of these multidimensional partial differential equations needs to be done with implicit methods. But this generally means that one is faced with solving banded systems of equations in which the diagonals are widely separated from each other. The fill-in that would occur during Gaussian elimination makes solution of the system of equations by a direct method prohibitive. ADI gets around this problem by solving in only one dimension at a time. Since just one dimension is considered unknown in these "sweeps," only tridiagonal systems need to be solved. Thus, the solution of many tridiagonal systems, for which there is no fill-in penalty, approximates the solution of a wider banded system.

There are several ways to implement ADI on a hypercube. Lim [87] and Thanakij study the performance of six different implementations on a model heat flow problem. All of the methods are based upon a rectangular decomposition of the two-dimensional problem domain that is just like the data decomposition in the transonic flow application discussed earlier. But ADI is more complicated since it requires that tridiagonal systems, which stretch over the data spaces of several processors, be solved.

As might be expected, most of the implementations concentrate on a parallel algorithm for solving a tridiagonal system. In these implementations, groups of processors cooperate to solve a single tridiagonal system at a time. Two of these methods are the well-known serial and parallel variants of cyclic reduction. The remaining three are variants of substructured Gaussian elimination in which each processor independently attempts to perform Gaussian elimination on its portion of the tridiagonal matrix. Since they do this in parallel rather than in the usual serial fashion, fill-in destroys the upper bidiagonal structure that would normally occur. This fill-in, however, can be arranged so that a tridiagonal system, equal in size to the number of processors used, decouples from the rest of the equations. Once this smaller system is solved, the remainder of the solution may be found by a totally parallel backsubstitution. The three variants arise from the method used to solve the intermediate tridiagonal system: serial cyclic reduction, parallel cyclic reduction, or a pipelined version of the serial Thomas algorithm.

The last implementation they study is called *scattered decomposition*. This method is like a two-dimensional version of the card deal used to distribute matrix rows for LU factorization that was used in the vortex method. Scattered decomposition is important because it has been shown to be effective in parallelizing problems on irregular domains [Morrison 85]. In this decomposition strategy, instead of giving each processor just one subdomain of the problem, each processor receives p smaller subdomains that have been scattered about the original problem domain, where p is the number of processors. An example of this for four processors is shown in Fig. 6.7.

In each sweep, all processors along one edge of the problem domain begin solving tridiagonal systems using the usual Thomas sequential algorithm. When they reach the far side of their subdomains, the processors hand off the problem to the processor across the edge. Since

3	0	1	2
2	3	0	1
1	2	3	0
0	1	2	3

Figure 6.7 Scattered decomposition for ADI.

rings can be embedded in hypercubes, it is always possible to arrange the subdomain locations so that only nearest neighbor communications in the hypercube are required. Once the handoff is completed, the solution of the tridiagonal systems continues, only now the processors go on with different systems than they started with. This handing-off procedure continues across the problem domain and then retraces its steps for the back substitution. Note that one can save considerable communications costs by not handing off until each processor has performed a partial factorization on all of its tridiagonal systems. A communication at this time will only incur the cost of one overhead time, rather than one for each triadiagonal system as would have otherwise been the case.

One final implementation, which was not studied in Lim [87], is a pipelined technique developed by Johnsson, Saad, and Schultz [Johnsson 85]. Here, the normal rectangular decomposition is used. For the case of an x-sweep, each processor on the left edge of the problem domain begins solving its first tridiagonal system. Note that this leaves most of the processors idle. When the far side of the subdomain is reached, they hand these problems off to their neighbors to the right. These neighbors can now continue the original problem while the left edge processors start on their second tridiagonal systems. Clearly, a pipeline is being set up, and once it is full, all processors are working in parallel. When all the systems have been factored, the pipeline is reversed for the backsubstitution.

At this point note that the first five implementations represent a straightforward parallelization of a sequential algorithm. The sequential algorithm consists of a series of tridiagonal systems to be solved. The parallel implementation merely parallelizes the solution of each of these systems; no effort is made to alter the main flow of the algorithm. On the other hand, the last two implementations are of quite a different nature. They offer an alternative approach by considering the problem from a bigger frame of reference. They attempt to parallelize an entire sweep rather than just the individual components of a sweep. This is a very significant difference since frequently one needs to look at the problem as whole, rather than its individual pieces, in order to devise an efficient parallel algorithm.

We now look at the performance of the implementations studied in Lim [87]. Figure 6.8 is a plot of which method provides the best performance as a function of problem size and number of processors based on theoretical performance formulas for a processor like the AMETEK System 14. What we see is quite interesting and is supported by performance measurements on the actual hardware. No single implementation is best. Along a ray heading from the origin toward the lower right-hand corner of the plot is a region we might term the fine-grain limit. Here, very few grid points are assigned to each processor. The

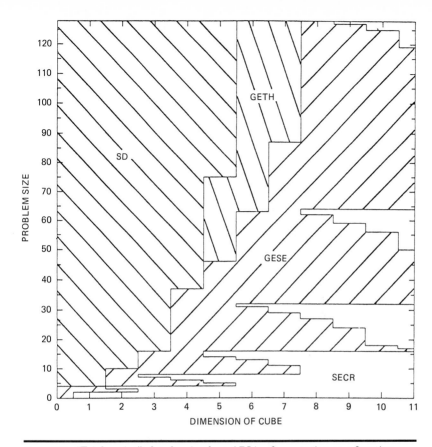

Figure 6.8 "Triple-point" plot showing best ADI implementation as a function of problem size and number of processors.

best performer in this region is substructured Gaussian elimination with the serial cyclic reduction variation. (The theoretical results predicted that serial cyclic reduction would be the best performer. On the hardware, however, GESE performed best, the one discrepancy between the theory and the measured results.) Along a ray to the upper right-hand corner, a region in which each processor contains moderate numbers of grid points, one finds medium-grain parallelism. Here, substructured gaussian elimination with the Thomas algorithm variation has the best performance. And finally, along the left-hand side of the plot, which is the course-grain limit, the best performer is the scattered decomposition.

Since hypercubes are new, it would make life much easier for them and their users (and their manufacturers) if one algorithm were clearly the best. But it seems that this multigrain type of behavior is going to be more often the rule than the exception. Depending on the problem being solved, users will have to choose from many possible algorithms. If they are to attain the best possible performance, they will have to choose wisely.

6.3.5   Solving matrix equations: LINPACK

Jack Dongarra's LINPACK benchmark [Dongarra 86] is by now a standard measure of computer performance. This is more a consequence of the hard work Dongarra has put into collecting the results than an indication that the benchmark truly reflects the performance of computers on real scientific problems.† Nevertheless, the benchmark is a well-understood piece of code, and as such, one can extrapolate key elements of machine performance from it.

The benchmark consists of solving a matrix equation by gaussian elimination.‡ The algorithm consists of two parts: the factorization, in which the matrix is factored into the product of a lower triangular matrix and an upper triangular matrix; and the backsolve, in which the triangular matrix systems are solved.

Suggested parallel decompositions of this problem usually distribute either the rows or columns of the matrix among the processors. In the vortex calculations presented above, a row decomposition was used. But for this study we have chosen to use the column-oriented algorithm described by Moler [86] since it should be a bit more efficient. Here, each processor is assigned columns of the matrix as if they were dealt out like playing cards. Thus, if n is the size of the matrix and p the number of processors, each processor receives approximately $[n/p]$ columns; we will denote the number of columns a given processor receives by m.

To study the performance of the parallel algorithm, we simply tally up the time it takes to execute the algorithm. For this we need to look at the code. The node program for the factorization is shown in Fig. 6.9. Note that the part in the then clause of the if statement is executed sequentially in one node. Thus, even if internode communication required no time, this algorithm could not be 100 percent efficient in parallel. Nevertheless, the algorithm is still very good since the remainder of the code, the k and j loops, can be executed in parallel with almost perfect load balance, and the majority of the work is in this section of the code.

To calculate the factorization time, we assume that all arithmetic operations take the same amount of time, $\frac{1}{2}f$, where f is the time to

---

†In fact, in just one of our previous examples, the vortex method, was a LINPACK-like routine used, and even there it contributed only a negligible amount to the total running time of the code.

‡For a description of the sequential algorithm, we refer the reader to Dongarra [79].

```
l = 1
for i = 1 to n - 1 do
  if (mynode() = (i - 1 mod p)) then
    find pivot in column l
    col = {column l} / pivot (for rows j = i + 1 to n)
    l = l + 1
    broadcast col
  else
    receive broadcast of col
  end if
  for k = 1 to m do
    for j = i + 1 to n do
      a(j,k) = a(j,k) - a(i,k)*col(j)
    end loop on j
  end loop on k
end loop on i
```

Figure 6.9   Parallel matrix factorization algorithm.

perform 1 FLOP (the operation $y_i = y_i + ax_i$, see Dongarra [86]). Furthermore, we make the assumption that each processor has exactly the same number of columns, $m = n/p$. Finally, we denote the message overhead by α and the time required to send one floating-point word (exclusive of overhead) by β, and we use the fact that a hypercube broadcast takes $\log_2 p$ messaging steps. After a little algebra, we find

$$T_{\text{fact}} = \frac{f}{p} [\ \frac{1}{3}(n-1)^3 + \frac{1}{2}(n-1)^2 + \frac{1}{6}(n-1)] + \frac{3}{4} fn(n-1) + f(n-1) +$$

$$\frac{\beta}{2} n(n-1) \log_2 p + (n-1)(\alpha + \beta) \log_2 p$$

For the backsolve we abandon Moler's algorithm in favor of the much more efficient *cube fan-in algorithm* described by Heath and Romine [Heath 87b]. Like all backsolve algorithms, it consists of two parts: the forward elimination and the backward elimination. The basic operation of this algorithm is an inner product of part of a row of a triangular matrix with part of the right-hand side vector. In contrast, the factorization's basic operation is a saxpy (the loop on index j).

This algorithm is parallelized by distributing the dot product. The code is shown in Fig. 6.10. Here, we have used the routine sdot (vector1, vector2, length) to calculate the dot product of the parts of the vectors that each processor contains. These values are combined in the fan-in to produce the final scalar value for the dot product of the entire vectors. A little more algebra yields the time for the backsolve:

$$T_{\text{back}} = \frac{f}{p} n(n-1) + 2(n-1)(\alpha + \beta + \frac{f}{2}) \log_2 p + \frac{f}{2}n$$

In order to compute how many MFLOPS the hypercube is achieving in

```
/* Forward Elimination */
  for k = 2 to n do
    sdot(b,a(k),(k − 1)/p)
    fan-in to processor holding column k
    b(k) = b(k) − dot_product
  end loop on k
  /* Backward Elimination */
  b(n) = b(n)/a(n,n)
  for k = n − 1 downto 1 do
    sdot(y,a(k),(n − k)/p)
    fan-in to processor holding column k
    b(k) = (b(k) − dot_product)/a(k,k)
  end loop on k
```

Figure 6.10   Parallel backsolve algorithm.

this problem, we need to know how many floating-point operations there are in the LINPACK benchmark. We obtain this figure simply by setting $f = 2$ (since a flop requires two operations) and $p = 1$ (to reduce to the sequential algorithms) in the above formulas. From the factorization time we obtain

$$\text{NOPS}_{\text{fact}} = \frac{2}{3}(n - 1)^3 + \frac{3}{2}(n - 1)^2 + \frac{11}{6}(n - 1)$$

for the backsolve, we have

$$\text{NOPS}_{\text{back}} = 2n^2 - n$$

To calculate the MFLOP rate, we just divide the sum of these two operation counts by the time calculated from the formulas for the factorization and backsolve.

With these formulas, we can now study the performance of LINPACK on arbitrary hypercubes (or any concurrent processor than can broadcast in $\log_2 p$ stages). Speedup curves show the same behavior characteristics that we have seen previously for the vortex method and transonic flow, so we will not present those curves here. Instead, we choose to look at the effect of the messaging rate on the performance.

Figure 6.11 shows the performance of a 64-node hypercube solving a 1000×1000 matrix system for various message overheads and a range of message per byte rates. The overheads cover the span from a poor first-generation time of 1000 μs down to a perfect 0 μs; the per byte rates range from a good first-generation speed of 0.5 Mbyte/s up to the ideal of ∞ Mbyte/s. These curves were calculated assuming a single-node double-precision calculation rate of 3 MFLOPS, a figure typical of what we expect real throughput to be for this type of problem on present or upcoming vector accelerators for concurrent computers.

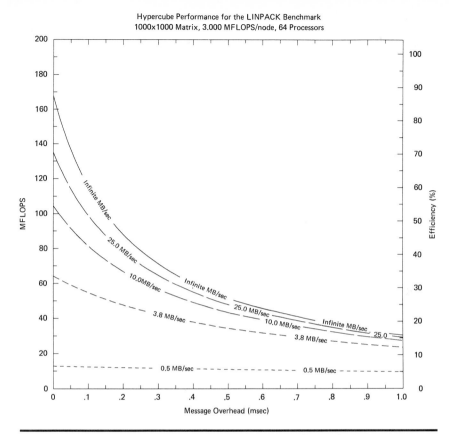

Figure 6.11   Effect of hypercube messaging rate on LINPACK performance.

The performance is quite startling. We see immediately that it makes no sense to put such an accelerator on a first-generation hypercube; there simply is not enough message throughput to support the calculation rate. Note, though, that message overhead has virtually nothing to do with the poor performance; it is simply a matter of link speed.

For a second-generation hypercube, one would expect overheads to drop to the 100- to 200-μs range due to the increased MIPS of faster microprocessors, and a typical per byte rate is anticipated to be about 4 Mbytes/s. Such a machine fares better than its first-generation cousin, but efficiencies are still only about 25 percent, and this is for a fairly large problem. To achieve 50 percent efficiency, one would need a machine with a 100-μs overhead and a per byte rate of about 20 Mbytes/s.

This performance, however, should not be considered typical. Most large scientific problems no longer employ Gaussian elimination to

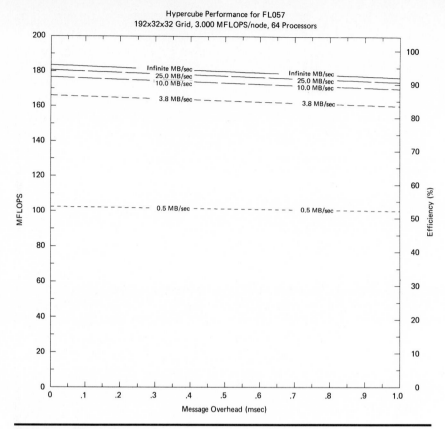

Figure 6.12   Effect of hypercube messaging rate on FLO57 performance.

solve their matrix systems since much faster techniques, such as multigrid or preconditioned conjugate gradient, are now available. These algorithms are very similar in structure to the transonic flow algorithm presented in Sec. 6.3.2, and their performance is likewise similar.

As a contrast to the LINPACK results, Fig. 6.12 shows the effect of messaging rate on the performance of the transonic flow code. The curves were computed from formulas derived in Bassett [87]. As before, the results presented are for a 64-node hypercube with a 3-MFLOPS vector accelerator,† and the problem size was chosen to be similar to the 1000 × 1000 matrix considered in the LINPACK model.

The performance here is dramatically better than that for LINPACK. Even a first-generation hypercube is not completely over-

---

†We have ignored the fact that the increased complexity of the arithmetic operations in this case would probably allow the accelerator to run faster on this problem than on LINPACK.

powered by the floating-point rate as it exceeds 50 percent efficiency on this problem. Second-generation machines do quite well at better than 80 percent efficiency. And a hypercube with a messaging rate of 10 Mbytes/s would exceed 90 percent efficiency for all but the highest message overheads. While the LINPACK benchmark results may not show the full performance of first- or second-generation machines, on most full-scale scientific applications we are likely to see much more impressive efficiencies and performance.

6.4   Second-Generation Systems

It has been shown that hypercubes perform well for a wide range of scientific and engineering computations. The experience at AMETEK and other sites such as Caltech, JPL, and Oak Ridge National Laboratory further indicates that porting existing software to hypercubes is not a formidable task. Once ported it has been shown that the executed codes compete favorably against their sequential counterparts.

The first-generation machines that have been described have been suitable for research into these new software techniques. However, these first-generation machines have been limited in many ways and are often not suitable for continuous on-line problem solving. It will be the second-generation machines that deliver enough power, flexibility, and usability to be selected for "production" applications.

6.4.1   Hardware evolution

The hypercube is a powerful and effective parallel computer architecture. But it is unfortunate that these computers have so far derived their name from the topology of the interconnection network. The effectiveness of these machines has more to do with the message-passing paradigm as implemented on a distributed memory multicomputer than with the wires that carry the messages. Further, the second-generation systems will see both significant enhancement to and departure from the hypercube model. In fact, some second-generation systems have since been introduced. The AMETEK System 14 has been discontinued and replaced by the Symult (AMETEK) Series 2010. The Intel IPSC has been succeeded by the Intel IPSC/2. The FPS T Series, however, has been discontinued with no replacement.

The next generation of multicomputers will have more balanced processing, include vector floating point, have increased memory, have more flexible I/O capabilities, and faster message passing capability. The high level of replication inherent in multicomputers will result in the increasing application of VLSI [Seitz 84*a*]. This will take place in the integration of concurrent computer functions, or as in the case of NCUBE, to the concurrent computer node itself. As a result, nodes will become cheaper and smaller. This will also encourage the use of inherent redundancy for fault tolerance [Armstrong 81].

Most of these gains will be as a result of trickle-through technology improvements, such as faster 32-bit processors, integrated floating-point accelerators, or denser RAM. However, one of the most important advancements that will appear specific to the concurrent computers of the second generation is vastly improved message-passing capabilities, both in reduced message overhead and message passing rate. As noted previously, a severe weakness of the first-generation machines is the poor ratio of computation to communication times, typically no better than 1:10 and often worse. Thus, an order of magnitude improvement in this area will be needed to deliver on the promise of concurrent computers. Two areas that are being examined in order to improve message-passing performance are network topology and message-passing mechanisms.

Some new work has demonstrated that though hypercubes are a good compromise of many conflicting needs, they are not necessarily the best compromise. There is a broad class of networks, including particularly k-ary n-cubes, which offer opportunities to restrain connectivity growth while retaining comparable or improved performance. Consider that wires, interconnections, and communications circuits are not free; otherwise we would certainly choose a fully connected network. In this case, a figure of merit for technology and cost tradeoffs can be reflected in the bisection bandwidth. The bisection bandwidth can be computed by cutting the network along an axis of symmetry and computing the number of wires crossing the cut times the bandwidth that each wire is able to support. For example, a binary 4-cube with 8-Mbit/s serial channels interconnecting the nodes has the same bisection bandwidth as a binary 4-cube with 1-Mbit/s byte-wide channels interconnecting the nodes. In considering bisection bandwidth, and also including real effects such as capacitance and propagation delays, Dally [86] has shown that lower dimensionality networks with higher bandwidths per channel perform much better than the comparable hypercube.

Other new work has also indicated the efficacy of utilizing wormhole routing at the hardware and network level to transport messages between nodes [Dally 87]. Wormhole routing is a variation on packet switching. Rather than passing data through intermediate nodes to a destination node, as is done with the store-and-forward approach on first-generation hypercubes, data are passed through a series of interconnected switches. Data passed through these switches are first formed into discrete packets; then each packet is affixed with a header containing destination address information. When this packet is inserted into the network of switches, the address information is interpreted and causes each switch to set so that a complete route is allocated from the source to the destination. If there should be contention for a switch somewhere along the path, then arbitration is performed and one path is allowed to complete while the other path is blocked until the first path is relinquished. With this technique, message latency in the network remains almost constant, up to network congestion, regardless of the distance between the source and destination nodes.

Both these ideas have been implemented in a second-generation message-passing concurrent computer, the Symult (AMETEK) Series 2010. This new machine is a k-ary 2-cube[†] interconnection network that implements wormhole routing for message passing. The use of reduced connectivity allows higher parallelism in the channel leading to a higher message rate per channel. The reduction in connectivity allows the integration of the message-passing function into VLSI, leading to an even higher message rate and lower parts count. The new wormhole routing mechanism leads to significantly lower message overhead and latency due to minimization of resource utilization in the network and the nodes.

The resulting message-passing network of this new system has such high bandwidth and low latency for message passing that, from the point of view of the programmer, the network is essentially fully connected. Thus, the hypercube interconnection topology can be thought of as a subset of the network, which means that hypercube programs can run unmodified on the new machine. Initial measurements on this new network technology show performance in excess of 20 Mbytes/s independent of distance from source to destination, an improvement of two orders of magnitude over the capabilities of the first-generation networks. This meets the goal of balancing the computation to communication performance ratio: one order of magnitude is needed to obtain balance with computation and another order of magnitude is needed to keep up with the next generation processor technology that is being used in the new systems.

6.4.2 Software revolution

The greatest challenge to bringing these second-generation concurrent computers to market is without a doubt the software. As noted above, users of first-generation machines are primarily researchers interested in exploring a new technology. As such they have been very forgiving of the spartan programming environments available on the

---

[†]That is, a two-dimensional mesh network. In the future, larger systems could implement a k-ary 3-cube interconnection. This will allow higher connectivity and bandwidths as systems grow.

machines. But second-generation machines must support tools and software that are commonly available to users of more traditional computer architectures.

Fortunately, good progress is being made in this area. Since the release of its first machine, AMETEK has been delivering a simulator and multiprocess debugger to aid programmers in correcting the subtle bugs that can occur in parallel programming. While very useful, not all program bugs can be detected with a simulator, so AMETEK has subsequently added rudimentary hardware debugging capabilities to their software. NCUBE and Intel have taken this one step further by making on-node debugging available on their processors; Intel's debugger even supports full symbolic capabilities.

At Tufts University, software called SEECUBE [Cybenko 87] has been developed which allows one to play back hypercube statistics in slow motion in order to study message flow. This type of graphic profiler is extremely useful in determining communication bottlenecks in algorithms. The Trillium project at Cornell [Brown 87] and the MACH project at Carnegie-Mellon [Rashid 86] offer the promise of putting a well-known operating system, namely UNIX, on concurrent computer nodes themselves, instead of just the host. This has the potential for opening up concurrent computers to a vast base of existing software.

However, it is not enough to move a familiar operating system to a concurrent computer. These machines have problems unique to their architecture, and existing operating systems are not designed to address those issues. One such problem is that of balancing the workload of multiple processes on these processors. Current applications must make this effort internally to the program and usually apply some heuristic that may or may not work. The capability to perform automatic load balancing belongs in the operating system. Applications programs just cannot be guaranteed access to all the system metrics that are necessary to effectively make such decisions. One recently developed technique that shows promise in this area is simulated annealing [Steele 85]. Simulated annealing is a heuristic which treats some metric or set of metrics as an artificial temperature. In a process analogous to annealing in materials, processes are allowed to move around in the hypercube with the goal of reducing the artificial temperature.

But the most important software needed for these machines, parallelizing compilers, is still an area of active research. Much work looks promising, but it is clear that success is still several years away. Fortunately, there is now a growing base of machines on which to perform this research; this can only hasten the development.

Bibliography

[Agarwal 83]   R.K. Agarwal and J.E. Deese. *Transonic Wing-Body Calculations Using Euler Equations.* AIAA Paper 83-0501, 1983.

[Armstrong 81]   J.R. Armstrong and F.G. Gray. "Fault Diagnosis in a Boolean n-Cube Array of Microprocessors." *IEEE Trans. Computers,* vol. C-30, no. 8, pp. 587–590, August 1981.

[Bassett 87]   M.E. Bassett and C.J. Catherasoo. *Simulation of Transonic Flow on a Hypercube.* AMETEK Computer Research Division Tech. Rep. TR-87-012, May 28, 1987.

[Brown 87]   A.A. Brown. "Trillium OS for the FPS T-Series." In M.T. Heath (ed). *Hypercube Multiprocessors 1987.* SIAM, Philadelphia, 1987.

[Catherasoo 87]   C.J. Catherasoo. *Separated Flow Simulations Using the Vortex Method on a Hypercube.* AIAA Paper 87-1109-CP, 1987.

[Christiansen 73]   J.P. Christiansen. "Numerical Solution of Hydrodynamics by the Method of Point Vortices." *J. Computational Physics,* vol. 13, pp. 363–379, 1973.

[Colanna 86]   J.D. Colanna. "ACRD Charges onto the Scene with Super-Fast Parallel Processor." *Information Week,* July 14, 1986.

[Cybenko 87]   G. Cybenko. "Visualizing Hypercube Computations." In M.T. Heath (ed). *Hypercube Multiprocessors 1987.* SIAM, Philadelphia, 1987.

[Dally 86]   W.J. Dally. *A VLSI Architecture for Concurrent Data Structures.* Caltech Tech. Rep. 5209:TR:86, March 13, 1986.

[Dally 87]   W.J. Dally and C.L. Seitz. "Deadlock-Free Message Routing in Multiprocessor Interconnection Networks." *IEEE Trans. Computers,* vol. C-36, no. 5, pp. 547–553, May 1987.

[Dongarra 86]   J.J. Dongarra. *Performance of Various Computers Using Standard Linear Equations Software in a Fortran Environment.* Argonne National Laboratory Mathematics and Computer Science Tech. Mem. No. 23, July 24, 1986.

[Dongarra 79]   J.J. Dongarra, C.B. Moler, J.R. Bunch, and G.W. Stewart. *LINPACK Users' Guide.* SIAM, Philadelphia, 1979.

[Dunnigan 87]   T.H. Dunigan. *Performance of Three Hypercubes.* Oak Ridge National Laboratory Tech. Rep. ORNL/TM-10400, May 1987.

[Durham 86]   T. Durham and T. Johnson. *Parallel Processing: The Challenge of New Computer Architectures.* Ovum Ltd., London, England, 1986.

[Ezsih 86]   I.P. Ezsih. "Vector Processing Boosts Hypercube's Performance." *Electronics,* pp. 30–31, April 14, 1986.

[Fox 86]   G.C. Fox. *Caltech Concurrent Computation Program Annual Report 1985–1986.* Caltech Concurrent Computation Program Tech. Rep. C³P-290B, October 13, 1986.

[Fox 84]   G.C. Fox and S.W. Otto. "Algorithms for Concurrent Processors." *Physics Today,* pp. 13–20, May 1984.

[Gustafson 86]   J.L. Gustafson, S. Hawkinson, and K. Scott. "The Architecture of a Homogeneous Vector Supercomputer." *Proc. 1986 International Conference on Parallel Processing,* IEEE Computer Society Press, Washington D.C., pp. 649–652, 1986.

[Hayes 86]   J.P. Hayes, T.N. Mudge, Q.F. Stout, S. Colley, and J. Palmer. "Architecture of a Hypercube Supercomputer." *Proc. 1986 International Conference on Parallel Processing,* IEEE Computer Society Press, Washington D.C., pp. 653–660, 1986.

[Heath 87a] M.T. Heath. "Hypercube Applications at Oak Ridge National Laboratory." In M.T. Heath (ed). *Hypercube Multiprocessors 1987.* SIAM, Philadelphia, 1987.

[Heath 87b] M.T. Heath and C.H. Romine. *Parallel Solution of Triangular Systems on Distributed-Memory Multiprocessors.* Oak Ridge National Laboratory Tech. Rep. ORNL/TM-10384, March 1987.

[Hillis 85] W.D. Hillis. *The Connection Machine.* MIT Press, Cambridge, MA, 1985.

[Jameson 84] A. Jameson, W. Schmidt, and E. Turkel. *Numerical Solutions of the Euler Equations by Finite Volume Methods Using Runge-Kutta Time-Stepping Schemes.* AIAA Paper 84-0430, 1984.

[Johnsson 85] S.L. Johnsson, Y. Saad, and M.H. Schultz. *Alternating Direction Methods on Multiprocessors.* YALEU/DCS/RR-382, Yale University, October 1985.

[Jurasek 86] D. Jurasek, W. Richardson, and D. Wilde. "A Multiprocessor Design in Custom VLSI." *VLSI Systems Design,* pp. 26–30, June 1986.

[Lim 87] D.S. Lim and R.V. Thanakij. "A Survey of ADI Implementations on Hypercubes." submitted to *Parallel Computing.*

[Locanthi 80] B.N. Locanthi. *The Homogeneous Machine.* Caltech Tech. Rep. 3759:TR:80, January 1980.

[Moler 86] C.B. Moler. "Matrix Computation on Distributed Memory Multiprocessors." In M.T. Heath (ed). *Hypercube Multiprocessors 1986.* SIAM, Philadelphia, 1986.

[Morrison 85] R. Morrison and S. Otto. *The Scattered Decomposition for Finite Elements.* Caltech Concurrent Computation Program Tech. Rep. C^{3}P-286, May 1985.

[Pease 77] M.C. Pease III. "The Indirect Binary n-Cube Microprocessor Array." *IEEE Trans. Computers,* vol. C-26, no. 5, pp. 458–473, May 1977.

[Rashid 86] R.F. Rashid. "From RIG to Accent to MACH: The Evolution of a Network Operating System." *Proc. 1986 Fall Joint Computer Conference,* IEEE Computer Society Press, pp. 1128–1137, 1986.

[Rosenberg 85] R. Rosenberg. "Supercube." *Electronics Week,* pp. 15–17, February 11, 1985.

[Seitz 84a] C. Seitz. "Concurrent VLSI Architectures." *IEEE Trans. Computers,* vol. C-33, no. 12, pp. 1247–1265, December 1984.

[Seitz 84b] C. Seitz and J. Matisoo. "Engineering Limits on Computer Performance." *Physics Today,* pp. 5–12, May 1984.

[Seitz 85] C. Seitz. "The Cosmic Cube." *Communications of the ACM,* vol. 28, no. 1, pp. 22–33, January 1985.

[Steele 85] C.S. Steele. *Placement of Communicating Processes on Multiprocessor Networks.* Caltech Tech. Rep. 5184:TR:85, April 1985.

[Spalart 83] P.R. Spalart, A. Leonard, and D. Baganoff. *Numerical Simulation of Separated Flows.* NASA TM-84328, 1983.

[Walton 87] S.R. Walton. "Fast Fourier Transforms on the Hypercube." In M.T. Heath (ed). *Hypercube Multiprocessors 1987.* SIAM, Philadelphia, 1987.

Parallel Architectures for Implementing Artificial Intelligence Systems

Kai Hwang

University of Southern California, Los Angeles, CA

Raymond Chowkwanyun

Symult Systems Corporation, Monrovia, CA

Joydeep Ghosh

University of Texas, Austin, TX

7.1 Introduction

This chapter assesses advanced architectures, technological bases, and knowledge engineering requirements for developing a new generation of computers for *artificial intelligence* (AI) applications [Hwang 87b]. Basic design issues of multiprocessors for AI applications have been introduced in Chap. 4. We focus here on parallel AI machine architectures including (1) *multiprocessors* which support interactive MIMD operations through a shared memory space; (2) *multicomputers* for supporting multiple SISDs via message passing among distributed processors with local memories; and (3) massively parallel architectures consisting of a large number of processor-memory nodes cooperating in an SIMD or multiple SIMD or MIMD fashion. AI machines are classified into four processing paradigms in Table 7.1. We start with some assessment of symbolic processing requirements, AI machine characteristics, and knowledge engineering. Then we proceed to evaluate different categories of AI machines.

TABLE 7.1   Major AI Machine Paradigms

Processing paradigm	Representative systems
AI language processing	Symbolics and ALICE
Knowledge engineering	Connection Machine and FAIM-1
Connectionist computations	Hypernet and Boltzmann machine
Vision and pattern recognition machines	Butterfly and Warp

7.1.1 Symbolic processing in AI

The acquisition, representation, and intelligent use of information [Wah 86] and knowledge is fundamental to AI processing. A system can acquire information from varied external sources: visual, vocal, and written. These inputs are often incomplete, imprecise, or even contradictory. Proper recognition and understanding of speech and images is required. At a higher performance level, intelligent machines should learn on their own by applying their cognitive capabilities to accumulated knowledge and experiences.

Knowledge representation involves encoding information regarding objects, relations, goals, actions, and processes into data structures and procedures. The encoding should facilitate the addition, alteration, and manipulation of knowledge. Prominent among current approaches to knowledge representation are *semantic nets, frames, scripts, objects, production systems, predicate logic,* and *relational databases* [Brachman 83].

AI processing is required for problem solving, making logical deductions, and retrieving information. Methods to achieve these include *state space traversal, problem reduction, forward and backward chaining, resolution, planning, heuristic search,* and *pruning* [Nilsson 80]. Most of these are I/O-bound; i.e., the amount of memory accesses and I/O activities required outweighs computational needs. Furthermore, the operations are often global and are carried out over large knowledge bases. Table 7.2 provides a summary of symbolic processing characteristics.

7.1.2 AI-oriented computers

A von Neumann architecture with centralized control presents a processor/memory bottleneck to intensive and irregular memory access patterns. The von Neumann bottleneck leads directly to a *hardware crisis* where we can foresee a time when the limitations of technology will prevent uniprocessors from delivering the execution speed demanded by future AI and other applications. *Parallel* and *distributed processing* offers one solution to this crisis. Many AI algorithms are *nondeterministic* in nature. Dynamic resource allocation and load balancing become crucial for AI information processing. Management

TABLE 7.2   Major Characteristics of Symbolic Processing

Knowledge representations:
 Lists, relational databases, scripts, semantic nets, frames, blackboards, objects, production rules, logic.

Commonly used operations:
 Search, sort, pattern matching, filtering, contexts and partitions,
 transitive closure, unification, retrieval, set operations, reasoning.

Memory requirements:
 Large memory with intensive access patterns. Addressing is often content-based. Locality of reference may not hold.

Communication patterns:
 Message traffic varies in size and destination; granularity and
 format of message units changes with application.

Properties of algorithms:
 Nondeterministic, possibly parallel and distributed computations. Data dependencies may be global and irregular in pattern
 and granularity.

I/O requirements:
 User-guided programs; user-oriented, intelligent person-machine
 interfaces; inputs could be graphical and audio as well as from
 keyboard; access to very large on-line databases.

Architecture issues:
 Consistent parallel update of large, possibly distributed knowledge bases; dynamic load balancing; intense global memory accesses; dynamic memory allocation; hardware-supported garbage
 collection.

of large knowledge bases is often required. Key issues in developing
AI-oriented computers include AI programming languages and their
applications, parallel algorithms for unification and logic programming, multiprocessing of combinatorial search problems, functional
programming systems, logic machine architectures, parallel production systems, semantic networks, distributed problem solving, logic
inference mechanisms, and intelligent person-machine interfaces. At
present, most AI architectures are software-oriented. Many new approaches to computer architecture have been proposed or experi-
mented with for AI systems. Candidate architectures include
*dataflow, reduction, direct-execution of high-level languages, data/
knowledge-base machines,* and *logic machines* [Wah 86].

We need intelligent computers for automated reasoning, automatic
programming, planning, problem solving, and theorem proving. In the
process of developing such systems, we hope to improve our understanding of cognition, learning, and reasoning in humans as well. Machines for knowledge base management and expert systems for consulting and computer-aided instruction help us in managing, pooling,
and using our huge warehouse of knowledge more easily and effec-

tively. The largest expert systems manipulate huge knowledge bases involving extremely complex interrelationships at an expert level. Such systems rely heavily on the use of efficient knowledge representations and inferencing mechanisms. Critical to these systems is the ability to capture and maintain the knowledge base and to explain its decisions to the human user. At present, the implementation of such systems is closely tied to the application domain. We would eventually like to create general expert systems capable of functioning in any application domain.

Our discussion will focus primarily on the execution mechanisms of AI machines at the expense of memory management. Principally this means a lighter coverage of the topic of garbage collection. In languages like Pascal and C, the user is responsible for run-time memory management. In Pascal this means allocating memory with the command *new* and reclaiming it with *release*. The corresponding C commands are *alloc* and *free*. AI systems relieve the user of such memory management chores to allow concentration on higher level concepts. As a result, AI systems generate a large number of objects at a high rate during run time. Moreover these objects tend to have short lifetimes; therefore efficient garbage collection is important to the smooth functioning of AI systems. The two major systems for garbage collection are *marking* and *reference counting*. A marking garbage collector traces the pointers from some group of known "live" objects, marking the objects as it goes. Unmarked objects are garbage and may be added to the free memory list. A reference-counting collector maintains a reference count for each object to track the number of pointers to the object. A reference count of zero indicates the object is garbage. Reference counting trades off memory for computation time as compared to marking [Cohen 81].

7.2   A Taxonomy of AI Machines

Four major classes of AI machines are identified below:

- Language-based machines
- Knowledge-based machines
- Connectionist machines
- Intelligent interface machines

Language-based AI machines are designed to efficiently execute Lisp, Prolog, or a functional language. *Knowledge-based* machines support a particular knowledge representation such as semantic networks, rules, frames, or objects. *Connectionist* machines take a radically different approach to knowledge representation: on such machines, knowledge is not represented by symbols, but by direct encoding into the pattern of interconnections between processing elements. *Intelligent interface* machines are specialized for person-machine interface applications.

The language-based paradigm is a conservative approach to AI machine design. In the case of Lisp and Prolog machines, the intent is to capitalize on the large libraries of existing software written in these languages. These libraries allow the machines to be applied rapidly without the need to first develop expensive software. Language-based machines are also flexible in supporting a wide variety of knowledge representations and heuristic search procedures. Applications developed on language-based machines are also more transportable. Any machine supporting the language of development can be used to execute the application.

The disadvantage of the language-based approach is that knowledge representations have to be written in the supported language. Therefore the language represents an extra layer of software between the application and the hardware. This extra layer exacts a penalty in the form of slower execution time. This observation leads to architectures in which knowledge representations are supported directly by the hardware, and the advantages of flexibility and transportability are traded off for faster execution time. Within this revolutionary approach to AI machine design, we have observed three distinct approaches which are discussed below.

The knowledge-based approach uses coarse-grained knowledge representations such as frames or objects. The inference steps are correspondingly large during the search for a solution. By contrast, a connectionist machine uses very fine grained knowledge representations. The inference steps are smaller and more numerous than for the knowledge-based approach. There is also a critical concept of cooperation and competition in the connectionist approach that is absent in the knowledge-based paradigm [Amari 82]. The processing elements in a connectionist architecture cooperate to solve a problem, but at the same time they may also compete with each other in proposing alternative solutions. The final solution to a problem is the end result of a complex process of cooperating and competing interactions between the processing elements of the connectionist machine. Finally, intelligent interface machines are specialized for person-machine interfaces. A variety of knowledge representations may be used by such a machine. These machines potentially represent the largest societal impact of all the AI machines, providing easy access to computers through the use of graphics and spoken language. For the computer professional, these machines may also play a vital role in solving the *software crisis* by providing hardware support for the burgeoning new trend in visual computing [Raed 85]. Orthogonal to the issue of whether an AI machine follows the language-based, knowledge-based, or intelligent interface paradigm is the implementation issue.

As shown in Fig. 7.1, an AI machine can be designed with a *top-down, middle-out,* or *bottom-up* methodology, which was treated in

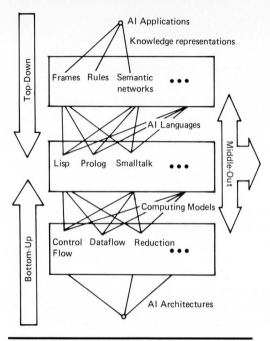

Figure 7.1 Three approaches to designing AI machines. [Wah 86]

Chap. 4. The top-down methodology is analogous to the life cycle model [Balzer 83] found in software engineering and begins with requirements' specification for the application being implemented and gradually works down to finer details until the hardware level is reached. The middle-out methodology is a shortcut to the top-down method. It starts with a well-established language or knowledge representation scheme. Working in the upward direction, the language is modified to fit the application. At the same time, work is done in the downward direction to design the hardware architecture support for the language. In the bottom-up method, the computer architect first selects a computational model (such as control flow, dataflow, or reduction). An architecture is then designed to implement the computational model, and finally software is built on top of the hardware to support the application.

7.2.1 Language-based AI machines

In the language-based approach the hardware supports a higher level language such as Lisp [Steele 84] or Prolog [Clocksin 84], and knowledge representations and inference mechanisms must be written in that language. Table 7.3 shows language-based machines characterized by the supported language and the implementation method. The most widely used AI machines at present are commercial Lisp machines such as Symbolics which are dominated by middle-out designs.

TABLE 7.3   Language-Based AI Machines

	Lisp	Prolog	Functional languages
Top-down approach	—	PIM [Tanaka 86]; PIE [Murakami 85]	—
Middle-out approach	Symbolics 3600 series [Moon 87]; Concert [Halstead 86]; Xerox 1100 series [Manuel 83]; TI Explorer [TI 84]; Fujitsu ALPHA [Hayashi 83]; SPUR [Hill 86]	Xenologic X-1 [Dobry 87]; PLM (Aquarius) [Dobry 85]	ALICE [Cripps 86]; C-Lisp machine [Vegdahl 84]
Bottom-up approach	Scheme 79 [Sussman 81]; Common Lisp chips [Hindin 86]	Tamura machine [Tamura 84]	Rediflow [Keller 84]; ZAPP [Vegdahl 84]

Important exceptions are the so-called Lisp on a chip implementations which are based on very large scale integration (VLSI) architecture. Scheme 79 was a university-based implementation of the Scheme dialect of Lisp. Texas Instruments (TI), Xerox, and Symbolics have all developed commercial VLSI implementations of the Common Lisp dialect. Preliminary reports suggest that the chips represent an application of VLSI technology to implement proven Lisp architectures rather than a major architectural innovation. We therefore believe the major impact of these chips will be to increase the availability of Lisp machines by lowering their cost while increasing their performance. The TI chip is a 32-bit processor clocked at 40 MHz which delivers 60 percent of the functionality of the Explorer. It is claimed to execute one Lisp instruction every clock cycle and to have five times the performance of the Explorer. The Symbolics chip is a 40-bit processor that implements a complete Lisp machine on a single chip. It is claimed to require only commercial memory chips to build a fully functional machine. A major feature of this chip is the implementation of 32-bit addresses allowing access to gigabyte-sized memories.

The only top-down implementations among the language-based machines are the Japanese Fifth-Generation Computer System project's PIM [Tanaka 86] and PIE [Murakami 85] architectures. The Xenologic X-1 [Dobry 87] is a coprocessor board for the Sun workstation that implements Prolog with extensions for Lisp. The PLM [Dobry 85] was the prototype for the X-1 and was developed as a coprocessor for the Aquarius machine. The Tamura machine implements Prolog on a conventional multiprocessor. The ALICE implements the functional language HOPE using graph reduction on a shared-memory multiprocessor [Cripps 86]. The C-Lisp machine

[Vegdahl 84] implements a version of pure Lisp in which operators with side effects have been removed and a number of operators to support parallel programming have been added. The Rediflow [Keller 84] uses graph reduction on a mesh-connected multicomputer. The ZAPP also uses graph reduction but with a hypercube as the machine architecture [Vegdahl 84].

7.2.2 Knowledge-based AI machines

There are three types of knowledge-based AI machines as summarized in Table 7.4. Rule-based expert systems use a knowledge base of *if-then* conditional rules together with a method for manipulating the

TABLE 7.4   Knowledge-Based AI Machines

Rule-based	Semantic networks	Object-based
DADO2 [Stolfo 87]; NON-VON [Shaw 85]; PSM [Gupta 86]	Connection Machine [Hillis 85]; NETL/Thistle [Fahlman 83]; SNAP [Moldovan 85]	FAIM-1 [Anderson 87]; Dorado [Deutsch 83]; SOAR [Ungar 87]

rules. Well-known systems include R1 and XSEL, which are used to configure VAX systems. Such systems are considered forward-chaining because they drive forward from facts to conclusions. The OPS5 language and its descendents were designed to implement a type of forward-chaining rule-based system known as production systems. The forward chaining is executed in a three-phase cycle of *match, select,* and *fire*. In the match phase, the *if* part of each rule is matched against a *working memory* of facts. The *if* part may have multiple conditional clauses, and more than one rule may match resulting in a set of *candidate* rules. One rule is selected from the candidate set in the select phase. The rule is then fired by adding the facts in its *then* clause to the working memory. The DADO2 exploits the inherent parallelism in the match phase where many rules must be matched against the facts in the working memory. The working memory is stored in a tree architecture, and matches are carried out in parallel as is updating the working memory after a rule has been fired. While exhibiting good support for production systems, the NON-VON supercomputer is proposed as a general-purpose AI machine [Shaw 85]. This claim is based on its capability for concurrent symbolic manipulation on a per-record basis, made possible by incorporating logic into memory. Both the DADO2 [Stolfo 87] and NON-VON are massively parallel machines which are intended to be implemented with tens of thousands of 8-bit processors. The PSM [Gupta 86] takes a diametrically opposed approach and is based on 32 to 64 very powerful ECL-based processors. The PSM reflects the influence of the Rete algorithm [Forgy 82], which speeds up sequential processing of OPS5 but reduces parallelism and the need for a large number of processors.

A semantic network is a directed graph in which nodes represent objects and the links specify relationships. A subset of such a network might read "elephant is a mammal" where "elephant" and "mammal" are nodes and "is a" is a link from "elephant" to "mammal." Knowledge retrieval from a semantic net can involve searching the entire network. If the desired fact is not stored explicitly, it may have to be deduced from other stored information. Programs for knowledge retrieval often spend most of their time repeating a few basic operations such as logic operations on sets, sorting, pattern matching against a set of assertions, and deducing facts from semantic inheritance networks. Speedup can be obtained by simultaneously initiating these operations from many nodes of the network. Ideally, each concept (node) should be allocated to a distinct processor and the interconnections between these processors should be flexible enough to represent the relationships between the corresponding concepts. The Connection Machine [Hillis 85] and NETL [Fahlman 83] are massively parallel fine-grain machines. The SNAP [Moldovan 85] is an array-structured machine for processing semantic networks and is designed for VLSI implementation.

The concept of objects [Stefik 85] has become increasingly important in software engineering as part of the response to the *software crisis.* Object-oriented facilities have been added to such languages as C with C++ [Stroustrup 86] and Objective-C [Cox 86] and to Lisp with Loops [Bobrow 86] and Flavors. Object-oriented software systems are characterized by four features:

- Information hiding
- Data abstraction
- Dynamic binding
- Inheritance

Information hiding refers to the bundling of related code and data into modules. To the external world the module appears as a black box, performing certain functions but with the internal implementation hidden. The external world is also barred from manipulating the internal data variables of a module. This prevents undesired side effects which result when distant parts of a program manipulate the same data objects. Information hiding is an important concept in software engineering and the realization of such goals as reuseable software modules. *Data abstraction* refers to user-defined data types which aid in compile-time detection of programming errors. Languages such as Modula-2 and Ada have the features of information hiding and data abstraction but lack dynamic binding and inheritance.

Dynamic binding is necessary to implement message passing and still have maintainable code. In object-oriented languages there are no procedure calls. Instead messages are sent to objects (modules) whose behaviors (internal code) then act on internal data objects and/or produce more messages. An example would be sending the message *write* to the objects *printer* and *CRT*. Each object contains the appropriate device drivers for their hardware equivalents, and the programmer is freed from attending to implementation-specific details. Dynamic binding facilitates the addition of new behaviors to an object because the language automatically binds messages to the appropriate code. Thus while a statically bound language like Modula-2 could implement message passing, the interface between the module and the outside world would have to be rewritten every time a new behavior is added, severely complicating the maintenance task. The flexibility characteristic of AI environments is also greatly curtailed, thus discouraging the freedom to experiment.

All objects are hierarchically organized into classes. Subclasses inherit the behaviors of their superclass. The *inheritance* feature can reduce the inferencing effort required of a system. For example we can infer many of the properties of a car through inheritance from the superclass of vehicles. This kind of inferencing cannot be accomplished in a flat knowledge base that is not hierarchically organized.

The FAIM-1 [Anderson 87] is a multicomputer system with a unique hexagonal mesh topology chosen for its fault tolerance, scalability, and planar characteristics. The FAIM-1 implements logic programming and procedural programming within an object-oriented framework. The Dorado [Deutsch 83] and SOAR [Ungar 87] both implement Smalltalk-80, the archetypical object-oriented language. We did not include these machines within the language-based machine category because of the highly object oriented nature of Smalltalk. The Dorado is a microcoded ECL-based single-user workstation. The SOAR is a RISC-based microprocessor with the same functionality and speed as the Dorado.

7.2.3 Connectionist systems

Connectionist systems [Fahlman 87] offer a radically different approach to AI problem solving. All other architectures described in this chapter are based on *symbolic processing,* where knowledge is represented by complex structures such as frames or rules. The structures are stored in memory, and the machines operate by reading and writing to memory. The connectionist school observes that applications such as image and speech understanding have not been well supported by symbolic manipulation. While symbolic systems have been built that support these activities, they do not deliver adequate performance and response times are long. The connectionist school believes that the symbolic approach is fundamentally flawed and that a new approach is needed.

Connectionist models and artificial neural systems are inspired by biological systems such as the brain, where knowledge is stored and processed by a large number of interconnected neurons. Neurons have elementary computational capabilities, but they operate in a highly parallel fashion. The cooperative and competitive processing of aggregates of neurons is fundamental to the functioning of the brain. Some of these approaches are explored in Chap. 16.

A connectionist architecture is distinguished by the use of connections, rather than memory cells, as the principal means of storing information. A connectionist system consists of a very large number of interconnected "neurons" or cells. Each connection has a *weight* associated with it, and the pattern of weights forms the knowledge representation. The connections connect a huge number of processing cells, each cell capable of performing only very basic operations such as bit comparison. The strength of connectionism is that the entire knowledge base can be brought to bear on a problem, since computation is explicitly governed by the interconnection weights. By contrast a symbolic machine can only bring to bear those representations which can be retrieved from memory.

Each cell or neuron in a connectionist system computes a weighted sum of the states of its neighbors. The new state of the cell is a function of this weighted sum and the previous state of that cell. Some of the popular models used for state update are given in Chap. 16. Typically, a *thresholding function* [Feldman 82] is used because they dampen spurious input signals. Thus each cell only needs to perform very simple arithmetic operations. The power of a connectionist system comes from its ability to simultaneously apply the entire knowledge base to the problem at hand. All the cells are concurrently active, and the computations are directly affected by the knowledge base encoded in the network links. Ideally, a connectionist system will return an answer in constant time regardless of problem size. However this presupposes that the ratio of the number of cells to the number of actual processing units remains bounded, irrespective of the size of the system.

Connectionist systems are inherently fault-tolerant. Since knowledge is encoded in the entire network of cells rather than in particular memory locations, the system is able to withstand the loss of individual cells without significant performance degradation. Fault tolerance also makes wafer scale integration possible since the system can automatically adjust to bad areas on the wafer [Bailey 87].

Connectionist architectures are weak in the area of programmability. The abandonment of symbolic representation means that encoding knowledge into a connectionist machine becomes very difficult. Maintenance also becomes difficult for the same reason. With possibly millions of cells and their connections forming the knowledge representation, it is clearly infeasible to modify knowledge directly by manipulating the individual cells. The solution proposed by the connectionist school is *self-learning,* whereby the machine itself encodes the knowledge using Hebb's rule, for example, or with the help of training sessions such as in backward propagation methods [Rumelhart 86]. Unfortunately the learning schemes that have been devised are either too slow to be practical or are unscalable to larger machine sizes. Further development of connectionist machines waits on the invention of an efficient scalable learning mechanism.

The difficulty of devising a good self-learning mechanism has forced a partial retreat in the connectionist position. They now admit that a machine that totally abandons symbolic representation may not be feasible. Symbolic representations may have to be used at an intermediate level. It is also conjectured that the human mind may use symbolic representations but that these representations are not accessible to the conscious mind.

A connectionist system can either be fully or virtually implemented in hardware. A full implementation provides a dedicated processor for each neuron or cell, and a dedicated physical link for each connection. Modest sized fully implemented analog systems have been realized on VLSI chips [Hecht-Nielsen 86]. Virtual systems time multiplex several neurons on each processor. The interconnection pattern, weights, and other system parameters are stored in local memories. The entire network is partitioned into groups, one for each processor. Connections among these groups are multiplexed over the physical interprocessor links. Thus, virtual systems take advantage of the much faster speeds of electronic systems as compared to biological systems in order to counter the complexities of the latter.

Connectionist systems can be hierarchical as in the Hypernet [Hwang 87a], which is a class of modularly extensible multicomputers. The Boltzmann machine [Fahlman 83], on the other hand, is nonhierarchical. It applies simulated annealing [Kirkpatrick 83] to allow the connectionist network to acquire new knowledge. Architecturally, they are also distinguished by being either *marker-passing* or *value-passing* machines. Markers are 1-bit tokens which get passed around from cell to cell. Values are atomic numbers such as integers. Structures such as arrays are not allowed. Machines could also be based on *message passing,* in which case the message could contain complex data structures. Message-passing machines are not generally considered to be connectionist in nature because the possibility of complex data structures requires each processing cell to provide a considerable amount of memory. This violates the basic assumption of connectionism that only very simple processing cells will be used.

7.2.4   Intelligent interface machines

AI systems often provide speech analysis, natural-language under-standing, image processing, and computer vision as intelligent inter-faces between people and computer. While proposed schemes for natural-language understanding are implemented in software at present, computer architectures have already emerged to support speech-understanding and image-understanding applications. Some of these systems are highlighted in Table 7.5. These systems are not

TABLE 7.5   Intelligent Interface Machines

Speech recognition	Pattern recognition and image processing	Computer vision
Harpy [Torrero 85]	Cytocomputer [Hwang 83]	Warp [Annaratone 86]
Hearsay-II [Torrero 85]	PIPE [Kent 85]	Butterfly [Crowther 85]
Dialog System 1800 [Torrero 85]	Pyramid [Tanimoto 84]	VICOM-VME [Pratt 85]
NEC DP-100 [Torrero 85]	Tospics [Hwang 83]	
	Pumps [Hwang 83]	
IBM Nat. Task [Torrero 85]	Zmob [Weiser 85]	

pure symbolic processors. Some carry out low-level processing of speech and images involving substantial numerical computation; pro-cessing of symbolic representations of phonemes and images is carried out at higher levels.

7.3   Language-Based Machines

Three language-based machines for Lisp, Prolog, and functional pro-gramming respectively are now presented in greater detail.

7.3.1   Lisp machines: Symbolics 3600 series

A Lisp program can be viewed as a set of functions in which data are passed from function to function. The concurrent execution of these functions forms the basis for parallelism. The applicative and recur-sive nature of Lisp requires an environment that efficiently supports stack computations and function calling. The use of linked lists as the basic data structure makes an automatic storage allocation mecha-nism with efficient garbage collection vital [Moon 87]. AI programs such as MACSYMA, which consists of about 230 kwords of compiled Lisp code, need a large memory space. Conventional computers fail to meet the above requirements. They also do not recognize untyped data objects efficiently. Thus, fast execution of Lisp necessitates novel architectures tailored to its specific requirements.

The Symbolics family of 3600 series machines provides a good example of the middle-out approach to AI machines [Symbolics 85]. Architecture development proceeds along three levels: *systems architecture, instruction architecture,* and *processor architecture* [Moon 87]. The systems architecture is the topmost level, the instruction architecture is at the middle level, and the processor architecture is the layout of hardware components. Each higher level is shielded from the level below it, so that upgrades can be incorporated without disturbing the expensive software assets accumulated at higher levels. In keeping with the middle-out approach, the systems architecture extends the basic Lisp language to provide a complete environment for program development with an overall goal of allowing safe programming practices without sacrificing speed. An example is type checking for compile-time error detection. Languages such as Pascal, Modula-2, and Ada provide the safety of type checking but at the expense of slower development because programmers must specify types explicitly. The Symbolics system's architecture guarantees automatic type checking but without the need for explicit user intervention. Safety is provided without compromising speed. The architecture also provides for incremental compilation so that each new function can be compiled independently of the rest of the program of which it is a part. This means that it is possible to rewrite a program in one display window while watching it execute in another window. Any modifications to the code are immediately reflected in the running program. Incremental compilation provides the rapid feedback and ease of debugging of interpreters without sacrificing the speed of compilers.

The instruction architecture must provide for fast function calling and efficient representations of lists in order to support Lisp. Fast function calling encourages programmers to structure their programs into small modular units which are interlinked by function calling to form the complete application program. Modular programming eases program maintenance, which accounts for the major share of software costs and the "software crisis." Without fast function calling, efficiency-minded programmers will collect their programs into large code blocks to minimize expensive function calls. These programs will be fast but difficult to maintain and test. Fast function calls are implemented by basing the instruction call architecture on a *stack machine* model. The control information needed to run a function is contained in a stack frame. Function calling is implemented by simply pushing another stack frame onto the control stack which takes one machine cycle (currently about 200 ns) [Symbolics 85]. Compiler design is considerably simplified since there is only one function calling

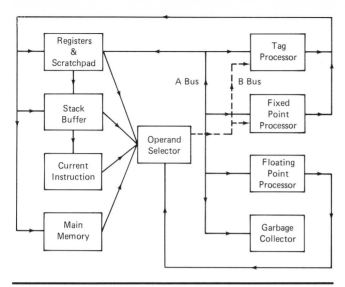

Figure 7.2 Symbolics 3600 series architecture. [Moon 87; Symbolics 85]

mechanism, there are no general-purpose registers to save, and there are no complex indirect addressing modes. Instructions are either 0-address or 1-address instructions. The 1-address instructions access operands from within a stack using an offset from the stack pointer register. Lists are the fundamental data structure in Lisp, and their implementation must allow for rapid access and compact storage. When memory is used for list representation, a 2-bit data tag is used as the *cdr* code.† This data tag halves the amount of data required to store a list representation. In effect a list is stored contiguously in memory instead of requiring that each cons cell store the address of its *cdr*.

The processor architecture is shown in Fig. 7.2. This is a stack-oriented machine rather than the pure stack machine assumed in the instruction architecture; i.e., most instructions fetch their operands from the stack but a few do not. The division of the overall machine architecture into layers allows the use of a pure stack model to simplify instruction set design while implementation is carried out with a stack-oriented machine. Nevertheless most operands will be fetched from the stack so the stack buffer and scratch-pad memories are implemented as fast caches to main memory.

Instruction prefetching is provided in all models. The most sophis-

---

†In Lisp terminology, the car of a list returns the first element of the list, while the *cdr* returns all elements except the first. A list is stored as a linked list of cons cells. Each cons cell contains a list element and a pointer to its *cdr*.

ticated model, 3675, provides a 1K-word instruction cache which is equivalent to 2K instruction words since two 17-bit instruction words are packed into each 34-bit logical word. This cache is sufficient to ensure that the execution pipeline is almost always busy.

The Symbolics executes most Lisp instructions in one machine cycle. An example is the addition of two 32-bit integers. To execute the addition, the operands are fetched from the stack buffer and the duplicate top of stack in the scratch-pad memory (Fig. 7.2). Dual buses allow both operands to be delivered simultaneously to the functional units. Floating-point add, garbage collection, data type checking by the tag processor, and fixed-point addition are carried out in parallel. The result of the floating-point unit will be discarded since the operands are integers in this example. Likewise the result of the fixed-point unit would be discarded if either operand were floating-point. Any errors cause a trap to the exception handler; e.g., the detection of arithmetic overflow would trigger a call to an addition routine for 64-bit integers. The stack pointer and frame pointer are contained in the miscellaneous registers structure.

The instruction set is designed to work with 36-bit words which are implemented in physical memory as 44-bit words. Seven of the extra bits are used for single error correction and double error detection with one spare bit. The maximum virtual memory is 256 Mwords with a maximum real memory of 7 Mwords. The stack buffer contains 1K words and the instruction cache on the 3675 model contains 1K words equal to 2K instruction words.

7.3.2   Prolog machines: PIM in japan

Interest in Prolog machines has increased because of the selection of Prolog as the prototype kernel language for the Japanese Fifth-Generation Computing System (FGCS) project. The execution of a *Prolog*-based program can be speeded up by exploiting various kinds of parallelism. *AND-parallelism* refers to the simultaneous execution of logically ANDed clauses. If two goals have variables in common, then a successful execution requires such variables to be bound to the same set of values in both clauses. This requires a consistency check, which in the worst case makes parallel execution as slow as a sequential one. Chapter 13 discusses *restricted* AND-parallelism, which exploits AND-parallelism without the overhead of consistency checking. Parallel evaluation of clauses is restricted to clauses which do not share a variable that has not been instantiated. In such cases, consistency errors cannot occur. It is estimated that this approach could yield parallelism on the order of hundreds of processors.

Alternatively, ANDed clauses with common variables can be

chained together in producer-consumer relationships to speed up serial AND evaluation. This *stream parallelism* is essentially macro-pipelining of variable binding to avoid the need for consistency checking. In the Tamura machine [Tamura 84], a parent process executing the query ? − p(X),q(X,Y). first spawns a child process p(X). While the child executes, the parent process goes into a wait state. Suppose the child now succeeds by binding X to the constant a. The child wakes the parent up and parallelism begins as the parent spawns a second child q(a,Y), which executes in parallel with the first child p(X). Further instantiations of X found by p are stored in a buffer, and when the second child eventually fails, the parent reads the next value of X from the buffer and restarts the second child. The parent always goes to a wait state after spawning or restarting the last created child, which is known as the youngest child. In this machine, only this youngest child may wake the parent up from the wait state. In our example this ensures that all possible Y solutions for X = a are found by q before going on to any new values of X found by p. X will be consistent across all clauses.

When the eldest child process p(X) fails, the parent continues to send any X values remaining in the buffer to the youngest child until the buffer is exhausted, at which time the youngest child fails and parent fails too. The PIM-R [Murakami 85] implements stream parallelism using message blackboards to hold the common variables and lists of suspended processes.

OR-parallelism refers to the concurrent search for alternate solution paths. The paths and their respective variable bindings are independent so no consistency check is required. In the earlier stages of research into logic machines, most designs were based on OR-parallelism rather than on AND-parallelism. OR-parallelism was believed to offer more parallelism and would also avoid the overhead of consistency checking. With more experience, it appears that a high degree of parallelism may not be possible [Onai 84], so the research emphasis is switching to AND-parallelism.

Finally, one can implement *unification parallelism,* which refers to the parallel matching of clauses in the Prolog database with the goal clause and the parallel instantiation of variables to constant values. The PIM and PIE [Tanaka 86] provide hardware for parallel matching goal clauses to clause heads in the knowledge base, as well as for parallel instantiation of variables.

The PIM is a multicomputer under development at ICOT in Japan. The PIM will implement OR-, AND-, and unification parallelism. The system consists of multiple inference modules, each with its own process pool and unification unit as shown in Fig. 7.3. The inference modules are linked by a dedicated network which allows for process

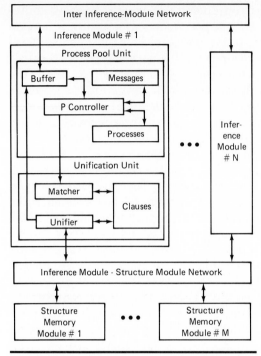

Figure 7.3 Parallel inference machine (PIM) in Japan. [Murakami 85]

migration. A separate network links the inference modules to multiple-structure memory modules which hold constant data that are lists, vectors, matrices, or other structured data.

7.3.3 Functional programming machines: ALICE

Functional programming languages have been proposed as solutions to both the *software crisis* and the *hardware crisis*. From this viewpoint, the software crisis arises from an overemphasis on the minutiae of *how to solve a problem* that is present in all imperative style languages such as Fortran. Programs become divorced from their specifications by the bulkiness of the code necessary to spell out in detail the steps to achieve a solution. As a result, program verification and maintenance become enormously expensive. Functional programming languages emphasize the question of *what is the problem?* rather than *how do you solve the problem?* A declarative style of programming is practiced where the specification itself becomes the program. The computer is expected to implement the necessary solution from a correct problem specification. This approach considerably simplifies the tasks of program verification and maintenance, which together make up the major portion of the software crisis.

The hardware crisis refers to the technological limitations on the speed of uniprocessor machines so that parallel machines must be used to achieve further speedup gains. Functional languages offer a solution because they are free of side effects and so allow the maximum exploitation of available parallelism. In a functional programming language there is no concept of state, time dependence, or storage. Instead functional languages are *referentially transparent* so that the meaning of a program statement can be determined entirely from its lexical (written) context without reference to the history of computation. Subprocedures may be evaluated on different processors without the need for costly synchronization. Moreover referential transparency makes possible powerful transformation techniques for code optimization. While optimizing compilers are also available for procedural languages like Fortran, the transformation techniques for functional languages have a stronger theoretical foundation and can more confidently be relied upon to preserve the meaning of the code during translation.

Functional languages become attractive for AI applications because they provide a friendly development environment coupled with fast execution speed. Programs can be written at a higher level, using a compact and lucid notation. However, they present efficiency problems when implementing inherently sequential algorithms and I/O operations, and handling of arrays. This, coupled with the high frequency of function calls, the garbage collection overhead, and the lack of destructive memory updating due to a single-assignment† policy, have given functional programs a reputation for running slowly. Whether parallel architectures and compiler techniques can exploit the inherent parallelism of functional programs to a degree sufficient to compensate for these problems remains an open research issue.

In demand-driven or lazy evaluation, a function is only evaluated when its result is needed as an argument by another function. The alternative is a bottom-up approach which evaluates a function as soon as all its arguments are available, and is called data-driven computation. Demand-driven evaluation requires more overhead than data-driven evaluation but allows better control of parallelism, more selective evaluation, and a natural way of handling infinite structures.

The *Applicative Language Idealised Computing Engine* (ALICE) is a middle-out design for a functional language machine [Darlington 81]. The target language is a purely functional language called HOPE [Pountain

---

†Single assignment means a variable can only be written once within a function call.

85], which has no side effects. A program consists of a set of function definitions. The user then proposes a function $f(x)$ to begin the evaluation.

At the logical level, the ALICE uses demand-driven graph reduction to evaluate functions. The history of function invocations is represented by a directed acyclic graph whose root is the original function given for evaluation. This function is *reduced* by *rewriting*. It is replaced by its code which is stored in the function-definition database. A node in the graph represents a function invocation and the directed arcs leading out of it point to its arguments. The graph reduction process ends when all leaf nodes can be evaluated to constants. These are then passed back to their parents until the final result is obtained at the root.

At the implementation level, the graph is represented by a set of packets. Each packet corresponds to a node in the logical graph. The format of a packet is shown below:

Identifier	Function	Argument list	Secondary fields

The identifier is a unique packet identifier, implemented as the memory address of the packet, so this field is actually empty. The function is implemented as the memory address of the function code. The argument list is a list of the identifiers of the function's arguments. Since an argument's identifier is its address, the identifier effectively serves as a pointer to the argument. The secondary fields contain control information such as status bits indicating whether the packet is reducible, and signaling information used to communicate when arguments have been evaluated. The logical evaluation graph can therefore be represented by a physical set of packets with the logical nodes mapped onto physical packets and the directed arcs represented by the argument lists of the nodes. If a very complex expression is required as the argument for multiple nodes, it would be expensive to duplicate the expression. Therefore common subexpressions are referenced by all parent packets (nodes) and are not copied.

The ALICE architecture is designed to implement efficient execution of graph reduction; the prototype is illustrated in Fig. 7.4a. Each processor contains five high-speed Transputers together with some cache memory. The interconnection network is a full crossbar implemented as a delta network using four-way crossbar switches as basic building blocks. The memory units have one Transputer and contain 2 Mbytes of storage. The prototype has 16 processors and 24 memory units. The ratio of processors to memory units was determined based on analytical modeling to determine the optimum balance. Informally, the processors can perform the simple rewrite operations very fast and

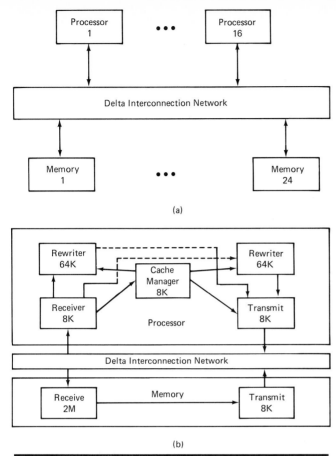

Figure 7.4   The ALICE multiprocessor. (*a*) The ALICE architecture; (*b*) Transputer implementation. [Cripps 86]

so are generally waiting on the availability of data which must be fetched via the network if there is a miss in the cache. Therefore a higher number of memory units is required to balance the processing and memory bandwidths.†

The internal structure of the processors and memories is shown in Fig. 7.4*b*. Two Transputers are dedicated to packet rewriting and each has 64K caches. A third Transputer is dedicated to managing the caches and guarantees that the code required for packet rewriting will be in the cache when a packet is rewritten. A fourth and fifth Transputer are dedicated to communicating through the interconnec-

---

†Older ALICE designs included two rings that connected the processors. These rings were separate from the main interconnection network. One ring was dedicated to circulating free packet identifiers and the other was dedicated to circulating the identifiers of rewritable.

tion network. One handles incoming packets and the other handles outgoing packets. The memory units are much simpler in design and contain only one Transputer.

HOPE is compiled into ALICE Compiler Target Language (CTL), which contains instructions for rewriting packets and generating argument packets. The Transputer with its RISC-based high-processing-rate design is the best off-the-shelf component to execute the simple CTL language and handle the high volume of dataflow involved in graph reduction. Nevertheless the Transputer is not ideal in that it has its own machine language OCCAM which must be used to interpret CTL instructions. Therefore it is envisaged that future versions of ALICE will be built from processor chips dedicated to executing the CTL language. In addition to HOPE a compiler is being built for the PARLOG [Clark 84] dialect of Prolog, which will compile into HOPE.

7.4   Knowledge-Based Machines

We will examine knowledge-based machines by considering three representative systems. DADO2 is designed to support production systems. It is based on a complete binary tree topology and features fast root to leaf communication. The Connection Machine is based on semantic networks. A fine-grained hypercube topology is used. The FAIM is a general-purpose AI machine based on both Lisp and Prolog. A fault-tolerant hexagonal mesh topology is used.

7.4.1   Rule-based production machines: DADO2

DADO2 is a top-down design for a production system machine [Stolfo 87]. A production system is rule-based and forward-chaining and has found widest application in expert systems. The system drives forward from facts, using a database of rules, to derive conclusions. The database of facts is called the *working memory* (WM), rules are known as *productions,* and the database of productions is called the *production memory* (PM). Productions have the form of if-then rules, but the conditional element of the *if* may consist of a complex compound condition. Similarly the *then* clause may consist of a complex compound of actions, all of which add or delete facts from the WM. The forward chaining is accomplished by a three-phase cycle:

1. *Match.*   The production memory is searched for productions whose conditions satisfy the facts in the working memory. More than one production may match.

2. *Select.*   The set of matching productions is called the *conflict set* and one element from the set is selected for execution.

3. *Fire.*   The actions in the then part of the selected production are taken, resulting in additions and deletions to the facts in the working memory.

At the middle level, DADO2 uses OPS5 as the language in which to represent production systems. In addition, compilers have been developed for parallel versions of PL/M, C, and Lisp. A parallel Prolog compiler has also been proposed. At the bottom level, DADO2 provides direct execution of the three-phase forward-chaining cycle.

DADO is actually a class of machine architectures of which DADO2 is the second implementation. Other implementations are DADO1 and DADO [Stolfo 87]. The DADO class of machines is characterized by a binary tree topology, fast broadcast from root to leaf, fast resolution for searching, and the ability to segment the tree into subtrees working in multiple SIMD fashion. Different implementations differ in the number of PEs and the granularity, memory capacity, and processing power of each PE. For example, the DADO2 is oriented toward execution of production systems and has medium grain, while the DADO/DSP is designed for speech recognition and has fine granularity.

The architecture of the DADO2 is shown in Fig. 7.5. DADO2 has 1023 nodes arranged in a 10-level binary tree. Figure 7.5 provides a functional representation of the tree and how it carries out its computation. Each node consists of an 8-bit microprocessor, 64K of RAM, and a switch. The switches can broadcast 1 byte from root to leaf in one instruction cycle. The speed of these switches is critical to the efficient running of the DADO2. In earlier DADO implementations, the microprocessor handled the switching tasks, and 14 instruction cycles were consumed at each level during the broadcast of a byte [Stolfo 84].

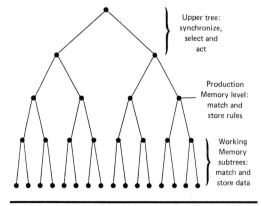

Upper tree: synchronize, select and act

Production Memory level: match and store rules

Working Memory subtrees: match and store data

Figure 7.5   Conceptual architecture of DADO.
[Stolfo 87]

DADO2 can segment itself into subtrees which can then work independently on matching productions. Each node can operate in either MIMD or SIMD mode. In MIMD mode a node will ignore all instructions from nodes higher up in the tree. In SIMD mode it obeys those instructions. SIMD is somewhat of a misnomer since the subtrees do not execute in synchronous lockstep as in true SIMD execution. Rather all nodes in the subtree execute the same instruction but at their own rate so that some nodes will finish before others. Figure 7.5 shows the upper levels of the tree performing the select and fire phases, together with synchronization. The middle level of the tree operates in MIMD mode during the match phase, and the leaves store the facts and carry out the lower level pattern matching. When the leaves complete their task, the results of successful matches are sent back up the tree. In effect DADO2 can function as a multiple-SIMD machine.

In addition to production systems, DADO2 has been proposed for any instance of the wider class of problems characterized as *almost decomposable searching problems*. As well as suggesting additional applications, the concept of almost decomposable problems gives some theoretical basis for the operation of DADO2. This approach is a generalization of the *decomposable searching problem* suggested for solution by systolic arrays of opposing trees [Bentley 78]. The searching problem is defined as answering queries about a set F of N objects organized into data structure D. The problem is characterized by the parameters S, the storage required by D to store F; P, the time required to construct D; and Q, the time required to answer a query by searching D. Therefore to find if x is in F, where F is a set of totally ordered integers and has the parameters $S = N$, then $P = O(N \log N)$ and $Q = O(\log N)$. Decomposable searching problems are amenable to solution by a divide-and-conquer strategy and so are well suited to the DADO class of architectures. The query is written as

$$Query(x,F) = B\ q(x,f)\ \text{for f in F}$$

B is the repeated application of a commutative binary operator; e.g., $Member(x,F) = OR\ equal(x,f)$ for f in F. The strategy in this case would be to evaluate the equal(x,f) in parallel and then combine the answers through the OR operator.

The benchmark test in Table 7.6 was a search of a relational database with 32-byte records. Both computers had about 16 Mbytes of main memory, and the 4381 was running IBM's SQL query language under the VM/CMS operating system. The timings are strictly for the search operation; all I/O times have been excluded. This is significant because it may take a considerable time to load the data into the DADO2 since data

TABLE 7.6   Comparative Performance of IBM 4381 and DADO2 in Database Search Excluding I/O Times

Number of records	IBM 4381, s	DADO2, s	Speedup
1000	0.042	0.0056	7
4000	0.141	0.0224	6
8000	0.265	0.0448	6

SOURCE: Stolfo [87].

transfers take place a byte at a time.† In these examples the problem size matches the machine size so that the number of records is an integral multiple of the number of DADO2 PEs. There is a possibility of performance degradation near the boundaries when the problem size does not match machine size so neatly. That is, if 1050 records were to be searched, about 20 PEs would have 2 records and the remaining 1000 or so would have 1 record.

Do the low speedup times imply nonlinear speedup? That is, why is the DADO2 with 1023 PEs not 1000 times faster than the IBM 4381? The IBM 4381 is a large minicomputer, whereas the DADO2 PEs are 8-bit microprocessors. Therefore it is not possible to conclude from this test whether speedup is linear or not.

In Table 7.7, the DADO2 is compared to the VAX 750 in the execution of production systems. The VAX 750 had a 6-Mbyte main memory running OPS5 under Unix 4.2. (We assume that I/O times have again been excluded, although the report does not explicitly state this.) In addition to the speedup data, the number of productions, facts, and PEs utilized is also shown. In general, the greater the ratio of facts to productions, the greater the degree of parallelism in the match phase and the greater the speedup. The Mud production system has a low ratio of facts to productions and has the lowest speedup. However, this relationship is not absolute since the Waltz system has a higher ratio of facts to productions than Mud but the speedup is no greater.

Several researchers have suggested that massive parallelism in the style of DADO2 is ineffective in speeding up the execution of production systems [Gupta 84]. They observe that the new facts added by the firing of a production results in only minor changes in the *conflict set* of rules selected during the match phase. The change in the conflict set is called the *affect set*. The Rete algorithm [Forgy 82] was invented to exploit this behavior and speed up sequential execution of production systems. The algorithm calculates the affect set at each rule fir-

---

†If we assume a cycle time of 1.8 μs [Stolfo 84], it would take 57.6 s to load one thousand 32-character records or approximately 10,000 times longer than the actual searching time. $57.6 = 0.0018 \times 1000 \times 32$.

TABLE 7.7   Relative Performance of VAX 750 and DADO2 for OPS5

System name	No. of rules	No. of facts	DADO PEs Used	VAX 750, s	DADO2, s	Speedup
Mapper	237	528	287	68.119	6.696	7
Monkeys	13	12	13	2.240	754	3
Puzzle1	13	65	137	313.344	28.663	11
Puzzle2	13	65	137	313.344	17.850	18
Puzzle3	13	65	438	313.344	10.028	31
Waltz	33	50	50	77.350	34.873	2
Mud	884	241	943	675.172	338.844	2

SOURCE: Stolfo [87].

ing and avoids searching through the entire database during the match phase. The typical size of the affect set is about 30 productions for the 2000-production R1 system. The size of the affect set and the potential parallelism is almost constant and does not increase significantly as the number of productions increases. Therefore the conclusion is that production systems are best speeded up by using 50 to 100 very fast processors to exploit the parallelism available [Forgy 84]. Additional processors would only remain idle.

The DADO team's response to these observations has been to develop program transformation techniques that increase the available parallelism. Complex productions requiring more processing time than other productions are duplicated with additional control information [Ishida 85]. Work is also under way to develop parallel rule firing production systems. The team also suggests that a style of programming weighted toward exploiting the sequentially oriented Rete algorithm may also result in less parallelism. A style of programming oriented toward the massive parallelism style of DADO2 would more fully be able to exploit its potential.

7.4.2   Semantic network machine: Connection Machine

The Connection Machine was conceived at MIT's AI Laboratory [Hillis 85] for concurrent manipulation of knowledge stored in semantic networks. Figure 7.6a shows the block diagram of the system constructed by Thinking Machines Corporation at Cambridge, Massachusetts [TMC 87]. This is an SIMD machine having 64K simple processor/memory cells linked by a 12-dimensional hypercube network. The hypercube topology is distinguished by its symmetry, small diameter, and multiplicity of paths between any two nodes and is amenable to a layout with high packing density and short average wire length. Each vertex of the hypercube consists of a custom CMOS chip containing 16 processors and a hardware router. Each processor has 4K bits of memory for a total system memory of 32 Mbytes

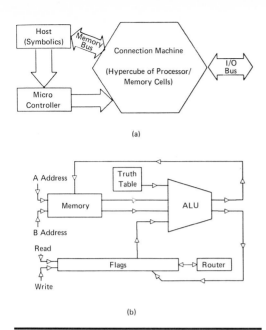

Figure 7.6   The Connection Machine. (*a*) Connection Machine system architecture; (*b*) single processing cell. [Thinking Machines Corp. 87]

[Waltz 87]. The processing cells are logically connected in data-dependent patterns which are used to both represent and process the data. The external host computer stores these data structures in the connection machine, orchestrates their activities, and reads the results. The connection machine can also transfer data to and from peripheral devices directly by using a high-bandwidth I/O channel.

The microcontroller converts high-level instructions from the host into sequences of simpler instructions that can be executed directly by the processors. For example, the host might specify a 32-bit addition sequence by a single command to the microcontroller, which would translate it into 32 individual bit operations to be executed directly by the cells. Thus the microcontroller acts effectively as a bandwidth amplifier for the instruction stream coming from the host. Figure 7.6*b* shows the interior design of a single processor cell [Hillis 85]. All data paths are 1 bit wide. Each processor has only 16 bits of state information, stored in 16 one-bit flags. The processor cell has an extreme RISC architecture with only one simple but powerful instruction. This instruction takes in three 1-bit operands, two from the 4K-bit external memory and one flag, and produces two output bits, one to be written in the external memory and the other to update a flag. The outputs are found by a memory/flag table lookup. One of 256 possible functions is chosen from each table. All processors receive the same instruction from the control unit, but each processor can be independently masked off, if so desired. The chip control unit decodes nanoinstructions received through the instruction pins and produces signals to control the processor array and the router, using an externally supplied clock for synchronization.

Within a chip, the processors are connected by a 4 × 4 mesh. Each processor cell can communicate directly with its north, east, west, and south neighbors. The router is responsible for routing messages between chips. Suppose a processor P(i,j) on chip i wants to communicate with processor P(k,l) on chip k. It first sends the message to the router R(i) on its own chip, using a simple hand-shaking mechanism. This router forwards the message to router R(k) on chip k. Finally, R(k) delivers the message to the appropriate memory location. The routing algorithm used by the router moves messages across each of the 12 dimensions of the hypercube in sequence. If there are no conflicts, a message will reach its destination within one cycle of this sequence, since any vertex of the cube can be reached from any other by traversing no more than 12 edges.

Programs for knowledge retrieval often spend most of their time repeating a few basic operations such as logic operations on sets, sorting, pattern matching against a set of assertions, and deducing facts from semantic inheritance networks. Speedup can be obtained by simultaneously initiating these operations from many nodes of the semantic network. Ideally, each concept (semantic node) should be allocated to a distinct processor and the interconnections between these processors should be flexible enough to represent the relationships between the corresponding concepts. This requires a large number of processor elements with programmable logical connections so that the topology can be configured to suit the problem. If the silicon area is limited, the processors must be simple and have little local memory, and the interconnection network should be regular. However, the memory is now distributed throughout the machine and is more intelligent because it can modify itself in many places simultaneously through the local processors. The fundamental inefficiency of the von Neumann memory, where only a few locations can change state at any given time, is thus avoided. The above considerations are reflected in proposed massively parallel, fine-grained architectures.

Reflecting the above logical scheme, the Connection Machine assigns a semantic node to a logical cell. This might be the same as one physical processor/memory cell for simple nodes with little representational or processing requirements, or a set of interconnected cells serving as a logical unit to represent a more complicated semantic node. Relationships among nodes are represented by logical connections among the corresponding processor/memory cells using pointers stored in the memory. Problems which are not expressed in the semantic network framework but require massively parallel searching/matching are also suitable for the Connection Machine. Thus for the object recognition problem, the entire tree of possible object interpretations is loaded into the Connection Machine before run time and the search done in one step (constant time). In case the problem size is too large to fit in the Connection Machine, it can be solved by dynamically allocating and deallocating processors as follows: The connection machine is loaded with as many levels of the tree as can fit. A parallel pruning is done, and the processors which are pruned out are deallocated and are utilized in the next iteration as new branches of trees from the processors which still represent consistent pairings. For fast execution of such large problems, the Connection Machine should have enough processing cells to match their size. The Connection Machine, once fully completed, may use over a million cells to handle some AI problems.

Since each cell can perform only extremely simple tasks, the real power of the Connection Machine derives from its ability to store information in the reconfigurable virtual interconnection patterns among the cells, and from the concurrent execution of the same simple operation on a very large number of cells. The Connection Machine has been used for object recognition [Stanfill 86a] and unstructured text retrieval [Stanfill 86b]. While these problems were not expressed in terms of a semantic network, they require sorting and searching on the same intensive scale as for processing semantic nets. There is also a profound change in the type of algorithms which are meaningful for this machine. For example, one may no longer need to presort a large set of data in the order in which it is needed, since the Connection Machine can sort its entire memory in 30 ms.

7.4.3   Object-oriented machines: FAIM-1

The FAIM-1 is an object-oriented machine implemented with the middle-out approach [Anderson 87]. The middle-level language paradigm selected is an object-oriented programming language called Our Intermediate Language (OIL). The motivation for the design of OIL is the observation that some AI problems are best expressed in a logic programming language while others are best expressed in a procedural language. OIL attempts to bring both programming styles together within an object-oriented framework.

Two major object classes are *logical OIL,* a Prolog-like language, and *procedural OIL,* a Lisp-like language. Logical OIL excludes operations with side effects such as *assert* and *retract* in order to preserve the maximum parallelism. Parallel execution of logical OIL is based on OR-parallelism and limited AND-parallelism. AND-parallelism is only allowed when the variables in the ANDed clauses are independent and expensive consistency checking is not required. In addition the user can specify consumer and producer variables so that stream parallelism can be implemented. (See Sec. 7.3.2 for a discussion of OR- and AND-parallelism). Logical OIL also provides a packaging mechanism for rules which is not available in regular Prolog. Packages are in keeping with the object-oriented style of programming and are important for modular software development and good software engineering. Procedural OIL is a modification of the lexically scoped T dialect of Lisp. In procedural OIL, T is extended with parallel control and data structures, operations on parallel data structures, and user-specified parallel evaluation strategies.

At the top level, the FAIM-1 is intended to be a general-purpose AI machine capable of addressing a wide range of applications. At the bottom level, the FAIM-1 is a message-passing multicomputer with no shared memory. The multicomputer nodes are connected in a hexagonal mesh topology chosen for its fault-tolerant characteristics [Gordon 84]. Such a hexagonal mesh is shown in Fig. 7.7a for an E-3 *surface,* where the 3 indicates the number of nodes on each hexagonal edge. The basic mesh is augmented with wraparound connections which reduce mesh diameter and make the mesh symmetrical so that every node has exactly six neighbors. An E-n surface has a diameter of n-1, and each wrap is twisted by n-1 increments. In the figure only one of the three sets of wraparound connections is shown. These wraparound connections are implemented by means of three-way switches attached to the edge nodes and shown as triangles in the figure. The corner nodes have three switches, and the other edge nodes have two switches.† Each switch has one internal port connected to its node, one external port that can either function as an I/O port or a connect to another surface, and one port for the wraparound connection.

Several hexagonal surfaces may be joined together as in Fig. 7.7b. There are wraparound connections internal to each surface as discussed above. In addition there are wraparound connections external to each surface that connect the surfaces together. These external wraparound connections are implemented by connecting the external ports of the switches on the outer edges of each surface. These external wraparound connections are necessary to keep the network diameter small. A smaller diameter can be achieved by constructing a large network out of smaller surfaces than by building a single monolithic surface. A 58,381-processor E-140 surface has a diameter of 139, while a 58,807 processor built from 217 E-10 surfaces has a diameter of 89.

---

†This is because each node must have exactly six neighbors. A corner node is internally connected to three nodes; therefore the remaining three nodes must be connected by wraparounds. Similarly the internal edge node has four internal neighbors and so must be connected to two other nodes by wraparound.

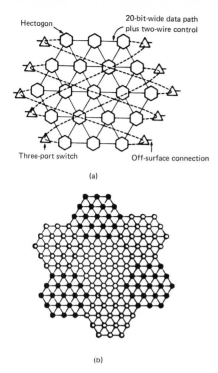

Hectogon

20-bit-wide data path
plus two-wire control

Three-port switch

Off-surface connection

(a)

(b)

Figure 7.7 The architecture of FAIM-1. (*a*) A wrapped hexagonal E-3 surface; (*b*) an S-2 tessalation of E-3 surfaces.

Each node consists of six bus-connected coprocessors which are briefly described here. The *evaluation processor* is a stack processor oriented toward Lisp and Prolog processing. (For a discussion of stack processors for Lisp see Sec. 7.3.1.) The *switching processor* manages rapid context switching for saving and restoring register memory. The *instruction stream memory* is a specialized memory that performs retrieval and partial instruction decoding as well as conventional storage duties. The scratch random-access memory is the basic local memory for the node and is multiported for access by the evaluation processor, switching processor, bus, and *post office*. The *pattern-addressable* memory is an associative memory used to support unification in Prolog. (For a discussion of unification see Sec. 7.3.2.) The post office handles all communications for the node and is the only topology-dependent coprocessor. Thus with appropriate modification of the post office, it would be possible to use the basic node architecture to build multicomputers with other topologies such as trees and hypercubes. The node is designed for efficient evaluation of logical and procedural OIL. All coprocessors operate asynchronously.

FAIM-1 relies on a host processor such as a Lisp machine to perform compilation of OIL programs. The compiler has the primary responsibility for allocating code to nodes. The philosophy of FAIM-1 is that programmer-directed resource allocation is unrealistic for large programs while extensive dynamic load balancing incurs too much overhead. Therefore the primary focus is on static load-balancing techniques with limited dynamic load balancing and some programmer provided directives.

7.5   Connectionist and Intelligent Interface Machines

Most connectionist systems are currently implemented by simulating their behavior on a uniprocessor or on bus-based architectures using a small number of off-the-shelf processors. Massively parallel machines that exploit the high degree of concurrency in connectionist models are being explored at several research centers [Hammerstrom 86]. The hypernet series of massively parallel architectures for connectionist computations [Hwang 87*b*] is presented below. We also present the BBN Butterfly processor to illustrate the use of an intelligent interface machine for vision applications.

7.5.1   Connectionist machine: Hypernet

To exploit the high parallelism inherent in the connectionist models of computation, a connectionist machine should not only have a large number of fine-grained processors, but should also have an interconnection network capable of catering to the high volume of interprocessor communication. A modular and extensible architecture makes it possible to choose a system size commensurate with anticipated problem sizes so that the goal of constant time computation is met.

The influence of the design goals mentioned above is clearly seen in a class of modularly extensible architectures called *hypernets,* which can be synthesized from identical VLSI modules. Figure 7.8 shows two such modules, namely, *buslets* and *cubelets.* Each node consists of an elementary processing unit, a small local memory, and a switch for communicating with other nodes through bidirectional links or shared buses. If a link is used for connecting to another node within the same module, it is an *internal link;* otherwise it is called an *external link.* When a basic module is incorporated as part of a bigger network, the external links are used for a direct linkage with another module, or for interfacing with the external world. Each such module is targeted for implementation on a small chip set using VLSI/WSI technology, so that a medium-sized hypernet built out of these modules can be fabricated on a few PC boards.

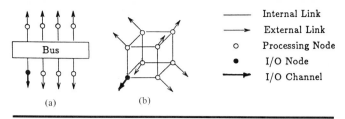

Figure 7.8 Building blocks for hypernet. (*a*) A buslet; (*b*) a 3-cubelet. [Hwang 87]

An *n-cubelet* is obtained by augmenting an *n*-dimensional hypercube with one extra "external" link per node. A (*d,h*)-*net* is a hypernet constructed with *d*-cubes and having *h* hierarchical levels. Figure 7.9 shows a (3,3)-net. This hypernet has three levels of hierarchy. It is constructed by interconnecting eight (3,2)-subnets, such that there is exactly one direct link between any two of these subnets. Each (3,2)-subnet is in turn constructed from four 3-cubelets in a similar fashion, as can be seen from the expanded view of subnet 011 in Fig. 7.9. A (3,3)-net thus uses a total of 32 cubelets to yield a multicomputer network with 256 nodes. Note that some external links have not been used for interconnecting nodes within the (3,3)-net. These links are available for making connections with other (3,3)-nets to form a (3,4)-net, or as extra I/O links.

Hypernets built with identical blocks have a *constant node degree*. Links once connected are left undisturbed when the network grows in size. Hypernets offer dense local connectivity. In the synthesis process, exactly half of the external links of a cubelet are used for connections within the same (3,2)-subnet or as a dedicated I/O channel for that subnet. Similarly, half of the remaining links are used to connect to nodes belonging to other (3,2)-subnets, when forming a hypernet at the next hierarchical level. Thus the *connectivity among nodes* in a hypernet *decreases in higher dimensions,* unlike in a hypercube where the connectivity is constant for all dimensions. This implies a significant reduction in hardware.

Nodes dedicated to I/O are provided in a systematic manner. Not only does every cubelet have a dedicated I/O node, but there is an additional node with a dedicated I/O channel for each (*d,i*)-subnet ($2 \leq i < h$) of a (*d,h*)-net. These nodes can link with secondary storage devices, a host computer, or other multicomputer systems. Communication efficiency is improved by traversing local links more often than remote connections.

A layout of a hypernet aims to keep all modules belonging to the same subnet as physically close as possible. Suppose we want to build

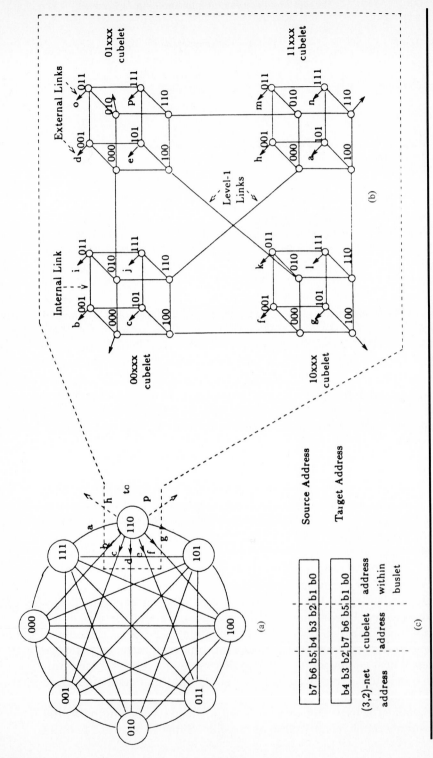

Figure 7.9 Construction of a (3,3)-net with eight (3,2)-nets. (a) Topology of a (3,3)-net consisting of eight (3,2)-subnets; (b) (3,2)-subnet with 110 prefix; (c) address mapping. [Hwang 87]

a hypernet with 64K nodes, using 5-cubelets as building blocks. In view of current technology, the following limits are assumed:

Maximum nodes/clip   =   32   (area-limited)

Maximum I/O pins/chip   =   256   (pin-limited)

Maximum chips/board   =   256   (area-limited)

Maximum I/O ports/boards = 2400   (connector-limited)

Under the above limitations, a (5,1)-net can be implemented on a chip. Suppose each bidirectional link needs two I/O pins, namely serial-in and serial-out. Then four (5,2)-nets can be implemented on a single board, and 32 boards are required to accommodate all 64K nodes, as shown in Table 7.8. In contrast, consider a hypercube of the same size and with 2-bit-wide links. Only a 3-cube is implemented on a chip since a 4-cube will require $16 \times 2 \times 12 = 384$ I/O pins, which exceeds the limit. A 7-cube can be accommodated on a board by barely meeting the I/O connector limit. The total number of boards required is 16 times, and the number of interboard connections is almost 18 times that for the hypernet. This is largely because pinout limitations become crucial, which further underscores the importance of reducing the number of off-chip and off-board connections.

When highly interconnected, fine-grain units are used as the basic modules, the resulting hypernets have attractive features for supporting distributed connectionist models and as a virtual neurocomputer [Hecht-Nielsen 86]. Examples of such modules would be high-dimensional cubelets, buslets, and a set of nodes connected as a complete graph or a complete bipartite graph. The modules should have as many links per node as practically feasible under the state-of-the-art technology and economic constraints. The local memory of each node is used to store the states and the weighted connectivity matrix of all

TABLE 7.8   Processor Distribution and I/O Demands in Hypercube vs. Hypernet Multicomputers with 64K PEs

Size	No. of processing elements		No. of I/O pins or off-board connectors used	
	Hypernet	Hypercube	Hypernet	Hypercube
Per chip	32 (one (5,1)-net)	8 (one 3-cube)	64 (pins)	208 (pins)
Per board	2048 (four (5,2)-nets)	128 (one 7-cube)	2164 (connectors)	2304 (connectors)
Overall system	2^{16} (32 boards)	2^{16} (512 boards)	69,248	9×2^{17}

the neurons assigned to it. The states are updated using multiplexing and pipelining.

When layered value-passing networks are mapped onto hypernets, clusters within the same layer are mapped onto nearby nodes. Most connectionist models exhibit a high degree of spatial locality [Bailey 87]. Local broadcast communication can efficiently handle the large fan-out of local communications. Point-to-point communication is resorted to for the few remaining long-distance connections. The subnets form natural broadcast domains. The natural communication patterns for hypernets corresponds to a low, uniform traffic superimposed on a high volume of traffic local to each module. Thus they provide a good match for neural networks within current technological constraints. The presence of I/O nodes throughout the hypernet is useful for supporting the intensive I/O operations needed for error detection and feedback.

Sophisticated cognition models involve simultaneous and mutually reinforcing recognition of features at multiple levels of abstraction. In visual recognition, for example, high-level and low-level routines cooperate and compete with each other in coming to a global comprehension of a scene. Connectionist networks corresponding to such situations involve *layers* of nodes with arbitrary *interlevel constraints* and interactions. In a simple pyramidal structure, nodes in one layer are directly connected only to nodes in the two layers directly below and above them. This is clearly inadequate for complicated multilevel interactions. When a hypernet is viewed as a multilevel hierarchy, some nodes serve as virtual nodes at several levels. These nodes are prime candidates for mapping connectionist units which are simultaneously operative at various levels.

A major drawback of distributed connectionist representations is that they are hard for an outside observer to understand or to modify. This necessitates some *automatic learning* scheme. Learning schemes employed at present use *backward error propagation* or stochastic methods. They are extremely slow, even for modest examples, and scale poorly. A practical solution is to partition large networks into smaller modules that can learn more or less independently of one another. Hypernets provide subnets of various sizes within which one can constrain error propagation or simulated annealing search to speed up the learning process.

7.5.2 Vision machine: BBN Butterfly

The BBN Labs in Cambridge, Massachusetts, have developed a tightly coupled, shared-memory multiprocessor system for numerical supercomputing as well as computer vision applications. This system, called the Butterfly Parallel Processor, is an MIMD computer with up to 256 processor nodes [BBN 85]. The processor nodes are identical, each consisting of a Motorola 68020 with 68881 floating-point coprocessor and 4 Mbytes of local memory on a single board. The processor is rated at 1 MIP, giving a total peak system throughput of 256 MIPs and a 1-Gbyte system memory [Rettberg 86]. Each processor can access its local memory directly, and when accessed through a multistage butterfly switching network, the local memories collectively form a globally shared memory space. Typically it takes about 2 μs to complete a local memory access and about 6 μs to access a remote memory via the network.

The Butterfly's operating system, Chrysalis, provides a distributed execution environment in which tasks can be distributed among the processors without much concern about the physical distribution of the data sets. The system is designed to support C, Lisp, and Modula-2 languages.

In 1987, the Butterfly switch had a bandwidth of 32 Mbits/s. The computing power is attained through a balanced match among the processor/memory nodes, switch, and I/O capacities. The system performance is almost linearly scalable with the number of processors [Rettberg 86]. The Butterfly does not suffer from universal performance degradation due to *hot spot* [Phister 85] memory contention. A hot spot is a slight nonuniformity in memory reference patterns on the order of 0.125 percent. Such hot spots cause severe performance degradation in shared-memory multiprocessors with a multistage network. Moreover, the tree saturation effect causes performance degradation even for accesses to cold spots. The Butterfly has a nonblocking switch so that in case of a memory access conflict one of the memory accesses is rerouted rather than having to wait for the chosen memory access to complete [Thomas 86]. No tree saturation effect results, and so cold spot access remains unimpaired.

The Butterfly switch uses packet switching techniques to support interprocessor communication. Each switching node is a 4×4 crossbar switch implemented on a VLSI chip. Eight VLSI switch chips are packaged on a single board to form a 16×16 switch. These boards can be combined to form a fully connected packet switching network of the desired size. For example, four 16×16 Butterfly switches and 16 additional 4×4 switch elements can be used to form a three-stage Butterfly switch for a system of 64 processor/memory nodes as shown in Fig. 7.10 [Crowther 85].

Research with the Butterfly multiprocessor is presently being conducted within BBN, Inc., and at the University of Rochester under an NSF/CER grant. The BBN researchers are concentrating on the development of distributed hardware/software systems and on the efficient programming of such a parallel system. Efforts at Rochester include artificial intelligence and computer vision. The Butterfly machine is especially attractive for solving large-grain problems which demand

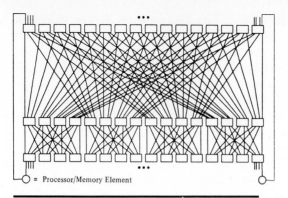

= Processor/Memory Element

Figure 7.10   The architecture of a 64-node Butterfly multiprocessor. [BBN 87]

general interconnects among the processors. The Connection Machine also supports general connect, but it is more tuned toward fine-grain problems.

Real-time computer vision has been identified as one of the major applications of the Butterfly processor [Brown 85]. Real-time vision demands ultra-high speed. The vision process involves image processing at a lower level and pattern recognition at a higher level. The former demands extensive fine-grain numerical computation, whereas the latter demands a high degree of symbolic processing via some syntactic or semantic analysis of the feature-extracted images. Both levels of vision algorithms are being implemented on the Butterfly machine. Research topics include vision control mechanisms, special data structures such as resolution pyramids, and the development of a distributed programming environment. A connectionist model has been suggested to simulate human vision processing on the Butterfly machine. A Lisp-based ISCON simulator is under development for this purpose. Besides vision and AI, the Butterfly is also being considered for solving simultaneous linear equations and the implementation of finite-element methods. Other reported benchmark results for a 256-node Butterfly include matrix algebra, histogramming, region relabeling, two-dimensional convolution, and integer selection and summation [BBN 85].

7.6   The Future of AI Machines

The development of AI machines takes place against the larger backdrop of software and hardware crises. The term *software crisis,* first coined in the late 1970s, refers to the decline in programmer productivity with increasing project size. A large program in this frame of reference means more than 1 million lines of code for present technologies. Examples include the software for the space shuttle and the proposed Strategic Defense Initiative (SDI) Star Wars control system. By contrast, UNIX 4.2 consists of about 300,000 lines of code and would be considered only a medium-sized system. Hardware crisis refers to a time when VLSI circuit technology will no longer be able to deliver further increases in uniprocessor speed. That day can already be foreseen.

AI machines may be able to contribute to the solution of both crises. A good system specification is widely recognized as one of the keys to successfully building a large software system [Basili 84]. AI machines can provide a platform for rapid prototyping of large software systems in an environment rich with support tools and safety mechanisms. Programmers can work out system specifications quickly and with confidence in the correctness of their work. An example of a system developed in this way is KEE, which was originally developed on Lisp machines and then ported to the C language for execution on conventional architectures [Fikes 85]. At the same time techniques developed to solve the software and hardware crises may also be of use in the development of AI machines. Both conventional computers and AI machines would benefit from a cross-fertilization of ideas. From this point of view, knowledge engineering is more than software engineering, but only by a little bit. In fact, software engineers have expressed serious concerns about the reliability of knowledge engineering systems [Parnas 85]. Developers of knowledge engineering systems and the AI machines which support them should not lose sight of the benefits of techniques employed in more mundane disciplines.

The AI machine designs that we have surveyed concentrate on providing hardware support for the inferencing mechanism even though knowledge representation is recognized to be the central element of AI systems. Few results have been obtained in the area of efficient representation of knowledge structures. We therefore expect to see more efforts directed toward this area. This issue was addressed with the introduction of the hypernet class of hierarchically structured architectures. The hypernet architecture is designed to accommodate the software structure of object-oriented knowledge systems.

Connectionist systems represent an alternative approach to AI which does not rely on symbolic processing. Instead intelligent behavior is elicited from the interactions of a large number of fine-grained processors. There is no direct mapping of symbols onto processors. It is the combined action of the processors according to learned behavior patterns that leads to intelligent behavior. Connectionist systems are a promising approach in the areas of image and speech understanding, which seem to resist the symbolic approach [Feldman 82]. The major research challenge for connectionism is to discover efficient learning mechanisms. Current learning algorithms are too slow for practical use.

There is a strong trend toward trying to exploit VLSI technology in building AI machines. Machines such as FAIM-1 are being designed with planar topologies to make *wafer scale integration* (WSI) possible. The DADO2 uses simple 8-bit microprocessors which could also be implemented with WSI. VLSI implementation faces a *scaling bottleneck*, which means that as the number of internal components rises, the ratio of control lines to internal elements decreases. This implies that off-chip controls must be at a higher level and that the internal hardware will self-organize and self-repair in response to internal hardware failures.

The trend toward highly parallel architectures as a solution to the von Neumann processor/memory bottleneck may cause a new bottleneck, the *I/O bottleneck,* to surface. The problem of how to load possibly thousands of nodes with code and data has not been addressed in the literature, yet it represents a major practical problem in the operation of highly parallel machines. The issue is usually ignored with the researchers concentrating exclusively on execution performance without regard for I/O processing time. While it is conceivable that each node be accorded its own mass storage system, at some point there is always the bottleneck of the single human user. When the machine needs to communicate interactively with the user, there always exists a situation of multiple outputs converging on a single point and the need to distribute inputs to multiple destinations.

The development of fifth-generation computers was motivated by the combination of parallel processing hardware with AI software. It has been projected that the sixth-generation computer will be based on cooperative efforts in AI, brain theory, and cognitive science [Arbib 87]. Forty years have passed from the early days of using computers for data processing to today's knowledge processing. It may take several more generations of coordinated human efforts to develop machines with AI approaching natural intelligence. In Chap. 16, emerging new computing technologies aimed at this long-term goal will be presented.

Bibliography

[Amari 82]   S. Amari. "Competitive and Cooperative Aspects in Dynamics of Neural Excitation and Self-Organization." In M.A. Arbib (ed). *Competition and Cooperation in Neural Nets.* Springer-Verlag, New York, NY, 1982.

[Anderson 87]   J.M. Anderson, W.S. Coates, A.L. Davis, R.W. Hon, I.N.Robinson, S.V. Robison, and K.S. Stevens. "The Architecture of the FAIM-1." *IEEE Computer,* vol. 20, no. 1, pp. 55–65, January 1987.

[Annaratone 86] M. Annaratone, E. Arnould, T. Gross, H.T. Kung, M.S. Lam, O. Menzilcioglu, K. Sarocky, and J.A. Webb. "Warp Architecture and Implementation." *Proc. 13th Annual International Symposium on Computer Architecture,* pp. 346–356, June 1986.

[Arbib 87] M.A. Arbib. *Vision, Brain and Cooperative Computation.* MIT Press, Cambridge, MA, 1987.

[BBN 85] BBN Labs., Inc. "Benchmark Results for a 256-Node Butterfly Parallel Processor." *Newsletter, Computer Architecture Technical Committee,* pp. 121–124, IEEE Computer Society, September/December 1985.

[Bailey 87] J. Bailey, D. Hammerstrom, and M. Rudnick. "Interconnect Architectures for WSI Neurocomputers." *Tech. Report,* Oregon Graduate Center, Beaverton, OR, May 1987.

[Balzer 83] R. Balzer, T.E. Cheatham, and C. Green. "Software Technology in the 1990's: Using a New Paradigm." *IEEE Computer,* vol. 16, no. 11, pp. 39–45, November 1983.

[Basili 84] V.R. Basili and B.T. Perricone. "Software Errors and Complexity: An Empirical Investigation." *Communications of the ACM,* January 1984.

[Bentley 78] J.L. Bentley. "Decomposable Searching Problems." *Information Processing Letters,* pp. 244–250, June 1978.

[Bobrow 86] D.G. Bobrow, K. Kahn, G. Kiczales, L. Masinter, M. Stefik, and F. Zdybel. *Common Loops: Merging Lisp and Object-Oriented Programming,* Xerox Palo Alto Research Center, 1986.

[Brachman 83] R.J. Brachman and B.C. Smith (eds). *Special Issue on Knowledge Representation, IEEE Computer,* vol. 16, no. 10, October 1983.

[Brown 85] C.M. Brown, C.S. Ellis, J.A. Feldman, T.J. LeBlanc, and G.L. Petersen. "Research with the Butterfly Multicomputer." *Newsletter, Computer Architecture Technical Committee,* pp. 46–66, IEEE Computer Society, September/December 1985.

[Clark 84] K. Clark and S. Gregory. "Note on System Programming in PARLOG." *Proc. International Conference on Fifth Generation Computer Systems,* pp. 299–306, ICOT and North-Holland, 1984.

[Clocksin 84] W.F. Clocksin and C.S. Mellish. *Programming in Prolog,* Springer-Verlag, New York, NY 1984.

[Cohen 81] J. Cohen. "Garbage Collection of Linked Data Structures." *ACM Computing Surveys,* pp. 341–367, September 1981.

[Cox 86] B. Cox. *Object-Oriented Programming: An Evolutionary Approach.* Addison-Wesley, Reading, MA, 1986.

[Cripps 86] M.D. Cripps, A.J. Field, and M.J. Reeve. "The Design and Implementation of ALICE: A Parallel Graph Reduction Machine." In S. Eisenbach and C. Sadler, (eds). *Functional Programming: Languages, Tools and Architectures,* Ellis Horwood Ltd., London, England, 1986.

[Crowther 85] W. Crowther, J. Goodhue, R. Gurwitz, R. Rettberg, and R. Thomas. "The Butterfly Parallel Processor." *Newsletter, Computer Architecture Technical Committee,* pp. 18–45, IEEE Computer Society, September/December 1985.

[Darlington 81] J. Darlington and M. Reeve. "ALICE: A Multiprocessor Reduction Machine for the Parallel Evaluation of Applicative Languages." *ACM/MIT Conference on Functional Programming Languages and Computer Architecture,* 1981.

[Deutsch 83] L.P. Deutsch. *The Dorado Smalltalk-80 Implementation: Hardware Architecture's Impact on Software Architecture.* Addison-Wesley, Reading, MA, 1983.

[Dobry 85]   T.P. Dobry, A.M. Despain, and Y.N. Pratt. "Performance Studies of a Prolog Machine Architecture." *Proc. 12th Annual International Symposium on Computer Architecture,* pp. 180–190, June, 1985.

[Dobry 87]   T. Dobry. "A Coprocessor for AI; LISP, Prolog and Data Bases." *COMPCON Spring,* pp. 396–403, 1987.

[Fahlman 83]   S.E. Fahlman and G.E. Hinton. "Massively Parallel Architectures for AI: NETL, THISTLE and BOLTZMANN Machines." *Proc. National Conference on Artificial Intelligence,* pp. 109–113, 1983.

[Fahlman 87]   S.E. Fahlman and G.E. Hinton. "Connectionist Architectures for Artificial Intelligence." *IEEE Computer,* vol. 20, no. 1, pp. 100–109, January 1987.

[Feldman 82]   J.A. Feldman and D.H. Ballard. "Connectionist Models and Their Properties." *Cognitive Science,* vol. 6, no. 3, pp. 205–254, 1982.

[Fikes 85]   R. Fikes and T. Kehler. "The Role of Frame-Based Representation in Reasoning." *Communications of the ACM,* pp. 904–920, September 1985.

[Forgy 82]   C.L. Forgy. "Rete: A Fast Algorithm for the Many Pattern/Many Object Pattern Match Problem." *Artificial Intelligence,* pp. 17–37, September 1982.

[Forgy 84]   C.L. Forgy, A. Gupta, A. Newell, and R. Wedig. "Initial Assessment of Architectures for Productions Systems." *National Conference on Artificial Intelligence,* pp. 116–120, August 1984.

[Gordon 84]   D. Gordon, I. Koren, and G.M. Silberman. *Fault-Tolerance in VLSI Hexagonal Arrays,* Computer Science Technicon, Haifa, Israel, 1984.

[Gupta 84]   A. Gupta. "Implementing OPS5 Production Systems on DADO." *International Conference on Parallel Processing,* pp. 83–91, 1984.

[Gupta 86]   A. Gupta, C. Forgy, A. Newell, and R. Wedig. "Parallel Algorithms and Architectures for Rule-Based Systems." *Proc. 13th Annual International Symposium on Computer Architecture,* pp. 28–39, June 1986.

[Halstead 86]   R. Halstead, Jr., T. Anderson, R. Osborne, and T. Sterling. "Concert: Design of a Multiprocessor Development System." *Proc. 13th International Symposium on Computer Architecture,* pp. 40–48, June 1986.

[Hammerstrom 86]   D. Hammerstrom, D. Maier, and S. Thakkar. "The Cognitive Architecture Project," *Computer Architecture News,* vol. 14, pp. 9–21, 1986.

[Hayashi 83]   H. Hayashi, A. Hattori, and H. Akimoto. "ALPHA: A High-Performance LISP Machine Equipped with a New Stack Architecture and Garbage Collection System." *Proc. 10th Annual International Symposium on Computer Architecture,* pp. 154–161, 1983.

[Hecht-Nielsen 86]   R. Hecht-Nielsen. "Performance Limits of Optical, Electro-Optical, and Electronics Neurocomputers." *Internal Report,* TRW Rancho Carmel AI Center, San Diego, CA, 1987.

[Hill 86]   M. Hill et al. "Design Decisions in SPUR." *IEEE Computer,* vol. 19, no. 11, pp. 8–22, November 1986.

[Hillis 85]   W.D. Hillis. *The Connection Machine.* MIT Press, Cambridge, MA, 1985.

[Hindin 86]   H.J. Hindin. "Silicon Software Tackles AI Problems." *Computer Design,* pp. 42–50, March 15, 1986.

[Hwang 83]   K. Hwang (ed). "Special Issue on Computer Architectures for Image Processing." *IEEE Computer,* vol. 16, no. 1, January 1983.

[Hwang 87a]   K. Hwang and J. Ghosh. "Hypernet: A Communication-Efficient Architecture for Constructing Massively Parallel Computers." *IEEE Trans. Computers,* vol. C-36, no. 12, pp. 1450–1466, December 1987.

[Hwang 87b]   K. Hwang, J. Ghosh, and R. Chowkwanyun. "Computer Architectures for Artificial Intelligence Processing." *IEEE Computer,* vol. 20, no. 1, pp. 19–27, January 1987.

[Ishida 85]   T. Ishida and S.J. Stolfo. "Towards the Parallel Execution of Rules in Production System Programs." *International Conference on Parallel Processing,* pp. 568–575, August 1985.

[Keller 84]   R.M. Keller, F.C.H. Lin, and J. Tanaka. "Rediflow Multiprocessing." *Proc. COMPCON Spring,* pp. 410–417, July 1984.

[Kent 85]   E.W. Kent, M.O. Shneier, and R. Lumia. "PIPE: Parallel Image-Processing Engine." *J. Parallel and Distributed Processing,* pp. 50–78, February 1985.

[Kirkpatrick 83]   S. Kirkpatrick, C.D. Gelatt, and M.P. Vecchi. "Optimization by Simulated Annealing." *Science,* vol. 220, no. 4589, pp. 671–680, 1983.

[Manuel 83]   T. Manuel. "Lisp and Prolog Machines are Proliferating." *Electronics,* pp. 266–271, November 1983.

[Moldovan 85]   D.I. Moldovan and Y.W. Tung. "SNAP: A VLSI Architecture for Artificial Intelligence Processing." *J. Parallel and Distributed Processing,* vol. 2, no. 2, pp. 109–131, May 1985.

[Moon 87]   D.A. Moon. "Symbolics Architecture." *IEEE Computer,* vol. 18, no. 6, pp. 43–52, January 1987.

[Murakami 85]   K. Murakami, K. Kakuta, R. Onai, and N. Ito. "Research on Parallel Machine Architecture for Fifth-generation Computer Systems." *IEEE Computer,* vol. 18, no. 6, pp. 76–92, June 1985.

[Nilsson 80]   N.J. Nilsson. *Principles of Artificial Intelligence.* Tioga Press, Palo Alto, CA, 1980.

[Onai 84]   R. Onai, H. Shimizu, K. Masuda, and M. Aso. *Analysis of Sequential Prolog Programs,* ICOT Research Center, Tokyo, Japan, 1984.

[Parnas 85]   D.L. Parnas. "Software Aspects of Strategic Defense Systems." *Communications of the ACM,* pp. 1326–1335, December, 1985.

[Phister 85]   G.F. Phister and A. Norton. "Hot Spot Contention and Combining in Multistage Interconnection Networks." *1985 International Conference on Parallel Processing,* pp. 790–797, August 1985.

[Pountain 85]   D. Pountain. "Parallel Processing: A Look at the ALICE Hardware and HOPE Language." *Byte,* vol. 10, no. 5, pp. 385–395, May 1985.

[Pratt 85]   W.K. Pratt. "A Pipeline Architecture for Image Processing and Analysis." *Proc. Workshop for Computer Architecture for Pattern Analysis and Image Database Management,* pp. 516–520, November 1985.

[Raed 85]   "A Survey of Current Graphical Programming Techniques." *IEEE Computer,* vol. 18, no. 8, pp. 11–25, August 1985.

[Rettberg 86]   R. Rettberg and R. Thomas. "Contention Is No Obstacle to Shared-Memory Multiprocessing." *Communications of the ACM,* pp. 1202–1212, December 1986.

[Rumelhart 86]   D.E. Rumelhart, G.E. Hinton, and R.J. Williams. "Learning Internal Representations by Error Propagation." In D.E. Rumelhart, J.L. McClelland and the PDP Research Group (eds). *Parallel Distribution Processing: Explorations in the Microstructure of Cognition,* Bradford Books/MIT Press, Cambridge, MA, 1986.

[Shaw 85]   D.E. Shaw. "NON-VON's Applicability to Three AI Task Areas." *Proc. 9th International Joint Conference on Artificial Intelligence,* pp. 61–70, August 1985.

[Stanfill 86a]   C. Stanfill and D. Waltz. "Toward Memory-Based Reasoning." *Communications of the ACM,* pp. 1213–1228, December 1986.

[Stanfill 86*b*]   C. Stanfill and B. Kahle. "Parallel Free-Text Search on the Connection Machine System." *Communications of the ACM,* pp. 1229–1239, December 1986.

[Steele 84]   G.L. Steele, Jr. *Common LISP.* Digital Press, Bedford, MA, 1984.

[Stefik 85]   M. Stefik and D. Bobrow. "Object-Oriented Programming: Themes and Variations." *AI Magazine,* pp. 40–61, Winter 1985.

[Stolfo 84]   S.J. Stolfo and D.P. Miranker. "DADO: A Parallel Processor for Expert Systems." *International Conference on Parallel Processing,* pp. 74–82, August 1984.

[Stolfo 87]   S.J. Stolfo. "Initial Performance of the DADO2 Prototype." *IEEE Computer,* vol. 20, no. 1, pp. 75–83, January, 1987.

[Stroustrup 86]   B. Stroustrup. *The C++ Programming Language.* Addison-Wesley, Reading, MA, 1986.

[Sussman 81]   G.J. Sussman, J. Holloway, G.L. Steele, Jr., and A. Bell. "Scheme 79— Lisp on a Chip." *IEEE Computer,* vol. 14, no. 7, pp. 10–21, July 1981.

[Symbolics 85]   *Symbolics Technical Summary.* Symbolics, Inc., Cambridge, MA, October 1985.

[TI 84]   *TI Explorer Technical Summary.* Texas Instruments, Dallas, TX, 1984.

[TMC 87]   *Connection Machine Model CM-2 Technical Summary.* Thinking Machines Corp., Cambridge, MA, April 1987.

[Tamura 84]   N. Tamura and Y. Kaneda. "Implementing Parallel Prolog on a Multiprocessor Machine." *Proc. International Symposium on Logic Programming,* pp. 42–48, May 1984.

[Tanaka 86]   H. Tanaka. "A Parallel Inference Machine." *IEEE Computer,* vol. 17, no. 5, pp. 48–54, May 1986.

[Tanimoto 84]   S.L. Tanimoto. "A Hierarchical Cellular Logic for Pyramid Computers." *J. Parallel and Distributed Processing,* vol. 1, no. 1, pp. 105–132, August 1984.

[Thomas 86]   R. Thomas. "Behaviour of the Butterfly Parallel Processor in the Presence of Memory Hot Spots." *1985 International Conference on Parallel Processing,* pp. 46–50, August 1986.

[Torrero 85]   E.A. Torrero. *Next-Generation Computers.* IEEE Press, New York, NY, 1985.

[Ungar 87]   D. Ungar and D. Patterson. "What Price Smalltalk?" *IEEE Computer,* vol. 20, no. 1, pp. 67–74, January 1987.

[Vegdahl 84]   S.R. Vegdahl, "A Survey of Proposed Architectures for the Execution of Functional Languages." *IEEE Trans. Computers,* vol. C-33, no. 12, pp. 1050–1071, December 1984.

[Wah 86]   B. Wah and G.-J. Li (eds). *Computers for Artificial Intelligence Applications.* IEEE Computer Press, Washington, D.C., 1986.

[Waltz 87]   D.L. Waltz. "Applications of the Connection Machine." *IEEE Computer,* vol. 20, no. 1, pp. 85–97, January 1987.

[Weiser 85]   M. Weiser, S. Kogge, S. McElvany, R. Pierson, R. Post, and A. Thareja. "Status and Performance of the ZMOB Parallel Processing System." *COMPCON Spring,* pp. 71–73, 1985.

8

Comparison of the Cray X-MP-4, Fujitsu VP-200, and Hitachi S-810/20[†]

Jack J. Dongarra and Alan Hinds

Argonne National Laboratory, Argonne, IL

8.1   Introduction

In the fall of 1985 we ran a set of programs, gathered from major Argonne computer users, on the then current generation of supercomputers: the Cray X-MP-4 at Cray Research Inc. in Mendota Heights, Minnesota; the Fujitsu VP-200 at the Fujitsu plant in Numazu, Japan; and the Hitachi S-810/20 at the Hitachi Ltd. Kanagawa Works in Kanagawa, Japan. Recently the NEC corporation provided us with timings of the same set of programs on their NEC SX-2 computer. We have included architectural data and program timings for the SX-2 in our tables, but we received the SX-2 data too late to include in our comparative analysis. We have updated our tabular data and descriptions of the Cray X-MP-4 and Fujitsu VP-200 computers to reflect the models offered in the fall of 1987. But all our program timings and conclusions are based on the models we actually benchmarked in 1985.

8.2   Architectural Overview

The Cray X-MP, Fujitsu VP, and Hitachi S-810 computers are all high-performance vector processors that use pipeline techniques in

†Work supported in part by the Applied Mathematical Sciences subprogram of the Office of Energy Research, U.S. Department of Energy, under Contract W-31-109-Eng-38.

both scalar and vector operations and permit concurrent execution by independent functional units. All three machines use a register-to-register format for instruction execution. Each machine has three vector load/store techniques—contiguous element, constant stride, and indirect address (index vector) modes. All three are optimized for 64-bit floating-point arithmetic operations. Outstanding features and major differences in these machines are discussed below and summarized in Table 8.1 at the end of this section.

8.2.1   Cray X-MP

The Cray X-MP-4 (Fig. 8.1) is the largest of the family of Cray X-MP computer models, which range in size from one to four processors and from 4 to 16 million words (Mwords)† of central memory. The Cray X-MP/48 computer consists of four identical pipelined processors, each with fully segmented scalar and vector functional units with an 8.5-ns clock cycle. All four processors share in common an 8-Mword, high-speed (34-ns cycle time) bipolar central memory, a common input/output (I/O) subsystem, and an optional integrated solid-state storage device (SSD). Each processor contains a complete set of registers and functional units, and each processor can access all of the common memory, all of the I/O devices, and the single (optional) SSD. The Cray X-MP-4 vector register set—512 words per processor—is the smallest in this study.

The four Cray central processing units (CPUs) can process four separate and independent jobs, or they can be organized to work concurrently on a single job. This document will focus on the performance of only a single processor of the Cray X-MP-4, as none of our benchmark programs were organized to take advantage of multiple processors. Thus, in the tables and text that follow, all data on the capacity and the performance of the Cray X-MP-4 apply to a single processor, except for data on the size of memory and the configuration and performance of I/O devices and the SSD.

The Cray X-MP-4 has extremely high floating-point performance for both scalar and vector applications and both short and long vector lengths. Each Cray X-MP processor has a maximum theoretical floating-point result rate of 235 MFLOPS for overlapped vector multiply and add instructions. With the optional solid-state storage device installed, the Cray X-MP-4 has an I/O bandwidth of over 2.4 Gbytes/s, the largest in this study; without the SSD, the I/O bandwidth is 424 Mbytes/s, but only 68 Mbytes/s is attainable by disk I/O. The Cray DD-49 disks have the fastest single disk data transfer rate (9.6 Mbytes/s) in this study. The Cray permits a maximum of four disk de-

---

†Throughout this chapter the term *word* always means a 64-bit unit of storage.

TABLE 8.1   Overview of Machine Characteristics

Characteristic	Cray X-MP-4	Fujitsu VP-200	Hitachi S-810/20	NEC SX-2
Number of processors	4	1	1	1
Machine cycle time	8.5 ns vector; 8.5 ns scalar	7.0 ns vector; 14 ns scalar	14 ns vector; 28 ns scalar	6 ns
Memory addressing	Real	Modified virtual	Modified virtual	Modified virtual
Maximum memory size	16 Mwords	128 Mwords	32 Mwords	32 Mwords
Optional SSD memory	32–512 Mwords	n*64 Mwords	32–128 Mwords	16–1024 Mwords
SSD transfer rate	256 Mwords/s	1.5 Mwords/s	128 Mwords/s	167 Mwords/s
I/O-memory bandwidth	50 Mwords/s	12 Mwords/s	12 Mwords/s	12 Mwords/s
Per processor:				
CPU-memory bandwidth	353 Mwords/s	570 Mwords/s	570 Mwords/s	1333 Mwords/s
Scalar buffer memory	64 words, T register	8192 words cache	32,768 words cache	8192 words cache
Vector registers	512 words	8192 words	8192 words	10,240 words
Vector pipelines:				
Load/store pipes	2 load; 1 store	2 load/store	3 load; 1 load/store	8 load/4 store
Floating-point multiply and add	1 multiply; 1 add	1 multiply/add; 1 add	2 add; 2 multiply/add	4 add; 4 multiply
Peak vector (multiply and add)	235 MFLOPS	855 MFLOPS	855 MFLOPS	1333 MFLOPS
Cooling system type	Freon	Forced air	Air and radiator	Water
Operating systems	Cray-OS (batch); CTSS (interactive); UNICOS	VSP (batch); MVS/XA; MVS/TSO	HAP OS	SXOS
Front ends	IBM; CDC; DEC; Data General; Univac; Apollo; Honeywell	IBM-compatible	IBM-compatible	Built-in (control processor)
Vectorizing languages	Fortran 77; C	Fortran 77	Fortran 77	Fortran 77 (on arithmetic processor)
Other high-level languages	Pascal, Lisp	Any IBM-compatible	Any IBM-compatible	Pascal, Lisp, Prolog (on control processor)
Vectorizing tools	Fortran compiler	Fortran compiler; FORTUNE; interactive vectorizer; batch vectorizer	Fortran compiler; Vectorizer	Fortran compiler; Vectorizer/SX; Analyzer/SX; Optimizer

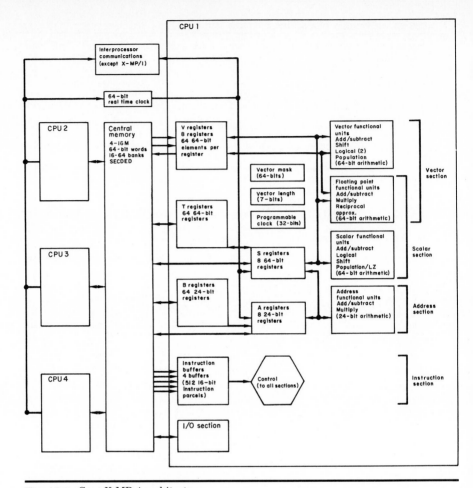

Figure 8.1 Cray X-MP-4 architecture.

vices on each of eight disk control units, the smallest disk subsystem and disk I/O bandwidth in this study. The cooling system for the Cray X-MP-4 is refrigerated liquid freon.

The Cray X-MP-4 operates with the Cray operating system (COS), a batch operating system designed to attach by a high-speed channel or hyperchannel interface with a large variety of self-contained, general-purpose front-end computers. All computing tasks other than batch compiling, linking, and executing of application programs must be performed on the front-end computer. Alternatively, the Cray X-MP-4 can operate under UNICOS (derived from AT&T UNIX System V) or CTSS (Cray Time-Sharing System, available from Lawrence Livermore National Laboratory), both full-featured interactive systems with background batch computing. The primary programming languages for the Cray X-MP are Fortran 77 and Cray assembly language (CAL); the Pascal, C, and Lisp programming languages are also available.

The Cray X-MP-4 model timed in this study had a 9.5-ns CPU clock cycle and 8 Mwords of 38-ns cycle time bipolar memory. The theoretical floating-point result rate of the timed machine was only 210 MFLOPS (per processor), about 90 percent of the result rate of the currently offered model.

8.2.2 Fujitsu VP-200 (Amdahl 1200)

The Fujitsu VP-200 (Fig. 8.2) is midway in performance in a family of four Fujitsu VP computers, whose performance levels range to over 1.7 GFLOPS. In North America, the Fujitsu VP-200 is marketed and maintained by the Amdahl Corporation as the Amdahl 1200 Vector Processor. Although we benchmarked the VP-200 in Japan, the comparisons in this document will include the configurations of the VP-200 offered by Amdahl in the United States.

The Fujitsu VP-200 is a high-speed, single-processor computer, with up to 128 Mwords of fast (56-ns cycle time) static MOS central memory. The VP-200 has separate scalar (14-ns clock cycle) and vector (7.0-ns clock cycle) execution units, which can execute instructions concurrently. Memory over 32 Mwords is only addressable by the vec-

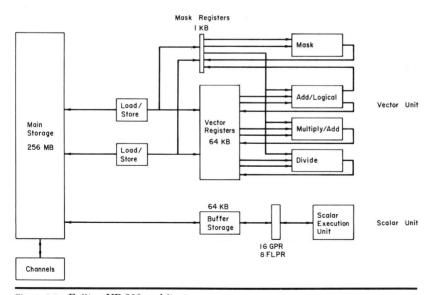

Figure 8.2 Fujitsu VP-200 architecture.

tor execution unit. A unique characteristic of the VP-200 vector unit
is its large (8192-word) vector register set, which can be dynamically
configured into different numbers and lengths of vector registers.

The VP-200 has a maximum theoretical floating-point result rate of
855 MFLOPS for overlapped vector multiply and add instructions (two
multiply and four add results per cycle). The VP-200 system is cooled
entirely by forced air.

The Fujitsu VP-200 scalar instruction set and data formats are fully
compatible with the IBM 370 instruction set and data formats; the
VP-200 can execute load modules and share load libraries and
datasets that have been prepared on IBM-compatible computers. The
Fujitsu VP-200 uses IBM-compatible I/O channels and can attach all
IBM-compatible disk and tape devices and share these devices with
other IBM-compatible mainframe computers. Fujitsu does not offer an
integrated SSD for the VP computer series; but optional Fujitsu SSDs
can attach to standard VP channels and emulate standard IBM-
compatible disk devices. Also, central memory can be used for virtual
I/O at full memory speed. The total I/O bandwidth of the VP-200 is 96
Mbytes/s, the smallest in this study. The entire 96 Mbytes/s can be
used for disk I/O. The maximum single-disk data transfer rate is 3
million bytes/s, but each Fujitsu SSD can transfer data over four channels concurrently, a bandwidth of 12 Mbytes/s. The VP-200 can attach
over 4000 disk devices.

The Fujitsu VP-200 operates with the FACOM VP control program,
a batch operating system designed to interface with an IBM-
compatible front-end computer via a channel-to-channel (CTC) adaptor in a tightly coupled or loosely coupled network. In North America
and Europe, Amdahl is using the IBM MVS/XA operating system for
the vector processor; the Amdahl 1200 vector processor can be configured with or without a front-end computer. The front-end computer
operating system may be Fujitsu's OS-IV (available only in Japan) or
IBM's MVS, MVS/XA, or VM/CMS. To optimize use of the VP vector
hardware, Fujitsu encourages VP users to perform all computing
tasks, other than executing their Fortran application programs, on
the front-end computer.

Of the three machines in this study, Fujitsu (Amdahl) provides the
most powerful set of optimizing and debugging tools. With the VSP
operating system, interactive tools must be run on the front-end computer system, but batch versions of the tools can run on either the
front-end or the vector processor. (The IBM MVS/XA operating system
permits interactive computing on the vector processor in MVS/TSO,
but Amdahl recommends that most interactive computing should be
done on a front-end computer system if available). Fujitsu Fortran
77/VP and IBM assembly language (extended with vector macros) are
the only programming languages that take advantage of the Fujitsu

VP vector capability, although object code produced by any other compiler or assembler available for IBM scalar mainframe computers will execute correctly on the VP in scalar mode.

The Fujitsu VP-200 model timed in this study had a 15-ns scalar clock cycle, a 7.5-ns vector clock cycle, and 8 Mwords of 60-ns cycle time static MOS memory. The theoretical floating-point result rate of the timed machine was only 533 MFLOPS, about 60 percent of the result rate of the currently offered model.

8.2.3 Hitachi S-810/20

The Hitachi S-810/20 (Fig. 8.3) computer is the more powerful of two Hitachi S-810 computers, which currently are sold only in Japan. Little is published in English about the Hitachi S-810 computers; consequently, some data in the tables and comparisons are inferred and may be inaccurate.

The Hitachi S-810/20 is a high-speed, single-processor computer, with up to 32 Mwords of fast (70-ns bank cycle time) static MOS central memory and up to 128 Mwords of extended storage. The computer has separate scalar (28-ns clock cycle) and vector (14-ns clock cycle)

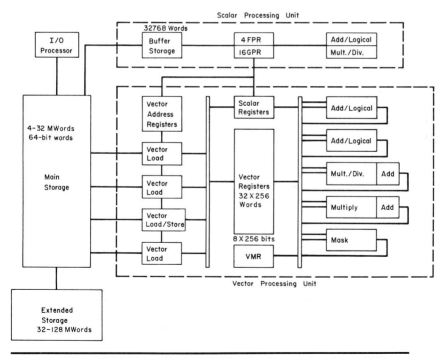

Figure 8.3 Hitachi S-810/20 architecture. FPR = floating-point registers; GPR = general-purpose registers; VMR = vector mask registers.

execution units, which can execute instructions concurrently. The scalar execution unit is distinguished by its large (32,000 words) cache memory. The S-810/20 vector unit has 8192 words of vector registers, and the largest number of vector functional units and the most comprehensive vector macro instruction set of the three machines in this study. The Hitachi S-810 family alone has the ability to process vectors that are longer than their vector registers, entirely under hardware control.

The Hitachi S-810/20 has a maximum theoretical floating-point result rate of 855 MFLOPS for overlapped vector multiply and add instructions (two multiply and four add results per cycle). The S-810/20 computer is cooled by forced air across a closed, circulating-water radiator.

Like the Fujitsu VP, the Hitachi S-810/20 scalar instruction set and data formats are fully compatible with the IBM 370 instruction set and data formats; the S-810/20 can execute load modules and share load libraries and datasets that have been prepared on IBM-compatible computers. The Hitachi S-810/20 uses IBM-compatible I/O channels and can attach all IBM-compatible disk and tape devices and share these devices with other IBM-compatible mainframe computers. Hitachi's optional, extended storage offers extremely high performance I/O. With the extended storage installed, the Hitachi S-810/20 has an I/O bandwidth of 1.1 Gbytes/s; without extended storage the I/O bandwidth is 96 Mbytes/s. All 96 Mbytes/s can be used for disk I/O; the maximum single-disk data transfer rate is 3 Mbytes/s. The Hitachi can attach over 4000 disk devices.

The Hitachi S-810/20 operates either with a batch operating system designed to interface with an IBM-compatible front-end computer via a channel-to-channel (CTC) adaptor in a loosely coupled network, or with a stand-alone operating system with MVS-like batch and MVS/TSO-like interactive capabilities. The primary programming languages for the Hitachi S-810 computers are Fortran 77 and assembly language, although object code produced by any assembler or compiler available for IBM-compatible computers will also execute on the S-810 computers in scalar mode.

8.3 Comparison of Computers

The Fujitsu VP-200 and Hitachi S-810 supercomputers evolved from similar predecessors—IBM-compatible general-purpose computers with attached floating-point array processors. The VP-200 and S-810 supercomputers reflect this heritage in their large, general-purpose instruction sets; many instruction data types and sizes; large main memories with byte-level virtual addressing; high-speed cache memories; separate scalar and vector execution units; extremely high vector result rates; and large, modest-speed, disk I/O subsystems. The Cray X-MP, by contrast, has a small instruction set; few data types and only two data sizes; fast main memory with word-level real addressing; a high-speed instruction buffer; common execution units for both scalar and vector instructions; balanced scalar and vector result rates; and a small, but fast, disk I/O subsystem.

8.3.1 IBM compatibility of the Fujitsu and Hitachi machines

Both the Fujitsu and Hitachi computers run the full IBM System 370 scalar instruction set, but neither of these machines can run the IBM 3090 Vector Facility instruction set. Also, neither Japanese computer system is fully compatible with the IBM XA extensions to System 370; each vendor has its own 31-bit address architecture that provides an XA-equivalent 2-Gbyte address space. (Amdahl is running MVS/XA on the Amdahl 1200 computer, which Amdahl upgraded to be compatible with XA architecture.) The Japanese operating systems provide IBM MVS system functions at the SVC level. MVS load modules created on Argonne's IBM 3033 computers ran without modification on both the Fujitsu and Hitachi machines in scalar mode.

The Fujitsu and Hitachi computers can share datasets on direct-access I/O equipment with IBM-compatible front-end computers. Programs can be developed and debugged on the front end computers with the user's favorite tools, then recompiled and executed on the vector processors. All software tools for the vector processors will run on IBM-compatible front ends. Currently the interactive software tools are MVS TSO/SPF oriented.

The Fujitsu and Hitachi Fortran compilers are compatible with IBM VS/Fortran; the full ANSI X3.9 (Fortran 77) standard and most IBM extensions are implemented.

8.3.2 Main storage characteristics

The main storage requirements of compute-intensive processors are considered in detail in Chap. 5. The main storage characteristics of the three machines in this study are compared in Table 8.2. All three machines have large, interleaved main memories, optimized for 64-bit-word data transfers, with bandwidths matched to the requirements of their respective vector units. Each machine permits vector accesses from contiguous, constant-stride-separated, and scattered (using indirect list vectors) memory addresses. All three machines use similar memory error-detection and error-correction schemes. The text that follows concentrates on those differences in main memory that have significant performance implications.

The Cray X-MP-48 uses extremely fast bipolar memory, while the

TABLE 8.2 Main Storage Characteristics

Memory item	Units	Cray X-MP-4	Fujitsu VP-200	Hitachi S-810/20	NEC SX-2
Memory type	SECDED	16K-bit bipolar	64K-bit S-MOS	64K-bit S-MOS	64K-bit S-MOS
Addressing:					
Type	Type	Extended real	Modified virtual	Modified virtual	Modified virtual
Paged		No	System only	System only	Yes (4 kbytes, 1 Mbyte)
Address word	Bits	24	24 or 31	24 or 31	31
Address space	Mwords	4(inst); 16(data)	2; 256	2; 256	256
Address boundary:					
Instructions	Bit	16	16	16	32
Scalar data	Bit	64	8	8	8
Vector data	Bit	64	32; 64	32; 64	32; 64
Vector addressing					
Modes		Contiguous Constant stride; indirect index	Contiguous Constant stride; indirect index	Contiguous Constant stride; indirect index	Contiguous Constant stride; indirect index
Memory size	Mwords	4–16	8–128	4–32	4–32
	Mbytes	32–128	64–1024	32–256	32–256
Interleave	Sections	4	8	8	—
	Ways	16–32	32–256	128	256
Cycle time:					
Section	CP†, ns	1 CP, 8.5 ns	2 CP, 14 ns	1 CP, 14 ns	1 CP, 6 ns
Bank	CP, ns	4 CP, 34 ns	8 CP, 56 ns	5 CP, 70 ns	13 CP, 78 ns
Access time:					
Scalar	CP, ns	14 CP, 119 ns	From cache: 2 CP, 28 ns	From cache: 2 CP, 28 ns	From cache: 2 CP, 12 ns
Vector	CP, ns	17 CP, 144 ns	?	?	36 CP, 216 ns

Transfer rate:					
Scalar L/S	Words/CP	1 word/17 ns‡	2 words/28 ns	2 words/28 ns	1 word/6 ns
Inst. Fetch	Words/CP	8 words/8.5 ns‡	2 words/28 ns	1 words/28 ns	4 words/6 ns
Vect. Load	Words/CP	2 words/8.5 ns‡	8 words/14 ns	8 words/14 ns	8 words/6 ns
Vect. Store	Words/CP	1 word/8.5 ns‡	8 words/14 ns	2 words/14 ns	4 words/6 ns
Vect. Total	Words/CP	3 words/8.5 ns‡	8 words/14 ns	8 words/14 ns	8 words/6 ns
I/O	Words/CP	1 word/8.5 ns‡	?	1 words/14 ns	?
Vector bandwidth:					
Load/store pipes	Pipes	2 load; 1 store‡	2 load/store	3 load; 1 load/store	2 load; 1 store
No. of sectors	Sectors		× 2 sectors	× 2 sectors	× 4 sectors
Vector bandwidth:					
Stride	Stride	One; odd; even	One; odd; even	One; odd; even	One; odd; even (2)
Maximum load	Mwords/s	235; 235; 235	570; 285; 143	570; 570; 570	1333; 1333; 1333
Maximum store	Mwords/s	118; 118; 118	570; 285; 143	143; 143; 143	667; 667; 667
Total load/store	Mwords/s	353; 353; 353	570; 285; 143	570; 570; 570	1333; 1333; 1333
Scalar buffer memory:		*T registers*	*Cache memory*	*Cache memory*	*Cache memory*
Size	Words	64	8192	32768	8192
Block load	Words/CP	1 word/8.5 ns	8 words/56 ns	8 words/70 ns	16 words/24 ns
Access time	CP, ns	1 CP, 8.5 ns	2 CP, 14 ns	2 CP, 28 ns	2 CP, 12 ns
Transfer rate	Words/CP	1 word/8.5 ns	1 word/14 ns	1 word/28 ns	4 words/6 ns
Instruction buffer:		*128 words I-stack*	*Cache memory*	*Cache memory*	*256 words I-stack*
Block load	Words/CP	8 words/8.5 ns	8 words/56 ns	8 words/70 ns	64 words/96 ns

†CP = clock period.
‡Per CPU.

Fujitsu and Hitachi computers use relatively slower-static MOS memory (see Table 8.2). Cray's choice of the faster but much more expensive bipolar memory is largely dictated by the need to service four processors from a single, symmetrically shared main memory. Fujitsu and Hitachi selected static MOS for its higher chip circuit density, lower cost, and lower heat dissipation. These MOS characteristics permit much larger memory configurations without drastic space, cost, and cooling penalties. Fujitsu and Hitachi compensate for the relatively slower speed of their MOS memory by providing much higher levels of memory banking and interleaving. (It is noteworthy that Cray only offers bipolar memory on the four-processor model of the Cray X-MP; currently, the one- and two-processor Cray X-MP models use 68-ns MOS memory.)

8.3.3 Memory address architecture

The Fujitsu VP and Hitachi S-810 computers share the complex, byte-oriented virtual-address architecture of IBM System 370 general-purpose computers. The Cray X-MP, by contrast, has a simple, word-oriented real-address architecture, typical of compute-intensive processors (Chap. 5).

Memory address word and address space. The Cray X-MP uses a 24-bit address, which it interprets as a 16-bit "parcel" address when referencing instructions and as a 64-bit word address when referencing operands. This addressing duality leads to a 4-Mword address space for instructions and a 16-Mword address space for operands.

The Fujitsu and Hitachi machines use similar memory addressing schemes, owing to their mutual commitment to IBM compatibility. Both Japanese computers allow operating-system selection of IBM 370–compatible 24-bit byte-level addressing or IBM XA-like 31-bit byte-level addressing. These addressing alternatives provide a 2-Mword address space or a 256-Mword address space, respectively. The address space is identical for both program instructions and operands.

Operand sizes and operand memory boundary alignment. Cray X-MP computers have only two hardware operand sizes: 64-bit integer, real, and logical operands; and 24-bit integer operands, used primarily for addressing. The 24-bit integers permit faster arithmetic, but no savings in memory. All Cray operands are stored in memory on 64-bit word boundaries. Cray program instructions consist of one or two 16-bit parcels, packed four to a word. Cray instructions are fetched from memory, 32 parcels at a time beginning on an 8-word memory boundary, into an instruction buffer that in turn is addressable on 16-bit parcel boundaries.

The Fujitsu and Hitachi computers provide all of the IBM 370 architecture's operand types and lengths, and some additional ones. The Fujitsu and Hitachi scalar instruction sets can process 8-, 16-, 32-, 64-, and 128-bit binary-arithmetic and logical operands; 8- to 128-bit (in units of 8 bits) decimal-arithmetic operands; and 8- to 32,768-bit (in units of 8 bits) character operands. Scalar operands may be aligned in memory on any 8-bit boundary. However, the Fujitsu and Hitachi vector instruction sets can process only 32- and 64-bit binary-arithmetic and logical operands, and these operands must be aligned in memory on 32- and 64-bit boundaries, respectively. Most of the Fujitsu and Hitachi incompatibilities with IBM Fortran programs arise from vector operand misalignment in COMMON blocks and EQUIVALENCE statements.

Memory regions and program relocation.   The Cray X-MP uses only real memory addresses. The operating system loads each program into a contiguous region of memory for instructions and a contiguous region of memory for operands. The Cray X-MP uses two base registers to relocate all addresses in a program; one register uniformly biases all instruction addresses, and the second register uniformly biases all operand addresses.

In contrast, the Fujitsu and Hitachi computers use a modified virtual-memory addressing scheme. The operating systems and user application programs are each loaded into a contiguous region of "virtual" memory, although each may actually occupy noncontiguous "pages" of real memory. Every virtual-address reference must undergo dynamic address translation to obtain the corresponding real-memory address. As in conventional virtual-memory systems, operating-system pages can be paged out to an external device, allowing the virtual-memory space to exceed the underlying real-memory space. However, user application program pages are never paged out. Application program address translation is used primarily to avoid memory fragmentation.

Main memory size limitations.   The Cray X-MP is available with up to 16 Mwords of main memory, the maximum permitted by its 24-bit address architecture. This is restrictive compared to the Japanese offerings, especially as the memory must be shared by four processors. Currently, the Fujitsu computers permit a maximum of 128 Mwords of main memory, and the Hitachi computers offer a maximum of 32 Mwords of main memory. However, Fujitsu memory over 32 Mwords is not addressable by the scalar execution unit and the I/O channels; this memory is usable only by the vector execution unit and for virtual I/O. Both Japanese computers could accommodate expansion to 256 Mwords within the current 31-bit virtual-addressing architecture.

The memory size requirements of a number of scientific and engineering applications are also discussed in Chaps. 1, 2, 5, and 6.

8.3.4 Memory performance

The studied computers incorporate a wide range of features to enhance memory performance, including large numbers of memory banks, instruction buffers, cache memory, intermediate staging registers, and multiple streaming pipelines between main memory and vector registers.

Memory bank structure. The computers on which we ran the benchmark problems were all equipped with 8 Mwords of main memory. The Cray X-MP-48 memory was divided into 64 independent memory banks, organized as 4 sections of 16 banks each (current models of the Cray X-MP are limited to 32 memory banks). Both the Fujitsu and Hitachi computer memories were divided into 128 independent memory banks organized as 8 sections of 16 banks each (Cray and Fujitsu have reduced the banking of 8 Mword memories on their current offerings, to 4 sections of 4 banks and 8 sections of 4 banks, respectively). In general, larger numbers of memory banks permit higher bandwidths for consecutive block memory transfers and fewer bank conflicts from random memory accesses.

Instruction access. The Cray X-MP has four 32-word instruction buffers that can deliver a new instruction for execution on every clock cycle, leaving the full memory bandwidth available for operand access. Each buffer contains 128 consecutive parcels of program instructions, but the separate buffers need not be from contiguous memory segments. Looping and branching within the buffers are permitted; entire Fortran DO loops and small subroutines can be completely contained in the buffer. An instruction buffer is block-loaded from memory, 32 words at a time, at the rate of 8 words per 8.5-ns cycle.

The Fujitsu and Hitachi processors buffer all instruction fetches through their respective cache memories (see "Scalar memory access" below). The cache bandwidths are adequate to deliver instructions and scalar operands without conflict.

Scalar memory access. The Cray X-MP does not have a scalar cache. Instead, it has sixty-four 24-bit intermediate-address B registers and sixty-four 64-bit intermediate-scalar T registers. These registers are under program control and can deliver one operand per 8.5-ns clock cycle to the primary scalar registers. The user must plan a program carefully to make effective use of the B and T registers in Cray Fortran; variables assigned to B and T registers by the compiler are never stored in memory.

The Fujitsu VP-200 and Hitachi S-810/20 automatically buffer all scalar memory accesses and instruction fetches through fast cache memories of 8192 words and 32,768 words, respectively. The Fujitsu and Hitachi cache memories can each deliver 1 word per scalar clock cycle (14 and 28 ns, respectively) to their respective scalar execution units, entirely under hardware control.

Vector memory access.   The computers studied all have multiple data-streaming pipelines to transfer operands between main memory and vector registers. Each processor of a Cray X-MP has three pipelines, two dedicated to loads and one dedicated to stores, between its own set of vector registers and the shared main memory. (A fourth pipe in each X-MP processor is dedicated to I/O data transfers.) The Fujitsu VP-200 has two memory pipelines, each capable of both loads and stores. The Hitachi S-810/20 has four memory pipelines, three dedicated to loads and one capable of both loads and stores.

Each Cray X-MP pipe can transfer one 64-bit word between main storage and a vector register each 8.5-ns cycle, giving a single-processor memory bandwidth (excluding I/O) of 353 Mwords/s and a four-processor memory bandwidth of 1412 Mwords/s. Each Fujitsu and Hitachi pipe can transfer two 64-bit words each memory cycle (7 and 14 ns, respectively), giving each machine a total memory bandwidth of 570 Mwords/s.

For indirect-address operations (scatter/gather) and for constant strides different from one, the Fujitsu computer devotes one of its memory pipelines to generating operand addresses; its maximum memory-to-vector register bandwidth is 285 Mwords/s for scatter/gather and odd-number constant strides, and 143 Mwords/s for even-number constant strides. For constant strides, the Hitachi and Cray X-MP computers can deliver full memory-to-vector register bandwidth, except when the stride is a multiple of the number of memory sections (eight on the Hitachi S-810 and four on the Cray X-MP). The Cray X-MP can have only one scatter/gather active at a time, but scatter/gather and constant-stride accesses can take place concurrently.

All three machines can automatically "chain" their load and store pipelines with their vector functional pipelines. Thus, vector instructions need not wait for a vector load to complete but can begin execution as soon as the first vector element arrives from memory. And vector stores can begin as soon as the first result is available in a vector register. In the limit, pipelines can be chained to create a continuous flow of operands from memory, through the vector functional unit(s), and back to memory with an unbroken stream of finished results. In this "memory-to-memory" processing mode, the vector registers serve as little more than buffers between memory and the functional units. The Cray X-MP's three memory pipes permit memory-to-memory operation with two input operand streams and one result stream. With only two memory pipes, the Fujitsu VP-200 can function in memory-to-memory mode only if one of the input operands is already in a vector register, or if one of the operands is a scalar, and not at all if the vector stride is different from one. The Hitachi, with four memory pipes, can function in memory-to-memory mode with up to three input operand streams and one result stream; add to this the Hitachi's ability to automatically process vectors that are longer than its vector registers, and the Hitachi can be viewed as a formidable memory-to-memory processor.

8.3.5 Input/output performance

Table 8.3 summarizes the input/output features and performance of the Cray X-MP, the Fujitsu, and the Hitachi. This information is entirely from the manufacturers' published machine specifications; no I/O performance comparisons were included in our tests.

Both the Cray and Hitachi I/O subsystems have optional integrated SSDs, with data transfer rates of 2048 (up to two 1024-Mbyte channels) and 1024 Mbytes/s, respectively, over specialized channels. The I/O bandwidth of one of these devices dwarfs the I/O bandwidth of the entire disk I/O subsystem on each machine. The optional Fujitsu solid-state storage devices emulate standard IBM disk devices; each can attach to from one to four standard Fujitsu 3-Mbyte/s channels, for a maximum single device data transfer rate of 12 Mbytes/s. Like disk devices, many Fujitsu SSDs can be attached to the VP channels and shared with the front-end and other IBM-compatible computers. Also, the Fujitsu VP can use main memory (up to 128 Mwords) for virtual I/O at full vector memory bandwidths.

The IBM-compatible disk I/O subsystems on the two Japanese computers have a much larger aggregate disk storage capacity than the Cray. The Cray can attach a maximum of 32 disk units, while Fujitsu and Hitachi can each attach over 4000 disks. Cray permits a maximum of 8 concurrent disk data transfers, while Fujitsu and Hitachi permit as many concurrent disk data transfers as there are channels (up to a maximum of 32). Individually, Cray's DD-49 disks can transfer data sequentially at the rate of 9.6 Mbytes/s, compared with only 3 Mbytes/s for the IBM 3380-compatible disks used by Fujitsu and Hitachi. But the maximum concurrent Cray disk data rate (four DD-49 data streams on each of two I/O processors) is only 68 Mbytes/s, compared with 96 Mbytes/s for the two Japanese computers. The disks used on all three computers should have very similar random access performance, which is dominated by access time rather than data transfer rate.

Cray includes up to 32 Mwords of I/O subsystem buffer memory be-

TABLE 8.3 Input/Output Features and Performance

I/O features	Cray X-MP-4	Fujitsu VP-200	Hitachi S-810/20	NEC SX-2
Disk I/O channels:				
Disk I/O processors	2 I/O processors	2 I/O directors	2 I/O directors	1 I/O director
Channels per IOP	1	16	16	32
Maximum channels	2	32	32	32
Data rate/channel	100 Mbytes/s	3 Mbytes/s	3 Mbytes/s	3 Mbytes/s
Total bandwidth	200 Mbytes/s	96 Mbytes/s	96 Mbytes/s	96 Mbytes/s
Disk controllers:	DCU-5	6880	3380-equivalent	N7265
Max. per channel	4	8	16	1
Max. controllers	8	128	256	32
Disks/controller	4	4–64	4–16	8
Data paths/controller	1	2	2	2
Bandwidth/controller	12 Mbytes/s	6 Mbytes/s	6 Mbytes/s	6 Mbytes/s
Disk devices:	DD-39; DD-49	6380	3380-equivalent	N7765
Storage capacity	1200 Mbytes; 1200 Mbytes	600 Mbytes; 1200 Mbytes	600 Mbytes; 1200 Mbytes	2.6 Gbytes; 5.2 Gbytes
Data transfer rate	6 Mbytes/s; 10 Mbytes/s	3 Mbytes/s	3 Mbytes/s	3 Mbytes/s
Average seek time	18 ms; 16 ms	15 ms	15 ms	15 ms
Average latency	9 ms; 9 ms	8 ms	8 ms	8 ms
Maximum striping	5; 3	24	?	32
Maximum disk bandwidth	45 Mbytes/s; 68 Mbytes/s	96 Mbytes/s	96 Mbytes/s	96 Mbytes/s
Optional SSD:				
Capacity (Mwords)	Integrated 32; 64; 128	Channel attached 16; 32; 64/device	Integrated 32; 64; 128	Optional 16; 32;...;1024 (16-Mbyte increments)
Data transfer rate	256 Mwords/s	1.5 Mwords/s	128 Mwords/s	167 Mwords/s

tween its CPUs and its disk units. This I/O buffer memory permits 100-Mbyte/s data transfer between the I/O subsystem and a single Cray CPU. The IBM 3880-compatible disk controllers used by the two Japanese machines permit up to 16 Mwords of cache buffer memory on each controller. This disk controller cache does not increase peak data transfer rates but serves to reduce average record access times.

All three machines permit "disk striping" to increase I/O performance; the data blocks of a single file can be interleaved over multiple disk devices to allow concurrent data transfer for a single file. Cray allows certain disks to be designated as striping volumes at the system level; striped and nonstriped datasets may not reside on the same disk volume. A single Cray file may be striped over a maximum of three DD-49 or five DD-39 disk units. Fujitsu and Hitachi permit striping on a Fortran dataset basis; striped and nonstriped datasets may reside on the same disk volume. A single Fujitsu dataset may be striped over as many as 24 disk volumes. Fortran programs compiled by the Japanese Fortran compilers in scalar mode can use disk striping on any IBM-compatible computer; and striped datasets can be shared between the vector processors and their front-end computers.

8.3.6 Vector processing performance

Table 8.4 shows the vector architectures of the three computers studied. All three machines are vector register based, with multiple pipelines connecting the vector registers with main memory. All three have multiple vector functional units, permit concurrency among independent vector functional units and with the load/store pipelines, and permit flexible chaining of the vector functional units with each other and with the load/store pipelines. Although Fujitsu and Hitachi permit both 32-bit and 64-bit vector operands, all vector arithmetic on all three machines is performed in and optimized for 64-bit floating point. The three vector units differ primarily in the numbers and lengths of vector registers, the numbers of vector functional units, and the types of vector instructions.

Of the three machines, the Cray has the smallest number and size of vector registers. Each Cray X-MP processing unit has 8 vector registers of 64 elements, while the Fujitsu and Hitachi computers each have 8192-word vector register sets. The Fujitsu vector registers can be dynamically configured into different numbers and lengths of vector registers (see Table 8.4), ranging from a minimum of 8 registers of 1024 words each to a maximum of 256 registers of 32 words each. The Fujitsu Fortran compiler uses the vector-length information available at compile time to try to optimize the vector register configurations for each loop. The Hitachi has 32 vector registers, fixed at

Total capacity	512 words/CPU	8192 words	8192 words	12,040 words
Number × size	8 × 64 words/CPU	8 × 1024 words 16 × 512 words 32 × 256 words 64 × 128 words 128 × 64 words 256 × 32 words	32 × 256 words	8 × 256 words (fixed) 8192 words (reconfigurable)
Mask registers	64 bits/CPU	8192 bits	8 × 256 bits	8 × 256 bits
Vector pipelines:	(per CPU)			
Load	2 load; 1 store	2 load/store	3 load; 1 load/store	8 load/4 store
Floating point	1 multiply; 1 add; 1 recip. approx.	1 multiply/add; 1 add/logical; 1 divide	2 add/shift/logic; 1 multiply/add; 1 multiply/divide/add	4 add; 4 multiply
Other	1 shift; 1 mask; 2 logical	1 mask	1 mask	4 shift; 4 logical; 1 mask
Maximum vector result rates (64-bit results):				
Floating-point multiply	118 MFLOPS	285 MFLOPS	285 MFLOPS	667 MFLOPS
Floating-point add	118 MFLOPS	570 MFLOPS	570 MFLOPS	667 MFLOPS
Floating-point divide	39 MFLOPS	60 MFLOPS	71 MFLOPS	83 MFLOPS
Floating multiply & add	235 MFLOPS	570 MFLOPS 855 (M + 2A)	570 MFLOPS 855 (M + 2A)	1333 MFLOPS
Vector data types:				
Floating point	64-bit	32-bit; 64-bit	32-bit; 64-bit	32-bit; 64-bit
Fixed point	64-bit	32-bit	32-bit	32-bit
Logical	64-bit	1-bit; 64-bit	64-bit	64-bit
Vector macroinstructions:				
Masked arithmetic	No	Yes	Yes	Yes
Vector compress/expand	Yes	Yes	Yes	Yes
Vector merge under mask	Yes	No	No	Yes
Vector sum (S = S + Vi)	No	Yes	Yes	Yes
Vector product (S = S*Vi)	No	No	Yes	Yes
Dot product (S = S + Vi*Vj)	Chain	Chain	Yes	Chain
DAXPY (Vi = Vi + S*Xi)	Yes	Yes	Yes	Chain
Iteration (Aj = Ai*Bi + Ci)	No	No	Yes	Yes
Max/min (S = Max(S,Vi))	No	Yes	Yes	No
Fix/float (Vi = Ii;Ti = Vi)	Chain	Yes	Yes	Yes

256 elements each, but with the unique ability to process longer vectors without the user or the compiler dividing them into sections of 256 elements or less; the Hitachi hardware can automatically repeat a long vector instruction for successive vector segments. The HAP Fortran compiler decides when to divide vectors into 256-element segments and when to process entire vectors all at once, based on whether intermediate results in a vector register can be used in later operations.

The Hitachi has more vector arithmetic pipelines than the Cray and Fujitsu computers. Depending on the operation mix, the Hitachi can drive two vector add and two vector multiply-and-add pipelines concurrently, for an instantaneous result rate of 855 MFLOPS. If the program operation mix is inappropriate, however, the extra pipelines are just expensive unused hardware. The HAP Fortran "pair-processing" option often increases performance by dividing a vector in two and processing each half concurrently through a separate pipe. For long vectors, pair processing can double the result rate; but for short vectors, startup overhead can result in reduced performance. The HAP Fortran compiler permits pair processing to be selected on a program-wide, subroutinewide, or individual loop basis. Pair-processing was the compiler default for all our timings. Previous S-810 benchmarks that reported relatively poorer performance were done without pair processing [Lubeck 85].

The Fujitsu and Hitachi computers have larger and more powerful vector instruction sets than the Cray. These macroinstruction sets make these machines more "compilable" and more "vectorizable" than the Cray. Especially valuable are the macroinstructions that reduce an entire vector operation to a single result, such as the vector inner (or dot) product. Lacking such instructions, the Cray must normally perform these operations in scalar mode, although vectorizable algorithms exist for long Cray vectors. The Hitachi has the richest set of vector macroinstructions, with macrofunctional units to match. Both Fujitsu and Hitachi have single vector instructions or two instruction chains to extract the maximum and minimum elements of a vector, to sum the elements of a vector, to take the inner product of two vectors, to perform the DAXPY multiply-and-add sequence, and to convert vector elements between fixed-point and floating-point representations. To these, the Hitachi adds a vector product reduction and a vector iteration useful in finite-difference calculations.

The only Cray masked vector instructions are the vector compress/expand and conditional vector merge instructions; the Cray Fortran compiler uses these instructions to vectorize loops that contain only a single IF statement. The Cray can hold logical data for only a single vector register. Both Japanese computers, on the other hand, have masked arithmetic and assignment instructions that permit straightforward vectorization of loops with IF statements. The Fujitsu and Hitachi computers have mask register sets that can hold logical data for every vector register element. These large mask register sets, and vector logical instructions to manipulate these masks, should make the Japanese machines strong candidates for logic programming. These machines can hold the results of many different logical operations in their multiple mask registers, eliminating the need to recompute masks that are needed repeatedly, and permitting the vectorization of loops with multiple, compound, and nested IF statements.

8.3.7 Scalar processing performance

Table 8.5 compares the scalar architectures of the three machines studied. All three computers permit scalar and vector instruction concurrency; Cray permits concurrency among all its functional units. The Fujitsu and

TABLE 8.5   Scalar Architecture

Scalar processing item	Cray X-MP-4	Fujitsu VP-200	Hitachi S-810/20	NEC SX-2
Scalar cycle time	8.5 ns	14 ns	28 ns	6 ns
Scalar registers:				
General/ addressing	8 × 24-bit	16 × 32-bit	16 × 32-bit	128 × 64-bit
Floating point	8 × 64-bit	8 × 64-bit	4 × 64-bit	128 × 64-bit
Scalar buffer memory:	T registers	Cache memory	Cache memory	Cache memory
Capacity	64 words	8192 words	32,768 words	8192 words
Memory bandwidth	118 Mwords/s	70 Mwords/s	112 Mwords/s	667 Mwords/s
CPU access time	1 CP,† 8.5 ns	2 CP, 28 ns	1 CP, 28 ns	2 CP, 12 ns
CPU transfer rate	1 word/8.5 ns	1 word/14 ns	1 word/28 ns	2 words/12 ns
Scalar execution times:				
Floating-point multiply	7 CP, 59.5 ns	4 CP, 56 ns; 3 CP, 42 ns‡	3 CP, 84 ns	9 CP, 54 ns
Floating-point add	6 CP, 51.0 ns	3 CP, 42 ns	2 CP, 56 ns	6 CP, 36 ns
Scalar data types:				
Floating point	64-bit	32; 64; 128-bit	32; 64; 128-bit	32; 64; 128-bit
Fixed point	24; 64-bit	16; 32-bit	16; 32-bit	16; 32-bit
Logical	64-bit	8; 32; 64-bit	8; 32; 64-bit	64-bit
Decimal	None	1 to 16 bytes	1 to 16 bytes	None
Character	None	1 to 4096 bytes	1 to 4096 bytes	1 byte

†CP = clock period.
‡32-bit results.

Hitachi computers are compatible with IBM System 370; they implement the complete IBM 370 scalar instruction set and scalar register sets (Fujitsu added four additional floating-point registers).

Cray computers use multiple, fully segmented functional units for both scalar and vector instruction execution, while Fujitsu and Hitachi use an unsegmented execution unit for all scalar instructions. Cray computers can begin a scalar instruction on any clock cycle; more than one Cray scalar instruction can be in execution at a given time, in the same and in different functional units. Fujitsu and Hitachi, on the other hand, perform their scalar instructions one at a time, many taking more than one cycle. Thus, even though many scalar instruction times are faster on the Fujitsu than on the Cray, the Cray will often have a higher scalar result rate because of concurrency. In our benchmark set, a single processor of the Cray X-MP-4 outperformed both the Fujitsu VP-200 and the Hitachi S-810/20 on most of the programs that were dominated by scalar floating-point instruction execution.

The Fujitsu and Hitachi computers have larger and more powerful general-purpose instruction sets than the Cray, and more flexible data formats for integer and character processing. Also, the large variety of data sizes on the Fujitsu and Hitachi computers reduce the need for packing and unpacking of small bits of data in larger words to conserve storage. Thus, applications that are predominately scalar but use little floating-point arithmetic may well execute faster on these IBM-compatible computers than on a Cray. We had no applications in our benchmark to measure such performance.

8.4 Benchmark Environments

We spent 2 days at Cray Research in December 1985 compiling and running the benchmark on the Cray X-MP-4. The Cray programs were one-processor tests; no attempt was made to exploit the additional processors. The Cray had 8 Mwords of memory in 64 banks, and a CPU cycle time of 9.5 ns, 11 percent slower than the models now offered and described in our tables.

For the Japanese benchmarkings, we sent ahead a preliminary tape of our benchmark source programs and some load modules produced at Argonne. At both Fujitsu and Hitachi the load modules ran without problem, demonstrating that the machines are in fact compatible with IBM computers on both instruction set and operating-system interface levels. (Of course, these tests did not use the vector features of the machines.)

The VP-200 tests were run at the Fujitsu plant in Numazu, Japan, during a 1-week period in August 1985. We had as much time on the

VP-200 as needed. The front-end machine was a Fujitsu M-380 (approximately twice as fast as a single processor of an IBM 3081 K).

The VP-200 we timed differed from the current model we describe in this document. The test machine had a CPU cycle time of 7.5 ns, 7 percent slower than the current 7.0-ns model. More importantly, the tested VP-200 had a multiply-only pipeline, rather than the multiply-add pipeline of the current model. Thus the tested VP-200 had a peak vector result rate of only 533 MFLOPS, compared with 855 MFLOPS for the current model.

The Hitachi S-810/20 tests were run at the Hitachi Kanagawa Works, during two afternoons in August 1985. The Hitachi S-810/20 benchmark configuration had no front-end system. Instead, we compiled, linked, ran, and printed output directly on the supercomputer.

The physical environment of the Hitachi S-810/20 at Kanagawa is noteworthy. The machine room was not air-conditioned; a window was opened to cool off the area. The outside temperature exceeded 100°F on the first day, and we estimate that the computer room temperature was well above 100°, with high humidity; yet the computer ran without problem.

8.5 Benchmark Codes and Results

Subsequent to performing the benchmark timings, we learned that the measured systems collect CPU time differently. The Japanese operating systems attempt to charge back to a job all CPU time for all services on that job's behalf. The Cray COS system, however, does not charge CPU time for system services back to the job requesting those services. The impact is greatest for jobs with heavy disk I/O, with overlayed programs, with large print output, and with many internal timing calls. We did not discover this discrepancy in time to measure or control for its effect on our results.

8.5.1 Codes

We asked some of the major computer users at Argonne for typical Fortran programs that would help in judging the performance of these vector machines. We gathered 20 programs, some simple kernels, others full production codes. The programs are itemized in Table 8.6.

Four of the programs have very little vectorizable Fortran (for the most part they are scalar programs): BANDED, NODAL0, NODAL1, SPARSESP. Both STRAWEXP and STRAWIMP have many calculations involving short vectors. For most of these programs the Cray X-MP performed fastest, with the Fujitsu faster than the Hitachi. Below we describe some of the benchmarks and analyze the results.

TABLE 8.6   **Programs Used for Benchmarking**

Code	No. of lines	Description
APW	1448	Quantum mechanics antisymmetric plane wave calculations for solids.
BANDED	1539	Band linear algebra equation solver, for parallel processors.
BIGMAIN	774	Vectorized Monte Carlo algorithm, for SU(2) lattice gauge theory.
DIF3D	527	One-, two-, and three-dimensional neutron diffusion theory kernels.
LATFERM3	1149	Statistical-mechanical approach to lattice gauge calculations.
LATFERM4	1149	Statistical-mechanical approach to lattice gauge calculations.
LATTICE8	1149	Statistical-mechanical approach to lattice gauge calculations.
MOLECDYN	1020	Molecular dynamics code simulating a fluid.
NODAL0	345	Kernel of three-dimensional neutronics code using nodal method.
NODAL1	345	Kernel of three-dimensional neutronics code using nodal method.
NODALX	345	Kernel of three-dimensional neutronics code using nodal method.
BFAUCET	5460	Variational Monte Carlo for drops of He-4 atoms; Bose statistics.
FFAUCET	5577	Variational Monte Carlo for drops of He-3 atoms; Fermi statistics.
SPARSESP	1617	ICCG for nonsymmetric sparse matrices based on normal equations.
SPARSE1	3228	MA32 from the Harwell library sparse matrix code using frontal techniques and software run on a 64×64 problem.
STRAWEXP	4806	Two-dimensional nonlinear explicit solution finite element structural program.
STRAWIMP	4806	Same as STRAWEXP but implicit solution.

APW. The APW program is a solid-state quantum mechanics electronic structure code. APW calculates self-consistent field wave functions and energy band structures for a sodium chloride lattice using an antisymmetrized plane wave basis set and a muffin-tin potential. The majority of loops in this program are short and are coded as IF loops rather than DO loops; they do not vectorize on any of the benchmarked computers. The calculations are predominantly scalar.

This program highlights the Cray X-MP advantage when executing "quasivector" code (vectorlike loops that do not vectorize for some reason). The Cray executes scalar code on segmented functional units and can achieve a higher degree of concurrency in scalar than either the Fujitsu or Hitachi machines, which execute scalar instructions one at a time.

BIGMAIN. BIGMAIN is a highly vectorized Monte Carlo algorithm for computing Wilson line observables in SU(2) lattice gauge theory. This program has the longest vector lengths of the benchmarks. All the vectors begin on the same memory bank boundary, and all have a stride of 12. The only significant nonvectorized code is an IF loop, which seriously limits the peak performance.

The superior performance of the Cray on BIGMAIN reflects both the Cray's insensitivity to the vector stride and its greater levels of concurrency when executing scalar loops. The Fujitsu performance reflects a quartering of memory bandwidth when using a vector stride of 12. The Hitachi performance reflects its slower scalar performance.

BFAUCET and FFAUCET. BFAUCET and FFAUCET compute the ground state energies of drops of liquid helium by the variational Monte Carlo method. The BFAUCET codes involve Bose statistics, and a table-lookup operation is an important component of the time. The FFAUCET cases use Fermi statistics and are dominated by the evaluation of determinants using LU decomposition. The different cases correspond to different sized drops, as shown in Table 8.7.

TABLE 8.7   Average Vector Length for
BFAUCET and FFAUCET

Case	Average vector length
BFAUCET1	10
BFAUCET2	35
BFAUCET3	56
BFAUCET4	120
BFAUCET5	10
BFAUCET6	35
FFAUCET1	10
FFAUCET2	17
FFAUCET3	10

BFAUCET1, 2, and 3 and FFAUCET1 and 2 perform only a single Monte Carlo iteration each; these cases are typical of checkout runs and are dominated by nonrepeated setup work. BFAUCET4, 5, and 6 and FFAUCET3 are long production runs.

LINPACK. The LINPACK timing is dominated by memory reference as a result of array access through the calls to SAXPY. For this problem the vector length changes during the calculation from length 100 down to length 1 (see Table 8.8).

TABLE 8.8   LINPACK Timing for a Matrix of Order 100

Machine	MFLOPS	Seconds
Cray X-MP	21	0.032
Fujitsu VP-200	17	0.040
Hitachi S-810/20	17	0.042

Fujitsu's and Hitachi's performance reflects the fact that they do not do so well as the Cray with short vectors.

LU, Cholesky decomposition, and matrix multiply. The LU, Cholesky decomposition, and matrix multiply benchmarks are based on matrix vector operations. As a result, memory reference is not a limiting factor since results are retained in vector registers during the operation. The technique used in these tests is based on vector unrolling [Dongarra 84], which works equally well on Cray, Fujitsu, and Hitachi machines. The depth of unrolling which gives the optimum performance varies from machine to machine. On the Fujitsu the loop unrolled to a depth of 2 provides the maximum execution rates; on the Hitachi the optimal depth is 4; and on the Cray the more the loop is unrolled, the better the performance (for these tests the loops were unrolled to a level of 16 on the Cray).

The routines used in Tables 8.9 through 8.11 have a very high percentage of floating-point arithmetic operations. The algorithms are all based on column accesses to the matrices. That is, the programs reference array elements sequentially down a column, not across a row. With the exception of matrix multiply, the vector lengths start out as the order of the matrix and decrease during the course of the computation to a vector length of one.

TABLE 8.9   LU Decomposition Based on Matrix Vector Operations

	MFLOPS		
Order	Cray X-MP (1 CPU)	Fujitsu VP-200	Hitachi S-810/20
50	24.5	20.5	17.9
100	51.6	51.8	47.5
150	72.1	84.6	76.3
200	87.4	117.1	102.2
250	99.2	148.8	126.4
300	108.4	178.8	147.8

TABLE 8.10   Cholesky Decomposition Based on Matrix Vector Operations

	MFLOPS		
Order	Cray X-MP (1 CPU)	Fujitsu VP-200	Hitachi S-810/20
50	29.9	25.8	18.8
100	65.6	70.6	60.1
150	91.9	117.6	104.9
200	107.7	162.2	144.9
250	119.1	202.2	179.7
300	132.3	238.1	211.8

TABLE 8.11   Matrix Multiply Based on Matrix Vector Operations

	MFLOPS		
Order	Cray X-MP (1 CPU)	Fujitsu VP-200	Hitachi S-810/20
50	98.4	112.9	100.0
100	135.7	225.2	213.3
150	149.0	328.1	279.3
200	156.2	404.5	336.8
250	165.9	462.2	366.7
300	167.9	469.2	390.4

For low-order problems the Cray X-MP is slightly faster than the VP-200 and S-810/20, because it has the smallest vector startup overhead (primarily due to faster memory access). As the order increases, and the calculations become saturated by longer vectors, the Fujitsu VP-200 attains the fastest overall execution rate.

With matrix multiply, the vectors remain the same length throughout; here Fujitsu comes close to attaining its peak theoretical speed in Fortran.

8.5.2   Results

Table 8.12 contains the timing data for our benchmark codes. We also include the timing results on other machines for comparison.

8.6   Fortran Compilers and Tools

Fortran 77 is the primary application programming language for the three computers in this study. And the Fortran compiler is the primary vectorizing tool on these computers. Fujitsu and Hitachi offer additional source-level software tools to help users optimize their programs.

TABLE 8.12 Timing Data (in seconds) for Various Computers and Compilers

Program name	Cray X-MP-4 using 1 proc. and CFT 1.15 compil.[1,15]	Fujitsu VP-200 and V1L10 compil.[2]	Hitachi S810/20 and HAP V02-00 compil.[3]	Hitachi S810/20 and FORTVS compil.[4]	Hitachi S810/20 and H EXT compil.[4]	IBM 370/195 and H EXT compil.	IBM 3033 and FORTVS compil.	IBM 3033 and H EXT compil.	Amdahl 5860 and f77 compil.	SX-2 400 and FORT77/SX compil.
APW	30.69	40.58	54.37				171		62	17.04
BANDED	24.3	34.15	38.3				102.65		35	15.09
BIGMAIN	10.86	23.49	34.36	41.0	157.66			5.75		
DIF3DS1/1	23.71	20.31	21.9	45.1	39.2	74.82	151.81	134.2	62	8.36
DIF3DS2/1	19.0	21.93	21.9	47.4	41.5	81.27	157.44	142.	67	8.38
DIF3DV0/1	9.31	16.37	11.8	50.1	39.5	73	168	138	73	6.08
DIF3DV1/1	9.37	16.59	12.1	49.3	38.7	74	167	137	70	6.03
LATFERM3	6.1	6.2	6.6	15.8	33.3				18	2.56
LATFERM4	121.8	65.29	65.3	345.2	820.6		52.07	87.8	640	53.81
LATTICE8	10.2	5.54	6.7	16	19.4		46.38	53.8	17	3.06
MOLECDYN	8.68	9.07	15.78	16.6	17.2	36.26	51.44	51.74	17	4.49
NODAL0	6.41	14.31	20.1	19.5	19.7	28.36	45.53	45.5	27	4.69
NODAL1	6.45	14.47	19.8	19.3	19.5	27.58	45.35	45.	23	4.70
NODALX	.25	.14	.20		1.14	1.45	1.57		.07	
BFAUCET1	11.2	16.13		22.9	22.8		74	73	31	6.11
BFAUCET2	8.96	11.66		23.9	24.2		79	78	34	5.28
BFAUCET3	10.6	18.48		38.7	38.9		130	128	405	9.02
BFAUCET4	259.4	551.2			621.0		2100	2048	920	197.1
BFAUCET5	787.4	923.04			1529.4				2351	394.8
BFAUCET6	727.5	823.98							2786	397.7
FFAUCET1	13.6	19.45			26.7		94	82	35	7.3
FFAUCET2	44.4	42.31			114.3		419	397	150	18.1
FFAUCET3	1144.0	1691.83							2440	614.7
SPARSESP	1200	1361	1264.29						1484	710.5
SPARSE1	2.51	6.74	9.85	14.26			33.06		26	2.2
STRAWEXP	37.3	45.74	59.2						51	24.1
STRAWEXP2	153.4	179.37	231.13		273.9	116.28	143.35	142.28	216	99.6
STRAWIMP	151.5	151.51	172.61		?	382.73	381.51	360.55		73.7

[1] The tested Cray had a 9.5-ns cycle time and 8 Mwords in 64 banks.
[2] The tested VP-200 had a 7.5-ns cycle time and 8 Mwords in 128 banks and lacked the multiply/add pipeline of the current models.
[3] The tested S-810/20 matched the description in the text and tables.
[4] Scalar runs from load modules created on an IBM machine using VS Fortran version 1.3.

8.6.1 Fortran compilers

The three compilers tested exhibit several similarities. All three tested systems include a full Fortran 77 vectorizing compiler as the primary programming language. The Cray compiler includes most IBM and CDC Fortran extensions; the two Japanese compilers include most IBM extensions to Fortran 77. All three compilers can generate vectorized code from standard Fortran; no explicit vector syntax is provided. All three compilers recognize a variety of compiler directives—special Fortran comments that, when placed in a Fortran source code, aid the compiler in optimizing and vectorizing the generated code. Each compiler, in its options and compiler directives, provides users with a great deal of control over the optimization and vectorization of their programs. On the Cray X-MP we used a prereleased version of CFT 1.15; on the Fujitsu the compiler was version V1L10; and on the Hitachi the compiler was release FORT77/HAP V02-00.

The two Japanese compilers provide a wider choice of floating-point precision (32-, 64-, and 128-bit) than does the Cray. And the Japanese computers implement all three precisions in hardware. See Chap. 5 for a discussion of the precision requirements of many scientific and engineering applications.

Optimization and vectorization.   All three compilers provide excellent optimization of scalar code. The compilers differ primarily in the range of Fortran statements they can vectorize, the complexity of the DO loops that they vectorize, and the quantity and quality of messages they provide the programmer about the success or failure of vectorization.

All three Fortran compilers have similar capabilities for vectorizing simple inner DO loops and DO loops with a single IF statement. The two Japanese compilers can also vectorize outer DO loops and loops with compound, multiple, and nested IF statements. The Fujitsu compiler has multiple strategies for vectorizing DO loops containing IF statements, based on compiler directive estimates of the IF statement true ratio. The Japanese compilers can vectorize loops that contain a mix of vectorizable and nonvectorizable statements; the Cray compiler requires the user to divide such code into separate vectorizable and nonvectorizable DO loops.

The vector macroinstructions (e.g., inner product, MAX/MIN, iteration) on the two Japanese computers permit their compilers to vectorize a wider range of Fortran statements than can the Cray compiler. And the Japanese compilers seem more successful at using information from outside a DO loop in determining whether that loop is vectorizable.

All three compilers convert loops with small iteration counts to scalar code when the advantages of vectorization will not repay the loop vector startup times. The Cray compiler can completely unroll inner DO loops with constant iteration counts less than 10, eliminating entirely the scalar loop overhead. Often an unrolled inner loop will then vectorize on an outer loop index, with dramatic performance improvement. The Fujitsu compiler can double the statements and halve the iteration count of all DO loops. This loop doubling improves scalar performance, but usually degrades vector performance by converting each vector operation to two new operations with half the vector length and double the stride of the original. The similar Hitachi option—"pair processing"—usually improves performance because the two new vector operations can execute concurrently on separate functional units.

In their output listings, all three compilers indicate which DO loops vectorized and which did not. The two Japanese compilers provide more detailed explanations of why a particular DO loop or statement does not vectorize. The Fujitsu compiler listing is the most effective of the three: in addition to the vectorization commentary, the Fujitsu compiler labels each DO statement in the source listing with a V if it vectorizes totally, an S if the loop compiles to scalar code, and an M if the loop is a mix of scalar and vector code. Each statement in the loop itself is similarly labeled. The Fujitsu compiler also suggests ways to vectorize loops that did not vectorize, and to further improve performance of loops that did vectorize.

The Fujitsu and Hitachi compilers make all architectural features of their respective machines available from standard Fortran. As a measure of confidence in their compilers, Fujitsu has written all and Hitachi nearly all of their scientific subroutine libraries in standard Fortran.

Integer arithmetic.   Cray Fortran provides a 64-bit default integer type and an optional 24-bit integer type (Table 8.13). The 24-bit integer offers fast scalar arithmetic. Only 64-bit integer add and subtract are vectorizable. The 64-bit integer multiply and all integer divide arithmetic are performed by software. Overflow of integer arithmetic results is not detected on the Cray.

The Fujitsu and Hitachi Fortran compilers provide a 32-bit default integer type and an optional 16-bit integer type. All integer arithmetic is performed by hardware. Short integers save memory, but not execution time. Only 32-bit integer arithmetic is vectorizable. Overflow of integer arithmetic results is detectable, but normally disabled.

Floating-point arithmetic.   All three vendor Fortran compilers use similar floating-point formats, consisting of a biased binary exponent and

TABLE 8.13   **Integer Arithmetic and Data**

	Cray X-MP-4	Fujitsu VP-200 and Hitachi S-810/20
Default integer:		
Representation	2's complement	2's complement
Length	64 bits	32 bits
Binary range	-2^{63} to $2^{63} - 1$	-2^{31} to $2^{31} - 1$
Decimal digits	19	9
Vectorizable	Add/subtract only	Yes
Overflow detection	No	Optional
Optional integers:		
Representation	2's complement	2's complement
Length	24 bits	16 bits
Binary range	-2^{23} to $2^{23} - 1$	-2^{15} to $2^{15} - 1$
Decimal digits	6	4
Vectorizable	No	No
Overflow detection	No	Optional

a signed, normalized fraction (Table 8.14). Cray uses a 15-bit exponent with a binary radix (base 2); the others use a 7-bit exponent with a hexadecimal radix (base 16). None of the floating-point formats conform to the IEEE standard.

Cray Fortran provides two floating-point data types—64-bit single-precision and 128-bit double-precision, while Fujitsu and Hitachi provide three—32-bit single-precision, 64-bit double-precision, and 128-bit extended-precision. All Cray double-precision arithmetic and all Cray floating-point division are performed by software. All Fujitsu and Hitachi floating-point arithmetic (except extended-precision divide) is performed by hardware; there is scalar (but not vector) hardware for

TABLE 8.14   **Floating-Point Arithmetic and Data**

	Cray X-MP-4	Fujitsu VP-200 and Hitachi S-810/20
Data formats	64 bits; 128 bits	32 bits; 64 bits; 128 bits
Exponent:		
Representation	Biased binary	Biased binary
Size	15 bits	7 bits
Radix	2	16
Range	2^{-8291} to 2^{8291}	16^{-65} to 16^{63}
Decimal range	10^{-2466} to 10^{2466}	10^{-79} to 10^{75}
Fraction:		
Representation	Signed binary, normalized	Signed binary, normalized
Size	48 bits; 96 bits	24 bits; 56 bits; 112 bits
Decimal digits	14; 28	7; 16; 33
Hardware	Yes; no	Yes; yes; yes
Vectorizable	Yes; no	Yes; yes; no
Guard digits	1 bit	4 bits

128-bit arithmetic. Although the 32-bit floating-point data type offers storage economy and scalar performance advantages, both Japanese machines' vector execution units are optimized for 64-bit floating-point arithmetic; vector floating-point operations are performed in 64-bit precision regardless of the precision of the operands. Thirty-two-bit precision is adequate for many engineering applications (Chap. 5).

Cray single- and double-precision floating-point representations provide 48- and 96-bit normalized binary fractions, exceeding 14 and 28 decimal digits of precision, respectively. Fujitsu and Hitachi single-, double-, and extended-precision floating-point representations provide 6, 14, and 28 normalized hexadecimal digit fractions, exceeding 7, 16, and 33 decimal digits of precision, respectively. Fujitsu and Hitachi carry one hexadecimal (4 bits) guard digit during all floating-point arithmetic instructions. Cray carries one guard bit during floating-point add and subtract only. Cray floating-point multiply hardware and divide software use approximate algorithms that are in error as much as one-half decimal digit.

The valid range of Cray floating-point magnitudes, 10^{-2466} to 10^{2466}, is large enough to accommodate the full spectrum of scientific and engineering computation; while the smaller range of Fujitsu and Hitachi floating-point magnitudes, 10^{-79} to 10^{75}, may require the programmer to scale intermediate results to avoid exponent range errors. Programming errors can lead to floating-point range errors on all three machines, which may cause interrupts, or be masked by the programmer. Floating-point interrupts, if enabled, terminate program execution on the Cray, while they invoke standard system or programmer fixup routines on the Fujitsu and Hitachi systems. Floating-point exponent underflow is not detected on the Cray. Floating-point exponent overflow stores a result with an invalid (too large) exponent on the Cray; the overflow is not detected until the invalid result is used in a subsequent calculation. Floating-point exceptions, if enabled, cause precise interrupts in Fujitsu and Hitachi scalar floating-point arithmetic; in vector floating-point arithmetic, the interrupt is held until all active vector instructions complete, complicating attempts to pinpoint the offending data and fix the results.

8.6.2 Fortran tools

All three systems include tools to trace program execution and identify the most time-consuming program areas for tuning attention. In addition, Fujitsu and Hitachi provide Fortran source program analysis tools which guide the user in optimizing program performance. The Fujitsu interactive vectorizer is a powerful tool for both the novice and the experienced user; it allows one to tune a program despite an unfamiliarity with vector machine architecture and programming practices. The interactive vectorizer (which runs on any IBM-compatible system with MVS/TSO) displays the Fortran source with each statement labeled with a V (vectorized), S (scalar), or M (partially vectorized), and a static estimate of the execution cost of the statement. As the user interactively modifies a code, the vectorization labels and statement execution costs are updated on-screen. The vectorizer gives detailed explanations for failure to vectorize a statement, suggests alternative codings that will vectorize, and inserts compiler directives into the source based on user responses to the vectorizer's queries. Statement execution cost analyses are based on assumed DO loop iteration counts and IF statement true ratios. The user can supply his own estimate of these values, or run the FORTUNE execution analyzer to gather run-time statistics for a program, which can then be input to the interactive vectorizer to provide a more accurate dynamic statement execution cost analysis.

The Hitachi VECTIZER runs in batch mode; it provides additional information much like the Hitachi Fortran compiler's vectorization messages.

8.7 Conclusions

The results of our benchmark show the Cray X-MP-4 to be a consistently strong performer across a wide range of problems. The Cray was particularly fast on programs dominated by scalar calculations and short vectors. The fast Cray memory contributes to low vector startup times, leading to its exceptional short-vector performance. The Cray scalar performance derives from its segmented functional units; the X-MP achieves enough concurrency in many scalar loops to outperform the Japanese machines, even though individual scalar arithmetic instruction times are longer on the Cray than on the Fujitsu.

The Fujitsu and Hitachi computers perform faster than the Cray for highly vectorizable programs, especially those with long (\ 50) vector lengths. The Fujitsu VP achieved the most dramatic peak performance in the benchmark, outperforming a single Cray X-MP processor by factors of two to three on matrix-vector algorithms, with the Hitachi not far behind. Over the life cycle of a program, the Fujitsu and Hitachi machines should benefit relatively more than the Cray from tuning that increases the degree of program vectorization. The recent upgrade to the VP, in which the multiply pipe was replaced by a multiply/add pipe, should increase the dominance of this computer on highly vectorized programs.

The Cray has I/O weaknesses that were not probed in this exercise. With an SSD, the Cray has the highest I/O bandwidth of the three machines. However, owing to severe limits on the number of disk I/O paths and disk devices, the total Cray disk storage capacity and aggregate disk I/O bandwidth fall far below that of the two Japanese machines. The Cray is forced to depend on a front-end machine's mass storage system to manage the large quantities of disk data created and consumed by such a high-performance machine.

Several weaknesses were evident in the Fujitsu VP in this benchmark. The Fujitsu memory performance degrades seriously for nonconsecutive vectors. This was particularly evident in the BIGMAIN, DIF3D, and FAUCET benchmark programs. Even-number vector strides reduce the Fujitsu memory bandwidth by 75 percent, and a stride proportional to the number of memory banks (stride = $n*128$) reduces the memory bandwidth about 94 percent. Fujitsu users will profit by ensuring that multidimensional-array algorithms are vectorized by column (stride = 1) rather than by row.

Fujitsu's vector performance is substantially improved if a program's maximum vector lengths are evident at compile time, whether from explicit DO loop bounds, array dimension statements, or compiler directives. For example, the order-100 LINPACK benchmark improves by 12 percent to 19 MFLOPS, and the order-300 matrix-vector LU benchmark improves by 23 percent to 220 MFLOPS, when a Fujitsu compiler directive is included to specify the maximum vector length (numbers from the LINPACK benchmark paper [Dongarra 85]). The Fujitsu compiler's vectorization messages indicate where performance could be improved by inserting vector length directives or explicit array dimensions. When maximum vector lengths are known, the Fujitsu compiler can optimize the numbers and lengths of the vector registers and frequently avoid the logic that divides vectors into segments no larger than the vector registers. Fujitsu's short-loop performance, not strong to begin with, is particularly degraded by unnecessary vector segmentation ("stripmining") logic. None of the benchmark problems had explicit vector length information.

In many ways, the Hitachi computer seems to have the greatest vector potential. Despite its slower memory technology, the Hitachi has the highest single processor memory bandwidth, owing to its four memory pipes. Also, Hitachi has the most powerful vector macroinstruction set and the most flexible set of arithmetic pipelines; in addition, the Hitachi is the only computer able to process vectors longer than its vector registers, entirely in hardware. The vectorizing Fortran compiler is impressive, although the compiler is rarely able to exploit fully the potential concurrency of the arithmetic pipelines. The Hitachi performs best on the benchmarks with little scalar content; its slow scalar performance, about half that of the Fujitsu computer, burdens its performance on every problem.

At present the Japanese Fortran compilers are superior to the Cray compiler at vectorization. Advanced Fujitsu and Hitachi hardware features provide opportunities for vectorization that are unavailable on the Cray.

For example, the Japanese machines have macroinstructions to vectorize dot products, DAXPY, simple recurrences, and the search for the maximum and minimum elements of an array; and they have multiple mask registers to allow vectorization of loops with nested IF statements. Thus, a wider range of algorithms can vectorize on the Japanese computers than can vectorize on the Cray. Also, the Japanese compilers provide the user with more useful information about the success and failure of vectorization. Moreover, there is no Cray equivalent to the Fujitsu interactive vectorizer and FORTUNE performance analyzer. These advanced hardware features, compilers, and vectorizing tools will make it easier to tune programs for optimum performance on the Japanese computers than on the Cray and will extract greater performance from programs that no one takes the time to tune.

Cray Fortran offers programmers the convenience of a more than adequate floating-point exponent range, but the IBM-compatible floating-point arithmetic on the Japanese computers is superior numerically. Lack of Cray integer hardware also favors the Japanese machines for integer arithmetic performance. The failure of the Cray to provide floating-point interrupts at the time that the floating-point exceptions occur, and the Cray's complete lack of fixed-point overflow detection, are major debugging nuisances.

The Cray X-MP and the Japanese computers require different tuning strategies. The Cray compiler does not partially vectorize loops. Therefore, Cray users typically break up loops into their vectorizable and nonvectorizable parts. The Japanese compilers, however, automatically segment loops into their vectorizable and nonvectorizable parts. It is advantageous to merge smaller loops together on the Japanese computers, to take maximum advantage of their large vector register sets.

Acknowledgment

We would like to thank Gail Pieper for her excellent help in editing this chapter.

Bibliography

[Dongarra 1984]   J.J. Dongarra and S.C. Eisenstat. "Squeezing the Most out of an Algorithm in CRAY Fortran." *ACM Trans. Math. Software,* vol. 10, no. 3, pp. 221–230, 1984.

[Dongarra 1985]   J.J. Dongarra. *Performance of Various Computers Using Standard Linear Equations Software in a Fortran Environment.* Argonne National Laboratory Report MCS-TM-23, October 1985.

[Lubeck 1985]   O. Lubeck, J. Moore, and R. Mendez. "A Benchmark Comparison of Three Supercomputers: Fujitsu VP-200, Hitachi S-810/20 and CRAY X-MP-2." *IEEE Computer,* pp. 10–23, December 1985.

Multicomputer Load Balancing for Concurrent Lisp Execution

Raymond Chowkwanyun

Symult Systems Corporation†, Monrovia, CA

Kai Hwang

University of Southern California, Los Angeles, CA

9.1 Introduction

Concurrent Lisp processing requires different computing architectures from numeric processing as discussed in Chaps. 3 and 4. In Chap. 7, irregular memory access and a high demand for processing power were identified as the two major features of Lisp execution. Much work has already been done on *dynamic memory management* to support Lisp processing with various garbage collection schemes [Hayashi 83, Moon 84]. In this chapter, we explore dynamic load balancing as a solution to the problem of allocating processes to processors. *Dynamic* and *run time* are taken to have the same meaning in the text, as are *compile time* and *static*. We use the term *multicomputer* to mean a message-passing multiprocessor in which distributed local memory is attached to each processor as introduced in Chap. 2.

Load balancing can be characterized as either *sender-initiated* [Lin 86] or *receiver-initiated* [Ni 85], depending on the way in which process migration is initialized. Process migration always goes from the busy processor to the lightly loaded or idle processor. Thus the busy processor is the *sender*, while the idle processor assumes the role of *receiver*. While process migration always proceeds in one direction, the

---

†Formerly AMETEK Computer Research Division.

flow of control could be in either direction. Either the sender or the receiver initiates the process migration. This exactly defines the difference between the sender- and receiver-initiated types of load balancers.

We introduced a *hybrid* load balancing method in Hwang [87a] that adapts to rapidly changing run-time conditions by switching between sender-initiated and receiver-initiated modes of operation depending on the system load. Sender-initiated mode is used when the system load is light, and receiver-initiated mode is used when the system load is heavy. System load refers to the total processing load on the entire multicomputer at one time. It includes all currently executing processes and processes waiting to be run in the ready queue. Cybenko [88] has proposed a dynamic load balancing scheme restricting load migration to immediate neighbors. Our system is not restricted by this constraint.

In this chapter, hardware and software architectures are presented for implementing the hybrid load balancer with special emphasis on concurrent Lisp processing. Both architectures are based on *macro dataflow* execution with the insertion of operating system directives to interface with the applications code. Consequently, applications programs can be ported between the two architectures without modification. The software design needs less hardware and is suitable for the current generation of multicomputers such as the Intel iPSC. However, a run-time overhead is imposed to execute the load balancer. To relieve the central processing unit (CPU) of this overhead, a hardware design is developed for direct execution of the hybrid load balancer. Specialized hardware units execute the load balancer in parallel with the CPU, which promises to yield improved performance over the software approach.

A pure functional language has no side effects such as writing to global variables. Thus all functions can be executed in parallel [Vegdahl 84, Darlington 81]. A subset of the Lisp language could be defined that would be a pure functional language. However the full Common Lisp standard has many side-effect constructs that prevent us from exploiting full parallelism [Steele 84]. DeGroot has proposed a method of dealing with side effects using *synch-blocks,* which is described in Chap. 13. While he deals with side effects in the context of logic programming, we believe the same concept could be used for Lisp.

Closely related to the issue of side effects is that of how to handle large data structures in a hardware environment with no shared memory between processors. This issue has been dealt with elsewhere, as for example in FAIM-1 [Anderson 87], in Arvind's I-structure for dynamic dataflow machines [Heller 83], and in Dally's object-oriented multiprocessor [Dally 86]. We concentrate here on the solution to the mapping problem as it pertains to processes.

9.2   Load Balancing in Multicomputers

Our load balancing methodology is directed toward message-passing multicomputers whose features are summarized below. We discuss the process-mapping problem as it relates to Lisp processing on multi-computers and conclude that a dynamic solution is desired.

9.2.1   Message-passing multicomputers

In a message-passing multicomputer, as defined in Chap. 2, multiple *processors* are connected by an interconnection network. Each processor consists of a CPU, local memory, and a switch connecting it to the network. In Fig. 9.1, the circles represent processors and the lines represent communications links. The processors do not have shared memory and communicate by message passing. The entire ensemble is controlled by a *distributed operating system,* and the processors work together on one problem. It is important to distinguish this from a *network operating system,* which links computers that typically work on different problems [Hwang 82]. In other words, a distributed operating system implies intrinsic MIMD operation, whereas a network operating system typically implies multiple SISD operations, which are independent of each other [Stankovic 84].

The interconnection network may assume any topology. Figure 9.1 shows a ring, a tree, and a hypercube, but other topologies may also be used. Any processor can send messages to any other processor. However, the message may have to pass through several *links* or *hops.* A link is a direct connection between two processors. Two processors connected by a link are referred to as *neighbors.*

Examples of hypercube multicomputers, described in Chap. 6, in-

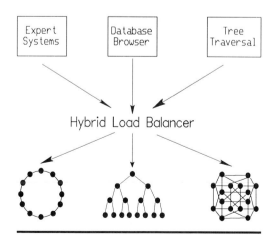

Figure 9.1   Load balancing for mapping Lisp programs onto message-passing multicomputers.

clude the Intel iPSC, NCUBE, FPS T Series, Caltech/JPL Mark III. The AMETEK 2010 is based on a mesh [Hwang 87*c*]. The DADO is an example of a tree-based multicomputer [Stolfo 87]. Hypernets are a class of hierarchically structured multicomputers [Hwang 87*b*]. Recently Texas Instruments has announced a board-level product which allows multiple Lisp machine chips to be supported on computers with a *NuBus*, such as the Apple Macintosh.

9.2.2   Control-level parallelism

We focus on exploiting *control-level parallelism* rather than data-level parallelism as in the Connection Machine [Steele 86]. Figure 9.2 gives an example of control-level parallelism. It shows the *function invocation tree* of a Lisp program, where functions are represented by circles and the arrows indicate function invocation. Processing begins at the root of the tree and spreads downward as more subprocesses are invoked. In control-level parallelism, these subprocess calls are evaluated in parallel on different processors. Generally we expect that the number of processes in such a system would significantly exceed the number of processors. Consequently, a fundamental problem of such systems is the allocation of processes to processors; this is called the *mapping problem*. A good solution to this problem is required if the multicomputer system is to realize its full potential. A poor solution

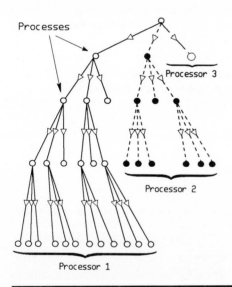

Figure 9.2   Imbalance in creating Lisp processes (function calls) among three processors in a system.

may result in idle processors, low utilization, and low speedup compared to uniprocessor designs.

The problem of finding a good mapping becomes acute for Lisp processing because the programs have highly unpredictable run-time characteristics. For example, the function invocation tree shown in Fig. 9.2 is dense and highly unbalanced. The leftmost branch off the root has the largest number of function calls, the middle branch somewhat less, and the rightmost branch terminates with only one call. In general the shape and depth of these trees is highly data dependent and can display tremendous variations between data sets.

For example, when the Gabriel benchmark Tak is invoked with arguments (18 16 15), it results in 9 function calls. With arguments of (18 16 6), 648,305 function calls result. A small change in a single argument has caused the computational load to increase on the order of 10,000 times. Such variability limits the usefulness of static solutions [Chu 87, Wah 86] to the mapping problem because these solutions depend on reliable predictions of run-time characteristics. For the same reason we use a nonpreemptive system since preemption presumes prior knowledge of run-time behavior. Thus Lisp processing demands a dynamic solution to the mapping problem just as it demands a dynamic solution to the memory management problem.

To illustrate the problems that can result from a bad mapping, consider the example shown in Fig. 9.2 again. Suppose each of the three branches from the root was mapped onto one of three processors with the leftmost branch going to processor 1, the middle branch to processor 2, and the rightmost branch to processor 3. Assuming roughly equal processing times for each function invocation, processor 3 would finish executing first and remain idle while the other two processors performed most of the work. A shorter processing time could be achieved if processes were migrated from the busy processors to the idle processor 3 for execution. (We use the terms *processes* and *functions* interchangeably.) Such run-time process migration and architectural designs for its support are the basic concepts we explore in this chapter.

9.3 Operating System Directives for Process Migration

The use of run-time process migration requires that we choose between a policy of *complete copying* and one of *code migration*. In complete copying, a copy of the application's code is kept on every processor. The operating system code must necessarily reside on every processor. Application's functions are represented by *process control blocks* (PCBs), and it is these PCBs which are migrated rather than the actual application code itself. In code migration, the code itself is moved when a process is migrated for evaluation on a remote proces-

TABLE 9.1   Memory Demands and Major Functions of the Load Balancer and Benchmark Programs

Program	Percentage of memory occupied	Major function
Hybrid	1.99	Load balancing
Tak	0.03	Boundary test
Boyer	1.27	Unification
Browse	0.16	Pattern matching
Traverse	0.31	Searching

sor. The selection of an appropriate policy is orthogonal to dynamic load balancing because either policy may be used with a dynamic load balancer. The choice regarding which policy to pursue then becomes an engineering decision.

Our architecture uses complete copying. Given that communication takes more time than memory access, it makes sense to trade off memory for communications. When this relationship is reversed, we can switch to a policy of code migration. Fortunately Lisp code is very compact, so the price we pay for complete code copying is low. Table 9.1 shows the percentage of total memory on each iPSC processor that is occupied by the code for the hybrid load balancer and four applications programs. Each processor has 4.5 Mbytes of memory with 4.0 Mbytes available for Lisp. The largest application, Boyer, occupies less than 1.3 percent of memory.

9.3.1 Process control blocks

A function is either executable or suspended. If it is executable, it can be sent to the Lisp interpreter for execution. The PCBs for executable functions are maintained in a *ready queue* and are termed *run* PCBs. A function is suspended if it is waiting for its arguments to be evaluated. The PCBs for a suspended function are stored in a *suspend heap* and are referred to as *suspend* PCBs. The ready queue and suspend

Run PCB

Executable Form	Parent ID

Suspend PCB

Process Address	Function Name	Parent ID	Argument Ports

Parent ID

Parent Processor	Process Address	Port ID

Figure 9.3   Process control block (PCB) structures.

heap are separate data structures. Only run PCBs are migrated in the hybrid architecture. Suspend PCBs always remain on the processor on which they were created. The structures of the run and suspend PCBs are shown in Fig. 9.3. The *parent ID* field is common to both and is shown as a separate display.

The following example shows how the suspend and run PCBs are used to represent the function invocation tree corresponding to the execution of a program. Figure 9.4 shows a function invocation tree for

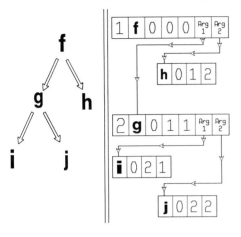

Figure 9.4   Process control block (PCB) representation of a function invocation tree.

the function f, which we have assumed is being invoked on processor #0. The two arguments to f will be returned as the result of evaluating g and h. g also takes two arguments which are the result of evaluating i and j. On the right is the corresponding tree of PCBs.

When a function has arguments that need to be evaluated, such as f, a suspend PCB is created for it in the suspend heap, in this case at *process address* 1. f's arguments are then spawned as run PCBs, and the parent ID fields of the spawned functions act as pointers back to the parent. When the child process has completed evaluation, the system returns the result back to the parent. The parent ID identifies the processor on which the parent resides so the child may be sent to a remote processor for evaluation and the result will still be returned to the correct parent.

For example, if h is evaluated on processor #15, the result is sent back to processor #0 and placed in the suspended process at address #1 because the first two elements of h's parent ID are 0 and 1. (Recall that suspended processes do not migrate, so the parent processor field is always correct). The *port ID* indicates the parent's position in the argument list, i.e., g and h occupy the first and second positions (ports) in the argument list of f and so have port IDs 1 and 2, respectively. When a function is suspended, the system sets the number of *argument ports* in the function's suspend PCB equal to the length of the function's argument list.

A suspend PCB remains in the suspend heap until all its arguments have been evaluated, at which time it is fired in dataflow style by adding it back to the ready queue. We emphasize that our system differs from dataflow in two crucial aspects. First, dataflow exploits very fine grain parallelism at the instruction level. For example, a dataflow actor could perform addition on two integers. We exploit parallelism at the level of Lisp programs, each of which is the equivalent of many dataflow actors. Therefore we are able to amortize the overhead of returning results to parent processes over a much larger number of instructions than is possible in dataflow. Second, tag matching is not required when returning the results. A suspend PCB never moves so it can be located by its address in the suspend heap. Address decoding is used to return results instead of the expensive tag matching operation used in dataflow.

9.3.2 Operating system directives

We provide the user with two operating system directives: SUSPEND and RUN, which act together as a *fork* operation. When inserted into the applications program, they direct the hybrid load balancer to evaluate the application in parallel. This style of interfacing between applications and operating system (O/S) is similar in concept to Halstead's *futures* [Halstead 85]. We did not use futures because the SUSPEND/RUN system is simpler to implement and we wanted to concentrate on load balancing rather than the application-O/S interface.

SUSPEND adds its argument to the suspend heap as a suspend PCB. The syntax of SUSPEND is

  (SUSPEND *function numArgs groundedArgs*)

function is the name of the function to be suspended. It can be either a user-defined function or a built-in Common Lisp function. *numArgs* is the total number of arguments for *function*. SUSPEND will establish an empty association list† of this length as the *arguments* field of suspend PCB. *groundedArgs* is an optional list of grounded arguments. A grounded argument is already bound to a constant which can be inserted into the argument list in the appropriate port.

RUN converts the Lisp form given as its argument into a run PCB form and adds it to the ready queue. The syntax of RUN is

  (RUN *form portID*)

---

†An association list is a list of pairs of tags and data.

form is the Lisp form that is to be evaluated. RUN and SUSPEND are used in conjunction so that a RUN always follows a SUSPEND. RUN creates a run PCB, which is stamped with a parent ID pointing to the function just SUSPENDed. SUSPEND writes the process address assigned to the suspended function into a global variable, which is read by RUN into the parent ID of the run PCB which it creates. The *portID* argument to RUN is written to the *port ID* field of the run PCB. The *parent processor* field of the run PCB is assigned the ID of the processor on which the RUN is being executed.

9.4   Hybrid Load Balancing Method

We describe below critical issues in implementing the hybrid method by defining the receiver- and sender-initiated modes. Each processor has a static list of neighboring processors lying within a neighborhood diameter of hops (links) from the processor. Typically the neighborhood diameter would be one or two hops in order to minimize the network traffic incurred during the exchange of load information. Ferrari [86] has developed a theoretical approach to determining the load index. However, this requires predictions of program behavior which are presumed to be unavailable, so we simply measure the *internal load* of a processor as the length of the ready queue. The *external load* of a processor is the load information broadcast by a processor to its neighbors. Various thresholds and system parameters to be used in the hybrid load balancing method are summarized in Table 9.2.

9.4.1   Sender- vs. receiver-initiated modes

Receiver-initiated mode. The receiver-initiated mode is based on a *drafting protocol* proposed by Ni and associates [Ni 85]. The idle processors initiate load balancing by requesting work from the busy processors. The drafting protocol is a modification of the *bidding method* by Smith [80] but avoids the excessive message traffic caused by broadcasting requests. Each processor only sends requests for work and exchanges load information with its neighbors. In addition, a process may be migrated only once to avoid the possibility of circulating processes.

The external load is obtained by banding the range of the internal load into three bands: *light-load, normal-load,* and *heavy-load* according to a threshold and saturation level denoted by R and S. When the internal load falls below R, the processor is in light-load state. If the internal load falls between R and S, the processor is in normal-load state. When the internal load exceeds S, the processor is in heavy-load state.

A heavy-load processor is a candidate for migrating processes. A

TABLE 9.2   Various Thresholds and Saturation Parameters Used in Hybrid Load Balancing

Threshold	Use	Description
R	Receiver-initiated mode	A processor whose internal load falls below R is in L-load state.
S	Receiver-initiated mode	A processor whose internal load exceeds S is in H-load state, a processor whose internal load falls in between R and S is in N-load state.
T	Sender-initiated mode	A processor's internal load must exceed T before it can export load.
D	Sender-initiated mode	When a processor's external load exceeds D, it may not export load. A processor's external load measures the number of hops to the nearest lightly loaded processor. Setting D to the network diameter shuts down load migration when all processors are heavily loaded.
H	Hybrid system	Processor operates in sender-initiated mode when the number of heavily loaded neighbors falls below H and in receiver-initiated mode when H is exceeded.
L	Hybrid system	A neighbor in sender-initiated mode whose external load exceeds L is considered heavily loaded.

normal-load processor does not participate in load balancing. A light-load processor requests work from heavy-load processors in its neighborhood using a *drafting protocol*. A timing diagram for the drafting protocol is shown in Fig. 9.5 with time increasing as we move down the vertical axis. The time line of a light-load processor is shown in the center flanked by the time lines of two heavy-load processors. The dots indicate events.

The light-load processor requests work from the heavy-load processors. This request is called a *draft*. The heavy-load processor rejects the draft if its load state has changed to normal-load or light-load and broadcasts its new status to its neighborhood. All eligible heavy-load processors return their *draft age* to the drafting processor. This draft age may be measured in several ways. We use the internal load of that processor. The drafting processor will then request a process from the processor with the highest draft age among those responding. The process is then migrated to the drafting processor.

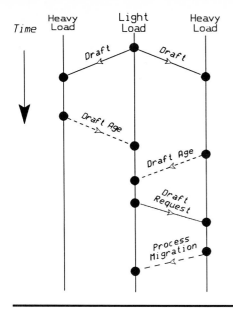

Figure 9.5 Timing diagram for the drafting protocol.

Sender-initiated mode. The *sender-initiated mode* is based on a *gradient* method of load balancing by Lin and Keller [Lin 86]. As compared to the receiver-initiated method, the roles of the idle and busy processors are reversed, so that the busy processors now initiate the load balancing. As before, the internal load of a processor is the length of the ready queue. The external load indicates the number of hops to the nearest idle processor. A processor is considered idle if its internal load drops below a static systemwide threshold T. If its load exceeds T, it takes the minimum external load of its neighbors and increments it by one. The external load is bounded by the diameter of the network to prevent circulating processes. The equation below summarizes the definition of external load:

$$\text{External load} = \begin{cases} 0 & \text{if internal load} < T \\ \min\{\Delta,\ 1 + \min\ \{\text{external loads of neighbors}\}\} \\ \text{otherwise} \end{cases}$$

where Δ is the network diameter.

The external load is zero if the internal load of processor P_j is less than T. An external load of zero signals the rest of the system that processor P_j is lightly loaded and is available to take on work from busier processors. If the internal load on the processor is greater than

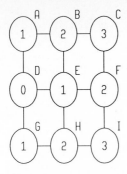

Figure 9.6 External loads in sender-initiated mode.

T, the processor picks the lowest of the external loads propagated by the neighboring processors, increments it by one, and passes it on. The propagation of these external load values provides an implicit routing to the nearest lightly loaded processor.

Figure 9.6 provides a snapshot of such an external load grid. Processor D is the only idle processor with an external load of 0. All the other processors have internal loads greater than the threshold, so they propagate the external load value, incrementing by one at each hop. The external load indicates the number of hops to the nearest processor with load 0. A processor always picks the neighbor with the least external load when exporting a process. The exported process follows the gradients provided by the external load values until it ends up at a 0 loaded processor. The gradients also ensure that the shortest path is used; e.g., processor F would always route to processor E since processors C and I have heavier external loads. Then processor E would forward to processor D since processors B and H have heavier external loads. In this way the process is forwarded by the shortest path between processors F and D.

9.4.2 The hybrid method

In a very heavily loaded system, the receiver-initiated mode has the advantage of minimizing network traffic since processes are only allowed to migrate once. There is also less possibility of all the heavily loaded processors migrating all their work to one lightly loaded processor and overwhelming its communications ports. However, in a lightly loaded system the sender-initiated mode has the advantage of beginning process migration as soon as a processor enters a heavily loaded state. There is no necessity to wait for lightly loaded processors to send requests and to engage in a lengthy protocol before migration begins. We therefore propose a hybrid method using the receiver-initiated mode when system load becomes excessive and using the sender-initiated mode when system load is light.

The hybrid method requires a distributed mechanism to manage the switching between sender-initiated and receiver-initiated modes of operation. The use of distributed control cannot guarantee that the entire system is in either one or the other mode exclusively. Instead each processor will operate in either sender-initiated or receiver-initiated mode depending on its local environment. All processors are initialized to sender-initiated mode. When more than a threshold number of a processor's neighbors become heavily loaded, the system becomes *congested* and the processor switches to receiver-initiated mode. We refer to this as the *hybrid threshold H* to distinguish it from the threshold value T that defines low and heavy load. If the number of heavily loaded neighbors falls below the hybrid threshold, the processor switches back to sender-initiated mode. Table 9.3 summarizes these changes. Processors can service messages and processes received from processors operating under the other mode, providing a smooth interface between the sender-initiated and receiver-initiated parts of the system.

TABLE 9.3   Switching Modes of Each Processor for Hybrid Load Balancing

Condition/mode	Processor is in receiver-initiated mode	Processor is in sender-initiated mode
System becomes congested	No change	Switch to receiver-initiated mode
System becomes uncongested	Switch to sender-initiated mode	No change

9.4.3   Macro dataflow execution model

Figure 9.7 shows the macro dataflow execution model which is the basis for implementing the hybrid load balancer. The figure shows the ready queue and suspend heap for a single processor. The components of the hybrid load balancer are shown as boxes with italic labels. The *decision maker* pops the next process off the ready queue and decides whether to evaluate it remotely or locally. The decision depends on whether the processor is in sender or receiver-initiated mode which is also controlled by the *decision maker*. These actions have all been described above.

PCBs destined for remote evaluation are sent to the *migrator* and are routed to a remote processor for evaluation. The returned values are picked up by the *mailman* and forwarded to *awake* which matches up the value with its parent in the suspend heap. When all arguments

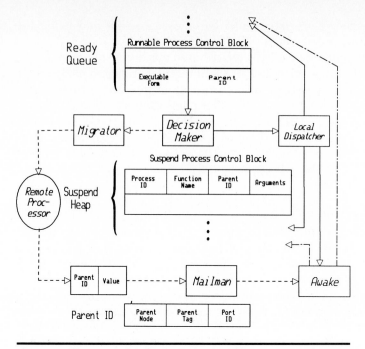

Figure 9.7   The macro dataflow execution model.

are present, the parent will be returned to the ready queue. If the *decision maker* decides on local evaluation, then the run PCB is sent to the *local dispatcher* and evaluated. This may cause additional functions to be suspended and added to the suspend heap and spawned functions which are added to the ready queue. Results are either sent to the local *awake* or the remote *awake* on which the parent process resides. As discussed in Sec. 9.3, the *parent ID* field of the PCB acts as a pointer back to the parent, allowing the result to be returned.

9.5   Multicomputer Architectural Support

Recent advances in very large scale integration (VLSI) technology make possible multicomputer Lisp machines which are an order of magnitude faster than current architectures [Sugimoto 83]. Lisp CPUs are available from Texas Instruments, Xerox, and Symbolics which provide faster Lisp processing than the general-purpose CPUs used in present Lisp multicomputers. Also available are fast switching chips capable of handling 100-Mbits/s interprocessor communications—10 times faster than current rates. Dynamic load balancing solves the mapping problem but can impose a severe run-time over-

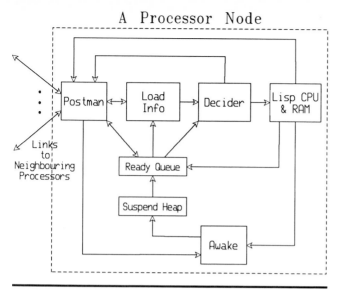

Figure 9.8   A processor node with hybrid load balancing.

head on CPU resources. Hardware designs are given below for alleviating overhead.

9.5.1   A single processor architecture

Figure 9.8 shows the architecture of a single processor. The fast switching chip is embedded in the *postman* module and the Lisp CPU [Sussman 81] is shown on the right. The hybrid load balancer is implemented in the *postman, load info, decider,* and *awake* modules. In a software implementation, these functions are executed sequentially by the CPU. The advantage of the hardware design is that these three units operate in parallel. Messages arriving at the *postman* are handled without waiting for CPU intervention. The *decider* module can begin exporting processes without waiting for the CPU to finish executing. The CPU can continuously evaluate applications programs without waiting for the load balancer to complete execution.

The hardware design also dedicates memory to the *ready queue* and *suspend heap,* speeding up access to these structures. In a software implementation, these structures are part of the general address space, and access may be delayed while the CPU accesses the same memory space.

9.5.2   The postman and awake modules

The *postman* module handles all communications functions and is shown in Fig. 9.9. The *switch* handles all message-routing functions.

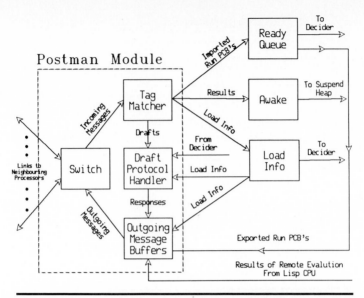

Figure 9.9 The *postman* module for a hardware load balancer.

We do not concern ourselves here with the design of this switch and assume that it can handle all incoming and outgoing messages.

All messages are tagged, allowing the *tag matcher* unit to sort incoming messages and forward them to the appropriate modules. Imported run PCBs are sent to the *ready queue* where they are either executed locally or exported depending on the actions of the *decider* module. Results of remote evaluation are sent to the *awake* module and returned to the corresponding parent in the *suspend heap*. Load information messages are sent to the *load info* module. This information is used by the *decider* module and the *draft protocol* unit. The draft protocol is part of the receiver-initiated mode defined in Sec. 9.4. A signal from the *decider* module activates a new draft protocol. Draft and response messages are all handled by the dedicated protocol unit.

The strategy of complete code copying results in a large number of short messages on the order of 50 bytes. To accommodate this type of traffic, the *outgoing message buffer* unit is designed to handle a large number of short messages rather than longer messages. The continuing decline in the cost of memory means that providing 10,000 to 100,000 buffers is feasible, and our experience running programs on the iPSC indicates that provision of buffers on this scale is required.

Figure 9.10 shows the *awake* module which controls the interaction of the *ready queue* and *suspend heap*. The *ready queue* accepts run PCBs from three sources: imports from neighboring processors, the Lisp CPU, and processes activated by the *awake* module. Run PCBs are exported under the control of the *decider* and *draft protocol unit*.

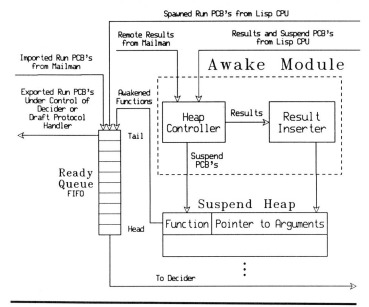

Figure 9.10 The *awake* module for a hardware load balancer.

The *local dispatcher* unit takes run PCBs from the head of the queue for evaluation by the Lisp CPU.

The *awake* module shown in Fig. 9.10 consists of the *heap controller* and *result inserter* units. The *heap controller* adds new suspended PCBs from the Lisp CPU to the *suspend heap*. When all the arguments to a suspended PCB have been returned, the *heap controller* reactivates the PCB as a run PCB and moves it to the *ready queue*. Results arriving at the *heap controller* are passed on to the *result inserter,* where they are matched with the corresponding parent process.

9.5.3 Load information and decider modules

The *load information* module shown in Fig. 9.11 consists of *load information registers* and a *load calculator* unit. The registers hold the external load data broadcast by neighboring processors. The *load calculator* monitors the *ready queue* and the registers to calculate the internal and external loads for this processor.

The *decider* module shown in the center of Fig. 9.11 consists of the *decision maker, migrator,* and *local dispatcher* units. These hardware units perform the same functions as their counterparts in the macro dataflow model. The *decision maker* switches the processor between sender- and receiver-initiated modes of operation. In sender-initiated

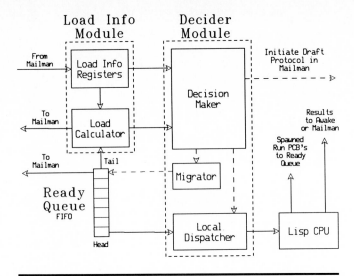

Figure 9.11 The *load info* and *decider* modules for a hardware load balancer.

mode, the *decision maker* can signal the *migrator* to begin load migration. In receiver-initiated mode, the *decision maker* can initiate a draft protocol by signaling the *draft protocol* unit in *mailman*. The *local dispatcher* is invoked if local processing is to be used.

The *ready queue* is a first-in, first-out (FIFO) queue. Access to the queue causes the length of the queue to be signaled to the *load calculator*. The execution of SUSPEND and RUN directives in the Lisp CPU spawns run PCBs which are added to the *ready queue*. The results of evaluation are sent to *awake* when the parent process resides in the same processor. When the parent resides on a remote processor, the result is sent to the *mailman* for forwarding.

9.5.4 Hybrid software architecture.

In this section, we present a software implementation of the hybrid load balancer based on the macro dataflow execution model. The implementation is characterized by a high degree of modularity for understandability, maintainability, portability, and reliability. Figure 9.12 shows the architecture of the software design. The identical architecture is duplicated on every processor and there are no client/server relationships between processors. The hybrid load balancer is therefore a true distributed operating system with no central master. This gives the hybrid load balancer the desirable property of *scalability,* meaning that even as the number of processors in the system is increased, the hybrid load balancer will continue to perform. It has no master component to become a bottleneck that eventually chokes the system.

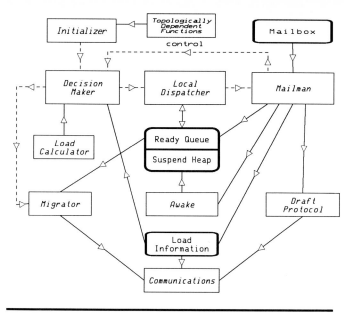

Figure 9.12   Components of a software load balancer.

In Fig. 9.12, functions are shown in plain boxes with italic labels, while data structures are shown in heavy boxes with plain labels. The basic *kernel* is a tight loop consisting of the *decision maker, local dispatcher,* and *mailman.* The kernel is entered through an *initializer* which configures the hybrid load balancer according to information contained in a file of *topologically dependent functions.* In this way we are able to isolate the hybrid load balancer from the topology of the underlying hardware allowing it to be ported to multicomputers of any topology.

The architecture is centered around three data classes: the run PCB, the suspend PCB, and a class of messages consisting of seven types (Table 9.4). Each data class is contained in a separate *package*

TABLE 9.4   Message Types in the Hybrid Load Balancer

Package	Message types
Local dispatcher	Run PCB
Awake	Suspend PCB
Mailman	Message:
	Result of evaluation
	Sender-initiated mode load information
	Receiver-initiated mode load information
	Receiver-initiated mode draft
	Receiver-initiated mode response to draft
	Receiver-initiated mode final call
	Kill kernel

which defines that data class and all functions that access that class. A package is an information hiding mechanism. Only names declared within the package as *exported* can be accessed by objects outside the package. For example, the run PCBs are stored in the ready queue which obeys a first-in, first-out discipline. All ready queue access functions have been concentrated in the *local-dispatcher* package. Any access to the ready queue must be made using the functions defined in the *local-dispatcher* package. Functions outside the *local-dispatcher* package cannot access the queue directly.

The run PCB and suspended PCB data classes have been treated in Sec. 9.3. The discussion therefore centers on the data types defined in the *mailman* package. All data types in the *mailman* are messages and are passed back and forth between the processors. In an object-oriented system, we would have defined each message type as a *subclass* of a class *message*.

Structures of the type *result of evaluation* are used to return the results of function evaluation back to the parent process. Instances of this type are produced by *local dispatcher* and consumed by *awake*. The structure of a *result* is shown in Fig. 9.13. The *parent address* and *port ID* allow *awake* to place the *return value* in the correct *argument port* of the correct suspended process.

Load information messages for sender-initiated mode and receiver-initiated mode carry the external load information defined in Sec. 9.4. The structure of this type is shown in Fig. 9.13. The *processor ID* field identifies the processor whose load information is being broadcast to the neighboring processors.

The three receiver-initiated mode types *draft, response-to-draft,* and *request-process* are used to implement the drafting protocol defined in Sec. 9.4. The stages of the drafting protocol and the corresponding message types are shown in Fig. 9.5. A new drafting protocol is initi-

Result Type

Parent Address	Port ID	Return Value

Load Information Type

Processor ID	Load Value

Draft and Request-Process Types

processor ID

Response-to-Draft Type

processor ID	Internal Load

Figure 9.13 Message types.

ated when the *decision maker* signals the *draft protocol* module. This module generates and handles all messages related to the protocol. The structures of the *draft, response-to-draft,* and *request-process* messages are shown in Fig. 9.13. When sending a draft or a request for process it is only necessary to identify the sender of the message. The *response-to-draft* requires two fields, one to identify the sender and another to hold the internal load information.

The *kill-kernel* message type is used to terminate the kernel when the application has finished executing. The kernel knows when to terminate by the following mechanism. The *parent address* 0 is reserved for use as the parent of the root process of the application. Therefore when *awake* receives a result destined for a parent with address 0, we know that processing has completed. An instance of the *kill-kernel* type is broadcast to all processors and the kernel shuts down. The *kill-kernel* consists simply of an empty dummy field.

9.6   Parallelism in Executing Lisp Programs

We discuss below how the hybrid load balancer exploits four classes of parallelism in Lisp programs: AND-parallelism, OR-parallelism, parallel evaluation of list structures, and parallel evaluation of arguments to functions.

9.6.1   AND-parallelism

AND-parallelism may occur in a conditional statement. The arguments to the AND can then be evaluated in parallel. An example is given below. If the functions f or g evaluates to true, then the function h will be executed.†

```
(cond ((AND (f) (g))
       (h)))
```

Care must be taken when employing AND-parallelism because the semantics of the parallel AND can be different from the sequential AND. In Common Lisp evaluation stops at the first failure, so if f failed, g would not be evaluated. With AND-parallelism, all parts of the condition would be executed. If g gave rise to some side effect, then the semantics of the parallel AND would be different from the sequential AND. AND-parallelism may also incur heavy overhead. Continuing our example, suppose g gives rise to a lot of computation and f is

---

†In Lisp syntax (f a) means calling the function f with the argument a and is equivalent to the Pascal function call f(a). Therefore (f) is equivalent to calling a function f, which takes no arguments.

false. In the sequential AND, g would not get executed and the computational overhead of g is avoided but in the parallel AND, g would be evaluated and the overhead incurred. When we converted the application programs for parallel execution, we avoided AND-parallelism in situations where it would give rise to different semantics or where there was a possibility of incurring heavy overhead.

9.6.2 OR-parallelism

OR-parallelism may also occur in a conditional statement. The arguments to the OR can then be evaluated in parallel. An example is given below. If either of the functions f and g evaluates true, then the function h will be executed.

    (cond ((OR (f) (g))
            (h)))

The remarks above about the potentially different semantics of sequential and parallel ANDs apply to ORs as well. Here the Common Lisp OR stops at the first success. Note that the sequential and parallel versions are not necessarily different; they are only potentially different. Necessary and sufficient conditions for the semantics to be different are that an interruption in execution should occur, for ANDs a failure, for ORs a success, and that one of the remaining forms that would not have been executed in the sequential version has a side effect. In the absence of side effects the semantics would be exactly the same, although run times may differ. As we mentioned in Sec. 9.1, side effects are beyond the scope of this chapter.

9.6.3 List and argument parallelism

List parallelism means the parallel application of a function to all the elements of a list. For example, the code below causes f to be applied to each element of longList. These multiple calls to f can all be evaluated in parallel.†

    (mapcar #'f longList)

Argument parallelism is a special case of list parallelism where the list happens to be the argument list of a function. In the example below, the function f has two arguments which are the result of the evaluation of g and h. In argument parallelism, g and h are evaluated in parallel

    (f (g) (h))

---

†If longList were bound to (a b c), execution of the above code would give rise to 3 calls to f: (f a) (f b) (f c).

When exploiting parallelism in existing sequential programs, care must be taken when the sequential program uses a shared global variable to pass data between subprocesses. We use the more common term *global variable* instead of the Common Lisp terminology, *special variable*. In the example below, the function f writes its argument to the global variable channel using the Lisp assignment function SETQ. The function g reads channel, wraps up the result of the read and its argument into a list, and prints out the result. Thus, channel serves as a channel for information from f to g. We shall denote such global variables as *channel variables*.

```
(defun f (y)
       (setq channel y))

(defun g (y)
       (format t "~ % ~ a" (list channel y))
```

Continuing with this example, we declare a temporary function using LAMBDA. The MAPCAR then causes the LAMBDA body to be applied to each element of targetList. If the evaluation of f is true, then g will be evaluated.

```
(mapcar #'(lambda (z)
              (cond ((f z)
                     (g z))))
        targetList)
```

If targetList consisted of the list (a b), then executing the code fragment above would result in two calls to the LAMBDA body:

```
(cond ((f a)
       (g a)))

(cond (f b)
      (g b)))
```

The MAPCAR cannot be evaluated using list parallelism because each call to f causes a value to be written to the channel variable channel. This may not then be read by the correct call to g. In our example, the value of channel written by the call to (f a) could be read by (g b) instead of the call to (g a). The problem results from a single global variable channel being used as a channel by multiple copies of f and g, and there is contention for the use of the channel. The solution is to localize channel so that each f and g pair has its own private channel.

```
(defun h (y)
       (let (channel)
            (cond ((setq channel y)
                      (format t "~%~ a" (list channel y))))))

(mapcar #'(lambda (z)
              (h z))
          targetList)
```

We define a new function h that combines the code of f and g. The LET causes channel to be treated as a local variable. The body of the LAMBDA in the MAPCAR is now changed to a call on h. List parallelism may now be applied to the MAPCAR without danger of conflict in the use of the channel variable channel.

9.7   Parallelization of Lisp Programs

We now show how the RUN and SUSPEND directives are used to exploit the four parallelism classes defined in Sec. 9.6.

9.7.1   Parallelization of AND/OR-parallelism

We begin with an example of AND-parallelism. The sequential AND is converted to parallel form by first suspending the AND. An argument of 2 is given to SUSPEND to indicate that the AND is expecting 2 arguments. These arguments are supplied by evaluating the functions f and g. f is RUN with a port ID of 1 so that the result of evaluating f will be returned to position 1 of the argument list of the suspended AND. g is RUN with a port ID of 2, and its result is returned to position 2 in the argument list. Recall that RUN does not cause its argument to be executed immediately. Rather RUN causes its argument to be added to the ready queue for later evaluation. f and g would then be evaluated in parallel if one of them is migrated to another processor.

Sequential AND:

(and (f) (g))

Parallel AND:

(SUSPEND 'and 2)
(RUN '(f) 1)
(RUN '(g) 2)

OR-parallelism can be exploited in the same way as AND-parallelism.

Sequential OR:

(or (f) (g))

Parallel OR:

(SUSPEND 'OR 2)
(RUN '(f) 1)
(RUN '(g) 2)

9.7.2 Parallelization of list and argument parallelism

List parallelism may be exploited by spawning a run PCB for each operation on a list element as in the example below. We first suspend a LIST to accumulate the results of the spawned functions. This duplicates the semantics of MAPCAR, which returns a list of the results of the successive calls to the function. One call to f will be made for each element of longList so the argument list of the suspended LIST is set to the length of longList. MAPCAR is used to execute RUN once for each element of longList. The macro statement '(f ,x) corresponds to an application of f on each list element.†

Sequential list operation:

(mapcar #'f longList)

Parallel list operation:

(SUSPEND 'list (length longList))
(let ((i 0))
    (mapcar #'(lambda (x)
            (RUN '(f ,x) (setq i (1+ i))))
        longList))

Argument parallelism can be exploited in a straightforward way. First the calling function f is suspended. Then each of its arguments is RUN with the appropriate port ID.

Sequential evaluation of arguments:

(f (g) (h))

Parallel evaluation of arguments:

(SUSPEND 'f 2)
(RUN '(g) 1)
(RUN '(h) 2)

---

†If longList is bound to '(a b c), the macrostatement corresponds to (f a) (f b) (f c).

9.7.3   Parallelization of Gabriel benchmarks programs

We decided to use benchmarks from the Gabriel suite [Gabriel 85] rather than write our own benchmarks because the semantics and profile of Lisp operations for these programs are well known and they have been used on a wide variety of computers. The Gabriel suite contains benchmarks oriented toward both numerical and AI processing. Since our interest is primarily in AI processing, we selected four benchmarks from this area: Tak, Boyer, Browse, and Traverse. Because the semantics and profile of these programs are published elsewhere, we concentrate on discussing the degree of parallelism found in these programs and on the *translation effort* required to prepare the sequential code for parallel execution. The following parallelization examples show that very little translation effort is required to obtain a high degree of parallelism.

The Tak program.   As a functionally oriented language, Lisp makes heavy demands on the function calling capabilities of an implementation. Tak generates many function calls and is a good test of the extent of overhead incurred by an implementation in setting up function calls. Moreover, Tak has a function invocation tree that is bushy and, at the same time, unbalanced. This makes it an ideal test of the load balancing capabilities of the hybrid method. The function invocation tree for this program was shown in Fig. 9.2. We reproduce below the sequential and parallel codes of Tak for comparison purposes:

Sequential Tak:

```
(defun tak (x y z)
      (if (not ( <  y  x))
                z
                (tak (tak (1-  x) y z)
                (tak (1-  y) z x)
                (tak (1-  z) × y))))
```

Parallel Tak:

```
(defun tak (x y z)
      (if (not ( <  y x))
                z
                (progn
                      (SUSPEND 'tak 3)
                      (RUN '(tak ,(1-  x) ,y ,z) 1)
                      (RUN '(tak ,(1-  y) ,z ,x) 2)
                      (RUN '(tak ,(1-  z) ,x ,y) 3))))
```

The sequential Tak consists of an *if* statement. If (not ($<$ y x)) suc-ceeds, i.e., if $y \leq x$, then Tak terminates, returning the value z. The *else* part consists of a recursive call on Tak whose arguments are three fur-ther calls on Tak. These may be parallelized by SUSPENDing the first call to Tak and then RUNning the three remaining calls to Tak. This is an example of the *argument parallelism* discussed in Sec. 9.6. The num-bers 1, 2, and 3 shown as arguments to RUN indicate that the results of the respective calls to Tak should be returned to the first, second, and third places in the argument list of the SUSPENDed Tak.

The Boyer program.   Boyer is a theorem-proving program. The inner loop of this program is unification, which is also the inner loop process of the Prolog language. We identified three levels of granularity and decided to exploit the two coarsest levels.

The coarsest granularity exploits the list parallelism defined in Sec. 9.6. The Boyer program is given a logical term to prove correct. This term is a compound term constructed from simpler terms. We can ap-ply list parallelism to break up the compound term into simpler terms and apply unification to each simple term. An example of a compound term is (equal (implies x y) (equal z w)). This may be broken up into the simpler terms (implies x y) and (equal z w) with unification being applied to each. The Lisp prefix syntax is being used here so (implies x y) represents the logical term $x \supset y$. All logical terms are constants, so we need not be concerned about consistency checking when apply-ing parallel unification to ANDed terms.

At the medium granularity, a term derived using the coarsest gran-ularity can be unified against multiple axioms in parallel in a form of OR-parallelism. For example, we attempt to unify the term (equal z w) with the four axioms shown below:

```
(equal (plus a b) (zero))
(equal (plus a b) (plus a c))
(equal (zero) (difference x y))
(equal x (difference x y))
```

At the finest granularity, atomic terms such as z and w can be uni-fied in parallel. We conjectured that this level of parallelism would be too fine grained to justify the overhead required to exploit it. Another reason for not exploiting this kind of fine-grain parallelism is that it results in code that is harder to understand, harder to maintain, and harder to test and debug because the parallelization process results in greater code complexity at such fine granularity.

The Browse program.   Browse performs pattern matching operations indicative of the inner loop operations found in expert systems. Two levels of granularity were identified and used in Browse as discussed below.

At coarse granularity, the *match* subroutine is multitasked 1200 times. Each run is independent of the others, so in the parallel version we run all 1200 in parallel. The semantics of the serial version requires that the result of the last *match* be returned. In order to duplicate this effect in the parallel version, we wrote a new function *last-elt* that returns its last argument. *last-elt* is SUSPENDed and then serves as the parent to the 1200 runs of *match*.

At the next level of granularity, we made use of OR- and AND-parallelism arising in conditional statements. We show an example for OR-parallelism below. The exploitation of AND-parallelism, which is not shown, is similar and was discussed in Sec. 9.7.

Sequential OR:

```
(OR (match (cdr pat) dat alist)
    (match (cdr pat) (cdr dat) alist)
    (match pat (cdr dat) alist))
```

Parallel OR:

```
(SUSPEND 'OR 3)
(RUN '(match ,(cdr pat) ,dat ,alist) 1)
(RUN '(match ,(cdr pat) ,(cdr dat) ,alist) 2)
(RUN '(match ,pat ,(cdr dat) ,alist) 3))
```

The parallel code has almost the same syntax as the serial version. This promotes understandability and maintainability. We first SUSPEND the OR, which then serves as the parent to the three parallel invocations of *match*.

The Traverse program. Traverse is a graph traversal program. The graph has 100 nodes and the edges are directed. Multiple edges can exist between graph nodes. The graph also has cycles and reflexive edges. However the graph does have a root. Traverse visits every node in the graph, marking visited nodes. The program operates by writing these marks to a global graph structure. In all, 250 graphs are traversed. To run all 250 traversals in parallel requires that we provide a private copy of the graph to each traversal, otherwise each copy of Traverse would mark the same data structure. This is done by having a list of 250 graphs on each processor. Each graph in the list has a unique ID, and each copy of the traversal program works on its own graph. Information about which graph nodes have been visited is exchanged between processors using an *environment* field in the *run PCB* and *result* structures. In this way processors working on the same graph can sometimes avoid marking the same node. However, we cannot guarantee that the same node will not be marked twice by different processors working simultaneously on the same graph. The semantics of the serial and parallel traverses are therefore different. In the serial version each node is marked exactly once; in the parallel version at least once, but perhaps more. Now whether visiting at least once is acceptable depends on the purpose of the traversal. If the purpose is simply to mark every node, then the semantics are the same. It is only when we require that each node be marked exactly once that the parallel version fails.

We emphasize that the hybrid operating system knows nothing about the contents of the environment field. The use of this field is completely the responsibility of the applications programmer, so the operating system is totally insulated from the application. The operating system only knows that the application will provide a function called *update-environment* which must be run every time a *run PCB* or *result* structure arrives at the *mailman*. Two levels of granularity were exploited in Traverse. At the coarsest level, all 250 graphs are traversed simultaneously.

At the next level, list parallelism is exploited within each graph traversal. When an unmarked node is encountered, it is marked and then all of the sons of that node are visited in turn. In list parallelism, all the sons are visited in parallel. The sequential and parallel codes are shown below.

Sequential processing of sons list:

```
(do ((sons (node-sons node) (cdr sons)))
    ((null sons) ())
    (travers (car sons) mark))
```

Parallel processing of sons list:

```
(SUSPEND 'AND (length (node-sons node))
(do ((sons (node-sons node) (cdr sons))
      (port ID 1 (1+  portID)))
    ((null sons) ())
    (RUN '(par-travers ,(car sons), graphID) port ID))
```

We review the sequential version first. The first argument to the do is a list declaring loop variables, in this case ((sons (node-sons node) (cdr sons))), which initializes the loop variable sons to the sons list of node. On subsequent iterations, sons will be set to its CDR, which returns all the elements of sons except the first. The main body of the do loop applies *travers* to the head of the sons list. In this way all of the elements of the sons list are processed until the sons list is empty, the exit condition ((null sons) ()) is met, and the loop is exited.

In the parallel version, we SUSPEND an AND to serve as the parent. The do loop is run in much the same fashion as the serial version. Only now, instead of executing *par-travers* immediately, we place it in the ready queue with RUN for later, possibly parallel, execution. The *travers* function in the serial version was renamed *par-travers* to avoid confusion.

9.7.4   Compile-time overhead

Table 9.5 below shows the number of operating system directives, SUSPEND and RUN combinations, required as a percentage of the lines of code in the benchmark programs. This percentage gives an idea of the amount of translation effort required by indicating roughly how many lines of code need to be changed out of the total lines of sequential code. In the "Number of SUSPEND/RUNs" column, we count each SUSPEND and its related RUNs as one unit since they logically go together. For example, the Tak program has 1 SUSPEND followed by 3 RUNs, and this is counted as one logical unit in the table below. In the "Number of lines of code" column, we count the lines of code in the sequential version of the test programs, excluding comments and blank lines. This gives a slightly more conservative estimate of the conversion effort than if we had used the lines of code in the parallel versions which have more lines of code.

TABLE 9.5   Operating System Directives in Percentage of Lines of Code

Program	Number of SUSPEND/RUNs	Number of lines of code	Percentage
Tak	1	6	17
Boyer	5	501	1
Browse	3	96	3
Traverse	2	116	2

The percentage of directive insertions required for Tak is abnormally high because it is such a short program to begin with. The percentages for the other programs are more representative, ranging from 1 to 3 percent. These low figures suggest that the translation effort is not unduly onerous.

Comparing these percentages with the degree of parallelism extracted from these programs, we see that we are able to elicit a high degree of parallelism for a small translation effort. In Browse and Traverse we extracted 1200 and 250 degrees of parallelism at the first level alone, with the lower levels adding more degrees of parallelism. While our sample is too small to represent a scientific sampling, we believe it gives a reasonable picture of the parallelism to translation ratio. These are standard benchmarks written originally for sequential machines without any thought for parallelism. That we were able to extract parallelism from such programs suggests the same would be true of other sequential programs. Furthermore, in Sec. 9.6, we indicated four general sources of parallelism commonly found in Lisp programs. This suggests that the hybrid load balancer would be an efficient means of providing for the parallel execution of existing software libraries.

9.8   Concurrent Lisp Benchmarking and Analysis

This section presents results of running the Gabriel benchmarks Tak, Boyer, Browse, and Traverse on an Intel iPSC multicomputer. Results were also obtained for tree and ring topologies which were simulated on the hypercube. Both applications and the hybrid load balancer itself are easily ported between topologies. The applications can be moved without modification. The hybrid load balancer needs only simple modifications to the set of topology dependent files which specify the list of neighbours for each processor. Different machine sizes can also be handled in the same way. Such portability would have required expensive maintenance had the applications been written directly to the hardware.

9.8.1   Gabriel benchmark results

In these experiments, we used *speedup* as the performance measure. To calculate speedup we first timed the execution of the serial benchmark program on a single processor of the multicomputer. We then timed the execution of the benchmark using multiple processors to obtain the parallel execution time. The speedup is then obtained by dividing the serial timing by the parallel timing. Table 9.6 summarizes the threshold and saturation parameters used in the four benchmark experiments.

TABLE 9.6   Threshold and Saturation Parameter Used in the Benchmarks

Threshold	Hybrid	Sender	Receiver
R	14	n/a	14
S	20	n/a	20
T	10†	10†	n/a
D	Network diameter	Network diameter	n/a
H	2	n/a	n/a
L	1	n/a	n/a

†3 for Boyer.

The Tak benchmark.   Figure 9.14*a* shows the speedup obtained for the Tak benchmark on the hypercube multicomputer with 4, 8, and 16 processors. The large number of functions spawned and the highly unbalanced function invocation tree make Tak a good boundary test of load balancing capabilities. Figure 9.14*b* through *c* show results for ring and tree topologies

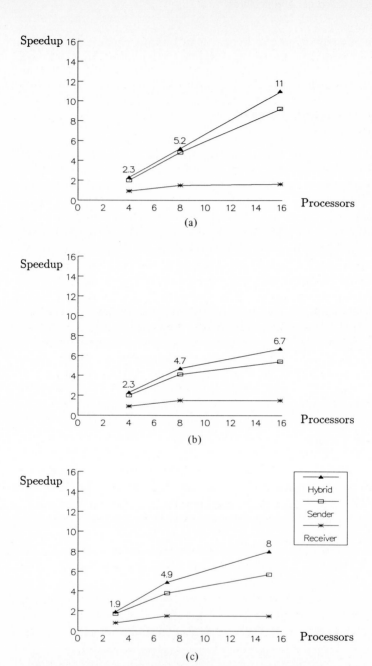

Figure 9.14 Results for the benchmark Tak. (a) iPSC hypercube; (b) ring topology simulated on the iPSC; (c) tree topology simulated on the iPSC.

which were simulated on the hypercube. With 16 processors, the hypercube performs best, followed by the tree and ring. At this machine size, the hypercube has greater connectivity with each processor having four neighbors, whereas in a tree a processor may have between one and three neighbors and in a ring each processor has only two neighbors. The hypercube does not have this advantage for smaller machine sizes, and so performance values are similar.

The Boyer benchmark. Figure 9.15 shows the speedups for the Boyer benchmark. These results are similar to the Browse benchmarks. The sender-initiated method can lead to load migration between busy processors when the system is heavily loaded. The penalty for this overmigration becomes greater as the network diameter increases. Therefore we see a more severe flattening off of the performance curve for the pure sender-initiated method for the ring and tree topologies than for the hypercube.

The Browse benchmark. Figure 9.16 shows the benchmark results for Browse. The hybrid method produces the best performance across all topologies and machine sizes. However, we noticed a severe flattening of the performance curve for the ring and tree topologies. We attribute this flattening to the uneven pattern of process generation in this program. The hypercube is better able to redistribute the load with its superior connectivity.

The Traverse benchmark. As revealed in Fig. 9.17, Traverse shows the least speedup of all the benchmarks. We attribute this to the possibility of duplicate work occurring during the execution of this program. Recall that Traverse causes all processors to traverse the same graphs in parallel. The processors exchange information about which graph nodes have been visited, but multiple processors can still visit the same graph node.

The iPSC running the hybrid system is shown to be scalable for the four benchmarks. In all cases the best performance is obtained under the hybrid method of load balancing. The low performance of the receiver-initiated method is attributed to the high overhead incurred during system initialization. Processing begins at a single root processor and must propagate throughout the system. Under the receiver-initiated method, process migration must wait for load information to propagate first since receivers must have knowledge about busy processors before they can begin drafting. During initialization, only the root processor is doing useful work. The receiver-initiated method should be reserved for the most heavily loaded stages of the computa-

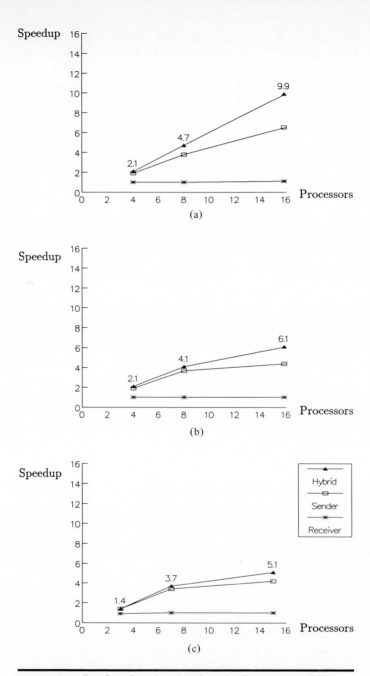

Figure 9.15 Results for the benchmark Boyer. (*a*) iPSC hypercube; (*b*) ring topology simulated on the iPSC; (*c*) tree topology simulated on the iPSC.

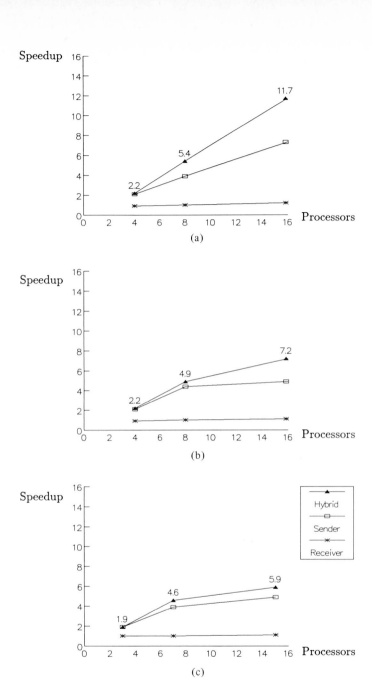

Figure 9.16 Results for the benchmark Browse. (*a*) iPSC hypercube; (*b*) ring topology simulated on the iPSC; (*c*) tree topology simulated on the iPSC.

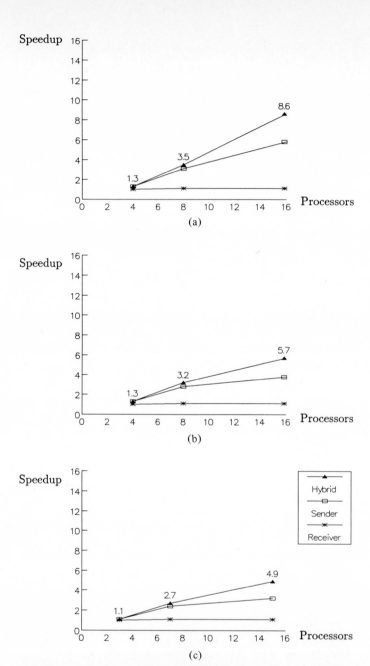

Figure 9.17 Results for the benchmark Traverse. (*a*) iPSC hypercube; (*b*) ring topology simulated on the iPSC; (*c*) tree topology simulated on the iPSC.

tion, during which its conservative approach can best help to reduce overhead.

The sender-initiated method works well during the initial stages of computation when load is light and the primary need is to propagate processes. During the later stages of computation this method produces excessive process migration as all the processors become heavily loaded and attempt to migrate processes to each other. The ability of the hybrid method to switch to the less expensive receiver-initiated method accounts for its better performance.

9.8.2 Performance analysis

Figure 9.18 compares dynamic load balancing with the hybrid method and static load balancing for Tak. For the static case we made a random allocation of processes to processors, and processes do not migrate at run time. Given the assumption that run-time behavior cannot be predicted, we cannot apply more sophisticated static methods which assume some knowledge of run-time characteristics. These results indicate that faster processing times can be achieved with dynamic methods.

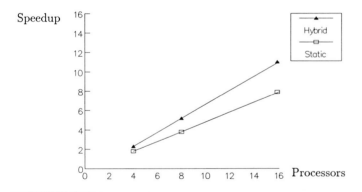

Figure 9.18 Relative performance of dynamic versus static load balancing.

The hybrid load balancer has pairs of threshold/saturation parameters for both the sender-initiated and receiver-initiated modes. These parameters are set globally before run time and remain constant during the execution of the program. We interpret the results for Tak shown in Figs. 9.19 and 9.20 as indicating that the performance of the hybrid load balancer is reasonably insensitive to the setting of these parameters. All experiments were performed with a hypercube topology.

Recall that the T value in Fig. 9.19 determines when processors will begin load migration in sender-initiated mode. When a processor's internal load exceeds T, it begins load migration. The four graphs differ

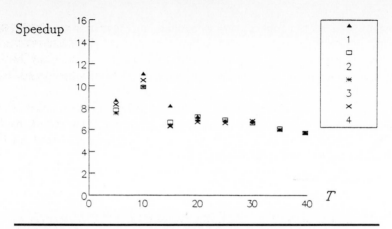

Figure 9.19 Relative performance of the hybrid load balancer on a 16-processor hypercube for different sender-initiated threshold values.

in the value of D which is set at values of 1 to 4. Lower D levels increase the probability of switching to receiver-initiated mode.

At extremely high settings for T, load migration never occurs, and the load balancer is effectively operating on one processor. Therefore we would expect to see lower speedup for greater values of T as indicated in Fig. 9.19. The decline is gradual, indicating the desired insensitivity to the setting of T for a wide range of values. There is a peak in the curves which we attribute to the use of the hybrid load balancer to initialize the system. Consider that processing begins on the root processor and spreads to the other processors with load migration. A high value for T delays this initialization process with consequent lower speedup. On the other hand too low a value for T results in excessive load migration and communications overhead which also reduces the speedup. Peak performance is achieved at a T value which balances these two effects. Since the peak results from using the dynamic load balancer to initialize the system, we could eliminate the peak by using a static initialization system. We do not explore this topic here because it has been investigated elsewhere [Chu 87].

The graphs in Fig. 9.20 were obtained for different values of the gap between the R and S levels in receiver-initiated mode. Recall that when a processor's internal load falls below R, it begins to request load from its neighbors. The neighbors do not participate in load balancing if their load falls in between the R and S levels. Only if their load exceeds the S level do they become candidates for load migration. The four graphs in Fig. 9.20 are obtained by setting the gap to values from 5 to 20.

The general pattern in these results is for low R settings to adversely affect performance. If the request for more load is delayed until the internal load is low, there is greater chance of the processor running out of processes and becoming idle. In general, once the R

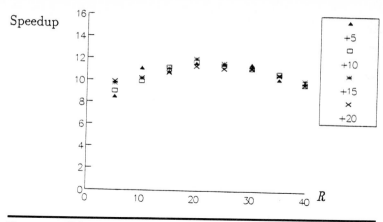

Figure 9.20 Relative performance of the hybrid load balancer on a 16-processor hypercube for different receiver-initiated threshold values.

reaches a reasonably high value, the speedup displays the required insensitivity to the threshold settings.

9.9 Conclusions

The hybrid load balancer is a distributed operating system that allows all the processors in a multicomputer to cooperate together on the solution of a single problem. The system's major features are its dual modes of operation that allow it to adapt to changing system loads and a completely distributed mechanism for deciding which mode should be used. The hybrid load balancer allows sequential Common Lisp programs, which have been properly translated, to be run in parallel. This is an important feature since it allows the hybrid load balancer to preserve the investment in existing software libraries.

Hardware supports presented for direct execution of the hybrid load balancer are implementable with state-of-the-art VLSI components. The hardware design runs the Lisp processing, communications, and load balancing functions in parallel, while the software implementation runs them serially. The greater parallelism of the hardware approach promises higher throughput but at the expense of additional hardware.

A software implementation of the hybrid load balancer on the Intel iPSC hypercube was used to obtain benchmark Lisp processing results. These results confirm the superiority of dynamic over static methods for programs with unpredictable run-time characteristics. The hybrid method also produced better results than the sender-initiated or receiver-initiated methods. We also demonstrated the ability of the hybrid load balancer and the applications which it supports to port between multicomputers of different size and topology.

The hybrid load balancer also appears relatively insensitive to the setting of internal parameters and so performs well without the need for extensive tuning.

We have focused on Lisp as applied to AI rather than numerical problems because AI programs generally exhibit more run-time unpredictability and therefore are in greater need of dynamic resource management. However, there is nothing in the design of the hybrid load balancer that restricts it to AI. The hybrid load balancer is also suitable for numerical applications with similarly unpredictable run-time characteristics. Functional languages, for example, could be a candidate for execution under the hybrid load balancer. On the other hand, highly structured numerical algorithms with predictable run-time characteristics are best handled by compile-time resource management or should be run on special-purpose architectures. Running the fast Fourier transform on a BBN Butterfly is an example. Matrix operations are another example of the highly structured class of numerical algorithms. It has been conjectured that 80 percent of the numerical codes being executed belong to the class of structured algorithms. Therefore it was natural that we should focus our attention on the AI area where there are more programs that are suitable for dynamic load balancing.

Four classes of parallelism in Lisp programs are exploited: AND-parallelism, OR-parallelism, list parallelism, and argument parallelism. The hybrid load balancer constructs SUSPEND and RUN can be used to direct the hybrid load balancer to exploit such parallelism. Based on our experience with the Gabriel benchmarks we believe most sequential programs would respond well to such translation.

Future research is encouraged for integrating the various systems for load balancing, handling side effects and structures into a single coherent system. Ongoing efforts to develop automatic serial to parallel code translators and distributed debuggers need to be continued. All these systems are required if we are to succeed in making parallel hardware accessible to the user community.

Acknowledgments

We would like to acknowledge the inputs of Dr. Les Gasser and Mr. Carl Braganza of the University of Southern California distributed AI group [Gasser 87] and thank them for the use of several communications primitives they have developed for the iPSC. We also appreciate the comments of Dr. DeGroot which greatly improved the presentation of this chapter.

Bibliography

[Anderson 87]   J. Anderson, W. Coates, A. Davis, R. Hon, I. Robinson, S. Robison, and K. Stevens. "The Architecture of the FAIM-1." *IEEE Computer,* vol. 20, no. 1, pp. 55–65, January 1987.

[Chu 87]   W.W. Chu and L.M-T. Lan. "Task Allocation and Precedence Relations for Distributed Real-Time Systems." *IEEE Trans. Computers,* vol. C-36, no. 6, pp. 667–679, June 1987.

[Cybenko 88]   G. Cybenko. "Dynamic Load Balancing for Distributed Memory Multiprocessors. *J. Parallel and Distributed Computing,* December 1988.

[Dally 86]   W. Dally. *A VLSI Architecture for Concurrent Data Structures.* Ph.D. thesis, Caltech Tech. Rep. No. 5209:TR:86, March 1986.

[Darlington 81]   J. Darlington and M. Reeve. "ALICE: A Multiprocessor Reduction Machine for the Parallel Evaluation of Applicative Languages. *ACM/MIT Conference on Functional Programming Languages and Computer Architectures,* 1981.

[Ferrari 86]   D. Ferrari and S. Zhou. "A Load Index for Dynamic Load Balancing. *Proc. Fall Joint Computer Conference,* pp. 684–690, November 1986.

[Gabriel 85]   R.P. Gabriel. *Performance and Evaluation of Lisp Systems.* MIT Press, Cambridge, MA, 1985.

[Gasser 87]   L. Gasser, C. Braganza, and N. Herman. "Implementing Distributed AI Systems Using MACE." *Proc. 3rd IEEE Conference on AI Applications,* February 1987.

[Halstead 85]   R. Halstead, Jr. "Multilisp: A Language for Concurrent Symbolic Computation." *ACM Trans. on Programming Languages and Systems,* vol. 7, no. 4, pp. 501–538, October 1985.

[Hayashi 83]   H. Hayashi, A. Hattori, and H. Akimoto. "ALPHA: A High-Performance Lisp Machine Equipped with a New Stack Architecture and Garbage Collection System." *Proc. 10th Annual International Symposium on Computer Architecture,* pp. 154–161, 1983.

[Heller 83]   S.K. Heller. *An I-Structure Memory Controller.* Master's thesis, Dept. of Electrical Engineering and Computer Science, MIT, June 1983.

[Hwang 82]   K. Hwang, W. Croft, G. Goble, B. Wah, F. Briggs, W. Simmons, and C. Coates. "A UNIX-Based Local Computer Network with Load Balancing." *IEEE Computer,* vol. 15, no. 4, pp. 55–66, April 1982.

[Hwang 87a]   K. Hwang and R. Chowkwanyun. *Dynamic Load Balancing for Distributed-Memory Multiprocessors.* Technical Report, Computer Research Institute, University of Southern California, Los Angeles, CA, August 1987.

[Hwang 87b]   K. Hwang and J. Ghosh. "Hypernet: A Communication-Efficient Architecture for Constructing Massively Parallel Computers." *IEEE Trans. Computers,* vol. C-36, no. 12, pp. 1450–1466, December 1987.

[Hwang 87c]   K. Hwang. "Advanced Parallel Processing with Supercomputer Architectures." *Proc. IEEE,* vol. 0C-75, no. 10, pp. 1348–1379, October 1987.

[Lin 86]   F.C. Lin and R.M. Keller. "Gradient model: A Demand-Driven Load Balancing Scheme." *IEEE Conf. on Distributed Systems,* pp. 329–336, 1986.

[Moon 84]   D. Moon. "Garbage Collection in a Large Lisp System." *1981 ACM Symposium on Lisp and Functional Programming,* pp. 235–246, August 1984.

[Ni 85]   L.M. Ni, C. Xu, and T.B. Gendreau. "A Distributed Drafting Algorithm for Load Balancing." *IEEE Trans. Software Engineering,* vol. SE-11, no. 10, pp. 1153–1161, October 1985.

[Smith 80]   R.G. Smith. "The Contract Net Protocol: High-Level Communication and Control in a Distributed Problem Solver." *IEEE Trans. Computers,* vol. C-29, no. 12, pp. 1104–1113, December 1980.

[Stankovic 84]   J.A. Stankovic. "A Perspective on Distributed Computer Systems." *IEEE Trans. Computers,* vol. C-33, no. 12, pp. 1102–1115, December 1984.

[Steele 84]   G. Steele, Jr. *Common Lisp.* Digital Press, Bedford, MA, 1984.

[Steele 86]   G.L. Steele, Jr., and W.D. Hillis. "Connection Machine Lisp." *1986 ACM Conference on Lisp and Functional Programming,* pp. 279–297, August 1986.

[Stolfo 87]   S.J. Stolfo. "Initial Performance of the DADO2 Prototype." *IEEE Computer,* vol. 20, no. 1, pp. 75–83, January 1987.

[Sugimoto 83]   S. Sugimoto, K. Agusa, K. Tabata, and Y. Ohno. "A Multimicroprocessor System for Concurrent Lisp." *Proc. International Conference on Parallel Processing,* pp. 135–143, 1983.

[Sussman 81]   G. Sussman, J. Holloway, G. Steele, Jr., and A. Bell. "Scheme 79—Lisp on a Chip." *IEEE Computer,* vol. 14, no. 7, pp. 10–21, July 1981.

[Vegdahl 84]   S. Vegdahl. "A Survey of Proposed Architectures for the Execution of Functional Languages." *IEEE Trans. Computers,* vol. C-33, no. 12, pp. 1050–1071, December, 1984.

[Wah 86]   G-J. Li and B. Wah. "Optimal Granularity of Parallel Evaluation of AND Trees." *Proc. Fall Joint Computer Conference,* pp. 297–306, November 1986.

Parallel Processing Software

Parallel Programming Environment and Software Support

Kai Hwang

University of Southern California, Los Angeles, CA

Doug DeGroot

Texas Instruments, Dallas, TX

10.1 Parallel Processing for Performance

Parallel processing has emerged as a hot field of research and development by computer professionals during the last decade. Various classes of parallel and vector supercomputers have appeared in the past two decades [Hwang 87]. However, the claimed performance was not always delivered as promised by the vendors. This is due to the fact that today's supercomputers are one generation behind the user's needs and yet one generation ahead of the popular programming skills. In other words, we really need *supersoftware* to help boost the performance. This chapter presents advanced software techniques that can help the creation of a parallel programming environment in which real ultrahigh performance can be delivered.

Usually, the effective performance of a supercomputer ranges between only 5 to 35 percent of its peak performance [Dongarra 87]. Such a pessimistic show of the delivered performance motivates many computer specialists to search for better algorithms, languages, hardware, and software techniques to yield higher performance. We examine below the requirements of parallel, vector, and scalar processing. Basic performance measures and benchmarking concepts are introduced first. In subsequent sections we address critical issues on languages, compilers, processor, memory, input/output (I/O) resources, programming, and various performance enhancement methods for parallel processing on various classes of supercomputers.

10.1.1 Advanced parallel processing

Parallelism refers to the simultaneous execution of jobs, job steps, programs, routines, subroutines, loops, or statements as summarized in Table 10.1. The higher the level, the finer the *granularity* of the soft-

TABLE 10.1   Five Levels of Parallelism in Program Execution

Level	Parallelism
1	Independent jobs and programs
2	Job steps and related parts of programs
3	Routines, subroutines, and coroutines
4	Loops and iterations
5	Statements and instructions

ware processes. In general, *parallel processing* refers to parallelism exploited at any or a combination of these levels. So far, *vector processing* is parallel execution of iterations of loops at level 4. Parallel execution of independent scalar statements at level 5 has been implemented in many machines with the look-ahead technique using multiple functional units [Thornton 70]. Most of today's computers support *multiprogramming,* which provides for the sharing of processor resources among multiple, independent software processes. Multiprogramming is practiced in most uniprocessor systems, in which concurrent CPU, and I/O activities are interleaved.

Multiprocessing is a mode of parallel processing that provides a generalized multiprogramming among two or more processors. Independent uniprocessing exploits parallelism at level 1 in multiple-SISD mode. *Multitasking* is a special case of multiprocessing defining a software process (a task) to be a job step or subprogram at levels 2 and 3 [Cray 84]. For machines with a small number of very powerful processors (such as the Cray X-MP) parallelism is mainly performed at the high levels (1, 2, and 3) across the processors. However, within each processor, parallelism levels 4 and 5 are still practiced. For massively parallel machines (such as the MPP [Batcher 80]) parallelism is mainly pushed at the lower levels. The general trend is pushing the granularity down. Concurrent scalar processing, vector processing, and multiprocessing are often desired in a modern supercomputer, if one has to satisfy the demands from various application domains.

10.1.2 Performance benchmarking

Understanding the benchmarks is of fundamental importance to measuring the performance of supercomputers. Only preliminary benchmark data from existing supercomputers are becoming available now. The key problem is the use of benchmarks in assuring comparability. Benchmarking intends to indicate the relative performance of various machines under the same workload. By definition, a computer benchmark is a set of key programs or sections of key programs that are executed for timing purposes. The subsets of key programs, called *kernels,* often represent the most time consuming portion of the major codes. Kernels must be converted to run on the target machines. Using the workload fractions as weights, multiple runs are timed and compared. The kernels are real and tractable and thus often used as standard tests. However, kernels may be too simple to reveal the limitations of the target machines [Lubeck 85].

The *Livermore kernels* are often used in evaluating the performance of scientific computers. Important steps in using kernel benchmarks have been summarized in Worlton [84]. Besides using the kernels, Jack Dongarra of Argonne National Laboratory compared the performance of about 100 different computers (ranging from supers to micros) using the standard linear system solver LINPACK in a Fortran environment [Dongarra 87]. More recent data appear in Dongarra [88]. Table 10.2 shows part of the performance data that were reported by Dongarra in 1987. The timing results that were released by him reflect only the relative performance on one problem area. To judge the overall performance of a computer system, one should test both kernels and specific application problems. Such benchmarking performance may change with respect to software and hardware changes. The operating system and compiler used can make a subtle difference, even running on the same machine. Further differences can be found in the direct use of assembly language coding or in the use of compiler directives.

10.2 Parallel Languages and Intelligent Compilers

We address below languages and system software issues for parallel processing on supercomputers. We review the development of concurrent programming languages and their compilers. Then, we discuss

TABLE 10.2   Performance of Various Computers Using LINPACK in Solving a System of Linear Equations of Order 100

Computer	Performance, MFLOPS
NEC SX-2	43
Cray X-MP-4	39
CDC Cyber 205	17
Fujitsu VP-200	17
IBM 3090/200 VF	12
Alliant FX/8	7.6
CONVEX C-1/XL	2.9
ELXSI	1.1
CDC Cyber 180-810	0.17
VAX 11/780 FPA	0.14
Sun-3/260	0.11
Encore Multimax	0.055
IBM PC/AT	0.033

SOURCE: Excerpt from Dongarra [87].

advanced methods in developing intelligent compilers for parallel/ vector as well as scalar computers.

10.2.1   Concurrent programming languages

To implement fast algorithms on supercomputers, we need a high-level programming language possessing the following features:

- *Flexibility*.   The language should make it easy for the programmer to specify various forms of parallelism in application programs.
- *Efficiency*.   The language should be efficiently implementable on various parallel/vector computer systems.

Three approaches that have been used in trying to solve this language problem (see Fig. 10.1) are described below.

The compiler approach.   Most existing application software packages are coded with sequential languages such as Fortran. Intelligent compilers are needed to detect parallelism in sequential programs and to convert them into parallel machine code, as illustrated in Fig. 10.1a. Good examples include the *CFT compiler* used in the Cray X-MP and the *KAP/205* compiler designed for the Cyber 205 [Huson 86]. An advantage of this approach is that software assets accumulated in conventional sequential codes can be used on parallel computers with

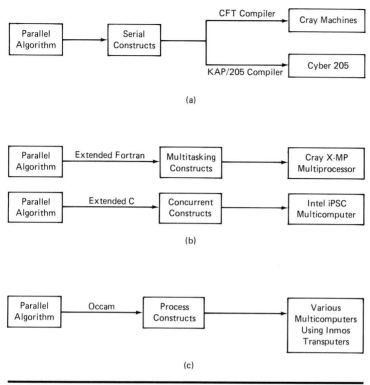

Figure 10.1   Three approaches to concurrent scalar/vector programming. (*a*) Smart compiler approach; (*b*) language extension approach; (*c*) new language approach.

only minor modifications. However, the sequential language forces the programmer to code parallel algorithms in sequential form. Due to the difficulty in detecting parallelism in a complex program mix, a compiler can enhance the performance by only a limited factor. Additionally, the types of parallelism that can be detected are usually limited to iterations over regular data structures, such as vectors, matrices, or lists.

The language extensions approach.   Sequential languages can be extended with architecture-oriented constructs to support concurrent programming. Usually, only one type of parallelism is supported in each extended language, as illustrated in Fig. 10.1*b*. For instance, Fortran has been augmented with commands like EVWAIT, LOCKON, and TASKSTART on the Cray X-MP to enable multitasking [Cray 84]. The *Concurrent C* language has been extended from C for the Flex/32 multicomputer [Fenner 87]. Other extensions include *Vectran* [Paul 82], *Actus-2* [Perrot 87], and *Vector C* [Li 85] for supporting vector processing on pipeline or array processors. Because the extensions are machine-oriented, they are often efficiently implemented. However, machine dependence implies poor portability. When the target machines are changed, users may have to recode the parallel algorithm in another extended language. And if a given application contains parallelism, but not of the specific kind supported in the language, the parallelism cannot be easily extracted.

The new languages approach.   With this approach, new concurrent languages are developed for supporting parallel processing. Quite a few concurrent languages have been proposed in recent years, including *Concurrent Pascal* [Hansen 75], *Modula-2* [Wirth 82], *CSP* [Hoare 72], *Occam* [Inmos 84], and *Ada* [DoD 81]. Unlike an extended language, these new languages contain some application-oriented parallel constructs. However, each of these languages is usually designed to support only one form of parallelism, as illustrated in Fig. 10.1c.

Comparing these three approaches, we observe an application barrier. On the one hand, parallel algorithms and supercomputers manifest a variety of computation modes. On the other hand, each of the proposed languages supports only one or two computation modes. This barrier is the major source of inflexibility and inefficiency in using conventional sequential languages to code parallel algorithms on supercomputers. Various languages and compilers used in modern supercomputers are summarized in Table 10.3.

Advanced programmers are searching for an ideal programming language for parallel/vector computers. Such a high-level language should be easy to learn and flexible to apply in major scientific/ engineering applications. The language should be architecture-independent. In other words, it can be used in various computation modes such as SIMD, MIMD, pipelining, and dataflow, etc. Such an ideal programming language may have to be developed with a combination of the above approaches, perhaps starting with a smart compiler, then adding some extensions to existing popular languages, and then gradually moving toward the development of a new language as a long-term effort. Recently, a *parallel programming language* (PAL) for supporting multimode concurrent parallel programming was proposed [Xu 89]. A new language construct, called *molecules,* is proposed there for programmers to specify *typed procedures* explicitly in various modes of parallel computation.

10.2.2   Intelligent compiler and directives

Both vectorization and concurrentization need to be supported by an intelligent compiler for a supercomputer. So far, most Fortran compil-

TABLE 10.3   Operating System, Programming Languages, and Compilers Used in Modern Supercomputers

System model	OS†/language/compiler	Remarks
Cray X-MP	COS/CFT (Fortran), CTSS	CTSS supports interactive mode
Cray 2	UNIX System V/CFT2, C	Macro assembler CAL 2 supported
Cyber 205	Virtual OS/FTN 200	Fortran compiler, ANSI 77 with vector extension
ETA-10	Virtual OS/Fortran, Pascal, C	Also V SOS, UNIX planned
NEC SX	ACOS/Fortran 77/SX, Pascal, C, Lisp, Prolog	Only Fortran in vector mode
Fujitsu VP	FACOM VSP/Fortran 77	Also appear in Amdahl 1200 Series
IBM 3090/VF	XA/VS Fortran V2	Economic analyzer supports interactive vectorization
Univac 1194/ISP	1100 Executive/UCS Fortran 77	ANSI Fortran 8X standard included
Cyberplus	Host NOS2/ANSI 77 Fortran	Cross compiler with host
HEP-1	UNIX III/Fortran 77, C, Pascal	Production suspended
Convex C-1	Unix 4.2 bsd/Fortran 77, C	Accepts VAX/VMS Fortran inputs
SCS-40	CTSS/Fortran 77 (CFT Civic)	COS and UNIX System V and C compiler under development
Alliant FX	Concentrix/FX Fortran, C, Pascal	OS based on UNIX 4.2
Elxsi 6400	EMBOS/Fortran 77, Pascal, Cobol 74, C, MAINSAIL	Also run UNIX system V.2
Balance 21000	DYNIX/C, Fortran 77, Pascal, Ada	Similar to UNIX 4.2 bsd
Encore/Multimax	UMAX 4.2/C, Fortran, Pascal, Ada, Lisp	Support multiprocessing also UMAX V/OS
FLEX/32	MMOS/Fortran 77, C, Ada, Concurrent C, and Fortran	Ada supports multiprocessing, also run UNIX System V
iPSC-VX	XENIX/C, Fortran, Common Lisp	OS run on Intel 310 host
AMETEK 14	Hypernet OS/C, Fortran	Host run on UNIX 4.2 bsd or VMS
FPS-T	Host OS/OCCAM	OS run on INMOS Transputers
FPS 164/MAX	Ultrix/Fortran 77, C	Ultrix is the DEC's version of UNIX
Connection Machine	Host OS/CM-C, CM-Lisp	Connection Machine extensions of C and Lisp
ICL/DAP	ICL Perq/DAP Fortran	Running under UNIX; similar to Fortran 8X
BBN Butterfly	Chrysalis/C, Common Lisp	OS similar to UNIX
IBM RP3	UNIX/C, Fortran, Pascal	OS modified from UNIX 4.2 bsd
Culler PSC	UNIX 4.2 csd/Fortran 77, C	Culler Expert Compiler
NCUBE E/10	AXIS/VERTEX/FORTRAN 77, C	AXIS run on host board; VERTEX run on nodes

†OS = operating system
SOURCE: HWANG [87]

ers developed for supercomputers have some vectorization capability. Very few compilers have been fully developed to exploit parallelism for multiprocessing. What is needed is an intelligent compiler that automatically detects the potential for both vector and parallel processing in standard Fortran (or any other high-level language) code and generates object code that uses the parallel and vector features of the hardware to full advantage. The compiler analyzes source code for data, control, and storage dependencies at the process, loop, and instruction levels. The goal is to generate optimized codes which can be executed in *concurrent scalar, vector, multitasked scalar,* or *multitasked vector* processing modes. The optimization process is aimed at enhanced vectorization and concurrency exploitation.

Generally speaking, the innermost DO loop is vectorized and the next outer loop should be concurrentized. Nested DO loops and multidimensional array operations can thus run in multitasked vector mode. Other situations, like DO WHILE loops, can run in current scalar mode. It is often very desirable to have an *interactive compiler* to achieve this goal.

An *interactive compiler* allows a programmer to fine-tune the code during the optimization process. Such a fine tuning can be conducted at a higher programming level (global), such as subroutines and tasks where optimization needs feedback information from the programmers. Such a compiler should provide facilities for programmers to monitor and modify the code optimizations. Messages and listings notify the user of conditions that affect optimization and summarize the scope of optimization. Programmers then modify the optimization with inserted compiler directives.

Compiler directives are often very helpful in achieving better optimization on a global basis. The intelligence of most compilers is presently restricted to local optimization. In order to increase the degree of multiprocessing or multitasking, compiler directives can be used to achieve global or subglobal optimizations. The directives allow the programmer to override the compiler where optimization does not enhance performance or may cause invalid results. For example, a directive can be added to suppress vectorization when the vector length is too short, and to suppress multitasking, if the overhead is too high.

Knuth has stated that less than 4 percent of a Fortran program generally accounts for more than half of its running time [Knuth 71]. Certainly, DO loops often play this role. The best performance results are often obtained by vectorizing and/or multitasking such loops. Loops containing data dependencies or recurrences may not be vectorizable. For such loops the compiler should perform one or more loop transformations to make the successive iterations multitaskable. This has been done in the Cray X-MP as well as in Alliant FX series multiprocessors [Alliant 87, Test 87]. The example shown in Fig. 10.2 illus-

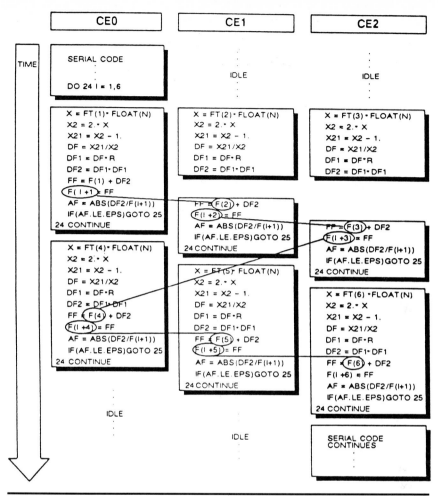

Figure 10.2 Parallel execution of a DO loop with data dependency on an Alliant FX system with three processors. (Courtesy of Alliant Computer Systems Corp.)

trates how concurrent processing of a DO loop, called *Doacross,* can be achieved in an Alliant system with three processors (computation elements). The data dependencies are synchronized by a hardware concurrency control bus across the processors.

Compiler technology plays a crucial role in the performance of vector supercomputers. Most vectorizing compilers are designed for specific machines such as the FX/Fortran used in Alliant FX/8. A significant need exists for *retargetable* vectorizers which require low software conversion costs when switched among different machines [Kuck 80]. The compiler must be designed to exploit not only vectorization but also parallelism at higher levels as treated in Chaps. 11 and 12.

Important capabilities of an intelligent compiler include vectorization, concurrentization, and general and directive optimizations. Conventional compilers can support only the general optimization. Vectorizing compilers and concurrentizing compilers may be developed separately or jointly. The joint approach is more useful to general-purpose applications. However, its development is much more involved. At present, the FX/Fortran compiler [Alliant 87] and the compiler developed for the Warp processor at Carnegie-Mellon University have some limited extent of these combined capabilities. The Cray CFT compiler supports automatic vectorization and multitasking by adding some initiation and synchronization routines to user programs [Cray 84, Sydow 83].

10.2.3 Trace scheduling for scalar parallelism

The presence of vectorizing or multiprocessing compilers can enhance the supercomputer performance only if a high percentage of the code is vectorizable or parallelizable. In real-world applications, many codes have low vectorization ratios or low degrees of parallelism. In other words, arbitrarily structured scalar programs cannot necessarily run in parallel using conventional intelligent compilers. In this section, we introduce the *trace-scheduling compacting compiler* developed by Fisher [81]. It supports overlapped execution of scalar operations without vectorization. The *very long instruction word* (VLIW) architecture for supercomputing will be introduced along with the Multiflow trace computer [Fisher 87] that has been built for exploiting parallelism in randomly structured programs we called *scalar parallelism*.

Trace scheduling was originally proposed to compact sequential microcode into parallel (horizontal) microcode. The Bulldog compiler [Ellis 86] and Multiflow's TRACE [Fisher 87] compacting compiler are based on trace scheduling. The technique uses global compaction through traces over many *straight-line code blocks* (SLCBs). A *trace* is a loop-free execution sequence of instructions selected at compile time by an intelligent compiler, which predicts conditional branches at the end of each SLCB. Breaking the conditional branch barrier allows the machine to overlap many operations for simultaneous execution. In each trace the compiler finds the most frequently used part of the program. The predictions at conditional branches are based on some heuristics or statistics gathered automatically by program profiling. The compiler may add a small amount of "compensation code" at every branch to guarantee that the program will always perform correctly. The compiler then proceeds to the most frequently used part of the remaining code (the second trace) and so on, until it has compiled the entire program.

The concept of trace scheduling is illustrated in Fig. 10.3. Part a shows a loop-free program flow graph, where each square represents a SLCB. Part b shows the first trace picked from the most frequently used code blocks by predicting branches at the ends of SLCBs A, B, and C. In part c, the trace has been compacted but has not been relinked to the rest of the code. Preprocessing adds special link instructions to the trace to prevent the scheduler from making illegal code motions between the SLCBs. After the selected trace is scheduled, postprocessing inserts compensation codes at the trace exits (S's) and rejoins (R's) to ensure the correct linkage to the remaining unscheduled code as shown in part d. Then we look for the second trace the same way. Eventually, this process works its way out, a code with little probability of execution. Trace scheduling on loops can be done by unrolling the loop for many iterations. The unrolled loop is a stream, all intermediate loop tests are conditional branches, and the stream gets compacted similarly as a loop-free stream. The process requires no user intervention, which implies that no program rewriting or compiler directives are needed. All the traces are handled by the TRACE compiler.

In a conventional, sequential CPU, each instruction performs only one operation. Only a small percentage of the functional elements are in use at any one time. Overlapped executions of multiple instructions can be added to a sequential CPU to increase resource utilization, but at the expense of more complex hardware for look-ahead capability. The programmer or compiler must ensure that data dependence and resource constraints have been met. In a VLIW machine many instructions are grouped together into wide instructions and issued in a single memory cycle. In addition to data dependence and resource constraints, a compiler for a VLIW architecture must find enough parallelism to use the hardware to its full capacity. In building such a machine, additional functional units are desirable, as are significantly broader data communication paths. The trace scheduling method appeals very favorably to such a VLIW computer architecture.

The VLIW architecture has been built into the Multiflow TRACE computer. The entry-level TRACE system packs 7 different operations into each 256-bit instruction word. The most powerful model packs 28 into each 1024-bit instruction word. Fine-grained parallelism is exploited at the level of individual additions, multiplications, loads, stores, and other primitive operations. Highly overlapped execution of these primitive operations gives high performance independent of the amount of parallelizable code. Each part of the wide instruction word controls a different arithmetic and logic unit (ALU) in the central pro-

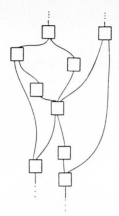

(a) A program flow graph, with blocks representing SLCBs (all edges are directed downward).

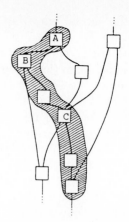

(b) A trace picked from the flow graph by predicting jumps at the ends of SLCBs A, B, and C.

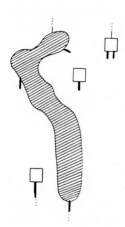

(c) Preprocessing adds new special edges to the flow graph to prevent illegal code motions between SLCBs.

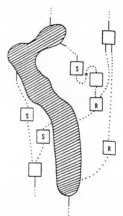

(d) Insertion of compensation code for relinking with the unscheduled code outside the trace.

Figure 10.3 Trace scheduling for parallel processing of straight-line code blocks (SLCBs). (*a*) A program flow graph, with blocks representing SLCBs (all edges are directed downward); (*b*) a trace picked from the flow graph by predicting jumps at the ends of SLCBs *A, B,* and *C;* (*c*) preprocessing adds new special edges to the flow graph to prevent illegal code motions between SLCBs; (*d*) insertion of compensation code for relinking with the unscheduled code outside the trace. (Courtesy of Fisher [87].)

cessor. Of course, the memory and I/O must match in bandwidth. The TRACE system allows up to 8 simultaneous memory references; it provides over 490-Mbytes/s memory bandwidth. Auxiliary I/O processors are used to relay data between peripherals and main memory.

The Multiflow TRACE architecture allows modular growth by simply plugging additional boards into the cabinet. Adding more processing hardware increases the width of the instruction word. At present, the TRACE compiler can support highly overlapped code from standard Fortran and C. The system runs a TRACE/UNIX operating system. The peak performance of the TRACE system is 215 VLIW MIPS on the 1024-bit architecture, in which 28 operations can be executed in parallel per each cycle. Figure 10.4 shows an example of packing highly parallel codes from two successive traces. By assuming that the program will actually take the predicated path, the compiler finds large amounts of fine-grained parallelism. The compensation code inserted at exits from the trace achieves two objectives. First, operations that should have been done before the branch, but were not, are done there. Second, operations that should not have been moved up above the branch in the scheduled trace are undone or ignored.

Where the code deviates from the predicated path, it carries out the unwanted computation. It would seem, at first glance, that some portion of the performance gain would be lost. However, the process is an iterative one, as shown in Fig. 10.4b. The subsequent traces may contain both compensation code and still-unprocessed original source code. In this way, high performance is sustained whichever path is taken, as long as the code is usually following the predicted path. This is done in a single linear pass through the source program, with original source operations each appearing on only one trace. It does not unwind all the possible execution paths. In a way, the trace scheduling converts an exponential process (in program flow) into essentially a linear one.

According to recently released benchmark performance from Multiflow, the TRACE 7/200 can deliver 6 MFLOPS in 64-bit precision when running a compiled LINPACK program. This performance is comparable with those of IBM 3090/200 and of Alliant FX/8-8 in running the same LINPACK program. The combined VLIW architecture and trace-scheduling compiler have made the Multiflow machine an attractive alternative to conventional parallel systems. The key distinction lies in the fact that Multiflow optimizes nonparallel code, where conventional vectorizing or multiprocessing computers cannot perform well. To prove that the system is indeed effective demands much more performance data. The argument by Multiflow is that the majority of the application markets are using "junk" code

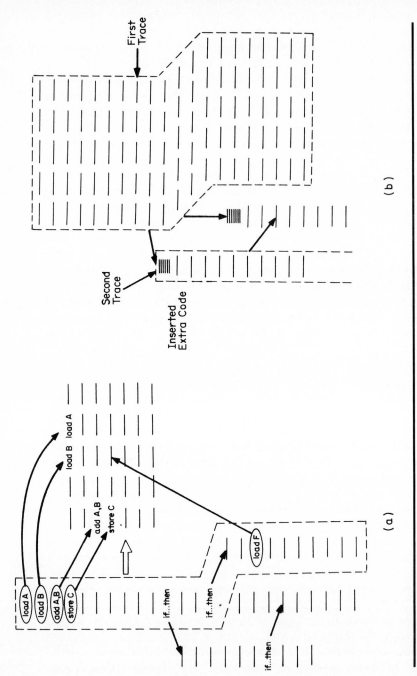

Figure 10.4 Code compaction for a VLIW architecture based on the trace scheduling compiling. (*a*) Picking the most likely execution path and packing the primitive instructions into wide instruction words on the right for highly overlapped execution; (*b*) inserting compensation code and picking the second most likely trace and compacting it; each trace produces several VLIWs. (Courtesy of Fisher [87].)

which cannot be easily parallelized or vectorized; that is exactly where the scalar parallelism can be exploited by trace scheduling.

10.3 Vectorization and Multitasking Software

In this section, we consider regularly structured or well-partitioned tasks, which use vectorization on vector processors and software support for multitasking among multiprocessors. We shall also study the tradeoffs between vectorization and multitasking. Vectorization exploits fine-grain parallelism through pipelining, while multitasking exploits coarse-grain parallelism using multiple processors.

10.3.1 Vectorization and migration techniques

Many supercomputers are equipped with vector hardware pipelines. Described below are the key concepts of vectorization and application migration methods associated with the effective utilization of vector facilities. Our objectives are to develop techniques for exploiting the vector facility, to derive methods of improving vector execution performance, and to look for vectorizable code. The *relative performance P* of vector processing over scalar processing is a function of the *vectorization ratio f* and of the *vector/scalar speedup ratio r* as plotted in Fig. 10.5.

$$P = \frac{1}{(1 - f) + f/r} \tag{10.1}$$

The performance P is very sensitive to the variation of f, which indicates the percentage of code which is vectorizable. When the vectorization ratio is low, the relative performance cannot be increased by increasing the hardware. The speedup ratio r is primarily determined by hardware factors.

The term *vectorization* refers to the compiler's role in analyzing user programs and producing object codes to execute on the vector hardware. The portion of the compiler which carries out the vectorization is called a *vectorizer*. *Vector migration* refers to the process of modifying and adapting an application program in order to reveal its vector content and to improve its performance. This implies that migration will assist the vectorizing compiler in exploiting the vector hardware for that program. Hazards may occur in which an apparent lack of data independence may prevent vectorization in certain loop types.

The basic unit of vectorization is the DO loop. Due to the size restriction of the vector registers, it is always necessary to split long vec-

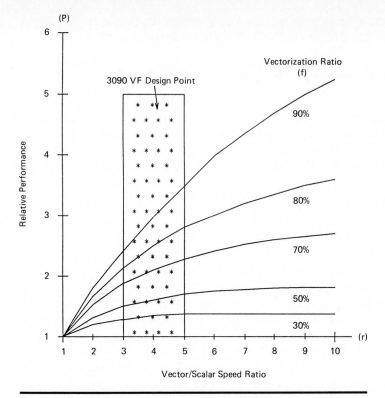

Figure 10.5 Speedup performance of vector processing over scalar processing in IBM 3090/VF. (Courtesy of IBM Corporation.)

tors into segments, called *sections*. For example, the Cray X-MP has section size 64, and the IBM 3090/400 VF has 128 elements in a section (Fig. 10.6) [Tucker 86]. Vectorizable loops must first be sectionized. *Data independence* in loops is a key factor in enabling the vectorization. A *recurrence* carries a dependence between the elements of a vector which prevents it from being vectorized [Kogge 73].

Indirect addressing refers to addressing an array by using subscripts which are themselves subscripted. As long as the array which is indirectly addressed does not appear on both sides of the equal sign in a Fortran statement, vectorization is possible. In other words, indirectly addressed variables may be vectorized, if there are only loads, or only stores of the variables, but not if there are both. *Vector reduction* refers to a vector operation which produces a scalar result, such as the dot product of two vectors or finding the maximum of an array of elements. Vector reduction arithmetic demands special pipeline hardware support [Ni 85].

Local vectorization techniques are centered on DO loops. It should be noted that not all DO loops are appropriate for vectorization. In fact,

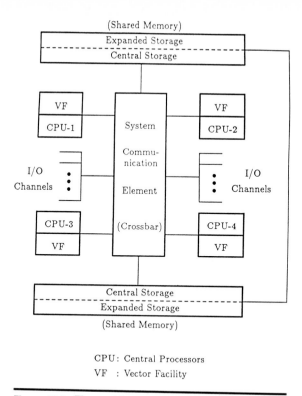

(Shared Memory)

CPU: Central Processors
VF : Vector Facility

Figure 10.6 The architecture of IBM 3090 Model 400/VF.

not all loops are DO loops, such as a loop containing an IF statement. Some DO loops iterate too few times or have unknown iteration counts. These may not be worth the effort to vectorize. The *stride* of a vector is the addressing increment between successive elements. Stride-1 addressing often results in better performance than addressing with longer strides. Therefore, *stride minimization* is often practiced to enhance local vectorization. Reorganizing data may improve the stride distribution among nested DO loops.

Prolonging the innermost DO loop makes it more appropriate for vectorization. Other local vectorization techniques include the use of *temporary variables, linearized multidimensional subscripts and auxiliary subscripts, statement reordering, loop segmentation, simplifying subscripts, reverse unrolling, loop distribution, IF conversion, improving vector density,* and the use of *equivalence* for longer vectors [Soll 86]. One should isolate nonvectorizable constructs, such as *CALL, recurrences, I/O, relationals,* and other *hazards,* in application programs [Gibson 86].

Global vector migration requires the global restructuring of application programs. This is often more difficult than local vectorization. One global technique is to incorporate loops across several computation modules or subroutines. Another approach is to change the solution method. At present, most vectorizers can perform only local vectorization. Only exceptionally smart vectorizers can perform a limited global vector migration. Most of the global program restructuring operations are still done by skillful programmers, perhaps through the help of an *interactive vectorizer*, which allows the user to tune programs as supported by the Fujitsu VP-200 compiler [Tamura 85]. The IBM 3090/VF system offers an *economic analyzer* in its VS Fortran compiler that estimates the number of cycles (cost) needed to execute given sections of code, including the vectorization overhead. This analyzer helps users fine-tune their programs with both local vectorization and global restructuring to enhance performance.

Multipipeline *chaining* as introduced in the Cray X-MP supports the fast execution of a sequence of vector operations. On the other hand, *systolic arrays* offer multidimensional pipelines for direct execution of certain vectorized algorithms. Recently, a dynamic systolic approach was proposed for fast execution of vector compound functions directly by *pipeline nets*. These are advanced hardware facilities for supporting large-grain vector computations. The pipeline nets are more attractive than linear pipeline chains or static systolic arrays in the area of programmability and flexibility for general-purpose applications. For example, it has been verified that the execution of most Livermore loops can be speeded up greatly if they run on a reconfigurable pipeline net [Hwang 88]. We shall describe how to convert program graphs into pipeline nets in Sec. 10.4.1. To explore these advanced hardware features, even more intelligent compilers are needed.

10.3.2 Multiprocessing and multitasking

Ultimately, we want to use a supercomputer that can support intrinsic multiprocessing at the process level. Such a tightly coupled computer uses shared memory among multiple processors. The Denelcor HEP was designed as such an interactive MIMD multiprocessor [Jordan 86, Kowalik 84]. HEP was suspended from marketing due to the lack of multiprocessing software. The main lesson learned from HEP is that fancy hardware alone is not enough to stretch for better performance. Multiprocessing at the process level must be supported by the following capabilities:

- Fast context switching among multiple processes resident in processors.

- Multiple register sets to facilitate context switching.

- Fast memory access with conflict free memory allocations.
- Effective synchronization mechanisms among multiple processors.
- Software tools to achieve parallel processing and performance monitoring.
- System and application software for interactive users.

In a multitasking environment, the tasks and data structures of a job must be properly partitioned to allow parallel execution without conflict. However, the availability of processors, the order of execution, and the completion of tasks are functions of the run-time conditions of the machine. Therefore, multitasking is generally *nondeterministic* with respect to time. On the other hand, tasks themselves must be generally deterministic with respect to results. To ensure successful multitasking, the user must precisely define each task, add the necessary communication and synchronization mechanisms, and provide the protection of shared data in critical sections. *Critical sections,* being accessed by only one task or one process at a time, may reside in shared memory, I/O files, subroutines, or other shared resources. One can use *lock* and *unlock* mechanisms to monitor the operation of critical sections.

Reentrancy is a useful property which allows one copy of a program module to be used by more than one task in parallel. *Nonreentrant code* can be used only once during the lifetime of the program. Reentrant code, if residing in a critical section, can be used only in a serial fashion, called *serially reusable code.* Reentrant code, which is called many times by different tasks, must be assigned with local variables and control indicators stored in independent, task-specific locations, each time the routine is called. *Stack* mechanisms have been employed in the Cray X-MP to support reentrancy. The Cray X-MP has developed software support to realize multitasking at several levels as illustrated in Fig. 10.7.

Dataflow analysis is often performed to reveal parallelism contained in application programs. The major constraint of parallelism is the various forms of data dependency [Bernstein 66]. The computational dependence is caused by either *data dependence* or *control dependence.* The nodes represent statements, processes, or even tasks. The arcs show the dependence relationship among them. Either multiprocessing or multitasking will introduce overhead that increases overall execution time. To reduce overhead, parallelism should be exploited at the lowest level (fine granularity) possible. The *storage dependence* is caused by memory conflicts. Each task or process must use independent or protected storage areas to guarantee the shared data integrity. For multitasking, storage dependence is often caused by a data dependence between the iterations of loop. When the extent of a left-hand-side array variable is less than the index range of the loop, such a storage dependence may occur.

Speedup from multitasking may occur only when the time saved in exe-

1. Multitasking at the job level

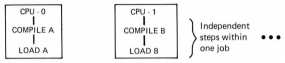

2. Multitasking at the job-step level

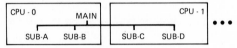

3. Multitasking at the program level

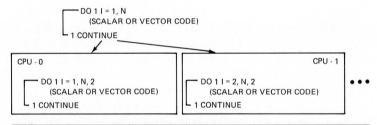

4. Multitasking at the loop level

Figure 10.7   Four possible multitasking modes in a Cray X-MP-2 multiprocessor system. (Courtesy of Cray Research, Inc.)

cuting parallel tasks outweighs the overhead penalty. The overhead is very sensitive to task granularity. The overhead includes the initiation, management, and interaction of tasks. These are often accomplished by adding additional code to the original code as exemplified below.

Consider a sequential code run on a uniprocessor (Cray X-MP-1):

```
PROGRAM MAIN
  .
  .
DO 100 I = 1, 50
  .
  .
    DO 10 J = 1, 2
      CALL SUB (J)
10    CONTINUE
  .
  .
100 CONTINUE
  .
  .
STOP
END
```

The following multitasked code runs on a dual-processor system (Cray X-MP-2):

```
PROGRAM MAIN
COMMON/MT/ISTART, IDONE, JOB
CALL TSKSTART(IDTASK, T)          SUBROUTINE T
JOB = 1                           COMMON/MT/ISTART, IDONE, JOB
DO 100 I = 1, 50                1 CALL EVWAIT(ISTART)
    CALL EVPOST(ISTART)           CALL EVCLEAR(ISTART)
    CALL SUB(1)                   IF ( JOB.NE.1 ) GO TO 2
    CALL EVWAIT(IDONE)            CALL SUB(2)
    CALL EVCLEAR(IDONE)          CALL EVPOST(IDONE)
100 CONTINUE   GO TO 1
    JOB = 2                     2 RETURN
    CALL EVPOST(ISTART)           END
    CALL TSKWAIT(IDTASK)
STOP
END
```

This program can benefit from multitasking, depending on the execution time of the subroutine SUB(J) and the overhead introduced in the service routines. Before one attempts to convert a serial code into multitasked code, the expected performance should be predicted to ensure a net gain. Factors affecting performance include the *task granularity, frequency of calls, balanced partitioning of work,* and *programming skill* in the choice of the multitasking mechanisms [Calahan 85, Larson 84].

The above program is analyzed below to predict performance. The 100 loop has dependent iterations which cannot be executed in parallel. The 10 loop has independent iterations, which are being attempted for multitasking. The execution time of the original program on one CPU consists of two parts:

$$\text{Time (1 CPU)} = \text{Time (Main)} + \text{Time (SUB)}$$

$$= (0.04 + 0.96) * (20.83 \text{ s})$$

$$= 20.83 \text{ s}$$

where Time (SUB) accounts for the 96 percent of the time spent in subroutine SUB and Time (Main) for 4 percent spent on the remaining portion of the program. The total run time on 1 CPU is assumed to be 20.83 s. To execute the multitasked program on 2 CPUs requires:

$$\text{Time (2CPUs)} = \text{Time (Main)} + \frac{1}{2} \text{Time (SUB)} + \text{Overhead}$$

because the subrouting SUB was equally divided between 2 CPUs. The overhead is calculated below with some approximation on the delays caused by workload imbalance and memory contention. The service routines TSKSTART, TSKWAIT, EVPOST, EVCLEAR, and EVWAIT are used in Cray X-MP to establish the multitasking structure [Cray 84].

Overhead = Time (TSKSTART) + Time (TSKWAIT)

$$+ 51 * \text{Time (EVPOST)} + 50 * \text{Time (EVCLEAR)}$$

$$+ 50 * \text{Time (EVWAIT)} + (\text{Workload imbalance delay})$$

$$+ (\text{Memory contention delay})$$

$$= 1500000 \text{ CP} + 1500 \text{ CP} + 51 * 1500 \text{ CP} + 50 * 200 \text{ CP}$$

$$+ 50 * 1500 \text{ CP} + (0.02 * 50 * 0.2 \text{ s}) = 0.216$$

where the CP (clock period) is equal to 9.5 ns. Therefore, Time (2−CPU) = (0.4 * 20.83) + ½ * (0.96 * 20.83) + 0.216 = 11.05 s. We thus project the following speedup:

$$\text{Speedup} = \frac{\text{Time (1CPU)}}{\text{Time (2CPUs)}} = \frac{20.83}{11.05} = 1.88$$

This speedup helps decide whether multitasking is worthwhile. The actual speedup of this program as measured by Cray programmers was 1.86. This indicates that the above prediction is indeed very close.

Multitasking offers a speedup which is upper-bounded by the number of processors in a system. Because vector processing offers a greater speedup potential over scalar processing (in the Cray X-MP, vectorization offers a speedup in the range of 10~20), multitasking should not be employed at the expense of vectorization. In the case of short vector length, scalar processing may outperform vector processing. In the case of a small task size, vector processing (or even scalar processing) may outperform multitasking. Both scalar and vector-codes may be multitasked, depending on the granularity and the overhead paid. For coarse-grain computations with reasonably low overhead (as is the above example), multitasking is appropriate and advantageous.

10.4   Parallel Algorithms and Application Software

We examine below computational techniques needed to enhance system performance. These include algorithm design, granularity trade-offs, resource sharing, synchronization schemes, asynchronous parallelization, I/O behavior, memory contention, miscellaneous OS services, software conversion considerations, and the development of efficient software packages in key application areas.

10.4.1   Mapping algorithms onto parallel architectures

Algorithm design usually involves several phases of development. The physical problem must first be modeled by a mathematical formulation such as differential equations or algebraic systems. In most cases, these equations or systems are defined over the real domain such as continuous time functions. In order for the computer to solve these systems, some form of discretization and numerical approximation must be employed. For example, in solving problems described by *partial differential equations* (PDEs), either *finite-difference* or *finite-element methods* can be used in the discretization process. Then numerical schemes are sought such as using iterative or direct methods in solving PDEs. Finally, one needs to partition the algorithm in order to map with parallel or vector architectural configurations. We concentrate below on the last phase in mapping decomposed algorithms onto parallel architectures.

Three approaches have been identified in designing parallel algorithms. The first is to convert a given sequential algorithm into a parallel version. This process is often not straightforward. Careful dataflow analysis must be employed to reveal all data/program dependencies. The inhibitors for parallelization or vectorization must be checked to avoid inefficiency in the programming. Very often the problem size does not match the machine size. Algorithmic transformation may be needed to establish a perfect match between the two sides of the problem. The second approach is to invent a new parallel algorithm. This looks more difficult. However, it is often more fruitful, because the new algorithm can be specifically tailored to the target machine. Most algorithm designers choose a combined approach by starting with a parallel algorithm for a similar problem and then modifying it for the problem at hand.

The mapping problem arises when the communication structure of a parallel algorithm differs from the interconnection architecture of the target parallel computer. This problem will be worsened when the number of processes created in the algorithm exceeds the number of processors available in the architecture. The implementation complexity of the algorithm depends on the degree of parallelism, granularity, communication and synchronization overheads, I/O demands, and other implementation overheads. For regularly structured architectures, such as *arrays* [Snyder 84], *prisms* [Rosenfeld 86], *pyramids* [Tanimoto 83], *hypercubes* [Seitz 85], and *trees,* the algorithm is more sensitive to architecture topology and machine size. A good match may make a big difference in performance. Recently, several design methodologies for synthesizing parallel algorithms and VLSI architectures have been proposed in Chen [86]. Program transformation is the key in establishing a perfect or a good match.

Algorithm designers must be aware that communication complexity could outweigh the computational complexity. If one adds the complexities from I/O and memory contention, the problem could be even more severe. This brings us to the concept of *balanced* parallel com-

TABLE 10.4   Candidate Algorithms for Parallelization or Vectorization

Category	Algorithms and Computations
Vector/matrix arithmetic	Matrix multiplication; matrix decomposition; conversion of matrices; sparse matrix operations; linear system solution; eigenvalue computations; least squares problems
Signal/image processing	Convolution and correlation; digital filtering; fast Fourier transforms; feature extraction; pattern recognition; scene analysis and vision
Optimization processes	Linear programming; sorting and searching; integer programming; branch and bound algorithms; combinatorial analysis; constrained optimization
Statistical analysis	Probability distribution functions; variance analysis; nonparametric statistics; multivariate statistics; sampling and histogramming
Partial differential equations	Ordinary differential equations; partial differential equations; finite-element analysis; domain decomposition; numerical integration
Special functions and graph algorithms	Power series and functions; interpolation and approximation; searching techniques; graph matching; logic set operations; transitive closures

putations, in which the effective bandwidths of all subsystems are matched to yield the best possible performance. In a message-passing multicomputer, the communication complexity may dominate the performance. The confronting goal is to minimize all the complexities coming from computation, communication, I/O and memory access in a balanced manner. Simply chasing the bottlenecks will not be sufficient if implementation efficiency becomes a major concern.

We list some candidate algorithms for parallel processing in Table 10.4. For algorithms which emphasize local operations, as seen in most low-level image and signal processing applications, the array (mesh) and pyramid are more suitable. For large-grain computations with global or unknown dependence, the algorithm is better implemented on shared-memory multiprocessors. Mapping algorithms onto array processors has been treated by many researchers [Chen 86, Hwang 88]. In Fig. 10.8 we illustrate a method which will convert a *dataflow graph* into a *pipeline net,* for vector processing a compound vector function consisting of six operators. The numbers in the dataflow graph represent nodal and edge delays. The nodes correspond to operations and the edges indicate the partial ordering relationships among the operations. Through a sequence of graph transformations, we obtain the pipeline net as shown.

Developing algorithms for multiprocessors or multicomputers demands a balanced partition of the algorithm. Partitioned algorithms

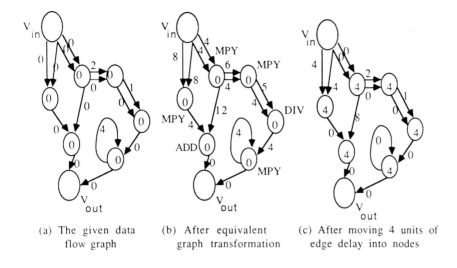

(a) The given data flow graph

(b) After equivalent graph transformation

(c) After moving 4 units of edge delay into nodes

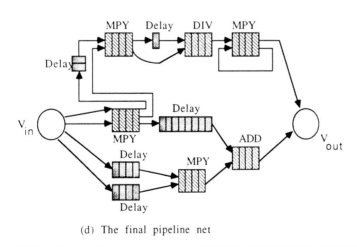

(d) The final pipeline net

Figure 10.8 Designing a pipeline net with a sequence of graph transformations on a synchronous dataflow graph. (*a*) The given data flow graph; (*b*) after equivalent graph transformation; (*c*) after moving four units of edge delay in nodes; (*d*) the final pipeline net. (Courtesy of Hwang and Xu [88].)

must be synchronized, because different granularities may exist in subprograms as discussed in Hwang [82 and 87]. Partitioned algorithms can be further divided into *prescheduled* or *self-scheduled* ones. In order to do this correctly, some prediction of the computation times and resource demand patterns of various subprograms must be known in advance. The self-scheduled algorithms obtain their resources at run time. Such a dynamic allocation of resources depends on an optimizing scheduler in the OS kernel. All ready-to-run subprograms are queued to match with the availability of resource types, such as processors or memories.

Another important class is *asynchronous algorithms,* in which no forced synchronization is conducted among concurrent subprograms [Hwang 87, Kung 80, Quinn 87]. This is based on a relaxation principle, in which each processor will not wait for another processor to provide it with data. Instead, each processor works with the most recently available data wherever it may come from. Because of this relaxation, asynchronous algorithms are difficult to validate. Race conditions may exist to produce untraceable results. One can design a parallel algorithm which consists of synchronized and asynchronous portions. Such a combined mode can be constructed in a hierarchical manner, so that the best match can be established between the programming levels and the underlying resource architecture. Divide-and-conquer algorithms can be used for this purpose [Stout 87].

To overcome the difficulty associated with I/O-bound problems, one can overlap computation with data transfer, such as using *double buffering* to isolate the input and output of a large volume of data movement. To reduce transfer time, extended main memory (such as the SSD in Cray 2 and the communication buffer in ETA-10) can be used to close up the speed gaps. One can also trade serial I/O for small-grain problems with parallel I/O for large-grain problems. The memory contention can be alleviated by skewed memory allocation schemes to avoid access conflicts or to use smart conflict resolution logic with multiported memory banks.

10.4.2   Mathematical software and application packages

Mathematical software serves as the bridge between numerical analysts who design algorithms and computer users who need application software. The creation, documentation, maintenance, and availability of software products are crucial to the effective use of supercomputers. We examine below five major classes of software libraries that have been developed in recent years. Representative application software packages are summarized in Table 10.5. Most of these packages are coded in Fortran, only a few have versions also in Pascal, Algol, Ada, or C. The formation of a typical application software organization is illustrated in Fig. 10.9. This demonstrates how a software library is used in selecting special computing modules to form an application package which is callable from the user's main program. Such systematized collections of software modules have inspired the creation of many useful software packages.

TABLE 10.5   Some Software Packages and Their Applications

Software package	Special applications
LINPACK	Solving linear systems of equations
MG3D	A seismic three-dimensional integration code for oil exploration
SPECTRAL	Short-term weather forecasting
PICF	A particle-in-cell simulation program for plasma research experiments
AIR 3D	A Navier-Stokes code for three-dimensional aerodynamic simulation
NASTRAN	A PDE solver for finite-element analysis
ELLPACK	Elliptic PDE solver
FUNPACK	Routines for computing special functions and integrals
EISPACK	Eigenvalue problem solvers
MINPACK	Routines for unconstrained and constrained optimizations
SPARSPAK	Package for solving large-scale spare matrices
ESSL	An IBM library for vector/matrix computations
BCSLIB	A core library supplied by Boeing Computer Services Center
SLATEC	A common math library jointly developed by several national laboratories
Math advantage	A mathematical package which is runable over 30 computer systems

Major numerical software libraries.   Several software libraries that have played major roles in scientific computations are commonly known as IMSL, PORT, NAG, and NATS [Cowell 84]. IBM has developed the Scientific Subroutine Package (SSP), which was later also used in Univac and CDC machines. Today IMSL (International Mathematical and Statistical Libraries) supports most mainframes and superminis at various computer centers [IMSL 80]. There are 495 user-callable Fortran subroutines in IMSL, which perform basic mathematical functions, differential equations, matrix arithmetic, and linear programming, etc. The PORT mathematical subroutine library, emphasizing portability among heterogeneous machines, was developed at the Bell Labs. The NAG (Numerical Algorithms Group) library was developed in both Fortran and Algol 60 versions. Both PORT and NAG routines have been used in Cray 1 benchmarking experiments. The NATS (National Activity to Test Software), backed by NSF and

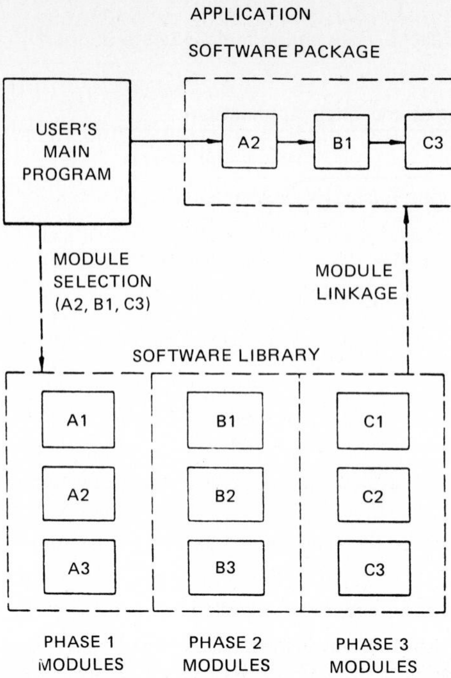

Figure 10.9 Application software packaging and a typical mathematical software library. (*a*) Forming an application software package with modules selected from a software library; (*b*) major software categories in the Boeing Software Library.

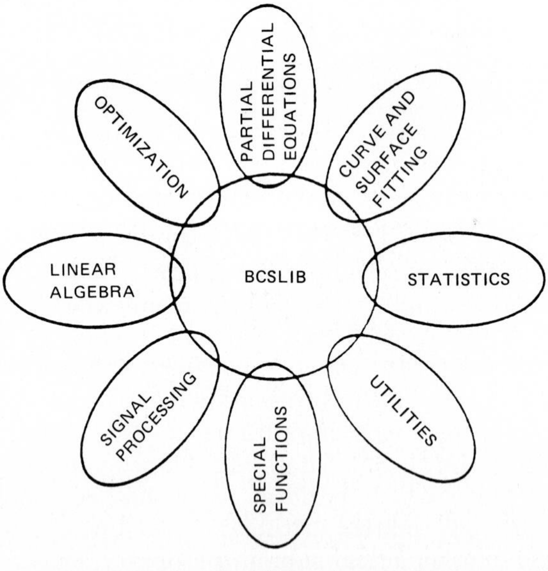

DOE, has promoted the development of the several scientific software packages [Boyle 72].

Important scientific software packages.   LINPACK is a package for solving linear systems whose matrices are general, banded, symmetric indefinite, symmetric positive, definite triangular, or triangular [Dongarra 84]. FUNPACK is a package of special function routines, such as Bessel functions and exponential integrals, etc. EISPACK, a package for solving eigenvalue problems, consists of 58 subroutines. These routines are being altered with Fortran 77 extensions to take account of vector machine architectures and a paging OS. MINPACK is a systematized collection of software for unconstrained, linearly constrained, and large-scale optimizations. These PACKs are among many other application software packages that are currently in use [Cowell 84].

Software for solving differential equations.   Many scientific/engineering problems are characterized by *ordinary differential equations* (ODEs) or PDEs. Mathematical software for ODEs includes the DEPAC developed at Sandia National Laboratories. Elliptic PDE problems are being attacked by the ELLPACK and the FISHPAK for fluid dynamics modeling. Since many ODE or PDE problems resort to the solution of large-scale sparse matrices, the SPARSPAK and the Yale package [Cowell 84] have been developed to meet this demand. Efforts in developing parallel PDE machines are reviewed in Ortega [85].

Software routines supplied by vendors.   Major mainframe and supercomputer manufacturers have each developed some scientific/engineering routines. Cray offers SCLILIB with functions microcoded for fast execution on the Cray computers. Besides using the vectorizing compiler CFT, Cray application groups have also developed impressive multitasking software tools [Cray 84]. These tools have been applied in running some benchmark codes, such as the SPECTRAL for short-term weather forecasting. This multitasked SPECTRAL code shows a speedup of 3.77 running on a Cray X-MP-4 as compared with a Cray X-MP-1. IBM has supplied the ESSL (Engineering and Scientific Subroutine Library) for a vector facility attached to the 3090 mainframe [Tucker 86]. FPS has a math library of 500 routines for their array processor families. The vendor-developed libraries are mostly machine dependent. Portability is potentially a serious problem with these packages. To help alleviate this portability problem, the Math Advantage [Smith 87] was commercially developed to supply over 200 routines in Fortran, C, and Ada versions runnable on over 30 computer systems, including some parallel and vector architectures.

Software development by user groups. The Boeing Mathematical Software Library is being upgraded to support CDC, IBM, FPS, and Cray computers. The Boeing library structure is shown in Fig. 10.9b, where the BCSLIB is the core library containing basic computing modules and some utility software. The outer software includes the dense matrix software form LINPACK, general sparse matrix routines, and other software routines mentioned earlier. This multilevel library structure is being optimized toward a vector library for the CDC Cyber 205 and Cray machines through a conversion approach. For example, the CRAYPACK is being developed with *Cray Assembly Languages* (CAL) to exploit the Cray architecture. Another interesting effort is the SLATEC Common Math Library, which provides a means for several National Laboratories (Sandia, Los Alamos, AF Weapons Lab., LLNL, NBS, etc.) to foster the exchange of software experiences in using supercomputers [Buzbee 84].

Most of the above Fortran-coded software packages were originally written for conventional scalar processors. Some software libraries have responded to the call for vectorization and multiprocessing. However, the conversion from serial codes to parallel codes has been limited in isolated cases. These application software libraries are presently taking very little advantages of the parallel hardware. Attempts to achieve vectorization have been made more often than those for multitasking or distributed computing. This is due to the fact that vector uniprocessors appeared at least 5 years ahead of their multiprocessor extensions. However, this time lag in development is being shortened. Most minisupers start as uniprocessor systems and upgrade to multiprocessor versions in later years. The extensions from Alliant FX/1 to FX/8 [Test 87] and from Convex C-1 to CXS are good examples [Convex 87].

Toward the parallelization and vectorization of application software, most supercomputers choose the intelligent compiler approach or restructure the underlying algorithms or mathematical model used. One has to realize that mathematical software is application-driven. Many of the above software libraries should be unified or standardized toward better portability, model sharing, routine sharing, and extended applicability. Proprietary restriction should be minimized and software documentation should be improved to benefit both designers and users of parallel/vector computers.

10.5 Creating a Parallel Programming Environment

We address next the issues related to the creation of a parallel programming environment for supercomputers. An ideal programming environment is outlined, in which the users are aided with system tools and visual aids for program trace, resource mapping, and analysis of data structures. Then we examine various techniques needed to enhance concurrent programming and thus system performance. These include algorithm design, granularity tradeoffs, load balancing, resource sharing, deadlock avoidance, synchronization schemes, and asynchronous parallelization, I/O behavior, memory contention, miscellaneous OS services, and software conversion considerations. Finally, we elaborate on multidiscipline interactions toward the development of efficient software packages in key application areas.

10.5.1 User-friendly programming environment

The advent of multiprocessor or multicomputer systems poses new problems for the software designers. Three problems stand out as crucial for optimizing performance of parallel algorithms: *memory contention, problem decomposition,* and *interprocessor communication.* Contention refers to the attempt to simultaneously access memory by different processes. Problem decomposition refers to the problem of allocating code to the various processors. Interprocessor communication refers to the messages that must be sent between processors to coordinate their operation. Below we describe several methods to establish a programming environment that aids in the solution of these problems.

A *programming environment* is a collection of software tools and visualization aids that can be used to develop software. Well-known programming environments are UNIX and C, Interlisp, and Smalltalk. With the advent of parallel architectures new issues in programming environment design arise. There are three key issues that must be adequately addressed. The *first* is what information is going to be collected. The *second* is how is the information recorded and displayed. The *third* is what mechanisms should be provided to alter execution. One must be able to monitor the performance of all functional units of the system. For many systems, a fixed processor topology is used, such as a ring, mesh, cube, cube-connected cycles, or hypercube. For these systems, problem decomposition to fit the network is essential. For other systems, e.g., Cedar and RP3, it is possible to dynamically reconfigure the processors in different ways. In this latter case, problem decomposition is enhanced by the ability to reconfigure processor interconnectivity.

To help determine what should be displayed and accessible with respect to the executing software, one should include on the screen all of the traditional views of a program. A system such as PECAN presents on the screen the following: the program listing, data type schema, parse tree, symbol table, flow graph, execution stack, and I/O dialogue. The ability to instantly view and access all of this information substantially improves the programmer's ability to understand what is going on with his program.

For multiprocessor systems the problem of data collection is exacerbated by the volume of material that may be produced during an execution. The traditional "table of numbers" can easily swamp any person's ability to determine performance factors. One approach to solving this problem is the display of data using graphical techniques. The second part of the data display problem is the sheer volume of material. It is not possible to view all this data in real time, nor is it desirable to run test cases multiple times. Thus we need a new medium that can store large volumes of data and have it displayed in a graphical form.

The goal is to design and construct a programming environment that would be used by creators of parallel algorithms. The hardware would consist of a supercomputer coupled to a high-resolution color display, a mouse, a keyboard, a videodisk recorder, and a player. The software contains support for the color graphics monitor plus associated windowing software. There must be software for manipulating the videodisk, both for recording and playback. All of these components would be obtained from current industrial sources. An ideal programming environment should be user-friendly. Listed below are the desired features in such an environment:

- It will display a map of the multiprocessor architecture that is available. Elements of the map can be examined separately using a zoom-in feature.

- For each functional element it will display an instantaneous picture of its activity. For each processor one can see its wait/active states, access to memory, and I/O activity.

- Each processor can indicate the code segment that is executing. Identical code segments are identified by color. It will permit the tracking of memory accesses, whether there is local memory or shared memory or both.

- Collection of graphical data in the form of video images are stored on disk. Video disk segments can be referenced, examined and played back.

- Statistical routines are available for analysis of the digital form of the data. The program can be edited, recompiled, and reexecuted in the environment.

Given such a visual programming environment, we expect a *balanced system* where all processors appear to be active. Queues for memory access are nonempty, and input and output processors are active. An *un-*

balanced system is immediately perceived as one or more processors are idle and memory accesses are wasted. Another information factor is the rate of transfer of the external media. These may not be capable of sustaining the rate required by the processors. This should be visible in the environment. Another common situation is when processors are divided into several levels. Each level may contain a cluster of processors that act in conjunction, but on different levels the processors behave entirely differently. Thus any attempt at balancing must also focus on the interaction across levels of processors.

10.5.2 Techniques of concurrent programming

Concurrent programming is inherently a nondeterministic process. The tradeoffs lie in vector processing vs. parallel processing. Asynchronous parallelization of codes seems to be conceptually simpler than vectorization. Furthermore, synchronized parallelism is much easier to implement than asynchronous parallelism. A race situation may exist in parallel branches of an asynchronous algorithm. Parallel processing demands the scheduling of parallel works among multiple processors. We discuss below the use of counting semaphores for deadlock avoidance and process synchronization.

Counting semaphores are used for *lock, unlock, deadlock prevention,* and *synchronization* of asynchronous processes. A simple definition of the $P(S)$ and $V(S)$ operators is given below, where S is a semaphore representing the availability of a specific resource type:

$P(S)$: 1 IF $S = 0$ THEN GOTO 1
    ELSE $S: = S - 1$
    $V(S)$: $S: = S + 1$

The value of S is typically initialized as 0 in the creation of concurrent processes, as exemplified below, where S_1 and S_2 are two resource types being shared by two processes:

Process one	Process two
.	.
· Serial	· Serial
· Work	· Work
.	.
$V(S_1)$	$P(S_2)$
.	.
· Parallel	· Parallel
· Work	· Work
$P(S_1)$	$V(S_2)$
.	.
· Serial	· Serial
· Work	· Work

If the value of a semaphore is initialized as 1, it can be used as a lock for specifying a critical section as follows:

$P(S)$

· Critical
· Section

$V(S)$

Dijkstra has indicated three basic requirements for the execution of critical sections [Dijkstra 65]. Knuth [71] has reenforced statement 3 as stated in 4:

1. At any given time, only one process is in the critical section.

2. Stopping one process outside the critical section has no effect on other processes.

3. The decision as to which process enters the critical section cannot be postponed indefinitely.

4. Every process wanting to enter the critical section will eventually be allowed to do so.

Another form of shared variable for interprocess synchronization is the use of *monitors,* a structured way of implementing mutual exclusion. Besides having variables representing the state of some resource, a monitor also contains procedures that implement operations on that resource and the associated initialization code, which initializes the values of variables before the monitor is called. Monitors are used to implement mutual exclusion. Concurrent Pascal [Hansen 75] supports monitors for this purpose.

System deadlock refers to the situation in a multiprocessor when multiple processes are holding resources and preventing each other from completing their executions. In general, a deadlock can be prevented if one or more of the following necessary conditions are removed:

1. *Mutual exclusion.*   Each process has exclusive control of its allocated resources.

2. *Nonpreemption.*   A process cannot release its allocated resources until completion.

3. *Wait for.*   Processes can hold resources while waiting for additional resources.

4. *Circular wait.*   Multiple processes wait for each other's resources in a circular dependence situation.

The example shown in Fig. 10.10 shows a circular wait situation among four concurrent processes as listed below:

Process 1	Process 2	Process 3	Process 4	Process 4 Modified
.	.	.	.	.
.	.	.	.	.
$P(S_1)$	$P(S_2)$	$P(S_5)$	$P(S_5)$	$P(S_1)$
.	.	.	.	.
.	.	.	.	.
$P(S_2)$	$P(S_4)$	$P(S_3)$	$P(S_6)$	$P(S_6)$
.	.	.	.	.
.	.	.	.	.
$P(S_3)$	$P(S_5)$	$V(S_5)$	$P(S_1)$	$P(S_5)$
.	.	$V(S_3)$	.	.
.	.	.	.	.
$V(S_1)$	$V(S_5)$		$V(S_6)$	$V(S_6)$
$V(S_2)$	$V(S_4)$		$V(S_1)$	$V(S_1)$
$V(S_3)$	$V(S_2)$		$V(S_5)$	$V(S_5)$

By modifying the resource claim ordering in process 4, the deadlock can be prevented, since there is no circular wait loop in the dependence graph, where S_1, S_2,..., S_6 are six resource semaphores being shared by the four processes. Each resource is assumed to have a single copy. *Static deadlock prevention* as outlined above may result in poor resource utilization. *Dynamic deadlock avoidance* depends on the run-time conditions, which may introduce a heavy overhead in detecting the potential existence of a deadlock. Although dynamic detection may lead to better resource utilization, the tradeoffs in detection and recovery costs must be considered.

At present, most parallel computers choose a static prevention method due to its simplicity to implement. Sophisticated dynamic avoidance or a recovery scheme for the deadlock problem requires one to minimize the incurred costs to justify for the net gains. The gain lies in better resource utilization, if those static deadlock prevention constraints are removed. To break a deadlock by aborting some non-critical processes should result in a minimum recovery cost. A meaningful analysis of the recovery costs associated with various options is very time consuming. This is the main reason why a sophisticated deadlock recovery system has not been built into current multiprocessors. The static prevention may be rather primitive, but it costs very

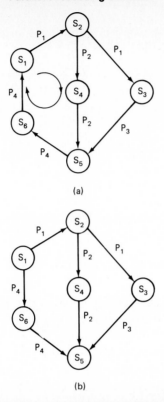

(a)

(b)

Figure 10.10 Resource allocation graph showing the sharing of six resources (represented by semaphors $S_1, \bullet, S_6$) by four concurrent processes (represented by $P_1, \bullet, P_4$). (*a*) Deadlock is possible with the existence of a circular wait among S_1, S_2, S_3, S_4, S_5, and S_6 by processes P_1, P_2, and P_4; (*b*) breaking the deadlock possibility by changing the order of resource requests by process P_4.

little to implement. Further research is needed to make the dynamic recovery system more cost-effective.

10.6 Conclusions

We have addressed the parallel programming and software issues in the context of delivering real supercomputer performance. Most existing supercomputers choose the vectorizing compiler approach, except the multiflow computer chooses the nonvectorized, trace-scheduling compacting compiling for scalar parallelism. The tradeoffs between vector and scalar processing do exist. Only through a large number of benchmark experiments can one prove the superiority of one approach over the other. Nevertheless, both approaches are exciting and have room for further improvement.

Besides the aforementioned issues, we would like to conclude this chapter by pointing out the following challenges in the research and development of systematic *software engineering* for parallel computers:

- The software development process should be systematically developed for parallel computers.

- Software conversion costs must be reduced between different machine architectures.

- Distributed program debugging is greatly in demand for multicomputer systems.

- Program validation procedures and systematic trace scheduling should be developed jointly.

- Application and system programmers should work together to achieve high performance.

- Visualization through the use of high-performance color graphics is needed for displaying the results in real-time supercomputers.

It may take several generations of programming experience before we can accept a universal programming language for a variety of parallel computers. Until then, we have to overcome the difficulty by using more intelligent compilers, better scheduling methods, optimized instruction sets (RISC vs. CISC), and concurrent programming techniques. More research and development efforts are needed to create a parallel programming environment which is truly user-friendly. Recently, a special issue entitled "Languages, Compilers, and Environments for Parallel Programming" has appeared in the *Journal of Parallel and Distributed Computing* [Kuck 88]. Interested readers are referred to that issue for additional new development.

Bibliography

[Alliant 87]   *Alliant FX/Series: Product Summary.* Alliant Computer Systems Corp., Acton, MA, June 1987.

[Batcher 80]   K.E. Batcher. "Design of a Massively Parallel Processor." *IEEE Trans. Computers,* vol. C-29, no. 9, pp. 836–840, September 1980.

[Bernstein 66]   A.J. Bernstein. "Analysis of Programs for Parallel Processing." *IEEE Trans. Computers,* vol. E-15, no. 10, pp. 746–757, October 1966.

[Boyle 72]   J.M. Boyle et al. "NATS: A Collaborative Effort to Certify and Disseminate Mathematical Software." *Proc. NCCC,* pp. 630–635, 1972.

[Buzbee 84]   B. Buzbee. "The SLATEC Common Mathematical Library." In W.R. Cowell (ed). *Sources and Development of Mathematical Software,* pp. 302–320, Prentice-Hall, New York, 1984.

[Calahan 85]   D.A. Calahan. "Task Granularity Studies on a Many-Processor Cray X-MP." *Parallel Computing,* pp. 109–118, June 1985.

[Chen 86] M. Chen. "A Design Methodology for Synthesizing Parallel Algorithms and Architectures." *J. Parallel and Distributed Computing,* vol. 3, no. 4, pp. 462–491, December 1986.

[Convex 87] *Convex C1 Series: XP Processors.* Convex Computer Corporation, Richardson, TX, technical notes edition, 1987.

[Cowell 84] W.R. Cowell (ed). *Sources and Development of Mathematical Software.* Prentice-Hall, New York, 1984.

[Cray 84] *Multitasking User Guide.* Tech. Note SN-0222, Cray Research Inc., February 1984.

[Dijkstra 65] E.W. Dijkstra. "Solution of a Problem in Concurrent Programming." *Comm. of ACM,* vol. 8, no. 9, pp. 569–570, September 1965.

[DoD 81] U.S. DoD. *Programming Language Ada: Reference Manual,* vol. 106. Springer-Verlag, New York, NY, 1981.

[Dongarra 84] J.J. Dongarra and G.W. Stewart. "LINPACK—A Package for Solving Linear Systems." In W.R. Cowell (ed). *Sources and Development of Mathematical Software,* pp. 20–48, Prentice-Hall, New York, 1984.

[Dongarra 87] J.J. Dongarra. "Performance of Various Computers Using Standard Linear Equations Software in a Fortran Environment." In W.J. Karplus (ed). *Multiprocessors and Array Processors,* pp. 15–33, Simulation Councils Inc., San Diego, CA, January 1987.

[Dongarra 88] J.J. Dongarra (ed). *Experimental Parallel Computing Architectures.* North-Holland, Elsevier, 1988.

[Ellis 86] J.R. Ellis. *Bulldog: A Compiler for VLIW Architectures.* MIT Press, Cambridge, MA, 1986.

[Fenner 87] P.R. Fenner. "The Flex/32 for Real-Time Multicomputer Simulation." In W.J. Karplus (ed). *Multiprocessors and Array Processors,* pp. 127–136, Simulation Councils, Inc., San Diego, CA, January 1987.

[Fisher 81] J.A. Fisher. "Trace Scheduling: A Technique for Global Microcode Compaction." *IEEE Trans. Computers,* vol. C-30, no. 7, pp. 478–490, July 1981.

[Fisher 87] J.A. Fisher. "VLIW Architectures: Supercomputing Via Overlapped Execution." *Proc. Second International Conference on Supercomputing,* May 3–8, 1987.

[Gibson 86] D.H. Gibson, D.W. Rain, and H.F. Walsh. "Engineering and Scientific Processing on the IBM 3090." *IBM System Journal,* vol. 25, no. 1, pp. 36–50, January 1986.

[Hansen 75] P.B. Hansen. "The Programming Language Concurrent Pascal." *IEEE Trans. Software Engineering,* vol. SE-1, no. 2, pp. 199–206, June 1975.

[Hoare 72] C.A.R. Hoare. "Toward a Theory of Parallel Programming." In C.A.R. Hoare (ed). *Operating Systems Techniques,* Academic Press, New York, 1972.

[Huson 86] C. Huson, T. Mache, J. Davies, M. Wolfe, and B. Leasure. "The KAP-205: An Advanced Source-to-Source Vectorizer for the Cyber 205 Supercomputer." *Proc. International Conference on Parallel Processing,* pp. 827–832, August 1986.

[Hwang 82] K. Hwang and Y.H. Cheng. "Partitioned Matrix Algorithms for VLSI Arithmetic Systems." *IEEE Trans. Computers,* vol. C-31, no. 12, pp. 1215–1224, December 1982.

[Hwang 87] K. Hwang. "Advanced Parallel Processing with Supercomputer Architectures." *Proc. IEEE,* vol. OC-75, no. 10, pp. 1348–1379, October 1987.

[Hwang 88] K. Hwang and Z. Xu. "Pipeline Nets for Compound Vector Supercomputing." *IEEE Trans. Computers,* vol. C-37, no. 1, pp. 33–47, January 1988.

[IMSL 80]   *IMSL Library Reference Manual.* IMSL, Inc., Houston, TX, 1980.

[Inmos 84]   *OCCAM Programming Manual.* Inmos Ltd., Prentice-Hall, Englewood Cliffs, NJ, 1984.

[Jordan 86]   H.F. Jordan. "Structuring Parallel Algorithms in an MIMD, Shared Memory Environment." *Parallel Computing,* vol. 3, no. 2, pp. 93–110, May 1986.

[Kogge 73]   P.M. Kogge and H.S. Stone. "A Parallel Algorithm for Efficient Solution of a General Class of Recurrence Equations." *IEEE Trans. Computers,* vol. C-72, pp. 786–793, June 1973.

[Kowalik 84]   J. Kowalik, R. Lord, and S. Kumar. "Design and Performance of Algorithms for MIMD Parallel Computers." In J. Kowalik (ed). *Proc. NATO Workshop on High-Speed Computations,* pp. 257–276, Springer-Verlag, West Germany, 1984.

[Knuth 71]   D.E. Knuth. "An Empirical Study of Fortran Programs." *Software Pract. Exper.,* vol. 1, no. 2, pp. 105–133, April–June 1971.

[Kuck 80]   D.J. Kuck, R.H. Kuhn, B. Leasure, and M. Wolfe. "The Structure of an Advanced Retargetable Vectorizer." *Proc. COMPSAC,* October 1980.

[Kuck 88]   D.J. Kuck and C.D. Polychronopoulos (guest eds). Special issue on "Languages, Compilers, and Environments for Parallel Programming." *J. Parallel and Distributed Computing,* vol. 5, no. 5, pp. 457–653, October 1988.

[Kung 80]   H.T. Kung. "The Structure of Parallel Algorithms." In M. Yovits (ed). *Advances in Computers,* pp. 65–112, Academic Press, New York, 1980.

[Larson 84]   J. Larson. "Multitasking on the Cray X-MP/2 Multiprocessor." *IEEE Computer,* vol. 12, no. 7, pp. 62–29, July 1984.

[Li 85]   K.C. Li and H. Schwetman. "Vectorizing C: A Vector Processing Language." *J. Parallel and Distributed Computing,* vol. 2, no. 2, pp. 132–169, May 1985.

[Lubeck 85]   O. Lubeck, J. Moore, and R. Mendez. "A Benchmark Comparison of Three Supercomputers: Fujitsu VP-200, Hitachi S810/20, and Cray X-MP/2." *IEEE Computer,* vol. 13, no. 12, pp. 10–29, December 1985.

[Ni 85]   L.M. Ni and K. Hwang. "Vector Reduction Techniques for Arithmetic Systems." *IEEE Trans. Computers,* vol. C-34, no. 5, pp. 404–411, May 1985.

[Ortega 85]   J.M. Ortega and R.G. Voigt. "Solutiuon of PDEs on Vector and Parallel Computers." *SIAM Review,* vol. 27, pp. 149–240, June 1985.

[Paul 82]   G. Paul. "VECTRAN and the Proposed Vector/Array Extensions to ANSI FORTRAN for Scientific and Engineering Computations." *Proc. IBM Conference on Parallel Computers and Scientific Computations,* Rome, Italy, March 1982.

[Perrot 87]   R.H. Perrot, R.W. Lyttle, and P.S. Dhillon. "The Design and Implementation of a Pascal-Based Language for Array Processor Architecture." *J. Parallel and Distributed Computing,* vol. 4, no. 3, pp. 266–287, 1987.

[Quinn 87]   M. Quinn. *Designing Efficient Algorithms for Parallel Computers.* McGraw-Hill, New York, 1987.

[Reed 87]   D.A. Reed and R.M. Fujimoto. *Multicomputer Networks: Message-Passing Parallel Processing.* MIT Press, Cambridge, MA, 1987.

[Rice 85]   J. Rice and R.F. Boisvert. *Solving Elliptic Problems Using ELLIPACK.* Springer-Verlag, New York, 1985.

[Rosenfeld 86]   A. Rosenfeld. "The Prism Machine: An Alternative to Pyramid." *J. Parallel and Distributed Computing,* vol. 3, no. 3, pp. 404–411, September 1986.

[Seitz 85]   C.L. Seitz. "The Cosmic Cube." *Comm. of ACM,* vol. 28, no. 1, pp. 22–33, January 1985.

[Smith 87]   W.R. Smith. "Quantitative Technology Corporation Math Advantage: A Compatible, Optimized Math Library." In W.J. Karplus (ed). *Multiprocessors and Array Processors,* Simulation Councils, Inc., San Diego, CA, January 1987.

[Snyder 84]   L. Snyder. "Supercomputers and VLSI." In *Advances in Computers,* pp. 1–33, Academic Press, New York, 1984.

[Soll 86]   D.B. Soll. *Vectorization and Vector Migration Techniques.* Tech. Bull., IBM Publishing Services, Irving, TX, June 1986.

[Stout 87]   Q. Stout. "Divide and Conquer Algorithms for Parallel Image Processing." *J. Parallel and Distributed Computing,* vol. 4, no. 2, pp. 95–106, February 1987.

[Sydow 83]   P.J. Sydow. *Optimization Guide.* Tech. Rep. SN-0220, Cray Research, Inc., Cheapawa Falls, WI, 1983.

[Tanimoto 83]   S.L. Tanimoto. "A Pyramidal Approach to Parallel Processing." *Proc. 10th Annual Symposium on Computer Architecture,* pp. 372–378, 1983.

[Tamura 85]   H. Tamura, S. Kamiya, and T. Ishigai. "FACOM VP-100/200: Supercomputers with Ease of Use." *Parallel Computing,* vol. 2, no. 3, pp. 87–108, June 1985.

[Test 87]   J. Test, M. Myszewski, and R.C. Swift. "The Alliant FX/Series: Automatic Parallelism in a Multiprocessor Mini-Supercomputer." In W.J. Karplus (ed). *Multiprocessors and Array Processors,* pp. 35–44, Simulation Councils, Inc., San Diego, CA, January 1987.

[Thornton 70]   J.E. Thornton. *Design of a Computer: The Control Data 6600.* Scott, Foresman, Glenview, IL, 1970.

[Tucker 86]   S.G. Tucker. "The IBM 3090 System: An Overview." *IBM Systems Journal,* vol. 25, no. 1, pp. 4–19, January 1986.

[Wirth 82]   N. Wirth. *Programming in Modula-2.* Springer-Verlag, New York, 1982.

[Worlton 84]   J. Worlton. "Understanding Supercomputer Benchmarks." *Datamation,* pp. 121–130, September 1984.

[Xu 88]   Z. Xu and K. Hwang. "Molecules: A Language Construct for Layered Development of Parallel Programs." *IEEE Trans. Software Engineering,* vol. SE-15, no. 5, May 1989.

Automatic Vectorization, Data Dependence, and Optimizations for Parallel Computers

Michael Wolfe

Oregon Graduate Center, Beaverton, OR

11.1 Introduction

As shown in Chap. 10, a compiler is an important part of a super-computer system. All manufacturers of vector supercomputers and minisupercomputers provide automatic vectorizing Fortran compilers to allow access to the vector hardware; at least one multiprocessor manufacturer also provides concurrentization in its compiler to distribute a job over multiple processors. Data dependence, the theoretical basis for parallelism detection, has many applications in compilers today and in the future. This paper discusses data dependence and some of its applications, vectorization in particular.

Most programmers do not worry much about performance except at the algorithmic level. They choose an algorithm and a programming language and trust the compiler to get good performance from the program. If the program is too slow, the programmer may look at improving the algorithm—replacing a bubble sort with a quick sort, for example; even the best compiler will not get good performance from a bad program. Most programs, however, will not run even twice as fast by any manual improvements without algorithmic changes. Compiler optimizations can improve the performance of most numerical programs to approach the performance of the best hand-coded machine language programs.

With supercomputers, however, a large program speedup is possible by simply recoding parts of the program. This is due to the vector or parallel architecture of today's supercomputers and the relative weakness of many optimizing compilers for these machines. Users are often required to consider the capabilities of the compiler as well as the machine when writing a program.

In this chapter, we consider what special compiler optimization techniques are appropriate for vector and parallel supercomputers. We discuss vectorization and other optimizations for vector computers. We develop data dependence and other tools for vectorization and apply these tools for other types of parallelism discovery.

Many vector computers are available today, and vectorizing Fortran compilers are available for all of them. Some of these compilers also accept explicit vector syntax, such as the hardware-dependent vector notation used by the FTN200 compiler [Control Data 84] for the Cyber 205, or the Fortran 8x [ANSI 87] array assignments accepted by the FX/Fortran [Alliant 86] compiler for the Alliant FX/8, but most compilers rely entirely on automatic vectorization.

Vectorization translates a serial **do** loop into vector code. The loop below

```
do I = 1,N
   A(I) = B(I) + 2
   C(I) = A(I) + D(I)
enddo
```

can be vectorized and expressed in Fortran 8x array notation as

```
A(1:N) = B(1:N) + 2
C(1:N) = A(1:N) + D(1:N)
```

Both the serial loop and the vector assignments generate the same answer; the values assigned to A in the first statement are used properly in the second statement. The following loop

```
do I = 1,N
   A(I) = B(I) + 2
   C(I) = A(I + 1) + D(I)
enddo
```

exhibits a different data usage pattern. Here the second statement reads the old value of A(2) on the first iteration, after which a new value is assigned to A(2) in the first statement on the next iteration. Simple-minded vectorization of this loop

```
A(1:N) = B(1:N) + 2
C(1:N) = A(2:N + 1) + D(1:N)
```

would violate this data usage pattern; in the vectorized version, A(1), A(2), A(3), and so on, are all assigned first; the second statement gets the wrong value for A(2) through A(N). The loop can be vectorized if the statements are reordered:

C(1:N) = A(2:N + 1) + D(1:N)
A(1:N) = B(1:N) + 2

Now the original data usage pattern is preserved since the assignment to C comes first. The conditions that need to be tested when vectorizing loops can be expressed in terms of *data dependence relations*.

11.2   Data Dependence

In this section we define and give examples of data dependence relations between statements in a program. We begin with some definitions. The notation S_n denotes a statement in a program. To make the definitions easy, the examples contain only assignment statements, but the ideas obviously apply to **if** statements, **read** and **write** statements, etc.

Definition: Input and output sets.   We use $OUT(S_1)$ to denote the set of output items (scalar variables or array elements) of statement S_1 (items whose values may be changed by S_1), and $IN(S_1)$ to denote the set of input items of S_1 (items whose values may be read by S_1).

The IN and OUT sets for the assignment statement in the loop

   do I = 1, 10
S_1: X(I) = A(I + 1)*B
   enddo

are

$IN(S_1)$ = {A(2), A(3), A(4),..., A(11), B}
$OUT(S_1)$ = {X(1), X(2), X(3),..., X(10)}

The IN and OUT sets are equivalent to the *use* and *gen* sets used in classical compiler optimization, except that each array element is considered distinct in the IN and OUT sets. In practice, IN and OUT sets will be approximated by a compiler, since the actual loop bounds or **if** branches are frequently unknown at compile time.

Definition: execution ordering.   If S_1 is enclosed in a loop with index I, we will write $S_1^{I'}$ to refer to the instance of S_1 during the particular iteration when I = I'. We define the relation θ to represent the execution order of the statements. We will write $S_1 \theta S_2$ if some instance of S_1 can be executed before an instance of S_2 in the normal execution of the program. If both S_1 and S_2 are enclosed in the loop, we will write

$$S_1^{I'} \theta S_2^{I''}$$

if $S_1^{I'}$ can be executed before $S_2^{I''}$ in the normal execution of the program. While in real programs the loop index can have an arbitrary increment, here we will assume an increment of one. If the loop increment is something else, such as

> **do** I = L,N,3
>   A(I) = A(I − 1) + A(I + 2) + B(I)
> **enddo**

we will *normalize* the loop by replacing the loop index I with the expression I*3 + L and adjusting the loop bounds:

> **do** I = 0, (N − L)/3
>   A(I*3 + L) = A(I*3 + L − 1) + A(I*3 + L + 2) + B(I*3 + L)
> **enddo**

In the loop

> **do** I = 1, 10
>   **do** J = 2, 20
> S_1: A(I,J) = B(J − 1) + C(I,J)
> S_2: B(I,J) = A(I,J) + B(I,J)
>   **enddo**
> **enddo**

both $S_1 \theta S_2$ and $S_2 \theta S_1$ hold (for example, $S_1^{1,2} \theta S_2^{1,2}$ and $S_2^{2,3} \theta S_1^{3,2}$). In fact, $S_1^{I',J'} \theta S_2^{I'',J''}$ whenever $I' < I''$ or $I' = I''$ and $J' <= J''$. Also, $S_2^{I',J''} \theta S_1^{I',J''}$ whenever $I'' < I'$ or $I'' = I'$ and $J'' < J'$.

These concepts are sufficient to define the basic idea behind data dependence.

Definition: data dependence relations. Given two statements S_1 and S_2, the following *data dependence relations* may hold true or the statements may be data independent:

1. If some item $X \in$ OUT(S_1) and $X \in$ IN (S_2) and S_2 is to use the value of X computed in S_1, then we say that S_2 is *data flow dependent* on S_1 and denote this with $S_1 \delta S_2$.

2. If some item $X \in$ IN(S_1) and $X \in$ OUT(S_2), but S_1 is to use the value of X before it is changed by S_2, then we say that S_2 is *data antidependent* on S_1 and denote this with $S_1 \bar{\delta} S_2$.

3. If $X \in$ OUT(S_1) and $X \in$ OUT(S_2) and the value computed by S_2 is to be stored after the value computed by S_1, we say S_2 is *data output dependent* on S_1 and denote this with $S_1 \delta^\circ S_2$.

Definition: indirect data dependence. Statement S_2 is data dependent on S_1, denoted $S_1 \delta^* S_2$, if $S_1 \delta S_2$, $S_1 \bar{\delta} S_2$, or $S_1 \delta^\circ S_2$. Statement S_2 is *indirectly data dependent* on S_1, denoted $S_1 \Delta S_2$, if there are statements $S_{k_1}, \ldots, S_{k_n}$, $n \geqslant 0$, such that $S_1 \delta^* S_{k_1} \delta^* \ldots \delta^* S_{k_n} \delta^* S_2$.

A data dependence relation is a precedence relation. If $S_1 \delta^* S_2$, then execution of some instance(s) of statement S_1 must precede execution of some instance(s) of statement S_2. The data flow dependence relations show the flow of data between the statements in a program. Data antidependence and data output dependence relations are sometimes caused by coding practices used by programmers. These "false" dependences can often be removed automatically [Allen 82, Kuck 78]. The following lemma is used to find a first approximation to the data dependence graph.

Lemma:

1. If $S_1 \delta S_2$, then $S_1 \theta S_2$ and $\text{OUT}(S_1) \cap \text{IN}(S_2) \neq \emptyset$.
2. If $S_1 \bar{\delta} S_2$, then $S_1 \theta S_2$ and $\text{IN}(S_1) \cap \text{OUT}(S_2) \neq \emptyset$.
3. If $S_1 \delta^\circ S_2$, then $S_1 \theta S_2$ and $\text{OUT}(S_1) \cap \text{OUT}(S_2) \neq \emptyset$.

Note that the converse conditions do not hold; for instance, in the serial program segment

$$S_1: A = B + D$$
$$S_2: C = A * 3$$
$$S_3: A = A + C$$
$$S_4: E = A / 2$$

the following data flow dependences hold:

$$S_1 \delta S_2 \qquad S_1 \delta S_3 \qquad S_2 \delta S_3 \qquad S_3 \delta S_4$$

Note that $S_1 \delta S_4$ does not hold, even though $S_1 \theta S_4$ and $\text{OUT}(S_1) \cap \text{IN}(S_4) = \{A\} \neq \emptyset$, because S_4 is not to use the value of A computed in S_1, but rather the value of A computed in S_3.

In practice, testing for execution order and set intersection is conservative (no dependences will be missed). Extra dependences may be computed by using this method, but most often (as in the example above) the extra dependences cause no extra precedence relations (by transitivity, $S_1 \Delta S_4$ anyway).

11.2.1   Data dependence directions

In loops we are interested in the particular instances of the statements involved in a data dependence relation. If there is a data dependence relation

$$S_1^{I'} \delta^* S_2^{I''}$$

then the value of $I' - I''$ is called the *dependence distance*. In multiple loops there is a distance associated with each loop. For instance, in the loop

```
do I = 2,N
  do J = 1,M
S₁:      A(I,J) = B(I,J) + C(I,J + 1)
S₂:      C(I,J) = A(I − 1,J) + 2
  enddo
enddo
```

there is a dependence $S_1^{2,1} \, \delta \, S_2^{3,1}$ due to assignment and use of the variable A; the dependence distance for the I loop is -1 and for the J loop is 0. These are often saved in a dependence distance vector as $(-1, 0)$. Likewise, there is a dependence $S_1^{2,1} \, \bar{\delta} \, S_2^{2,2}$ due to the use and reassignment of C, with the dependence distance vector of $(0, -1)$. For the optimizations that we discuss here for parallel and vector computers, we only need to save the sign of the dependence distance vector elements.

Definition: data dependence direction vector. Suppose statements S_1 and S_2 are nested in d loops with indices $I_1, I_2, \ldots, I_d$, and $S_1 \, \delta^* \, S_2$. We define the *data dependence direction vector* (or just direction vector) to be $\Psi = (\psi_1, \psi_2, \ldots, \psi_d)$ (where $\psi_1 \in \{ <, =, >, <=, >=, \neq, <=> \}$), and we say $S_1 \, \delta^*_{(\psi_1, \ldots, \psi_d)} \, S_2$, or $S_1 \, \delta^*_\Psi \, S_2$, when both of the following conditions hold:

1. There exist particular iterations of S_1 and S_2 such that

$$S_1^{I'_1, \ldots, I'_d} \, \delta^* \, S_2^{I''_1, \ldots, I''_d}$$

2. The following inequalities hold simultaneously:

$$I'_1 \, \psi_1 \, I''_1$$

$$I'_2 \, \psi_2 \, I''_2$$

$$\ldots$$

$$I'_d \, \psi_d \, I''_d$$

where $I <=> J$ means that the relation between I and J is unknown. The "$<=>$" direction is usually printed "*".

In the previous example loop, we have the dependences $S_1 \, \delta_{(<, =)} \, S_2$ due to the variable A, and $S_1 \, \bar{\delta}_{(=, <)} \, S_2$ due to the variable C.

The direction in each dimension is independent of the direction in any other dimension. Each dimension has one of three basic directions, or a combination of these. The forward direction ($<$) means the dependence crosses an iteration boundary forward (from iteration I to iteration I + 1, for example). A backward direction ($>$) means that the dependence crosses an iteration boundary backward; in serial **do** loops, a backward direction can only occur if there is a forward direction in an outer loop [from iteration (I,J) to (I + 1,J − 1)], because of the way the loops are traversed. An equal direction (=) means that the dependence does not cross an iteration boundary. The other four directions are combinations of these three basic directions, which occur for nontrivial subscript functions or when using imprecise data dependence tests. We can also add direction vectors to the θ execution ordering relation.

Definition: execution ordering direction vector. With S_1, S_2, and Ψ defined as above, we say $S_1 \, \theta_{(\Psi 1,\ldots,\psi d)} \, S_2$, or $S_1 \, \theta_\Psi \, S_2$, when both the following conditions hold:

1. There exist particular iterations of S_1 and S_2 such that

$$S_1^{I'_1,\ldots,I'_d} \; \theta \; S_2^{I''_1,\ldots,I''_d}$$

2. The following relations hold simultaneously:

$$I'_1 \, \psi_1 \, I''_1$$

$$I'_2 \, \psi_2 \, I''_2$$

$$\ldots$$

$$I'_d \, \psi_d \, I''_d$$

Notice that the relation $S1 \, \delta^*_\Psi \, S_2$ can hold only if $S_1 \, \theta_\Psi \, S_2$ also holds.

Not all direction vectors are possible. In Fortran **do** loops without jumps, the rules are simple. In a single loop,

```
do I = L, U
S₁:    ...
S₂:    ...
   enddo
```

$S_1 \, \theta_{(=)} \, S_2$ holds because, for a single iteration of I, execution of S_1 precedes execution of S_2. Across iterations, both $S_1 \, \theta_{(<)} \, S_2$ and $S_2 \, \theta_{(<)} \, S_1$ hold, because execution of a statement in one iteration precedes execution of any statement in a later iteration; note that $S_1 \, \theta_{(<)} \, S_1$ and $S_2 \, \theta_{(<)} \, S_2$ also hold. Notice that no (>) direction is plausible here.

Conditional statements in the loop can affect the possible direction vectors. The **if** statement in the loop

```
do I = L, U
      if(...)then
S₁:    ...
      else
S₂:    ...
      endif
   enddo
```

eliminates $S_1 \; \theta_{(=)} \; S_2$, since for any iteration of I only one of S_1 and S_2 will be executed.

For an inner loop, the rules are the same as for a single loop when direction vector elements for outer loops are all (=):

> **do** I = LI, UI
>   **do** J = LJ, UJ
> S_1: A(I,J) = B(I,J) + C(I,J)
> S_2: D(I,J) = A(I − 1,J + 1) + 2
>   **enddo**
> **enddo**

Here, $S_1 \; \theta_{(=,<=)} \; S_2$ and $S_2 \; \theta_{(=,\,<)} \; S_1$ hold; as long as the direction for the I loop is (=), the J loop can be treated as a single loop. When the direction for any outer loop is (<), then any direction for an inner loop is allowed. Thus, $S_1 \; \theta_{(<,\,*)} \; S_2$ and $S_2 \; \theta_{(<,\,*)} \; S_1$ also hold, since execution of any statement for one iteration of I precedes execution of any statement for a later iteration of I regardless of the relative values of J. The data dependence relation $S_1 \; \delta_{(<,\,>)} \; S_2$ holds in this loop due to the variable A. Note that the (>) direction is plausible for the J loop because of the (<) direction in the outer I loop.

Details of finding the data dependence relations are given later in this chapter. The concepts we have described are sufficient to proceed with the discussion of vectorization and other optimizations.

11.3 Vectorization Methods

In order to vectorize a serial loop, all the dependences of the serial loop must be satisfied by the corresponding vector code. Because vector code has no loops, the only dependences that can be satisfied by vector code are downward dependences (to statements following the source of the dependence); thus only serial loops with no upward dependences (or whose upward dependences can be removed by statement reordering or other methods) can be vectorized. For example, the loop below:

> **do** I = 2,N
> S_1: A(I) = B(I) + C(I)
> S_2: D(I) = A(I + 1) + 1
> S_3: C(I) = D(I)
>   **enddo**

has the following data dependence relations:

$$S_1 \; \overline{\delta}_{(=)} \; S_3 \qquad \text{due to C}$$

$$S_2 \; \overline{\delta}_{(<)} \; S_1 \qquad \text{due to A}$$

$$S_2 \; \delta_{(=)} \; S_3 \qquad \text{due to D}$$

Statement reordering must be used to vectorize the loop because of the upward dependence from S_2 to S_1. The vector code can be expressed as the Fortran 8x array assignments:

S_2: D(2:N) = A(3:N + 1) + 1
S_1: A(2:N) = B(2:N) + C(2:N)
S_3: C(2:N) = D(2:N)

Statement reordering can be used to change any upward dependence into a downward dependence unless there is a data dependence cycle; a data dependence cycle means that there is some statement such that $S_j \Delta S_j$. The following efficient algorithm [Tarjan 72] can be used to find data dependence cycles:

```
integer I, P;
procedure FINDCYCLE(V);
  P = P + 1; STACK(P) = V; INSTACK(V) = true;
  I = I + 1; LOWLINK(V) = I; NUMBER(V) = I;
  for W such that S_V δ* S_W do
    if NUMBER(W) = 0 then
      FINDCYCLE(W);
      LOWLINK(V) = min(LOWLINK(V),LOWLINK(W));
    else if NUMBER(W) < NUMBER(V) then
      if INSTACK(W) then
        LOWLINK(V) = min(LOWLINK(V),LOWLINK(W));
      end if;
    end if;
  end for;
  if LOWLINK(V) = NUMBER(V) then
    if STACK(P) = V then
      if S_V δ* S_V then
        S_V is a single statement data dependence self-cycle;
      else
        S_V is not involved in any data dependence cycle;
      endif;
      P = P - 1; INSTACK(V) = false;
    else
      S_V is in a multi-statement data dependence cycle;
      while NUMBER(STACK(P)) >= NUMBER(V) do
        W = STACK(P);
        S_W is part of this data dependence cycle;
        P = P - 1; INSTACK(W) = false;
      end while;
    end if;
  end if;
end procedure;
  P = 0; STACK(P) = 0;
  for S = 1 to NUMBER_STATEMENTS do
    INSTACK(S) = false; NUMBER(S) = false;
  end for;
  I = 0;
  for S = 1 to NUMBER_STATEMENTS do
```

```
    if NUMBER(S) = 0 then
       FINDCYCLE(S);
    end if;
  end for;
```

Many single-statement data dependence cycles can be recognized as simple reduction operations. The following loop:

```
    do I = 1,N
S₁:    A(I) = B(I) + C(I)
S₂:    S = S + A(I)
S₃:    AMAX = MAX(AMAX,A(I))
    enddo
```

has the following data dependence relations:

$$S_1 \ \delta_{\ (=)}\ S_2 \qquad S_1 \ \delta_{\ (=)}\ S_3 \qquad S_2 \ \delta^*_{\ (<)}\ S_2 \qquad S_3 \ \delta^*_{\ (<)}\ S_3$$

Statements S_2 and S_3 are single-statement data dependence cycles; however, each of these statements can be recognized as a reduction. The following Fortran 8x array assignments can be generated:

S_1: A(1:N) = B(1:N) + C(1:N)
S_2: S = S + SUM(A(1:N))
S_3: AMAX = MAX(AMAX,MAXVAL(A(1:N)))

Vectorizing arithmetic reductions (such as SUM, PRODUCT, and DOT-PRODUCT) can produce different answers due to different roundoff error accumulation. Some vector machines (such as the Cyber 205) accumulate these results in longer precision, so the different answers may be better. Nonarithmetic reductions such as MAX and MIN do not suffer from this problem.

When inspecting the data dependence relations of a loop, certain dependences can be ignored for vectorization. Any dependence relation that is satisfied by an outer serial loop need not be considered, as shown in the loop below:

```
    do I = 2,N − 1
       do J = 2,N − 1
S₁:       T(I,J) = A(I − 1,J) + A(I + 1,J)
S₂:       A(I,J) = T(I,J) * 2
       enddo
    enddo
```

This loop has the dependence relations

$$S_1 \ \delta_{\ (=,=)}\ S_2 \qquad S_1 \ \bar{\delta}_{\ (<,=)}\ S_2 \qquad S_2 \ \delta_{\ (<,=)}\ S_1$$

Even though there is a dependence cycle involving both statements, the inner **do** J loop can be vectorized. The $S_2 \delta_{(<,=)} S_1$ and $S_1 \bar{\delta}_{(<,=)} S_2$ dependence relations are satisfied by the $<$ direction on the serial **do** I loop; only the $S_1 \delta_{(=,=)} S_2$ dependence needs to be considered when vectorizing the **do** J loop.

Some self-antidependence and self-output dependence cycles can also be ignored when vectorizing loops. If fetches for right-hand side operands for iteration I' are guaranteed to complete before the stores of any iteration I'' ($I'' > I'$), then any data antidependence from the right-hand-side expression to the left-hand-side variable can be ignored. Also, since most vector computers that allow indexed scatter operations will store the operands in index-set order, self-output dependences can also be ignored. For instance, the dependence relations for the loop

```
    do I = 1,N
S₁:    A(I) = A(I + 1) − 1
S₂:    B(IP (I)) = A(I)
    enddo
```

are

$$S_1 \delta_{(=)} S_2 \qquad S_1 \bar{\delta}_{(<)} S_1 \qquad S_2 \delta^\circ_{(<)} S_2$$

However, the $S_1 \bar{\delta}_{(<)} S_1$ dependence will usually be satisfied by the way code is generated [fetches for $A(I + 1)$ will be performed before stores for $A(I)$]. The data dependence cycle $S_2 \delta^\circ_{(<)} S_2$ occurs because without more knowledge about the index array IP, the compiler must assume that there may be multiple stores to the same element of B. On many vector machines with indexed scatter instructions, this dependence will be satisfied by the hardware by completing the store for S_2^I before the store for $S_2^{I + 1}$.

Other data dependence cycles can be broken by prefetching some array. The data dependence relations for the loop

```
    do I = 2, N
S₁:    T(I) = A(I − 1) + A(I + 1)
S₂:    A(I) = B(I) + C(I)
    enddo
```

are

$$S_1 \bar{\delta}_{(<)} S_2 \qquad S_2 \delta_{(<)} S_1$$

The data dependence cycle can be broken by splitting S_1 into two parts:

```
    do I = 2, N
S₁ₐ:    X(I) = A(I + 1)
```

S_1: $T(I) = A(I - 1) + X(I)$
S_2: $A(I) = B(I) + C(I)$
      enddo

The new loop has no data dependence cycle and can be vectorized using statement reordering:

S_{1a}: $X(2:N) = A(3:N + 1)$
S_2: $A(2:N) = B(2:N) + C(2:N)$
S_1: $T(2:N) = A(1:N - 1) + X(2:N)$

This method, known as *node splitting*, can split data antidependences and data output dependences into auxiliary statements, thereby breaking the dependence cycle.

Some data dependence cycles cannot be resolved and cannot be vectorized:

      do $I = 2, N$
S_1: $A(I) = B(I - 1) * C(I) + A(I) * 2$
S_2: $C(I) = A(I) + 2$
S_3: $B(I) = A(I) * 5 - E(I)$
      enddo

The loop above has the data dependence relations

$$S_1 \, \delta_{\,(=)} \, S_2 \qquad S_1 \, \delta_{\,(=)} \, S_3 \qquad S_3 \, \delta_{\,(<)} \, S_1$$

The data dependence cycle involving S_1 and S_3 cannot be broken. Usually this means that the statements involved in the cycle must be executed serially; the other statements in the loop can still be vectorized, however:

      do $I = 2, N$
S_1: $A(I) = B(I - 1) * C(I) + A(I) * 2$
S_3: $B(I) = A(I) * 5 - E(I)$
      enddo
S_2: $C(2:N) = A(2:N) + 2$

By looking more carefully at the data dependence graph of the loop and the expression tree, even some subexpressions of the statements in the dependence cycle can be vectorized:

S_{1a}: $X(2:N) = A(2:N) * 2$
      do $I = 2, N$
S_1: $A(I) = B(I - 1) * C(I) + X(I)$
S_3: $B(I) = A(I) * 5 - E(I)$
      enddo
S_2: $C(2:N) = A(2:N) + 2$

Loops containing **if** deserve special mention. Most vector computers have some method to handle conditional vector operations, either by compressing the operands, masking out some elements, or merging two vectors under the control of a mask vector. For purposes of dependence calculation, the control dependence from the **if** statement to the conditional statements can be considered equivalent to a data dependence:

```
    do I = 1, N
S₁:     A(I) = B(I) + C(I)
S₂:     if(A(I) < 0) then
S₃:         E(I) = B(I) − C(I)
        endif
    enddo
```

A compiler would consider the above loop to have the dependence relations:

$$S_1 \, \delta_{(=)} \, S_2 \qquad S_2 \, \delta^c \, S_3$$

The δ^c relation is the control dependence relation. Control dependences, like dataflow dependences, cannot be broken by simple means such as node splitting, as shown in the following loop:

```
    do I = 2, N
S₁:     if( A(I − 1) > 0 )then
S₂:         A(I) = B(I) − C(I)
        endif
    enddo
```

The two statements form a dependence cycle:

$$S_1 \, \delta^c \, S_2 \qquad S_2 \, \delta_{(=)} \, S_1$$

This cycle cannot be broken, and so the loop cannot be vectorized [Allen 83].

Many **if** statements can be specially handled. When the condition being tested is invariant in the loop, the vectorized code will contain a scalar **if** statement:

```
    do I = 1, N
S₁:     A(I) = B(I) + C(I)
S₂:     if( A(I) < 0 )then
S₃:         E(I) = B(I) − C(I)
        endif
S₄:     if( X > 0 )then
```

S_5:   E(I) = E(I) + X
        endif
    enddo

Here S_4 tests a loop-invariant condition, while S_2 tests a vector condition. The vectorized form of this loop would be

S_1: A(1:N) = B(1:N) + C(1:N)
S_2: **where**(A(1:N) < 0)**do**
S_3:   E(1:N) = B(1:N) − C(1:N)
    endwhere
S_4: **if**(X > 0)**then**
S_5:   E(1:N) = E(1:N) + X
    endif

Some forms of **if** statements can be translated into intrinsic function calls, such as

    do I = 1, N
S_1:   **if**(A(I) > AMAX)**then**
S_2:   AMAX = A(I)
        endif
    enddo

which is equivalent to the simpler loop

    do I = 1,N
S_2:   AMAX = MAX(AMAX,A(I))
    enddo

Some other **if** statements can be eliminated altogether:

    do I = 1,N
S_1:   **if**(X(I) ≠ 0)**then**
S_2:   A(I) = A(I) + X(I)*B(I)
        endif
    enddo

Removing the **if** statement from this loop will produce the same result, and the loop can be vectorized:

$$S_2: A(1:N) = A(1:N) + X(1:N)*B(1:N)$$

The ease with which vectorization can be described and implemented in a compiler is entirely due to the elegance of dealing with the problem at the level of data dependence relations. Research on automatic discovery of parallelism at the University of Illinois [Kuck 80, 81], Rice University [Allen 82], and other places has produced a solid foundation which can be used in many contexts. It is surprising to see vectorizing compilers even today that still cannot perform such simple vectorizing transformations as statement reordering and partial loop vectorization [Control Data 84, Cray 84].

11.4   Loop Concurrentization

When multiple processors are available, a loop can be spread across the processors by assigning different iterations to each processor. We use the **doacross** statement to represent a loop that will be so executed. In fact, any loop can be translated into a **doacross** if the proper synchronizations are inserted. In the worst case there will be a synchronization from the end of each iteration to the beginning of the next iteration and the iterations will execute serially, resulting in no speedup. The goal is to find loops that can be executed concurrently with little or no synchronization.

In order to execute a loop in concurrent mode, all the data dependence relations must be satisfied. If all the data dependence relations in a loop have an $(=)$ direction for that loop, then the iterations of that loop can be executed concurrently with no synchronizations between the iterations, since there are no dependences between different iterations. As with vectorization, data dependences that are satisfied by a $(<)$ direction in an outer serial loop need not be considered. The loop below:

```
     do I = 2,N
        do J = 2,N
S₁:        A(I,J) = (A(I,J − 1) + A(I,J + 1))/2
        enddo
     enddo
```

has the data dependence relations

$$S_1 \; \delta_{(=,<)} \; S_1 \qquad S_1 \; \overline{\delta}_{(=,<)} \; S_1$$

Because all the dependence relations have an $(=)$ direction for the I loop, that loop can be executed in concurrent mode with no synchronization between the iterations:

```
     doacross I = 2,N
        do J = 2,N
S₁:     A(I,J) = (A(I,J − 1) + A(I,J + 1))/2
        enddo
     enddoacross
```

Synchronization between iterations is required when a dependence exists with a $(<)$ direction for that loop. Optimization of synchronizations is important for the best performance of the generated code [Midkiff 86]. When the dependence is downward, the synchronization will (in the best case) not reduce the parallelism in the loop except for the overhead of synchronizing. When the dependence is upward, then part of the loop may effectively be executed serially. For example, the loop

```
    do I = 2, N
S₁:    A(I) = B(I) + C(I)
S₂:    D(I) = A(I) + E(I − 1)
S₃:    E(I) = E(I) + 2 * B(I)
S₄:    F(I) = E(I) + 1
    enddo
```

In order to execute this loop in concurrent mode, the relation $S_3\ \delta_{(<)}$ S_2 must be synchronized. One method to execute this loop is

```
    doacross I = 2, N
S₁:    A(I) = B(I) + C(I)
       if (I > 2) wait(I − 1)
S₂:    D(I) = A(I) + E(I − 1)
S₃:    E(I) = E(I) + 2 * B(I)
       signal(I)
S₄:    F(I) = E(I) + 1
    enddoacross
```

This concurrent loop will effectively execute statements S_2 and S_3 serially, resulting in a small speedup over leaving the whole loop serial. However, there is no data dependence cycle in this loop, so the statements can be reordered:

```
    doacross I = 2, N
S₁:    A(I) = B(I) + C(I)
S₃:    E(I) = E(I) + 2 * B(I)
       signal(I)
       if (I > 2) wait(I − 1)
S₂:    D(I) = A(I) + E(I − 1)
S₄:    F(I) = E(I) + 1
    enddoacross
```

This second concurrent loop has more potential parallelism since there is no critical section. However, if one of the processors gets held up for any reason (such as a memory conflict or external interrupt), then other processors may also have to wait for that one processor. One way to reduce such effects is to maximize the distance between the **signal** and **wait:**

```
    doacross I = 2, N
S₃:    E(I) = E(I) + 2 * B(I)
       signal(I)
S₁:    A(I) = B(I) + C(I)
S₄:    F(I) = E(I) + 1
       if (I > 2) wait(I − 1)
```

S_2: $D(I) = A(I) + E(I - 1)$
      enddoacross

When there are no data dependence cycles in a loop, all synchronization can be removed by the proper use of *loop alignment* and *code replication* [Allen 85]. Using these techniques, this loop can be translated into

      $A(2) = B(2) + C(2)$
      $D(2) = A(2) + E(1)$
      do $I = 2, N - 1$
S_1: $A(I + 1) = B(I + 1) + C(I + 1)$
S_3: $E(I) = E(I) + 2 * B(I)$
S_2: $D(I + 1) = A(I + 1) + E(I)$
S_4: $F(I) = E(I) + 1$
      enddo
      $E(N) = E(N) + 2*B(N)$
      $F(N) = E(N) + 1$

Now the loop has no ($<$) dependences and can be executed in concurrent mode with no synchronization.

Concurrentization is more flexible than vectorization in that even loops that do not meet the requirements of completely independent iterations can be concurrentized, and loops at any nest level can be concurrentized. In fact, outer loops are preferred for concurrent execution, since the overhead of starting and stopping the multiple processors will happen only once for an outer loop, but will happen many times when an inner loop is executed concurrently.

As with vectorization, recognition and translation of reduction operations, which appear as single-statement cycles in the data dependence graph, can produce more efficient code. For instance, one method to generate parallel code for the loop

      do $I = 1, N$
S_1: $A(I) = B(I) + C(I)$
S_2: $D(I) = A(I) * 2.$
S_3: $ASUM = ASUM + A(I)$
      enddo

is for each processor to execute the code

      $ASUMX(p) = 0$
      do $I = p,N,P$
S_1: $A(I) = B(I) + C(I)$
S_2: $D(I) = A(I) * 2.$
S_3: $ASUMX(p) = ASUMX(p) + A(I)$
      enddo

and then add the partial sums ASUMX into ASUM at the end of the loop. This way, most of the loop can be executed in concurrent mode (again, with possible differences in roundoff error accumulation). If there are a large number of processors, then associative reductions like this can be accumulated with a fan-in tree in logarithmic time.

11.4.1 Multivector computers

New computers are now appearing with multiple processors, each of which has vector instructions. The Alliant FX/8 is the best current example; while the Cray X-MP fits this class, its multiple processors are usually used to increase multiprogramming throughput. With multiple vector processors, the compiler has two levels of parallelism to handle. The most efficient mode of operation would be to concurrentize an outer loop and vectorize an inner loop. Single loops can be executed in *concurrent-vector* mode [Alliant 86] by splitting the loop into P independent vectors and assigning one vector to each processor. In either case, the same rules for vectorization and concurrentization apply.

11.5 Loop Interchanging

Sometimes the inner **do** loop cannot be vectorized or would generate inefficient vector code. For example, on the Cyber 205, vector references to array elements that are not contiguous in memory require vector gathers or scatters to be generated; these extra gather or scatter operations can seriously reduce vector performance. Another case where a noninner loop would be more efficient is where the loop bounds are small. Since the execution time of a vector instruction consists of a certain fixed startup time plus an additional incremental time per result generated, vector machines are more efficient for long vectors. If the vector length is small, vectorization of some other loop may be more efficient. Loop interchanging can be used by compilers to bring a noninner loop to the innermost nest level to be vectorized.

Loop interchanging is useful for concurrent loops as well. Because concurrentizing outer loops is more efficient than concurrentizing inner loops, interchanging a concurrent loop to the outer nest level will produce more efficient code.

Two perfectly nested loops can be interchanged if there is no data dependence with a $(<,>)$ direction vector [Wolfe 78, 82; Kuck 82; Allen 82, 84]. The **do** loop nest

```
    do I = 2,N
      do J = 2,N
S₁:      A(I,J) = (A(I,J − 1) + A(I,J + 1))/2
      enddo
    enddo
```

has the data dependence relations

$$S_1\ \delta_{(=,<)}\ S_1 \qquad S_1\overline{\delta}_{(=,<)}\ S_1$$

Because of the data dependence cycle, the inner J loop cannot be vectorized. However, since there is no $(<,>)$ data dependence direction, the loops can be interchanged:

```
       do J = 2,N
         do I = 2,N
S₁:          A(I,J) = (A(I,J − 1) + A(I,J + 1))/2
         enddo
       enddo
```

Now the data dependence relations are

$$S_1\ \delta_{(<,=)}\ S_1 \qquad S_1\ \overline{\delta}_{(<,=)}\ S_1$$

This dependence is satisfied by the $<$ in the outer loop and thus the inner I loop can be vectorized.

When the loop bounds of the inner loop depend on the outer loop index, loop interchanging must modify the loop bounds [Wolfe 86]. For instance, interchanging the loops

```
       do I = 1,N
         do J = 1,I
         A(I,J) = A(J,I) / A(I,I)
         enddo
       enddo
```

must modify the loop bounds to become

```
       do J = 1,N
         do I = J,N
         A(I,J) = A(J,I) / A(I,I)
         enddo
       enddo
```

When the loop bounds of the inner loop are some nonlinear function of the outer loop index, loop interchanging may not be possible.

A loop that has all $(=)$ directions can always be interchanged with another loop [since there clearly cannot be a $(<,>)$ direction]; in addition it can be vectorized if it is at the innermost level and it can be executed in concurrent mode without synchronization at any nest level.

The data dependence tests for loop interchanging can often be relaxed for reductions. For example, the loop below:

```
    do I = 1,N
       do J = 1,N
S₁:    A(I,J) = B(I,J) + C(I,J)
S₂:    AMAX = MAX(AMAX,A(I,J))
       enddo
    enddo
```

has the data dependence relations

$$S_1 \, \delta_{(=,=)} \, S_2 \qquad S_2 \, \delta^*_{(\leq,*)} \, S_2$$

Even though the dependence relation $S_2 \, \delta^*_{(<,>)} \, S_2$ holds, we will allow loop interchanging here because the dependence appears only in a reduction. As with vectorization, interchanging around arithmetic reductions may affect the answers due to roundoff error differences.

11.6 Applications to Parallel Languages

The Fortran 8x [ANSI 87] proposed standard which includes array assignments and other proposals for new parallel syntax [Guzzi 87] will likely gain acceptance in the future. Parallel syntax is convenient for expressing some algorithms more naturally (using vector/matrix notation, for example) and is often necessary to achieve the desired high performance. Translation of parallel constructs into serial code will be important for running these codes on serial machines and for program checkout. Data dependence testing can tell when a parallel loop construct can be converted into serial code.

Vector code can have downward data dependences with any direction. The only downward dependences that can be satisfied by a serial **do** are those with forward or equal directions. For instance, the vector code

```
S₁:    A(2:N − 1) = B(2:N − 1) + C(2:N − 1)
S₂:    D(2:N − 1) = A(2:N − 1)
S₃:    E(2:N − 1) = D(1:N − 2)
```

is equivalent to the vector block **forall** construct:

```
    forall ( I = 2:N − 1)
S₁:       A(I) = B(I) + C(I)
S₂:       D(I) = A(I)
S₃:       E(I) = D(I − 1)
    endforall
```

which has the data dependence relations

$$S_1 \, \delta_{(=)} \, S_2 \qquad S_2 \, \delta_{(<)} \, S_3$$

Since all the data dependences have forward or equal directions, they can be satisfied by a serial **do.** Thus conversion of the **forall** into a serial **do** is legal. On the other hand, the block **forall:**

> **forall** (I = 2:N − 1)
> S_1:   A(I) = B(I) + C(I)
> S_2:   D(I) = (A(I − 1) + A(I + 1)) / 2
>   **endforall**

has the dependences

$$S_1 \; \delta_{(<)} \; S_2 \qquad S_1 \; \delta_{(>)} \; S_2$$

All values of A are assigned in S_1 before any values of A are used in S_2. Direct translation into a serial **do** would be incorrect, since a **do** loop would be reading "old" values for A(I + 1) instead of "new" values. The $S_1 \; \delta_{(>)} \; S_2$ data dependence relation would not be preserved in a **do** loop. Scalarization can be accomplished by distributing the loop into two **do** loops:

> **do** I = 2, N − 1
> S_1:   A(I) = B(I) + C(I)
>   **enddo**
>   **do** I = 2, N − 1
> S_2:   D(I) = (A(I − 1) + A(I + 1)) / 2
>   **enddo**

Even a single statement **forall** can exhibit a data dependence that is not preserved in a **do** loop; the code below:

> S_1: **forall** (I = 2:N) A(I) = (A(I − 1) + A(I + 1)) / 2

has the dependence relations

$$S_1 \; \bar{\delta}_{(<)} \; S_1 \qquad S_1 \; \bar{\delta}_{(>)} \; S_1$$

Direct translation into a **do** would change the backward antidependence into a forward flow dependence. Correct scalarization again requires loop distribution and introduction of a temporary to break the cycle:

> **do** I = 2, N − 1
>   T(I) = (A(I − 1) + A(I + 1)) / 2
>   **enddo**
>   **do** I = 2, N − 1
>   A(I) = T(I)
>   **enddo**

Another alternative when the backward dependence distance is a constant is to introduce a *wrap-around variable:*

> A1 = A(1)
> **do** I = 2, N − 1

```
    A2 = A1
    A1 = A(I)
    A(I) = (A2 + A(I + 1)) / 2
enddo
```

Scalarizing a **doall** may be somewhat easier. Since the only valid dependences in a **doall** without synchronization have " = " directions, all such **doall** can be executed as serial **do** loops. Even when synchronization primitives are added, if the synchronization is always to a later iteration, then the **doall** may be safely executed serially. Only when there is a synchronization that can cause a backward dependence, such as

```
    doall ( I = 2:N )
S₁:      A(I) = B(I) + C(I)
         signal (I)
         wait (I - 1, I + 1)
S₂:      D(I) = (A(I - 1) + A(I + 1)) / 2
    enddoall
```

will direct scalarization be inhibited; here, the **wait** statement blocks further execution of that iteration until the corresponding **signal** statements for the previous and next iterations have been completed (we assume proper resolution of boundary conditions). As in scalarization of a vector **forall,** an equivalent serial version of this **doall** would require two **do** loops.

11.7 Computing Data Dependence Relations

To compute data dependence relations we use hierarchical data dependence [Burke 86]. Given two array references (with s dimensions):

$$S_1:\quad X(f_1(I_1,\ldots,I_d),f_2(\bar{I}),\ldots,f_s(\bar{I}))$$

$$S_2:\quad X(g_1(I_1,\ldots,I_d),g_2(\bar{I}),\ldots,g_s(\bar{I}))$$

we test for both $S_1\ \delta^* \ S_2$ and $S_2\ \delta^* \ S_1$ simultaneously. The particular kind of dependence $(\delta, \bar{\delta}, \text{or } \delta^o)$ that results will be determined by whether the variable references are changes (left-hand side) or uses (right-hand side).

We will first test to see under what conditions the regions accessed by the two array references intersect. Intersection will occur when the subscript functions are equal simultaneously:

$$f_1(I'_1,\ldots,I'_d) = g_1(I''_1,\ldots,I''_d)$$

$$f_2(I'_1,\ldots,I'_d) = g_2(I''_1,\ldots,I''_d)$$

$$\ldots$$

$$f_s(I'_1,\ldots,I'_d) = g_s(I''_1,\ldots,I''_d)$$

The conditions of intersection are a direction vector $(\psi_1,\ldots,\psi_d)$ relating the indices:

$$I'_1 \; \psi_1 \; I''_1$$

$$I'_2 \; \psi_2 \; I''_2$$

$$\ldots$$

$$I'_d \; \psi_d \; I''_d$$

We first test for intersection with the direction vector $(*,*,\ldots,*)$. If independence can be proved with this direction vector, then the regions accessed by the two references are disjoint. If independence is not proved, then one $*$ direction vector element is refined to $<$, $=$, and $>$. Thus, intersection testing is done on a hierarchy of direction vectors. The hierarchy for two loops is shown in Fig. 11.1. If independence can be proved at any point in the hierarchy, the direction vectors beneath it need not be tested.

We define the complement of a direction vector $\Psi = (\psi_1,\ldots,\psi_d)$ to be $\psi^{-1} = (\psi_1^{-1},\ldots,\psi_d^{-1})$, where each ψ^{-1}_i is computed from ψ_i as follows:

ψ_1	$<$	$=$	$>$	$\leq$	$\geq$	$\neq$	$*$
ψ^{-1}_i	$>$	$=$	$<$	$\geq$	$\leq$	$\neq$	$*$

Ψ^{-1} is the same as Ψ with the $<$ and $>$ reversed. We also define the intersection of two direction vectors as follows: Given two direction vectors $\Psi^1 = (\psi_1^1,\ldots,\psi_d^1)$ and $\Psi^2 = (\psi_1^2,\ldots,\psi_d^2)$, we find $\Psi = (\psi_1,\ldots,\psi_d) = \Psi^1 \times \Psi^2$ by computing

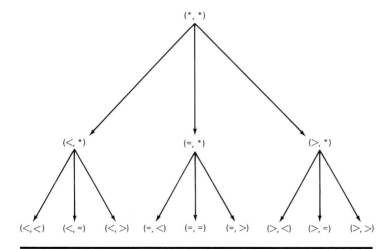

Figure 11.1   Hierarchy of direction vectors for two loops.

$$\psi_1 = \psi_1^1 \times \psi_1^2$$

$$\psi_2 = \psi_2^1 \times \psi_2^2$$

$$\cdots$$

$$\psi_d = \psi_d^1 \times \psi_d^2$$

where the $\times$ operation on the direction vector elements is defined as follows:

$\times$	$<$	$=$	$>$	$\leq$	$\geq$	$\neq$	$*$
$<$	$<$	$.$	$.$	$<$	$.$	$<$	$<$
$=$	$.$	$=$	$.$	$=$	$=$	$.$	$=$
$>$	$.$	$.$	$>$	$.$	$>$	$>$	$>$
$\leq$	$<$	$=$	$.$	$\leq$	$=$	$<$	$\leq$
$\geq$	$.$	$=$	$>$	$=$	$\geq$	$>$	$\geq$
$\neq$	$<$	$.$	$>$	$<$	$>$	$\neq$	$\neq$
$*$	$<$	$=$	$>$	$\leq$	$\geq$	$\neq$	$*$

The "." entries in the table mean that the result is a null direction vector element.

When we perform intersection testing, we test each subscript individually; this produces one direction vector Ψ^i for each subscript. Since dependence requires simultaneous intersection in all subscripts, we combine the subscript intersection direction vectors to get one direction vecto Ψ:

$$\Psi = \Psi^1 \times \Psi^2 \times \ldots \times \Psi^s$$

If this combination produces any "." entries, then there is no simultaneous intersection at all and so there can be no dependence.

To convert this subscript intersection into a data dependence, we must also take into account the execution ordering. So we must find the direction vectors $\Omega_{1 \to 2}$ and $\Omega_{2 \to 1}$ that satisfy

$$S_1 \, \theta_{\Omega_{1 \to 2}} \, S_2$$

$$S_2 \, \theta_{\Omega_{2 \to 1}} \, S_1$$

To find the data dependence direction vector for dependence from S_1 to S_2 we intersect Ψ with $\Omega_{1 \to 2}$ to get $\Psi_{1 \to 2}$:

$$\Psi_{1 \to 2} = \Psi \times \Omega_{1 \to 2}$$

If this combination produces any "." entries, there is no dependence from S_1 to S_2. If all entries are valid, we add the data dependence relation

$$S_1 \, \delta^*_{\Psi_{1 \to 2}} S_2$$

to our data dependence graph. Similarly, to compute dependence from S_2 to S_1 we intersect Ψ^{-1} with $\Omega_{2 \to 1}$; we must use Ψ^{-1} here since Ψ is computed for intersection from S_1 to S_2:

$$\Psi_{2 \to 1} = \Psi^{-1} \times \Omega_{2 \to 1}$$

If all entries are valid we add the data dependence relation

$$S_2 \, \delta^*_{\Psi_{2 \to 1}} S_1$$

11.7.1 Data dependence decision algorithm

The decision algorithm used here will decide whether two linear subscript functions can intersect under the constraints of a direction vector and the loop bounds. The method shown here is from Banerjee [76, 79] but has been adapted to use direction vectors. In this section we use the following notation: Let S_1 and S_2 be nested in d loops with indices $\bar{\imath} = (i_1, \ldots, i_d)$, such that

$$L_k \Lleftarrow i_k \Lleftarrow U_k$$

Let f and g be functions of $\bar{\imath}$ used as some subscript function of some array X in S_1 and S_2, and suppose

$$f(\bar{\imath}) = A_0 + \sum_{k=1}^{d} A_k i_k \qquad g(\bar{\imath}) = B_0 + \sum_{k=1}^{d} B_k i_k$$

Finally let $\Psi = (\psi_1, \ldots, \psi_d)$ be a direction vector. So we have a program segment like

> **do** $i_1 = L_1, U_1$
>   . . .
>   **do** $i_d = L_d, U_d$
> S_1:   ...X(...,f(i_1,...,i_d),...)...
> S_2:   ...X(...,g(i_1,...,i_d),...)...
>   **enddo**
>   . . .
> **enddo**

We try to find solutions $\bar{\imath}'$ and $\bar{\imath}''$ for $\bar{\imath}$ that satisfy the dependence equation

$$f(\bar{\imath}') = g(\bar{\imath}'')$$

such that the direction vector is also satisfied:

$$i'_k \, \psi_k \, i''_k$$

Definition. If Ψ is a direction vector and $\omega \in \{<, =, >, \leq, \geq, \neq, *\}$, we define

$$\Gamma(\Psi, \omega) = \{k \mid 1 <= k <= d \text{ and } \psi_k = \omega\}$$

The greatest common divisor (GCD) test [Banerjee 76, Allen 82] provides a simple means of detecting independence and is included here for completeness.

GCD test. The dependence equation is satisfied only when

$$\text{GCD}(\{A_k - B_k : k \in \Gamma(\Psi, =)\}, \{A_k, B_k : k \notin \Gamma(\Psi, =)\}) = B_0 - A_0$$

Proof. The dependence equation is equivalent to

$$\sum_{k=1}^{d} (A_k i'_k - B_k i''_k) = B_0 - A_0$$

or

$$\sum_{k \in \Gamma(\Psi, =)} (A_k - B_k) i'_k + \sum_{k \notin \Gamma(\Psi, =)} (A_k i'_k - B_k i''_k) = B_0 - A_0$$

By the theory of Diophantine equations [Griffin 54] this has an integer solution only if

$$\text{GCD}(\{(A_k - B_k) : k \in \Gamma(\Psi, =)\}, \{A_k, B_k : k \notin \Gamma(\Psi, =)\}) \mid (B_0 - A_0)$$

The GCD test is quick, but in practice it is relatively ineffective. In most subscripts the loop index multipliers $A_k = B_k = 1$, so the GCD is 1. It is useful in cases such as

```
    do I = 1, 10
S₁:    X(2*I)  = ...
S₂:     ... =  X(2*I + 1)
    enddo
```

Here, the GCD is 2, which does not divide the difference, which is 1; since there are no integer solutions, there can be no dependence.

The next decision algorithm depends on the definition and properties of the positive and negative parts of a number.

Definition: Positive and negative parts of a number. Let r be a real number. We define the positive part of r, r^+, and the negative part of r, r^-, as

$$r^+ = \begin{cases} 0 & r < 0 \\ r & r \geq 0 \end{cases}$$

$$r^- = \begin{cases} r & r \leq 0 \\ 0 & r > 0 \end{cases}$$

These have the following properties: Let r, s, and z be real numbers such that $0 <= z <= s$. Then

1. $r^+ \geq 0, r^- \leq 0$
2. $r = r^+ + r^-$
3. $r^- s \leq rz \leq r^+ s$
4. $r^- \leq r \leq r^+$
5. $-r^- s \geq -rz \geq -r^+ s$

The following inexact decision algorithm is based on the work of Banerjee [Banerjee 76, 79] and has been extensively studied elsewhere [Wolfe 82; Allen 82, 84].

Banerjee's equations. Given functions f and g and a direction vector as above, we try to show whether $f(\bar{i}') = g(\bar{i}'')$ can hold for any $\bar{i}',\bar{i}''$ under the constraints of the direction vector Ψ and the loop bounds. The dependence equation is

$$\sum_{k=1}^{d} (A_k i'_k - B_k i''_k) = B_0 - A_0$$

For each value of k, we find a lower and upper bound such that

$$LB_k^{\psi_k} \leq A_k i'_k - B_k i''_k \leq UB_k^{\psi_k}$$

By summing these bounds, we have the inequality:

$$\sum_{k=1}^{d} LB_k^{\psi_k} \leq \sum_{k=1}^{d} (A_k i'_k - B_k i''_k) \leq \sum_{k=1}^{d} UB_k^{\psi_k}$$

or, equivalently

$$\sum_{k=1}^{d} LB_k^{\psi_k} \leq B_0 - A_0 \leq \sum_{k=1}^{d} UB_k^{\psi_k}$$

If either $\sum_{k=1}^{d} LB_k^{\psi_k} > B_0 - A_0$ or $\sum_{k=1}^{d} UB_k^{\psi_k} < B_0 - A_0$ can be shown, then the functions f and g cannot intersect under the constraints of the direction vector.

$\psi_k \equiv <$

$$LB_k^< = (A_k^- - B_k)^- (U_k - L_k - 1) + (A_k - B_k)L_k - B_k$$

$$UB_k^< = (A_k^+ - B_k)^+ (U_k - L_k - 1) + (A_k - B_k)L_k - B_k$$

$\psi_k \equiv =$

$$LB_k^= = (A_k - B_k)^- (U_k - L_k) + (A_k - B_k)L_k$$

$$UB_k^= = (A_k - B_k)^+ (U_k - L_k) + (A_k - B_k)L_k$$

$\psi_k \equiv >$

$$LB_k^> = (A_k - B_k^+)^- (U_k - L_k - 1) + (A_k - B_k)L_k + A_k$$

$$UB_k^> = (A_k - B_k^-)^+ (U_k - L_k - 1) + (A_k - B_k)L_k + A_k$$

$\psi_k \equiv *$

$$LB_k^* = (A_k^- - B_k^+)(U_k - L_k) + (A_k - B_k)L_k$$

$$UB_k^* = (A_k^+ - B_k^-)(U_k - L_k) + (A_k - B_k)L_k$$

11.7.2 Examples of dependence computation

As an example of Banerjee's equations, take the loop

```
    do I = 1, 10
      do J = 2, 20
S₁:      A(I*20 + J) = B(I,J)
S₂:      C(I,J) = A(I*20 + J − 1)
      enddo
    enddo
```

To compute the dependence in this loop due to the variable A we have

$$L_1 = 1 \qquad U_1 = 10 \qquad A_1 = 20 \qquad B_1 = 20$$

$$L_2 = 2 \qquad U_2 = 20 \qquad A_2 = 1 \qquad B_2 = 1$$

$$A_0 = 0 \qquad B_0 = -1$$

We first test for intersection with the direction vector $\Psi = (*,*)$:

$$LB_1^* = -180 \qquad UB_1^* = 180$$

$$LB_2^* = -18 \qquad UB_2^* = 18$$

Since $LB_1^* + LB_2^* = -198 \le -1 \le 198 = UB_1^* + UB_2^*$ does hold, we refine Ψ; first we refine ψ_1 to " $<$ ":

$$LB_1^< = -180 \qquad UB_1^< = -20$$

Notice that $UB_1^< + UB_2^* = -2 < -1 = B_0 - A_0$, so there is no intersection with the $(<, *)$ direction vector; we need not refine ψ_2 any further here. Likewise, if we refine ψ_1 to " $>$ ", we get

$$LB_1^> = 20 \qquad UB_1^> = 180$$

Here, $LB_1^> + LB_2^* = 2 > -1 = B_0 - A_0$, so there is no intersection with the $(>, *)$ direction vector. Refining ψ_1 to "$=$", however, we get

$$LB_1^= = 0 \qquad UB_1^= = 0$$

Now $LB_1^= + LB_2^* = -18 \leqslant -1 \leqslant 18 = UB_1^= + UB_2^*$ does hold, so we refine ψ_2 further. We find that $LB_2^= = 0$ and $LB_2^> = 1$, thus disproving intersection with $(=, =)$ or $(=, >)$ direction vectors. However,

$$LB_2^< = -18 \qquad UB_2^< = -1$$

so $LB_1^= + LB_2^< = -18 \leqslant -1 \leqslant -1 = UB_1^= + UB_2^<$ does hold. We are left with the direction vector $\Psi = (=, <)$. Since $S_1\ \theta_{(=,<)}\ S_2$ holds, we have the data dependence $S_1\ \delta_{(=,<)}\ S_2$; flow dependence is used here since $A \in OUT(S_1) \cap IN(S_2)$. Dependence from S_2 to S_1 does not exist since $\Psi^{-1} = (=, >)$ and $S_2\ \theta_{(=,>)}\ S_1$ is not valid.

The beauty of Banerjee's equations is that in many actual cases, some of the terms will drop out altogether. For instance, the $(A_k - B_k)L_k$ term in many of the inequalities will be zero when $A_k = B_k$, which happens much of the time. Many of the inequalities still require knowledge of the loop upper and lower bounds. Even so, Banerjee's equations may still be useful when some of the bounds are not known. LB_k and UB_k are independent of the loop bounds when $A_k = B_k$ for certain directions Ψ_k; for instance, when $\Psi_k \equiv <$, then UB_k is independent of the loop bounds. If all the LB_k or all the UB_k can be found without knowing all the loop bounds, then one of the sums $\Sigma_{k=1}^d\ LB_k$ or $\Sigma_{k=1}^d\ UB_k$ can be found and tested against $B_0 - A_0$.

For example, if we replace $U_1 = 10$ in the previous example loop with an unknown variable N, then some of the LB and UB bounds become unknown also. However, when we refine Ψ_1 to "$<$", we have

$$LB_1^< = -20(N-2) - 20 \qquad UB_1^< = -20$$

Since $UB_1^<$ is independent of the unknown variable, it can still be used to disprove intersection with a $(<, *)$ direction vector.

For a loop with both loop bounds unknown,

```
    do I = 1, N
      do J = 2, M
S₁:       A(I*20 + J) = B(I,J)
S₂:       C(I,J) = A(I*20 + J - 1)
      enddo
    enddo
```

We test the following matrix of inequalities depending on the values of Ψ_1 and Ψ_2; all the entries are of the following form:

$$\mathrm{LB}_1^\psi + \mathrm{LB}_2^\psi \leq \mathrm{B}_0 - \mathrm{A}_0 \leq \mathrm{UB}_1^\psi + \mathrm{UB}_2^\psi$$

	$\psi_2 \equiv \; <$	$\psi_2 \equiv \; =$	$\psi_2 \equiv \; >$
$\psi_1 \equiv <$	$21 - M - 20N \leq -1 \leq -21$	$20 - 20N \leq -1 \leq -20$	$21 - 20N \leq -1 \leq M - 21$
$\psi_1 \equiv =$	$1 - M \leq -1 \leq -1$	$0 \leq -1 \leq -1$	$1 \leq -1 \leq M - 1$
$\psi_1 \equiv >$	$21 - M \leq -1 \leq 20N - 21$	$20 \leq -1 \leq 20N - 20$	$21 \leq -1 \leq 20N + M - 21$

By inspecting this matrix we can find many invalid inequalities, such as $-1 \leq -21$ for $\Psi = (<, \; <)$. In fact, only three direction vectors have valid inequalities: $(<, \; >)$, $(=, \; <)$ and $(>, \; <)$. Therefore a compiler would use the data dependence relations:

$$S_1 \, \delta_{(<, \; >)} S_2 \qquad S_1 \delta_{(=, \; <)} S_2 \qquad S_2 \, \overline{\delta}_{(<, \; >)} S_1$$

when optimizing the loop. This example shows the generality and power of Banerjee's equations even with unknown variables.

11.8 Summary

Data dependence is the theoretical basis for vectorization and other loop transformations used for parallel computers. We have described data dependence from a practical standpoint and have shown how to use data dependence in a compiler. The theory described here has been successfully implemented in a variety of settings, including the Parafrase translator at the University of Illinois [Kuck 80, 81], the PFC at Rice University [Allen 82], and KAP, a vectorizing and concurrentizing translator available from Kuck and Associates, Inc., and has also been used in several commercial compilers. Further research in this area will focus on additional transformations for new machine architectures, especially for distributed computing environments. Chapter 12 describes how some of these techniques can be retargeted to new architectures.

Bibliography

[Allen 82]   J.R. Allen and K. Kennedy. *PFC: A Program to Convert Fortran to Parallel Form*. Tech. Rep. MASC TR82-6, Rice University, Houston, TX, March 1983.

[Allen 83]   J.R. Allen, K. Kennedy, C. Perterfield, and J. Warren. "Conversion of Control Dependence to Data Dependence." *Conference Record of the 10th Annual ACM Symposium on Principles of Programming Languages,* pp. 177–189, Austin, TX, January 1983.

[Allen 84]   J.R. Allen and K. Kennedy. "Automatic Loop Interchange." *Proc. ACM SIGPLAN '84 Symposium on Compiler Construction,* pp. 233–246, Montreal, Canada, June 17–22, 1984, SIGPLAN Notices, vol. 19, no. 6, June 1984.

[Allen 85]   J.R. Allen and K. Kennedy. "A Parallel Programming Environment." *IEEE Software,* vol. 2, no. 4, pp. 21–29, July 1985.

[Alliant 86]   Alliant Computer Systems Corp. *FX/Fortran Language Manual,* vol. 2: *Specifications,* PN: 302-0003-B, Acton, MA, January 1986.

[ANSI 87]   American National Standards Institute, X3J3 Committee. *Fortran 8x.* Intermediate document for standard proposal, version 101, February 1987.

[Banerjee 76]   U. Banerjee. *Data Dependence in Ordinary Programs.* University of Illinois at Urbana-Champaign, Department of Computer Science, Rep. No. 76-837, November 1976.

[Banerjee 79]   U. Banerjee, S.-C. Chen, D. Kuck, and R. Towle. "Time and Parallel Processor Bounds for Fortran-like Loops." *IEEE Trans. Computers,* vol. C-28, no. 9, pp. 660–670, September 1979.

[Burke 86]   M. Burke and R. Cytron. "Interprocedural Dependence Analysis and Parallelization." *Proc. SIGPLAN '86 Symposium on Compiler Construction,* Palo Alto, CA, June 25–27, 1986; also available as *SIGPLAN Notices,* vol. 21, no. 7, pp. 162–175, July 1986.

[Control Data 84]   Control Data Corp. *Fortran 200 Reference Manual.* Pub. No. 60480200, Rev. D, March 1984.

[Cray 84]   Cray Research, Inc. *Cray-1 and Cray X-MP Computer Systems Fortran (CFT) Reference Manual.* Cray Research, Inc., Pub. No. SR-0009, Rev. J-02, Mendota Heights, MN, August, January 1984.

[Griffin 54]   H. Griffin. *Elementary Theory of Numbers.* McGraw-Hill, New York, 1954.

[Guzzi 87]   M.D. Guzzi. *Cedar Fortran Programmers' Manual.* Center for Supercomputing Research and Development, Doc. No. 601, University of Illinois, Urbana, IL, January 1987.

[Kuck 78]   D. Kuck. *The Structure of Computers and Computations,* vol. 1. Wiley, New York, 1978.

[Kuck 80]   D. Kuck, R.H. Kuhn, B. Leasure, and M. Wolfe. "The Structure of an Advanced Vectorizer for Pipelined Processors." *Proc. of COMPSAC 80, The 4th International Computer Software and Applications Conference,* pp. 709–715, Chicago, IL, October 28–31, 1980.

[Kuck 81]   D. Kuck, R. Kuhn, D. Padua, B. Leasure, and M. Wolfe. "Dependence Graphs and Compiler Optimizations." *Proc. 8th ACM Symposium on Principles of Programming Languages (POPL),* pp. 207–218, Williamsburg, VA, January 1981.

[Kuck 82]   D.J. Kuck, R.H. Kuhn, B. Leasure and M. Wolfe. "The Structure of an Advanced Retargetable Vectorizer." In Kai Hwang (ed). *Supercomputers: Design and Applications,* pp. 163–178, IEEE Computer Society Press, Silver Spring, MD, 1982.

[Midkiff 86]   S.P. Midkiff and D.A. Padua. "Compiler Generated Synchronization for DO Loops." *Proc. 1986 International Conference on Parallel Processing,* pp. 544–551, St. Charles, IL, IEEE Computer Society Press, Washington, D.C., August 19–22, 1986.

[Tarjan 72]   R. Tarjan. "Depth-First Search and Linear Graph Algorithms." *SIAM J. of Computing,* vol. 1, no. 2, June 1972.

[Wolfe 78]   M. Wolfe. *Techniques for Improving the Inherent Parallelism in Programs,* M.S. Thesis, Department of Computer Sciences, Rep. No. 78-929, University of Illinois, Urbana, IL, July 1978.

[Wolfe 82]   M. Wolfe. *Optimizing Supercompilers for Supercomputers,* Ph.D. Thesis, Department of Computer Science, Rep. No. 82-1009, University of Illinois, Urbana, IL, October 1982.

[Wolfe 86]   M. Wolfe. "Advanced Loop Interchanging." *Proc. of the 1986 International Conference on Parallel Processing.* pp. 536–543, St. Charles, IL, IEEE Computer Society Press, Washington, D.C., August 19–22, 1986.

12

Applying AI Techniques to Program Optimization for Parallel Computers

Ko-Yang Wang

Purdue University, West Lafayette, IN

Dennis Gannon

Indiana University, Bloomington, IN

12.1 Introduction

12.1.1 The trend toward parallelism

Perhaps the most important trend in supercomputer design is the reliance on parallelism to achieve performance improvements over our fastest sequential processors. During the 3-year period from 1984 to 1987, the number of commercially available general-purpose parallel processing systems jumped from a couple to over a dozen. The number of ways in which different architectures exploit parallelism is almost as large as the number of different companies. This is a healthy situation for computer architecture. Many good ideas are emerging. Unfortunately, each different machine presents a different architectural model to the programmer. A program that has been optimized for one system may not be well suited to another. At first glance, the differences may appear to be due to the fact that each machine supports a different set of extensions to Fortran, or even a different base programming language. But a deeper analysis shows that the architectural difference between machines plays a fundamental role in the organization of the computation. Surface-level syntactic changes are not enough to port a program optimized for a Cray X-MP to good code for a MIMD hypercube design. While this is an extreme case, it illustrates the problems faced by the small, but growing, cadre of programmers who have taken up the task of putting these machines to productive use.

Because of these problems, it has become clear that the greatest need in supercomputer development is a new generation of software tools that can help in the task of optimizing code for new architectures.

In this chapter, we describe a project under development at Purdue University and Indiana University, which is an experiment in integrating expert systems technology with the advanced compiler optimization research conducted over the last 10 years by Kuck, Wolfe, and their associates in Urbana, Illinois [Abu-Sufah 79; Kuck 80, 81, 84; Padua 79, 80; Polychronopoulos 86; Wolfe 82], Kennedy [80] and his students at Rice [Allen 83], and Allan, Cytron, and Burke [Burke 86; Cytron 84] at Yorktown Heights. There are three key ideas that are guiding our work:

- Interactive program restructuring tools are essential in helping users move programs to new machines.

- Expert knowledge about how to choose a sequence of restructuring transformations that optimize performance can be organized as an "advice giving" system. Furthermore, performance models of the target architecture can be incorporated into a rule-based system to guide the transformation process.

- New architectural models and expert programming heuristics for new target machines must be easily incorporated into such a system in a uniform manner.

Of course, interactive tools already exist. For example, FORGE from Pacific-Sierra Research provides an excellent user interface. PTOOL from Rice University [Allen 84] has an elegant way to help users identify data dependence in programs. And all automatic program restructurers, such as VAST, KAP, and Parafrase, employ powerful heuristics to retarget user code. The goal of this research is to show that an expert systems approach is a more flexible and extensible model than the conventional parallel compilers for designing a tool that can be rapidly adapted to new target machines and new heuristics for parallel program optimization.

12.1.2 Automatic program parallelism optimization

The program parallelism optimization problem is the following: given a program and a target parallel machine, how can a parallel program that is both functionally equivalent to the original program and optimal for the target machine be generated?

The basic algorithm for program parallelism optimization can be outlined as the following:

Basic Program
Input: a sequential or parallel program and the description of the target machine.
Output: a parallel program that is optimal for the target machine.
Begin
    repeat
        pick the "best" transformation from the set of
                all applicable transformations;
        apply the selected transformation to the program;
    until the resulting program is optimal for the target machine
End;

This algorithm is superficial in the sense that it does not specify how to determine either which transformation is the best or when the program is optimal. However, this is the algorithm that most parallel computer users use when they hand-optimize their programs. Picking the "best" transformation requires expert intelligence.

Our goal is to design an intelligent system that can perform the program parallelism optimization process for different classes of target machines automatically. Several fundamental issues must be addressed before such an intelligent system can be constructed.

Machine knowledge representation. Conventional program restructurers hide the impact of machine knowledge on the decisions made during program restructuring as a part of the process of selecting the heuristics used in the system. Only heuristics that are effective for the target machine are included. This is possible because only one target machine is considered. However, when the program parallelization system is designed to handle different classes of architectures, the features of the parallel computers that affect program parallelism must be abstracted and represented in a uniform structure. Separating the machine features from the heuristic acquisition process allows the description of the heuristics to be based on the machine features as well the program features. In this way, a heuristic can be applied to any target machine that has the appropriate set of features.

Program representation. The program representation problem is to define internal data structures that can encode the program's semantic and parallelism constraints. A good program representation must preserve the exact semantic and parallelism constraints of the original program. The program representation scheme must also allow easy and efficient accesses and modifications.

Transformation techniques.   Transformation techniques are the essential elements of program restructuring systems. Many transformation techniques have been studied during the past two decades by a number of pioneering researchers. Rather than going through the details of the mechanical techniques for modifying program structures, in this chapter we will emphasize the heuristics for applying the transformations and the effects of the transformations on program parallelism.

Restructuring heuristics.   The optimal sequences of transformations needed to get good performance from a section of code is very dependent on the program and the target machine. There are no algorithms that provide the optimal sequence of transformations for all circumstances. Heuristics are usually used to perform the task, and these heuristics are usually based on the particular application and make assumptions about the target machine. In order to make the heuristic general the special features of the program and the assumptions about the machine must to be made clear.

The representation and organization of transformation knowledge.   The representation, organization, and integration of the transformation knowledge are the central issues for an automatic program parallelizing system. They actually determine the effectiveness and efficiency of the system.

Parallelism metrics.   Parallelism metrics are used to compare the effects of different transformations and to decide when to terminate the optimization process. Measuring the achievable parallelism of a program on a target machine must be based on the parallelism features that the machine provides and the matching between the program structure and the target machine.

The remainder of this chapter is organized into three sections. In Sec. 12.2, we formally define the program parallelism optimization process and discuss the machine knowledge representation problem. The program representation problem and the problem of defining parallelism metrics are also briefly discussed. In Sec. 12.3, the transformation knowledge representation problem and some program restructuring heuristics are presented. Examples that describe the work of the inference engine are also included. In Sec. 12.4 we give a brief summary and describe the status of the project.

12.2   Abstracting the Machine Features and Building the Knowledge Base

In this section, we define the program parallelism optimization process. A machine feature abstraction scheme is introduced, and a function to estimate the matching between the program level parallelism and the machine level parallelism is also given.

12.2.1 Parallelism and program parallelization

Parallelism can be exploited at three different levels: the algorithm level, the program level, and the machine level. Each of these three levels has a conceptual concurrency model of computation, and we call this model the *virtual machine* for that level.

At the algorithm level, the virtual machine is the computational model (e.g., mesh, hypercube, etc.) that the parallel algorithms are based upon. *Algorithm-level parallelism* can be characterized as the number of virtual processors, the complexity of interprocessor communications, and the complexity class of the parallel execution time on the virtual machine model when expressed as a function of problem size.

At the program level, each parallel programming language defines a virtual machine by the semantics of its parallel control constructs. *Program-level parallelism* can be characterized by the control and data dependence constraints imposed by the language and the user's choice of data structures.

Machine-level parallelism is the maximum concurrent execution capacities of the architecture and can be characterized by various machine features.

When mapping problems from the algorithm level to the program level or from the program level to the machine level, the differences in the computational models of the two levels may cause parallelism to be lost. For example, when an algorithm is translated into a program, the concurrent properties of the algorithm may be serialized by the dependence relations inherited from program constructs and data synchronization. In some cases, the concurrency is lost because the limited parallel constructs provided by the programming language simply can not express the full parallelism in the algorithm. The problems encountered in translating parallelism from the algorithm level to the program level fall into the scope of parallel programming language design and will not be discussed in this chapter.

When the program is mapped from the program level to the machine level, the programs may have to be restructured, since some specific program structures or data structures may suit the target machine better than others. *Program restructuring* is the process of improving the match between the program-level parallelism and the machine-level parallelism by applying a sequence of program transformations to restructure the program.

12.2.2 Program realization and restructuring

The process of optimizing program parallelism consists of two steps: the program restructuring process and the program realization process. The program restructuring process improves the program parallelism by modifying the structure of the program representation. The program realization process maps the programs onto the computational model of the target machine by effectively utilizing the concurrency potential of the machine.

Program-level parallelism can be divided into three concurrency levels: *task, microtask,* and *operation.* At the task level, a program is decomposed into large processes which may be run on different processors. At the operation level, vector operations or scalar operations are the units of computation. The size of the vector operation represents the degree of concurrency of this level. The microtask level is the level between task level and operation level and is often characterized by loop bodies. More specifically, inside a task, operations are grouped into microtasks, which are the blocks of code that are executed between synchronization points.

Based on the dependence constraints of the program and the feature descriptions of the target machine, the program realization process partitions the program into operation blocks and composes them to form vector operations, microtasks, tasks, and processes. Abstractly, the process can be viewed as a function:

$$Program\_realization: Computational\_model \times Programs \to Program_A$$

where elements of $Program_A$ are programs that are augmented with parallelism and run-time information such as processor assignments, synchronization, vectorizable or parallelizable loops, etc.

The program realization process does not actually improve the true parallelism of the program. It simply takes the current form of the computation, as represented by the program, and based on the features of the target machine, applies a mapping to realize the program into parallel form. For example, for multiprocessor systems, the outermost parallelizable loop is always used to generate tasks. For machines with vector capability, the innermost loop is the one that is vectorized (if it is legal to do so). The synchronization technique that is provided by the computational model is used to satisfy any data dependence not already satisfied by sequential execution of parts of the program.

The *program restructuring process* improves the match between the program-level parallelism and the machine-level parallelism by modifying program structure and improving the data locality in the program. In particular, it involves techniques such as changing the in struction execution order (by forward substitutions, statement reordering, etc.), modifying program control (by loop interchange, loop distribution, etc.) and eliminating unnecessary data accesses and modification (by data localization, block transfer, cache optimization, dead code elimination, etc.). Each individual technique used to modify the structure of the program is called a *transformation*.

Abstractly, a program transformation T is a mapping:

$T: Program \rightarrow Program$

that maps a program representation to a new program representation that has the same input/output semantics. The *precondition* of a transformation is the list of conditions that must be satisfied so that the result of the transformation will have the same meaning as the original program. If a program satisfies the precondition of a transformation, we say that the transformation is *applicable* to the program.

Program transformations are just mechanical techniques for changing the structure of the program. To have a positive effect on the performance, the transformations must be chosen based on the full knowledge of the program, the target machine, and a set of effective heuristics. The program restructuring process is a composite function of a sequence of transformations. It uses heuristics that are based on features of the program and the machine to guide the transformations and effectively translate the program into optimal form. Abstractly, it takes the form

$Program\_Restructuring: Program \times Computational\_model \times Heuristics$
$\rightarrow Program$

At the heart of the program restructuring is the set of rules in the knowledge base that represents the expertise about program constructs, transformation techniques, machine parallelism, and heuristics for improving the matching between programs and machines. These rules decide the effectiveness of the program restructuring process.

12.2.3 Problems in program parallelism optimization

Corresponding to the concurrency levels of the program parallelism, the task of improving program parallelism can be subdivided into the following problems:

Partitioning problem.   How does one partition a problem into tasks and microtasks and form good vector operations? If the current structure of the program does not suit the hardware, various transformation techniques should be used to improve the program structures and to achieve a better partition.

Synchronization problem. When mapping a sequential program to a multiprocessor machine, the proper synchronization operations must be inserted in the code to preserve the meaning of the original program. Synchronization costs penalize the program performance, and, in the worst case, it may serialize the whole computation. Fewer synchronization points mean less processor idling time and better system performance. Grouping closely related microtasks into one task, copying repeatedly used data into local memories, and changing data access patterns may have a positive effect on minimizing the synchronization cost.

Scheduling problem. The scheduling of the processes is another important factor in obtaining optimal performance. Traditionally, this problem is viewed as the task of the operating system. However, studies have shown that static estimates done at compile time can simplify the task of the operating system at run time [Cytron 84]. There are techniques (e.g., do-across) that can estimate the required minimum process delay time and significantly reduce the amount of time the processor spends in "busy-wait" loops. Run-time tests can also be generated at compile time to guide the execution of the process.

Memory utilization problem. Since the data access time for different components of the memory hierarchy may be different, the utilization of fast memory components (like cache) and the removal of unnecessary data accesses will shorten the access time and speed up the computation. Array decomposition, data copying, scalar gathering, stride mining, loop interchanging, loop blocking, and other transformations can be used to achieve a lower cache miss ratio and improve locality.

Due to the complexity of the task, most algorithms used in solving the above problems are heuristic-driven. Some useful heuristics for program restructuring are discussed in Sec. 12.3, and others can be found in the literature on program transformations.

12.2.4 Program representation

The state of the program can be represented by *program dependence graphs,* which consist of the *control flow subgraph* [Ferante 83] and the *data dependence subgraph* [Kuck 81, Wolfe 82] of the program. The data dependence subgraph represents the set of essential constraints on the execution order of the operations. The control flow subgraph specifies the preconditions on the operations which are required for them to be actually executed. Together, these two subgraphs form a complete summary of the semantics of the program. The dependence relations in the program dependence graph specify the sequential order that the program parallelization process must respect. Violating the dependence relations may cause data access and modifications to happen in the wrong order which will change the meaning of the program. Program dependence graphs have been studied extensively; details of the representation and computation of the graph can be found in Ferante [83], Kuck [81], Burke [86], Wang [88], Wolfe [82].

12.2.5   The representation of machine structures

One of the major advantages of multitarget optimization systems over dedicated single-target optimization systems is that the heuristics can be shared among all target machines that have the same properties. When a heuristic is synthesized, the influences of the target machine must be distilled to identify the properties of the target machine that actually affect the heuristic. These properties of the machine must be represented in a uniform structure so that different parallel computers can be easily characterized. The properties of the target machines that affect program parallelism optimizations are called *machine features*.

The space of all possible values of a feature is called the *feature space*. A feature space may be either a subspace of the reals or a discrete space. The cross product of all the feature spaces forms the space of all possible computational models, which we call the *Computational_Model*. An element in the Computational_Model represents the computational model of a particular target machine. The computational model is the abstraction of the properties of the target machine that influence program parallelism optimization. It represents the program restructuring system's understanding of the target machine.

Since the intelligent program restructuring system can reason, not all of the hardware properties need to be included in the computational model. Instead, properties that can be derived from other features can be omitted from the computational model, since they can be derived by the system when they are needed. This helps keep the size of the feature list manageable.

We represent the Computational_Model as a frame "slot filler" model. This frame model of representing the computational model is called the *raw model*. Each individual feature is a slot of the raw model to be filled. The computational model of a target machine can be defined by filling the feature space attributes in the raw model with the correct values. Not all the slots have to be filled when abstracting a machine feature. A set of rules can be used to derive default values for the unfilled slots.

The computational model of the target machine can be divided into the following four categories:

1. Processor hierarchy

2. Processing units

3. Memory hierarchy

4. Networks/buses

Each of these four subspaces consists of a list of features. In the following three subsections, we examine the elements of these features and discuss their attributes in the program restructuring process.

Processor hierarchy and processing elements. The set of processing elements (PEs) in a parallel computer can be characterized by the following components of the feature space:

1. Number of processors

2. Modes of computation (SIMD, MISD, MIMD, etc.)

3. Methods of scheduling (data-driven, dataflow, demand-driven, control flow)

4. CPU scalar speed

5. CPU scalar instruction type (stack, two-address, three-address, etc.)

6. Vector instructions (diadic, triadic-vec-vec-vec, triadic-vec-vec-scalar, etc.)

7. Vector instruction speed

8. Vector startup time

9. Vector operands (register, memory)

10. Vector results (register, memory)

11. Number of vector registers

12. Size of vector registers

13. Chaining

14. Cost of nonuniform stride

15. Cost of scatter-gather

16. Vector reductions (max, add, inner-product, etc.)

17. Horizontally coded multiple function units

18. Special restrictions/features (list)

The number of processors affects the way in which a program is partitioned into tasks. For example, when partitioning a nested loop, the best way to create tasks is to first match the number of iterations of the outermost loop with the number of processors, then block the loop to form tasks. Loop interchange can be used to cause the best matching loop to be the outermost loop.

For processors with vector processing capabilities, issues such as where the operands are stored (in memory or in register), whether it has vector registers, and the size of vector registers affect the way that data are decomposed and how vector operations are formed. The vector operation start-up time and the relative speed of vector/scalar operations are critical in justifying whether a loop should be translated into vector operations. In addition, the use of special vector instructions (e.g., triadic vector operations, inner-product reductions, vector operand gathering) can be more important than the absolute speed of the vector processors.

The processors may have a special hierarchy that the programmer must keep in mind. This processor hierarchy, usually based on processor clustering, affects task decomposition. Features in this category include

1. Cluster size

2. Shared resources within clusters (memory, synchronization hardware, etc.)

3. Task switching time within a cluster

4. Processor scheduling within a cluster (loop-oriented, data-driven, etc.)

5. Special topological constraints (mesh, cube, etc.)

6. Cluster task granularity

7. Cluster scheduling policy (users or special operation system policy)

A cluster can be viewed as a collection of processors that is capable of executing a collection of very finely grained tasks in a tightly coupled manner which is not possible by the set of all processors. For example, the computational complex (CEs) of the Alliant FX/8 forms a cluster that is distinct from the interactive processors (IPs) system. A system may support multiple clusters with multiple processors per cluster (as in the Cedar system), or it may be viewed as one tightly coupled cluster of processors (as in the Connection Machine) or a loosely coupled system of one-processor clusters (as in the Cray X-MP). In a machine with multiple clusters, there will often be two levels of scheduling: a "microtask" level that manages jobs within each processor and a "process" level that assigns processes to each cluster.

Memory hierarchy. The memory hierarchy of a parallel computer consists of global memory, local memory, and cache memory, as well as the networks or buses that connect these components. Global memory is shared by all processors and can be either physically centralized in one memory module (as in the Alliant FX/8) or distributed among processor units (as in the BBN Butterfly and the IBM RP3). Local memory is owned exclusively by individual processors. Processors are not allowed to access other processors' local memories directly. However, some computers have a centralized controller which can access all local memories (as in the Pringle [Kapauan 84a, 84b] or the Connection Machine). The feature space for the memory hierarchy consists of the following items:

1. Size of cache

2. Cache sharing (shared cache, private cache, etc.)

3. Cache coherence strategy (compiler-managed, snoopy cache, etc.)

4. Cost of cache data fetch relative to register fetch

5. Size of local memory

6. Cache shared by cluster

7. Cost of local memory data fetch relative to register fetch

8. Size of global memory

9. Interleaved or noninterleaved global memory

10. Centralized or distributed global memory

11. Cost of "near" global fetch relative to register fetch

12. Cost of "far" global fetch relative to register fetch

13. Vector prefetch mechanism (from global to local, from global to cache, none)

14. Special synchronization memory commands (fetch-add, locks, memory tags, etc.)

Normally, accessing data from the global memory is slower than accessing data from a local memory, which is in turn slower than accessing data from a cache. In multiprocessor systems, an excessive amount of shared data access and synchronization might cause network contention and, as a result, saturate the entire system. For example, on the BBN Butterfly, if all processors make frequent references to the same critical section lock or data structure, a memory "hot spot" is created. If the data are not a critical section lock, then a local copy can be made. This can double performance on many algorithms.

Management of cache and local memory is also critical. If the cache miss ratio or the locality of an algorithm is bad, then the system utilization will be low since most of the processing power will be wasted waiting for data. On the Alliant FX/8, cache is shared by all computational elements. Because the cache is twice the speed of main memory, bad cache management can cut performance in half.

Although better locality always means better memory utilization, the cost ratios of data accesses from different components of the memory hierarchy play an important role in resolving conflicts between improving data locality and decreasing the number of instructions. We will discuss this issue in more detail in the next section.

Different machines may have different memory hierarchies. On some machines, one or more components in the memory hierarchy may be missing. For example, the Connection Machine has no cache; most MIMD hypercubes have only local memory; message-passing strategies are the basis of all synchronization and access to shared information. Dataflow machines have a completely different memory model. The Pringle has no shared memory; processor communication is done by message passing through reconfigurable processor-to-processor routing switches. Each processor in the Pringle has only eight ports, so a message routed to another processor might need to go through a couple of hops, and setting up an optimal message-routing network for a given algorithm is a nontrivial task. Although some heuristics for data allocation and routing on nonshared-memory machines like the Pringle do exist, the data decomposition problem for nonshared memory remains largely unsolved. More effort is needed before an optimal result can be achieved.

On the other extreme are the IBM RP3 and Cedar, both of which have a complete memory hierarchy that includes cache, local memories, and global memories. On the RP3, global memories and local memories reside in the same memory modules that belong to individual processing elements. The same mechanism is used in the BBN Butterfly Uniform system. On the RP3, a sophisticated memory-addressing scheme allows the boundaries between global and local memories to be adjustable. On both machines, it is more expensive for a PE to access another PE's global memory than it is for the PE to access its own. Therefore, it is very important that the locality is explored on these machines. The Butterfly provides a block transfer operation which makes localizing frequently used data attractive.

The Alliant FX/8 has no local memory, and its two 32K-byte caches are shared by eight processors. The shared cache is connected to the processors by an 8×8 crossbar switch and is connected to memory through a high-speed bus (188 Mbytes read-access per second). Therefore, cache utilization for the Alliant is important. Examples of data utilization for the Alliant are discussed in the next section.

Interconnection networks and buses. The connections between processors, or between processors and the memory hierarchy, or between the components of the memory hierarchy may utilize either buses or complicated networks. There are a number of factors that are very important to understand:

1. Network topology (bus, ring, cube, mesh, tree, banyan, etc.)
2. Network bandwidth
3. Delay per network stage
4. Packet or circuit switched
5. Packet size
6. Maximum pending memory references a processor can have in the network
7. Routing type (self-routing, compiler routing, both)
8. Performance penalty of self-routing

Network topology plays an important role in the way data structures are distributed around the system. On networks with a low bisection width, such as a tree, certain data movements are notoriously slow. For example, a matrix transpose is extremely slow on trees and rings. A complete study of the role of topology in parallel algorithm design is found in Gannon and Van Rosendale [Gannon 84].

From the point of view of a program restructurer, there are two issues which are more critical. First, if the network is not self-routing, then the compiler needs to plan a path and generate switch settings for the network. Many non-shared-memory machines require that each intermediate processor be programmed to intercept and forward cross network traffic as part of the target code. Second, if the network is such that some processors are "nearer" than others, and if the message delay from a far processor is significantly more than from a near processor, optimal data structure decomposition becomes critical. Not only is this problem NP-complete, there are also very few good heuristics for it. In addition, for dynamic allocation of new processes, it may cost more for a processor to start up a new process on a remote processor than it does for it to do the computation itself. The program restructuring system has to consider all these differences in network implementation before it can actually perform task and data decompositions.

Some interconnection networks have special properties to enhance the capabilities of the system. For example, the IBM RP3 has a combining network which supports fetch-and-op kinds of operations, making the implementation of system primitives much easier; in particular, it supports the implementation of task queues and makes self-scheduling loops possible. (On the Cedar and BBN Butterfly these same operations exist, but they are done by the memory controllers rather than the network.) For machines that support self-scheduling loops, the program restructuring system can leave the task scheduling problem to the operating system of the machine by transforming the outermost loop into a self-scheduling loop. However, the self-scheduling loop makes the global array decomposition almost impossible, since it can only be known at run time which loop will be run by which processor. Our experience shows that the data decomposition is usually more important than the loop scheduling, so in programs that have decomposable arrays (i.e., arrays that can be allocated into the local memories of the processing units) data decomposition should be favored.

In multistage networks, nonuniform network traffic, known as "network hot spots," is typically (but not uniquely) produced by shared locks or data synchronization. This can generate effects that severely degrade the network traffic. Studies have shown that combining data access requests within the switches is an effective technique for dealing with a hot spot contention problem that is caused by global shared locks [Phister 85]. For machines that have no combining network, balancing the operation load is one of the major challenges to the program restructuring system.

12.2.6 Program and machine feature abstraction

As discussed above, the program parallelism abstraction process bases its decisions on the features of the program at hand and the target machine. The features of the program and target machine are abstracted into concepts that can be used by various heuristics. In the case of program representation, this feature abstraction can be done by either matching patterns or checking program dependence relations to find out whether the program region under consideration matches some predefined concepts. For example, an inner-product operation can be recognized by matching the pattern that a statement inside a loop accumulates the product of corresponding elements of two arrays into a variable. A more complicated example is the concept of "vectorizable": a loop is vectorizable if each statement S in the loop can be executed for all values of the index set of the loop before executing any of the statements in the loop following S, and this alternate execution order will compute the same result. The vectorizable concept can be captured by examining the dependence relations of the loop. A procedure (or rule) that does the test inserts the fact "the current loop is vectorizable" into the solution space if the test is true.

As for the machine, we should note that there are usually some heuristics which accompany the features of the machine. These heuristics are the methodologies of utilizing the properties of the machine. Examples of this are "improve locality if the machine has cache or local memories," and "generate P(= number_of_processors) tasks if task creation cost is high." It is the collection of these methodologies that really defines the computational model of the machine.

There is a fundamental difference between the abstraction of features of the program and the abstraction of features of the machine. That is, the features of the machine are static, but the features of the program are dynamic. The facts that are derived by the feature abstraction process will stay true throughout the optimization process for the machine, but the facts about the program may be changed as the structure or data distribution of the program is changed. Therefore, the feature abstraction process for the machine is done at the time the target machine is chosen, but the feature abstraction process is done during the program restructuring process. Another dynamic aspect of the feature abstraction process is that only the features of the program that are currently important are abstracted. For example, it would make no sense for the restructuring system to check whether a loop is vectorizable when it is trying to figure out how to create tasks from a simple loop. However, if the loop is a nested loop and the machine supports both multiprocessing and vector processing, then the loops will be checked for vectorizability since the best way to schedule the loops is to create vector operations from the innermost loop and create most tasks out of the outermost loop.

12.2.7   The parallelism metric

In order to justify the merit of a particular transformation, a valuation function which evaluates both the degree of program parallelism and the matching between the program and the machine is needed. The valuation function

$$Matching: Computational\_Model \times Program \to R$$

returns a simple real valued index that estimates the matching between the computational model and the current structure of the program. The matching function is a weighted linear combination of several factors. Among these are how well the size of the program structure fits the size of the target machine (size matching); how well the data access pattern matches the data distribution on the memory hierarchy (data access matching); and how much synchronization delay is needed (scheduling matching). Each of these factors can be defined as a *match function* that maps the cross product of the spaces of the computational model and the program into a subset of the real space.

The size matching function quantifies the structure matching between the program and the target machine. For example, an outer loop that generates only two tasks on a machine with 100 processors would get a rather low score. For machines with vector instructions, the size matching function estimates the efficiency of the vector instructions.

Data access patterns are also measured. If possible, data that are repeatedly referenced should be kept in local memory or cache to reduce the network traffic. The most common example of repeatedly referenced data is the array references inside loops. The subscripts of the references, plus the loop bounds, give a good estimate of the number of array references in the loop. Nonunit stride array references are discriminated against when cache size is relatively small since these references will generate a much higher cache miss ratio than unit-stride array references.

Shared data accesses might cause memory contentions and serialize the data accesses and thus degrade the system performance. The more shared data references that a program has, the higher its synchronization cost will be. So the shared data synchronization factor can be defined to be the reciprocal of the number of shared data accesses in the program region under consideration.

Task scheduling and synchronization are also modeled by the match function. Based on a do-across schedule [Cytron 84], an estimate is made of processor utilization. This estimate contributes to the final value.

Once processor assignment is completed, only the cross-task dependence may produce interprocessor synchronization. Another source of synchronization cost is the serialized access of shared variables. This kind of data synchronization can also be characterized by intertask data dependence.

The number of intertask dependences (IDEPs) can then be used to quantify the effectiveness of the synchronization factor. The fewer of these dependences there are, the better the matching is. Let NDEP be the total number of dependences in the focused program region. The synchronization matching factor SYNC is defined as

$SYNC = (NDEP - IDEP)/NDEP.$

A large number of other factors go into the evaluation of the match function. A much more detailed discussion is given in Wang [88].

The weighted-combination approach of computing the match function has the following advantages:

Dynamism: Weights of the components can be adjusted dynamically and this makes the matching function very flexible and powerful. Different architectures can have different weights to suit their particular configurations. For example, on a vector machine that has vector registers, the weight of the size matching can be increased so that longer vector operations will be generated, and bad stride vector operations will be avoided. During the program transformation process, some factors can be intentionally ignored to resolve conflicts, or to allow alternative paths to be explored.

Simplicity: Each individual matching function focuses on the matching between the program and a set of particular features of the machine, making it easier to compute.

Modularity: When new factors that affect matching are introduced, they are very easy to be added into the matching function. One only needs to define the subfunction and give it a weight that represents its importance in matching parallelism.

Topics discussed in this section form the foundation of the program parallelism optimization process. However, what really decide the effectiveness of the program parallelism optimization systems are the heuristics which are based on this foundation and the program transformation techniques which are used to restructure the program to match the machine. In the next section, we discuss the mechanism used to organize the heuristics that deal with program transformation theory and we describe the operation of the inference engine.

12.3 Intelligent Program Transformations

In this section, the organization, integration, and interpretation of program transformation knowledge are discussed. An example of optimizing a matrix-vector multiply program for three different parallel machines (BBN Butterfly, Alliant FX/8, and Purdue Pringle) is given to describe the operation of the inference engine.

12.3.1 System organization

There are three major components in the expert systems organization: the knowledge base, the inference engine, and the user interface mechanism. The knowledge base contains the domain-dependent rules, facts, heuristics, and procedural knowledge. The inference engine is the mechanism used to select and apply the rules in the knowledge base to solve the problem. The user interface mechanism contains the utilities to build user-friendly interfaces. These include a menu selection mechanism, graphics interface utilities, an explanation mechanism, and help utilities. The inference engine and the user interface are domain-independent, and they can be used to construct other expert systems by adding a domain-dependent knowledge base.

The organization of the system components is shown in Fig. 12.1. As the figure shows, the inference engine analyzes the machine feature

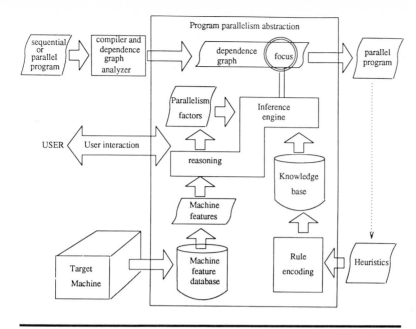

Figure 12.1   System organization.

list to form the *parallelism factors,* which are the key components of the computational model discussed in the last section. It selects part of the dependence graph as the *program focus,* and it analyzes and restructures the focus region based on the parallelism factors and the heuristics in the knowledge base. The structure of the knowledge in the knowledge base is discussed in the next two sections. Figure 12.2 illustrates the process of building the domain-dependent knowledge base.

12.3.2   Heuristic hierarchy

While the modularity and integratability of the rule-based expert system make modifying the knowledge base easy, its inefficient execution and the opacity of the knowledge are the major drawbacks. For example, translating a heuristic into a set of rules causes the knowledge to be fragmented; this makes the maintenance and modification of the knowledge difficult. Even though there are still strong relations between many of the rules, the fragmentation causes an unfortunate loss of coherence.

In order to improve the integration and modularity of the knowledge and the efficiency of the system, we have devised a new hierarchical structure to organize the heuristics. This *heuristic hierarchy* is used to integrate the rules into conceptually and logically related units. Since this is a new concept, we devote the remainder of this sec-

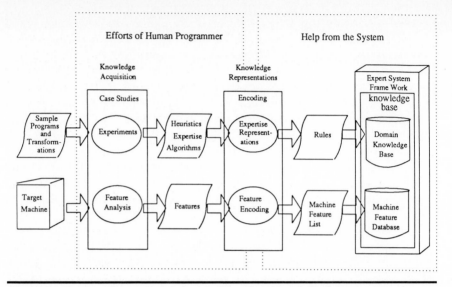

Figure 12.2   Process of constructing domain-dependent knowledge base.

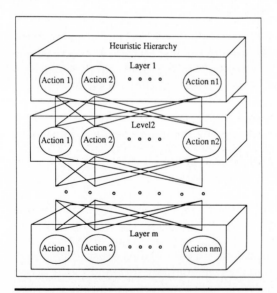

Figure 12.3   Heuristic hierarchy.

tion to a general description of heuristic hierarchies. In Sec. 12.3.3 we detail the organization of the hierarchy for the program restructuring system.

As shown in Fig. 12.3, a heuristic hierarchy consists of one or more *layers;* rules in the same layers are divided into groups that we call *actions.* Each heuristic hierarchy has a goal and some rules associated with it to accomplish the goal. The actions in the topmost layer represent possible solution steps that the hierarchy can use in trying to accomplish its goal. In other words, the rules of a heuristic hierarchy can use any actions of the top layer in attempts to satisfy the goal of the hierarchy. For each action, there is a goal for the rules in the action to accomplish. The rules in the action can select among the actions in the lower layer to satisfy its goal. Similarly, the actions in the lower layer may in turn select the actions in the next layer when trying to satisfy their goals. There are no goals associated with the layers because a layer represents a conceptual level of the problem-solving process in which different actions can be applied to achieve the goal of the control flow that calls the action.

A complicated action can be organized into a heuristic hierarchy. This recursive definition makes the heuristic hierarchy very flexible, and it can be constructed corresponding to the stepwise refinements in a top-down problem-solving approach. In a top-down problem-solving process, the problem is divided into multiple stages that represent the problem-solving steps of the process. Each stage can be refined stepwise as the system is implemented.

The inference engine of the heuristic hierarchy works as follows: the process tries to satisfy its goal by executing the rules of the hierarchy. The rules may select any of the actions in the top layer. An action works just like a hierarchy, except that the actions in the next layer may be called by any rules in the action. When a rule fails to satisfy the goal, other rules in the group are tried until either the goal is accomplished or all the rules have been tried. In either case, the control goes back up one level to the previous layer. If the selected action fails to satisfy the goal, an alternative action in the lower layer is selected. This process is repeated until the goal of the hierarchy is either satisfied or failed, and the control flow goes back to the caller of the hierarchy.

This hierarchical structure organization of the heuristics is actually a simplified hierarchical production system. It has the following advantages:

Modularity: Conceptually related rules can be grouped together. Grouping related rules together makes implementing, understanding, maintaining, and updating the knowledge base easier. The knowledge representation process that translates heuristics into rules can be done in either a top-down or a bottom-up fashion.

Efficiency: Only a small subset of the knowledge base needs to be considered at any given instance. The size of the knowledge base for real problems is usually very large. It is very inefficient to perform rule selection and backtracking when a flat structure knowledge base is used.

Flexibility: The order of the actions to be taken can be decided dynamically.

Note that the purpose of introducing the hierarchical structure is not to impose a tightly coupled structure onto the knowledge base, because not all knowledge can be represented in structured or procedural form. Also, if the structure of the rules is too tight, then the flexibility of the rule-based system may be lost. The purpose of the hierarchical structure is to provide a knowledge organization structure that matches the hierarchical structures in top-down problem solving processes. The hierarchical structure preserves all the advantages of a rule-based system but has better efficiency, modularity, and flexibility in the way it represents knowledge.

The hierarchical structure of the rules can be specified by the following declaration:

*hierarchy(name, [layer(name, [action] *)] *);*

where the notation *[expression]** represents a list of one or more expressions of the same type. Examples of this will be shown in the next section.

The lexical order of the layers represents the level of the layers from top down. The lexical order of the rules decides the default ordering of the rules to be applied. This default ordering can be overwritten by explicit rules. The order of the actions is irrelevant, since they are selected by the rules in the upper layer.

In the system, knowledge and heuristics are represented as rules of the following form:

```
[Rule, [action_name*]]:
   If
      {condition list}
   then
      {action list}.
```

The action_name* is used to label the action(s) in the hierarchy to which the rule belongs. These hierarchy declarations provide an easy way for the system engineer to specify the structure of the heuristics and keep closely related rules together.

12.3.3 Program transformation with heuristics

The program restructuring process is an iterative process. At each step, the dependence graph of the program focus region is analyzed, and a transformation that can improve the parallelism matching between the program and the machine is chosen and carried out. There are two difficulties with this process. The first problem is, *When and how does one apply which transformation?* Different sequences of transformations may lead to different results. Also, a transformation may have different effects when it is applied to different program states.

The second problem is, *How does the system detect that the program is in its optimal form and stop the transformation process?* Unlike some other AI problems, there is no good description of the goal states. The goal of performing the transformations is to optimize the matching between the program and the computational machine model. For the same program, there may be many different representations of the program that have the same input/output semantics. The problem is to find a sequence of transformations that transforms the current representation of the program into a representation that allows maximum parallelism on the target machine.

Since it is expensive to test the applicability of the transformations and apply the transformations, and since there may be many different applicable transformation sequences for a given program, it is impractical to try all of the sequences and then to choose the best way to restructure the program. Heuristics, and some kind of metric, must be employed in order to find the most promising transformation to apply at each step. The matching functions described in Sec. 12.2 can be used to measure the effectiveness of the transformations. But we should also note that the matching function can only be used to compare the relative merit of the transformations since an optimal form can only be found after we try all the possible transformation paths.

On the other hand, the user-selectable optimization degree indicates how deep the user wants the system to explore. The user can control the optimization depth by choosing the optimization degree or by stopping the process during an interactive session. The optimization degree is a real number between 0 and 1. If the user specifies an optimization degree of 1, the system tries all possible transformation sequences and selects the best sequence to apply. If the optimization degree is set to 0, no program restructuring effort will be tried; the system takes the program as it is and applies the program realization process to parallelize the program. When the optimization degree is set to some number between 0 and 1, the heuristics will be applied in selecting transformations. The higher the optimization degree is, the more aggressive the system is in trying different transformations. The optimization degree also sets a limit for the parallelism matching index to compare against. The attempt at restructuring the program is stopped when the parallelism matching index passes a certain limit, or when the heuristics are exhausted. Another advantage of using a user-selectable optimization degree is that different optimization degrees can be set for different regions of the program. During an interactive session, the user can concentrate the attention of the system (as well as his or her own) on parts of the program that he or she considers more critical.

Empirical studies of the sequences of transformations have been reported by Kuck and his associates. A number of fixed sequences of transformations, tailored for different architectures, have been investigated and built into the Parafrase project [Abu-Sufah 79; Kuck 80, 81; Padua 80]. Although these sequences work well for certain programs on the architectures and problems for which they are designed, the inflexibility of the fixed sequence of transformations may limit potential optimization. In fact, recognizing the shortcomings of fixed sequences of transformations, the Parafrase system relies on the user to provide the sequences of transformations as options for particular applications that the user knows well. Also, the user can provide assertions or directives to help the compiler recognize the parallelism that it overlooked.

In our system, heuristics are organized into heuristic hierarchy structures. The heuristic hierarchy and other user interface mechanisms are built on top of the UNIX C-Prolog. In the following subsections we explain the organization of the heuristics and illustrate the operation of the inference engine with an example.

12.3.4 Organization of transformation heuristics

There are three kinds of transformation heuristics: the heuristics to define program parallelism and machine parallelism, the heuristics to restructure the program to match parallelism between the program and the machine, and the heuristics to control the parallelism matching process. These three kinds of heuristics correspond to the three layers in the heuristic hierarchy which we call the *parallelism-defining* layer, the *parallelism-matching* layer, and the *parallelism-matching control* layer. Each of these three layers is further divided according to the purpose and effects of the heuristics. The hierarchy structure of the transformation heuristics is shown in Fig. 12.4.

The parallelism-defining layer is the basis of the program restructuring process. It defines the program parallelism and the machine parallelism by asserting facts about parallelism into the solution state. The computational model represents the machine parallelism, and its construction is based on the machine features and the heuristics of utilizing them. The program parallelism is represented by program dependence graphs. The parallelism-matching functions and the heuristics (for analyzing the matching between the program and the computational model) are included in this layer. Customized conflict

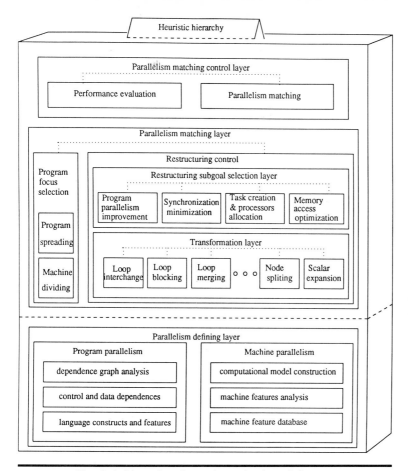

Figure 12.4   Heuristic hierarchy of transformation knowledge.

resolution strategies and inference rules can be added to this layer as well.

The program parallelism optimization process improves the matching between the program and the machine by repeatedly selecting program regions and restructuring them. Corresponding to this process, the parallelism-matching layer consists of two actions that are implemented as hierarchies: the *program focus selection* and the *program restructuring control*. The program focus selection process is responsible for selecting the program fragment to optimize, and the program restructuring control process utilizes heuristics to optimize the program focus.

The program restructuring control process is the part of the heuristic hierarchy that actually selects and performs the transformations. Corresponding to the problems of parallelism optimization discussed in Sec. 12.2, the purposes of the transformations can be classified into the following four categories: improving program parallelism, minimizing synchronization, creating tasks and allocating processors, and utilizing memory usages. Since each transformation may fit into several categories, we separate the heuristics in the program restructuring control layer into two layers: the *program restructuring subgoal selection* layer and the *transformation* layer. The restructuring subgoal selection layer contains the heuristics for solving the four problems mentioned above, and the transformation layer contains the transformation techniques which we termed *transformation modules*.

Each transformation module consists of the description of the transformation technique, the conditions for the transformation to be applicable, and the procedures to carry out the transformation. Also included in the module are the heuristics about the feasibility of the transformation under various circumstances, short-cut rules in applying the transformation, methods of estimating the effects of the transformation, etc. As an example, the module for "loop interchange" is outlined below. The direction vector notation is taken from Wolfe [82].

Module Name: Loop interchange

Purpose: Change the order of headers of
    nested loops into 'optimal' ordering.

Description: Based on heuristics, compute the loop order
    that matches the computational model best.
Restrictions: Loop orders that cause a dependence to
    have direction vectors in the form of
    (..., < , ..., > ,...) is prohibited.

Test Algorithm: Procedure legal_order(L, ORD)
    Given a loop order ORD,
     for each dependence DEP in the loops do
      if the direction vector of DEP has the form
       (..., < , ..., > ,...) according to ORD
      then return(fail);
     end for
    return(true); /* The order is legal */

Applying Algorithm: /* find the best ordering of the loops. */
    procedure best_loop_order(L)
    old-ord = generate-loop-order(L);
    while ((new-ord = generate-loop-order(L)) ! = NULL) do
     old-order = better-order(old-ord, new-ord);
    return(old-ord);

Transformation Algorithm: Loop_interchange(Outmostlp, Norder)
    change all distance vector according to Norder;
    update control dependence of the loop headers;

Heuristics:
    if has_IO(FOCUS)
    then fail.

    if (is_loop(FOCUS)) and (not nested(FOCUS))
    then apply loop_distribution(FOCUS).

    if (nested_loops(L1, L2)) and
        (in(S1, L1) and in(S2, L2)) and
        (dep(S1, S2, [< , >]))
    then not interchangeable(L1, L2).

    if ('memory optimization dominates instruction minimization')
    then
        (set(weight, size-matching, light)) and
        (set(weight, memory-access-matching, heavy))
    ...

The program restructuring process can be divided into the following stages that we term the *program restructuring subgoals*. These include the *program parallelism improvement subgoal*, the *synchronization minimization subgoal*, the *task creation and processor allocation subgoal*, and the *memory-access optimization subgoal*. A transformation might be applied in different situations for different reasons. Therefore, each subgoal category may select any of the transformations in the underlying transformation layer. Rules in each of the program restructuring subgoals select the appropriate transformations to apply. The selection of the transformations is based on the heuristics in the transformation layer and the parallelism-defining layer.

The program parallelism improving subgoal consists of rules about the methods of improving program structures. This goal is achieved by restructuring the program to cut down on the amount of data or control dependence presented in the program dependence graph. The synchronization minimization subgoal contains the heuristics for trying to decrease the cost of interprocessor synchronization. The task creation and processor allocation subgoal is formed by the heuristics for both decomposing the program into tasks and matching the tasks against the target machine. The memory-access optimization subgoal is aimed at utilizing the memory hierarchy. Issues considered here include array decomposition and allocation, cache utilization, intertask communications minimization, and locality improvement.

The program focus selection layer cooperates with the parallelism matching control layer in selecting the appropriate program focus. It consists of rules to select a portion of the program to serve as the current focus of program restructuring. Depending on the size and the structure of the program, as well as the optimization degree that the user sets, the size of the program focus ranges from a loop to the whole program. If the program is complicated, a divide-and-conquer strategy is used to subdivide the program. The program is divided into several "supertasks" and each supertask is restructured separately. Then the restructured portions are combined based on global considerations. Depending on the dependence relations, the supertasks of programs can be executed either sequentially or simultaneously. If these supertasks are to be executed sequentially on the target machine, then each part is restructured based on the computational model of the original machine. On the other hand, if some supertasks of the program are to be executed simultaneously, then the machine is subdivided into several independent virtual machines (or clusters) and the supertasks are assigned to the virtual machines.

Note that when a program is divided into subprograms, and the subprograms are restructured separately, the memory-accesses optimization subgoal will try to optimize the memory accesses and decompose the array storages based on the program focus and the machine model to which it is assigned. The array decompositions chosen in the subgoal may be changed when global consideration and adjustments are made.

The parallelism-matching control layer is the topmost layer of the hierarchy and it represents the process that controls the overall optimization of the program. It uses the subgoals in the parallelism-matching layer to decompose the program into tasks which we call *program* focuses. It then matches them with the machine model individually, and finally it adjusts the results based on global considerations.

The hierarchy structure significantly improves the flexibility and efficiency of the transformation process. The rules in a layer may select any of the actions (subgoals) in the lower layers. Thus no fixed ordering for applying the actions needs to be specified. This allows the system to be very flexible in deciding the sequences of the transformations. Unrelated rules do not need to be checked, since only the set of rules in the subgoal selected by the upper layer needs to be evaluated. Furthermore, backtracking only occurs within the set of rules in the same layer.

12.3.5 Applying a transformation hierarchy to program transformation

The program restructuring process starts by examining the rules on the top layer of the hierarchy. After the focus of the program is chosen, the transformation subgoals on the next layer are selected and the rules associated with the subgoal are involved in selecting the applicable transformations. Similarly, when a transformation is chosen, the rules associated with it are applied to decide the merits and methods of performing the transformation on the program focus.

The flow of control is decided by the rules in the heuristic hierarchy. We will illustrate the decision-making process of the system with a simple example. A matrix-vector multiply is a nice illustration of the ideas behind the system, since very few data dependences are involved and many transformations are possible. The program is a simple nested iteration:

```
for i in [1 .. n] do
  for j in [1 .. m] do
    y[i] = y[i] + a[i,j]*x[j];
  end for;
end for;
```

To simplify the discussion we assume that the result vector y has been previously initialized to zero. We seek to transform this program to programs suitable for three different machines: the BBN Butterfly, the Purdue Pringle, and the Alliant FX/8. The rules used in this example are listed in the Appendix at the end of this chapter.

Mapping onto the BBN Butterfly.   First, we consider the Butterfly. As we discussed in Sec. 12.2, the machine feature database is first consulted in the construction of the virtual computational model. For example, the fact "parallelize outermost loop without blocking" is added by rule 12.a.1 (listed in the Appendix) because the Butterfly provides a mechanism, *GenOnIndex,* which can schedule the loops automatically. The system discovers, among other facts, that memory optimization dominates instruction minimization (rule 12.a.5), locality is important, and local memory should be used whenever possible (rule 12.a.6). These facts are added to the system's state space in the working memory.

Next, the transformation heuristic hierarchy is used to optimize the program. First, the parallelism-matching control layer is involved to control the restructuring of the program. In this example, it is trivial to select the program focus. By rule 12.b.1, the whole subroutine is chosen as the program focus, since the original program consists only of a single statement inside the doubly nested loop.

The next step is for the program restructuring control layer to decide which sequence of program restructuring subgoals to achieve. Due to the simplicity of the dependence graph of this program, none of the transformations which are used to break the data dependence cycles are needed. Thus, the parallelism improvement subgoal is skipped (rule 12.c.1). For the sake of flexibility, it is best to do processor assignment toward the end of the transformation process. However, array decomposition can be done only after tasks are created. So there is a conflict in deciding which of the two subgoals, *task creation and processor allocation subgoal* or *memory-access optimization subgoal,* should be done first. Our solution to this problem is as follows. First, we find the tentative process allocation scheme and block the outermost loop to create "processes." The newly created outermost loop is marked but is not actually parallelized. The loop instances of this marked loop form the tentative processes, and this information will be used to guide the array decompositions in memory access optimization subgoal. The actual processor allocation is carried out at the end of the transformation process if the marked loop remains marked by then. This heuristic is encapsulated in the default ordering of rules 12.c.4, 12.c.5, and 12.c.7.

After the task creation and processor allocation subgoal is picked, the system concentrates its restructuring efforts on the loop structures. At this stage, applicable transformations include loop interchanging and loop blocking (to create processes). According to the heuristic (rule 12.e.1), if the program focus is a nested loop, then loop interchanging is checked to find the best order of the loops before the processes are created.

Therefore, the control goes down to the lower level transformation layer, and rules associated with loop interchanging are applied. We assume that the arrays in Butterfly are stored in row order. There are no dependence relations that prevent us from interchanging the loop, so the loop is interchangeable. However, if loop j is changed to be the outermost loop, the array a will be accessed in columns no matter how we block the outer loop to form processes. This is not attractive because it increases the intertask communications significantly. Therefore, based on the rules associated with loop interchange, the system decides that the original loop order is the best and that no loop interchange is needed.

The next step is to find a tentative way of allocating the processes to the processors. Since the Butterfly has an instruction *GenOnIndex* that can schedule the loops automatically, we can parallelize the outermost loop without blocking (rule 12.a.1). As a result, the outer loop i is marked to form tasks (rule 12.e.4). There are n instances of the loop i, so n tasks are formed if each loop instance is viewed as a task. This information will be used to guide the array decompositions when the memory access optimization subgoal is involved.

After the processor allocation phase, rule 12.c.3 chooses the memory-access optimization subgoal. Since local memory access is faster than global memory access on the Butterfly, locality is important (rule 12.a.6). Also, the Butterfly supports a "block-transfer" instruction, which allows a block of memory to be transferred to, or from, the local memory to speed up the data transfer. This makes copying array references inside loops into local memory beneficial. In the matrix-vector multiply program, there are two array references in the nested loops. Each element of array x is accessed once by every instance of the loop j. Also, elements of the *ith row of the array a* are accessed exclusively by loop instance *i*. Since loop *i* is marked to be parallelized in the "processor allocation" subgoal, every processor that runs loop instance *i* will have to access every element of the array *x* and the *i*th row of array *a* once. Rule 12.f.1 suggests we copy array *x* and array *a* into local memory with block transfer operations. Since the *i*th iteration accesses only the *i*th row of the array *a*, there is no need to copy the whole array. The block transfer operation on array *a* is later changed by rule 12.f.2 into a block transfer operation on row *i* of the array *a* in loop *i*. This gives us (by applying rule 12.f.3):

```
for i in [1 .. N] do
  block_transfer(x, x_local, sizeof(x));
  block_transfer(a[i, *], a_local, sizeof(a[i, *]));

  for j in [1 .. M] do
    y[i] : = a_local[j] * x_local[j];
  end for
end for
```

Since the block transfer statement of copying array *x* does not depend on loop *i*, it can be moved outside loop *i* to form another parallelized loop of *P* instances, where *P* is the number of the processors (rule 12.f.4). In this way, the array is copied *P* times instead of *N* times, as it was in the original form.

After the memory allocations are complete, the parallelism improving subgoal is tried. This is to see if there is any chance to improve the program further. It is relatively easy for the system to recognize that the inner loop *j* is an inner-product operation (rule 12.d.1), so the loop is replaced by an inner-product operation (rule 12.d.2). The final step involves the processor allocation subgoal again. Since no transformation that might prevent the parallelizing of the outermost loop *i* (which is marked for parallelizing) has been performed, the loop is directly parallelized as shown below:

```
coprocess k in [1 .. P] do
  block_transfer(x, x_local, sizeof(x));
end coprocess

coprocess i in [1 .. N] do
  block_transfer(a[i, *], a_local, sizeof(a[i, *]));
  y[i] : = inner-product(a_local[*], x_local[*]);
end coprocess
```

Mapping onto the Pringle/CHiP. The Pringle/CHiP architecture consists of an array of 64 processors which communicate with each other via a packet-switched message network. There is no shared memory, and each processor runs one process. The communication pattern of messages between processors, defined at compile time as a communication graph, is used to configure the switch network at load time. Each of the memory modules is dual ported. One port goes to the processor while the other goes to a global bus, this allows the local memory of each processor to be a page of the global address of the front-end host. Downloading programs and data to each processor and loading the results of a computation to the host is done over this bus.

For the same reason as in the case of Butterfly, the system decides not to change the original order of loops after the rules in the transformation module, *loop interchange,* are used to decide the order of loop headers. Making the program restructuring task different here are the facts that process creation time on the Pringle is expensive, and no self-scheduling primitive is available. The best strategy for processor allocation on the Pringle is to create P processes to run on the P processors that the Pringle has (rule 12.a.2). So, the n instances of the outermost loop i are blocked to form P tasks (rule 12.e.3). The result is shown below:

```
coprocess k in [0 .. P − 1] do
  for i in [k*n/P .. (k + 1)*n/P] do
    for j in [1 .. m] do
      y[i] : =  y[i] + a[i,j] * x[j];
    end for;
  end for;
end coprocess;
```

Next, the memory-access optimization subgoal is invoked to allocate the data. Since the Pringle is a non-shared-memory machine, all the data must be distributed among the processors. Array decompositions are done by means of interprocess dependence analysis. By checking the bounds of the loops, the system discovers that the processor which runs process k (kth iteration of the coprocess loop) accesses only rows $k*n/P$ to $(k + 1)*n/P$ of the array a. In terms of the dependence relations, this means that no out-of-bounds dependence (dependence edge that has only one end in the loops) or cross-iteration dependence (dependence whose source and sink are in different loop iterations) of the array a exist. So, it is best to store these rows of the array in the local memory of the processor that runs the task. By rule 12.f.11, the array a is divided into P blocks according to the memory access pattern, and the P blocks are allocated to local memories in the corresponding processors. Similarly, array y can be blocked into P "chunks" and stored in the local memories of the processors. Therefore, each of the processors computes n/P components of the y vector.

Since each process uses all the elements of array x, the processor that runs the process needs to access the whole array x no matter where the array is allocated. If we are free to allocate the array x anywhere, the most direct method is to put it in one processor, say PEO, and then "broadcast" it to other processors by means of a pipeline process (rule 12.f.12). To accomplish this, each element of x is passed from one processor to the next by using a "channel" variable. This transformation is termed *pipelining,* which is a modified version of the transformation "scalar expansion" to pass the data through "channel_ variables" instead of temporary variables. The channel variable Ch_x [k] implements a communication channel between processor k and processor $k + 1$. Processor $k = 0$ reads the value of $x[j]$ and puts it in $Ch\_x[0]$. Processor $k = 1$ reads the value in $Ch\_x[0]$ and puts it into $Ch\_x[1]$, etc. The result of the transformation is shown below:

```
coprocess k in [0 .. p − 1] do
  local tmp;
  for j in [1 .. m] do
    tmp = if (k = = 0) then x[j] else Ch_x[k − 1];
    Ch_x[k] = tmp;
    for i in [k*n/p .. (k + 1)*n/p] do
      y[i] = y[i] + a[i,j] * tmp;
    end for;
  end for;
end coprocess;
```

On some non-shared-memory machines it is too costly to send a message consisting of only one word (for example, the Intel IPSC and the NCUBE). In this case, it is best to send large segments of the x vector through the pipeline at a time.

Perhaps the most important problem to be solved for both non-shared-memory machines and shared-memory machines which require that programs exploit locality is how to analyze a program and derive an optimal partition of the data structures.

Mapping onto the Alliant FX/8.   In the case of the Alliant FX/8 there are three important programming issues. First, because of the powerful vector instruction set in each processor, one should exploit as many vector operations as possible. Second, since cache access is twice as fast as a memory access, the programmer must force as many memory accesses to be from the shared data cache as possible. Third, because only one operand in a vector instruction may come from memory or cache, it is important to keep vector operands that are used repeatedly in vector registers.

Most parallel compilers can recognize the inner-product operation in the original matrix vector multiply program and translate the program into the following form:

```
for i in 1 .. n do
    y[i] = inner_product(A[i, *], x);
end for;
```

Although the Alliant supports fast inner-product operations, this transformation does not really utilize the parallelism capabilities of the Alliant FX/8. Each processor that runs the program accesses the array x n times, so the array x needs to be brought into the cache repeatedly. Since each vector register in the Alliant FX/8 can hold only 32 words of data, the vector x and the matrix a in the sample program need to be loaded into the vector registers repeatedly. This data traffic floods the bus and slows down the computations significantly.

In general, without intelligent program analysis, this communication bottleneck problem is hard to solve. Our system tries to improve the matching between the program and the computational model of the Alliant by examining and managing the memory accesses intelligently.

As in the case of the Butterfly, task creation and processor allocation is the first subgoal selected. Since the Alliant has a vector capability, both the vector processing parallelism in the innermost loop and the multiprocessing parallelism in the outermost loop need to be explored. Before the outer loop is blocked to form tasks and the inner loop is blocked to form vector operations, loop interchange is considered to find the best ordering of the loop headers (rule 12.e.1). So control goes down to the transformation layer, and the rules associated with the transformation "loop interchange" are applied. First, the nested loops i and j in the original source are checked, and the conclusion that they are interchangeable is reached. Next, rules about loop orders are applied to decide the best order of the loop headers. Program size matching and memory utilization matching indices can be used to select the loop order. Rule 12.a.5 suggests that memory optimization dominates the instruction minimization, so memory optimization matching is considered.

The matrix-vector multiply program accesses vector x n passes in total, one pass for each loop instance of loop i. Loop j is the loop that scans through vector x. If loop j is the inner loop, and loop i is the outer loop, then each value of the vector x will be accessed once by every loop instance of loop i. Therefore, the vector needs to be brought into cache repeatedly. On the other hand, if loop i is the inner loop and loop j is the outer loop, the value $x[j]$ is brought into the cache and used by all loop instances of the inner loop i for each loop instance of the outer loop j. In this loop order, the network traffic for references of vector x is decreased significantly. Therefore, the loop order where loop j is outside is preferred according to the memory allocation matching function. In other words, the loops need to be interchanged.

After the loops are interchanged, the innermost loop is blocked to form vector operations, and the outermost loop is translated into tasks and may be blocked to form processes. For the vector loop blocking, the inner loop i is blocked according to the vector register size of the Alliant (rule 12.e.2). The vector operation is created by vectorizing the innermost loop after the blocking. The resulting program is shown below. Each loop instance of the outermost loop *j* forms a task. Since the Alliant instruction set provides a means to automatically allocate the processes to the eight processors, no loop blocking is needed to match the number of processes with the number of processors (rule 12.a.1). Subsequently, loop *j* is marked to be parallelized:

```
for j in [1 .. m] do
    for k in [0 .. n/32 − 1] do
        k1 = k * 32 + 1;
        k2 = (k + 1) * 32;
        y[k1 .. k2] sum = a[k1 .. k2, j] * x[j];
    end for;
end for;
```

The next step is to perform memory access optimization. Rule 12.a.7 suggests that keeping one vector operand in a vector register is beneficial. Since vector segment y[k*32 + 1 .. (k + 1)*32] is used repeatedly by each instance of the outer loop *j*, it is best to keep this segment in the vector register. This can be accomplished by interchanging loops *j* and *k* (rule 12.f.13). Note that in the previous task creation and processor allocation subgoal, the loop *j* is marked as "to be parallelized." However, according to rule 12.f.14, the utilization of vector registers and vector operations is weighted to be more important. So the previous decision is revoked, and the loops are interchanged. Loop *k* becomes the outermost loop to be parallelized. The resulting program is

```
coprocess k in [0 .. n/32 − 1] do
    local k1, k2 : int;
    k1 = k * 31 + 1;
    k2 = (k + 1) * 32;
    for j in [1 .. m] do
        y[k1 .. k2] sum =  a[k1 .. k2, j] * x[j];
    end for;
end coprocess;
```

In the final version, each 32-word *y* vector segment can be saved in a register for the lifetime of the process and can be written to memory only at the end of the computation. Experiments performed in collaboration with Dan Sorensen at the Illinois Center for Supercomputer Research and Development [CSRD] have shown that this implementation of the program is the fastest version of a matrix-vector multiply available for the machine.

The matrix-vector multiply example described above served three purposes:

1. It demonstrated how the inference engine works.

2. It illustrated the fact that a different sequence of transformations was required to produce an optimal program for each machine.

3. It showed the complexity of the program parallelism optimization process.

Many heuristics were needed even for this simple program. This reinforces our view that an expert systems approach is a more flexible and extensible approach than the conventional hard-wired heuristics approach.

On the other hand, the example described above is far too simple to illustrate many of the most interesting and important issues in program restructuring. In particular, it fails to illustrate the issues relating to the introduction of synchronization needed in many problems to satisfy data dependence constraints between parallel tasks. This topic and many others are considered in greater depth in Wang [88].

12.4 Conclusions

Different parallel architectures use different properties of parallel algorithms to speed up computation. These properties require different programming methodologies and heuristics in order to be well utilized. Most users of scientific parallel computers use the following approach: they study the target parallel architecture extensively, then develop tricks and expertise to utilizing the architecture. From these experiences, they carefully code their applications to exploit the parallelism provided by the hardware. This "study and experience cycle" may need to be repeated many times before the resulting program achieves a satisfiable speedup. As a result, users need to pay a great deal of attention to the problem of matching program parallelism to machine parallelism for each application. Furthermore, algorithms tailored to suit the particular underlying hardware may not be easily ported to other machines without major modifications. It is clear that this approach is expensive in human terms; i.e., software development and maintenance grow as the diversity of parallel machines increases.

Although most program transformation techniques are machine independent, the heuristics of applying these techniques to the target machine are not. These heuristics are based on extensive study of the particular target machine and are usually hard-wired into a compiler. As a result, existing parallel compilers/restructurers can only generate parallel code for one particular target machine. Much effort must be spent in order to build compilers for different machines even though much of the knowledge can be transferred with minor modifications. Furthermore, the transformation sequence is often predefined by the compiler or specified by the user as an option to the compiler. Given the dynamic nature of programs, this approach is not flexible and may not be able to generate optimal code across a wide spectrum of algorithms.

Building an interactive program restructurer is an attempt to improve the programming environment to allow users to experiment with different program restructuring sequences interactively. But the user still has the burden of matching program parallelism with the underlying machine. From our point of view, what the user really needs is a user friendly environment that is capable of exploring program parallelism and providing expert advice for different architectures when it is requested to do so.

The expert systems approach of program parallelism optimization has the following advantages over the conventional hard-wired approach:

Modularity: The heuristic hierarchy structure provides a means to organize the program transformation heuristics into a modular form for easy understanding and maintenance of the system. Basing heuristics on both the program features and machine features can clean up the heuristics and allow the heuristics to be used for different parallel machines. It also makes modifying and expanding the system easy. New heuristics can be easily installed. Porting the system to new target machines is just a matter of specifying the machine features and providing a mechanism to generate target code for that machine.

Flexibility: The decision of which transformation to apply is made dynamically during the program optimization process. Both current program structures and the target machine features are considered as the program is optimized. This allows the system to select transformations that suit the particular program and target machine well.

Retargetability: The system can handle different kinds of target machines. It would be very difficult, if not impossible, to implement a program parallelism optimization system using the conventional hardwired approach.

In its current form, our system consists of three major components: an interactive incremental parser/structured editor for a simple functional language Blaze [Mehrotra 85] or Fortran; an interactive graphics based program restructurer that allows the user complete control over the program restructuring process; and the knowledge base and inference engine described in this chapter. All three components now work in prototype form only, and much work remains to be done before we will know if this experiment has been a success.

Appendix: Construction of the Computational Model

This Appendix contains the rules used in the examples.

Process creation

[Rule 12.a.1, ['computational model construction']]
if 'has self-scheduling-loop primitives'
then
    assert('parallelize outermost loop without blocking').

[Rule 12.a.2, ['computational model construction']]
if ('process creation cost'(high)) and
    (number-of-processors(P))
then
    assert('number of processes to create'(P)).

[Rule 12.a.3, ['computational model construction']]
if 'process creation cost'(low)
then
    assert('parallelize outermost loop without blocking').

Locality

[Rule 12.a.4, ['computational model construction']]
if has-cache
then
    assert('locality is important').

[Rule 12.a.5, ['computational model construction']]
if 'data access/process cost ratio'(large)
then
    assert('memory optimization dominates instruction minimization').

[Rule 12.a.6, ['computational model construction']]
if 'shared/local memory access ratio'(large)
then
    (assert('locality is important')) and
    (assert('use local variable whenever possible')).

[Rule 12.a.7 ['computational model construction']]
if ('has vector register')
then
    ('try to keep vector operand in register')

The program focus selection subgoal

[Rule 12.b.1, ['program focus selection']]
if ('nested loop'(PDG)) and

(nested-in(BB, PDG)) and
('single statement block'(BB))
then
    FOCUS = PDG.
....

The transformation selection subgoal

[Rule 12.c.1, ['program restructuring subgoal selection']]
if ('nested loop'(FOCUS)) and
    (nested-in(BB, FOCUS)) and
    ('single statement block'(BB))
then
    select('task creation and processor allocation').

[Rule 12.c.2, ['program restructuring subgoal selection']]
if ('compound statement'(Focus))
then
    select('parallelism improvement').

[Rule 12.c.3, ['program restructuring subgoal selection']]
if ('tasks created')
then
    select('memory access optimization').

[Rule 12.c.4, ['program restructuring subgoal selection']]
:- (select('task creation and processor allocation')).

[Rule 12.c.5, ['program restructuring subgoal selection']]
if (('has cache') or ('has arrays in'(Focus)) or ('locality is important'))
then
    select('memory access optimization').

[Rule 12.c.6, ['program restructuring subgoal selection']]
if 'multiple tasks are created'
then
    select('parallelism improvement').

[Rule 12.c.7, ['program restructuring subgoal selection']]
if (('task created'(FOCUS)) and (not 'parallelized'(FOCUS)))
then
    select('task-creation and processor allocation')

Parallelism improvement subgoal

[Rule 12.d.1, ['parallelism improving']]
if (is-a-loop(L)) and
(L = (for i in [RANGE] do A + = B[i] * C[i]; end for))
then
is-inner-product(L)

[Rule 12.d.2, ['parallelism improving']]
if ('has built-in fast inner product') and
    (is-in(L, FOCUS)) and
    (is-inner-product(L))

then
    apply(transformation(inner-product, L)).

[Rule 12.d.3, ['parallelism improving']]
if ('has fetch and op operatıons') and
    ('recurrence relation'(STMT))
then
    ('change into accumulation'(STMT)).

[Rule 12.d.4, ['parallelism improving']]
If ('nested-loops'(Focus)) and
    (not 'perfectly-nested-loops'(Focus)) and
    (('is-multi-processors' and high('task-creation-time')) or
    ('has vector operations'))
then
    apply('loop distribution').
....

Rules about task creation and processor allocation

[Rule 12.e.1, ['task creation and processor allocation']]
if (is-nested-loop(FOCUS))
then
    select(loop-interchange(FOCUS)).

[Rule 12.e.2, ['task creation and processor allocation']]
if (is-nested-loop(FOCUS)) and
    ('has vector operations') and
    ('size of vector registers'(V)) and
    $(V <> 0)$ and
    (innermost-loop(FOCUS, INNER)) and
    (num-of-iterations(INNER, N)) and
    $(V < N)$
then
    'loop blocking'(INNER, N).

[Rule 12.e.3, ['task creation and processor allocation']]
if (is-a-loop(FOCUS)) and
    (outermost-loop(FOCUS, OUTER)) and
    (num-of-iterations(OUTER, N)) and
    (number-of-processor(P)) and
    $(N > P)$
then
    'loop blocking'(OUTER, P).

[Rule 12.e.4, ['task creation and processor allocation']]
if ('parallelize outermost loop without blocking') and
    (is-nested-loop(FOCUS)) and
    (outermost-loop(FOCUS, OUTER))
then
    (parallelize(OUTER))
       ....

Memory access optimization

[Rule 12.f.1, ['memory access optimization']]
Assume L2 is the innermost loop that is nested in L1 such
that array references of X depend on the loop index of L2.
Also let X-sub be the part of the array X whose references
depend on the loops inside L2.

if (has-instruction(block-transfer)) and
    (shared-array(X)) and
    (parallelize(L1)) and
    (referenced-in(X, L1)) and
    (innermost-depends-on-loop(L1, X, L2)) and
    (sub-depends-on(X, X-sub, L2)),
    (N = sizeof(X)) and
    ('minimal number of references to justify cost of block-transfer' = B) and
    (N > B)
then
    (apply('block transfer'(X-sub, L2))).

[Rule 12.f.2, ['memory access optimization']]
if (apply('block transfer'(X, L)) and
    (parallelize(L)) and
    ('nested in'(L1, L)) and
    (sub-depends-on(X, X-sub, L1))
then
    (apply('block transfer'(X-sub, L1))).

[Rule 12.f.3, ['memory access optimization']]
if (apply('block transfer'(X, L))) and
    ('nested in'(L, LO))
then
    ('create temp array'(*amp*, LO) and
    ('create statement'(S, block-transfer(X, *tmp*, sizeof(X))) and
    ('insert in front of'(S, L2)) and
    (substitute(X, *tmp*, L)).

[Rule 12.f.4, ['memory access optimization']]
if (S = ('block transfer'(A, L, N))) and
    (shared(A)) and
    (local(L)) and
    (nested-in(S, L0)) and
    (parallelized(L0)) and
    ('not depends on'(A, L0)) and
    ('number of processors'(P))
then
    (create-loop(LL, 1..P)) and
    (add-stmt(LL, S)) and
    (parallelized(LL)) and
    ('insert in front of'(LL, L0)).

[Rule 12.f.5, ['memory access optimization']]
if (S = ('block transfer'(L, A, N))) and
    (shared(A)) and

   (local(L)) and
   (nested-in(S, L0)) and
   (parallelized(L0)) and
   ('not depends on'(A, L0)) and
   ('number of processors'(P))
then
   (create-loop(LL, 1..P)) and
   (add-stmt(LL, S)) and
   (parallelized(LL)) and
   ('append to'(LL, L0)).

[Rule 12.f.6, ['memory access optimization']]
if ('has cache') and
   ('mostly used array'(A, FOCUS))
then
   ('keep in cache'(A)).

[Rule 12.f.7, ['memory access optimization']]
if ('locality is important') and
   ('has local memory') and
   ('data accessing ratio of shared memory-local memory' > 2) and
   (shared-array(A))
then
   (allocate array A to the local memory of each processor).

[Rule 12.f.8, ['memory access optimization']]
if (has-local-memory)
   ('mostly used array'(A, FOCUS))
   (shared-array(A))
   (appears-in(A, S)) and
   ('in nested loops'(S, [L1.. Ln])) and
   ('not depends on loops'(A, L1))
then
   ('create tmp'(tmp, L1)) and
   ('create statement'(S1, (A : = tmp))) and
   ('insert in front of'(S1, S)),
   (substitute(A, tmp, L1)).

[Rule 12.f.9, ['memory access optimization']]
if ('mostly used array'(A, FOCUS)) and
   (shared(A)) and
   (appears-in(A, S)) and
   ('in nested loops'(S, [L1.. Ln])) and
   ('depends on loops'(A, L1))
then
   (find the plausible loop order ORD with most inner loops that A depends on)
and
   'loop interchange'(L1, ORD) and
   (innermost-depends-on-loop(L1, X, LL)) and
   ('create tmp'(tmp, LL)) and
   ('create statement'(S1, (A : = tmp))) and
   ('insert in front of'(S1, S)),
   (substitute(A, tmp, LL)).

[Rule 12.f.10, ['memory access optimization']]
if ('has local memory') and

('mostly used array'(A, FOCUS)) and
(shared(A)) and
('not modified'(A)) and
(cache-size(C)) and
(sizeof(A) > C)
then
    ('create tmp'(tmp, FOCUS)) and
    (scalarize(A, tmp)).

[Rule 12.f.11, ['memory access optimization']]
if ('non-shared memory') and
    (parallelized(L)) and
    (array(A)) and
    (appears-in(A, L)) and
    ('no inter task dependence exist'(A, L)) and
    (sub-depends-on(A, A-sub, L))
then
    allocate-local(A-sub, L).

[Rule 12.f.12, ['memory access optimization']]
if ('non-shared memory') and
    (parallelized(L)) and
    (array(A)) and
    (appears-in(A, L)) and
    ('has inter task dependence in'(A, L))
then
    'pipelining references'(A, L).

[Rule 12.f.13, ['memory access optimization']]
if ('has vector register') and
    ('is a vector'(V)) and
    (appears-in(V, S)) and
    ('in nested loops'(S, LList)) and
    (member(LL, LList)) and
    ('not depends on'(A, LL))
then
    'interchange loops to move LL into innermost'.

[Rule 12.f.14, ['memory access optimization']]
if ('has vector register')
then
    ('vector register optimization dominates memory access optimization').
....

Bibliography

[Allen 83]   J.R. Allen. *Dependence Analysis for Subscripted Variables and Its Appli-cation to Program Transformations.* Ph.D. Thesis, Rice University, Houston, TX, April 1983.

[Allen 84]   J. Allen and K. Kennedy. *A Parallel Programming Environment.* Tech. Rep., Rice COMP TR84-3, July 1984.

[Abu-Sufah 79]   W. Abu-Sufah, D. Kuck, and D. Lawrie. "Automatic Program Trans-formations for Virtual Memory Computers." *Proc. 1979 National Com-puter Conference,* pp. 969–974, June 1979.

[Burke 86]   M. Burke and R. Cytron, "Interprocedure Dependence Analysis and Parallelization." *Proc. 1986 Compiler Construction Conference,* pp. 52–64, August 1986.

[Cohen 81]   P. Cohen and E. Feigenbaum. *The Handbook of Artificial Intelligence,* vol. 3. William Kaufmann, 1981.

[Cytron 84]   R. Cytron. *Compile-Time Scheduling and Optimization for Asynchronous Machines.* Ph.D. Thesis, University of Illinois, Urbana-Champaign, August 1984, Report No. UIUCDCS-R-84-1177.

[Ferante 83]   J. Ferante, K. Ottenstein, and J. Warren. *The Program Dependence Graph and Its Uses in Optimization.* IBM Tech. Rep. RC 10208, August 1983.

[Gannon 84]   D. Gannon and J. Van Rosendale. "On the Communication Complexity of Parallel Numerical Algorithms." *IEEE Trans. on Computers,* vol. C-33, no. 12, pp. 1180–1194, December 1984.

[Kapauan 84a]   A. Kapauan, D. Gannon, L. Snyder, and T. Field. "The Pringle Parallel Computer." *Proc. 11th International Symposium on Computer Architecture,* pp. 12–20, 1984.

[Kapauan 84b]   A. Kapauan, K. Wang, D. Gannon, J. Cuny, and L. Snyder. "The Pringle: An Experimental System for Parallel Algorithm Design and Testing." *Proc. 1984 International Conference on Parallel Processing,* pp. 1–6, August 1984.

[Kennedy 80]   K. Kennedy. *Automatic Translation of Fortran Programs to Vector Form.* Tech. Rep. 476-029-4, Rice University, Houston, TX, October 1980.

[Kowalik 85]   J. Kowalik. *Parallel MIMD Computation: Hep Supercomputer and Its Applications.* MIT Press, Cambridge, MA, 1985.

[Kuck 80]   D. Kuck, R. Kuhn, B. Leasure, and M. Wolfe. "The Structure of an Advanced Vectorizer for Pipelined Processors." *Proc. 4th International Computer Software and App. Conference,* pp. 709–715, October 1980.

[Kuck 81]   D.J. Kuck, R.H. Kuhn, B. Leasure, D.H. Padua, and M. Wolfe. "Dependence Graphs and Compiler Optimizations." *Proc. 8th Annual ACM Symposium on Principles of Programming Languages,* Williamsburg, VA, January 1981.

[Kuck 84]   D. Kuck, M. Wolfe, and J. McGraw. "A Debate: Retire FORTRAN?" *Physics Today,* pp. 67–75, May 1984.

[Minsky 75]   M. Minsky. "A Framework for Representing Knowledge." In P. Winston (ed). *The Psychology of Computer Vision,* pp. 211–277, McGraw-Hill, New York, 1975.

[Mehrotra 85]   P. Mehrotra and J.R. Van Rosendale. *The BLAZE Language: A Parallel Language for Scientific Programming.* Rep. No. 85-29, ICASE, NASA Langley Research Center, Hampton, VA, May 1985.

[Nau 83]   D. Nau. "Expert Computer Systems." *IEEE Computer,* pp. 63–85, February 1983.

[Nilson 71]   N.J. Nilson. *Problem-Solving Methods in Artificial Intelligence.* McGraw-Hill, New York, 1971.

[Padua 79]   D. Padua. *Multiprocessors: Discussion of Some Theoretical and Practical Problems.* Ph.D. Thesis, University of Illinois, Urbana-Champaign, November 1979.

[Padua 80]   D. Padua and D. Kuck. "High-Speed Multiprocessors and Compilation Techniques." *IEEE Trans. on Computers,* vol. C-29, no. 9, pp. 763–776, September 1980.

[Phister 85]   G. Phister and A. Norton. "Hot Spot Contention and Combining in Multistage Interconnection Networks." *Proc. 1985 International Conference on Parallel Processing,* pp. 790–797, 1985.

[Polychronopoulos 86]   C. Polychronopoulos. *On Program Restructuring, Scheduling, and Communication for Parallel Processor Systems.* Ph.D. Thesis, University of Illinois Center for Supercomputer Research and Development, CSRD TR.595, August 1986.

[Schwartz 80]   J. Schwartz. "Ultracomputer." *ACM Trans. on Programming Languages and Systems,* vol. 2, no. 4, pp. 484–521, October 1980.

[Wang 85]   K. Wang. "An Experiment in Parallel Programming Environment: The Expert Systems Approach." In K.S. Fu (ed). *Some Prototype Examples for Expert Systems,* TR-EE 85-1, Purdue University, pp. 591–624, March 1985.

[Wang 88]   K. Wang. *A Program Transformation Expert System: Methodologies for Mapping Programs to Different Parallel Computers.* Ph.D. Thesis, Department of Computer Sciences, Purdue University, West Lafayette, IN 47907, 1988.

[Weiss 84]   S. Weiss and C. Kulilowski. *A Practical Guide to Designing Expert Systems.* Rowman and Allanheld, 1984.

[Winograd 75]   T. Winograd. "Frame Representations and the Declarative/Procedural Controversy." In Bobrow and Collins (eds). *Representation and Understanding: Studies in Cognitive Science,* pp. 185–210, Academic Press, New York, 1975.

[Wolfe 82]   M. Wolfe. *Optimizing Supercompilers for Supercomputers.* Ph.D. Thesis, Department of Computer Science, University of Illinois, Urbana-Champaign, IL, 1982, Rep. No. UIUCDCS-R-82-1105.

13

Restricted AND-Parallelism and Side Effects in Logic Programming

Doug DeGroot

Texas Instruments, Dallas, TX

13.1 Introduction

With the increasing reliance upon artificial intelligence (AI) to solve many of today's complex military, industrial, social, and business computer applications, the demands for ever higher performance in the area of symbolic computing continue to mount. More and more, researchers are looking for methods of executing AI languages in parallel. The majority of this attention has focused on models of parallel Lisp (see Chaps. 3 and 9) and parallel Prolog [Conery 81, Wise 86].

Several novel approaches have been developed recently for executing logic programming languages, such as Prolog, in parallel (Prolog is probably the most well-known logic programming language). Although several approaches are being pursued, the majority involve variations of two basic mechanisms: *AND-parallelism* and *OR-parallelism* [Conery 81]. Although Prolog is the most successful and most widespread logic programming language, many approaches to parallel logic programming have either abandoned the semantics of Prolog or have developed new language extensions or even new languages. Examples of these approaches include Concurrent Prolog [Shapiro 83], Parlog [Clark 86], GHC [Ueda 86], and Epilog [Wise 86].

Conery's model is a notable exception [Conery 87]. In his *And/Or Process* model, a set of run-time tests and algorithms are executed in order to derive a run-time ordering of goals within a Prolog clause and to produce a possibly-parallel execution graph based on this ordering. Although Conery's approach does retain the original Prolog syntax and semantics, it does so at a fairly considerable expense. A simpler and cheaper model was presented in DeGroot [84]. This simpler model, called the *Restricted AND-Parallelism (RAP)* model, also retains the original syntax and semantics of Prolog, but with significantly less run-time expense. The run-time expense is reduced through a set of approximation techniques which make certain assumptions about the possible execution traces of a clause. Because the techniques used are approximation techniques, they may in fact occasionally result in less parallelism than possible. Conery's model does not suffer from this fault; his approach remains the standard by which maximal parallelism can be achieved.

The RAP model trades maximal detection of parallelism for more efficient execution. As explained in DeGroot [84], it is believed that the RAP model will detect more than enough parallelism to keep a moderately sized parallel processor system busy. Recent empirical evidence certainly lends support to this thesis [Carlton 88]. Techniques may in fact be needed to limit the run-time detection of parallelism of RAP; consequently, the execution model of RAP allows parallelism-extraction code sequences to execute as if they were sequential code sequences [DeGroot 84].

This chapter describes the RAP model, and in particular, shows how it can efficiently support side-effect computations [DeGroot 87].

13.2   Parallel execution of Prolog programs

Many excellent introductory texts on logic programming and Prolog exist [Lloyd 84, Shapiro 86, Kluzniak 84], and so only a minimal description is provided here. The goal of the description is to focus on the execution semantics of Prolog rather than the language features, so that the parallel execution model presented below can better be appreciated.

First, Prolog defines only three types of statements: facts, rules, and queries. All three statement types are called *clauses*. Examples of each type of clause are shown below:

Facts:

isa(fido,dog).
father(john,mary).
part(partno(p2),pname(bolt),color(green),weight(17)).

Rules:

grandparent(X,Y) :- parent(X,Z), parent(Z,Y).
happy(D) :- isa(D,dog), has_a(D,X), isa(X,bone).

Queries:

```
?- grandparent(sue,C).
?- country(C), borders(C,mediterranean), country(C1),
       asian(C1), borders(C,C1).
```

Facts constitute the fundamental truths of the program. Each fact asserts that a certain specific relation holds between its arguments; the meaning of the relation is implicit except for certain predefined system relations. In the above, constants begin with lowercase letters; they refer to specific individual elements of the name space. Variable identifiers begin with uppercase letters and are universally quantified [Lloyd 84]. Variables may assume any value whatsoever, including the value of another variable. When this occurs, aliases may arise.

Rules express conditional truths. Each rule specifies a conditional *conclusion* to the left of the arrow (i.e., the ":-") and one or more *pre-conditions* to the right of the arrow. The conclusion is frequently called the *goal* (or *head*) of the clause, and the preconditions are called the *subgoals* (or *body*). To determine the truth of the conclusion of a rule, a Prolog system must recursively establish the truth of each of the preconditions in the rule.

Queries are the language mechanism used to activate the proof procedure on rules. As can be seen in the above examples, queries also contain one or more subgoals. Every subgoal in a query must be solved for the query to be solved (or proved).

The data structures appearing as arguments in goals, subgoals, and facts are called *terms*. Terms can be arbitrarily structured; they are defined inductively as follows:

1. A variable is a term.

2. An atomic element is a term (e.g., constants, integers, characters).

3. If f is an alphanumeric symbol (or, more precisely, a *functor* [Lloyd 84]), and $t1$ through tn are terms, then $f(t1,t2,\ldots,tn)$ is also a term.

Normal Prolog execution involves the sequential, left-to-right execution of the subgoals in a clause or query. A subgoal can be solved by finding a "matching" fact or by finding a rule whose head "matches" and whose body can be recursively solved, also in a left-to-right manner. The matching process referred to is called *unification* [Lloyd 84]. It is a recursive process in which each argument (*term*) of a subgoal is matched with the corresponding argument in the same position of the fact or rule head with which the match is to be attempted. Unification operates on two terms. The two terms unify if they are identical atomic symbols, if either or both are a variable, or if the terms have the same functor name and the same number of arguments and if these arguments are themselves recursively unifiable. During unifi-

```
p :- g, h.
p :- k.
g :- a, b, j.
g :- d, m, b.
h :- f.
j :- c, m, e.
m :- d.
a.
b.
c.
d.
e.
f.

?- p.
```

(a)

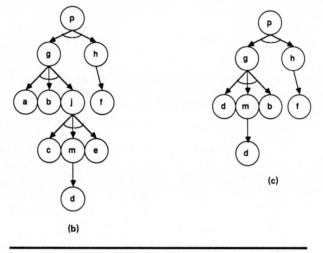

(b)

(c)

Figure 13.1   Possible execution trees from a query and program.

cation, assignment occurs if one or both of the terms to be unified is a variable. In such cases, one variable is assigned the value of the other term. The variable assigned the value of the other term can be either in the subgoal or in the fact or rule head. There is thus two-way assignment. The assignment is by reference and not by value; thus aliases can easily arise.

Every successful execution of a query results in an AND-execution tree, as illustrated in Fig. 13.1.† In these trees, leaf nodes represent

---

†Query execution can also be considered as producing AND/OR-execution trees. These are of interest mainly when considering OR-parallel execution models [Crammond 85] or combined AND/OR execution models, as in Conery [87]. In this paper, only AND-parallel execution models are considered, and so only AND-execution trees are of interest.

Prolog facts; internal nodes represent rules, where the node is labeled with the head of the rule represented by the node. In general, a query may be able to be solved in more than one way; each solution produces a possibly unique AND-execution tree. Figure 13.1 shows two possible AND-execution trees for the single query. AND-parallelism in logic programs is concerned with finding techniques to execute the nodes of the AND-execution tree in parallel, both internal and leaf nodes, rather than in the traditional, sequential manner.

Several problems arise when this is attempted. First, care must be taken to ensure that the values produced for variables are consistent among all executed goals. For example, consider the following simple program and query:

```
parent(bob,sally).
parent(jim,sue).
grandparent(X,Y) :- parent(X,Z), parent(Z,Y).

?- grandparent(bob,sue).
```

When the grandparent(bob,sue) query is executed, it matches the grandparent rule, giving the value of bob to the variable X and the value sue to the variable Y. To solve the grandparent rule then, the two subgoals must be solved with the assigned variable values. The two modified subgoals are thus parent(bob,Z) and parent (Z,sue). Suppose an attempt is made to execute these two subgoals in parallel. The first subgoal may succeed by matching the fact parent(bob,sally), thereby assigning the value sally to the variable Z; the second subgoal may succeed by matching the fact parent(jim,sue), thereby assigning the value sue to the variable Z.

Because both subgoals have succeeded, it is tempting to conclude that the entire rule has succeeded. But note that the two subgoals succeeded only by assigning two different values to the single variable Z. No single value of Z has been found such that bob is the parent of Z and sue is the child of Z. Consequently, the rule has not been successfully executed, and we do not know if bob is a grandparent of sue. When two different values are assigned to a single value, a *binding conflict* is said to have occurred.

Several techniques have been proposed to prevent this problem. One obvious technique is to have each subgoal produce all possible answers instead of just one and to then compute the relational join over the variables shared by the subgoals in the rule [DeGroot 88b]. This technique is examined in detail in Pollard [81]. If the empty set results from the join operation, no answer can be produced for the rule, and the rule fails. If the answer set is not null, this set is returned as the answer to the rule. Since the rule may have been invoked by some other rule, the answer set may be passed up the AND-execution tree as the answer to the rule's parent subgoal, helping constitute the answer for the parent rule.

As pointed out by Conery, this technique exhibits a few fundamental problems, one of which occurs simply when executing built-in arithmetic predicates and side-effect procedures that rely on Prolog's traditional sequential control flow [Conery 87]. This technique also suffers from certain performance anomalies which may make its parallel performance worse than sequential performance.

Several other approaches to AND-parallel execution of logic programs are currently being investigated; each exhibits significantly different performance characteristics, and no single model has yet emerged as "best" [Conery 87, DeGroot 88b, Wise 86].

13.3 Overview of the RAP Model

In this section, the RAP model of AND-parallel execution of logic programs is presented. It provides an efficient means of executing traditional Prolog programs in parallel while retaining the full semantics of sequential Prolog and hopefully offering the efficiency of single-answer execution [DeGroot 84]. The essential concept of the model is to compute at compile time a single execution graph expression which can at run time result in multiple, different parallel execution behaviors, and to do so with minimal run-time support. To do so, the execution procedure must monitor during run time all potentially executable subgoals and ensure that no two subgoals execute in parallel if they share one or more unbound variables. If this were allowed, the two subgoals might attempt to assign different values to the shared, unbound variable(s), and a binding conflict would have occurred.† This approach is exactly opposite that studied by Pollard.

The three main components of the RAP model are (1) the typing algorithm, (2) the independence algorithm, and (3) the execution graph expressions. Each of these is described below.

13.3.1 The typing algorithm

The *typing algorithm* is responsible for determining and maintaining the types of all terms (the data objects of Prolog) in an attempt to maintain an accurate indication of whether the term contains any unbound variables (unbound pointers) within it. A term may be of type

---

†In general, it is difficult to know for sure whether a binding conflict will occur, so the RAP model takes the conservative approach of simply assuming one will and therefore prevents parallel execution of such goals.

variable (the dereferenced pointer value is unbound), in which case it is assigned the type V; it may be a *ground term,* a term containing no unbound variables, in which case it is assigned the type G; or it may be a *nonground, nonvariable* term, in which case it is assigned the type N. The terms are typed recursively so that all terms and components of terms are typed. Figure 13.2 illustrates some simple examples of terms and their types.

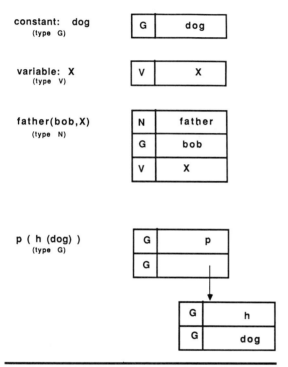

Figure 13.2   Examples of typing of terms.

During execution of a Prolog program, terms of type V (variables) may be bound to other terms of type V, G, or N; when variables become bound, they assume the type of the term to which they are bound. Terms of type N may become ground, and therefore of type G, by having their internal unbound variables bound to ground values. Terms of type G cannot change types (except through backtracking [Hermenegildo 87]).

Several possible typing algorithms are possible. A run-time checking algorithm was first described in DeGroot [84]. This algorithm attempts to lower the run-time overhead by making only a partial, top-level check of a term's contents instead of checking the term in depth. As a result of this partial check, a term may occasionally be typed too weakly; that is, it may be typed as nonvariable, nonground when, in fact, it may be ground. To make an asbolute determination of the type of a term, it would frequently be necessary to perform during run time a complete scan of the term to see if it contains any unbound variables. Because the term may be arbitrarily large, run-time scans are prohibitively expensive, especially when it is considered that in the worst case, these scans may occur following every successful subgoal invocation. The approximation to the typing is a compromise between run-time overhead and the need to make accurate type determinations.

Another typing algorithm based on a static data-dependency analysis is possible which incurs even less run-time overhead but which may occasionally have poorer performance [Chang 85, DeGroot 85]. This approach computes a set of possible activation "modes" for each clause and then settles for the worst-case mode in assigning types. In certain cases, this algorithm may make an accurate assessment of a term's type throughout the entire program execution, but in others, it may significantly underestimate the state of a term.

A very simple typing algorithm could simply use the terms' normal Warren Abstract Machine (WAM) type codes [Warren 83]—variable, constant, list, or structure. Variables would be assumed (naturally) to be of type V, constants would be type G, and lists and structures can simply be assumed to be of type N. No further typing overhead would then be required. The WAM's normal data type code assignments would be used to compute a RAP independence type code. Additional compiler directives, such as mode declarations or asserting that all lists contain only independent elements, would allow improved typing assumptions [DeGroot 88a]. The important point to note here is that all overhead can be eliminated from the typing algorithm component of the RAP model.

Other typing algorithms are clearly possible. The RAP model is defined independently of any particular typing algorithm.

13.3.2 The independence algorithm

The *independence algorithm* is responsible for determining when two terms are independent, that is, when neither shares an unbound variable with the other. The RAP execution model uses the independence algorithm to determine when two subgoals are independent: if two subgoals are invoked with arguments (terms) which are all independent from each other's, then the two subgoals are independent and may potentially execute in parallel; otherwise, they must execute sequentially in order to ensure that no binding conflicts occur. Figure 13.3 illustrates the independence algorithm.

```
function  INDEPENDENCE(arg1,arg2):boolean;
begin
 if  ground(arg1)  or  ground(arg2)  then
   INDEPENDENCE  :=  true
 else  if  (type(arg1)  =  type(arg2)  =  V)  and
   address(arg1)  ≠  address(arg2)  then
   INDEPENDENCE  :=  true
 else  {assume}  INDEPENDENCE  :=  false;
end;  {INDEPENDENCE}
```

Figure 13.3   The independence algorithm.

This independence constraint is sufficient but not necessary to ensure correct parallel execution: just because two subgoals are not independent, it cannot be concluded that a binding conflict *will* occur if they execute in parallel, only that one *might* occur. The RAP model is perhaps overly conservative in this respect. Significant opportunities exist for an optimizing compiler to assist in determining when this constraint can be relaxed [DeGroot 88*a*].

13.3.3 The execution graph expressions

The *execution graph expressions* are used to express the potential parallel execution sequences of the subgoals in a clause. Six expression types were originally defined, although others are possible. They are defined recursively as follows:

1. G   This is a simple goal (or subgoal); it is the simplest expression type.

2. (SEQ E1...En)   Execute expressions E1 through En sequentially.

3. (PAR E1...En)   Execute expressions E1 through En in parallel.

4. (GPAR(V1...Vk) E1...En)   If all the variables V1 through Vk are ground (have type G), then execute expressions E1 through En in parallel; otherwise, execute E1 through En sequentially.

5. (IPAR(V1...Vk)(Vm...Vp) E1...En)   If each variable V1 through Vk is independent of every variable Vm through Vp, then execute expressions E1 through En in parallel; otherwise, execute E1 through En sequentially.

6. (IF B E1 E2)   If expression B evaluates to true, execute expression E1; otherwise, execute expression E2.

The GPAR test simply examines the type fields of the specified terms to see if they are ground. The IPAR test simply invokes the independence algorithm on all pairs of variables in the IPAR expression; generally, the number of tests required is actually very small [DeGroot 88a].

13.4   Examples of Execution Graph Expressions

As examples of the types of execution graph expressions generated for typical Prolog clauses, consider the following clause:

f(X) :- g(X), h(X), k(X).

This clause may be compiled into the following execution graph expression:

f(X) :- (GPAR(X) g(X)
                (GPAR(X) h(X) k(X))).

This single execution graph expression can result in any of the three run-time execution graphs of Fig. 13.4. For example, if f is invoked

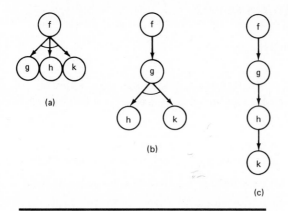

Figure 13.4   Examples of execution graphs.

with a ground value of X, as in "f(dog)", then the first GPAR test succeeds, thereby activating the two subexpressions in parallel. The first subexpression activates the subgoal g(X). The second subexpression simultaneously begins execution since the successful GPAR test guarantees that no binding conflicts can occur. This second subexpression also contains a GPAR test; it tests X again, finds it to be ground, and activates the two additional subexpressions in parallel.† Thus h(X)

---

†Note that this second GPAR test cannot fail. Since X was ground in the first test, it must still be ground. Terms of type G cannot change their types except through backtracking.

and k(X) begin parallel execution along with g(X). The resulting execution graph is shown in Fig. 13.4a. The GPAR tests assure that no binding conflicts will occur even though all three subgoals are executing in parallel with the same term.

Suppose now that the first GPAR test fails. Clearly then X is not ground and so contains an unbound variable somewhere within it. Consequently, no two of the subgoals can be allowed to execute in parallel, because otherwise a binding conflict might occur. Since the GPAR test failed, the two subexpressions must execute sequentially. So the first subgoal g(X) begins execution alone. When and if it successfully completes, the second subexpression can begin execution. Because the execution of g(X) may have resulted in X's becoming ground, the second subexpression retests X. If X is now ground, the GPAR test succeeds, and the two subgoals h(X) and k(X) can execute in parallel; the resulting run-time execution graph is shown in Fig. 13.4b. If the second GPAR test fails, X must still be nonground, and so h(X) and k(X) must execute sequentially, resulting in the run-time execution graph of Fig. 13.4c.

Note that three different run-time execution graphs are possible for the example Prolog clause but that only one RAP execution graph expression is needed to express all three execution graphs, and this is computed at compile time. Simple run-time tests are used to dynamically select one of a number of possible execution graphs given the execution graph expression. This is a significant advantage of the RAP model.

For another example, consider the following clause:

f(X,Y) :- p(X), q(Y), s(X,Y), t(Y).

This clause may be compiled into the execution graph expression

f(X,Y) :- (GPAR(X,Y)
            (IPAR(X,Y) p(X) q(Y))
            (GPAR(Y) s(X,Y) t(Y))).

or even into

f(X,Y) :- (GPAR(X) p(X)
            (GPAR(Y) q(Y)
              (GPAR(Y) s(X,Y) t(Y)))).

The first execution graph expression above can result in a slightly different set of run-time execution graphs than the second; it is interesting to compare the two.

The graph expression tests can be combined when necessary. For example, consider a variant of the popular grandfather clause:

grandfather(X,Y,Z) :- father(X,Y), father(Y,Z).

This clause can be compiled as

grandfather(X,Y,Z) :-
    (GPAR(Z) IPAR(X,Y) father(X,Z) parent(Z,Y).

Here, both the GPAR and IPAR tests must succeed for the two subgoals to execute in parallel.

It should be noted that the run-time tests are very simple and efficient. They can easily be implemented in hardware or firmware. Manuel Hermenegildo has in fact produced an extension to WAM for Prolog [Warren 83] that incorporates direct hardware support for the RAP model. The RAP graph expressions are easily compiled into this extended WAM model, and a sophisticated run-time kernel supports efficient parallel execution of the compiled Prolog program [Hermenegildo 87].

13.5 Backtracking in the RAP Model

To consider how normal Prolog backtracking can be implemented in the RAP execution model, a technique presented by Hermenegildo is described here [Hermenegildo 87]. Although it is not strictly necessary to understand backtracking to understand the following extension of the RAP model to include side effects, it is important.

First, it is important to consider how Prolog handles multiple clauses in a procedure. For example, consider the following simple procedure:

p :- a, b, c.
p :- g, h.
p :- q, r, s.

If we are given the goal p to solve, there are three different clauses that can be used in the proof. OR-parallel execution techniques proceed by attempting all three clauses in parallel; if any clause leads to success, then the query succeeds [Crammond 85]. AND-parallel execution, however, attempts only one clause at a time; but within the selected clause all subgoals may potentially execute in parallel. If the selected clause leads to failure, execution backs up to the most recent, previous execution point (subgoal) where untried clauses remain, and another clause is selected. If none of these remaining clauses lead to success, the next most recent execution point with remaining subgoals is examined, and so on. This process is called *backtracking*.

In WAM, Prolog execution maintains a run-time procedure-call stack. This stack contains procedure return addresses, actual parameter values, and other control information [Warren 83]. In particular, the stack contains *choice points* to mark those procedures that still contain one or more untried clauses. These choice points are used in backtracking. When AND-parallel execution is involved, the notion of backtracking to a "previous" subgoal is more complex. There is no chronological ordering that can be relied upon to implement normal backtracking. Consequently, additional information must be maintained in the stack.

In Hermenegildo's system, choice points are called *choice point markers* (CPMs). An additional marker type is defined called *parallel call markers* (PCMs). PCMs are used to record those points where a RAP execution graph expression resulted in the parallel execution of two or more subexpressions. As execution proceeds, CPMs and PCMs are recorded in the execution stack to record the execution points where clause choices were made and where parallel execution occurred. The backtracking algorithm can then be implemented as follows:

1. During normal, forward execution, record CPMs in the stack whenever a subgoal execution contains one or more untried program clauses. Record a PCM in the stack whenever an execution graph expression evaluates to true and produces parallel subexpressions. Mark each PCM as "inside" when it is created; change its value to "outside" if all subexpressions within the associated graph expression succeed.

2. If a subgoal fails, find the last (topmost) marker in the stack.
   a. If it is a CPM, all execution since that choice point has been sequential, so backtrack normally to that point and try one of the remaining untried clauses (as in sequential execution).
   b. If it is a PCM and its value is "inside," then several expressions are executing in parallel. Furthermore, at least one of these expressions has not yet completed. Cancel all unfinished subexpressions within the PCM's associated graph expression and recursively fail back (i.e., go to the previous marker).
   c. If it is a PCM and its value is "outside," then several expressions were executing in parallel, but all have finished. Find the last subexpression (using source-code textual order) that has remaining alternative clauses (represented by its associated CPM). Try these untried clauses one by one until one is found that succeeds; then restart in parallel all textually following expressions in normal, forward execution mode. If none of the untried clauses leads to success, fail back (i.e., go to the previous marker).

This simple, extended backtracking algorithm for RAP is easily implemented in Hermenegildo's extended abstract machine.

13.6   Side Effects

Unlike pure logic, logic programming languages such as Prolog have the curious aspect of occasionally having side effects as a result of, and during, execution of a logic program. Goals, subgoals, and predicates that produce side effects include those such as *assert* and *retract, read* and *write, cut,* and some other commonly used side-effect-producing procedures [Shapiro 86]. In addition, in the RAP model, goals that can produce possible machine-checks or system faults are also considered to be side-effect goals. Examples include *divide,* which might attempt to divide by zero and cause a program trap, and those that require a certain threshold in terms of the number of instantiated arguments, again, such as *divide,* which is required to have its first two arguments instantiated to nonvariable values, and arithmetic comparison predicates, such as *gt, lt,* and so on. Other examples include *var, plus, integer, is,* and the like. All of these are classified as side-effect goals within the RAP model.

The particular operational semantics of Prolog involve a simple, sequential execution model in which subgoals within a clause are tried in order, from left to right. In addition, multiple clauses within a single procedure are tried one at a time, from top to bottom (at least, within the domain of the selected, indexed clauses [Warren 83]). When coupled with the observed side effects, these two orderings produce a given program's observable behavior. To execute a Prolog program in parallel and retain its normal Prolog-defined semantics, it is necessary to retain the order of observable side effects in the program. As long as this order is retained, the goals themselves may execute in any order. Thus it is not really the left-to-right and top-to-bottom execution orderings of all goals and clauses that give Prolog its unique semantics, it is the induced ordering of the side effects produced. If, for example, a clause contains only subgoals which are side-effect-free, then the order of execution of these subgoals is irrelevant, and they may potentially execute in parallel (performance may differ, but the produced results will be identical [Warren 80]).

The semantics of Prolog then do not really require a sequential logic programming execution model; they only appear to with respect to the sequence of observable side effects. The side-effect goals must retain their left-to-right and top-to-bottom induced ordering; but all other goals are, to a certain extent (as explained below), order-independent. In fact, the goals in a side-effect-free Prolog program can be executed in any order whatsoever. It is only when side-effect goals are introduced that order becomes important. (Order independence should not be confused with the ability to execute in parallel.)

13.6.1 Side-effect goals—some terminology

For ease of discussion throughout the remainder of this chapter, an informal terminology is introduced. First, as previously mentioned there is a certain set of predefined, evaluable predicates in Prolog which when executed result in (or may result in) certain side effects to the normal execution. This set includes such evaluable predicates as *assert* and *retract, read* and *write, cut,* and so on. These predicates are referred to below as *side-effect built-ins.* A clause that contains a side-effect built-in is called a *side-effect clause,* and a procedure that contains at least one side-effect clause is called a *side-effect procedure.* A subgoal in a clause that calls a side-effect procedure is considered a side-effect goal, although it is more appropriately called a *potential side-effect goal.* Any clause containing such a potential side-effect goal is called a *potential side-effect clause,* or simply, a *side-effect clause.* A goal or subgoal that is neither a side-effect goal nor a potential side-effect goal is called a *pure goal* or *pure subgoal.* A clause that contains only pure subgoals is called a *pure clause,* and a procedure containing only pure clauses is a *pure procedure.* Clearly, a (potential) side-effect procedure may contain both side-effect clauses and pure clauses, and so may or may not produce a side effect when invoked. A potential side-effect goal may unify with the heads of both side-effect clauses and pure clauses, but a pure goal may call only pure procedures and thus may unify with only the heads of pure clauses.

A compiler can easily make a recursive traversal of the program source code and determine the type of every goal, clause, and procedure with respect to side effects. The required algorithm is similar to Mellish's automatic mode detection [Mellish 81] and to the static data-dependency analysis traversal algorithm of Chang [87] (see also O'Keefe [87]). Once the compiler has ascertained the type of each goal, clause, and procedure, the required synchronization code can be added to the RAP execution graph expressions, as described below.

13.6.2 Sequencing side-effect goals

As described in Sec. 13.2, successful execution of a Prolog query produces an AND-execution tree in which inner nodes represent rules and leaves represent either simple Prolog facts or built-in Prolog predicates. The successors of an internal node represent the subgoals of the rule. When considered as a list, in order, from left to right, the leaves of a tree represent all final subgoals that had to eventually be proven in order to prove the initial query. In Fig. 13.1*b*, this list is (a,b,c,d,e,f).

In general, consider the list of leaves in an execution tree that results from proving a query. If all the goals represented by these leaves are pure, then they can execute in any order. They may also possibly be executed simultaneously with full AND-parallelism (if they are all independent), or perhaps at least in any order using partial AND-parallelism (if they are at least partially independent). In any event, it is clear that the order of execution and the degree of parallelism are irrelevant with respect to the program's observable behavior since the program has no observable behavior except in the top-level reply to the query. Whether the program is executed in order or out of order, sequentially or with restricted AND-parallelism, the result is the same.

Consider now that some of the leaves represent side-effect goals, such as *write* predicates that write to a user terminal. Clearly, these write predicates must execute in their original, left-to-right, top-to-bottom order. If not, the resulting output stream might not appear the same as when the program is executed sequentially. So the write predicates must still execute in order. Since the remainder of the goals are pure goals, it might appear that they could execute in any order; but this is not so, as can be seen by considering the following example clause:

p(X) :- test(X), write(X).

It is tempting to compile this clause as:

p(X) :- (GPAR(X) test(X) write(X)).

But this would be wrong. On entry, if X is not ground, then the two subgoals execute sequentially, as in normal Prolog execution, and no problems can arise. But note that here, the first subgoal is intended to execute successfully before the write subgoal executes. If it fails, the write subgoal must not execute, for the write subgoal will exert an irrevocable side effect upon the program's observable behavior. If X is ground on entry, the GPAR test succeeds, and the two subgoals can execute in parallel; the write subgoal may precede the execution of the test subgoal, thereby leading to possible errors. This clause would then be correctly compiled as

p(X) :- (SEQ test(X) write(X)).

It can be seen by extension that all subgoals preceding a side-effect goal must execute successfully before the side-effect goal can execute (at least those that may potentially fail). What about pure goals following a side-effect goal? Can they execute in any order? Consider the following clause:

p(X) :- test(X), write(X), m(X).

Assume m is pure. Then if X is ground, m(X) can execute in any order whatsoever, even before either of the first two goals. Because m(X) has no side effects, it cannot affect the execution in any way whatsoever. Thus even if test(X) fails, m can still execute without changing the set of producible answers and observable behaviors. So this clause can be compiled as

p :- (SEQ   test(X)
            (GPAR(X) write(X) m(X))).

In fact, since it is certain that the write subgoal cannot affect the value of X, the clause can even be compiled as follows:

p :- (SEQ   test(X)
            (PAR write(X) m(X))).

Only the first of these last two expression formats can be used if the write(X) subgoal is replaced by a read(X) subgoal.

But consider the following clause:

p :- m, assert(n), n.

Assume subgoals m and n are pure; clearly assert is not. Because m may be checking some set of preconditions for the assert subgoal, m must execute successfully before the assert subgoal can execute, as above. But notice that the assert subgoal can affect the computation of the following pure subgoal n since it modifies the definition of n [Shapiro 86]. In this example then, the pure subgoal following the side-effect subgoal may execute only after the preceding side-effect subgoal has successfully completed. Although it is shown in Sec. 13.9 how to relax this constraint, for now the following rule is adopted:

Sequencing rule. All subgoals preceding a side-effect subgoal must complete successfully before the side-effect subgoal can execute. Further, all subgoals following a side-effect subgoal must not begin execution until the preceding side-effect subgoal has successfully completed.

Figure 13.5 illustrates this rule. Note that the leaves of the execution tree can be divided into alternating segments: pure, then a side-effect subgoal, then pure, then a side-effect subgoal, and so on. These segments must execute in order, but within a pure segment, the subgoals can execute in any order, and possibly in parallel. Because AND-parallelism is used within these segments, care must be taken to ensure that no two subgoals execute in parallel if they share a common, unbound variable; but this is easily accomplished with the normal RAP execution graph expressions.

13.7   Compiling Side-Effect Expressions

Given a clause to compile, if the clause is pure and thus contains only pure subgoals, these subgoals may execute in parallel, in any order, within the limits imposed by the normal execution graph expressions.

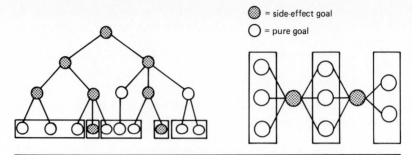

Figure 13.5   Alternating pure and side-effect segments.

In other words, the subgoals can execute in parallel except when they are not independent. The RAP graph expressions specify these conditions. But suppose one of the subgoals is a side-effect built-in. In particular, consider the clause

s2 :- a, s1, b.

where subgoals a and b are pure and s1 is a side-effect built-in. (For simplicity, assume also that these subgoals have no arguments and thus are independent.) Clearly, these three subgoals must execute sequentially (actually, as discussed above, we consider below cases where b can execute before s1, or even before a). Because these subgoals must execute sequentially, it is tempting to compile this clause into the graph-expression

s2 :- (SEQ a s1 b).

And indeed, this is correct to a point. But note that because s1 is a side-effect built-in, the s2 clause becomes a side-effect clause, and thus s2 becomes a side-effect procedure.
   Now consider the clause

s3 :- c, s2, d.

where c and d are again pure, but s2, from above, is a (potential) side-effect goal. Clearly then, the s3 clause is also a side-effect clause and s3 becomes a side-effect procedure. We can compile this clause in the same manner, which yields

s3 :- (SEQ c s2 d).

and if we then invoke the goal

?- s3.

all subgoals in the two clauses will execute sequentially and not in parallel.

Note that the resulting execution tree is that shown in Fig. 13.6. The left-to-right order of the leaves of the tree defines the normal execution sequence that is induced by a sequential Prolog. Note also that there are two pure subgoals preceding the single side-effect, leaf subgoal, and there are two following it. The two preceding it should be able to execute in parallel, as should the two that follow it, because they are clearly independent. The compiled clauses above do not allow this, but they are certainly correct and do provide a proper sequencing of side effects. But they unnecessarily limit the amount of parallelism. To correct this situation, the graph expressions need to be augmented with special synchronizing mechanisms. These mechanisms and their use are described below.

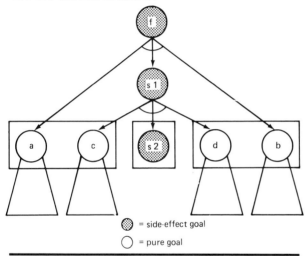

Figure 13.6   An AND-tree with totally sequential grouping.

13.7.1   Synchronization blocks

Simple two-part memory data structures are all that are required to implement the synchronization between the disjoint, parallel executing parts. These structures are called simply enough *synchronization blocks,* or *synch-blocks.* They can be implemented as two-word memory blocks, as shown in Fig. 13.7. The first word is used to maintain a

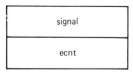

Figure 13.7   A synch-block.

count of expressions involved in the synchronization, while the second word is used for signaling the completion of a side-effect predicate.†

Five operations are defined for manipulating these synch-blocks: create, inc, dec, signal, and wait. Each of these is defined below.

First, *create* simply creates a synch-block in free memory. Two types of creation are allowed, one for creating input synch-blocks and one for creating output synch-blocks. The created synch-blocks are identical in both cases, but the fields are initialized to different values depending on which type of creation is invoked. The use of these two types of synch-blocks is discussed below.

A *create(sb,input)* operation creates a synch-block for the left part of the AND-execution tree preceding a side-effect predicate:

sb.ecnt : = 0 {indicates no unfinished, preceding, pure expressions}
sb.signal : = yes {indicates no unfinished, preceding, side-effect built-in}

A *create(sb,output)* operation creates a synch-block for the right part of the AND-execution tree following a side-effect predicate:

sb.ecnt : = 1 {indicates one unfinished, preceding side-effect built-in}
sb.signal : = no {indicates that the preceding side-effect built-in has not completed}

The expression-count (*ecnt*) field of a synch-block can be either incremented or decremented atomically. The statement *inc(sb)* is shorthand for

sb.ecnt : = sb.ecnt + 1;

where the addition must be performed atomically. Similarly, the statement *dec(sb)* is shorthand for the statement

sb.ecnt : = sb.ecnt − 1;

where the subtraction must also be performed atomically.

A signal field indicates whether the associated side-effect built-in has yet completed. A value of "no" indicates that the predicate has not yet completed, while a value of "yes" indicates that it has. A signal field may be changed to yes with the statement *signal(sb = yes)*.

A *wait(sb.ecnt = 0)* operation indicates that the expression-count field of the designated synch-block is to be checked for a value of zero. If the value is zero, the processor continues execution of the current expression. If the value is nonzero, the expression evaluation is suspended and the expression is placed in a suspended expression list. The manner in which suspended expressions are reawakened is discussed in Sec. 13.10.

Similarly, a *wait(sb.signal = yes)* operation tests the signal field of a synch-block for a value of yes. If a yes value is found, execution con-

---

†Actually, if not for soft side effects, a single word synch-block could be used.

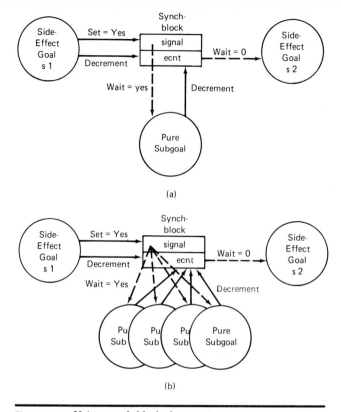

Figure 13.8 Using synch-blocks between segments.

tinues. Otherwise, execution is suspended, and the expression is placed in the suspended expression list.

13.7.2 Distributing synchronization blocks

Consider now a list of subgoals which are all pure except for a single subgoal in the middle of the list which has a side effect. As described above, the list must now be broken into three segments: (1) the pure subgoals preceding the side-effect subgoal, (2) the side-effect subgoal itself, and (3) the pure subgoals following the side-effect subgoal. These three segments must execute in order. When one segment finishes, it must somehow "signal" the following segment that it has completed. Similarly, each segment must wait for the preceding segment to signal it. Figure 13.8a illustrates the use of synch-blocks between segments to provide a correct sequencing of subgoals.

Clearly the synch-blocks must be properly distributed to the appropriate segments. To do this, the RAP execution graph expressions must be extended to carry along the required synch-blocks and pass them down the AND-execution tree in order to reach the appropriate segments. If not done properly, this can add significant additional overhead. In the technique discussed below, it is shown how this overhead is minimized.

Before considering the extensions to the RAP expressions, consider a single pure subgoal. It must (1) wait on the preceding side-effect goal to complete, and (2) it must signal the following side-effect goal when it itself completes. Call the preceding side-effect goal s1 and the following side-effect goal s2. The pure subgoal under consideration lies between s1 and s2. A single synch-block can be used by this pure subgoal to effect the required synchronization. The signal field of the synch-block will be used by the preceding side-effect goal s1 to signal its completion, and the ecnt field can be used by the pure subgoal to indicate to the following side-effect subgoal s2 when it has completed. This process is illustrated in Fig. 13.8*a*.

Generally, there are more than one pure subgoal between any two side-effect goals. They can all utilize a common synch-block, however, to synchronize their executions with the side-effect goals. Figure 13.8*b* illustrates this. It can be seen in this figure that the signal field can be a simple boolean value field, while the ecnt field must be an integer. Given this simple scheme, the number of side-effect goals can be increased; to do so, all that is required is to add one more synch-block between each pair of side-effect goals and to make this synch-block accessible to all intervening pure subgoals, as shown in Fig. 13.9. In this

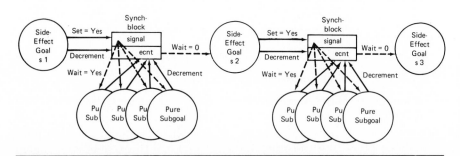

Figure 13.9   Using synch-blocks between several segments.

figure, it can be seen that a side-effect goal needs access to two synch-blocks—the preceding one and the following one. The preceding synch-block is called an *input* synch-block; the following synch-block is called an *output* synch-block. Pure goals need access to only one synch-block; this synch-block is called an *input* synch-block, although in fact it serves both an input and an output function (see the figures).

Now the extensions to the RAP expressions can be considered. These extended expressions represent code macros that are expanded in-line before actual code generation. In these expressions, *seg* stands for "side-effect goal", and *seb* stands for "side-effect built-in."

1. (pure(SI) e)   where e is a pure expression, gets expanded into the sequential code sequence

   wait(SI.signal = yes)
   e
   dec(SI)

2. (seb(SI,SO) s)   where s is a side-effect built-in or sequence of side-effect built-ins, gets expanded into the sequential code sequence

   wait(SI.ecnt = 0)
   s
   signal(SO.signal = yes)
   dec(SO)

If s is a sequence of side-effect built-ins, they execute sequentially.

3. (seg(SI,SO) p<args>)   where p is a potential side-effect goal but is not a side-effect built-in, gets expanded into

   call p(<args>,SI,SO)

4. f(<args>,SI,SO) :-   <graph expression for side-effect clause body>   If f is a side-effect procedure and this is a side-effect clause, then the clause head is extended to accept the two additional synchronization block parameters. All calls to f will have been extended to pass these two synch-blocks to f.

5. f(<args>,SI,SO) :- (pure(SI) e)   where f is a side-effect procedure but this clause is a pure-clause within f. Since this clause is pure, the clause body is pure, and a normal, simple RAP graph expression is compiled for the body. Because f is a side-effect procedure, all calls to f will be side-effect goals, and so they will have been augmented with the two extra synch-block parameters. The clause head must therefore be extended to accept these two extra parameters, even though only the SI synch-block is used. (Actually, an optimizing compiler can simply ignore the SO synch-block. It is included in the source code simply to maintain consistency between the use and declaration of a procedure.) Note, however, from the definition of a pure expression that neither synch-block is passed to any subgoal in the body expression. This is an efficiency advantage.

6. All pure procedures are compiled normally, without any induced overhead whatsoever.

These additional expressions, along with the statements for manipulating synch-blocks, are sufficient to ensure the correct sequencing of
pure code segments and side-effect goals.

Note that all nonpure expressions receive either one or two synch-
blocks. One is generally an input synch-block, denoted as SI, and one
is an output synch-block, denoted as SO. An input synch-block represents the preceding side-effect goal and the number of preceding pure
expressions that follow the preceding side-effect goal. The synch-
block's two components—ecnt and signal—represent these two pieces
of information. Since the synch-block must be distributed to the preceding side-effect goal, to each preceding pure expression, and to the
consuming side-effect goal, the ecnt field is used to count the number
of times the synch-block has been distributed. Each time the synch-
block is distributed, the ecnt field is incremented. When a pure expression or the preceding side-effect goal successfully completes, it
decrements the ecnt field. When the ecnt field reaches zero, all preceding pure expressions and the preceding side-effect goal have completed. At this point, the next side-effect goal can begin execution.
When a side-effect goal completes, it sets the signal field of its output
synch-block to yes, indicating that it has completed. At this point, the
following pure expressions which precede the next side-effect goal can
all begin execution.

13.8   Examples of Side-Effect Graph Expressions

To illustrate the handling of side-effect goals in the RAP model, this
section presents several examples of side-effect clauses and their corresponding side-effect graph expressions.

Example 1   First, consider the following clause and query:

f :- a, s, b.
?- f.

where a and b are pure but s is a side-effect built-in. Because s is a side-effect
built-in, the clause for f is a side-effect clause, and thus f is a side-effect procedure. The clause is therefore compiled as

f(SI,SO) :-
        (SEQ inc(SI)
              inc(SO)
              (PAR (pure(SI) a)
                    (seb(SI,SO) s)
                    (pure(SO)b))).

After macro expansion, this clause becomes

```
f(SI,SO) :-
    (SEQ inc(SI.ecnt)
          inc(SO.ecnt)
          (PAR (pure(SI) a)
                    wait(SI.signal = yes)
                    a
                    dec(SI.ecnt)
                (seb(SI,SO) s)
                    wait(SI.ecnt = 0)
                    s
                    signal(SO.signal = yes)
                    dec(SO.ecnt)
                (pure(SO) b)
                    wait(SO.signal = yes)
                    b
                    dec(SO.ecnt)))
```

Because f is a side-effect procedure, the query

?- f.

is compiled into the sequential code

```
(SEQ create(SI,input)
          SI.ecnt : =  0
          SI.signal : =  yes
      create(SO,output)
          SO.ecnt : =  1
          SO.signal : =  no
      call (f(SI,SO)).
```

When this query expression is executed, two synch-blocks are created and initialized. The SI signal field is initialized to yes as there is no unfinished, preceding side-effect goal, and the SI ecnt field is initialized to 0 since there are no unfinished, preceding pure expressions. The SO synch-block represents the side-effect goal and the following pure subgoals that precede the next side-effect subgoal, if any (here, there are none). The SO signal field is initialized to no since the side-effect goal s has not yet completed; the ecnt field is set to 1, representing the unfinished, preceding side-effect goal, namely f.

Following creation and initialization of the synch-blocks, the subgoal call is executed, and the procedure for f is entered. Upon entry, both synch-blocks have their ecnt fields incremented. This is because the clause has both a left and a right pure part, and because the corresponding synch-blocks will be passed into these expressions. These expressions must be counted before the expressions are entered and the synch-blocks passed in. This explains why the creation and incrementing occur sequentially before the parallel subgoal expressions begin.

Then the PAR expression is entered. Upon entry, the SI synch-block has SI.ecnt = 1 and SI.signal = yes, while the SO synch-block has SO.ecnt = 2 and SO.signal = no. Because a PAR expression was entered, all three subexpressions can begin executing in parallel. The second expression, the seb expression, suspends since SI.ecnt ≠ 0, and the third expression suspends since SO.signal ≠ yes. Only the first expression can execute since SI.signal = yes. Thus subgoal a begins execution. When and if a successfully completes, SI.ecnt is decremented to 0. This is the condition the second expression is awaiting. When SI.ecnt is found to be zero, the side-effect subgoal s begins execution. When and if it successfully completes, SO.signal is set to yes, and SO.ecnt is decremented to 1. When SO.signal is found to be yes, the third subgoal b can begin execution. Upon successful completion of b, SO.ecnt is decremented to 0. Since all three subexpressions completed successfully, the entire expression has completed and control returns to the top-level query processor. Both synch-blocks have their signal fields set to yes and their ecnt fields set to 0, indicating completion of all subgoals. (It should be obvious that the PAR expression can be replaced here by the more efficient SEQ expression. As described in Sec. 13.9, however, soft side effects benefit from the PAR expression. In order to hopefully minimize confusion, only PAR expressions are used throughout the remainder of this chapter.)

Note that subgoal a may invoke an arbitrarily complex subtree of subgoals, one perhaps containing several thousands of nested subgoals. But these subgoals are all pure and so are compiled into normal execution graph expressions. These expressions do not have to consider any synch-blocks, and no synch-blocks are passed in as parameters. Thus no overhead is introduced into this subtree for the required synchronization. The same is true for the third subgoal b. In fact, the only operations on the synch-blocks are those shown explicitly in the compiled expression above. It can be seen then that the root node of a pure subtree in an AND-execution tree handles the synch-block manipulation for the entire pure subtree below it. No overhead is introduced into the subtree except at the root node, and this overhead is minimal. This low overhead of passing and manipulating synch-blocks is a significant advantage of the RAP model.

If you consider the resulting macroexpanded code above, it can be seen that an optimizing compiler can easily make improvements. For example, reconsider the complete macroexpanded code for the clause

f :- a, s, b.

It is

```
f(SI,SO) :-
        (SEQ inc(SI.ecnt)
             inc(SO.ecnt)
             (PAR (pure(SI) a)
                     wait(SI.signal = yes)
                     a
                     dec(SI.ecnt)
                  (seb(SI,SO) s)
                     wait(SI.ecnt = 0)
                     s
                     signal(SO.signal = yes)
                     dec(SO.ecnt)
                  (pure(SO) b)
                     wait(SO.signal = yes)
                     b
                     dec(SO.ecnt)))
```

Careful consideration of this code shows that certain instructions can be omitted due to the fact that s is a side-effect built-in and that the PAR expression can be replaced by a SEQ expression. In the code below, the boldface parts are the required parts; the remainder can be optimized away:

```
f(SI,SO) :-
      (SEQ inc(SI.ecnt)
            inc(SO.ecnt)
            (PAR (pure(SI) a)
                        wait(SI.signal = yes)
                        a
                        dec(SI.ecnt)
            (seb(SI,SO) s)
                        wait(SI.ecnt = 0)
                        s
                        signal(SO.signal = yes)
                        dec(SO.ecnt)
            (pure(SO) b)
                        wait(SO.signal = yes)
                        b
                        dec(SO.ecnt)))
```

Extracting only the above boldface parts, the resulting optimized code is simply

```
f(SI,SO) :-
      (SEQ wait(SI.signal = yes)
            a
            wait(SI.ecnt = 0)
            s
            signal(SO.signal = yes)
            b
            dec(SO.ecnt))
```

The resulting optimized code is clearly more efficient. However, since the unoptimized code is clearly correct as well and since it easier to represent, the unoptimized code sequences are used throughout the remainder of this chapter. Additional optimization techniques based on data-dependency analysis are discussed in DeGroot [88a].

Example 2 Now consider the following query and two clauses:

```
?- f.
f :- a, s1, b.
s1 :- c, s2, d.
```

where subgoals a, b, c, and d are pure, and s2 is a side-effect built-in. Then s1 is a side-effect procedure, making f a side-effect procedure as well. As before, the query is compiled into

```
(SEQ create(SI,input)
      create(SO,output)
      call f(SI,SO)).
```

The two clauses are compiled nearly identically as

```
f(SI,SO) :- (SEQ inc(SI)
                 inc(SO)
                 (PAR (pure(SI) a)
                      (seg(SI,SO)s1)
                      (pure(SO) b))).†
s1(SI,SO) :-
        (SEQ inc(SI)
             inc(SO)
             (PAR (pure(SI) c)
                  (seb(SI,SO) s2)
                  (pure(SO) d))).
```

This example is possibly more interesting. Once again, when the query is activated, both an input and an output synch-block are created. Then the side-effect procedure f is called with these two synch-blocks, and the clause for f is entered. Upon entry, SI.ecnt is incremented to 1, counting the preceding pure expression for a, and SO.ecnt is incremented to 2, counting the following pure expression for b and the nested side-effect built-in. The PAR expression is then entered.

The third subexpression, for b, cannot execute since SO.signal≠yes. But the first two subexpressions can begin parallel execution. Suppose they do. The first subexpression invokes a pure execution subtree for subgoal a which begins immediate execution and does so without any overhead of the synchronization mechanism. The second subexpression begins parallel execution and immediately calls the side-effect procedure s1, passing in the modified input and output synch-blocks, SI and SO. This call results in the clause for s1 being executed.

When this clause begins execution, both synch-blocks are again incremented, thereby counting the left and right pure subexpressions in the clause. Now, SI.ecnt = 2 and SO.ecnt = 3, and SI.signal = yes and SO.signal = no. Consequently, when the PAR expression is entered, only the first subexpression can begin execution. The second and third subexpressions must suspend. When the first subexpression, for c, begins execution, c may also invoke an arbitrarily complex execution subtree. Note that this subtree can execute in parallel with the subtree invoked by subgoal a.

Before the side-effect subgoal s2 can execute, both subgoals a and b must complete. If the execution subtrees for a and b are executed successfully, control returns to the pure subexpressions containing them. These subexpressions then proceed to decrement the SI.ecnt field. Since SI.ecnt = 2 at this time, the two decrementings set SI.ecnt = 0. Because both subexpressions may be executing in parallel and may possibly attempt to simultaneously decrement SI.ecnt, the decrement operation must be atomic, using semaphores, test-and-set instructions, replace-add instructions, or others. Eventually, however, SI.ecnt = 0.

At that point, the second subexpression of the s1 clause can begin execution. This subexpression, with its macro expansion, is

```
(seb(SI,SO) s2)
        wait(SI.ecnt = 0)
        s2
        signal(SO.signal = yes)
        dec(SO)
```

---

†As just shown, the code for this clause can actually be significantly optimized.

After the wait instruction succeeds, the side-effect built-in s2 can execute. If successful, SO.signal is set to yes to indicate its completion to all following pure subgoal expressions, and SO.ecnt is decremented to 2.

When SO.signal is set to yes, the two subexpressions

(pure(SO) b)
     wait(SO.signal = yes)
     b
     dec(SO.ecnt)

in the clause for f, and

(pure(SO) d)
     wait(SO.signal = yes)
     d
     dec(SO.ecnt)

in the clause for s1, can both begin execution. This allows the two subgoals b and d to invoke their pure execution subtrees in parallel, and again without any overhead of the synchronization mechanism. Figure 13.10 illustrates the result-

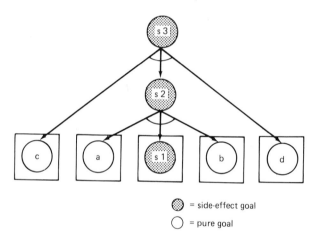

Figure 13.10   An AND-tree with parallel execution grouping.

ing parallel execution. Compare it with the sequential execution of Fig. 13.6, and compare the above execution expressions with the expressions in Sec. 13.7.

This example shows how, in a sequence of nested clauses, pure subgoals preceding a side-effect goal are all allowed to execute in parallel, then the side-effect built-in executes, and then the following pure subgoals are allowed to execute in parallel. Obviously, this example extends to nested clauses of any depth.

Example 3   As mentioned before, a side-effect procedure can contain both side-effect clauses and pure clauses. When a pure clause is contained within a side-effect procedure, it is compiled simply as follows:

f(SI,SO) :-
    (pure(SI) e).
        wait(SI.signal = yes)
        e
        dec(SI.ecnt)

Example 4   Consider the following example clauses and their compilations. In each clause, let a, b, and c be pure subgoals; let s1 and s2 be side-effect built-ins; and let g1 and g2 be non-built-in, side-effect subgoals. The clause

f :- a, s1, s2, b.

is compiled as

f(SI,SO) :-
    inc(SI.ecnt)
    inc(SO.ecnt)
    (PAR (pure(SI) a)
        (seb(SI,SO) s1 s2)
        (pure(SO) b)).

Here, the two side-effect built-ins execute sequentially as required.
The clause

f :- a, g1, b, g2, c.

is compiled into

f(SI,SO) :-
    create(SM,output)
    inc(SI.ecnt)
    inc(SM.ecnt)
    inc(SO.ecnt)
    (PAR (pure(SI) a)
        (seg(SI,SM) g1)
        (pure(SM) b)
        (seg(SM,SO) g2)
        (pure(SO) c)).

This example shows that some synch-blocks are created within a clause and not just at the query level. An optimizing compiler can combine the creation of SM with the incrementing of SM.ecnt.

Example 5   As discussed above, a side-effect clause that contains only a side-effect built-in can be compiled with a SEQ expression rather than with a PAR expression. The resulting code can even be highly optimized. When the side-effect goal is not a built-in, however, the PAR expression must be used in order to extract greater parallelism. Consider a complex clause containing both side-effect goals and side-effect built-ins:

f :- a, g1, b, s1, c, g2, d.

where, as before, a, b, c, and d are pure subgoals, g1 and g2 are side-effect subgoals (but not built-ins), and s1 is a side-effect built-in. This clause can be compiled as

```
f(SI,SO) :-
        create(SM1,output)
        create(SM2,output)
        inc(SI.ecnt)
        inc(SO.ecnt)
        inc(SM1.ecnt)
        inc(SM2.ecnt)
        (SEQ (PAR (pure(SI) a)
                   seg(SI,SM1) g1)
                  (pure(SM1) b))
              (seb(SM1,SM2) s1)
              (PAR (pure(SM2) c)
                   (seg(SM1,SO) g2)
                   (pure(SO) d))).
```

As above, significant code optimizations can be performed by an optimizing compiler. The entire clause body can instead be wrapped in a single PAR expression.

Example 6   Two examples are now shown for clauses that do not have pure parts preceding or following a side-effect goal. First, the clause

f :- a, s1.

is compiled as

```
f(SI,SO) :-
        inc(SI)
        (PAR (pure(SI) a)
              (seg(SI,SO) s1)).
```

The clause

f :- s1, b.

is compiled as

```
f(SI,SO) :-
        inc(SO)
        (PAR (seg(SI,SO) s1)
              (pure(SO) b)).
```

Example 7   Finally, consider an example in which both the side-effect expressions and independence-determination expressions are combined. Consider the clause

f(X) :- a(X), s(X), b(X), c(X).

Let a, b, and c be pure subgoals and s be a non-built-in, side-effect subgoal. This clause is compiled as

```
f(X,SI,SO) :-
    (SEQ inc(SI)
        inc(SO)
        (GPAR(X)
        (pure(SI)
        a(X))
        (GPAR(X)
        (seg(SI,SO) s(X))
        (pure(SO)
        (GPAR(X) b(X) c(X))) ))).
```

Here, if f is entered with X ground, all four subgoals will begin parallel execution. The additional side-effect synchronization code, however, will ensure that
the four subgoals, including all their descendant subgoals, execute in the proper
sequence. If X is not ground on entry, a executes first, sequentially. Subgoals s,
b, and c, must wait. In this case, s cannot be allowed to begin expansion into its
subtree, for any pure subgoals in the leftmost part of its tree must now wait for
a's subtree to complete and hopefully present a ground value for X. It can be
seen then that the normal RAP execution graph expressions provide data synchronization, while the synch-block–management code extensions provide side-
effect synchronization.

13.9   Soft Side-Effect Built-ins

It is possible to divide the set of side-effect built-ins into *soft side effects,*
those that cannot affect the following computation, and *hard side effects,*
those that can. Certainly, a write subgoal cannot affect the execution of
the following pure subgoals and so it is a soft side-effect goal. An assert
subgoal, however, may very well affect the following execution. Given
these definitions, the seb expression defined above is for hard side-effect
subgoals. A soft side-effect built-in s might be compiled as

```
(soft-seb(SI,SO) s)
    signal(SO.signal = yes)
    wait(SI.ecnt = 0)
    s
    dec(SO)
```

Here, because the signal operation occurs before the side-effect
subgoal s begins execution, the pure subgoals following s can immediately begin execution. The side-effect goals still execute in sequential
order, however, as required, and still, no-side-effect goal can execute
until all preceding goals have completed.

But there is no sense in waiting until just before s begins execution to
set the signal field to yes; instead, it can be set at the creation of the
synch-block. To see how, note that once side-effect built-ins are classified
as either hard or soft, the same classification applies to clauses and procedures. Then we need to be able to create both hard and soft synch-
blocks. A new *create_soft* operation is defined: *create_soft(sb,output)*

creates an output synch-block for a soft side-effect expression:

sb.ecnt : = 1; {indicates to the following side-effect goal that there
              is at least one preceding, incomplete side-effect goal,
              namely, the soft one for which this synch-block is
              being created}
sb.signal : = yes; {indicates to all following pure expressions that
                they do not have to wait on this soft-side effect
                goal}

The corresponding definition of *soft-seb* is then:

```
(soft-seb(SI,SO) s)
      wait(SI.ecnt = 0)
      s
      dec(SO)
```

The definition of *soft-seg* remains the same as *seg*. A clause containing both hard and soft side effects is considered to have only hard side effects. Now consider the following example:

```
f :- a, s1, b.
s1 :- d, write(foo), e.
?- f.
```

Let a, b, d, and e be pure subgoals. Clearly, write(foo) is a soft side-effect subgoal, and thus s1 and f are a soft side-effect procedures. The query is compiled as

```
?-
create(SI,input)
      SI.ecnt : =  0;
      SI.signal : =  yes;
create-soft(SO,output)
      SO.ecnt : =  1;
      SO.signal : =  yes;
call f(SI,SO).
```

The two clauses would be compiled as

```
f :- a, s1, b.
f(SI,SO) :-
      (SEQ inc(SI)
            inc(SO)
            (PAR (pure(SI) a)
                  (soft-seg(SI,SO) s1)
                  (pure(SO) b))).
s1 :- d, write(foo), e.
s1(SI,SO) :-
      (SEQ inc(SI)
            inc(SO)
            (PAR (pure(SI) d)
```

(soft-seb(SI,SO) write(foo))
(pure(SO) e)).

This will allow all of the pure subgoals a, b, d, and e to execute in parallel. However, the write subgoal can execute only when both a and b have successfully completed, as required.

Soft side-effect goals are those that cannot affect the computation of their following pure subgoals; as a consequence, the following pure subgoals do not have to wait for the preceding soft side-effect goal to complete. However, two or more soft side-effect subgoals must still maintain their proper sequence. For example, every read goal can be properly sequenced with the normal execution graph expressions, as demonstrated above. However, two read subgoals must not be allowed to execute out of order. The soft side-effect control constructs ensure that this does not occur.

As explained above, if a procedure contains both hard and soft side-effect subgoals, all are treated as hard side effects. This may possibly be improved. Other optimizations are possible and constitute future research efforts. For example, two reads from two different files do not need to be sequenced. Also, reads followed by writes may not need to be sequenced with synch-blocks, as the normal graph expressions will likely ensure correct sequencing.

13.10 Suspending Expression Execution

When a wait instruction is executed in an expression, a particular condition is checked. If the condition exists, execution of the expression may continue. If the condition does not exist, the expression execution must suspend. Later, when and if the condition becomes true, the suspended expressions may resume execution.

Clearly there must be an execution mechanism capable of providing this service. Many are possible. One possible mechanism is a simple *suspended expression list*. When an expression checks for a condition and finds it false, the expression is placed on the suspended expression list, and the processor looks for another expression to execute. As long as the processor has active expressions to execute, it will not be idle, and system utilization will not suffer. If a condition required by a suspended expression becomes true while the processor is executing other expressions, the condition does not need to be noted by the waiting processor. But when a processor runs out of active expressions to execute, it can then make a pass through the suspended expression list, rechecking the required conditions for each suspended expression. As soon as one condition is found to be true, execution of the associated expression can resume. If no condition is found to be true, the processor has run out of ex-

pressions to execute, and it can then volunteer to assist other processors in executing their overload of active expressions, if any. Although this model is a polling model, it will not flood the
communication system with condition-checking memory accesses
except when a processor is idle and no other processor will send it
additional work to do. But in such cases, the overall system activity
will most likely be low, and the communication network will thus
likely be underutilized. Other architectural implications of the required support mechanisms can be found in Hermenegildo [87].

13.11   Summary

An AND-parallel execution model for Prolog has been presented;
this model is called the Restricted AND-Parallelism (RAP) model.
A technique for extending the RAP model to handle side-effect computations has also been described. This technique ensures that the
normal, observable sequence of side effects that would occur in a
traditional, sequential execution of a Prolog program is retained
within the restricted AND-parallel execution of the same program.
To handle side effects within the RAP model, a new set of expressions is introduced into the execution graph expression language.
These additional expressions are sufficient to ensure proper sequencing of side effects.

The only data structures required are two-word synch-blocks. The
extended execution expressions operate on these synch-blocks to properly serialize the side-effect goals and the intervening pure subgoals.
The model described actually results in little additional overhead, as
the synch-blocks are distributed down into the AND-tree only as far
as required. Possible compiler optimizations were presented to further
reduce the overhead, and side-effect goals were divided into hard side
effects and soft side effects.

It should be pointed out that the model is not yet complete. At
present, the backtracking semantics and an efficient implementation
model are being investigated. An automatic graph expression compiler is also being extended to incorporate the side-effect expressions
[DeGroot 88a].

Bibliography

[Carlton 88]   M. Carlton and P. Van Roy. *A Distributed Prolog System with AND-Parallelism.* Department of EECS, University of California at Berkeley, CA, 1988.

[Chang 85]   J.-H. Chang, A. Despain, and D. DeGroot. "AND-Parallelism of Logic Programs Based on a Static Data-Dependency Analysis." *Proc. Spring Compcon 85,* pp. 218–225, 1985.

[Clark 86]   K. Clark and S. Gregory. "PARLOG: Parallel Programming in Logic." *ACM Trans. Programming Languages and Systems*, pp. 1–49, January 1986.

[Conery 81]   J. Conery and D. Kibler. "Parallel Interpretation of Logic Programs." *Proc. Conference on Functional Programming Languages and Computer Architecture*, pp. 163–170, ACM, New York, 1981.

[Conery 87]   J. Conery. *Parallel Execution of Logic Programs*. Kluwer Academic Publishers, Hingham, MA, 1987.

[Crammond 85]   J. Crammond. "A Comparative Study of Unification Algorithms for OR-Parallel Execution of Logic Languages." *Proc. 1985 International Conference on Parallel Processing*, pp. 131–138, 1985.

[DeGroot 84]   D. DeGroot. "Restricted AND-Parallelism." *Proc. of the International Conference on Fifth Generation Computer Systems 1984*, pp. 471–478, North Holland, 1984.

[DeGroot 85]   D. DeGroot and J.-H. Chang. "A Comparison of Two AND-Parallel Execution Models." *Hardware and Software Components and Architectures for the 5th Generation*, AFCET Informatique, pp. 271–280, Paris, March 1985.

[DeGroot 87]   D. DeGroot. "Restricted AND-Parallelism and Side Effects." *Proc. Symposium on Logic Programming*, San Francisco, 1987.

[DeGroot 88*a*]   D. DeGroot. "A Technique for Compiling Restricted AND-Parallelism Execution Graph Expressions." *Proc. 1987 International Supercomputing Conference*, Athens, June 8–12, 1987.

[DeGroot 88*b*]   D. DeGroot. "AND-Parallelism in Logic Programs." In G. Rabbat (ed). *Advanced Semiconductor Technology and Computer Systems*, Van Nostrand Reinhold, New York, 1988.

[Hermenegildo 87]   M. Hermenegildo. *A Restricted AND-Parallel Execution Model and Abstract Machine for Prolog Programs*, Kluwer Academic Press, Hingham, MA, 1987.

[Kluzniak 84]   F. Kluzniak and S. Szpakowicz. *Prolog for Programmers*, Academic Press, New York, 1984.

[Lloyd 84]   J. Lloyd. *Foundations of Logic Programming*, Springer-Verlag, New York, 1984.

[Mellish 81]   C. Mellish. *The Automatic Generation of Mode Declarations for Prolog Programs*. DAI Res. Paper 163, Department of Artificial Intelligence, University of Edinburgh, August 1981.

[O'Keefe 87]   R. O'Keefe. A Prolog Program to Detect Side-Effect Procedures. Personal correspondence. Quintus Computer Systems, Mountain View, CA, May 1987.

[Pollard 81]   G.H. Pollard. *Parallel Execution of Horn Clause Programs*. Ph.D. dissertation, University of London, Imperial College of Science and Technology, United Kingdom, 1981.

[Shapiro 83]   E. Shapiro. *A Subset of Concurrent Prolog and Its Interpreter*. ICOT Tech. Rep. TR-003, ICOT, Tokyo, February 1983.

[Shapiro 86]   E. Shapiro. *The Art of Prolog*, MIT Press, Cambridge, MA, 1986.

[Ueda 87]   K. Ueda. *Guarded Horn Clauses*, MIT Press, Cambridge, MA, 1987.

[Warren 80]   D.H.D. Warren. "Efficient Processing of Interactive Relational Database Queries Expressed in Logic." *Proc. 7th International Conference on Very Large Data Bases*, pp. 181–203, July 1980.

[Warren 83]   D.H.D. Warren. *An Abstract Prolog Instruction Set*. Tech. Note 309, SRI International, Menlo Park, CA, October 1983.

[Wise 86]   M. Wise. *Prolog Multiprocessors*, Prentice-Hall, Englewood Cliffs, NJ, 1986.

New Computing Technologies

Dataflow
Computation for
Artificial Intelligence

Jack B. Dennis

MIT Laboratory for Computer Science, Cambridge, MA

14.1 Introduction

Dataflow computation, conceived 20 years ago, has reached maturity and is ready for fruitful application, especially in the area of large-scale scientific computation. Many scientific computations have parts that are very regular—a rule of calculation is applied uniformly to all elements of a large data array, for example. Such computations are easily mapped onto the processing elements of a computer so each processor is kept fully busy doing productive work.

Nevertheless, computational problems are frequently irregular. Often many subproblems must be solved, each requiring an amount of calculation determined by data generated during program execution. Beyond the classic number-crunching scientific applications, problems of symbol manipulation usually involve treelike data structures that divide information into irregular units. The algorithms applied to these data structures are frequently "divide-and-conquer" methods or heuristic search strategies. The rules of calculation are applied in a number of instances that depends on the subtree being processed and therefore varies greatly with the actual data of the problem.

These characteristics are typical of the kinds of computations regarded as part of the artificial intelligence milieu. Our goal in this study is to illustrate how such computations can be performed efficiently on a dataflow computer. Because each dataflow processing element can exploit concurrency in computations through fully overlapped execution of instructions, and because interprocessor communication is done with no software overhead, a large dataflow multiprocessor offers a speedup of hundreds of times over what is currently possible with single processor machines of conventional organization. The advantage of dataflow is even greater for artificial intelligence problems than for number-crunching calculations; the latter often gain significant advantage from the vector pipelined capabilities of contemporary supercomputers, whereas other problems have little to gain from vector or array processing.

The computations of artificial intelligence are generally thought of as purely symbolic—as not involving numerical computation in any significant way. In contrast, the example we study in this chapter, speech recognition by maximum likelihood analysis, is both an illustration of artificial intelligence programming techniques and an application for high-performance numerical computation. Our goal is to show how a process for speech recognition, which involves the backtracking search characteristic of many artificial intelligence computations, can be executed very efficiently on a static dataflow computer. We will see that a static dataflow multiprocessor with 64 processing elements can be expected to achieve better than 300 MFLOPS performance in the speech recognition task—a speedup of roughly a hundred over present capabilities. This could bring quality real-time speech recognition much closer to reality.

The areas of symbol manipulation and heuristic search are application domains for which the static dataflow architecture has been thought to be too limited. The problems seem to require handling of recursion, backtrack programming, and load balancing—aspects of computing that have no specific support in the dataflow computer. It is commonly thought that only the more dynamic dataflow architectures have the generality of structure to support such computations. In fact, the material presented here shows how the problems of backtrack programming and load balancing can be solved for a simple dataflow multiprocessor. This is done within the context of speech recognition. The implementation of recursive processes such as divide-and-conquer algorithms on dataflow multiprocessors will be the subject of another publication.

We begin with a brief introduction to the principles of dataflow computation as developed under my direction at the MIT Laboratory for Computer Science [Dennis 87a]. Next, we note the nature of artificial intelligence computations and justify our concentration on the principles and techniques of heuristic search. We then present the sentence recognition task which serves as our illustrative problem. We have chosen the statistical approach used by the group led by Dr. Jelinek at the IBM Research Center [Jelinek 82, Bahl 83]. In the IBM methodology, speech generation and recognition processes are viewed as in statistical communication theory: statistical models are used to characterize the order of word appearances in sentences and the phonetic construction of individual words; and a backtracking search procedure is used to construct the sentence most likely to have been spoken.

Running the recognizer efficiently on a parallel processor requires a way of implementing the heuristic search process in parallel. Such a search process generates a set of candidates that represent the possible avenues for continued search. The key ingredient is the means for holding and organizing the pool of candidates. We introduce the *parallel priority queue* as a useful general mechanism for implementing the pool and for distributing the workload among the processing elements of a parallel computer. A major contribution of this study is an explanation of how the parallel priority queue can be implemented efficiently on a static dataflow multiprocessor.

Another important consideration arises because the statistical databases that drive the recognition process are very large. It is necessary to support access by a dataflow processing element to parts of the database stored at other processing elements. We describe a simple and efficient scheme for implementing remote access to a global database on the dataflow multiprocessor. Our scheme supports more throughput than is possible with other multiprocessor architectures. Conventional shared-memory multiprocessors suffer from expensive switching hardware and processor waiting time that becomes worse as the number of processor is increased; and distributed multiprocessor systems based on conventional processors suffer from the software overhead of message handling.

Next, we give a projection of the performance that may be expected when the speech recognition task is run on the dataflow multiprocessor. Using estimated parameters of the recognition process, we conclude that about 75 percent of the machine's instruction execution capacity and nearly two-thirds of the machine's floating-point addition capability will be utilized. This indicates a speedup factor of at least 100 over presently available general-purpose computers.

14.2   Dataflow Computation

The dataflow model of computation has been under study in the Computation Structures Group of the MIT Laboratory for Computer Science since 1966. In the dataflow model [Dennis 74], data values involved in a computation are carried by *tokens* placed on the arcs of a graph. The nodes of the graph are *actors* which respond to the presence of tokens on their input arcs by "firing", applying an operator to the values carried by the input tokens. The results are carried by tokens placed on each output arc of the actor. In the *static* dataflow model an arc may carry no more than one token. Other dataflow models allow more general behavior, for example, the *tagged token* model espoused by [Arvind 78]. The tagged-token model has been developed into an interesting architecture proposal [Arvind 80, 81]. It has been used by the Manchester University group as the basis for their experimental machine [Watson 82] and is also the basis of a more modern design implemented at the Electrotechnical Laboratory in Japan [Yuba 84].

In a dataflow model there is no notion of sequential flow of control as in conventional computers. Many actors of a dataflow graph may be ready to fire at the same time. To the extent permitted by the computational algorithm, this opens the possibility of large-scale parallelism in machines designed to execute programs represented by dataflow graphs—machines with hundreds or thousands of dataflow processing elements.

The general organization of a dataflow computer is shown in Fig. 14.1. There are many *processing elements* and a *packet routing network* that allows any processing element to send information packets to any other. The organization also includes *array memory* units for holding the large databases of information required in many problems, whether scientific, commercial, or artificial intelligence. The routing network provides a path for any processing element to send a result of instruction execution to serve as an instruction operand in any other processing element. Because throughput of the network is more important than latency, a routing network that has O (log n) stages and uses a store-and-forward protocol is very efficient, even with large numbers of processing elements.

The dataflow multiprocessor chosen for the present study has evolved from work on static dataflow architecture done at the MIT

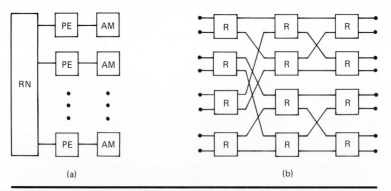

(a)   (b)

Figure 14.1   General organization of a dataflow computer. (*a*) Processing elements (PEs) with local array memories (AM) interconnected by a packet routing network (RN); (*b*) routing network for eight PEs having three stages each consisting of four 2×2 packet-routing modules R.

Laboratory for Computer Science [Dennis 80, 84] and is described in greater detail in Dennis [87b]. In this architecture each dataflow instruction is signaled by the completion of specific predecessor instructions and is activated when the right number of signals have been counted. The signals indicate that the data on which the instruction will operate are available at specific memory locations. At any time there can be at most one instance of execution of an instruction.

Each processing element has storage for dataflow instructions, data memory for the values on which instructions operate, functional units capable of performing the basic scalar operations, and a mechanism for controlling activation of instructions. Its principles of operation are illustrated in Fig. 14.2a. The processor holds a collection of dataflow instructions, some of which are marked as ready for execution. Instructions selected for execution are inserted into an *execution pipeline* by "fire" signals. The execution pipeline is similar to the instruction execution units of some conventional central processors and has stages for address calculation, operand fetch, operator application, and storage of results. Upon completion of its execution, an instruction generates a "done" signal that gives notice to successor instructions, possibly marking some of them as ready for execution.

The instruction format corresponding to this processing element structure (Fig. 14.2b) has three parts: the *execution part* specifies the operation to be performed, the data to be used, and the disposition of the result; the *signaling part* lists the successor instructions and specifies

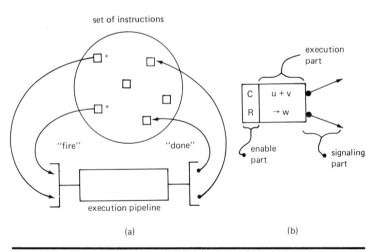

Figure 14.2 Elements of dataflow instruction execution. (a) Illustration showing how "fire" signals initiate execution of enabled instructions by feeding their indices to an instruction execution pipeline, and how "done" signals generated by instruction completion lead to the enabling of successor instructions; (b) dataflow instruction format showing execution part, signaling part, and enable part.

which of these are to be signaled upon instruction completion; and the *enable part* specifies how many signals must be received before the instruction is ready to fire. In the enable part, the C field indicates the number of signals that must yet be received from other instructions to make the instruction ready for execution; it decreases by one for each signal received. The R field specifies the count to be restored to C when the instruction is executed.

This description shows how the dataflow processing element is able to achieve sustained operation at nearly full performance. Scalar parallelism in the application task is sufficient to keep the execution pipeline filled with productive work. No other general-purpose architecture has been able to achieve this goal.

We see that a program represented as dataflow machine code is a directed graph in which the nodes are instructions and the arcs represent the sequencing information contained in the signaling parts of instructions. The group of four dataflow instructions shown in Fig. 14.3 illustrates an important principle of dataflow computing, that of *pipelining in dataflow programs*. The four instructions form three pipeline stages as labeled in the figure. Once stage 1 has executed, storing a value of t in data memory, signals are sent to the instructions of stage 2, indicating that a new value for t is available. Once the two instructions of stage 2 have executed, values of u and v have been stored and the value of t has been used. Then the instructions of stage 2 send signals to stage 3 to say that the values it needs are ready, and they also send signals to stage 1 to say that stage 1 may now store a next value for t. In this way, stage 2 can fire alternately with stages 1 and 3, processing streams of data in the same manner as a hardware pipeline. The reader may verify that the count and reset fields of the instructions have been properly specified.

It is important to know how often repeated execution of the instruc-

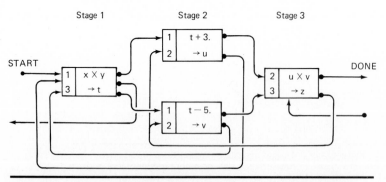

Figure 14.3   A group of four dataflow instructions arranged to operate as a software pipeline. In applications dataflow pipelines may contain hundreds or thousands of instructions.

tions of a dataflow pipeline may occur. This rate is determined by the longest simple cycle of instructions in the pipeline graph. The time interval taken by the complete execution of any one instruction is called the *instruction execution period*. This is the time interval from the instant an instruction becomes enabled to the time that signals have been delivered to its successor and predecessor instructions. The instruction execution period will depend on design details of the processing element and will vary for different classes of instructions. Present estimates based on preliminary designs for the dataflow processing element indicate that a 3- to 5-μs period may be expected. If the limiting cycles of a pipelined code block contain no more than three dataflow instructions, then the repetition interval of the pipeline may be expected to be about 10μ s, giving a maximum processing rate of 100 kHz for the pipeline. Given the 40-MHz rate estimated for the instruction execution pipeline, this figure implies that 400 instructions must be active concurrently at all times to keep the processor fully utilized. This should not be regarded as slow. At this rate a processing element holding 400 instructions in pipelined code would be running at the full 40 MIPS performance. If half of these instructions were floating-point operations, then 20 MFLOPS performance would be achieved.

How pipelined dataflow machine code supports high-performance numerical computation has been shown for an aerodynamic simulation code by Dennis [1987*b*]. In this and other scientific computations, most of the work may be viewed as the construction of array values. The form of these constructions is illustrated by the following program fragment written in the functional programming language VAL [Ackerman 79].

```
forall i in [1, n]
 X : =  if i = 1 then A[i]
        elseif i = n then A[n]
        else 0.5 * (A[i − 1] + A[i + 1])
        endif;
    construct X
    endall
```

For each value of i the body of this **forall** expression defines a value of X that is the ith element of the resulting array value. On the dataflow processing element, this computation could be carried out by reading the elements of A from the array memory, performing the evaluations of the conditional expression in a dataflow pipeline, and storing the elements of the constructed array in the array memory. For further details of dataflow computing for large-scale scientific applications, the reader is referred to Dennis [84, 87], which present detailed analyses of a global weather model and aerodynamic simulation, respectively.

14.3   Artificial Intelligence

The field of artificial intelligence has no simple characterization. One popular way of describing artificial intelligence is that it concerns the use of computers to perform tasks thought of as uniquely human. Traditionally, these include cognitive skills, problem solving, and organizing information for decision making. This notion runs immediately into the dilemma that once a challenging task, playing chess for example, has been mastered by the computer, it is no longer a uniquely human task. Consequently, we choose to regard artificial intelligence as *the study of problem solving by automatic means*. Artificial intelligence is the set of viewpoints, tools, and techniques used in the practice of computer-mediated problem solving [Barr 81, Nilsson 80].

The problem-solving approach of artificial intelligence generally involves a space of possibilities—all possible games of chess, and the set of possible interpretations of images of faces or of spoken words. The space is always so enormous that individual consideration of all possibilities must be ruled out. Instead, the problem solver must have some structural knowledge of the problem that permits the search for a solution to be focused and efficient. Most often the structure has the form of a tree in which each node represents a state—the accumulation of hypotheses made in reaching the node from the origin, the root node of the tree. A move away from the root node represents a choice among additional hypotheses, each one represented by an arc leading to a new node. Progress toward a solution of a problem is viewed as a search for the "best" path through the tree, one that achieves a specified goal or that is the best among acceptable paths according to some measure. In chess, the nodes of the tree are the arrangements of the chess pieces on the board; in speech recognition the nodes may denote the portion of a spoken utterance that has been successfully matched with the words of a hypothetical sentence. Problem solving in such a space of possibilities is often called *heuristic search,* for there is usually no guarantee that a solution will be found, even knowing that one exists, or that the search will find the best of all possible solutions.

The objective of heuristic search is to explore as many of the most promising paths as possible within the limits of computing resources. Generally, a depth-first search is not attractive because a deep search may explore many paths that would be ruled out with awareness of possibilities at a shallower level elsewhere in the tree. The popular search techniques maintain a *pool of candidates,* nodes worthy of exploration. Each candidate is tagged with a *heuristic value* that is an estimate of how promising a search of its subtree is for reaching the goal or finding the best solution.

On a sequential computer the best strategy for heuristic search is to pick the candidate tagged with the highest value. The expert designing the intelligence into the program must figure out how to assign values to states in a way that will lead the search quickly to successful paths.

In performing heuristic search on a parallel computer, the opportunities for concurrency lie on one hand within processing the chosen candidates, and on the other hand, in the possibility of processing many candidates simultaneously. By far the most promising source of concurrency is the processing of many candidates. In fact, several authors have implemented such schemes on hypercube multiprocessors [Anderson 87, Quinn 87, Felten 87]. In general, the idea is to permit concurrent processing of the candidates having the highest valued tags in the candidate pool. In large problems, one readily encounters consideration of thousands of candidates, so it is easy to anticipate that hundreds of candidates could be processed concurrently, leading to a large speedup over the performance of a single processor. The circumstances in which a speedup nearly equal to the number of processors that can be achieved have been discussed by Wah, Li, and Yu [Wah 85].

Dataflow technology provides a new framework in which to develop multiprocessing schemes for heuristic search. A dataflow processing element can achieve peak performance in computations offering only scalar (nonvector) parallelism. For this reason, dataflow computers are even more attractive for heuristic search problems than for the structured computations of engineering and physics: vector processing as performed by a Cray supercomputer offers little advantage in most heuristic search applications.

14.4   A Sentence Recognizer

Research in speech recognition concerns the automatic transcription of natural language utterances. The ultimate goal is recognition of continuous natural speech without restriction to particular speakers or to quiet environments. It is yet to be achieved because of insufficient knowledge and the lack of sufficient processing power. Any advance in our ability to apply higher computing performance to the speech recognition task will directly improve recognition capability and will also support the evolution of knowledge of the speech process that will lead to better methods of speech processing.

Speech recognition starts with the acoustic speech signal produced by the human vocal tract and modified by the environment separating the speaker and the sensing organ of the recognizer. There have been two major schools of thought on how speech recognition should be carried out by computer. One approach divides the process into "feature extraction" and "phoneme recognition," the former involving numerical computation but the latter being principally symbolic. In the second approach, the one adopted for the present study, the problem is treated as analogous to communication through a noisy channel, where the noise represents the different ways various speakers encode utterances as acoustic signals on different occasions and in different environments. The methods of statistical inference are used to estimate, on the basis of analysis of the acoustic signal, the sentence most likely to have been spoken.

As shown in Fig. 14.4, it is useful to model the generation of the speech signal by two components—the *text generator* and the *speaker*. The text generator emits the word sequence that is the spoken sentence, and the speaker component models the encoding of the word sequence into an acoustic signal.

The first step in recognition always involves processing the acoustic speech signal to extract information about the variation of its energy spectrum with time. In this way the high-bandwidth acoustic signal is reduced to streams of attribute values that encode significant features of the speech signal. This part of a speech recognizer is called the *acoustic processor*. The rest of the speech recognizer uses the derived features of the acoustic signal to discover the sentence that was spoken. The statistical approach to speech recognition is one of deciphering the code signal emanating from the acoustic processor. Appropriately, this part of the recognizer is known as the *linguistic decoder*.

It is convenient for the linguistic decoder to receive a sequence of symbols, each one characterizing a brief interval of the acoustic signal, usually about 10 ms. An acoustic processor that produces this sort of output is said to be *time-synchronous,* and the items in its output sequence are *phonetic labels*. In this case we may regard the combination of the text generator, speaker, and acoustic processor as a random source of *label sequences.*

The essence of linguistic decoding is finding that sentence, among the totality of all possible sentences, that best explains the observed output of the acoustic processor. What is "best" can be given meaning through the methods of statistical analysis, as follows.

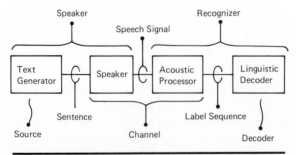

Figure 14.4 System model of the sequential decoding approach to speech recognition.

Suppose the language of interest has a vocabulary of N words, and the text generator emits a sequence of words

$$\mathbf{x} = x_1, \ldots, x_q \qquad \text{where } x_i \in \{1, 2, \ldots, N\}$$

Suppose the speaker and acoustic processor transform this word sequence into the label sequence

$$\mathbf{z} = z_1, \ldots, z_r \qquad \text{where } z_j \in \{1, 2, \ldots, L\}$$

where L is the number of distinct phonetic labels, typically several hundred. Consider the experiment of randomly choosing a sentence $\mathbf{x}$, presenting it to the *channel* (speaker model and acoustic processor), and observing the label sequence $\mathbf{z}$. Statistically, our experiment concerns the two dependent random variables $\mathbf{x}$ and $\mathbf{z}$. Thus the fundamental distribution function for this experiment is the joint probability density $Prob(\mathbf{x}, \mathbf{z})$.

The recognition task is to determine, for an observed label sequence $\mathbf{z}$, the sentence $\mathbf{x}$ most likely to have been spoken. In symbols, we must find the $\mathbf{x}$ for which

$$Prob(\mathbf{x}|\mathbf{z})$$

is greatest. However, note that this is the same problem as finding the $\mathbf{x}$ for which $Prob(\mathbf{x}, \mathbf{z})$ is greatest because

$$Prob(\mathbf{x}, \mathbf{z}) = Prob(\mathbf{z})Prob(\mathbf{x}|\mathbf{z})$$

and $\mathbf{z}$ is given and constant.

To go further, we must be more specific in our characterization of the language and the channel. For our language model we characterize the distribution of words in sentences by an $N \times N$ matrix of *digraph probabilities*:

$$DiGraph[i,j] \qquad 1 \leq i, j \leq N$$

This means that if word x_1 appears in a sentence, then the probability that the next word is x_2 is $DiGraph[x_1, x_2]$. We use the notation $DiGraph[\varepsilon, x]$ for the probability that the first word of a sentence is x. To illustrate, for this language model the probability that sentence $\mathbf{x}$ is spoken to the recognizer is

$$Prob(\mathbf{x}) = DiGraph[\varepsilon, x_1] \times \prod_{k=1}^{q-1} DiGraph[x_k, x_{k+1}]$$

To simplify our discussion of word models, we assume that the distribution of the label strings that characterize a particular word x is not dependent on its surrounding context in a sentence. Thus all statistical relationships between successive words are represented in the digraph probabilities.

Given the discrete nature of the label sequences, it is natural to represent each word x by a Markov chain $M[x]$ such that each transition sequence of $M[x]$ defines a label sequence that might be produced by the channel for the given word. Each transition sequence (and the corresponding label sequence) has a probability that is the product of the transition probabilities along the associated path through the Markov chain.

It will help to introduce one more piece of notation. If $\mathbf{z}$ is the observed label sequence for some sentence $\mathbf{x}$, then $\mathbf{z}$ may be divided into subsequences:

$$\mathbf{z} = \mathbf{w}_1 \bullet \ldots \bullet \mathbf{w}_q$$

such that each label subsequence $\mathbf{w}_i$ corresponds to a transition sequence of the Markov chain for word x_i.

The sentence recognition task may now be stated as follows: Given an observed label sequence $\mathbf{z}$, find the sentence $\mathbf{x}$ for which $Prob(\mathbf{x}, \mathbf{z})$ is maximum, where

$$Prob(\mathbf{x}, \mathbf{z}) = Prob(\mathbf{x}) \times Prob(\mathbf{z}|\mathbf{x})$$

$$= \underbrace{DiGraph[\varepsilon, x_1] \times \prod_{k=1}^{q-1} DiGraph[x_k, x_{k+1}]}_{Prob(\mathbf{x})} \times \underbrace{\prod_{k=1}^{q} PathProb(x_k, \mathbf{w}_k)}_{Prob(\mathbf{z}|\mathbf{x})}$$

where $PathProb(x_k, \mathbf{w}_k)$ is the probability of the most likely path in $M[x_k]$ that generates $\mathbf{w}_k$.

For the present discussion, we assume the simple form of Markov chain shown in Fig. 14.5. One may regard each state as corresponding to a portion of the sound spectrogram characteristic of a specific phoneme of the word; a transition to the next state means that the energy distribution has changed and should be matched by the next phoneme of the word if the present path is to have a good likelihood of success. Figure 14.5b gives the rule for calculating $PathProb(x_k, \mathbf{w}_k)$, which is explained below.

In principle one could calculate $Prob(\mathbf{x}, \mathbf{z})$ for every sentence $\mathbf{x}$ and select the one that yields the highest probability. This would, of course, be extremely wasteful because enormous numbers of sentences would be evaluated, of which only a tiny fraction would be reasonable candidates.

A better approach is to work with a collection of possible sentence prefixes. Each step of the recognition process consists of extending one

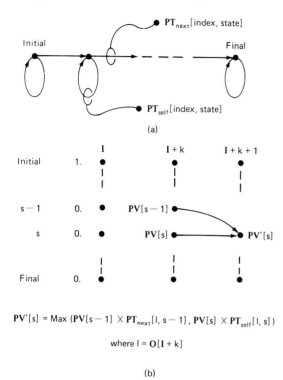

$$PV'[s] = \text{Max} \left(PV[s-1] \times PT_{next}[l, s-1], PV[s] \times PT_{self}[l, s] \right)$$

$$\text{where } l = O[I+k]$$

(b)

Figure 14.5 Simple Markov process model for the phonetics of words. (*a*) Markov graph with self- and next-state transitions; (*b*) calculation of the state probabilities for the next phonetic label.

of the candidate prefixes by one word and calculating its likelihood of eventually yielding the best overall match to the complete label sequence. In each step candidate prefixes that have too little chance of yielding a best match are dropped from further consideration. This is one kind of *heuristic search* process that is typical of the methods of artificial intelligence computation. It is also related to the *dynamic programming* concept promoted in Bellman [62]. In the more specialized area of communication technology, it is a variation on the "stack" implementation of the Viterbi sequential decoding algorithm [Forney 73, Jelinek 69].

It is convenient to start the process at the beginning of the observed label sequence and proceed forward in time considering only the word sequences most likely to have led to the observation. At any point in the process, there will be many partial sentences that match the processed prefix of the observation well enough to be in the running as the prefix of the most likely sentence. In more detail, a candidate C is represented by four data items. The sentence prefix C.history is the

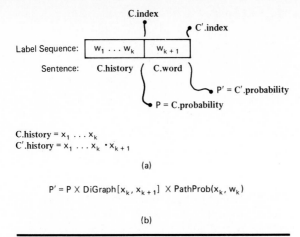

C.history = $x_1 \ldots x_k$
C'.history = $x_1 \ldots x_k \cdot x_{k+1}$

(a)

$$P' = P \times DiGraph[x_k, x_{k+1}] \times PathProb(x_k, w_k)$$

(b)

Figure 14.6 The basic step in the decoding process. (a) Forming a new candidate by extending the hypothesized word sequence by one of the selected possible next words; (b) calculation of the probability value for the new candidate.

history of word choices made so far in the recognition process. The portion of the label sequence matched by C.history may be represented by C.index, the index of the first unmatched label, since the observation is constant. The likelihood that this history is the best interpretation of the acoustic signal is the probability C.probability. Finally, C.word is one of the words estimated to be a plausible extension of the sentence prefix on the basis of the language model. The situation represented by a candidate is illustrated in Fig. 14.6.

Processing a candidate consists of two steps. The first is to determine which paths through the Markov model for the trial word provide the best match with the label sequence starting at I = C.index. For a Markov graph of the kind shown in Fig. 14.5a, determining the best paths involves computing successive probability vectors PV^0, PV^1,...corresponding to successive labels O[I], O[I + 1],....The computing rule is illustrated in Fig. 14.5b. The probability for state s' at label O[I + k + 1] is obtained by choosing the predecessor state s for which $PV^{I+k} \times PT_{s'}[l, s]$ is largest, where PT gives the matrix of state transition probabilities for the label $l = O[I + k + 1]$. In the case that a state has only two predecessor states, the rule reduces to the simple form given in the figure.

Any vector PV^k having a nonzero probability for the state final defines a path for further consideration. The corresponding extended history C.history • C.word has likelihood

$$P \times PathProb(x, \mathbf{w})$$

where P = C.probability

x = C.word

$\mathbf{w}$ = $< O[I], \ldots, O[I + k] >$

The new candidates to be considered will be defined by the set of words most likely to follow C.word in the sentence. If C′ denotes any one of these candidates, and C′.word = x', then the new candidate has likelihood

$$P \times PathProb(x, \mathbf{w}) \times DiGraph[x, x']$$

Only those candidates for which this computation yields a value exceeding a certain lower bound are entered into the pool of candidates.

When this process is implemented on a real computer with the usual limitations of precision, it must be recognized that the probabilities to be calculated will be extremely small numbers. To avoid the possibility of exponent overflow, it is usual practice to use the logarithms of probabilities instead of the probabilities themselves. The principal change in the mathematics is that all multiplications of probabilities become additions of the logarithms instead. In the programs presented below, we have used the probabilities rather than logarithms for the sake of clarity. However, when we discuss performance, we will simply count all multiplications as though they were additions.

14.5 Program Structure for the Search Process

Let us now turn to the structure of a computer program for performing this speech recognition process. The program examples that follow are written in the functional language VAL [Ackerman 78, McGraw 82], developed at MIT for use in evaluating the power and applicability of dataflow computers.[†] Some of the less familiar features of the VAL language are explained in the accompanying figure legends. The overall computation is performed by a function Recognize that returns a Sentence when given a Language and an Observation:

Recognize: Language × Observation → Sentence

The data types used in the process are defined in Fig. 14.7. If L is a Language, the integer L.N specifies that L has a vocabulary of N words. The second component L.DiGraph specifies the matrix of di-

---

†We have taken a few liberties with the VAL syntax as defined in Ackerman [78] to improve the readability of the examples.

```
type Language = record [
    N: integer;      % Number of words in vocabulary
    DiGraph: array [RankList];
                     % The digraph probabilities for pairs of words
    Words: array [WordModel] ];
                     % The statistical database for words of the language

type RankList = array [record [
    probability: real;
    word: integer ] ];

type Sentence = array[integer];
                     % A sequence of integers representing words

type Observation = array[integer];
                     % A sequence of phonetic labels

type WordModel = record [
    states: integer;              % number of states
    self: array[array[real]];     % self transition probabilities
    next: array[array[real]] ];   % next-state transition probabilities

type Candidate = record [
    probability: real;   % Probability for the above history
    history: Chain;      % Hypothesized word sequence
    index: integer;      % Index in observation
    word: integer ];     % Hypothesis for next word

type Chain = oneof [ empty: null; nonempty: record [
    element: integer; next: Chain ] ];

type PathList = array[ record [
    index: integer;      % end of word index in observation
    probability: real ]; % probability of the path

type CandidateList = array [Candidate];
```

Figure 14.7   Data types for the sentence recognizer.

graph probabilities. For each word x, L.DiGraph[x] is a RankList giving the words that might follow word x, ordered by decreasing probability. The third component L.words is the database of Markov models for each of the N words of the language. Since N may be several thousand or more and each word model may embody thousands of data values, the database for a language amounts to many millions of computer words.

The data type Sentence represents a sentence by a sequence of the integers that stand for the individual words. Similarly, the type Observation represents the sequence of phonetic labels emitted by the acoustic processor. Typically, the alphabet of phonetic labels distinguishes several hundred possibilities.

For each word of the language, the database contains a WordModel that describes a simple Markov model having a state graph of the form shown in Fig. 14.5a. In a word model M, the integer M. states gives the number of states. As indicated earlier, each state has a set of self-transitions and a set of next-state transitions for each possible phonetic label. This data are organized in the word model as a pair of two-dimensional arrays. For any label l and any state s, element M. self $[l, s]$ is the probability of a transition from state s to state s when the current label is l. Similarly, M. next $[l, s]$ is the probability of a transition from state s to state $s + 1$.

A member C of the type Candidate represents a further search possibility. The component C. history represents, as a linked list, the sequence of words that constitutes the sentence prefix under consideration. The likelihood that C. history is the best choice for further search is given by C. probability. The integer C. index is the index in the observed label sequence such that all earlier labels are accounted for by C. history. The last component C. word gives one choice of word to be considered for extending the history.

The history components of the candidates are linked lists representing word sequences. Note that the references in these lists will be to the preceding word in each case; when the search is complete the winning sentence will be read from end to beginning by following the linked list. Since a large number of sentence hypotheses will exist during the process, it is important that the implementation realize the sharing of list structure that is implicit in this data type.

The PathList data type is used for intermediate data generated in the processing of a candidate, and the CandidateList type is used to hold the new candidates generated.

The Recognize function (Fig. 14.8) uses the two operations Remove and Insert on the pool of candidates for processing. The pool is implemented as a *priority queue,* which means that the Remove operation always yields the candidate C having the highest value of C. probability.†

The Remove operation at the beginning of the ProcessCandidates function selects the best candidate in the pool for processing. The processing comprises two steps. First the function BestPaths is used to find the most likely transition sequences for word model L. words [X] starting at position I in the label sequence. Then the function Next Words is used to choose combinations of path and next word that yield new candidates having a likelihood better than a threshold value threshold. The final section of Recognize uses the Insert operation to put the candidates into the priority queue.

---

†In keeping with the requirements of functional programming, the Remove operation also returns the new (modified) queue explicitly.

```
function Recognize ( O: Observation, L: Language ) returns ( Sentence )
function ProcessCandidates ( Q: Queue ) returns ( Sentence )
      let  C, StartQ := Remove ( Q );
              I: integer := C.index;      % Current index in observation
              H: Chain := C.history;     % Candidate sentence prefix
              P: real := C.probability;  % Probability for the candidate
              X: integer := C.word;      % Hypothesis for next word

              WM: WordModel := L.Words [X];
              RL: RankList := L.DiGraph [X];
              NewH: Chain := make Chain [nonempty: record
                        [element: X; next: H] ];

              PL: PathList := BestPaths ( WM, I );

              CL: CandidateList := NextWords ( PL, RL, NewH, P );

              NewQ := for  Q := StartQ;
                            i := 1;
                      do   if i > size ( CL ) then Q
                           else iter
                                  Q := Insert ( Q, CL[i] );
                                  i := i + 1;
                                enditer
                           endif
                        endfor;
      in ProcessCandidates ( NewQ )
      endlet
endfun ProcessCandidate
      let BeginQ: Queue := InitialQueue ( L );
      in ProcessCandidates ( BeginQ )
      endlet
endfun Recognize
```

Figure 14.8   The `Recognize` function. The operation
make `T[t: v]` uses the value v to make a value of
union type T with tag t. The expression **size** (A)
gives the number of elements in array A. The brack-
ets `iter`...`enditer` indicate a rebinding of loop
variables initialized at the beginning of the **for** expression, followed by reevaluation of its body.

Figure 14.9 gives an implementation of the `BestPaths` function.
This routine computes a succession of probability vectors PV starting
with a vector (lines 4 to 6) that is null except for unity probability for
state initial. In lines 8 to 10 the transition probabilities of the word
model for the current phonetic label are defined. The computation of
the new probability vector is done in lines 11 to 19 and includes a test
of whether all state probabilities are now less than `Limit`. If the new
probability for the state `final` is not zero, a record is appended to the
path list (lines 22 to 24), which was initially empty (line 7). If `Test` is
true, the computation terminates with the current collection of paths
(line 26); otherwise the cycle is repeated with the new probability vector and path list, and with `index` advanced to the next phonetic label
(lines 27 to 31). The guts of the `BestPaths` function, and the entire

```
function BestPaths ( WM: WordModel; I: integer ) returns ( PathList )
     for  initial := 1;          % Initial and final                    1
          final := WM.states; % states of the word model               2
          index := I;                                                   3
          PV: array [real] := concatenate ( % initial vector            4
               fill ( initial, initial, 1. ),        % of state probabilities   5
               fill ( initial+1, final, 0. ) );                         6
          PL: PathList := empty;                                        7
     do   let   label: integer := O[I];                                 8
               Pt-self: array[real] := WM.self [label];                 9
               Pt-next: array[real] := WM.next [label];                10
               NewPV: array[real], Test: boolean :=                    11
                    forall s in [initial, final]                       12
                         P := if s = initial                           13
                              then PV[s] * Pt-self[s]                   14
                              else max ( PV[s] * Pt-self[s], PV[s-1] * Pt-next[s-1] )   15
                              endif;                                    16
                    construct P                                        17
                    eval and ( P < Limit )                             18
                    endall;                                            19
               NewPL :=    if NewPV[final] = 0.                        20
                           then PL                                     21
                           else add-high (PL, record [                 22
                                index: index;                          23
                                probability: NewPV[final] )            24
                           endif;                                      25
          in   if Test then NewPL                                      26
               else iter                                               27
                    PV := NewPV;                                       28
                    PL := NewPL;                                       29
                    index := index + 1;                               30
                    enditer                                           31
               endif                                                  32
          endlet                                                      33
     endfor                                                           34
endfun BestPaths
```

Figure 14.9   The `BestPaths` function. The operation **concate-
nate** (A, B) creates a new array with low index equal to that of
A and containing the elements of A and B; **fill** (a, b, v) creates an array having a and b as low and high index limits, and
each element equal to v; **empty** returns the array having no elements; **add-high** (A, v) creates a new array from A having its
high index one greater, and a new highest element with value v;
max (a, b) returns the larger of its two arguments.

recognition process for that matter, is the computation of the new
state probabilities.

An implementation of the NextWords function appears in Fig.
14.10. For each path in the path list PL, the words of L are considered,
working down the rank list of successor words. For each combination
of history (sentence prefix), path, and next word, the joint probability
is calculated in line 4 and compared with threshold. If the probability is above the threshold, a new candidate record is created (lines
6–10) and appended (line 12) to the candidate list CL, and the word
next lower in the rank list is considered (line 13). If the threshold is
not met, then attention moves on to the next path (line 16). Once all

```
function NextWords ( PL: PathList, RL: RankList, H: Chain, P: real ) returns ( CandidateList )
    for  p = 0; j = 0;                                                         1
         CL := empty;                                                          2
    do   if p = size ( PL ) then CL                                           3
         else let NewP := PL[p].probability * RL[j].probability * P;           4
              in   if NewP > Threshold                                        5
                   then let   R: Candidate := record [                        6
                              probability: NewP;                             7
                              history: H;                                     8
                              index: PathList[p].index;                       9
                              word: RL[j].word ];                             10
                        in   iter                                            11
                              CL := add-high ( CL, R );                       12
                              j := j + 1;                                     13
                              enditer                                        14
                        endlet                                               15
                   else iter p := p + 1; j := 0 enditer                       16
                   endif                                                     17
              endlet                                                         18
         endif                                                              19
    endfor                                                                  20
endfun NextWords
```

Figure 14.10   The NextWords function.

paths have been processed, the candidate list becomes the result value of NextWords (line 3).

14.6   Concurrency in Heuristic Search: The Parallel Priority Queue

The code described above illustrates one general form of heuristic search. The basic component is the pool of candidates to be considered for further exploration and evaluation. The pool of candidates is represented as an abstract data type (Queue) with two operations—Insert and Remove. The insert operation puts a candidate in the queue and associates the candidate with a value, in our example, its probability field. The remove operation removes the candidate having the highest value. Such an abstract data type is known as a *priority queue*.

The best way to implement a priority queue, even on conventional computers, is not immediately obvious. If candidates are added to a simple list as they are inserted, then finding the best one to remove requires time that grows directly with the length of the list. If such a list is kept in order, then the insert operation requires linear time. Neither scheme would be acceptable because the size of the candidate pool may be very large. Fortunately, a method developed by Crane and given by Knuth [73] succeeds in performing both insertion and removal using no more than $O(\log n)$ operations. To accomplish this the pool of candidates is organized as a tree structure and maintained so the entry having the highest value is always at the root node.

The Recognize function, implemented using a priority queue, requires that once a candidate has been removed from the queue for processing, no further candidates may be removed from the queue until the first candidate has been completely processed. This is because the queue insists that the best candidate be chosen; if the "best" candidate were selected before all insert operations had been performed, there would be no guarantee that the chosen candidate has the highest value.

Strictly honoring the priority queue discipline limits the parallelism to that which is possible within the processing of a single candidate. On the other hand, we have already noted that processing the top n candidates in the pool concurrently can yield a speedup of nearly n in many cases. One may readily imagine situations in which the pool holds many thousands of candidates and hundreds of these may be profitably explored in parallel.

For the implementation of the candidate pool on a machine having p processing elements, we need a system that can accept Insert commands from many sites and can statisfy Remove requests from many sites. Abstractly, such a system may be viewed as in Fig. 14.11a. It has p input ports for receiving candidates, and p output ports for delivering candidates to processing elements. We would like the delivered candidates to be those having the highest values of all candidates entered into the pool. Such a system is called a parallel priority queue (PPQ).

It is natural to refine the picture of Fig. 14.11a as shown in Fig. 14.11b. Since the candidate pool will of necessity occupy memory in each of the processing elements, this storage might as well be organized as a priority queue in each processing element so only the best choices possible will be considered for transfer to other processing elements. Then the function of the *selection/distribution* (S/D) system is

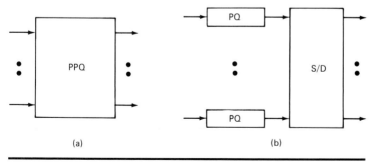

(a)   (b)

Figure 14.11   Parallel priority queue. (*a*) Regarded as a concurrent system; (*b*) composed of independent priority queues (PQ) with top element t and a selection/distribution (S/D) system.

to pick the best of the candidates presented to it and to distribute them to all processing elements at rates sufficient to keep them busy. To implement this scheme, one of the priority queues and a share of the S/D system would be allocated to each processing element.

It is attractive to design the S/D system so that the sequences of candidates processed by the separate processing elements have similar statistical properties, specifically their distributions of likelihood values. One reason is to prevent a situation in which one processor alone is generating all of the most worthy candidates, causing other processors either to be idle or to process less worthy possibilities. A second reason concerns disposal of the *tailings*—those candidates that have become so unlikely that they must be flushed from the pool to make room for better ones. This is a serious issue; for each candidate processed *many* new candidates will enter the pool and, in the steady state, an equal number must be thrown out. If the separate priority queues are statistically similar, each one can act independently in managing its share of the pool, and no interprocessor communication is needed for satisfactory handling of the tailings. For these reasons we require that the S/D system spread the candidates accepted from each input port evenly over all output ports.

We are uncertain about the precise specification of the parallel priority queue, or what will prove to be its most desirable realization on a dataflow multiprocessor. A simple or complex implementation may be called for, depending on how elaborate is the processing to be carried out on each candidate. If the processing is large, then additional complexity in the implementation of the candidate pool may be justified if it decreases the resources spent on unworthy candidates.

The packets that flow through the system of Fig. 14.11*b* would not contain all the data that make up a candidate record. Instead, all that is needed is the value of the candidate and a reference pointer that locates the remaining information. The reference pointer, of course, must be a global identifier; the ultimately receiving processor must be able to retrieve the data (by means to be discussed below) from whichever processor holds it. In addition, the packet must include the number of the source processor so that on each sort/select cycle each processor can be told whether or not to move a new candidate into the top of its queue. Thus a *Q-Packet* has the format

```
type Q-Packet = record[
    value: real;
    reference: integer;
    source: integer]
```

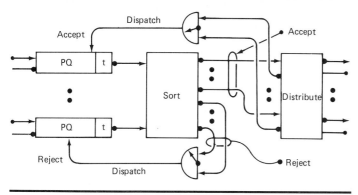

Figure 14.12   Scheme for implementing the S/D component of a parallel priority queue.

One implementation possibility is shown in Fig. 14.12. Each of the p priority queues holds a top entry t which is available to the sorting system. The outputs of the sorting system are divided into *high* and *low* groups. The Q-Packets in the high group are accepted and passed to the distribution system. For each Q-Packet accepted, an *accept* signal is sent to the priority queue from which the packet was obtained. This causes the priority queue to remove its top element and to present a new top element to the sorting system. For each of the remaining Q-Packets participating in the sort, a *reject* signal is sent to the corresponding priority queue. This signal gives the queue an opportunity to change its top element if a better candidate has arrived during the cycle of operation.

The sorting subsystem can be implemented as a *sorting network* [Knuth 73]. However, it is sufficient merely to separate the top ranking items—the elements of the high and low groups need not be ordered internally. Systems that perform this simpler task are called *selection networks* and their structure is discussed in Wah [84].

According to Knuth [73], sorting networks with p inputs can be built with a number of comparators no greater than $\frac{1}{4} \times p \times (\log_2 p)^2$. For $p = 64$, this yields $\frac{1}{4} \times 64 \times 6^2 = 576$. Since each set of 64 input packets is sorted by exactly one use of each comparator, and each use of a comparator operates on two packets, it follows that the sorting involves at most 2×576 operations on packets and therefore that an average packet is subject to no more than 18 comparison/swaps.

Figure 14.13 shows a two-input sorter, the building block for sorting and selection networks. This implementation is straightforward: instruction (1) fires when signals at inputs 1 and 2 indicate that packets A and B are available in storage; then instruction (2) or (3) is fired according to which packet has the greater value, and the two packets are moved to locations C and D so C holds the one of greater value.

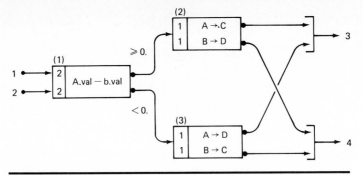

Figure 14.13 Dataflow implementation of the sorting section of a parallel priority queue.

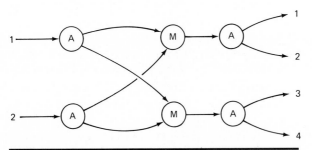

Figure 14.14 Implementation of the distribution section using a network of merge units and alternators.

The distribution system can be built as a network of *alternator* and *merge* units as shown in Fig. 14.14. An alternator delivers packets to its two output ports on demand—alternately if neither output is blocked; the merge unit passes packets received at its input ports on a first-come, first-served basis. At each input port of the distribution system, a stream of packets has access to a binary tree of alternators that provides a path to each output port of the distribution system and spreads the stream to all outputs equally.

The merge unit is very special. It requires careful design because the two input signals can occur closely in time, but different effects are required for the two orders of arrival. This is an example of a *nondeterminate system* in which an erroneous design can lead to occasional failures that are difficult to trace. An implementation is shown in Fig. 14.15. The merge unit has two input ports and one output port. A signal at an input port is a *request* to transfer a packet at that port

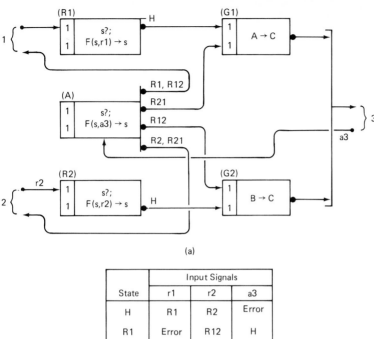

(a)

	Input Signals		
State	r1	r2	a3
H	R1	R2	Error
R1	Error	R12	H
R2	R21	Error	H
R12	Error	Error	R2
R21	Error	Error	R1

(b)

Figure 14.15   Implementation of the nondeterminate merge unit. This implementation uses a finite state machine in which each transition is performed by the firing of a dataflow instruction. Instructions (R1) and (R2) fire upon receipt of request signals r1 and r2, while instruction (A) fires once use of the merged result in location C has been signaled at a3. (*a*) Dataflow instructions; (*b*) table for state function F.

to the output port, and to send a signal at the output port. No further transfers are permitted until an (acknowledge) signal is returned at the output port. Thus the granting of a request from the other input must be deferred until any earlier request is completed. Here the logic of the service protocol is implemented by a state variable s shared and updated atomically by several instructions. An implementation of the alternator may employ the same principles of operation.

The dispatch of accept and reject signals to the proper processing elements can be done by a single dataflow instruction that sends a signal packet to a target processing element according to a computed processing element index.

14.7   Implementing Global Memory on a Dataflow Multiprocessor

There are several places in the recognizer where access to data that is most likely stored in the array memory of other processing elements is required. The primary information of this sort is the word model data and the digraph probabilities that characterize the language of interest. These databases are far too large to be replicated at each processing element. In addition, the candidate records themselves are stored in the array memory of the processor that creates them; each one must be fetched by remote access from by the processor that processes it.

The history field of each candidate record is a pointer to a linked list of word records which will be distributed over all of the processing elements. Managing the memory used by this collection of linked lists (which form a large tree) requires global memory accesses to maintain reference counts so that histories corresponding to abandoned paths of search may be released. Finally, note that the phonetic label sequence, being fixed and of small extent, can be held redundantly by each processor.

Two possible strategies for processing candidates yield very different problems of balance and communication. One possibility is to assign candidates to processing elements randomly, as would be the case using the parallel priority queue scheme just described. In this case, an even distribution of processing load over the processing elements will be obtained, but essentially all access to word model and digraph data will be done by remote access using the routing network of the machine. A second possibility is to assign each word to one or a few specific processors, each of which has a copy of the relevant portion of the linguistic data base. In this case all accesses to word model information will be local, but candidates must be sorted according to their assignment. Load balancing might be a serious problem since there is no guarantee that the assignment of words to processors will match their distribution in the recognition task.

Here we consider the first alternative and show how access to a global data base may be managed on the dataflow multiprocessor. For the speech recognizer, only read accesses need be supported. This may be generally true since it will usually be better to store information where it is created.

The problem to be solved is the following: one processing element (the *local* one, call it A) needs a data value resident at a second processing element (the *remote* one, call it B). The transaction will be carried out by a pair of packets sent between A and B. First A sends a request packet R of the form

type R-Packet = **record**[
    address: **integer**;
    source: **integer**]

The field R.address specifies the location in B's memory to be read; and R.source is the number of processing element A so B can reply correctly. The word packet returned by B has the form

type W-Packet = **record**[
    value: **real**]

The transfer of a packet is accomplished by special **Send** and **Re-ceive** specifiers that may be used in place of operand and result addresses, respectively, in dataflow instructions. Each such specifier is associated with one of several *packet ports* of a processing element. Figure 14.16 shows how the send and receive features are used to im-

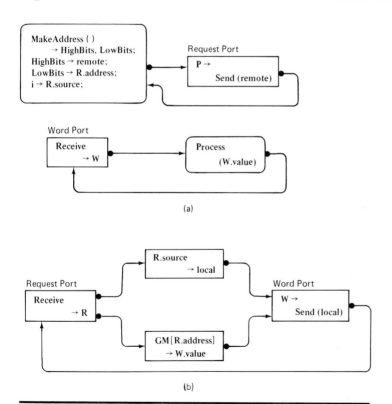

(a)

(b)

Figure 14.16 Implementation of global memory accesses on a dataflow multiprocessor. The enable parts of instructions have been omitted to simplify the figure. (*a*) Local processing element; (*b*) remote processing element.

plement remote memory access. The local processor A computes a global address, converts it into a processor number and a local address, and builds and sends an R-Packet to B using the Request Ports of both processors. Processor B uses the address to fetch the desired word and return it to A in a W-Packet using the Word Ports.

If a block of data is required by processor A, then instructions may be loaded in B that return a series of word packets in response to a single request. This is possible because the code installed in both A and B is produced by a compiler that is aware of the structure of the entire computation. For example, a request can be interpreted by the code in B as asking for the entire rank list of digraph data for a particular word.

Now, what are the problems? The most significant issue arises from the possibility that several requests may be directed to the same receiver concurrently. In the multiprocessor design under consideration, an input port has an associated buffer store in the data memory of the processing element. It is essential that no further packets be sent to the port once the buffer has become filled. Our global memory scheme must ensure that this cannot happen regardless of how much traffic in global memory accesses occurs, because packets that cannot be received can cause deadlock to occur unless they are discarded. One solution is simple: provide an input buffer of size equal to the number of processing elements that can send it packets and require that each processor have at most one unfilled request at a time.

Other solutions that offer more throughput may occur to the reader. The transaction rate of one port is about equal to the instruction repetition rate of the processing element or 100 kHz. Since this is a factor of 30 less than the word packet capacity of the routing network, it is possible to increase throughput to the extent needed by operating several ports concurrently.

14.8   Overall Performance Analysis

Evaluating performance of the dataflow multiprocessor for the speech recognition process is problematic because many parameters of the computation are not known with precision. In the following we do not draw any conclusion about the quality of speech recognition that will be achieved because the relation of performance to speed of execution is a matter of conjecture. We will be able to estimate the ratio of performance of the dataflow machine to that of a conventional machine for computations that can be supported by the strategies and mechanisms we have discussed.

An advantage the dataflow processor has over most other parallel computer architectures is its ability to process many parts of a program simultaneously, even within one processing element. The parts may be independent loops calling for floating-point calculations, or they may be parts involving various combinations of arithmetic, array memory access, and packet transmission through the routing network. Of course the total requirement of all concurrent activities cannot exceed the capacity of the processing elements; so in any specific computation there will be some one aspect (arithmetic, memory, or communication) that dominates and places a limit on performance achieved.

For the present projection of performance, reasonable performance limits for the key categories of dataflow instructions are shown in Table 14.1. The categories are mostly self-explanatory, but a few re-

TABLE 14.1   Activity Rate Limits for the Dataflow Multiprocessor

Activity	Maximum rate, in MHz (each processing element)
Instruction execution:	
Floating-point add	10
Floating-point multiply	10
All instructions	40
Array memory access:	
Reads and writes	20
Packet transmission (packet words):	
Sends	6
Receives	6

marks may help. We assume that independent limits apply to floating-point adds and multiplies because the two operations are likely to be implemented by separate hardware elements. The integer additions used to compute addresses and to count iterations are excluded from the limits on floating-point rates. Array memory accesses are assumed to be reads or writes of 32-bit data words. All packets sent through the routing network are built of 32-bit units called *packet words*. A data packet for a 32-bit value has two packet words, one for the header and one for the data; similarly, a 64-bit data packet has three packet words; and a signal packet consists of one packet word. According to the table, the maximum rate of executing either sends or receives is 6 million per second for each processing element.

The overall computation divides into two major parts: the processing of candidates and the parallel priority queue. A convenient measure of computational load is the number of candidates processed per unit time, for exactly as many candidates are processed by the ProcessCandidates function as are selected by the parallel priority queue. In the following we consider the various components of the computation in turn and summarize the results in Table 14.2.

TABLE 14.2   Summary of Performance Data

Component	Instructions	Adds	Array memory	Packet words
Process Candidate				
BestPaths	5400	1800	900	1440
NextWords	1500	150	750	600
Parallel Priority Queue				
Priority Queue	6050	550	6600	0
Sorting	108	18	0	108
Selection	4	0	0	2
Distribution	60	0	0	36
Remove	8	0	4	9
Total	13,130	2518	8254	2195
Rate, MHz	31.8	6.1	20.0	5.3

The biggest consumer of computing resources is the BestPaths function. The number of arithmetic operations executed by BestPaths in processing a candidate is determined by the number of states and the number of observations. We suppose that a word spans 30 observations on the average and that the average word model is a Markov chain with 15 states. The computation in line 15 of Fig. 14.9 is performed for each state and for each phonetic label, that is, about $15 \times 30 = 450$ times on the average. For each execution of line 15 there are two multiplications, plus one addition to implement the **max** operator. We will count the multiples as adds, recognizing that the logarithms of probabilities will be used, so the total count of additions per execution of line 15 is 1350. In addition, the test in line 18 is performed once for each label and each state yielding 450 more additions per candidate processed, giving a total of 1800 additions per candidate.

An important part of BestPaths is accessing the word model data WM.self and WM.next. For each cycle of the iteration, one of the several hundred pairs of transition probability vectors is needed and is most likely stored in the array memory of a remote processing element. We suppose that the data for each of 30 labels (some of which will be repeated) is obtained by sending one R-Packet to a remote processor and receiving 15 W-Packets of 64-bit double data words in return. This requires $30 \times 30 = 900$ array memory references by the remote processor and the transfer of $30 \times (3 + 15 \times 3) = 1440$ packet words.

An exact count of the number of dataflow instructions executed per candidate processed can be found by working out the detailed dataflow machine code. A close figure can be obtained by constructing the dataflow code for the **forall** expression in lines 12 to 19, counting the instructions and including the instructions required to remotely access the word model data. This analysis yields $12 \times 450 = 5400$.

The NextWords function uses the rank list of digraph probabilities which must be fetched from a remote processing element. This action can be done just once per candidate because the same probability data apply for each path in PL. We assume the average rank list contains 200 elements and that an average of 50 of these are considered for each path. Constructing the dataflow machine code for loops that retrieve the rank list and construct the new candidate records (lines 4 to 16) gives the numbers in the table.

Now we consider the candidate pool and the parallel priority queue. Most of the processing cycles are used in managing the local priority queue at each processing element. Inserting or removing a candidate from a priority queue is done by an iteration that makes two passes over the shortest path to a leaf node in the binary tree that holds the queue entries. Assuming that a candidate pool of 100,000 entries is distributed over 64 processing elements, the shortest path in one of the binary trees would have no more than 11 levels. Given our premise of 50 new candidates for each one processed, at most 550 loop cycles will be executed for each candidate processed by Process Candidates. The table shows that this function makes intensive use of the array memory, where the tree structure is held.

The components that make up the S/D system of the parallel priority queue make very small demands on resources. The numbers in Table 14.2 follow from consideration of the implementation diagrams in Figs. 14.13 and 14.15. Based on Knuth's complexity bound for sorting, a Q-Packet will pass through 18 sort modules, firing about 6 dataflow instructions for each module (including send and receive functions). The numbers in the table for sorting are doubled because we have assumed that only half of the sorted packets correspond to candidates that will be selected for processing. The selection function is performed by a few dataflow instructions in each processor that send the accept or reject signals through the routing network to the appropriate source processors. The distribution component consists of $\log_2 p = 6$ stages, each stage having at most one merge and one alternator module in the path followed by a Q-Packet. The table indicates that about 10 dataflow instructions will fire for each packet handled by any of the 6 stages.

The numbers in Table 14.2 are sensitive to two factors. One is the *branching degree* of the pool of candidates, the average number of new candidates created for each candidate processed. We have assumed a branching degree of 50, which leads to the machine devoting 46 percent of its instruction execution cycles to the individual priority queues. A smaller branching degree would substantially reduce resources consumed by the priority queues.

The second factor is the fraction of the rank list for a word that must be scanned to be certain of considering all reasonably likely next words. We have assumed that an average of 200 words from a vocabulary of 1000 words are retrieved for scanning by the NextWords function.

The totals show that, for the problem parameters we have chosen, performance is limited by the throughput capacity of the array memory modules. Assuming the array memory operates at its limit of 20 million accesses per second, the other activity rates turn out as listed in the bottom line of Table 14.2. The processing elements operate at about 75 percent of their peak performance and execute adds at 6.1 MFLOPS apiece or 390 MFLOPS for all 64. The routing network passes packets at 5.3 million word packets per second, which is less than half of capacity.

For these rates to be achieved, the machine code loaded into each processing element must provide for keeping at least 400 instructions active at all times. All program components must be continuously active, and several candidates must be in process concurrently in each processor. The most difficult aspect of realizing the projected performance lies in the priority queue, for we have assumed that all candidates handled by a processing element yield new candidates that are entered in the same priority queue.

These projections indicate that a dataflow computer having 64 processing elements will be able to process speech at least 200 times faster than a 20-MIPS conventional processor. It has been reported that a 3-MIPS computer is able to perform a recognition process similar to the one described here at the rate of one second of speech signal for each 60 s of computing time. On this evidence the dataflow machine should be able to achieve real-time recognition of speech.

14.9   Conclusions

Our principal conclusion is that speech recognition is a problem for which a dataflow multiprocessor is well suited. The analysis presented indicates that the statistical decoding approach to sentence recognition can be run on a 64-processor dataflow machine so that all processors are utilized performing essential elements of the computation. The fraction of instructions devoted to tasks not required in a single processor implementation is less than 1 percent. Although certain simplifications have been made in the language models used in this discussion, the use of more sophisticated statistical models for word sequences and the phonetic constitution of words would not change the results significantly since the major impact would be to increase the size of the data base of statistical parameters. The principal reason for the high performance is the very efficient interprocessor communication made possible by the dataflow instruction scheduling mechanism.

The sentence recognizer is an example of just one form of heuristic search, one in which each node of the search tree has a *heuristic* value that represents the likelihood that the best complete path will include that node. Other forms of heuristic search have wide application. A *branch-and-bound* algorithm [Lawler 66] is a problem-solving procedure in which each node of the search tree has both a *heuristic* value and a *performance* value that is an objective measure of goodness of a partial solution. For example, in the traveling salesman problem, a subproblem might be to find the best route from city A to city B that touches a specified subset of all cities. The performance value of a solution to the subproblem would be the length of a route proposed as a solution, whereas the heuristic value would estimate how worthy the partial solution is as a candidate for constructing the best route for all cities. An implementation of branch and bound, in addition to using the heuristic value to select candidates for processing, uses the performance values of nodes to eliminate nodes that cannot represent pieces of the best complete solution. If two nodes that represent the same subproblem have different performance values, then the one with the smaller value can be discarded because it cannot be part of a best solution to the whole problem. To implement branch and bound, it is necessary to provide for communication among activities developing solutions to the same subproblem. This may be done either by assigning all such activities to the same processing element of a multiprocessor, or by using a shared location in global memory to hold the *incumbent,* the currently best performance value for the subproblem.

Another heuristic search technique is alpha-beta pruning, which is used to find best moves in game trees [Knuth 75]. The parallel processing of this search principle is discussed in Finkel [82]. In Kumar [83,] it is shown that an alpha-beta search is equivalent to a branch-and-bound search, so similar implementation schemes will be effective.

These results suggest that the dataflow multiprocessor described in this chapter would perform well in a variety of applications utilizing artificial intelligence techniques. The feasibility of applying parallel processing to search problems has been demonstrated by the experience with hypercube architectures and by experiments with the Crystal multiprocessor [Finkel 87].

This study raises two fundamental questions that must be addressed to make the techniques discussed here more accessible to practitioners of artificial intelligence methods. The first issue concerns how a heuristic search process should be expressed in a high-level programming language. Although we presented code for the sentence recognizer in VAL, we cheated. Obeying the program would not permit exploiting the parallelism allowed by the parallel priority queue. Some means of describing the pool of candidates and the policies to be followed in its implementation is needed. Any such notation will be a notation for nondeterminate computation and will violate the purity of a functional language such as VAL. The *manager* concept discussed by Arvind [82] is one suggestion of a suitable extension of a functional programming language.

The second issue concerns whether it will ever be possible for a compiler to automatically generate the sort of machine code structures envisioned in this chapter. Much progress is being made on the mapping problem for allocating and scheduling large-scale scientific applications on multiprocessor computers, and these schemes are sure to find their way into future compilers intended for scientific computations. It is reasonable to expect that extensions of these techniques will eventually encompass programs and code structures such as those we have treated in this chapter.

Bibliography

[Ackerman 79]   W.B. Ackerman and J.B. Dennis. *VAL—A Value-Oriented Algorithmic Language: Preliminary Reference Manual.* Report MIT/LCS/TR-218, Laboratory for Computer Science, 545 Technology Sq., Cambridge, MA 02139, June 1979.

[Anderson 87]   S. Anderson and M. Chen. "Parallel Branch-and-Bound Algorithms on the Hypercube." In M. Heath (ed). *Hypercube Multiprocessors 1987,* pp. 309–317, Society for Industrial and Applied Mathematics, Philadelphia, 1987.

[Arvind 84]   Arvind and J.D. Brock. Resource Managers in Functional Programming. *J. of Parallel and Distributed Computing,* vol. 1, pp. 5–21, 1984.

[Arvind 78]   Arvind, K. Gostelow, and W. Plouffe. *The (Preliminary) Id Report: An Asynchronous Programming Language and Computing Machine.* Tech. Rep 114, Department of Information and Computer Science, University of California, Irvine, September 1978.

[Arvind 80]   Arvind, V. Kathail, and K. Pingali. *A Dataflow Architecture with Tagged Tokens.* MIT/LCS/TM-174, Laboratory for Computer Science, 545 Technology Sq., Cambridge, MA 02139, September 1980.

[Arvind 81]   Arvind and V. Kathail. "A Multiple Processor Dataflow Machine That Supports Generalized Procedures." *Proc. Eighth Ann. Symp. on Computer Architecture,* pp. 291–296, May 1981.

[Bahl 83]   L.R. Bahl, F. Jelinek, and R.L. Mercer. "A Maximum Likelihood Approach to Continuous Speech Recognition." *IEEE Trans. on Pattern Analysis and Machine Intelligence PAMI-5,* vol. 2, pp. 179–190, March 1983.

[Barr 81]   A. Barr and E.A. Feigenbaum. *The Handbook of Artificial Intelligence.* HeurisTech Press, Stanford, CA, 1981.

[Bellman 62]   R. Bellman and S. Dreyfus. *Applied Dynamic Programming.* Princeton University Press, Princeton, NJ, 1962.

[Dennis 87a]   J.B. Dennis. *Final Report: Data Flow Computer Architecture.* Report MIT/LCS/TR, Laboratory for Computer Science, 545 Technology Sq., Cambridge, MA 02139, 1987a.

[Dennis 87b]   J.B. Dennis. "Dataflow Computation: A Case Study." In V. Milutinovic (ed). *Computer Architecture: Concepts and Systems.* Elsevier, New York, 1987b.

[Dennis 74]   J.B. Dennis. "First Version of a Data Flow Procedure Language." In B. Robinet (ed). *Lecture Notes in Computer Science, Vol. 19: Programming Symposium,* pp. 362–376, Springer-Verlag, Berlin, Heidelberg, New York, 1974.

[Dennis 80]   J.B. Dennis. "Data Flow Supercomputers." *IEEE Computer,* vol. 13, no. 4, pp. 48–56, November 1980.

[Dennis 84]   J.B. Dennis, G-R. Gao, and K.W.R. Todd. "Modeling the Weather with a Data Flow Supercomputer." *IEEE Trans. on Computers,* vol. C-33, no. 7, pp. 592–603, July 1984.

[Felten 87]   E. Felten, R. Morison, S. Otto, K. Barish, R. Fatland, and F. Ho. "Chess on the Hypercube." In M. Heath (ed). *Hypercube Multiprocessors 1987,* pp. 327–332, Society for Industrial and Applied Mathematics, Philadelphia, 1987.

[Finkel 82]   R.A. Finkel and J.P. Fishburn. "Parallelism in Alpha-Beta Search." *Artificial Intelligence* vol. 19, no. 1, pp. 89–106, September 1982.

[Finkel 87]   R.A. Finkel and U. Manber. "DIB—A Distributed Implementation of Backtracking." *Trans. on Programming Languages and Systems,* vol. 9, no. 2, pp. 235–256, April 1987.

[Forney 73]   G.D. Forney, Jr. "The Viterbi Algorithm." *Proc. of the IEEE,* vol. 61, no. 3, pp. 268–277, March 1973.

[Heath 87]   M. Heath. Oak Ridge National Laboratory, Oak Ridge, TN, 1987. Presentations on artificial intelligence applications: S. Anderson and M. Chen. "Parallel Branch-and-Bound for NP Optimization on the Hypercube"; M.J. Quinn. "Solving Best-First Branch-and-Bound Algorithms on Hypercube Multicomputers; and S. Otto, E. Felten, and R. Morison. "Chess on the Hypercube."

[Jelinek 69]   F. Jelinek. "A Fast Sequential Decoding Algorithm Using a Stack." *IBM J. of Res. and Dev.,* vol. 13, pp. 675–685, November 1969.

[Jelinek 82]   F. Jelinek, R.L. Mercer, and L.R. Bahl. "Continuous Speech Recognition." In P.R. Krishnaiah and L.N. Kanal, (eds). *Handbook of Statistics,* pp. 549–573, North-Holland, Amsterdam, 1982.

[Knuth 73a]   D.E. Knuth. "Largest in, first out." In *The Art of Computer Programming, vol. 3: Sorting and Searching,* pp. 149–153, 220–235, Addison-Wesley, Reading, MA, 1973.

[Knuth 73b]   D.E. Knuth. "Networks for Sorting." In *The Art of Computer Programming, vol. 3: Sorting and Searching,* pp. 220–246, Addison-Wesley, Reading, MA, 1973.

[Knuth 75]   D.E. Knuth and R.W. Moore. "An Analysis of Alpha-Beta Pruning." *Artificial Intelligence,* vol. 6, pp. 293–326, 1975.

[Kumar 83]   V. Kumar and L. Kanal. "A General Branch-and-Bound Formulation for Understanding and Synthesizing AND/OR Tree Search Procedures." *Artificial Intelligence,* vol. 21, pp. 179–198, 1983.

[Lawler 66]   E.L. Lawler and D.W. Wood. "Branch-and-Bound Methods: A Survey." *Operations Research,* vol.14, pp. 699–719, 1966.

[McGraw 82]   J.R. McGraw. "The VAL Language: Description and Analysis." *Trans. on Programming Languages and Systems,* vol. 4, no. 1, pp. 44–82, January 1982.

[Nilsson 80]   N.J. Nilsson. *Principles of Artificial Intelligence.* Tioga Publishing Company, Palo Alto, CA, 1980.

[Quinn 87]   M.J. Quinn. "Implementing Best-First Branch-and-Bound Algorithms on Hypercube Multicomputers. In M. Heath (ed). *Hypercube Multiprocessors 1987,* pp. 318–326, Society for Industrial and Applied Mathematics, Philadelphia, 1987.

[Wah 84]   B.W. Wah and K.L. Chen. "A Partitioning Approach to the Design of Selection Networks." *IEEE Trans. on Computers,* vol. C-33, no. 3, pp. 261–268, March 1984.

[Wah 85]   B.W. Wah, G-j. Li, and C.F. Yu. "Multiprocessing of Combinatorial Search Problems." *IEEE Computer,* pp. 93–108, June 1985.

[Watson 82]   I. Watson and J. Gurd. "A Practical Data Flow Computer." *IEEE Computer,* vol. 15, no. 2, pp. 51–57, February 1982.

[Yuba 84]   T. Yuba, T. Shimada, K. Hiraki, and H. Kashiwagi. *Sigma-1: A Dataflow Computer for Scientific Computation.* Electrotechnical Laboratory, 1-1-4 Umesono, Sakuramura, Niiharigun, Ibaraki 305, Japan, 1984.

VLSI Array Processors
for Signal/Image Processing

S. Y. Kung

Princeton University, Princeton, NJ

15.1 Introduction

Digital signal and image processing encompasses a wide variety of
mathematical and algorithmic techniques, including transform techniques, convolution/correlation filtering, and some key linear algebraic methods. These algorithms possess common properties such as
regularity, recursiveness, and locality, which can be naturally exploited in array processor design. With very large scale integration
(VLSI) it becomes feasible to construct an array processor which
closely resembles the flow graph corresponding to the algorithm of interest. The most prominent examples are the *systolic arrays* [H.T.
Kung 82] and *wavefront arrays* [Kung 82]. These types of arrays are
highly regular, parallel, and pipelined, which maximize the strength
of VLSI in terms of intensive computing power and yet circumvent its
main limitation on communication. Therefore, they can offer a
throughput rate adequate for real-time signal/image processing.

Systolic arrays. A systolic array is a network of processors which
rhythmically compute and pass data through the system. It often represents an algorithm-oriented processor array and is used as an attached processor of a host computer. The systolic array features the
important properties of modularity, regularity, local interconnection,
high degree of pipelining, and highly synchronized multiprocessing.
Extensive literature on the subject of systolic array processing exists;
the reader is referred to Fisher [85] and the references therein.

Wavefront arrays. The data movements in the systolic arrays are controlled by global timing-reference "beats." The burden of having to

synchronize the entire computing network will become severe for very large scale arrays. A simple solution is to take advantage of the *dataflow computing* principle which is natural to signal processing algorithms, which leads to the design of the wavefront arrays. There are two approaches to deriving wavefront array algorithms: one is to trace and pipeline the computational wavefronts [Kung 82]; the other is based on a dataflow graph (DFG) model as proposed in Sec. 15-2. Conceptually, the requirement on correct "timing" in systolic array is now replaced by the correct "sequencing" in the wavefront array, opening up new flexibilities in many design aspects. In fact, the wavefront array can be viewed as a static dataflow array which supports the direct hardware implementation of regular dataflow graphs. By the dataflow principle, the parallelism extraction and programming for the wavefront arrays are relatively simpler.

Single-instruction-stream, multiple-data-stream (SIMD) computers, multiple-instruction-stream, multiple-data-stream (MIMD) computers, systolic arrays, and wavefront arrays are currently popular multiprocessors. To highlight the characteristic differences among these different architectures mentioned above, we propose a classification as shown in Fig. 15.1. Note that an SIMD array usually loads data into its local memories before the computation starts, while systolic and

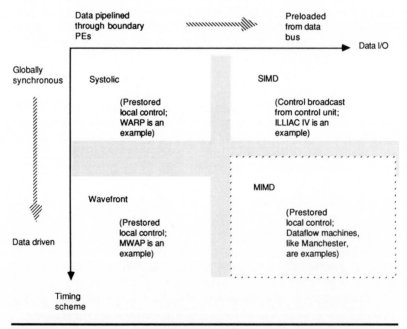

Figure 15.1   Classifications of SIMD and MIMD machines, systolic arrays, and wavefront arrays.

wavefront arrays usually pipe data from an outside host and also pipe the results back to the host. A systolic array has local instruction codes, and external data are piped into the array concurrently with the processing. SIMD and wavefront arrays can be regarded as somewhat more complex as compared with systolic arrays. An SIMD array has control (instruction) buses and data buses (in lieu of the local instruction codes adopted in the systolic arrays). Wavefront arrays, on the other hand, provide data-driven processing capability. MIMD multiprocessors in general offer all the features just mentioned, possibly with an additional feature of shared memories.

In Moore [87], Dew and Manning show comparisons of SIMD arrays and systolic arrays for vision preprocessing application. It was reported that local windowing operations can be effectively implemented on both systolic and SIMD arrays. However, for data-dependent operations such as the binary search correlator the utilization of the SIMD array will be inferior to the systolic array. The better efficiency of the systolic or wavefront array is due to the fact that the host is responsible for the image storage and can select the desired data and pipe them into the array.

Organization of the chapter.   The trends of special-purpose array processors have necessitated a systematic methodology of mapping computations onto systolic arrays. To facilitate the mapping, regular computations can be represented in some computational graphs. In Sec. 15-2, we introduce mapping methodology for mapping homogeneous computational graphs onto systolic and wavefront arrays. A more general methodology for mapping heterogeneous computational graphs onto systolic arrays can be found in Kung [87]. System design issues, such as array system organization, matching algorithms to a fixed array, partitioning a problem to fit into a given size array, and fault tolerance of array processors, are discussed in Sec. 5-3. Section 5-4 illustrates many systolic array design examples for signal/image processing applications, including the two-dimensional convolution for edge detection, shortest path problem, dynamic time warping for speech recognition, simulated annealing for image restoration, and artificial neural networks.

15.2   Mapping Algorithms to Systolic/Wavefront Arrays

The main concern in algorithm-oriented array processor design is, *Given an algorithm, how is an array processor systematically derived?* The ultimate design should begin with a powerful algorithmic notation to express the recurrence and parallelism associated with the description of the space-time activities. Next, this description will be converted into a VLSI hardware description or into executable array processor machine codes.

The methodology proposed in this section is an extension of graph-based mapping techniques investigated by many authors. For an extensive review, please see Fortes [85] and Rao [85]. These previous efforts all share as a common basis the work on uniform recurrence equations (UREs) by Karp, Miller, and Winograd [Karp 67]. Their approaches have recently been further popularized by Moldovan [83] and Rao [85].

The constraints governing the mapping to array processors of an algorithm are the data dependencies among the computations. To describe the data dependencies in an algorithm, we introduce the *dependence graph (DG)*. The DG is a directed acyclic graph, in which nodes represent the computations in the algorithm and its directed arcs specify the direct data dependencies in computations. If the computation of a variable at index point B depends on the value of a variable at index point A, then B is dependent on A and there is a directed arc from A to B in the DG. In order to obtain a locally connected array configuration, which is suited for VLSI, the arcs in the DG should be "local," i.e., the lengths of the arcs are not proportional to the size of the graph. Usually, the algorithms we are interested in are very "regular"; therefore, the variables in the algorithm can be represented by indices, such as $x(i,j,k)$. To derive the DG of an algorithm, it is very useful to express the algorithm in a *single assignment* form, in which every indexed variable is assigned a unique value in the entire computation. Then we can assign the computations associated with the same index point to a node in the DG, and assign the data dependencies between variables of different indices to the arcs in the DG.

In this chapter, we are mainly interested in the mapping of *shift-invariant (SI)* or uniform DGs, in which the dependence arcs appear to be the same for every node. In this case, the dependence arcs can be described by a set of *dependence vectors,* which correspond to the index differences of the end nodes of the arcs. However, there is a large class of problems that can be solved by algorithms that are "semiregular." We have developed a more general mapping methodology to cope with this class of problems [18].

For a shift-invariant DG, a simple linear mapping can be used to map the algorithm to a systolic or a wavefront array. This mapping is divided into *three stages,* which is shown pictorially in Fig. 15.2 and further described below.

Stage 1: Local DG design. In the first stage, a local DG is developed to perform the computation. Since the structure of a DG greatly affects

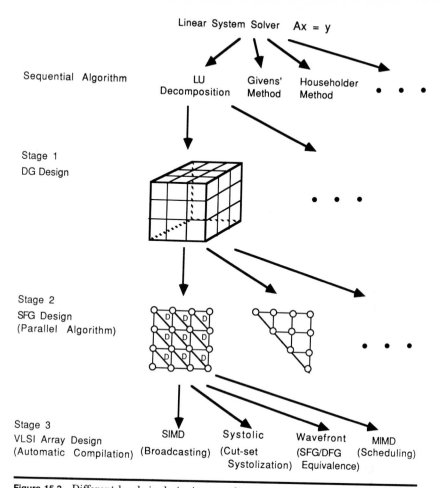

Figure 15.2 Different levels in designing systolic/wavefront arrays.

the final array design, either a very "good" DG is derived directly or further modifications on the DG are required in order to achieve a better design.

Stage 2: Signal flow graph design. In the second stage, the nodes of the DG are mapped onto an abstract processor array architecture, which is modeled by a *signal flow graph* (SFG). This mapping, involving both the assignment of DG nodes to processors and their scheduling in time, is guided by the structure of the DG. Since the DG treated is shift-invariant, linear mapping is used in this stage.

Stage 3: Systolic/wavefront array processor design. The third stage addresses the issues of implementing the SFG via a systolic/wavefront array. The progression through these stages is not strictly top-down. Factors at one stage may prompt a designer to backtrack to a previous stage. In general, any design effort will involve iterations through this cycle.

15.2.1   Stage 1: Local DG design

The question of how to develop a local DG is not easy to answer. It is much like trying to describe how to invent an algorithm. However, given a general approach to the problem, such as a serial algorithm or a set of recursive equations, there are several steps to go through in deriving a local DG:

1. Identify the individual primitive computations.

2. Define an index space structure that naturally fits these computations. Associate the intermediate result of each computation with a unique indexed variable, therefore generating the single assignment form. From this, a set of basic (possibly nonlocal) dependence relations can be determined. This generates the indexed single assignment form.

3. Localize the dependence arcs so that only local dependencies exist.

The first two steps are rather intuitive and it is difficult to give specific techniques that are helpful. In the last (localization) stage, however, several design options can be used if the nonlocal dependencies are of the *broadcast* type; i.e., there is a single data *source* and multiple data *receivers*. Since all these receiver nodes are dependent on the source data, this set of receiver nodes constitutes a *broadcast contour*. Localized data dependencies can be derived from the broadcast contour by using a *transmittent variable,* which propagates data without being modified. This localization technique can be illustrated by the following example.

Example: DG for Convolution Algorithm   The problem of convolution is defined as follows: Given two sequences $u(j)$ and $w(j), j = 0, 1,\ldots, N - 1$, the convolution of the two sequences is

$$y(j) = \sum_{k=0}^{j} u(k)w(j - k)$$

or

$$y_j = \sum_{k=0}^{j} u_k w_{j-k}$$

where $j = 0, 1, \ldots, 2N - 2$.

The first step of deriving the single assignment form is to introduce a recursive variable y_j^k. Then the convolution equation can be rewritten in terms of a recursive form:

$$y_j^k = y_j^{k-1} + u_k \bullet w_{j-k} \qquad (15.1)$$

where $k = 0, 1, \ldots, j$ when $j = 0, 1, \ldots, N - 1$; and $k = j - N + 1, j - N + 2, \ldots, N - 1$ when $j = N, N + 1, \ldots, 2N - 2$.

Note that Eq. (15.1) is now in a single assignment form. However, Eq. (15.1) is an expression with global data dependencies.

By replacing the broadcast contours with local arcs, the global DG can be easily converted to a localized version as shown in Fig. 15.3a. The localized DG has a corresponding (local) single assignment form, as follows:

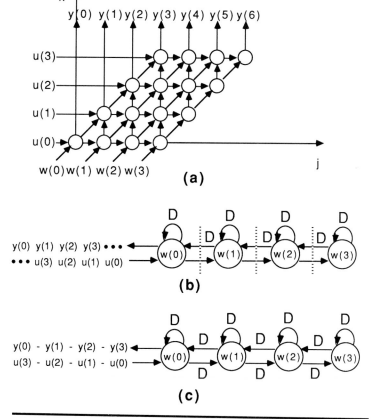

(a)

(b)

(c)

Figure 15.3 (a) Localized DG for convolution; (b) an SFG obtained by projection in $[1\ 1]^T$ direction; (c) a systolic array obtained by cut-set transformation of part b.

$$y_j^k = y_j^{k-1} + u_j^k \cdot w_j^k \qquad y_j^0 = 0$$

$$u_j^k = u_{j-1}^k \qquad u_0^k = u^k$$

$$w_j^k = w_{j-1}^{k-1} \qquad w_{j-k}^0 = w_{j-k}$$

where $k = 0, 1, \ldots, j$ when $j = 0, 1, \ldots, N - 1$; and $k = j - N + 1, j - N + 2, \ldots,$
$N - 1$ when $j = N, N + 1, \ldots, 2N - 2$.

15.2.2   Stage 2: Signal flow graph design

Definition: Signal flow graph.   A *signal flow graph* (SFG) is a directed graph consisting of *nodes* and *arcs* weighted with *arc delays*. The nodes model computations and the arcs communications. Time is explicitly modeled by the delays, since node computations and arc communications are assumed to take zero time. An SFG must have a nonnegative number of delays on every arc. A systolic array differs from an SFG only in that there should be a positive number of delays on every arc. An example of an SFG for convolution is shown in Fig. 15.3*b*.

We introduce the SFG to serve as an abstract representation of a processor array. Hence, the SFG can model the implementation, in time and space, of a computation described by a local DG. To obtain this implementation we *map* the DG onto the SFG. This mapping includes *assigning* the nodes in the index space to particular nodes of the SFG and *scheduling* the order in which these nodes are to be computed. Due to the more abstract nature and fewer timing constraints of the SFG, it is easier to map a DG onto an SFG than it is to map the DG directly to hardware. The SFG representation so obtained can then be transformed to a systolic or wavefront array. Basically the SFG represents an intermediate level which allows many of the structural and timing issues to be treated separately from each other.

Mapping from a DG to an SFG.   To implement an SI DG, a projection from the index space onto an array processor can be used. The meaning of projection is to assign the operations of all nodes along a line (corresponding to the projection direction $\vec{d}$) to a single processor (see Fig. 15.4*a*).

The projection should be accompanied by a specific schedule, which defines the sequence of operations in *all* the PEs. That is, we need to specify at what time each node of the DG is executed. Only linear schedule will be adopted here. A linear schedule is a linear mapping in which all nodes on an *equitemporal hyperplane* are mapped to the same integer and thus are executed at the same time. The set of integers then corresponds to a set of parallel hyperplanes. Mathematically, a linear schedule $L(\mathbf{i})$, denoted by a column vector $\vec{s}$, maps a node index $\mathbf{i}$ to an integer $L(\mathbf{i}) = \vec{s}^{\mathrm{T}}\mathbf{i}$ (see Fig. 15.4*b*).

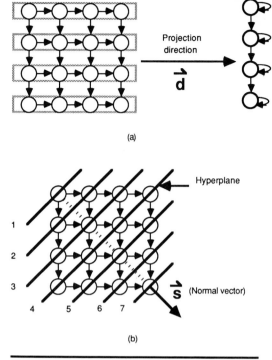

(a)

(b)

Figure 15.4 Illustration of (a) a linear projection with projection vector $\vec{d}$; (b) a linear schedule $\vec{s}$ and its hyperplanes.

To ensure an effective pipelining, the scheduling vector $\vec{s}$, which shows the normal direction of the equitemporal hyperplanes, must satisfy the following conditions:†

$$1.\ \vec{s}^{\,T}\vec{e} \geqslant 0 \qquad \text{for any dependence arc } \vec{e} \qquad (15.2)$$

$$2.\ \vec{s}^{\,T}\vec{d} > 0 \qquad\qquad\qquad\qquad\qquad\qquad (15.3)$$

where T denotes transpose.

A linear schedule, whose scheduling vector $\vec{s}$ satisfies these two conditions, is called a *permissible linear schedule*. Using a projection combined with a permissible linear schedule, an SFG can then be pro-

---

†These conditions can be checked by inspection. In fact, these conditions are true if and only if there exists a hyperplane whose normal vector $\vec{s}$ is not orthogonal to the direction $\vec{d}$, and all the dependency arcs are pointing in the same direction across the hyperplane.

duced where the schedule or time dimension is represented by the arc delays and the processors in the processor space by the indexed nodes.

The above graph-based projection procedure may be formally described in terms of linear transformation of the indices. Given a DG of dimension n, a projection vector $\vec{d}$, and a permissible linear schedule $\vec{s}$, then an SFG may be derived based on the following mappings:

1. *Node mapping:* This mapping assigns the node computations in the DG to processors. The set of nodes **P** of the SFG are represented by the mapping

$$\mathbf{P} : R \rightarrow I^{n-1}$$

where R is the index set of the nodes of the DG, and I_{n-1} is the cartesian product of $(n-1)$ integers. The mapping of a computation **c** in the DG onto a node **n** in the SFG is found by

$$\mathbf{n} = \mathbf{P}^{\mathrm{T}}\mathbf{c}$$

where the *processor basis* P, denoted by an $n \times (n-1)$ matrix, is *orthogonal* to $\vec{d}$. Mathematically,

$$\mathbf{P}^{\mathrm{T}} \vec{d} = \mathbf{0}$$

2. *Arc mapping:* This mapping maps the arcs of the DG to the arcs of the SFG. The arc $\vec{e}$ into each node of the SFG and the number of delays $D(\vec{e})$ on it are derived from the dependence $\vec{e}$ at each point in the (shift-invariant) DG by

$$
\begin{bmatrix} D(\vec{e}) \\ \cdots \\ \vec{e} \end{bmatrix} = \begin{bmatrix} \vec{s}^{\mathrm{T}} \\ \cdots \\ \mathbf{P}^{\mathrm{T}} \end{bmatrix} [\vec{e}]
$$

3. *I/O mapping:* The SFG node position **n** and time $t(\mathbf{c})$ of an input of the DG computation **c** is derived as

$$
\begin{bmatrix} t(\mathbf{c}) \\ \cdots \\ \mathbf{n} \end{bmatrix} = \begin{bmatrix} \vec{s}^{\mathrm{T}} \\ \cdots \\ \mathbf{P}^{\mathrm{T}} \end{bmatrix} [\mathbf{c}]
$$

A similar mapping applies to output nodes.

Remark. The elements of $\vec{s}$, $\vec{d}$, and **P** are integers. Clearly, it is desirable to have these vectors (matrices) represented by the smallest integers whenever possible. To avoid confusion, from now on the elements of $\vec{s}$ are restricted to be coprime. That is, *the greatest common divisor of all the elements of $\vec{s}$ is 1.* The elements of $\vec{d}$ are also assumed to be coprime, as are the elements of each column vector of **P**.

Example: SFGs for Convolution   The two-dimensional index space of convolution, as shown in Fig. 15.3a, can be decomposed into a direct sum of a one-dimensional *processor space* and a one-dimensional *schedule space*. With the projection direction $(\vec{d})$ $[1\ 1]^\mathrm{T}$ and the scheduling vector $(\vec{d})$ $[0\ 1]$, the SFG obtained is shown in Fig. 15.3b. Note that all the outputs $y(n)$ are obtained from the boundary processor.

15.2.3   Stage 3: Systolic/wavefront array processor design

Many issues are involved in the implementation of algorithms described by SFGs, and a number of previous works have focused on them [Kung 84, 87]. In brief, an SFG can be transformed to a systolic or a wavefront array.

Systolic array design.   Note that the SFG obtained from a local DG in stage 2 is always spatially localized but not necessarily *temporally localized*. That is, some arcs of the SFG contain no delay. An SFG is easily implemented as a systolic array once it is temporally localized. Temporal localization involves a *retiming* or *systolization* transformation of the SFG to an equivalent SFG (that performs the same computation) which has no zero delay arcs. A number of techniques exist to perform this transformation [Kung 87]. A systolic array can then be constructed with a PE corresponding to each SFG node and interconnections corresponding to the SFG arcs.

Cut-set systolization.   The cut-set systolization procedure is based on two simple rules:

Rule 1. Time-Scaling: All delays **D** may be scaled by a single positive integer α,† i.e., **D** can be replaced by $\alpha\mathbf{D}'$. Correspondingly, the input and output rates also have to be scaled by a factor of α (with respect to the new time unit $\mathbf{D}'$). The time-scaling factor (or, equivalently, the slowdown factor) α is determined by the slowest cycle in the SFG array [Kung 87].

Rule 2. Delay-Transfer: Given any cut-set of the SFG,‡ which partitions the graph into two components, we can group the arcs of the cut-set into *inbound arcs* and *outbound arcs,* depending upon the di-

---

†α is also known as the *pipelining period* of the SFG.

‡A cut-set in an SFG is a minimal set of arcs, which partitions the SFG into two parts.

rections assigned to the arcs. Rule 2 allows advancing $k(\mathbf{D}')$ time units on all the outbound arcs and delaying k time units on the inbound arcs, or vice versa. It is clear that, for a (time-invariant) SFG, the general system behavior is not affected, because the effects of lags and advances cancel each other in the overall timing. Note that the input/input and input/output timing relationships also remain exactly the same only if they are located on the same side of the cutset. Otherwise, they should be adjusted by a lag of $+k$ time units or an advance of $-k$ time units. If there is more than one cut-set involved and if the input and output are separated by more than one cut-set, then such adjustment factors should be accumulated.

The following statement guarantees that the basic cut-set rules are sufficient for the systolization procedure [Kung 84].

All computable SFGs can be made temporally local by following the cut-set systolization rules. Consequently, a spatially local and regular SFG array is always systolizable.

Example: Systolization of SFGs for Convolution   To systolize the SFG in Fig. 15.3*b*, rule 1 is applied with $\alpha = 2$, and then rule 2 is applied. The resulting systolic array is shown in Fig. 15.3*c*.

Wavefront array design.   Given an SFG, we can also implement it by a wavefront array. The SFG already defines the structure of the wavefront array, the only remaining thing to be specified is the initial token distribution. A general rule for initial token assignment is that *the number of initial tokens on an arc of the wavefront array is equal to the number of delays of the corresponding arc in the SFG* [Kung 84].

On the other hand, a wavefront array can be directly determined by the DG, without obtaining the SFG. This is explained next. Due to the dataflow nature, a wavefront array does not have a fixed schedule. Therefore, the operation of the wavefront array is dictated only by the data dependency structure and the initial data tokens. The wavefront array can be modeled by a *dataflow graph (DFG)* as explained below. A DFG is a *weighted, directed* graph:

$$\text{DFG} \equiv [N, A, D(a), Q(a), \tau(n)]$$

in which nodes N model computation and arcs A model communication links. Each node n has an associated nonnegative real weight $\tau(n)$ representing its computation time. Each arc a is associated with a nonnegative integer weight $D(a)$, representing the number of initial data tokens on the arc, and a positive integer weight $Q(a)$, representing the first-in, first-out (FIFO) queue size of the arc. A node is *enabled* when all input arcs contain tokens and all output arcs contain empty queues. A node *fires* after it has been enabled for its computation time. Whenever a node fires, each input arc is taken away one input token and each output arc from the node is assigned one more token.

There exists a systematic way to map DGs to DFGs. Recall that for a shift-invariant DG, some boundary nodes of the DG may appear to have different dependency structure (e.g., fewer dependency arcs) than that of the internal nodes. For our mapping, it is necessary to enforce a uniform appearance by assigning some initializing data (usually a constant, e.g., zero) to the boundary nodes of the DG. Now *all* the nodes should have the same dependency arcs (see Fig. 15.5*b*), and all the data input to boundary nodes are viewed as *input data*.

For the shift-invariant DG and a given projection direction $\vec{d}$, we can derive the DFG in a manner similar to the systolic mapping, except that the delay elements are now replaced by the initial tokens $D(a)$. Each input data token in the DG is mapped to an initial token on the corresponding arc in the DFG. Here the queue size for each DFG arc is assumed to be large enough to accommodate the target algorithms. An example of mapping a DG to a DFG (with its initial tokens) is shown in Fig. 15.5*b*. In contrast to the systolic mapping as shown in Fig. 15.5*a*, *the DFG mapping does not need any schedule vector* $\vec{s}$, since the data-driven computing nature of the wavefront array obviates the need of specifying the exact timing. Furthermore, based on the dataflow principle, an optimal schedule implied by the DG will be automatically followed. This is explained below.

Assume that each DG node is assigned to one PE and that all the input data are available, then minimum computation time can be achieved. Suppose that the projection direction $\vec{d}$ is chosen so that *there is a strict dependency among the nodes which are mapped to the same PE*. Thus the sequential processing among these nodes by the single PE should not in any way impose extra slowdown in the execution time, so the resulting DFG can compute the same computation in minimum time. This provides a simple guideline for the selection of the projection direction $\vec{d}$ (In fact, this rule is also useful for the systolic mapping.) Note that this guideline may be generalized to cover the inhomogeneous DG and/or the *nonlinear assignment* situations [Kung 87].

This section demonstrates the similarities between the mappings to systolic and wavefront arrays. In the following, we shall concentrate on the systolic array designs. However, most ideas apply equally well to the wavefront array design.

15.3 System Design Issues of Systolic/Wavefront Arrays

In the previous sections, we only treated the design and analysis of processor arrays. An important and more challenging subject is, *How*

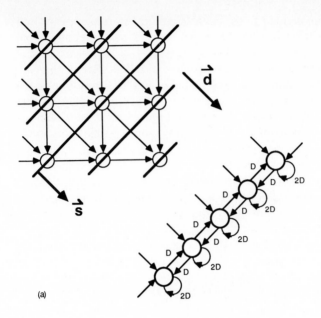

(a)

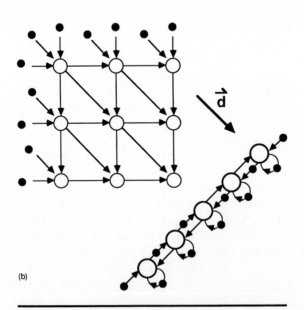

(b)

Figure 15.5 (*a*) Mapping a DG to a systolic array, and (*b*) mapping a DG to a DFG (wavefront array). Note that the DG represents a convolution-like algorithm.

to incorporate these arrays into an overall computing system? Generally speaking, in an overall array processor system, one seeks to maximize the following performance indicators: effective system organization, high-speed communication to enhance the computing power, programmability for adequate software support, flexibility on problem partitioning, and fault-tolerance to improve system reliability. In the following, we will address these issues.

15.3.1 Organization of systolic/wavefront array systems

A wavefront array processor may be used either as an attached processor interfacing with a compatible host machine or as a stand-alone processor equipped with a global control processor. In general, desirable features for an array processor system are (1) high speed, (2) flexibility, (3) reliability, and (4) cost-effectiveness. A possible overall system configuration of an array processor is proposed in Fig. 15.6. The system consists of the following major components:

- Processor array(s)
- Interconnection network(s)
- Host computer and interface unit

15.3.2 Matching algorithms to arrays

In the previous section, the issue addressed is *mapping* an algorithm onto a dedicated array. Recall that the main question addressed there is, *How is a (dedicated) array processor design affected by the data structure of the algorithm under consideration?* Now let us address a closely related question, *How is a set of algorithms best programmed and executed on a specific array processor?* This is referred to as the *algorithm matching* problem, in which the key parameters of the array such as the number of PEs, communication links, or memory size are assumed to be under certain constraints. In other words, matching is basically a "constrained mapping." If constraints are on the communication links, some special methods will be necessary to solve the problem. When the constraints are on the number of PEs or the size of memory, the matching problem basically becomes a partitioning issue. If the intended processor array structure is of a lower dimension, say a one-dimensional array, and the DG is of a higher dimension, say a three-dimensional DG, then it is possible to project the DG *multiple times* to obtain the intended array. This is the so-called multiprojection. These issues are discussed next.

Matching mesh algorithms to hypercube structures. In order to better understand the general methodology of matching algorithms with cer-

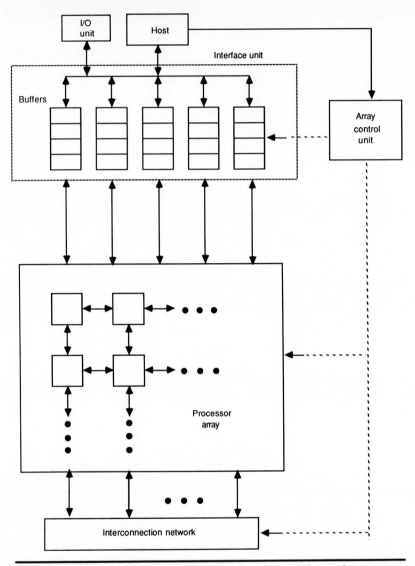

Figure 15.6 An array processor system consists of host/ACU, interface system, interconnection networks, and processor array.

tain structures, let us choose one case study example of matching mesh algorithms to hypercube structures.

Our aim here is to demonstrate that a mesh algorithm (of any dimension) may be embedded in a hypercube [Chan 86]. Combining this with the previous observation that any local DG can be matched to a mesh [Kung 87], it is concluded that all local DGs may be matched to a hypercube array.

An n-cube is a hypercube consisting of 2^n nodes. The nodes of an n-cube can be labeled by n-bit binary indices, from 0 to $2^n - 1$. *By the definition of hypernetwork, two processors are directly linked if and only if their binary index representations differ only by one bit.* For example, if $n = 3$, then the 8 nodes can be represented as the vertices of a three-dimensional cube as shown in Fig. 15.7*a*. To see how to embed meshes in a hypercube, let us consider a two-dimensional mesh of size 8×4 as shown in Fig. 15.7*b* and examine how it might be embedded into a 5-cube. (Note that $2^5 = 32$.) By using a 3-bit Gray code ($b_1 b_2 b_3$) for labeling the horizontal dimension and a 2-bit Gray code ($c_1 c_2$) for the vertical dimension, each node in the mesh may be labeled as a 5-bit representation ($b_1 b_2 b_3 c_1 c_2$) [Chan 86]. Due to the Gray coding, the corresponding indices between any two neighboring nodes in the mesh differ exactly by 1 bit. By the definition of *hypernetwork*, their corresponding nodes in the hypercube are thus directly connected. Thus, the embedding of this 8×4 mesh into a 5-cube is completed. By a similar manner, any algorithm executable in a mesh can be easily matched to (and executed by) a hypercube computer.

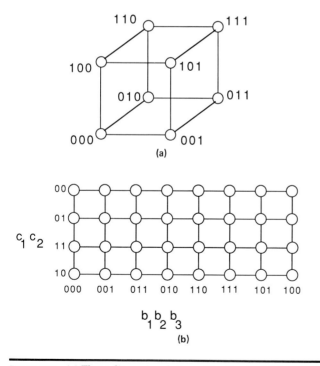

Figure 15.7   (*a*) Three-dimensional view of the 3-cube; (*b*) two-dimensional Gray code for an 8×4 mesh. (Adapted from [3].)

Note that each PE of an n-cube connects to n other PEs, and each PE of a mesh connects only to four neighboring PEs. In our method, the communication ability of a hypercube is not fully utilized. The method to further enhance the utilization is yet to be investigated.

Partitioning.   The partitioning problem is basically *mapping computations of a larger size problem to an array processor of a smaller size.* It is a basic requirement in many practical system designs, since no matter what special-purpose computing hardware is available, there is a computation too large for it [Heller 85]. There have been several works on this problem [Heller 85, Rao 85, Moldovan 86, Horiiki 87]. In general, the mapping scheme (including both the node assignment and scheduling) will be much more complicated than the regular projection methods discussed in the previous chapters. To design the partitioning scheme, the following factors should be taken into account [Moldovan 86]: *(1) minimize overall computation time, (2) minimize control overheads, (3) tradeoff between external communication and local memory.*

What to be specified is *at what time and in which PE the computation of each DG node takes place.* For a systematic mapping from the DG onto a systolic/wavefront array, the DG is regularly partitioned into many *blocks,* each consisting of a cluster of nodes in the DG. For convenience of presentation, we adopt the following mathematical notations. Suppose that an N-dimensional DG is (linearly) projected to an $(N-1)$-dimensional SFG array of size $L_1 \times L_2 \times \cdots \times L_{N-1}$. The SFG is partitioned into $M_1 \times M_2 \times \cdots \times M_{N-1}$ blocks, where each block is of size $Z_1 \times Z_2 \times \cdots \times Z_{N-1}$. Obviously, for $i = 1, 2, \ldots, N-1, Z_i = L_i/M_i$. As a simple example, we look at the computation of a matrix-vector multiplication $\mathbf{Ab} = \mathbf{c}$, where $\mathbf{A}$ is 6×6 and $\mathbf{b}$ and $\mathbf{c}$ are 6×1, with a linear array of 3 PEs. The DG of this problem is shown in Fig. 15.8a. Two partitioning of blocks are also shown in Fig. 15.8. In Fig. 15.8b, $L_1 = 6$, $M_1 = 3$, and $Z_1 = 2$. In Fig. 15.8c, $L_1 = 6$, $M_1 = 2$, and $Z_1 = 3$. There are two methods for mapping the partitioned DG to an array: the *locally sequential globally parallel* (LSGP) method and the *locally parallel globally sequential* (LPGS) method.

1. *LSGP scheme:*   In the LSGP scheme, one block is mapped to one PE. Thus, the number of blocks is equal to the number of PEs in the array, i.e., the product $M_1 \times M_2 \times \cdots \times M_{N-1}$ has to be equal to the array size. Each PE sequentially executes the nodes of the corresponding block. In order to store the node data in the block, local memory within each PE is needed, i.e., local memory size should be $Z_1 \times Z_2 \times \cdots \times Z_{N-1} \times c$, where c is a small constant (e.g., 1, 2, or 3) depending on the data dependencies. As long as the local memory is large enough for the computation under consideration, the LSGP ap-

proach is quite appealing. The LSGP scheme for the matrix-vector multiplication example is shown in Fig. 15.8d. The number of blocks M_1 is equal to the array size 3. The local memory size is $Z_1 = 2$.

2. *LPGS scheme:* In the LPGS scheme, the block size is chosen to match the array size, i.e., one block can be mapped to one array. All nodes within one block are processed concurrently, i.e., *locally parallel.* One block after another block of node data is loaded into the array and processed in a sequential manner, i.e., *globally sequential.* Hence the name LPGS. In this scheme, local memory size in the PE can be kept constant, independent of the size of computation. All intermediate data can be stored in certain buffers outside the processor array. Usually, simple FIFO buffers are adequate for storing and recirculating the intermediate data efficiently. In the above matrix-vector multiplication example for the LPGS scheme, the DG is partitioned into two blocks as shown in Fig. 15.8c.

Schedule strategies for LSGP scheme. The preceding discussion specifies only the node assignment scheme, i.e., the spatial mapping of a DG to the processor array. The scheduling part, i.e., at what time the computation takes place, is yet to be specified.

Given an N-dimensional DG and a projection direction $\vec{d}$, there is a corresponding processor basis matrix $\mathbf{P}$. Let $\mathbf{P}^T = [\vec{P}_1\ \vec{P}_2 \cdots \vec{P}_{N-1}]$ be a set of independent vectors, each orthogonal to $\vec{d}$. This set of vectors specifies the SFG space. From the *processor sharing* perspective there are $Z_1 \times Z_2 \times \cdots \times Z_{N-1}$ nodes in each block in the SFG, which share the same PE. An *acceptable* (i.e., *sufficiently slow*) linear schedule is chosen so that at any time instant, there is at most one active PE in each block. This problem can be formally stated as follows. Find a scheduling vector $\vec{s}$, which

$$\text{Minimizes } \alpha\ (= \vec{s}^T\vec{d}\ )$$

and satisfies the following constraints:

1. $\vec{s}^T\vec{e} > 0$ for all dependency arcs $\vec{e}$.
2. For all $\vec{m}$ which satisfies $\vec{m}^T\vec{s} = 0$ (i.e., $\vec{m}$ is on an equitemporal hyperplane), there exists i, such that $P_i^T\vec{m} \geq Z_i$.

Note that in the LSGP scheme, *the minimum α is very often determined by the number of processor-sharing nodes in the SFG;* i.e.,

$$\alpha = Z_1 \times Z_2 \times \cdots \times Z_{N-1}$$

Since the solution $\vec{s}$ should have its elements reasonably small, it is usually possible to obtain a solution by *enumeration* on $\vec{s}$ and $\vec{m}$. That

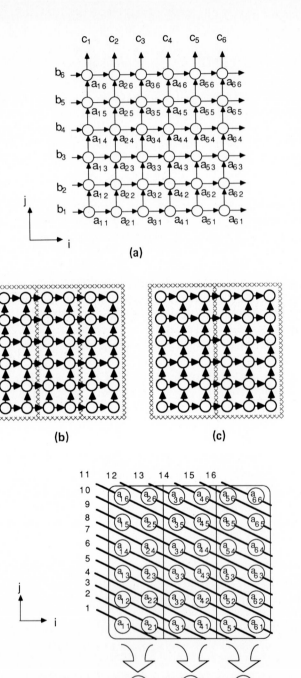

Figure 15.8 (*a*) DG for a matrix-vector multiplication; (*b*) DG being partitioned into three blocks; (*c*) DG being partitioned into two blocks; (*d*) LSGP partitioning of matrix-vector multiplication.

is, different $\vec{s}$ can be checked to see if the constraints are satisfied. Let us now look at two examples.

Example: LSGP for One-dimensional Array   In the previous matrix-vector multiplication problem,

$$\vec{d} = \begin{bmatrix} 0 \\ 1 \end{bmatrix} \qquad \vec{e}_1 = \begin{bmatrix} 1 \\ 0 \end{bmatrix} \qquad \vec{e}_2 = \begin{bmatrix} 0 \\ 1 \end{bmatrix} \qquad \text{and} \qquad \vec{P}_1 = \begin{bmatrix} 1 \\ 0 \end{bmatrix}$$

The lower bound of α is obviously $Z_1 = 2$. Thus if $[1\ 2]$ is used for $\vec{s}^{\mathrm{T}}$, we may find that it satisfies all the constraints, and the resulting α is 2 which is minimal. The result for LSGP partitioning using the linear scheduling is shown in Fig. 15.8d.

Schedule considerations for LPGS scheme.   As to the scheduling scheme for the LPGS method, a general rule is to select a (global) scheduling vector $\vec{s}^{\mathrm{T}}$, which does not violate the data dependencies. As a simple example, the result of the LPGS mapping method for matrix-vector multiplication is shown in Fig. 15.8e.

Note that the previous example can be handled by a simple scheme because there is no *reverse data dependence* for the chosen blocks so that the interblock dependencies have the advantage that blocks can be executed one after another in a *natural* order. In general, such advantageous property may not exist. Thus the choice of blocks depends on the data dependencies. A procedure to decide the blocks can be found in Moldovan [86].

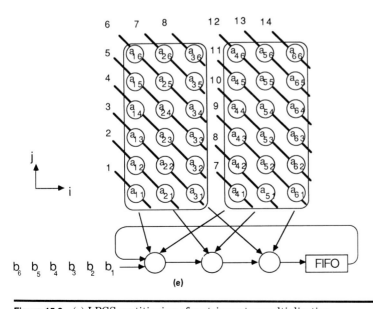

(e)

Figure 15.8   (e) LPGS partitioning of matrix-vector multiplication.

Multiprojection. In general, it is possible to map an N-dimensional DG directly onto an $(N - k)$-dimensional SFG $(k = 1, 2, ..., N - 1)$ [Rao 85]. In the previous section, we proposed a methodology that maps an N-dimensional DG to an $(N - 1)$-dimensional SFG. In principle, the method can be applied k times and thus reduces the dimension of the array to $N - k$. More elaborately, a similar projection method can be used to map an $(N - 1)$-dimensional SFG into an $(N - 2)$-dimensional SFG, and so on. This scheme is called the *multiprojection* method.

To simplify the discussion, let us assume that the SI DG is N-dimensional, and after one projection (say, in the i direction), the resulting SFG is $(N - 1)$-dimensional. The question is, *How to further project the SFG to an $(N - 2)$-dimensional SFG?*

The potential difficulties of this mapping are (1) the presence of delay arcs in the $(N - 1)$-dimensional SFG, and (2) the possibilities of loops or cycles in an SFG, although no loops or cycles can exist in a DG. Therefore, mapping this SFG to an $(N - 2)$-dimensional SFG will require additional care.

To handle the cycle problem, an *instance graph* (at certain time $t = t_0$) is defined as *the SFG with all the delay arcs removed*. Hence the *instance graph* has no loops or cycles. According to the SFG schedule, all the nodes in the instance graph are executed simultaneously at $t = t_0$. An activity instance (at t_0) can be defined as the nodes represented by the instance graph at $t = t_0$. According to the SFG schedule, there will be no overlap in time between two consecutive activity instances (one at $t = t_0$ and the next instance at $t = t_0 + D$).

Recall that a mapping methodology should consist of a projection part and a schedule part:

- As to the projection part, the same projection method previously proposed may be applied in the j direction. *The original SFG (with delay arcs included) is now projected along the $\vec{d}$-(i.e., j) direction.*

- The schedule part is somewhat more complicated. First, it is always possible to find a valid SFG schedule vector $\vec{s}$ for the instance graph, since there is no loop or cycle in an instance graph. To project the $(N - 1)$-dimensional instance graph to an $(N - 2)$-dimensional graph, it is necessary to create a new type of delay, denoted by τ. Note that the *global* delay D and *local* delay τ are intimately related. The relationship depends upon the constraints imposed by both the processor availability and the data dependency (i.e., data availability). *The original delay arcs with βD map to an arc bearing delay weight $\beta D + \vec{s} \cdot \vec{e} \, \tau$ (see Fig. 15.9b).*

Now let us more closely examine the relationship between D and τ. *First,* to ensure *processor availability,* an activity instance must have

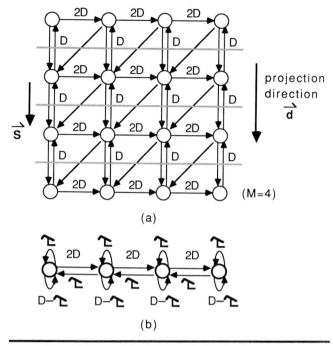

projection
direction
$\vec{d}$

(M=4)

(a)

(b)

Figure 15.9   (*a*) The original SFG; (*b*) the further projected SFG.

adequate time to be complete before the next activity instance starts. So the following condition is necessary:

(a) $D \geqslant \tau + (M - 1)(\vec{s} \cdot \vec{d})\tau$

where M is the maximal number of nodes along the $\vec{d}$-direction in the instance graph (see Fig. 15.9a). Note that this condition also guarantees that there is no time overlap between two activity instances.

Second, to ensure *data availability,* conditions (b) and (c) are necessary for all arcs $\vec{e}$:

(b) $\beta D + (\vec{s} \cdot \vec{e})\tau \geqslant 0$

(c) $\beta D + (\vec{s} \cdot \vec{e})\tau \geqslant \tau$ for at least one arc in every cycle

Condition (b) is necessary in order to satisfy the causality condition of the SFG. Condition (c) is necessary to ensure that every cycle in the new SFG has at least one delay element (τ) in the cycle. Note that these two conditions are necessary for a graph to be qualified as an SFG.

Conditions (a), (b), and (c) together guarantee both the processor and data availability for the new SFG. Therefore, the mapping is complete. Note that condition (a) is very often the dominant constraint. In fact, condition (a) would be sufficient to ensure conditions (b) and (c) whenever a locally interconnected SFG is considered.

Obviously, this mapping methodology may be directly applied to map from $(N - 2)$-dimensional SFG to $(N - 3)$-dimensional SFG. The method can be applied k times (i.e., using k steps of simple projection) to reduce the dimension of the array to $N - k$.

Example: Band Matrix Multiplication To demonstrate the procedure, a two-dimensional SFG for *band matrix multiplication* and its corresponding projected SFG are shown in Fig. 15.10a and b. In Fig. 15.10b, note that the matrix **B** is

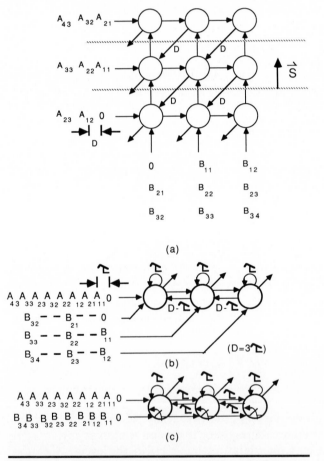

Figure 15.10 Multiprojection on band matrix multiplication. (*a*) A two-dimensional SFG and a "good" schedule; (*b*) the one-dimensional projected SFG; (*c*) the final SFG using **D** = 3*r*.

input in parallel and will lead to an I/O bandwidth of order M which is usually not desirable. Since there is only one datum in M time steps for each parallel input arc, these data can be interleaved and input from the boundary PE, as shown in Fig. 15.10c.

15.4   Signal/Image Processing Applications

A successful array processor design requires an understanding of the signal and image formation process, the algorithm class involved, and the specifications of the intended applicational system. Digital signal and image processing encompasses a wide variety of mathematical and algorithmic techniques. Two dominating aspects in signal and image processing requirements are enormous throughput rates and a huge amount of data and memory. On the other hand, most signal and image processing algorithms are dominated by transform techniques, convolution/correlation filtering, and some key linear algebraic methods. These algorithms possess common properties such as regularity, recursiveness, and locality, which can be naturally exploited in array processor design.

In this section, the systolic architectures for some important signal/ image and scientific processing algorithms are derived using the mapping methodology. These algorithms include two-dimensional convolution for two-dimensional edge detection, dynamic time warping (DTW) for speech recognition, shortest path solver for graph theory, simulated annealing for image restoration, and neuronal computation in artificial neural networks.

15.4.1   Edge detection by means of two-dimensional convolution

Edge detection via mask processing.   Two-dimensional convolution is the most common method for image edge detection. Assume that image $\mathbf{x}$ is to be edge detected; the two-dimensional convolution involves convolving a small window pattern $\mathbf{w}$ with the image $\mathbf{x}$. This is done by moving the window pattern $\mathbf{w}$ over the image. At each point the convolution is computed:

$$y(m,n) = \sum_i \sum_j w(i,j)x(m - i,n - j) \tag{15.4}$$

For two-dimensional convolution we define a $k_1 \times k_2$ matrix as a window. Since the size of an image may typically vary from 256×256 up to 8K $\times$ 8K pixels, we immediately see the necessity of extremely fast operation. For real-time applications, where the image is updated 30 to 60 times per second, the speed requirements are even more critical. In the following the systolic design of the two-dimensional convolution is described.

Array architecture design for two-dimensional convolution

DG design.   Without loss of generality, assume that the window size is 3×3 and the image size is $N \times N$. Then Eq. (15.4) can be rewritten as

$$y(m,n) = \sum_{j=0}^{2} \sum_{i=0}^{2} w(i,j)x(m-i,n-j)$$

Since there are four indices i, j, m, n in this equation, the DG for this algorithm is four-dimensional and the SFGs obtained via projection are three-dimensional. Because of the difficulties in drawing a four-dimensional DG, a three-dimensional DG for the image ($N \times N$) convolved with one row of the window pattern (1×3) is shown in Fig. 15.11a. Note that each two-dimensional ($3 \times N$) layer of the three-

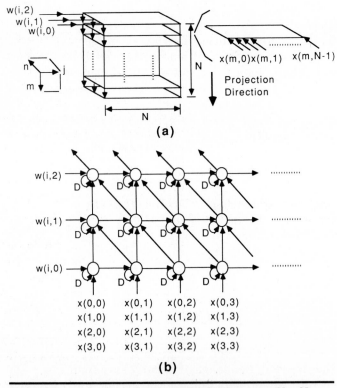

Figure 15.11   (*a*) A three-dimensional DG for the image ($N \times N$) convolved with one row of the window pattern (1×3). The four-dimensional DG may be constructed by summing up the outputs of three such three-dimensional DGs; (*b*) a two-dimensional SFG obtained by projecting the three-dimensional DG along *m* direction.

dimensional DG is the same as what was shown in Fig. 15.3a for the convolution of two one-dimensional signals. The four-dimensional DG may be constructed by summing up the outputs of three such three-dimensional DGs. Mathematically, this is equivalent to saying

$$y(m,n) = \sum_{j=0}^{2} w(0,j)x(m,n-j) + \sum_{j=0}^{2} w(1,j)x(m-1,n-j)$$

$$+ \sum_{j=0}^{2} w(2,j)x(m-2,n-j) \tag{15.5}$$

Note that each term in the right-hand side of Eq. (15.5) is represented by a three-dimensional DG.

SFG design. From the four-dimensional DG, we can generate three-dimensional SFGs. Here we consider only a three-dimensional SFG with (approximate) size $3 \times 3 \times N$. This three-dimensional SFG may be obtained by first projecting each three-dimensional DG onto one two-dimensional SFG (of size $3 \times N$) (see Fig. 15.11b) and then combining these three two-dimensional SFGs by summing up the outputs (see Fig. 15.11c).

If two-dimensional SFGs are preferred, then multiprojection can be adopted to project the three-dimensional SFG to two-dimensional SFGs. Figure 15.11d shows a two-dimensional SFG with size $3 \times N$. Different projection directions can also be applied if desired. For example, it is apparent that a 3×3 SFG can also be obtained.

Systolic array design. The SFGs shown in Fig. 15.11c and d can be easily systolized by applying cut-set procedure. For example, the two-dimensional SFG shown in Fig. 15.11d can be systolized by using rule 2 (delay-transfer) only. First, two delays are added to each arc of horizontal "cuts" (see Fig. 15.11d). Then, applying vertical cuts, one delay can be transferred from each diagonal arc to the horizontal arcs.

15.4.2 Shortest path problem

In this subsection, we consider a very important type of dynamic programming problem, i.e., the shortest path problems. We will present the design of an "optimal" systolic array for the shortest path problem using the Floyd algorithm.

The shortest path problem. The shortest path problem for a directed graph is to determine the lengths of the shortest paths between all pairs of nodes in the graph. The input is a distance matrix $\mathbf{A}$, which is defined as follows:

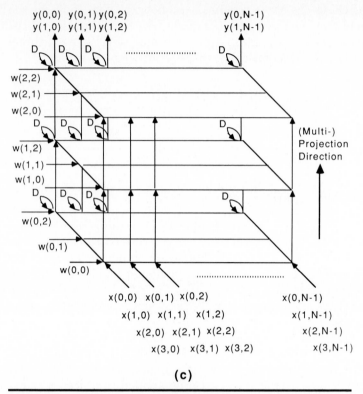

Figure 15.11   (c) The three-dimensional SFG obtained by summing the outputs of 3 two-dimensional SFGs.

1. a_{ij} = the distance from vertex i to vertex j if there is an arc from i to j.
2. $a_{ij} = \infty$ if there is no arc connecting i and j.
3. $a_{ij} = 0$ if $i = j$.

The shortest path problem is to compute the shortest path matrix $\mathbf{A}^+$, whose element a_{ij}^+ is the shortest path length from vertex i to j.

The Floyd algorithm.   Given the input matrix $\mathbf{A}$, the sequential Floyd algorithm to find $\mathbf{A}^+$ of the graph is quite well known and is as follows [Aho 74]:

$$x_{ij}^k \leftarrow x_{ij}^{k-1} \oplus x_{ik}^{k-1} \otimes x_{kj}^{k-1} \qquad \text{for } i,j,k \text{ from 1 to } N$$

where the initial $\mathbf{X}$ matrix $\mathbf{X}^0$ is equal to $\mathbf{A}$, and the output matrix $\mathbf{A}^+$ equals $\mathbf{X}^N$. The $\oplus$ operation is the minimum operation; the $\otimes$ operation is the addition operation.

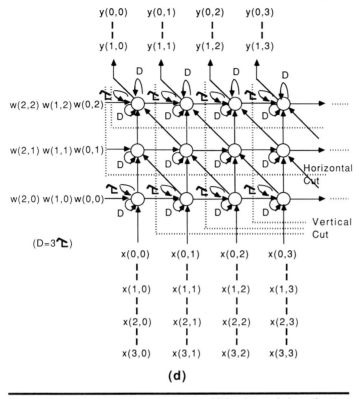

Figure 15.11 (*d*) The two-dimensional SFG obtained by adopting multiprojection.

Dependence graph. The Floyd algorithm can be easily converted to a single assignment form by introducing an iteration dimension k, and localized by adding propagating variables for the row variable r and column variable c at each level k:

$$c(i,j,k) \leftarrow \begin{cases} x(i,j,k-1) & \text{if } j = k \text{ \# distribute column } k \\ & \text{for } i,j,k \text{ from 1 to } N \\ c(i,j+1,k) & \text{if } j < k \text{ \# over row } i \\ c(i,j-1,k) & \text{if } j > k \end{cases}$$

$$r(i,j,k) \leftarrow \begin{cases} x(i,j,k-1) & \text{if } i = k \text{ \# distribute row } k \\ & \text{for } i,j,k \text{ from 1 to } N \\ r(i,j+1,k) & \text{if } i < k \text{ \# over column } j \\ r(i-1,j,k) & \text{if } i > k \end{cases}$$

$$x(i,j,k) \leftarrow x(i,j,k-1) + r(i,j,k) \times c(i,j,k) \qquad \text{for } i,j,k \text{ from 1 to } N$$

form kth connections

where the input is $x(i,j,0) \leftarrow a_{ij}$ and output is $a_{ij}^+ \leftarrow x(i,j,N)$.

The cubic DG is shown for the $N = 4$ case in Fig. 15.12a, with each ij plane drawn separately. What should have been included but not drawn are the additional dependence lines in the k direction that run from points (i,j,k) to $(i,j,k+1)$. In each plane the points which serve

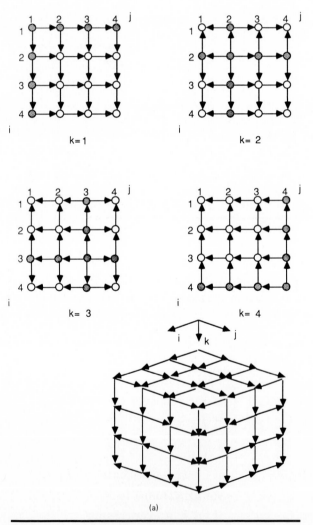

(a)

Figure 15.12 (a) Dependence graph of the Floyd algorithm for the case $N = 4$.

as the "source" of the row and column values are marked as dark nodes.

Reindexing the DG.   The DG in Fig. 15.12a is not totally regular. The source nodes in the DG move from row (column) k to row (column) $k + 1$ from the kth ij plane to the next one, and the transmittent data streams in the ij planes propagate in two opposite directions. These irregularities will create problems in the mapping. One way to get around this problem is by reindexing the nodes in the DG, thereby transforming it to a more regular DG. For this purpose, we would like to reindex the nodes in the DG such that it is shift-invariant in the i direction. The revised DG is shown in Fig. 15.12b.

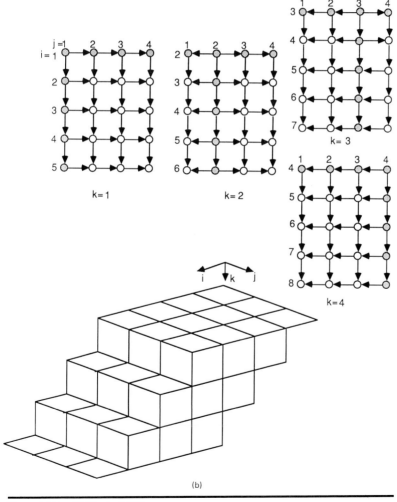

(b)

Figure 15.12   (b) Revised DG.

Projection in the *i* direction.   If we project the revised DG in the *i* direction and use a schedule vector also in the *i* direction, the resulting SFG is shown in Fig. 15.12*c*. This SFG can be systolized by the cut-set transformation along the (dashed-line) cuts shown in Fig. 15.12*c* and yields the systolic array in Fig. 15.12*d*.

Optimality of the design.   This orthogonal systolic array is an optimal one for the transitive closure problem. The array uses N^2 processors and $2N$ I/O ports. It supports a noninterleaved block pipeline period of N, so successive computations can be repeated every N steps. (Note that in Fig. 15.12*d*, the $\{b_{ij}\}$ data block follows immediately after the

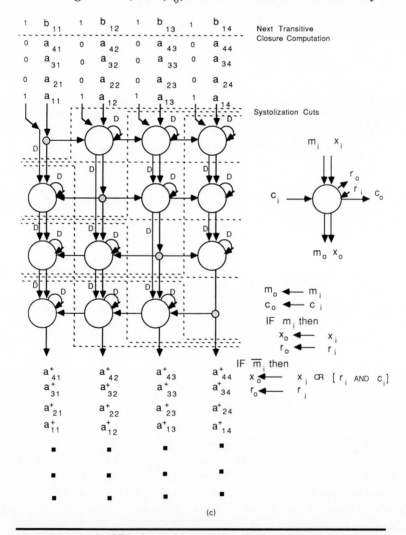

(c)

Figure 15.12   (*c*) An SFG obtained by projection in the *i* direction.

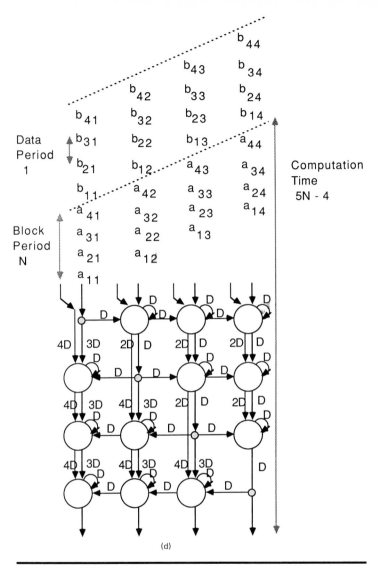

Data
Period
1

Block
Period
N

Computation
Time
5N - 4

(d)

Figure 15.12 (d) The optimal systolic array.

$\{a_{ij}\}$ data block.) Since N^3 computations must be performed with N^2 processors, N is the minimal period. This minimal period ensures 100 percent processor utilization for a series of pipelined computations. The total computation time of the systolic array is $5N - 4$. We can see from the original "parallelized" Floyd algorithm dependence graph that this is indeed optimal. In the DG in Fig. 15.12a we find that there exists a directed path of length $5N - 4$ along the path $(1, 1, 1) \rightarrow (N, 1, 1) \rightarrow (N, N, 1) \rightarrow (N, N, N) \rightarrow (1, N, N) \rightarrow (1, 1, N)$. Hence, any systolic implementation, in which all inputs must be calculated at least one step before they are used, have a computation time of at least $5N - 4$. Finally, we note that for a period of N we need to input N data and output N data at each step, and hence $2N$ is the minimal number of I/O connections required.

15.4.3 Dynamic time warping for speech recognition

Speech recognizers generally consist of four functional blocks: a feature extractor, a pattern matcher, a reference vocabulary memory, and a decision maker. Among them, the most crucial component is the pattern matcher, which involves the computation of a similarity measure between a test pattern and a reference pattern. The pattern-matching task here is considerably more complicated than the ordinary template-matching procedure; in fact, it may be regarded as a generalized version of the template-matching method. The main difference lies in the requirement of compensating the variation of speaking rates, i.e., the time misalignment between the original training reference pattern and the new input test pattern. Dynamic time warping (DTW) may be used efficiently to compensate for such nonlinear temporal distortion.

DTW algorithm via minimum cost path formulation

Unconstrained formulation. The DTW algorithm can be formulated by the following minimum cost path problem. We are going to travel through a two-dimensional cartesian grid, with size $m \times n$. Each node $V(i, j)$ has a specified cost $d(i, j)$. The nodes are connected by three types of arcs: up, right, and diagonal; and each type of arc has an associated multiplicative weight $\{w_i, i = 1, 2, 3\}$. The problem is to find a minimum cost path from the lower left corner node $V(1, 1)$ to the upper right corner node $V(m, n)$.

Let $[i(k), j(k)]$ denote the node visited at the kth step; then the cost function of a path is determined not only by the cost in the visited nodes $d(i(k), j(k))$ but also the multiplicative weight associated with the entering arc:

$$\min \sum_k d\,[i(k), j(k)]\, w\,(k) \tag{15.6}$$

where $d[i(k), j(k)]$ is the node cost visited at the kth step, and $w(k) \in \{w_i, i = 1, 2, 3\}$ is the weight at arc used to enter the node at the kth step.

In speech recognition, the input test speech consists of m frames of test feature vectors $\{\mathbf{t}_i, i = 1, 2, \ldots, m\}$. These feature vectors come from the need to characterize the speech waveform by a set of characteristic parameters, and these parameters can only be accurately extracted out in short time intervals (15 to 30 ms). In addition, we have Q sets of reference speech, each one consisting of n_q frames of reference feature vectors $\{\mathbf{r}_{qj}, q = 1, 2, \ldots, Q, j = 1, 2, \ldots, n_q\}$. The task of the speech recognizer is to match the input test speech string with all the Q sets of reference speech to find the most similar pattern; for the matching with each set of reference patterns we need to use Eq. (15.6) to find out the similarity measure. In a pattern-matching system, the node cost $d(i, j)$ stands for the distance between reference frame $\mathbf{r}_{qj}$ and test frame $\mathbf{t}_i$. If the frame parameters are LPC coefficients, then the distance is usually the Itakura distance, and the arc weighting in most cases is $w_1 = w_2 = 1$, $w_3 = 2$ [Rabiner 81].

Adding local constraints. To evaluate this function for all possible cost paths would, in general, be very computationally expensive. However, it is possible to derive constraints on the allowed path routes for the underlying physical problem. For example, a local path constraint might ensure that no more than two consecutive horizontal (or vertical) nodes can be visited. This implies that we do not allow too much replication of the same frame in the test or reference speech. The preceding local constraints can be expressed in the following formulation:

$$i(k) - i(k-1) = 0,1 \qquad \text{if } i(k-1) \neq i(k-2)$$
$$= 1 \qquad \text{if } i(k-1) = i(k-2)$$
$$j(k) - j(k-1) = 0,1 \qquad \text{if } j(k-1) \neq j(k-2)$$
$$= 1 \qquad \text{if } j(k-1) = j(k-2) \qquad (15.7)$$

Adding global constraints. We can also set global path constraints by limiting the path route to some area of the grid plane. This avoids useless computation when the two patterns are deviating too much or have one obviously different pattern; then the minimum cost path will go beyond the banded diagonal region, and we can skip this reference pattern without further effort. The mathematical formulation for this global constraint can be expressed as $|i(k) - j(k)| \leq B$, where $2B + 1$ is the effective matching area.

Recursive computation of path cost. Once local and global constraints have been set, the accumulated cost $G_q(i, j)$ between the test pattern and the qth set of reference speech of the minimum cost path ends at any candidate node (i, j) can then be calculated recursively, using the fact that the cost depends only on $d(i, j)$ and the accumulated cost of the minimum cost paths ending at the allowed predecessors node of (i, j). This recursive evaluation property relies upon the fact that no route reversing is permitted. The value $G_q(m, n)$, the minimum cost of all paths, is a measure of the global similarity between the two sets of speech.

Systolic design for the DTW algorithm. Several DTW algorithms have been used with similar performance [Rabiner 81]. If we adopt the algorithm with local constraints as mentioned in the previous section, then the single-assignment formulation can be written as in Eq. (15.8). Note that, because of the local constraints, we have two more weight values (w_4 and w_5). The DG with global constraint is shown in Fig. 15.13a, where node (i, j) may be reached from nodes $(i - 2, j - 1)$, $(i - 1, j - 1)$, and $(i - 1, j - 2)$. For i from 1 to m and for j from 1 to N, we have

$$G(i,j) = 0 \quad \text{for } i \leqslant 0 \quad \text{or} \quad j \leqslant 0$$

$$\mathbf{r}(i,j) = \mathbf{r}(i - 1, j)$$

$$\mathbf{t}(i,j) = \mathbf{t}(i, j - 1)$$

$$d(i,j) = \text{dist}\{\mathbf{r}(i,j), \mathbf{t}(i,j)\}$$

$$G(i,j) = \mathbf{min} \begin{cases} G(i-2,j-1) + w_1 d(i-1,j) + w_2 d(i,j) \\ G(i - 1, j - 1) + w_3 d(i,j) \\ G(i-1,j-2) + w_4 d(i,j-1) + w_5 d(i,j) \end{cases} \tag{15.8}$$

By setting the global constraints so that the warping path will not deviate too much, we confine the mapping to the interior of the global constraint window $|i - j| \leqslant B$. Also, to assure local communication be-

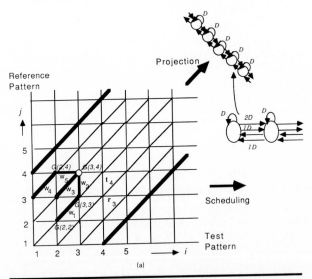

Figure 15.13 (a) The DG of DTW algorithm with local constraints and global constraint window.

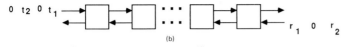

Figure 15.13   (*b*) A linear array for DTW algorithm.

tween PEs and obtain high efficiency, we project the DG onto an SFG in the (1, 1) direction, which yields a linear array configuration as shown in Fig. 15.13*b* [note that the detailed configuration of each PE is not illustrated; it will depend on the choice of distance measure and Eq. (15.8)]. After systolization of the SFG, the pipelining period α is equal to 2.

It is also possible to remove the local constraints and to further localize the DG by introducing some extra intermediate variables in the mathematical implementation of the single assignment code. There is still one remaining problem: the PEs work only half the time because of $\alpha = 2$. One possible solution to this is to process in parallel two sets of reference speech **r** and **r′** at the same time but interleave them, which will make the overall performance twice as fast.

15.4.4 Simulated annealing for image restoration

Problem formulation for MAP estimator. Image restoration is restoring images from various degradation mechanisms, e.g., blurring, nonlinear deformation, or multiplicative or additive noise. Mathematically, given a degraded image **g**,

$$\mathbf{g} = H(\mathbf{f}) \odot \mathbf{n} \qquad (15.9)$$

where **f** = image to be restored
H = (linear or nonlinear) blurring/deformation transformation over small window
$\odot$ = invertible operation, such as addition or multiplication
n = statistically independent noise

If only linear blurring mechanism and additive noise are considered, then the degraded image vector **g** in Eq. (15.9) can be rewritten as

$$\mathbf{g} = H\mathbf{f} + \mathbf{n} \qquad (15.10)$$

where **H** is a known blurring matrix.

Image restoration is recovering the original nonblurred image **f**, given the observed degraded image **g**, the transformation function of H, and some statistical properties of the noise **n**. The most straightforward method is to solve the least-squares problem, i.e., to find an estimate $\hat{\mathbf{f}}$ which minimizes the total estimation error:

$$\min (\mathbf{g} - \mathbf{H}\hat{\mathbf{f}})^{\mathrm{T}}(\mathbf{g} - \mathbf{H}\hat{\mathbf{f}}) \tag{15.11}$$

In many cases, however, a priori information about the image properties (e.g., smoothness, intensity distribution) is known. In order for the estimated solution also to reflect this information, a modified least-squares formulation should be adopted:

$$\min (\mathbf{g} - \mathbf{H}\hat{\mathbf{f}})^{\mathrm{T}}(\mathbf{g} - \mathbf{H}\hat{\mathbf{f}}) + \gamma\,(\mathbf{W}\hat{\mathbf{f}})^{\mathrm{T}}(\mathbf{W}\hat{\mathbf{f}}) \tag{15.12}$$

where the $\mathbf{W}$ matrix represents the intensity weighting for the overall smoothness measure of the image, and γ is a proper regularization parameter.

By generalizing this deterministic formulation, one of the most popular statistical estimation methods for image restoration, called the *maximum a posteriori* (MAP) approach, which is based on Bayes' theorem, can be derived. Let $\mathbf{F}$ denote the set of all possible solutions of $\mathbf{f}$, and assume that $P(\mathbf{f}) > 0$, for all $\mathbf{f} \in \mathbf{F}$. The MAP solution $\hat{\mathbf{f}} \in \mathbf{F}$ is the one which maximizes the conditional probability:

$$P(\hat{\mathbf{f}}|\mathbf{g}) \propto P(\mathbf{g}|\hat{\mathbf{f}})P(\hat{\mathbf{f}}) \tag{15.13}$$

If the linear blurring and additive gaussian noise are assumed, with the a priori probability $P(\hat{\mathbf{f}})$ being the Gibbs distribution (which will be discussed later), then the sum of two exponent terms on the right side of Eq. (15.13) is equal to the expression in Eq. (15.12). And the MAP estimated solution using the statistical approach is the same as the modified least-squares estimator using the deterministic approach as given in Eq. (15.12).

Assume that there are N pixels in the image and each pixel has L intensity/color levels, then the size of solution space is equal to L^N for such a discrete state case. Since there is no closed form solution to this problem, the computational load is clearly excessive. Therefore, iterative approaches which exploit the characteristics of locally dependent property of the image model appears to be more attractive [Besag 86].

Markov random field and neighborhood system.   Let the sites of all the pixels of an image be represented by a set $S = \{s_1, s_2, \ldots, s_N\}$, and a possible solution is represented by $\mathbf{f} = \{x_s, s \in S\}$. It is popular and practical to assume that the image can be modeled after a Markov random field (MRF). An MRF is characterized by the property that

$$P(x_s|x_{S-\{s\}}) = P_s(x_s|x_{\partial s}) \tag{15.14}$$

where the ∂s is called the *neighborhood* of pixel site s.

First-order and second-order MRFs are the most common examples of MRF representations defined in a finite grid model. In the first-order MRF, the neighborhood of a pixel s is defined as the set comprising its four nearest (north, south, east, and west) neighbors. The exceptions are the boundary pixels which have three neighbors, and the corners which have only two. In the second-order MRF, the neighborhood of a pixel s is defined as the set comprising its eight nearest neighbors (north, south, east, west, northeast, northwest, southeast, and southwest).

Simulated annealing via stochastic relaxation.   An iterative method to find a feasible bayesian estimator of Eq. (15.13) has been proposed [Besag 86]. By applying the updating iteratively, $P(\hat{\mathbf{f}}|\mathbf{g})$ should increase (nonstrictly) at each iteration and eventually converge to a steady-state solution. The main drawback, however, of this iterative method is that there is a high risk of converging to a local optimum. If it happens, it cannot get out of the "trap" due to its noncompromised commitment to nondecreasing $P(\hat{\mathbf{f}}|\mathbf{g})$ at each updating. Fortunately, the simulated annealing (SA) approach provides a means to circumvent such a difficulty.

The essence of SA for image restoration/reconstruction is a stochastic relaxation algorithm which generates a sequence of images that converges at an appropriate pace to the MAP estimate. The MRF assumption is again very crucial for deriving an effective SA algorithm. Basically, an iterative change is made on every pixel. Furthermore, such a change can be modeled as a random process depending on the pixels in its immediate neighborhood, and a local conditional probability distribution.

Geman and Geman [84] propose a method based on the SA method, which considers the conditional probability of any state $\mathbf{f}$, given $\mathbf{g}$, as

$$P(\hat{\mathbf{f}}|\mathbf{g}) \propto \{P(\mathbf{g}|\hat{\mathbf{f}})P(\hat{\mathbf{f}})\}^{1/T} \tag{15.15}$$

There are various iterative methods of constructing an updating process; the method adopted in Geman [84] is based on the *Gibbs distribution* assumption. An energy function E is defined on a finite set of states $\{f \in \mathbf{F}\}$. More precisely, a Gibbs distribution is a probability measure $P(\mathbf{f})$ with the following representation:

$$P(\mathbf{f}) = \frac{1}{Z} e^{-E(\mathbf{f})/T} \tag{15.16}$$

where Z is the normalizing constant.

To simplify the global dependency implied by Gibbs distribution, we can again take advantage of the MRF model. Based on this, Eq. (15.15) for pixel s can be rewritten as [Besag 86]

$$P_T(x_s|y_s, x_{S-\{s\}}) \propto \{P(y_s|x_s)P_s(x_s|x_{\partial s})\}^{1/T} \tag{15.17}$$

Because of the nature of stochastic updating, to ensure the convergence of the simulated annealing method by Geman and Geman, the pixels have to be updated under a prespecified schedule.† More specifically, for any parallel updating, no two neighboring pixels should be simultaneously updated. SA is especially simple to implement for a locally dependent a priori distribution $\{P(x_s|x_{\partial s})\}$, since only y_s and the current estimate of the neighbors are required in order to update the pixel s.

Systolic design for relaxation algorithms. We note that the ICM and SA methods share the same parallel processing and data transaction structure in the updating process. Therefore, the array architecture to be discussed below is suitable for both methods. The only distinction is on the function inside the node, which is dependent on the chosen relaxation algorithm. To allow efficient mapping of these relaxation algorithms onto array architectures, two important factors are crucial in determining the overall architecture pattern: (1) the order of the neighborhood system, (2) the size of the blurring window.

First-order MRF. The simplest example is the case when there is no blurring (nonlinear deformation on single pixel is allowed), and the first-order MRF is assumed. For this case, nodes in the DG can be embedded in a three-dimensional index space. The node with index (i,j,k) represents the kth updating of a pixel point (i,j). The initial guess of the relaxation process is simply the input image $(i,j,0)$. The DG is shown in Fig. 15.14a. In this graph, we have taken the maximum parallelism based on the "coding sets" updating procedure proposed in Besag [86]. (No two pixels that are neighbors should be updated at the same k index.) The single assignment code of this relaxation algorithm can be written as follows for k from 1 to infinity with an increment of 2 per step:

$$x(i,j,k) \leftarrow \begin{cases} \Phi\left\{x(i,j,k-1), x(i-1,j,k-1), x(i,j-1,k-1),\right. \\ \left. x(i+1,j,k-1), x(i,j+1,k-1)\right\} & \text{if } i+j = \text{even} \\ x(i,j,k-1) & \text{if } i+j = \text{odd} \end{cases}$$

$$x(i,j,k+1) \leftarrow \begin{cases} \Phi\{x(i,j,k), x(i-1,j,k), x(i,j-1,k), \\ x(i+1,j,k), x(i,j+1,k)\} & \text{if } i+j = \text{odd} \\ x(i,j,k) & \text{if } i+j = \text{even} \end{cases}$$

---

†Geman and Geman have shown that if the temperature $T(k)$ employed in executing the kth image in the iteration scheme satisfies the bound

$$T(k) \geq \frac{T_0}{\log(1+k)}$$

then the probability converging to one is $k \to \infty$ [10].

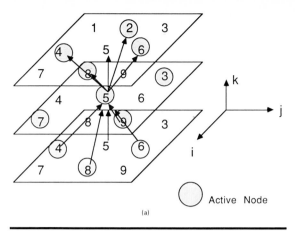

Active Node

(a)

Figure 15.14 (*a*) DG for relaxation algorithms with first-order MRF.

The Φ function is dependent on the different formulation of the Gibbs distribution for different applications. The difference between the even and odd cases comes from the constraints that no two neighboring pixels should be simultaneously updated. Because of the nondeterministic nature of the size of the DG in the k direction (the iteration number axis), the only permissible projection direction is in the k direction with schedule planes lying on each ij plane of different k indices. Note that each node in the SFG derived from this projection alternatively changes its function between an even and an odd index. For this, a special switch control is implemented inside the PEs. The resulting SFG and systolic array are shown in Fig. 15.14*b* and *c*. The systolic architecture is a mesh-connected array, with PEs being active for only 50 percent of the processing time due to the special data dependency. This inefficiency can be easily solved by PE sharing strategies.

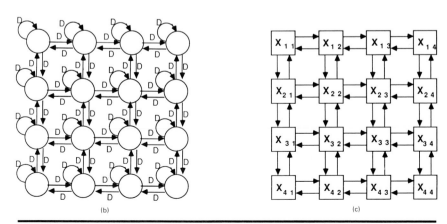

Figure 15.14 (*b*) SFG array; (*c*) systolic array.

The above type of architecture has been widely used in the parallel Jacobi method for solving two-dimensional elliptical PDE problems (also called the red/black partitioning approach). In fact, by slightly modifying the DG, the Gauss-Siedel and successive over-relaxation (SOR) algorithms for solving elliptical PDEs can be directly mapped onto two-dimensional systolic architectures. Even more complicated ad hoc SOR algorithms, from which one-dimensional architecture gains more popularity, can be easily derived through the process of multiple projections from three-dimensional DG to one-dimensional arrays.

Second-order MRF. A more complicated case is the second-order neighborhood system, and H is a blurring mechanism (plus nonlinear deformation) representing a 3×3 convolving blurring mask. By a similar idea, a mesh-connected array with diagonal interconnections can be derived by projecting the DG in the k direction. Note however, that each PE can be active only for 25 percent of the processing time.

The inefficiency of PE utilization and the complicated interconnection patterns motivated us to explore a one-dimensional linear array [Kung 87]. By using the piecewise linear schedule, a one-dimensional systolic array with 100 percent efficiency can be derived. For higher order neighborhood systems or larger size of convolving blurring matrix, it can be expected that the efficiency of two-dimensional array architectures will further degrade, and one-dimensional linear array will be the more amenable choice.

15.4.5 Systolic design of artificial neural networks

Neuroscientists have revealed that the massive parallel processing power in the human brain lies in the global and dense interconnections among a large number of identical logic elements or *neurons*. These neurons are connected to each other with variable strengths by a network of *synapses* [Takeda 86]. The original discrete-state Hopfield model and the continuous-state Hopfield-Tank model (including the proposed analog neural circuits) [Hopfield 85, 87] have recently become popular in the realization of artificial neural networks (ANNs). They can be programmed to perform computational networks for associative retrieval or for optimization problems. Several optical computing approaches, exploiting the global interconnectivity of optical signal flow, have been proposed [Farhat 85].

Both the analog neural circuits and the optical neural networks suffer from the disadvantages of low precision, difficulty of modifying the synaptic strengths, convergence to local optima, and global interconnectivity. In order to overcome the disadvantages mentioned above, a locally interconnected systolic architecture for an ANN is proposed [Kung 87].

Hopfield-Tank models. In order to imitate the continuous I/O relationship of real neurons, and also to simulate the integrative time delay due to the capacitance of real neurons, the continuous-state neural network model proposed by Hopfield and Tank can be approximated by the following dynamic equations [Hopfield 84, 85; Takeda 86]:

$$U_i(k) - U_i(k-1) = \sum_{j}^{N} T_{ij} V_j(k) + I_i \tag{15.18}$$

$$V_i(k+1) = g[U_i(k)] \tag{15.19}$$

where $g[x]$ is a nonlinear function, e.g.,

$$g[x] = \frac{1}{2}\left(1 + \tanh\frac{x}{x_0}\right) \tag{15.20}$$

which approaches a unit step function as x_0 tends to zero. The right-hand side of Eq. (15.18) can be considered as the new excitation source, which effects "modification" of the states as shown in the left hand side. An energy function is defined as [Hopfield 84]:

$$E = -\frac{1}{2}\sum_{i=1}^{N}\sum_{j=1}^{N} T_{ij} V_i V_j - \sum_{i=1}^{N} I_i V_i \tag{15.21}$$

Hopfield has shown that, if $T_{ij} = T_{ji}$, then neurons in the continuous-state model always change their states in such a manner that the energy function decreases in value [Hopfield 84].

The Hopfield model can be formulated as a consecutive matrix-vector multiplication problem with some prespecified thresholding operations [Farhat 85]. For example, a matrix-form expression of Eqs. (15.18) and (15.19) can be written as

$$\mathbf{u}(k) = \mathbf{T}\mathbf{v}(k) + \mathbf{i} + \mathbf{u}(k-1) \tag{15.22}$$

$$\mathbf{v}(k+1) = G[\mathbf{u}(k)]$$

where the $G[\mathbf{x}]$ function specifies the nonlinear thresholding of each element of the vector $\mathbf{x}$, and the vectors and matrices used are given as

$$\mathbf{u} = [U_1, U_2, \dots, U_N]^T$$

$$\mathbf{v} = [V_1, V_2, \dots, V_N]^T$$

$$\mathbf{i} = [I_1, I_2, \dots, I_N]^T$$

$$\mathbf{T} = \begin{bmatrix} T_{11} T_{12} \dots T_{1N} \\ T_{21} T_{22} \dots T_{2N} \\ \dots\dots\dots\dots\dots \\ T_{N1} T_{N2} \dots T_{NN} \end{bmatrix} \tag{15.23}$$

Example: Solving Image Restoration Problem   Artificial neural networks have been successfully applied to low-level vision processing [Koch 86]. Here, an image restoration example is given to illustrate how to map applicational problems onto ANNs.

As we mentioned in the previous section, the image restoration problem can be solved by using the modified least-squares formulation as given in Eq. (15.12). To formulate the regularized image restoration problem in terms of ANN, the key step is to derive an energy function so that the lowest energy state (the most stable state of the network) would correspond to the best restored image. Once the energy function is determined, the synaptic strengths and input can be immediately derived. Let each pixel of image f_i correspond to the neuron state V_i; then the derived energy function is equal to the expression given in Eq. (15.12). By comparing Eqs. (15.21) and (15.12), the corresponding $\mathbf{T}$ matrix and $\mathbf{i}$ vector are found to be

$$\mathbf{T} = -2(\mathbf{H}^T\mathbf{H} + \gamma\,\mathbf{W}^T\mathbf{W})$$

$$\mathbf{i} = 2\mathbf{H}^T\mathbf{g} \qquad\qquad (15.24)$$

Once $\mathbf{T}$ and $\mathbf{i}$ are determined, the ANN can be programmed accordingly to solve the image restoration problem.

Systolic design via cascade DG.   The consecutive matrix-vector multiplication array architecture design can be derived from a cascaded DG with nonlinear assignment [Kung 87]. By using the nonlinear assignment, a locally interconnected systolic array with bidirectional communication links can be obtained [Kung 87]. This systolic architecture requires some smart switches to change the operations of each PE at different time slots, and some T_{ij}s need to be repetitively stored in multiple PEs, and making the design unsuitable for adaptive modification of T_{ij}.

Modified cascade DG design.   Examining the DG design more closely, we note that many undesirable design aspects are due to the fact that the input direction of neuron states $V_i(k)$ is orthogonal to the output direction of the thresholded neuron states $V_i(k + 1)$. It is possible to rearrange the data ordering of the T_{ij} elements, so that the input direction $V_i(k)$ becomes parallel to the output direction of $V_i(k + 1)$. Such a modified DG is depicted in Fig. 15.15a. In this DG, for $i = 1,$ $2,\ldots, N$, the ith column of the T_{ij} data array is circularly shifted up by $i - 1$ positions. This DG is not totally localized due to the presence of the global spiral communication arcs. However, the input direction (from the top) and the output direction (from the bottom) are parallel. The advantage is that when many such DGs are cascaded top-down, the inputs and outputs data can be matched perfectly.

Ring array for ANN.   For the top-down cascaded DG, the projection can be taken along the vertical direction, which will result in a ring array

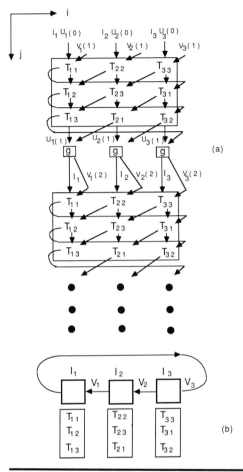

(a)

(b)

Figure 15.15 (a) Modified DG for consecutive matrix-vector multiplication formulation of Hopfield model; (b) ring systolic array for consecutive matrix-vector multiplication formulation of Hopfield model.

architecture as shown in Fig. 15.15b. In the ANN implementation, each PE, say the ith PE, is treated as a neuron, and the synaptic strengths $(T_{i1}, T_{i2},\ldots, T_{iN})$ are stored in it. At the kth iteration, the operation of the PE is as follows:

1. Each of the neuron outputs $(V_1, V_2,\ldots, V_N)$ is cycling through the ring array, and will pass through the ith PE once during the N clock cycles.

2. When V_j passes through the ith PE, it is multiplied with T_{ij}, and the result is added to the sum of $U_i (k - 1)$ and I_i [according to Eq. (15.18)].

3. After all N clock cycles, the computation for $U_i(k)$ is completed, and it is ready for the thresholding operation.

4. After the thresholding operations, the PE sends the thresholded neuron output $V_i(k + 1)$ to the left-side neighbor PE.

The above procedures are repeated until a convergence is reached. For implementing a large number of neurons, the problem of the long wraparound line can be solved by a special two-dimensional scheme [Kung 87].

Advantageous properties of systolic ANN. The advantages of this array architecture for ANN are summarized as follows:

- The pipelining period $\alpha = 1$, which implies 100 percent utilization efficiency during the iteration process.

- Only N synaptic strengths of T_{ij} are stored in each PE. This results in easier modification of the synaptic strengths, making the "learning" capability possible.

- Using this proposed systolic architecture, the gain parameters can be easily updated during the iterations. (It is observed that if the gain control parameter of the sigmoid I/O relation in the neuron can be dynamically changed, then a faster convergence and better performance can be obtained [Hopfield 85].)

15.5 Concluding Remarks

Array processors as implemented in VLSI offer a new and promising opportunity to the development of the state-of-the-art supercomputer. The heart of the matter lies in a systematic methodology of mapping applications and algorithms onto array architectures. In other words, the research essence of VLSI array processors hinges upon a vertical integration of *applications, algorithms, architectures,* and *technology.*

The emergence of new VLSI technology, along with modern engineering workstations, CAD tools, and other hardware and software advances in computer technology, virtually assures a revolutionary information processing era in the near future. In particular, the systolic and wavefront array processors have shown great promise for a broad range of applications in signal and image processing. The research and development of these array processors will play a key role in defining the trend of the future supercomputer technology.

Bibliography

[Aho 74]   A.V. Aho, J.E. Hopcraft, and J.D. Ullman. *The Design and Analysis of Computer Algorithms.* Addison-Wesley, Reading, MA, 1974.

[Besag 86]   J. Besag. "On the Statistical Analysis of Dirty Pictures." *J. Royal Statist. Soc., series B,* vol. 48, no. 3, pp. 192–236, 1986.

[Chan 86]   T.F. Chan and Y. Saad. "Multigrid Algorithms on the Hypercube Multiprocessor." *IEEE Trans. Computers,* pp. 969–977, November 1986.

[Dennis 80]   J.B. Dennis. "Data Flow Supercomputers." *IEEE Computer Magazine,* pp. 48–56, November 1980.

[Farhat 85]   N.H. Farhat, D. Psaltis, A. Prata, and E. Paek. "Optical Implementation of the Hopfield Model." *Applied Optics,* vol. 24, pp. 1469–1475, May 1985.

[Fortes 85]   J.A.B. Fortes, K.S. Fu, and B.W. Wah. "Systematic Approaches to the Design of Algorithmic Specified Systolic Arrays." *Proc. IEEE ICASSP'85,* pp. 300–303, Tampa, FL, March 1985.

[Fortes 85]   J.A.B. Fortes and C.S. Raghavendra. "Gracefully Degradable Processor Arrays." *IEEE Trans. Computers,* pp. 1033–1044, November 1985.

[Fisher 85]   A.L. Fisher and H.T. Kung. "Special-Purpose VLSI Architectures: General Discussions and a Case Study." In S. Y. Kung, H. J. Whitehouse, and T. Kailath (eds). *VLSI and Modern Signal Processing,* pp. 153–169, Prentice-Hall, Englewood, NJ, 1985.

[Geman 84]   S. Geman and D. Geman. "Stochastic Relaxation, Gibbs Distributions, and the Bayesian Restoration of Images." *IEEE Trans. Pattern Analysis and Machine Intelligence,* vol. 6, pp. 721–741, November 1984.

[Heller 85]   D. Heller. "Partitioning Big Matrices for Small Systolic Arrays." In S. Y. Kung, H. J. Whitehouse, and T. Kailath (eds). *VLSI and Modern Signal Processing,* Prentice-Hall, Englewood, NJ, 1985.

[Hopfield 84] J.J. Hopfield. "Neurons with Graded Response Have Collective Computational Properties Like Those of Two-State Neurons." *Proc. National Academy Science,* vol. 81, pp. 3088–3092, 1984.

[Hopfield 85] J.J. Hopfield and D.W. Tank. "Neural Computation of Decision in Optimization Problems." *Biological Cybernetics,* 1985.

[Horiike 87]   S. Horiike, S. Nishida, and T. Sakaguchi. "A Design Method of Systolic Arrays Under the Constraint of the Number of the Processors." *Proc. of ICASSP 87,* pp. 764–767, 1987.

[Hwang 84]   K. Hwang and F. Briggs. *Computer Architectures and Parallel Processing.* McGraw-Hill, New York, 1984.

[Karp 67]   R.M. Karp, R.E. Miller, and S. Winograd. "The Organization of Computations for Uniform Recurrence Equations." *J. of ACM,* vol. 14, no. 3, pp. 563–590, July 1967.

[Koch 86]   C. Koch, J. Marroquin, and A. Yuille. "Analog 'Neuronal' Networks in Early Vision." *Proc. National Academy Science,* vol. 83, pp. 4263–4267, 1986.

[H.T. Kung 82] H.T. Kung. "Why Systolic Architectures?" *IEEE Computer,* vol. 15, no. 1, January 1982.

[Kung 87]   S.Y. Kung. *VLSI Array Processors.* Prentice-Hall, Englewood Cliffs, NJ, 1987.

[Kung 86]   S.Y. Kung, C.W. Chang, and C.W. Jen. "Real-Time Reconfiguration for Fault-Tolerant VLSI Array Processors." *Proc. Real-Time Systems Symposium,* pp. 46–54, December 1986.

[Kung 84]   S.Y. Kung. "On Supercomputing with Systolic/Wavefront Array Processors." *Proc. IEEE,* vol. 72, no. 7, July 1984.

[Kung 82]   S.Y. Kung, K.S. Arun, R.J. Gal-Ezer, and D.V. Bhaskar Rao. "Wavefront

Array Processor: Language, Architecture, and Applications." *IEEE Trans. Computers, Special Issue on Parallel and Distributed Computers,* vol. C-31, no. 11, pp. 1054–1066, November 1982.

[Moldovan 83]   D.I. Moldovan. "On the Design of Algorithms for VLSI Systolic Arrays." *Proc. the IEEE,* vol. 71, no. 1, January 1983.

[Moldovan 86]   D.I. Moldovan and J.A.B. Fortes. "Partitioning and Mapping of Algorithms into Fixed Size Systolic Arrays." *IEEE Trans. Computers,* vol. 35, no. 1, pp. 1–12, January 1986.

[Moore 87]   W. Moore, A. McCabe, and R. Urquhart (eds). *Systolic Arrays.* Adam Hilger, Bristol, England, 1987.

[Rabiner 81]   L.R. Rabiner and S.E. Levinson. "Isolated and Connected Word Recognition—Theory and Selected Application." *IEEE Trans. Communication,* vol. C-29, no. 5, pp. 621–658, May 1981.

[Rao 85]   S.K. Rao. *Regular Iterative Algorithms and Their Implementations on Processor Arrays.* Ph.D. thesis, Stanford University Press, Stanford, CA, 1985.

[Sami 86]   M. Sami and R. Stefanelli. "Fault-Tolerance and Functional Reconfiguration in VLSI Arrays." *Proc. ISCAS 1986,* pp. 643–648, 1986.

[Sami 86]   M. Sami and R. Stefanelli. "Reconfigurable Architectures for VLSI Processing Arrays." *Proc. IEEE,* pp. 712–722, May 1986.

[Siewiorek 82]   D.P. Siewiorek and R.S. Swarz. *The Theory and Practice of Reliable System Design.* Digital Press, Bedford, MA, 1982.

[Takeda 86]   M. Takeda and J.W. Goodman. "Neural Networks for Computation: Number Representations and Programming Complexity." *Applied Optics,* vol. 25, pp. 3033–3046, September 1986.

Exploring Neural Network and Optical Computing Technologies

Scott T. Toborg

Hughes Aircraft Company, El Segundo, CA

Kai Hwang

University of Southern California, Los Angeles, CA

16.1 Introduction

Artificial neural networks and optical computing are two promising areas of research in computer science and engineering. While these two fields represent a wide diversity of principles, techniques, and applications, they are in some respects very complementary. In this chapter we explore the fundamental principles of each field, highlight potential advantages over conventional computing, and discuss important areas of application. The chapter gives an overview of important concepts that will help researchers and engineers evaluate the usefulness of these emerging technologies for solving their particular problems.

Sections 16.2 and 16.3 discuss the fundamentals of computing with neural networks. We describe some of the major principles, models, and applications. Sections 16.4 and 16.5 present the major concepts in optical computing including materials, devices, architectures and algorithms. Section 16.6 discusses how electronics and optics can be used to implement neural architectures. Finally, the conclusion summarizes the state of the art in both fields, and discusses critical areas for future research and experiment.

16.1.1   Limitations of conventional computers

Since the beginning of the computer age, scientists have dreamed of building a machine that mimics the human brain. However, limitations in both theory and hardware have so far led to less ambitious developments. Initially, computers were built to perform serial operations, that is, execution of one instruction at a time. This "von Neuman" approach has been extended with the introduction of pipelining, array processing, and multiprocessing. All of these approaches are based on what could be called "algorithmic architectures." That is, problems are solved by formulating algorithms that are directly mapped into machine instructions. Computation occurs by successive instruction fetch, decode, operand fetch, operand decode, and instruction execution. Results are precise and predictable.

In general, these architectures are very proficient with arithmetic/logic operations. However, there are some serious drawbacks. With increasingly complex parallel hardware it becomes more difficult to construct programming languages, compilers, and debuggers that fully exploit the resources. Problems also arise in parallel memory access, cache updating, and processor synchronization. Parallel processors are still limited in their ability to solve important real-time problems in areas like vision, pattern matching, speech recognition, optimization, and associative memory.

Scientists suspect that something must be fundamentally wrong in the way some of these problems are approached. This belief is substantiated by many examples in nature of biological systems (ranging from slugs to humans) that are capable of real-time solutions to problems beyond the capacity of the largest supercomputer. And this processing occurs using biological elements that are a million times slower than semiconductor devices.

Aside from structural weaknesses, coventional computers also face speed limitations due to properties of the semiconductor devices used. Optics may be able to alleviate some of these limits with its inherently parallel, noninterfering, speed-of-light computation. Together, neural networks and optical computing will open up many new possibilities for solving a wide variety of very hard problems. In the following sections we outline some properties that substantiate this claim and explain the motivation for continuing research in both fields.

16.1.2   The neural network paradigm

Artificial neural networks represent a fundamental shift in computer architecture and operation. Although the current interest in the subject is new, research into neural networks actually has a relatively long background. Neuroscientists were originally interested in understanding the electrical and chemical processes of the human brain. Early work by McCulloch and Pitts dates back to the 1940s [McCulloch 1943].

Much excitement was generated in the early 1960s when Rosenblatt [61] introduced the "Perceptron." Rosenblatt's theories suggested that quick advances could be made in machine learning and automatic feature recognition. Perceptrons simulated characteristics similar to biological learning. However, interest in neural network research waned in the late 1960s after a theoretical critique by Minsky and Papert uncovered fundamental weaknesses with Perceptrons [Minsky 68]. While this critique only applied to a limited definition of the Perceptron, it significantly quenched the pursuit of neural networks for computing. At that time AI research switched to the study of high-level processes based on symbols, frames, and schemas.

In recent years, several factors have combined to renew interest in neural network approaches. First, hardware advances now allow economic development of massively parallel computers. Second, theories about collective computation in neural networks have matured thanks to continued investigation by a number of dedicated researchers. Third, after nearly 20 years of AI research, it is clear what types of problems are best suited for symbolic approaches. Neural networks appear to complement conventional AI approaches by suggesting solutions to problems requiring associative searches, pattern recognition, classification, and optimization on fuzzy, incomplete, or unpredictable data.

Some of the major features that distinguish neural networks from conventional computing include

- *Massive parallelism:* Full-scale neural networks may have hundreds of thousands of individual processing cells.

- *High interconnectivity:* Some models require dedicated interconnects between each processor. Other models may be arranged in layers that require fewer interconnections. The amount of connectivity is dependent on the application, theoretical model, and desired performance.

- *Simple processors:* Each processor simply sums incoming signals and fires when those signals reach a threshold. There are no accumulators, registers, ALU, or memory as in conventional architectures.

- *Distributed representation:* The strengths of the connections are modified to include new information. Data are stored as a pattern of connections spread out over the entire network.

- *Fault tolerance:* If a neuron fails the system still performs. The accuracy of the network decreases gradually as more neurons fail.

- *Collective computation:* A neural network does not execute individual instructions; rather, all the cells in the network are trained to solve a particular problem collectively.

■ *Self-organization:* A neural network may autonomously adapt its structure to learn new patterns.

16.1.3   The state of optical computing

Optical computing refers to the use of optics to perform arithmetic, logic, and symbolic operations as often encountered in modern digital computers. This area has been driven by computationally intensive problems, which have been tackled by electronic computers with only limited speed and accuracy. To achieve optical computing, one demands major improvements in optical materials and devices, memory arrays, interconnection networks, arithmetic/symbolic algorithms, and new programming paradigms. Computation-intensive problems that can be more effectively solved by optical computers include signal/image processing, computer vision, pattern recognition, robotics control, supercomputing in scientific simulations, artificial neural computing, machine intelligence, and optimization.

Electronic technologies are rapidly approaching their limits in terms of switching speed and packaging (pin-out) requirements. As microcircuits become denser, the problems of clock skew, bandwidth, crosstalk, and capacitive loading are intensified. Optical interconnection networks are a promising alternative to electrically wired networks. The inherent parallelism, high bandwidth, and immunity from cross talk make optics a good source for implementing massively parallel computers. Some of the advantages of optics over electronics for computing include

■ Optical signals propagate in parallel channels without interference and without crosstalk due to negligible photon-photon interactions.

■ There are no parasitic reactances in optics to slow down the speed of the signal; as a result, the optical signal travels at nearly the speed of light.

■ Optical signals do not require high-speed ground planes.

■ Optics supports large fan-outs over long distances, and thus massive parallelism becomes possible.

■ Optics minimizes queuing delays due to its inherent speed.

■ Optics offers the capability of real-time reconfiguration using holograms.

■ Optical connectivity can be used for applications constrained by the limited number of pinouts provided by electronic packaging technologies.

- Optics offers the capability of broadcast communication for clock distribution and other global signals.

These potential advantages suggest that an optical computer has inherent parallelism contributed by large communication bandwidth (spatial and temporal), no planar constraints in three-dimensional volume systems, reduced capacitive loading and crosstalk, and no pin-out limitations, in contrast with electronic systems, which have low bandwidth, electromagnetic interferences, and pin-out constraints.

At present, optical computing is more a meaningful direction than a matured technology. Traditional computer engineers are developing digital optical computers by using optically coded binary information. More recently, there has been growing interest in developing analog optical systems for neural network computing, AI, and signal processing applications. In Table 16.1, we compare the major characteristics and capabilities of optical computers with their electronic counterparts. Many of the entries in this table are estimates yet to be verified by research and experiment.

16.2 Principles of Neural Network Computing

A general framework is presented below for describing neural networks. This framework is adapted primarily from Rumelhart [86]. Additional concepts and terminology are borrowed from Hecht-Nielsen

TABLE 16.1   Characteristics of Electronic and Optical Computers

Characteristics	Electronic computers	Optical computers
Switching speed	$O(10^{-9}) \sim O(10^{-11})$ s in Si, GaAs, JJ, HEMT	$O(10^{-12}) \sim O(10^{-15})$ s in optical gate arrays
Processor granularity and parallelism	Large-grain and $O(1) \sim O(10^2)$ processors per system	Fine-grain and massive parallelism
Communication bandwidth	$O(10) \sim O(10^3)$ Mbits/s	$O(1) \sim O(10^2)$ Gbits/s
Physical integration	$O(10^4) \sim O(10^5)$ transistors per CMOS chip	$O(10^2) \sim O(10^6)$ gates per optical array
Control complexity	Synchronous with digital clocking	Synchronous/asynchronous (absence of clock skewing)
Power requirements	$O(10^2)$ W per board at $O(10)$-MHz clock rate	$O(10^{-1})$ W per array at $O(10)$-MHz clock rate
Reliability and maintenance	Architecture and technology dependent	Less interference and could be very costly

SOURCE: Hwang [87].

[86]. By introducing this general framework, other specific models will be easier to understand and compare. We discuss neural network structure, state equations and stability, methods of computation and learning, and neural network design. These concepts represent only a few of the most important ideas necessary for an introductory understanding. In subsequent sections, we trace how these concepts are applied to specific models and how they affect the choice of applications and hardware implementations.

16.2.1 Structure and design considerations

In general, a neural network consists of two major parts: the individual neural processing units and the network of interconnections among processors. A neural network may have many processing units. Each unit receives different inputs from many other units and transmits an output to other units. The system has distributed control. This means there is no executive; each processor executes its operations autonomously without explicit knowledge of the system as a whole.

Neural processing elements accept incoming signals from other units, perform simple operations on those signals, and compute single-value outputs. These three functions correspond to three different parts of a general neural processing unit (Fig. 16.1). First, for a system of N processing units, there may be as many as $N - 1$ inputs into a single arbitrary unit u_i. These inputs come from the outputs o_j of other units. The output values are modified by a weighting factor w_{ij}, representing the relative strength of connection i to connection j. A *net input function* determines how the inputs should be combined to get a net input value net_j. For the simplest case, this function takes the weighted sum of all impinging signals. That is, $net_j = \Sigma w_{ij}o_j$. More complex combinations occur if there are different types of connections. For example, each connection type might have to be summed separately and then combined. In this case, let net_{ij} be the net input of connection type i to unit u_j. The most common case of multiple input types is for differentiating excitatory vs. inhibitory inputs. Often these types can be combined by simply using positive and negative weights.

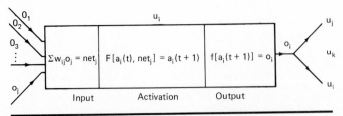

Figure 16.1 Functional specification of a neural processing unit.

Second, this net input value is used in calculating the activation value. The activation value for an arbitrary unit i at time t, $a_i(t)$, represents the current state of the unit. The set of activation values may be continuous or discrete. Continuous values are normally bounded between some interval, for example, 0 to 1. Discrete values are either binary, {0, 1} or {− 1, 1}; or range over a small set of values such as {1, 2,...,9}. The choice of activation values often has an important impact on the characteristics of computation. The state of the system is simply the vector $\vec{a}(t)$, representing the state of activation for each unit at time t. This state vector is also called the *pattern of activation*. We define a function F that takes $a_i(t)$ and net_{ij} and calculates a new state of activation. In equation form: $a_i(t + 1) = F[a_i(t), net_{ij}]$. The activation function may take on a number of different forms. The simplest case is where the activation value is simply the net input net_{ij}. More likely, F is some kind of threshold function with no activation until the net input exceeds a certain value. Stochastic, decay, and sigmoid functions have also been used to modulate the activation values.

Third, activation values are used to determine the final output value $o_i(t)$. An output function $f(a_i(t))$ maps the current state of activation $a_i(t)$ to an output value $o_i(t)$. This function may be an identity function, in which case $o_i(t) = a_i(t)$. Other common alternatives include thresholding or stochastic.

In a neural network, interprocessor connections are much more than simple communication links. The connections actually encode what patterns the network can identify. In addition to connectivity, the interconnections also have an associated weight or strength. A convenient way to represent this property is by using a weight matrix W. An element in W, w_{ij}, denotes the strength of connection i to j. For a simple case, positive weights represent excitatory connections while negative weights represent inhibitory connections. A value of 0 means there is no connection between the units.

More complex patterns may be needed for different types of connections. In this case, there would be a weight matrix W_i for each connection type. As mentioned above, the distinction between excitatory and inhibitory connections is only needed if they have different net input functions. Also, W could be more than two-dimensional. For instance, instead of the normal "biconnection" described above, there could be a "triconnection" between three units. In this case, each element in W would have three indices w_{ijk}. This idea can be extended to an arbitrary number of connections represented by higher dimensional weight matrices [Little 86].

The topology of neural network interconnections can be very diverse. In the simplest case there may be a single layer of fully interconnected processors. More often the network is divided into multiple layers with full interconnection between layers but not with every neuron. One layer of neurons may be used to input values into the network, while another layer may output the final results. In between the input and output layers may be many intermediate or *hidden* layers.

The process of designing a neural network consists of three major parts: problem definition, architecture design, and hardware implementation. These parts are sequential and iterative. That is, a designer starts out by defining the problem then developing the state equations to solve the problem and finally implementing these equations in hardware. But the process may iterate in that the equations may change the problem and the hardware limitations might change both the problem and the equations.

First, we must identify problems that can be reasonably solved using neural approaches. According to Hecht-Nielsen [86], some areas where neural networks perform well include

- Nearest neighbor classification of spatiotemporal patterns
- $O(1)$-time parallel search
- Self-organization of ordered spatial maps
- Knowledge storage, retrieval, and processing
- Robot effector commands

These general areas may apply across a wide variety of applications. Because this technology is so new, it is still very difficult to identify what problem areas are best suited for nerual networks. No doubt the areas listed above will change as experimental results clarify neural network capabilities.

Second, architectural design takes the problem definition and attempts to find neural equations that will define the mathematical architecture of the system. There may be several ways of defining these equations. The choice of which design to use may be very hardware dependent. Often the geometry of the problem leads to clues as to which equations to use and how to arrange the structure. As the technology matures, it will become easier to identify\which models work best for different problems.

Third, the appropriate hardware must be selected to implement neural network equations. Neural networks may be implemented in two general ways: full or virtual. A full implementation means that there is a dedicated processor and interconnect for every neuron described by the architecture state equations. A virtual implementation means that network equations may share the same resources. For example, the processing for many neurons may be multiplexed onto the same processor. There are also a number of different choices for hardware technologies. In general, these choices may be grouped into three major categories: electronic, electrooptical, and optical. Section 16.6

presents a more complete discussion of major issues for neural network implementation.

16.2.2   State equations and stability

Once the structure of a neural network is defined, the next step is to determine the exact form for the mathematical equations describing changes in individual neurons and changes in the network as a whole. In essence, we must write down specific relations for the net input, activation, and output functions described in the previous section. These equations may be either continuous or discrete depending on how the variables are represented in the system. For example, with a discrete representation, the activation value $a_i(t + 1)$ could be determined by simply summing the inputs and comparing them to some threshold θ. If the summed input is above the threshold, then the unit is given a positive activation. If below the threshold, then the activation is negative. In equation form,

$$a_i(t + 1) = \begin{cases} 1 & \text{if } \sum w_{ij} o_j > \theta \\ -1 & \text{otherwise} \end{cases} \qquad (16.1)$$

If the activation variables take on continuous (but bounded) values, then it may be possible to write the equations of state as a system of nonlinear, coupled differential equations. By carefully choosing these equations, the behavior of the system can be analyzed mathematically. Neural network equations are not arbitrary systems of differential equations. They normally have a form that exhibits convergence to stable states.

Stability is a major theorem of neural network processing. What we are saying is that a system of neurons can be constructed that will converge to some stable state regardless of the starting state. Useful computation in neural networks can occur only if the system tends toward stable states. Otherwise, a network would oscillate, or randomly fluctuate without giving consistent results. Cohen, Grossberg, and others have shown how arbitrarily many units computing arbitrary nonlinear transfer functions (i.e., input, activation, output functions) can interact asynchronously with complex nonlinear feedback yet still reach stable equilibrium points [Cohen 83].

One way of viewing network stability is in terms of a dissipative energy function. The equations of state converge to a finite set of equilibrium points that are minima of a "computational energy" function E. Another way of saying it is the equations of state change such that E is a nonincreasing function of time. And since E is bounded below, it must converge.

To visualize simplistically what is happening, imagine a very bumpy surface. The depressions correspond to local minima. A marble

MOUNTAIN PEAK ⊚   ─── HIGH ALTITUDE
                                       CONTOURS

SALT LAKE ⦿   ─ ─ ─ LOW CONTOURS

Figure 16.2 The surface of a "computational energy" contour describing the state space of a system of neurons is similar to a topological map
with valleys as local minima. [Hopfield 86]

placed on this surface would roll to the nearest depression and stay
(Fig. 16.2). Denker suggested a more accurate extension to the marble
analogy by imagining a massless marble moving through honey along
some complicated potential-energy surface in a space of a thousand dimensions [Denker 86]. However you view it, the behavior is still the
same: a neural network functions by starting from some initial state
and then stabilizing to the nearest equilibrium point.

   If these equilibrium points could be made to correspond to the values of desired memory locations, then the neural network would function as a _content-addressable memory_ (CAM). This CAM could start
with only partial information and move to the stable state (i.e., memory) that most closely resembles the input.

   It is interesting to note that while conventional computers can trace
memory to a specific hardware address, neural network memory is
represented as a pattern of connections spread across the entire system. New memories or patterns can be added to the system by adjust-

ing the interconnection weights. The process of changing connection weights to accommodate multiple stored patterns is discussed below.

16.2.3 Methods of learning and computation

Networks that can dynamically modify their interconnection weights are capable of "learning." A particular pattern/memory can be stored in the network by using one of a number of learning schemes that adapts the connection weights to recognize new patterns. Three of the most popular learning schemes are hebbian, delta, and backward error propagation.

Hebbian learning suggests that if two units are active—one unit u_i creating input to u_j, then the weight w_{ij} between i and j should be increased or strengthened. This approach was first introduced by Hebb in 1949. The simplest form of this equation is where the change in weight is proportional to the activation and output value:

$$\Delta w_{ij} = \eta a_i o_j \qquad (16.2)$$

with η as a proportionality constant representing the learning rate.

Another variation on general hebbian learning is called the *delta rule*. In this case, the change in connection strength is proportional to the difference between the actual and target activation given by the teaching input $t_i(t)$. These changes also act to minimize the mean-square error in the system:

$$\Delta w_{ij} = \eta \left[t_i(t) - a_i(t) \right] \qquad \text{or} \qquad \eta \delta_i o_j(t) \qquad (16.3)$$

where $\delta_i = t_i(t) - a_i(t)$.

The delta rule applies specifically to feedforward networks without hidden layers. A "generalized delta rule" has been developed to describe learning for multilayered feedforward and feedback networks. Three equations summarize how this rule is applied. With feedback networks, this rule is also called *backward error propagation*. First, as with the original delta rule, changes are proportional to the error signal δ_j and the output of the unit along the line $j \to i$:

$$\Delta w_{ji} = \eta \delta_j o_i \qquad (16.4)$$

where δ_j denotes the jth element of the error signal. This error signal is calculated differently for units at the output layer and units in the hidden layers. For the output layer the error signal for a particular unit is

$$\delta_j = (t_j - o_j) f_j' \, (\text{net}_j) \qquad (16.5)$$

where f_j' is the derivative of the semilinear output function which maps the total input to a unit to an output value $o_j(t)$. A semilinear function is a nondecreasing and differentiable function of the net total input. For example, sigmoid functions are semilinear, whereas linear threshold functions are not, since their derivative is infinite at the threshold and zero elsewhere. By using a semilinear function it has been shown that backward error propagation performs a gradient descent over the system of interconnection weights. This means that it minimizes the square of the difference between the desired outputs and all input/output pairs [Rumelhart 86, p. 318].

The error signals for the hidden units are determined recursively in terms of the error signals to which they are directly connected and their connection weights:

$$\delta_j = f_j' \,(\text{net}_j) \sum_k \delta_k w_{kj} \qquad (16.6)$$

That is, after δ has been calculated for the output layer, this value is used to calculate weight changes for units that feed into the output layer, which in turn are used to determine weights for successive layers until the process terminates back at the input layer.

This generalized delta rule is applied by first presenting the input and propagating forward to produce an output value o_j for each unit. This output is then compared with the desired output, and an error signal δ_j is calculated for each unit. Next, a backward pass through the network adjusts the hidden units according to the recursive formula described above.

A neural network operates by first defining the neural processing unit responses, interconnections, and learning rules. After definition, interconnection weights are initialized either to a predetermined starting state (perhaps all zero) or a random value. If the weights are adaptive, then the system can learn desired input patterns using perhaps hebbian or backward error propagation. After learning, the system is ready for recall. An input vector is presented and the network cycles (based on updates according to the state equations) until it reaches the nearest stable state. This stable state consists of activation values corresponding to the desired memory or pattern.

16.3   Neural Network Models and Applications

In this section we outline three popular models for neural networks developed by Hopfield, Fukushima, and Grossberg. These models are described according to the framework discussed in Sec. 16.2. Each model is illustrated with an example application.

16.3.1 Hopfield model and the traveling salesman problem

Hopfield's model is especially appealing because of its simplicity and mathematical consistency. Although the Hopfield model is limited in the kinds of problems it can describe [Takeda 86], it provides an excellent introduction to more complex models [Hopfield 82, 85, 86].

A distinguishing characteristic of a Hopfield network is its structure. The network generally consists of a single layer of completely interconnected processors. There are no self-connections ($w_{ii} = 0$) and the connections are symmetric ($w_{ij} = w_{ji}$). Each neural processing unit or "model neuron" has a single activation function that sums the inputs from other neurons, compares this sum to a threshold, and outputs a value to all other neurons. The gain on this function can be adjusted to give a smooth sigmoid monotonic response or act as a step function.

Hopfield networks can be represented by continuous and discrete variables. For instance, with continuous variables a Hopfield network can be described by a system of nonlinear coupled differential equations:

$$C_i \frac{du_i}{dt} = \sum_{j=1}^{N} T_{ij} V_i g(u_i) - \frac{u_i}{R_i} + I_i \qquad i = 1,\ldots,N \qquad (16.7)$$

where C_i = capacitance of neuron i
$\quad u_i$ = input potential
$\quad T_{ij}$ = synaptic strength between i and j represented by a conductance (same as w_{ij})
$\quad V_i$ = amplitude of the output voltage from neuron i
$\quad g(u_i)$ = sigmoid function describing how output voltage changes with input
$\quad R_i$ = internal resistance
$\quad I_i$ = external current

The model described above is continuous with time. That is, outputs from V_i have values over a range (say from 0 to 1). Interesting properties result by looking at a discrete version of Eq. (16.7). We allow V_i to take on values of 0 or 1 according to the following relations:

$$V_i = 0 \qquad \text{if} \sum_{ji}^{N} T_{ij} V_j + I_i < U_i \qquad (16.8)$$

$$V_i = 1 \qquad \text{if} \sum_{ji}^{N} T_{ij} V_j + I_i > U_i \qquad (16.9)$$

where U_i represents some threshold current. In this case each neuron samples its input at random times. The output voltages V_i are determined by the sum of the input currents. If the sum is greater than the threshold U_i, then $V_i = 1$; otherwise, $V_i = 0$.

An important property of Hopfield networks is that given a symmetric connectivity matrix with no self-connections (i.e., $T_{ij} = T_{ji}$, $T_{ii} = 0$), the output vector, $V^s = V_1, V_2, V_3, \ldots, V_n$, will converge to a set of stable states. The proof of this property comes following the construction of an appropriate energy function that always decreases regardless of the state changes produced by Eqs. (16.8) and (16.9). Consider the following function:

$$E = -\frac{1}{2} \sum_{i=1}^{N} \sum_{j=1}^{N} T_{ij} V_i V_j - \sum_{i=1}^{N} I_i V_i + \sum_{i=1}^{N} U_i V_i \qquad (16.10)$$

The change of E with respect to changes in state V_k is

$$\frac{\Delta E}{\Delta V_k} = -\frac{1}{2} \sum_{j=1}^{N} T_{ki} V_i - \frac{1}{2} \sum_{j=1}^{N} T_{jk} V_j - I_k + U_k \qquad (16.11)$$

Assuming symmetric strengths between connections, then $T_{ik} = T_{ki}$. Also i and j are dummy variables with identical ranges; therefore, the first and second terms of Eq. (16.11) combine to yield

$$\Delta E_k = -\left(\sum_{j=1}^{N} T_{kj} V_j + I_k - U_k \right) \Delta V_k \qquad (16.12)$$

The quantity in parentheses (call it S_k), is the original equation of state for the system. [Compare with Eqs. (16.8) and (16.9).] If $S_k > 0$, then according to Eq. (16.9), $\Delta V_k > 0$, and this implies that $\Delta E < 0$. Likewise, if $S_k < 0$, then $\Delta V_k < 0$ and $\Delta E_k < 0$. No matter how S_k changes, $\Delta E < 0$; therefore, E always tends to a minimum.

The problem can be represented as operating in an N-dimensional coordinate system. Each axis corresponds to a different V_i. The stable states of the system are points in V space. The problem could be visualized, for the two-dimensional case, as a topological map of hills and valleys. Stable system states correspond to valleys where there is a local minimum (Fig. 16.2).

The stable states of a Hopfield network can be determined primarily by adjusting the T_{ij} matrix. Depending on the application, this connection matrix may be constant or adaptable. For example, in the *traveling salesman problem* (TSP), the connections are static. If the network functions as an associative memory, the connections may be adapted using some learning rule (as described in Sec. 16.2.3).

A now classic example of the power of neural networks is Hopfield's solution to the TSP. This optimization problem has been frequently studied [Garey 79]. Because of the computational complexity, solutions to the TSP represent a major advance in computer science. If neural networks can be used to efficiently solve TSP, then possibly a wide variety of other optimization problems could be solved.

Simply stated, TSP consists of a salesman and a number of cities to be visited which are separated by various distances. The object is for the salesman to complete a circuit visiting each city once, returning to the starting point, and choosing a sequence of visits so that the total distance traveled is a minimum. In other words, suppose we have a set of cities $A, B, C,...$ and distances between each pair $d_{AB}, d_{AC}, d_{BC},...$. A tour would define a sequence of cities, $B, D, G, A,...$, for example, visiting each city and having a total distance, $d_T = d_{BD} + d_{DG} + d_{GA} +...$. Again, the quality of a valid tour is measured by the total distance needed to complete the circuit. The shorter the distance, the better the tour.

To map this problem onto a neural network, Hopfield suggests a simple representation consisting of a matrix of $N \times N$ neurons [Hopfield 85]. Rows in the matrix represent cities and columns represent positions in the tour. For example, active neurons in positions $A1, D2, F3$, would mean that the chosen circuit visits A then D, then F, etc. The final state of the network would be a permutation matrix; that is, one entry for each column and row. (For an $N \times N$ matrix there would be N final states.)

To formulate the equations of state for this problem our notation must be modified slightly. Since neurons are arranged in an $N \times N$ matrix, we describe them with double indices $V_{X,J}$. The row subscript is the city, and the column subscript has the position of the city in the tour.

In this problem, it is easier to first formulate the energy equation using the known constraints, and then determine the connection matrix and external inputs by correspondence with the original equations of state. The following energy equation represents a minimum total "cost" function based on problem constraints:

$$E = \frac{A}{2} \sum_x \sum_i \sum_{j \neq i} V_{xi} V_{xj} + \frac{B}{2} \sum_i \sum_x \sum_{x \neq y} V_{xi} V_{yi}$$

$$+ \frac{C}{2} \left(\sum_x \sum_i V_{xi} - N \right)^2 + \frac{D}{2} \sum_x \sum_{x \neq y} \sum_i d_{xy} V_{xi} (V_{Y,i+1} + V_{Y,i-1}) \quad (16.13)$$

where A, B, C, D are all positive constants. The first term has a minimum if and only if each row contains no more than one entry (with the rest of the entries 0). The second term is minimum when each column has no more than one entry. The third term is minimum if the entire matrix has only N entries. The square in this term is used to determine the absolute difference of the total entries from the desired number. The final term minimizes the length of the path corresponding to a given tour. With this equation the total energy for a stable state represents the length of the tour.

The network would operate by initializing V_{ij} and letting the states settle to a stable solution. In operation the network computes solutions that are very good but not necessarily optimal. For example, with a 30-city tour the estimated optimal path was around 4.26, while the network typically converges to paths around 6 to 7. Out of 10^{30} possible choices the network converges to one of the 10^7 best tours. Better performance is observed when random biases are injected into V_{ij} and gain control parameters are adjusted gradually. This acts to "kick" the system out of local minima by raising the "temperature" of the system and gradually relaxing into better solutions. This technique of *simulated annealing* comes from methods for annealing crystals and has been specifically used for optimization problems [Kirkpatrik 83].

The Hopfield model has weaknesses when used as an associative memory. First, the number of memories that can be stored in a system of N neurons is limited to around $0.15N$ [Hopfield 82]. Typically the number of memories is kept well below this value. Trying to store more memories than this leads to unpredictable recall because the energy minima are too close for proper resolution. Second, if two memories are very close to each other (in the Hamming sense), the network will not consistently stabilize to the correct memory. To eliminate this problem the input vectors must be orthogonal. In general, there are hardware implementation problems with any kind of Hopfield application because it requires full interconnection between neurons.

16.3.2 The Neocognitron and character recognition

The Neocognitron is a multilayered neural network model capable of recognizing arbitrary patterns that are shifted in position and distorted in shape. This model was developed by Fukushima and his colleagues at NHK Research Laboratories [Fukushima 80]. The Neocognitron is a feedforward network arranged into modules, layers, and planes of neural processing units or cells. For example, in Fukushima's 1983 version there are four modules plus the input plane [Fukushima 83]. Each module consists of two layers, and each layer contains many planes (ranging from 8 to 38). A cell plane is a square matrix of individual cells. The number of cells in a plane range from 19×19 at the input plane to 1×1 (a single cell) at the output. Figure 16.3 shows the overall cell topology. The numbers at the bottom tell how big the plane is and how many planes per layer.

The Neocognitron has a very complex interconnection scheme. In-

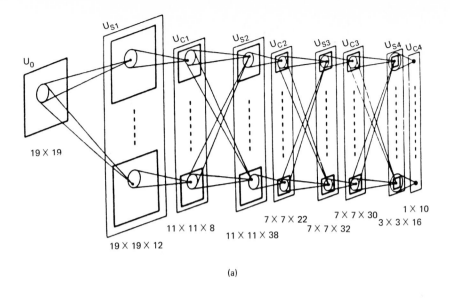

19 × 19

19 × 19 × 12

11 × 11 × 8

11 × 11 × 38

7 × 7 × 22

7 × 7 × 32

7 × 7 × 30

3 × 3 × 16

1 × 10

(a)

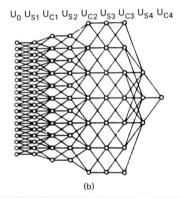

U_0 U_{S1} U_{C1} U_{S2} U_{C2} U_{S3} U_{C3} U_{S4} U_{C4}

(b)

Figure 16.3   Neocognitron network topology. (*a*) Synaptic connections between layers; (*b*) one-dimensional view of interconnections for different cell planes as seen from the top. Only one cell plane is drawn in each layer. [Fukushima 83]

side a module, the layers are differentiated into two cell types: S and C. The interconnections are different between S and C layers of different modules and S and C layers of the same module. Between module $l - 1$ and l, each S cell in plane k is connected to an area of C cells (or cells in the input plane for $l = 0$). For example, each cell in the U_{S1} layer is connected to a 3×3 area of cells in the input plane. The same cell in each S plane is connected to the same 3×3 area of C cells in every C plane. In addition to these excitatory connections between C and S planes, there is a single inhibitory connection to each S cell. In the same module, the S to C cell connections are all excitatory but arranged differently. In this case, each C cell is connected to a 5×5 area of cells in only one S plane.

There are three state equations for the system: S cell output, inhibitory cell output, and C cell output. The output response u_S for an arbitrary S cell with input stimulus $p(v)$ from an area of cells connected to u_S is

$$u_S = r \cdot \phi \left(\frac{1 + \sum_v a(v) \cdot p_{(v)}}{1 + \frac{r}{1+r} \cdot b \cdot v_{Ce-1}} - 1 \right) \qquad k = 1, 2, \dots, K_{Sl} \qquad (16.14)$$

where $\phi [x] = \max(x, 0)$

$a(v), b =$ connection weights between excitatory and inhibitory connections, respectively

$u_{Cl-1}, v_{Cl-1} =$ outputs from excitatory and inhibitory connections of previous layer

$r =$ constant controlling intensity of inhibition

The inhibitory cells receive inputs from the same group of cells as u_S and output a value proportional to the weighted root mean square of its inputs. The connection weights for the inhibitory cells are unmodifiable. The values decrease monotonically from the center of v (an area of cells connected from layers S to C).

The output of an arbitrary C cell is

$$u_C = \psi \left(\sum_{\kappa=1}^{K_{Sl}} j(\kappa, k) \sum_{v \in D_l} d(v) \cdot u_S \right) \qquad k = 1, 2, \dots, K_{Cl} \qquad (16.15)$$

where

$$\psi [x] = \begin{cases} x/(\alpha + x) & \text{if } x \leqslant 0 \\ 0 & \text{otherwise} \end{cases} \qquad (16.16)$$

In this equation α is a positive constant which determines the degree of output saturation. These values are fixed empirically during experiment. K_{Cl} and K_{Sl} are the number of C and S planes in the lth module. Also, $d(v)$ denotes the fixed connection strengths for the synapses leading from S cells, $j_l(\kappa, k)$ is a connectivity matrix indicating connections between the κth S plane to the kth C plane, D_l is the area of S cells covered by a single C cell.

The Neocognitron has four different types of synapses or connection weights: a, b, c, and d. Of the four types only a and b are modifiable. Both are inputs to S cells with a excitatory and b inhibitory. The connection strengths for a "representative" S cell are modified according to the following hebbian learning rule:

$$\Delta a(v) = q \cdot c(v) \cdot p(v) \qquad (16.17)$$

$$\Delta b(k) = q \cdot v$$

where q is a positive constant, set through experiment, to determine the amount of learning.

The modification of synaptic connections proceeds from the input plane to the deeper layers, one layer at a time. During the training process, the network is presented with a set of training patterns to the input layer, along with constraints telling which cells should respond to each of the training patterns. This approach is called *learning with a teacher*.

There are a number of planes in each layer. These planes are trained one at a time. A training pattern is given to the input layer, and simultaneously one S cell is chosen as the "representative" from the plane. The representative is reinforced depending on the inputs to its synapses. Only those synapses having nonzero signals are reinforced. After training the representative cell, all other cells in a cell plane have their input synapses modified identically to the representative.

Pattern recognition in the network operates according to the following process. The stimulus is presented to S cells in the first module. These cells act as local feature extractors. Each plane of S cells is trained to detect a very particular feature such as a line segment in a certain orientation. The C cells, on the other hand, allow for positional errors in the features detected by the S cells. C cells receive signals through fixed connections from a group of S cells and extract the same feature from slightly different positions. If just one S cell is activated in a particular C cell region, then the C cell is also activated. In intermediate stages of the network, local features are gradually combined into more global patterns. Finally, only a single cell is activated indicating which pattern was presented. The process of tolerating small amounts of position errors at each stage allows the network to be flexible in recognizing very distorted patterns.

Fukushima trained the Neocognitron to recognize hand-drawn Arabic digits. Figure 16.4a shows a number of patterns that were correctly identified by the system. Notice that identification occurs even when the patterns are distorted, shifted, or degraded with noise. Figure 16.4b shows a few examples of patterns that gave incorrect or inconclusive responses. Notice that even though these patterns are grossly distorted you can probably identify the pattern. While these results are extremely impressive, they also remind us that artificial systems still have a long way to go to match the flexibility and power of human pattern matching.

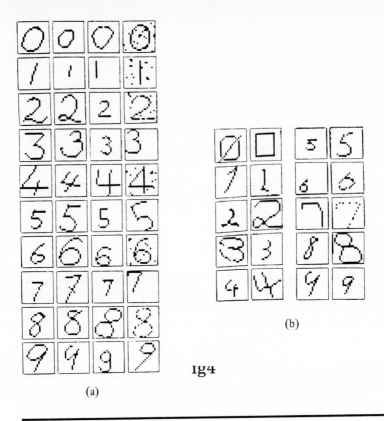

(a)

(b)

Ig4

Figure 16.4 (a) Patterns that the Neocognitron successfully identified;
(b) patterns that the Neocognitron did not correctly identify.

The feedforward cascade structure of the Neocognitron has been
modified by Fukushima's group to include feedback and lateral inhibition [Fukushima 87]. As a result of these structural enhancements,
the new model has the ability of selective attention. That is, when a
pattern is presented that consists of two previously trained patterns,
the network can selectively identify each pattern from the other. Another ability of this new model is to take very incomplete or noisy patterns and restore them to the originally trained pattern.

16.3.3 Adaptive resonance and pattern classification

Grossberg and associates have worked for nearly 20 years on theories
to explain human cognition in terms of neural network operations.
Their research has culminated in a model called *adaptive resonance
theory* (ART). This model is extremely rich and complex. It would be

impossible to fully describe it in a few pages. This section gives a few of the highlights of ART; see Carpenter and Grossberg [Carpenter 87a, 87b, 86] for more detailed descriptions.

The overall structure of the ART model is broken into two subsystems. Familiar or previously learned patterns are processed within the *attentional subsystem.* This subsystem establishes precise internal representations to familiar events. By itself this subsystem is unable to simultaneously maintain stable representations of familiar categories *and* create new categories for unfamiliar patterns. The second subsystem fills this inadequacy by resetting the attentional subsystem when unfamiliar events occur. This *orienting* subsystem is essential for determining whether a new pattern is familiar and has a recognition code or unfamiliar and in need of a new recognition code (Fig. 16.5).

The core structure of the ART model consists of two stages or layers plus some additional control connections. Figure 16.5 shows the overall anatomy of the ART model. The first layer F_1 contains enough nodes to encode the input pattern. For example, with binary inputs there would be one node or neural processing unit for each binary value in the pattern. The F_1 layer is normally completely connected to layer F_2. In both layers there are separate excitatory and inhibitory

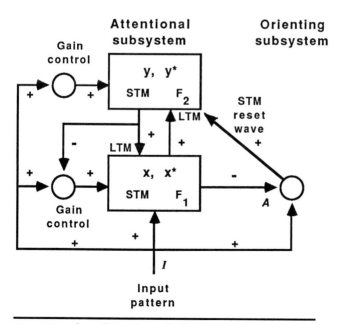

Figure 16.5 Overall topology of adaptive resonance system. [Carpenter 86]

connections. There are additional connections between layers to modulate the gain control and arousal control. Other versions of ART have extended this structure to include additional layers. For example, *masking fields* extend this architecture to higher levels $F_3, F_4, \ldots$ and have valuable properties for visual object recognition, speech recognition, and higher cognitive processes [Carpenter 87a]. For simplicity we discuss only the two-layer system.

In ART there are state equations for short-term memory (STM) and long-term memory (LTM). STM equations show the instantaneous activation of each neuron in the network. LTM equations describe how the network interconnection weights change during learning. In layer F_1 nodes are denoted by v_i, where $i = 1, 2, \ldots, M$. F_2 nodes, v_j, range between $j = M + 1, M + 2, \ldots N$. The STM equations for each layer obey a membrane equation of the following form:

$$\epsilon \frac{d}{dt} x_k = -x_k + (1 - Ax_k)J_k^+ - (B + Cx_k)J_k^- \qquad (16.18)$$

where x_k is the activation value for either layer F_1 or F_2. All parameters are nonnegative. J_k^+ is the total excitatory input to v_k, J_k^- is the total inhibitory input to v_k. If $A > 0$ and $C > 0$, then STM activity is bounded within the finite interval $[-BC^{-1}, A^{-1}]$.

The excitatory inputs to node v_i of F_1 are the sum of signals from the input pattern I_i and the previously learned top-down template V_i:

$$J_i^+ = I_i + V_i \qquad (16.19)$$

and

$$V_i = D\sum_j f(x_j)z_{ji} \qquad (16.20)$$

where D = constant
$\quad f(x_j)$ = signal generated by activity x_j on v_j
$\quad z_{ji}$ = LTM weight matrix from v_j to v_i

The F_2 layer chooses the largest weighted input from F_1 and as such approximates a binary switch. Also, the top-down template V_i is weight-enhanced according to

$$V_i = \begin{cases} Dz_{ji} & \text{if } F_2 \text{ node } v_j \text{ is active} \\ 0 & \text{if } F_2 \text{ is inactive} \end{cases} \qquad (16.21)$$

The inhibitory inputs J_i^- are simply the sum of signals generated by activity x_j on node v_j. There are no inhibitory signals when F_2 is inactive.

The LTM traces between F_1 and F_2 follow basically the same equation but have distinct connections for "bottom-up" and "top-down" pathways. A single equation is sufficient to show the form of the learning rule:

$$\frac{d}{dt} z_{ij} = Kf(x_j)[- E_{ij}z_{ij} + h(x_i)] \qquad (16.22)$$

Notice that the rules for LTM changes are *nonhebbian* and represent a learning rule not previously encountered.

ART uses a sophisticated series of feedforward and feedback phases to compare new inputs with previously learned patterns. If the new input matches previously learned templates (to the desired degree of accuracy), then the process terminates with a match. However, if there is sufficient mismatch between bottom-up inputs and top-down inputs and top-down templates, then the template is reset and a search continues for a better match or a new template is created. The amount of mismatch tolerated between new and previously learned patterns is modulated by the orienting subsystem. In this way the system is capable of very fine pattern classification resulting in many different categories or coarse classification using only a few categories. The following paragraphs give a very simplified overview of some of the processes involved.

Refering back to Fig. 16.5 we briefly trace the transformations that an input pattern experiences during recognition and learning in the network. The input pattern I is received at layer F_1. Pattern I is transformed into a pattern of activation across the F_1 nodes via the activation Eq. (16.18) described earlier. Next, this activation pattern X elicits a sequence of steps that eventually produces a new contrast-enhanced pattern Y that is stored in F_2.

After the bottom-up $I \rightarrow Y$ transformation takes place, F_2 uses Y to send a top-down excitatory signal pattern back to F_1. Only sufficiently large activities in Y cause feedback signals between layers F_2 and F_1. The resulting weighted and summed output pattern generates a new input pattern V on F_1. V is called a top-down template.

Two sources of input impinge on layer F_1: the bottom-up input pattern I and the top-down template V. As a result, the activity pattern X^* is produced which is the sum of I and V. X^* is typically different from the activity pattern X that was produced by I alone. The extent of this mismatch determines whether the input pattern I is classified as a new pattern or matched with a previously learned input.

In Fig. 16.5 the orienting subsystem A uses the mismatch between bottom-up input patterns and top-down templates to determine whether a new pattern category should be learned. Very simply stated, if the mismatch is greater than some threshold, then A fires an arousal burst. When A fires, all F_2 cells are excited. Nodes in F_2 react to this arousal signal in a state-dependent fashion. In a special case where F_2 chooses a single node for activation, the arousal burst acts to reset the number of active cells in F_2. This reset causes the top-down template V to be removed. At this point the process begins again with input pattern I inducing X across F_1, which again generates a new pattern Y^* at F_2. This new pattern reads-out a new top-down template V^*. If the mismatch between I and V^* is again greater than some threshold, then the activity pattern at F_2 is again reset. In effect, this reset mechanism is used to search for learned patterns. In the case where no previously learned pattern sufficiently matches the new input pattern, a new recognition category is formed.

The orienting subsystem described above allows ART to distinguish "critical features" in a pattern. Critical features are those patterns which are seen as relevant and important to the particular context. Features that are seen as critical in one context might be seen as noise in another. For example, Fig. 16.6a shows two input patterns composed of three features. There is a mismatch in one of the three features. In this case, the mismatch might be seen as significant so that two different categories would be learned for the two input patterns. Figure 16.6b shows another case where the same pattern of 31 dots is superimposed on the two previous patterns. As before, the patterns

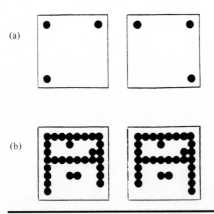

(a)

(b)

Figure 16.6 Critical feature detection. (a) Two patterns mismatch at one feature, which in this case is sufficient to encode two different pattern categories; (b) although these patterns mismatch at the same feature, both patterns are classified into the same category and the mismatch is treated as noise. [Carpenter 87a]

mismatch in one feature, but since this feature is not significant to the overall pattern, it could be viewed as noise. Thus a feature may be a critical feature in one instance and irrelevant noise in another.

The orienting subsystem uses a parameter called *vigilance* to determine whether a new pattern has critical features or sufficiently matches a known pattern. To quantify this parameter let $|I|$ denote the number of nodes that receive positive inputs when pattern I is presented. The input pattern, I, is modified by F_1 nodes to produce a pattern of activity X across the nodes. Let $|X|$ be the number of activated nodes after initial processing by F_1. The orienting subsystem is activated when

$$\rho > \frac{|X|}{|I|} \tag{16.23}$$

In other words, the proportion $|X|/|I|$ must exceed the vigilance threshold ρ, or the excitatory wave induced by A will force the system to reset F_2 activations and look for a new match or learn a new category.

In order for F_1 to distinguish between bottom-up and top-down signals, ART incorporates a mechanism called *attentional gain control*. When a bottom-up input pattern is being processed, F_1 receives both a specific input from pattern I and a nonspecific attentional gain control input. On the other hand, when matching simultaneous bottom-up and top-down patterns, the attentional gain control is inhibited by F_2. Nodes at F_1 must receive sufficiently large signals from both bottom-up and top-down patterns to reach the threshold of activation. As a result, mismatched patterns will not generate suprathreshold activities. There are three sources of signals: the bottom-up input, the attentional gain control, and the top-down template. The so-called two-thirds rule states that an F_1 node becomes active only when it receives signals from two of the three signal sources.

As an example of how ART might be used in pattern classification, we relate the results of Grossberg's two simulation experiments using alphabet letters as input patterns. Figure 16.7 shows the results of one presentation of each of the first 20 letters in the alphabet using two different vigilance levels. In the first test the vigilance parameter ρ was set at 0.5; in the second experiment $\rho = 0.8$.

With $\rho = 0.5$ the network grouped 26 letter patterns into 8 stable categories (only the first 20 trials are shown in the figure) in 3 presentations. For this simulation F_2 had 15 nodes; therefore, 7 nodes remained uncoded. Given $\rho = 0.8$ and 15 nodes at F_2, the network grouped 25 letters into 15 stable categories within 3 presentations. With ρ closer to 1, this network classified letters into 15 distinct categories within 2 presentations. In general, if an ART network has enough nodes in F_1 and F_2, it is capable of self-organizing an arbitrary

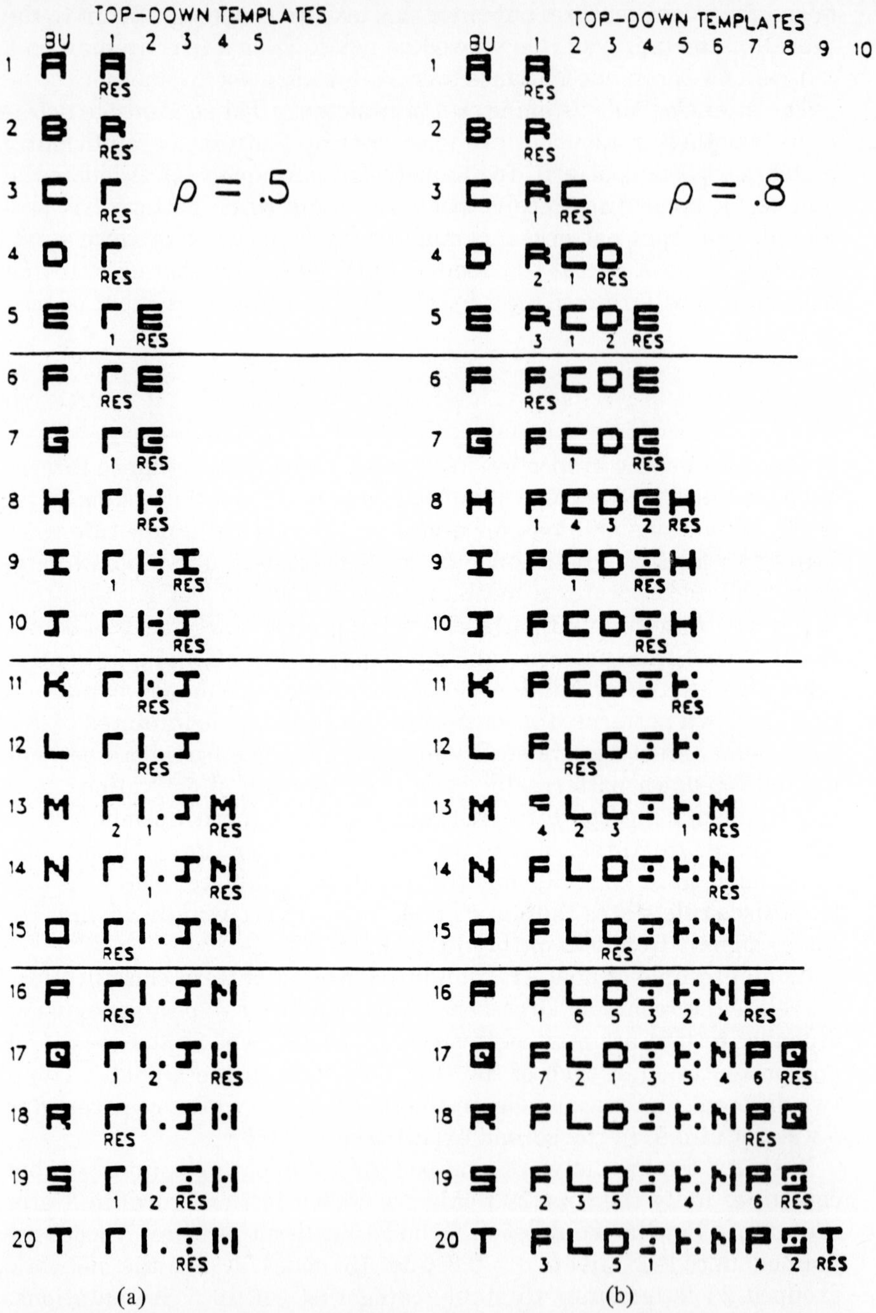

Figure 16.7 Alphabet pattern classification. (*a*) Pattern learning with a lower vigilance results in fewer categories or templates; (*b*) with higher vigilance more templates were formed. [Carpenter 87*a*]

ordering of arbitrarily many and arbitrarily complex input patterns into self-stabilizing categories.

The ART model was orginally intended to be used with binary inputs. Recently ART-2 has been introduced to overcome this restriction, and, while using the same basic principles as ART-1, it allows for analog signal inputs in a real-time environment [Carpenter 87*b*]. Paul Kolodzy and associates at MIT Lincoln Laboratories are using ART-2 with inputs from a laser range and velocity system to classify objects in a very complex scene [Kolodzy 87]. No doubt other important applications will be forthcoming.

The Hopfield, Fukushima, and Grossberg models are three of the more widely known and studied approaches. These models provide an example of the diversity of mathematical architectures possible for neural networks. It would be impossible to describe, and very difficult to list, all of the neural network models currently in use. Because of intense research new models and applications are growing at an astounding rate. Table 16.2 summarizes a few of the most popular models along with their applications and references.

TABLE 16.2   List of a Few Popular Neural Network Models, Potential Areas of Application and Sources for Further Information

Model	Applications	References
Hopfield model	Electronic and optical associative memory, resource allocation, TSP, A/D conversion, radar image recognition	[Hopfield 85, 86; Dunning 86; Farhat 85; Sivilotti 86; Tank 86]
Neocognitron	Pattern recognition	[Fukushima 83, 87]
Adaptive resonance	Pattern classification, machine vision, analog signal processing	[Cohen 83; Carpenter 86, 87*a*, 87*b*; Kolodzy 87]
Boltzmann machine	Associative memory, optimization, speech recognition, TSP	[Hinton 86; Prager 86; Ticknor 87]
Bidirectional associative memory (BAM)	Associative memory	[Kosko 87]
Counterpropagation network	Image compression, pattern classification	[Hecht-Nielsen 87]
Back propagation	Speech synthesis, pattern recognition, signal processing, expert systems	[Sejnowski 86; Castalez 87]
Grossberg avalanche network	Pattern recognition	[Grossberg 71]

16.4 Optical Computing Devices and Architectures

In the next two sections, we introduce basic optical devices, architectural choices, and arithmetic algorithms needed for developing digital optical computers. In Sec. 16.6 we discuss approaches for constructing optical or electrooptical neural computers.

To develop an integrated optical computer, we need extensive research in the following four areas: *materials, devices, architectures,* and *algorithms*. The fastest electronic transistors take several picoseconds $(10^{-12}$ s) to switch between on and off states. At AT&T Bell Laboratories, the shortest optical pulse can be switched in 0.008 ps [Hecht 87]. Light travels at 3×10^8 m/s, which makes the signal propagation delay much shorter than via electronic wires. Over the years, optical computing has been researched for image processing using spatial filtering or coherent light, pattern recognition using matched filters, signal processing using acoustooptic devices, and matrix-vector processors. All of these data processing applications are based on the development of a coherent light source such as the laser.

16.4.1 Optical computing devices

The early research in optical logic concentrated on gates that could be built from solid-state lasers. More recently, an experimental array of *bistable optical gates* became available. These gates can perform logical AND, NOR, or memory functions over inputs and outputs represented by light intensities as characterized in Fig. 16.8. The device is nonlinear with positive feedback to ensure bistability. The I/O characteristics follow a hysteresis cycle (Fig. 16.8a), in which logical **0** corresponds to the incident light intensity from I_1 to I_3 and logic **1** from I_4 to I_2. The switching states take place between I_1 and I_3 for $\mathbf{0} \rightarrow \mathbf{1}$ and between I_2 and I_1 for $\mathbf{1} \rightarrow \mathbf{0}$. Functionally, an optical bistable device with two light inputs x and y is shown. The control signal c decides the function, and power input p establishes the intensity bias value. The outputs q and $\bar{q}$ are related to the inputs by the following boolean equation:

$$Newq = \bar{c} \cdot q + c \cdot (x + y) \tag{16.24}$$

$$New\bar{q} = \bar{c} \cdot \bar{q} + c \cdot \overline{(x + y)}$$

This implies that the device can be used as a logical OR or a logical NOR gate when the control signal $c = 1$ and as a pure memory device, latch with $Newq = q$ and $New\bar{q} = \bar{q}$, when $c = 0$. In other words, an optical array of bistable devices can be used in performing both logic and memory functions. Of course, one may have to use multiple arrays

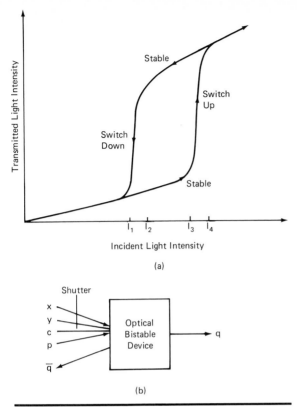

Transmitted Light Intensity

Stable

Switch
Up

Switch
Down

Stable

I_1 I_2 I_3 I_4

Incident Light Intensity

(a)

Shutter

x
y
c
p

$\bar{q}$

Optical
Bistable
Device

q

(b)

Figure 16.8 (*a*) Input/output characteristics of an optical bistable device; (*b*) implementation of an optical processing cell.

to implement multi-level logic or memory circuits. The above only provides a functional sketch of an optical logic gate/latch device. For physical details of the materials and technology used, see Tanguay [85].

Besides optical bistable devices and arrays, *spatial light modulators* (SLMs) are needed for storing, modifying, and amplifying digital optical signals. The SLMs can be electrically or optically controlled and can process optical signals in one-dimensional, two-dimensional, or three-dimensional formats. Available SLMs can be made with electrooptic, magnetooptic, photochronic, or acoustooptic means. Example functions for SLMs include incoherent-to-coherent conversion, wavelength conversion, serial-to-parallel conversion, and intensity-to-spatial frequency conversion. Hybrid SLMs use combined optics and the extensive signal conditioning capability of silicon or GaAs-based ICs. The advantages of such a hybridization include the capability of on-chip data coding and decoding, level restoration, spatial reformatting, rescaling, and base-line subtraction. SLMs are useful as pattern recognizers and pattern substitutors for symbolic substitution in optical arithmetic (described in Sec. 16.5). They are also used to perform thresholding of input signals in neural networks.

Detailed assessments of various materials and devices for optical computing can be found in Tanguay [85] and Gibbs [80]. In Sec. 16.4.2, we assess various means of constructing and operating optical interconnection networks that form the core communication architecture in any optical computer. In Sec. 16.5, we discuss optical digital arithmetic processors and assess their potential performance and advantages. Optical switching speed is $O(10^3)$ to $O(10^6)$ faster than electronic gates. Electronic computer architectures have primarily used a few coarse grain processors, whereas optical computers will most likely consist of fine-grain massively parallel systems [Hwang 87]. The control complexity, power requirements, and reliability of optical computers are potentially superior to their electronic counterparts. Optical computing is so near and yet far away in terms of cost-effectiveness and programmability. Until these and other issues are satisfactorily answered, it is too early to predict when optical supercomputers will appear. However, among the emerging new technologies, optics or hybrid optics/electronic is certainly the most promising approach to achieving a major breakthrough in the history of computing [Sawchuk 84].

16.4.2   Architecture of an optical computer

Optical computing research requires skills in computer architecture, signal/image processing, communication/system theory, quantum electronics, and optical material/devices. This section focuses on the architectural issues of developing a digital optical computer.

The architecture of an optical computer is illustrated in Fig. 16.9.

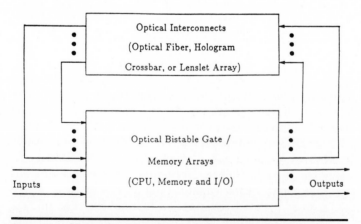

Figure 16.9   The architecture of an optical computer. [Hwang 87]

Optical bistable gate/memory arrays are used to build the CPU, the memory, and I/O interfaces. These functional arrays are interconnected by some form of optical network. In this section, we present various optical interconnection networks. These networks provide interprocessor and interprocessor-memory-I/O communications. Various optical networks for parallel processing are summarized in Table 16.3. Interconnection problems exist at various spatial scales ranging from 10 m between processors to 0.1 mm between boards, 0.01 mm between chips and 10^{-6} mm between gates.

Some important issues in designing optical interconnection networks include planar vs. volume (bulk), packet vs. circuit switched, guided wave vs. free space (using refractive or defractive elements), undirectional vs. bidirectional, optical vs. electronic control, and asynchronous vs. synchronized operations. Of course, the reconfiguration time, communication bandwidth (>1 GHz), propagation delay time, cascadability, and broadcast capability are other important parameters that affect the performance and efficiency. Electronic technologies are approaching their limits in terms of switching speed and packaging (pin-out) requirements. As microcircuits become denser, the problems of clock skew, bandwidth, cross talk, and capacitive loading are intensified. Using optical networks, many of these limitations can be lifted to allow the construction of large-scale networks to support massive parallelism.

Optical beams need to use drivers and detectors such as laser diodes, light-emitting diodes (LEDs), and optoelectrical transducers. The transmission media include free space, fibers, or planar waveguides. Other important optical devices are needed for beam steering, spatial light modulation, and holograph generation.

Optical buses cannot be used as mere 1:1 replacements of electrical buses. Significant increases in control complexity and power consumption may be encountered in using multiple optical buses. However, one can take advantage of the high density of optics by multiplexing. The *time division multiplexing* (TDM) allows one to carry $m \times n$ signals in an m-channel optical fiber. Multiplexing signals onto an optical bus reduces the number of interconnections, uses less power, and offers higher application flexibility. The major drawbacks in using multiplexed optical bus include fixed connections and no broadcast capability.

16.4.3   Optical crossbar and hologram networks

An optical crossbar switch can be constructed with free-space optics, input laser diodes, *variable grating mode* (VGM) devices, Fourier transform lens, spatial filters and detector arrays. The VGM device

TABLE 16.3 Characteristics of Optical Interconnection Networks

Networks	Bandwidth	Reconfiguration speed	Broadcast capability	Parallelism	Rearrangeability
Matrix-vector multiplication	Medium	Fast, control matrix	Yes	High	Yes, control matrix
VGM crossbar	Low	Slow, VGM device	No	High	Yes, voltage vector
Parallel optic bus	High	N/A	No	Medium	Not possible
Hologram	Medium	Fast, computer-generated hologram	No	High	Yes, computer-generated hologram
Optical perfect shuffle	Medium	Medium, dependent on number of stages	No	Low	$O(\log N)$ limited permutations

N = number of elements.

performs an intensity-to-frequency conversion over a two-dimensional field. The VGM directs input signals to one of the several spatially separate output channels. The spatial filter masks off the unwanted diffraction orders. The VGM network can be used in real time with nonblocking interconnections. Although the network is reconfigurable, the reconfiguration speed is rather slow (100 ms). It can be used in applications that require a large volume of block data transfers and demand a few reconfigurations such as image or graphic processing.

The VGM network consists of two Fourier transform lenses and a switching matrix made from a *liquid crystal light valve* (LCLV). The input vector consists of a row of LEDs. The control of the LCLV generates a matrix of light or dark spots. The input vector is "multiplied" (reflected or absorbed) by the LCLV matrix to form the output vector. The LCLV crossbar network has lower reconfiguration overhead and broadcast capability. (All other networks cannot broadcast.) However, the network has a loss efficiency, because most of the light from the sources is lost due to the reflecting matrix. This network appeals more to the construction of dynamically reconfigurable systems.

Instead of operating on a two-dimensional plane, hologram-based networks use the third dimension for free-space optical transmissions. A hologram is a beam-steering array used to establish arbitrary interconnections. Holograms can be used in two ways: as a defractor or as a deflector as shown in Fig. 16.10. The deflector is mainly used for board-to-board interconnections. The deflector is used for chip-to-chip or intrachip communications. The main advantage of a deflective hologram is that it uses the surface of a chip as a matrix of pinouts interconnecting internal circuits. The hologram interconnections can be computer generated and thus reconfigurable. The major drawback is its low tolerance for misalignment of light beams and deflectors.

Either free-space optics or integrated optics can be used for constructing an optical shuffle network. Holograms can be also used to construct the free-space shuffle network. The integrated perfect shuffle is implemented with a waveguide network using hybrid optical/electrical devices. The major drawback lies in the limited number of permutations that can be generated in one pass. Thus multiple stages may be needed, which may cause longer propagation time delays.

16.5 Optical Arithmetic Algorithms and Processors

In this section, we present the basics of optical digital arithmetic design including: number representation, algorithms for fast addition,

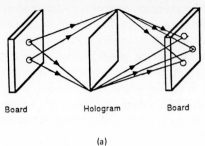

Board   Hologram   Board

(a)

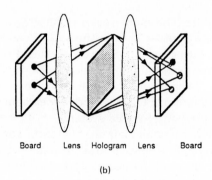

Board   Lens   Hologram   Lens   Board

(b)

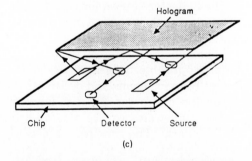

Chip   Detector   Source

(c)

Figure 16.10 Different types of holographic interconnection schemes. (*a*) Diffracting hologram; (*b*) diffractive hologram with focusing elements; (*c*) deflective hologram.

and processor architecture. Additional algorithms for multiplication and division with optics can be found in Hwang [89].

16.5.1 Optical symbolic arithmetic

Several methods have been proposed for performing digital arithmetic operations on optical data. The residue number system has been considered for its carry-free addition, subtraction, and multiplication [Hwang 79]. But this system suffers from the difficulties in performing division, comparing two numbers, and converting a residue number to a conventional representation. Another technique, called *symbolic substitution*, has been proposed for arithmetic and logic operations on optical data [Huang 83]. This technique involves the recognition of spatial patterns of binary coded data and replaces them according to a set of predefined symbolic substitution rules. Substitution rules for binary addition have been developed by Brenner [85, 86]. Unfortunately, these rules are based on the conventional number representation, which demands carry propagation and requires an $O(n)$ addition time, where n is the operand length.

The *signed-digit* (SD) number representation can be used in conjunction with symbolic substitution to take full advantage of what optics can offer. By doing so, one can significantly improve the speed, accuracy, and the dynamic range of digital arithmetic. The SD representation limits carry propagation only to adjacent digital positions for addition. Thus the addition time of two SD numbers becomes a constant. Thus totally parallel addition becomes possible with a digit set of $\{1, 0, \bar{1}\}$ [Avizienis 61]. The ability of implementing a symbolic substitution scheme with high-speed optical components and the provision of a carry-constrained arithmetic system permit us to develop an optical arithmetic processor which is potentially several orders of magnitude faster than any existing electronic counterparts.

16.5.2 Totally parallel addition in optics

Given an integer $Y = (y_{n-1} \ldots y_1 y_0)_{SD}$ in SD notation, the algebraic value is evaluated as $Y_v = \Sigma_{i=0}^{i=n-1} y_i 2^i$, where $y_i \in (1, 0, \bar{1})$. We use $\bar{1}$ to denote the digital value -1. Note that there is no need of an explicit sign digit in Y. In fact, the sign of the most significant digit y_{n-1} determines the sign of Y. Fractions can be similarly represented in SD notation. This scheme can be easily extended to floating-point arithmetic with only minor modifications. We present below algorithm for SD addition/subtraction.

The addition of two n-digit SD integers X and Y produces an $n+1$-*digit* SD integer $S = X + Y = (s_n \ldots s_1 s_0)_{SD}$. A totally parallel adder can be built with only three stages.

At the first stage, we perform $x_i + y_i = w_i + 2t_{i+1}$ at the ith digital position, where

$$w_i = \begin{cases} \bar{1} & \text{if } x_i + y_i = \bar{1} \\ 0 & \text{if } x_i + y_i = -2 \text{ or } 0 \text{ or } 2 \\ 1 & \text{if } x_i + y_i = 1 \end{cases} \qquad (16.25)$$

$$t_{i+1} = \begin{cases} 1 & \text{if } x_i + y_i \geq 1 \\ 0 & \text{if } x_i + y_i = 0 \\ \bar{1} & \text{if } x_i + y_i \leq \bar{1} \end{cases}$$

The second stage performs an interim addition, $w_i + t_i = 2t'_{i+1} + w'_i$, at the $i+1$-th digital position, where

$$t'_{i+1} = \begin{cases} 1 & \text{if } w_i + t_i = 2 \\ 0 & \text{if } w_i + t_i = \bar{1} \text{ or } 0 \text{ or } 1 \\ 1 & \text{if } w_i + t_i = -2 \end{cases} \tag{16.26}$$

$$w'_i = \begin{cases} 1 & \text{if } w_i + t_i = 1 \\ 0 & \text{if } w_i + t_i = -2 \text{ or } 0 \text{ or } 2 \\ \bar{1} & \text{if } w_i + t_i = -1 \end{cases}$$

The last stage performs the final addition to produce the final sum digit:

$$s_i = w'_i + t'_i = \begin{cases} 1 & \text{if } w'_i + t'_i \geq 1 \\ 0 & \text{if } w'_i + t'_i = 0 \\ \bar{1} & \text{if } w'_i + t'_i \leq \bar{1} \end{cases} \tag{16.27}$$

The digit set $\{1, 0, \bar{1}\}$ used in SD number representation is optically represented by spatial imagery symbols as shown in Fig. 16.11. Each signed digit is represented by two binary pixels, which can be easily obtained with the extreme variation of light intensity. The shaded square corresponds to a complete dark pixel and the unshaded square corresponds to a complete bright pixel. Three combinations are used in representing $1, 0$, and $\bar{1}$, respectively. The patterns for 1 and $\bar{1}$ complement each other. In other words, the negation of $\bar{1}$ is 1 and vice versa. There is no boolean negation used in the SD code. All the negations performed are arithmetic in nature. This means that the negative of 0 is still zero, because positive 0 and negative 0 means the same in SD notation. In this sense, the zero could be represented by either two dark pixels or by two bright pixels. To save light energy, we use two dark pixels.

These *symbolic substitution* (SS) rules can be easily implemented with optics. The left sides of the rules are the input light combinations, and the right sides are the output light patterns. It is rather straightforward to generate and to modify binary images consisting of these combinations, such as letting the light through or by blocking the light with a shutter. The change of these patterns can be electronically controlled in an electrooptical system.

We need to apply 17 rules for the SD addition specified in Eqs.

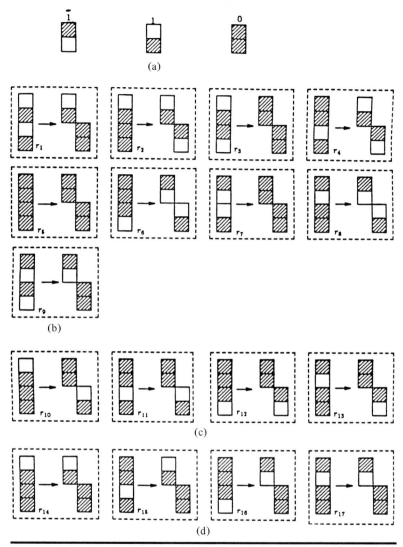

Figure 16.11 Optical substitution rules for signed-digit addition. (*a*) Image encoding of the digit set {1, 0, $\overline{1}$ }; (*b*) substitution rules used in stage 1; (*c*) substitution rules for stage 2; (*d*) substitution rules for stage 3.

(16.25) to (16.27). An example is shown in Fig. 16.12 to illustrate the sequence of imagery patterns being substituted in the addition of $X = (\overline{1}01\overline{1})_{SD}$ and $Y = (010\overline{1})_{SD}$ to produce the sum $S = X + Y = (000\overline{1}00)_{SD}$. Note only three stages of substitutions are performed. In fact, substitution operations on all digital positions are performed in parallel, and the 3 stages can be pipelined, if many pairs of numbers are to be added in a pipelined fashion. The SS subtraction

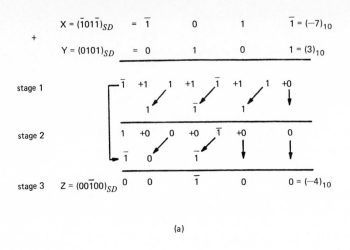

(a)

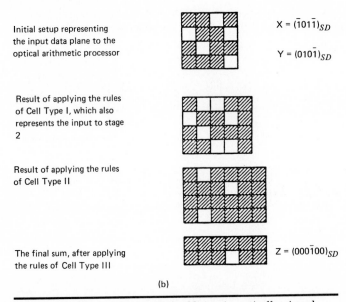

(b)

Figure 16.12 The totally parallel addition in optically signed digit code. (*a*) An example of totally parallel addition; (*b*) the image substitution in three stages. [Hwang 89]

needs an extra stage to perform digitwise arithmetic negation, before the SS addition is performed, and this extra stage needs only two more substitution rules. Algorithms have been also developed in Hwang [89] for performing multiplication and division using an extended set of SS rules.

16.5.3   An optical arithmetic processor

In order to execute many rules in parallel, we need to replicate the input data plane containing the optically coded SD operands according to the number of rules to be activated. For example, if we are at stage one of the SD addition, we need to replicate the input 9 times corresponding to the nine SS rules of the first stage. Then each copy goes through one of the single rule procedures outlined in parts *b* and *c* of Fig. 16.11. The output of each rule is then fed to a *pattern combiner* whose function consists of optically superimposing the output images from each rule to form the output plane (or the next input plane in case of iterations). A functional approach to developing such an optical arithmetic processor is illustrated in Fig. 16.13, where we define modules for SD *addition,* SD *shift/negate,* and SD *logical AND.*

These modules are arranged in a feedback loop. Each module performs a set of rules defined previously. The hardware components of each module consists of a *beam splitter* to replicate the input plane containing the operands as many times as there are rules applied; a set of *recognizers* and *substituters* that assume the functions of recognizing and replacing the spatial patterns; an *image combiner* and a *static-beam steering element* that directs the combined output image produced after the necessary processing to the processor output plane. The static-beam steering element can be implemented as an optically recorded hologram providing the space-invariant interconnections.

An optical arithmetic processor could outperform an electronic processor by a speedup factor of $O(10^2)$ to $O(10^4)$ depending on the optical devices, interface conversions, and the interconnection networks used. Design tradeoffs do exist in speed performance, power consumption, reconfigurability, and reliability.

16.6   Electronic and Optical Implementations

We have delayed discussion of neural network implementation because many of the principles described in Sec. 16.4 on optical computing are directly related to optical neural networks. For a complete view of neural network hardware implementation concerns we must examine the major features of not only optical and electro-optical but also purely electronic implementation. This section first discusses electronic implementations in the form of custom designed chips, and virtual coprocessors/simulators. Next, we show how optical and electrooptical devices can be used. Finally, we discuss some of the tradeoffs between different implementation approaches.

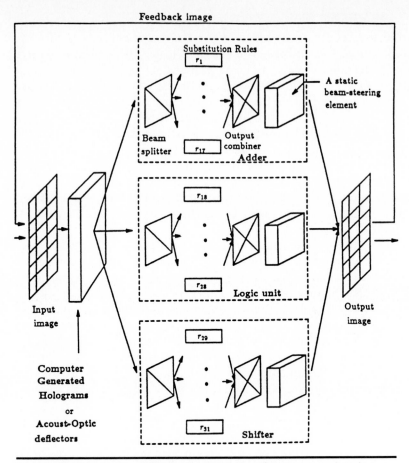

Figure 16.13 The functional blocks in an optical arithmetic processor using the signed-digit symbolic substitution rules. [Hwang 89]

16.6.1 Fully implemented neural network chips

Silicon VLSI implementations of neural networks will probably be the most common choice for near-term practical applications. VLSI technology is relatively inexpensive, widely available, and well understood. Also, new tools and environments are available for designing and constructing chips. The primary difficulty with fully implemented silicon networks is the limitations on wiring for each processor. Theoretically, wires could be spaced as closed as $\frac{1}{2}$ μm from each other. However, when putting the processing element on a planar array much more space is required. Spacing problems will probably limit the number of processors to a few thousand (for planar arrays). Research is continuing on three-dimensional networks, and three-dimensional wafer scale integration [Hughes 86]. Other significant research into fully implemented neural circuits is being done at AT&T, Caltech, and MIT Lincoln Laboratories.

At AT&T Bell Laboratories a 256-neuron associative memory chip has been built [Graf 86]. The memory was designed using 2.5-μm CMOS technology and consists of amplifier units, interconnection matrix, and I/O control with a total of nearly 25,000 transistors. The amplifiers have inverting and noninverting outputs to make inhibitory and excitatory connections. Connections between individual neurons are provided by amorphous-silicon resistors which are placed on the silicon chip in the last step of fabrication. The resistor values are fixed once fabrication is finished, but electron-beam direct writing is used to pattern the resistors and make it easy to change distributions from one chip to the next. All resistors have the same value or interconnection weight.

During operation, the circuit handles several hundred bits in parallel. This number was too large to bring in and off the chip in parallel so I/O circuits were designed to multiplex/demultiplex the data. The data flow over a 16-bit bus, are stored in a buffer, and loaded onto the amplifiers. Once the amplifiers are initialized, the circuit is enabled and the whole system settles down to a stable state.

The memory actually has 512 amplifiers on the chip, but the minimum line width available was too large to interconnect more than 256. These limitations should be overcome in future chips by using different geometries and moving to 1.25-μm designs. Also, a 54-neuron circuit has been designed with programmable connection weights. This increased flexibility greatly reduces the number of neurons that can be put on the chip.

To overcome the problems of building programmable synapes, researchers at MIT Lincoln Laboratories have built a Hopfield neural network circuit based on *charge-coupled device* (CCD) and *metal-nitride-oxide* (MNOS) technologies [Sage 86]. The group claims two significant features resulting from their design: (1) electrical programmability, and (2) analog storage.

With electronic programmability interconnection weights are not hard-wired (like the AT&T chip). New values can be established under electrical control at anytime. Also, the synaptic weights are not limited to binary or ternary values but can take on a wide range of continuous values (equivalent to 4 to 8 bits). Analog weights normally give superior performance and storage density. This is especially important when applying adaptive learning that requires incremental changes in connection weights.

CCDs are used to represent analog information transmitted through a synapse while the MNOS devices are used to store electronically changeable nonvolatile analog synaptic weights. New states in the system are updated synchronously (10-MHz clock). Current devices consist of very small fully interconnected networks that use the Hopfield model with simple hebbian learning.

Mead and colleagues at Caltech built a Hopfield associative memory chip with 22 neurons and a full interconnection matrix using 4-μm nMOS technology [Sivilotti 86]. They were able to demonstrate some interesting properties dealing with information storage density and fault tolerance. This design has been extended to a 289-neuron chip which has been fabricated and is being tested for use in character recognition. Mead's group has more recently designed and built chips that mimic parts of the choclea and early human vision [Mead 87].

16.6.2 Virtual coprocessors and simulators

The vast majority of neural networks currently in use fit into this category. Instead of directly implementing state equations and interconnects in hardware they are simulated on a conventional digital computer. These simulations are often too slow for investigating large networks. To counter this problem, conventional PCs and workstations are often enhanced with plug-in coprocessor boards or attached multiprocessor systems. There are a number of commercial products appearing that bundle simulation software with plug-in/attachable hardware.

In Table 16.4 we compare a few commercially available neural network simulators. The performance of these products is measured according to (1) interconnects per second (IPS), (2) number of nodes, and (3) number of connections. IPS are measured according to the minimum time it takes a single neuron to update its activation state. This definition is still vague and unstandardized. The number of nodes and connections are more a limit of the system memory. Of course, the more nodes and connections, the slower the system will perform. Consequently, these maximum numbers are never exercised in real simulations. Most products also offer a menu-driven environment for selecting models and setting-up experiments. In addition, simulations may have a special purpose language for defining neural network models not included in the standard environment.

16.6.3 Optical and electrooptical implementations

While electronic implementations hold great promise for near-term and special-purpose applications, optical components may have greater long-term potential. Optics seem to be a natural match for

TABLE 16.4   Comparison of Different Neural Network Simulators

Name, company	Processor type, Host	No. of nodes and connections	Interconnects, s	Comments
Mark V, TRW	16-68020/6881s, VAX/VMS	1.78M+	Up to 16M	Supports most neural net models
Sigma-1, SAIC	Havard pipeline, PC/AT	3.1M	11M	Supports 13 network models
ANZA plus, HNC	Havard pipeline, Zenith (80386)	2.5M	10M	5 neural net models, AXON descip. Lang.
NX-16, Human Dev.	16 RISC processors, Mac II	1.6M	8–32M	Runs Neuronics MacBrain 1.2
NDS, Nestor	Sun or Apollo	15M	500K	Pattern recognition using proprietary model
Prof II, NeuralWare	Sun	1.5M	100K	Supports 9 models +, Weitek coprocessor available
ODYSSEY, TI	DSP accelerators, TI Explorer	256K	20M	General-purpose neural network modeling
MX-1/16, MIT Lincoln Labs	16 DSPs, Lisp machine	50M	120M	Experimental machine, projected performance

neural networks. For instance, optical technology is capable of producing interconnects between large numbers of processing elements. This is possible because light from different sources can cross and overlap without interference. Also, light can communicate in free space, whereas conventional electronic components are limited to wires and channels.

Optics are not as good for constructing complicated logical functions. Again, this is acceptable because neural processors require only very simple operations. An optical implementation is an especially good match for problems that already use optical input devices such as vision, sensor processing, and pattern recognition. In these cases, the inputs do not need to be converted to electronic signals. The optical signals can be used directly in the network so that the computing process itself does the signal processing. These are some general properties that make optical implementations very favorable for neural networks.

Optical interconnect technologies are already being used in conventional computers for cabinet-to-cabinet and board-to-board communications. Development of package-to-package, chip-to-chip, and within-a-chip interconnects is progressing rapidly [Hutcheson 87]. Developers can draw on this rich technological interest for adaptation to neural networks.

In general, an optical interconnect requires a source, an optical waveguide, and a receiver. For optical neurocomputers the source is normally the input signal being analyzed, light emitting or laser diodes. The optical waveguide can be constructed from optical fibers, integrated optical channels or free-space propagation using lenses, holograms, or electrooptical/acoustooptical devices. The optical receiver could be made of nonlinear switching elements (e.g., GaAs).

Among the various types of optical networks (see Sec. 16.4.2), the hologram-based network is the most feasible one to implement using current technologies. Holograms have tremendous potential for directing optical signals. A planar hologram can be constructed to direct a signal from any point on one side to any point on the other. For free-space propagation, the number of signals is limited by diffraction effects on the spot size. Even with this restriction, it is possible to direct 100 million signals per square-inch of material. This means that 10,000 light sources could be fully connected to 10,000 receivers [Abu-Mostafa 87]. For volume holograms, using photorefractive crystals, perhaps several billion interconnects are possible [Hecht-Nielsen 86].

In addition to the possibility of massive interconnections, holograms can be reconfigured which make them very attractive in general-purpose applications. In fact, a crossbar network can be implemented with the defractive hologram network. The optical bus and perfect shuffle networks are both weak in reconfigurability and thus are less attractive. Much of the speed (bandwidth) of optical networks is severely compromised by the slow electrooptical and optoelectrical conversions. Totally optical networks are still in the research stage. All present computer-generated hologram networks are still too bulky in physical size. However, the advantages outweigh the shortcomings. In terms of communications bandwidth, optical networks support 1 Gbyte/s, as opposed to only 10 Mbytes/s per electronic line.

Optical processing elements require properties that perform thresholding, analog summation of multiple signals and feedback. Devices having some of these properties include phase conjugate mirrors [Dunning 86], light amplifiers, Fabry-Perot etalons, or quantum well superlattice structures [Hecht-Nielsen 86].

Most optical neurocomputers are fully implemented networks with very restrictive application areas. Applications have centered in pattern recognition and associative memory. Optical neural computers are expected to be capable of extreme speed and moderate cost. Unfortunately, very little hard data are available on specific performances. The cost for building optical neurocomputers will be primarily for the PEs. The interconnection network consisting of either holograms or optical fibers should be relatively inexpensive.

Electrooptical implementations of neural networks are very similar to optical implementations. The main difference is the use of electrooptical devices for the PEs. Both virtual and fully implemented networks have been constructed. Interconnects are usually optical with electrooptical switching and routing. Electrooptical components may be slightly slower and more costly than purely optical or electronic.

An example of a virtual electrooptical implementation is that of Psaltis and Farhat [Psaltis 85]. Their system implements a 64-PE nearest neighbor content addressable memory. Interconnection weights are expressed by a photographic transparency. A single Bragg cell is used for processing.

On the other extreme, Ravi Athale of BDM constructed a simple fully implemented neural network also for nearest neighbor memory searches. His system uses simple electronic PEs connected by LEDs and photoresistors with an optical attenuation mask in between to weigh the connections [Hecht-Nielsen 86].

Researchers at Honeywell and Rockwell have been developing technology to integrate optoelectronic devices with complex gallium arsenide circuits [Hutcheson 87]. This approach combines source (diode laser), waveguide (integrated channels) and receiver (photodector) into a monolithic chip. Much more development is needed before this approach matches the speed and density needed for practical circuits.

16.6.4   Implementation tradeoffs

Each implementation category (electronic, optical, electrooptical) has both advantages and disadvantages. No category appears as the clear and obvious candidate for all neural network applications. As can be expected, the implementation choice is dependent on the neural network architecture and application. It is also very difficult to make a quantitative comparison of the different types of implementation mediums because there are no standard benchmarks.

Electronic implementations have the advantages of using a well-known, stable technology assisted by automated development support tools. Both virtual and fully implemented networks have been produced. Also, the processing elements can be as simple or complex as desired. Densities may allow around a thousand PEs and several thousand interconnects. This number might be sufficient for simple applications or multilayered networks could be used with several chips. Electronics offer a near-term medium, while other technologies are still developing. The major disadvantage is density. There is a fundamental limit on the size of the interconnect structure. Also, other implementations may have higher bandwidth and faster signal propagation speeds.

Optical implementations have the potential for much higher density interconnects. Millions of PEs with billions of interconnects are conceivable. Signal propagation and computation could be extremely fast. Optics may be especially useful for problems that require processing of optical signals. Some problems include the fact that so far only fully implemented networks have been constructed. Scaling to high densities has not been proved. Costs will probably be greater than electronic circuits, and the technology for optical computing is less well understood.

Electrooptical approaches combine the features of both electronics and optics. For instance, PEs could have more complex functions. Large numbers of optical interconnects are possible. Both virtual and fully implemented networks have been built. However, the costs may be higher than any other approach and the overall technology is less well understood.

16.7   Critical R/D Issues and Future Trends

We have examined some of the major properties and capabilities of neural and optical computing technologies. As a result, we have shown the enormous potential of these technologies for augmenting current computing approaches. Much more research is needed before these concepts are realized. In this final section we suggest a few important directions for research and development and then project future trends.

16.7.1 Critical issues in research and development

In order for neural and optical technologies to make progress, a number of critical issues must be addressed. Some suggestions are listed below:

- *Improve understanding of the fundamental mechanisms of human brain function:* This research would clarify overall structure and individual neuron activity. Important discoveries are needed to tie low-level neuronal activity with high-level cognitive processes.

- *Enhance theoretical neural network models for biological and nonbiological systems:* Mathematical models should include results from brain mechanism studies but could also include promising nonbiological connectionist approaches.

- *Develop advanced simulation environments for testing and debugging neural network models and applications:* Critical issues include the development of architectures, languages, compilers, and graphics, as identified in Ghosh and Hwang [Ghosh 88].

- *Clarify and extend application areas:* Application domains should be carefully investigated to determine most suitable materials and architectures for neural and optical approaches.

- *Construct and experiment with large-scale networks:* New problems and behaviors may immerge by implementing networks of hundreds or thousands of neurons.

- *Experiment with interfaces between neural, optical and electronic computers:* Real systems will certainly be hybrids. Research should uncover potential bottlenecks.

- *Intensify research into optical materials and devices:* Hardware is needed that minimizes heat dissipation, size, weight, misalignment, and is easy to fabricate and package.

- *Develop practical optical arithmetic processors:* This represents a major step in construction of a digital optical computer.

- *Establish procedures for hardware implementation and commercial production:* This would include building the infrastructure for producing VLSI chips, monolithic optical-electronic processors, volume holograms, and other optical devices.

- *Integrate neural network and/or optical technologies into complete systems:* Some interfaces include robots, sensors, and other computers.

16.7.2   Future trends in supercomputing and AI

Artificial neural networks and optical computing are technologies that use approaches radically different from today's conventional electronic computers. Neural networks offer the possibility of self-organizing, fault-tolerant systems capable of real-time vision, pattern matching and optimization that not only improve their performance with experience but also require little or no software engineering/programming. Optical computing offers equally impressive hope for massively parallel, high-bandwidth, noninterfering, speed-of-light computation. These ideas signify major new paradigms for computing, all of which require the development of new principles, theories, mathematics, design and implementation approaches.

With this great promise we must also acknowledge the immense gap between concept and product. Many technological challenges must be overcome before neural and optical approaches will be effective and economical for commercialization. Both fields are in the early stages of research and development. Hopefully, the currently intense research by government, academic and industrial groups will accelerate development towards practical applications before the turn of the century. However, many uncertainties make it difficult to predict when these technologies will be matured enough to produce practical commercial products.

While neural networks and optical computing have great potential we must also be aware of their weaknesses and limitations. These approaches are not (and will never be) panaceas for all of the current problems in computing. They function best within carefully defined bounds. For instance, neural networks are not appropriate for high-precision, numeric processing; likewise, optics may not be reasonable for extremely complex operations on small sets of data. These systems will never completely replace electronics. Future systems will most likely be electronic/optical/neural hybrids where the behavior of the materials and devices are best matched to the problem domain.

In spite of current limitations, we believe these technologies will eventually result in systems that will revolutionize current approaches to supercomputing and AI applications. By exploring neural network and optical technologies we have looked into the future of computing. We have seen that concepts previously relegated to the realm of science fiction are now within the scope of engineering reality.

Bibliography

[Abu-Mostafa 87]   Y.S. Abu-Mostafa and D. Psaltis. "Optical Neural Computers." *Scientific American,* pp. 88–95, March 1987.

[Avizienis 61]   A. Avizienis. "Signed-Digit Number Representations for Fast Parallel Arithmetic." *Trans. Electronic Comp.,* vol. EC-10, pp. 389–398, 1961.

[Brenner 85]   K.H. Brenner and A. Huang. "An Optical Processor Based on Symbolic Substitution." *Tech. Digest, Topical Meeting on Optical Computing,* paper WA4.1-WA4.3, 1985.

[Brenner 86]   K.H. Brenner, A. Huang, and N. Streibl. "Digital Optical Computing with Symbolic Substitution." *Applied Optics,* vol. 25, no. 18, September 15, 1986.

[Castalez 87]   P. Castalez, J. Angus, and J. Mahoney. "Application of Neural Networks to Expert Systems and Command and Controls Systems." *Proc. IEEE WESTEX-87 Conference on Expert Systems,* pp. 118–125, Anaheim, CA, June 2–4, 1987.

[Carpenter 86]   G.A. Carpenter and S. Grossberg. "Associative Learning, Adaptive Pattern Recognition, and Cooperative-Competitive Decision Making by Neural Networks." *Proc. SPIE Conference on Optical and Hybrid Computing,* SPIE, vol. 634, pp. 218–247, 1986.

[Carpenter 87a]   G.A. Carpenter and S. Grossberg. "A Massively Parallel Architecture for a Self-Organizing Neural Pattern Recognition Machine." *Computer Vision, Graphics and Image Processing,* vol. 37, pp. 54–115, January 1987.

[Carpenter 87b]   G.A. Carpenter and S. Grossberg. "ART-2: Self-Organization of Stable Category Recognition Codes for Analog Input Patterns." *Proc. IEEE First Annual International Conference on Neural Networks,* San Diego, CA, June 21–24, 1987.

[Cohen 83]   M. Cohen and S. Grossberg. "Absolute Stability of Global Pattern Formation and Parallel Memory Storage by Competitive Neural Networks." *IEEE Trans. Systems, Man and Cybernetics,* pp. 815–826, September/October 1983.

[Denker 86]   J.S. Denker. "Neural Network Models of Learning and Adaptation." *Physica,* vol. 22D, pp. 216–232, 1986.

[Drake 86]   B.L. Drake, R.P. Bocker, M.E. Lasher, R.H. Patterson, and W.J. Miceli. "Photonic Computing using the Modified Signed-Digit Number Representation." *Optical Engineering,* vol. 25, no. 1, pp. 038–043, January 1986.

[Dunning 86]   G.J. Dunning, Y. Marom, Y. Owechko, and B. H. Soffer. "Optical Holographic Associative Memory Using a Phase Conjugate Resonator." *Optical Computing, SPIE,* vol. 625, pp. 205–213, 1986.

[Farhat 85]   N.H. Farhat, D. Psaltis, A. Prate, and E. Paek. "Optical Implementation of the Hopfield Model." *Applied Optics,* vol. 24, no. 10, pp. 1469–1475, May 15, 1985.

[Fukushima 80]   K. Fukushima. "Neocognitron: A Self-Organizing Multilayered Neural Network." *Biological Cybernetics,* vol. 36, pp. 193–202, 1980.

[Fukushima 83]   K. Fukushima, S. Miyake, and T. Ito. "Neocognitron: A Neural Network Model for a Mechanism for Visual Pattern Recognition." *IEEE Trans. Systems, Man, and Cybernetics,* pp. 826–834, September/October 1983.

[Fukushima 87]   K. Fukushima. "A Neural Network Model for Selective Attention." *Proc. IEEE First Annual International Conference on Neural Networks,* San Diego, CA, June 21–24, 1987.

[Garey 79]   M.R. Garey and D.S. Johnson. *Computers and Intractability.* Freeman, San Francisco, CA, 1979.

[Ghosh 88]   J. Ghosh and K. Hwang. "Critical Issues in Mapping Neural Networks onto Message-Passing Multicomputers." *Proc. 15th International Symposium on Computer Architecture,* pp. 3–11, Honolulu, HI, May 30 to June 2, 1988.

[Gibbs 80]   H.M. Gibbs, S.L. McCall, and T.N.C. Venkatesan. "Optical Bistable Devices: The Basic Components of All-Optical Systems?" *Optical Engineering,* vol. 19, pp. 463–468, 1980.

[Graf 86]   H.P. Graf et al. "VLSI Implementation of Neural Network Memory with Several Hundreds of Neurons." In J.S. Denker (ed). *Neural Networks for Computing,* pp. 182–187, AIP Conference Proceedings, 1986.

[Grossberg 71]   S. Grossberg. "Embedding Fields: Underlying Philosophy, Mathematics, and Applications to Psychology, Physiology, and Anatomy." *J. Cybernetics,* vol. 1, pp. 28–50, 1971.

[Hebb 49]   D.O. Hebb. *The Organization of Behavior,* Wiley, New York 1949.

[Hecht 87]   J. Hecht. "Optical Computers." *High Technology,* pp. 44–49, February 1987.

[Hecht-Nielsen 86]   R. Hecht-Nielsen. "Performance Limits of Optical, Electro-Optical, and Electronic Neurocomputers." *Optical and Hybrid Computing,* SPIE, vol. 634, pp. 277–306, 1986.

[Hecht-Nielsen 87]   R. Hecht-Nielsen. "Counterpropagation Networks." *Proc. IEEE First Annual International Conference on Neural Networks,* San Diego, CA, June 21–24, 1987.

[Hinton 86]   G.E. Hinton and T.J. Sejnowski. "Learning and Relearning in Boltzmann Machines." In D.E. Rumelhart and J.L. McClelland (eds). *Parallel Distributed Processing,* pp. 282–317, MIT Press, Cambridge, MA, 1986.

[Hopfield 86]   J.J. Hopfield and D.W. Tank. "Computing with Neural Circuits: A Model." *Science,* vol. 233, pp. 625–633, August 8, 1986.

[Hopfield 85]   J.J. Hopfield and D.W. Tank. "Neural Computation of Decisions in Optimization Problems." *Biological Cybernetics,* vol. 52, 1985, pp. 141–152.

[Hopfield 82]   J.J. Hopfield. "Neural Networks and Physical Systems with Emergent Collective Computational Abilities." *Proc. National Academy of Science, Biophysics,* vol. 79, pp. 2554–2558, April 1982.

[Huang 83]   A. Huang. "Parallel Algorithms for Optical Digital Computers." *Proc. IEEE Tenth International Optical Computing Conference,* pp. 13–17, 1983.

[Hughes 86]   Hughes Aircraft Company. *Development of a 3-D Processor.* Tech. Proposal 86M-0203/G1146, prepared for Rome Air Development Center, March 1986.

[Hutcheson 87]   L.D. Hutcheson, P. Haugen, and A. Husain. "Optical Interconnects Replace Hardware." *IEEE Spectrum,* pp. 30–35, March 1987.

[Hwang 79]   K. Hwang. *Computer Arithmetic: Principles, Arichitecture and Design,* Wiley, New York, 1979.

[Hwang 87]   K. Hwang. "Advanced Parallel Processing with Supercomputer Architectures." *Proc. IEEE,* vol. OC-75, no. 10, pp. 1348–1379, October 1987.

[Hwang 89]   K. Hwang and A. Louri. "Optical Multiplication and Division Using Signed-Digit Symbolic Substitution." *J. Optical Engineering,* special issue on optical computing, March 1989.

[Kirkpatrik 83]   S. Kirkpatrik, C.D. Gelatt, and M.P. Vecchi. "Optimization by Simulated Annealing." *Science,* vol. 220, no. 4598, pp. 671–680, May 13, 1983.

[Kolodzy 87]   P.J. Kolodzy. "Multidimensional Machine Vision Using Neural Networks." *Proc. IEEE First Annual International Conference on Neural Networks,* San Diego, CA, June 21–24, 1987.

[Kosko 87]   B. Kosko. "Competitive Adaptive Bidirectional Associative Memories." *Proc. IEEE First Annual International Conference on Neural Networks,* San Diego, CA, June 21–24, 1987.

[Lapedes 86]   A. Lapedes and R. Farber. "A Self-Optimizing, Nonsymmetrical Neural Net for Content Addressable Memory and Pattern Recognition." *Physica D,* vol. 22D, pp. 247–259, October/November 1986.

[Little 86]   M.J. Little and C.S. Bak. "Enhanced Memory Capacity of a Hopfield Neural Network." *SPIE Technical Symposium,* San Diego, CA, August 1986.

[Mead 87]   C.A. Mead. *Analog VLSI and Neural Systems,* Addison-Wesley, Reading, MA, 1987.

[Minsky 68]   M.L. Minsky and S. Papert. *Perceptrons,* MIT Press, Cambridge, MA, 1968.

[McCulloch 43]   W.S. McCulloch and W. Pitts. *Bulletin on Mathematics and Biophysics,* vol. 5, p. 115, 1943.

[Neff 87]   J.A. Neff. "Major Initiatives for Optical Computing." *Optical Engineering,* vol. 26, no. 1, pp. 2–9, January 1987.

[Prager 86]   R.W. Prager, T.D. Harrison, and F. Fallside. *Boltzmann Machines for Speech Recognition,* Cambridge University, Department of Engineering, NTIS PB87–1237 41, 1986.

[Psaltis 85]   D. Psaltis and N. Farhat. "Optical Information Processing Based on an Associative-Memory of Neural Nets with Thresholding and Feedback." *Optics Letters,* vol. 10, no. 2, pp. 98–100, February 1985.

[Ramamoorthy 87]   P.A. Ramamoorthy and S. Anthony. "Optical MSD Adder Using Polarization Coded Symbolic Substitution." *Tech. Digest, Topical Meeting on Optical Computing,* March 1987.

[Reilly 82]   D.L. Reilly, L.N. Cooper, and C. Elbaum. "A Neural Model of Category Learning." *Biological Cybernetics,* vol. 45, pp. 35–41, 1982.

[Rosenblatt 61]   F. Rosenblatt. *Principles of Neurodynamics: Perceptrons and the Theory of Brain Mechanisms,* Spartan Books, Washington, D. C., 1961.

[Rumelhart 86]   D.E. Rumelhart, G.E. Hinton, and R.J. Williams. "Learning Internal Representations by Error Propagation." In D.E. Rumelhart and J.L. McClelland (eds). *Parallel Distributed Processing,* pp. 318–362, MIT Press, Cambridge, MA, 1986.

[Rumelhart 86]   D.E. Rumelhart and J.L. McClelland (eds). *Parallel Distributed Processing: Explorations in the Microstructure of Cognition,* MIT Press, Cambridge, MA, 1986.

[Sage 86]   J.P. Sage, K. Thompson, and R.S. Withers. "An Artificial Neural Network Integrated Circuit Based on MNOS/CCD Principles." In J.S. Denker (ed). *Neural Networks for Computing,* pp. 381–385, AIP Conference Proceedings, 1986.

[Sawchuk 87]   A.A. Sawchuk, B. Jenkins, C.S. Raghavandra, and A. Varma. "Optical Crossbar Networks." *IEEE Computer,* vol. 20, no. 6, pp. 50–60, June 1987.

[Sawchuk 84]   A.A. Sawchuk and T.C. Strand. "Digital Optical Computing." *Proc. IEEE,* vol. 72, no. 7, July 1984.

[Sejnowski 86]   T.J. Sejnowski and C.R. Rosenberg. *NetTalk: A Parallel Network that Learns to Read Aloud.* Tech. Re. JHU.EECS-86/01, Johns Hopkins University, Electrical Engineering and Computer Science Departments, 1986.

[Sivilotti 86]   M.A. Sivilotti, M.R. Emerling, and C.A. Mead. "VLSI Architectures for Implementation of Neural Networks." *Neural Networks for Computing,* pp. 408–413, AIP Conference Proceedings, 1986.

[Takeda 86]   M. Takeda and J.W. Goodman. "Neural Networks for Computation: Number Representations and Programming Complexity." *Applied Optics,* vol. 25, no. 18, September 15, 1986.

[Tanguay 85]   A.R. Tanguay. "Material Requirements for Optical Processing and Computing Devices." *Optical Engineering,* vol. 24, no. 1, pp. 002–018, February 1985.

[Tank 86]   D.W. Tank and J.J. Hopfield. "Simple Neural Optimization Network: An A/D Converter, Signal Decision Circuit and a Linear Programming Circuit." *IEEE Circuits and Systems,* vol. 33, no. 5, p. 533, 1986.

[Thakoor 86]   A. P. Thakoor, J. L. Lamb, A. Moopenn, and J. Lamb. "Binary Synaptic Memory Connections Based on a-Si:H and SnOx:Sb." *Proc. Second Annual Conference on Neural Networks for Computing,* American Institute of Physics, 1986.

[Ticknor 87]   A.J. Ticknor and H.H. Barrett. "Optical Implementations of Boltzmann Machines." *Optical Engineering,* vol. 26, no. 1, pp. 16–21, January 1987.

[TRW 86]   TRW. *Mark III Artificial Neural System Processor, Product Description.* TRW AI Center, Rancho Carmel, CA, April 11, 1986.

[Widrow 62]   B. Widrow. "Generalization and Information Storage Network of Adeline Neurons." In M.C. Yovits (ed). *Self-Organizing Systems,* p. 435, Spartan Books, Washington, D.C., 1962.

Index

About the Editors in Chief

Kai Hwang is professor of electrical engineering and computer science at the University of Southern California. His teaching and research activities are in vector supercomputers, multiprocessors, VLSI and dataflow computing structures, and AI-oriented multiprocessors. He has served as a principal investigator, consultant, specialist, and lecturer on advanced computer architectures and high-technology applications for several federal, industrial, and international research organizations including the NSF, National Academy of Sciences, AFOSR, IBM, Academic Sinica, Fujitsu, and Nato. He has authored, edited, and co-edited several books including *Computer Architecture and Parallel Processing* published by McGraw-Hill in 1984. In addition, he is co-editor in chief of the *Journal of Parallel and Distributed Computing*. Dr. Hwang received his Ph.D. from the University of California at Berkekley.

Douglas DeGroot is senior researcher in the AI group at Texas Instruments.